The Concise Encyclopedia of
WORLD HISTORY

Edited by
JOHN BOWLE

The Concise Encyclopedia of
WORLD HISTORY

 Hutchinson of London

HUTCHINSON & CO (*Publishers*) LTD
London W1

London Melbourne Sydney
Auckland Johannesburg Cape Town
and agencies throughout the world

First published 1958
Second edition (revised in new format) 197

This book has been set in Bembo type, printed in Great Britain
on opaque wove paper by Anchor Press, and
bound by Wm. Brendon, both of Tiptree, Essex

ISBN 0 09 107500 9

CONTENTS

Contents

MAPS AND CHARTS

All the maps and charts were prepared by Dr. James Houston, except for 'African States in 1970' which was supplied by Geographia Ltd.

INTRODUCTION

Out of the twilight of prehistory and the dawn of recorded time civilisations have risen, flourished and fallen, their influence strictly bounded by the facts of geography. Massive societies emerged in the Middle East, in India, in China, in Mediterranean Europe, while exotic cultures developed in the Americas, completely unknown to the peoples of Europe and Asia, and the interior of Africa remained the Dark Continent until less than a century ago. A real world history was therefore impossible since no historian had a complete vision of all the societies of mankind. It is only today, when all the ends of the habitable earth have been explored and science is making the world technologically one, aircraft, rockets and radio are abolishing distance, and man has reached the moon, that we can discover, in the light of the world past, the tentative outlines of a future world civilisation. Saving nuclear catastrophe, its realisation is to be expected.

Apart from the impetus long provided by the nomads of Central Asia, it was mainly European initiative that set mankind on the move. The swift expansion of the Europeans which followed the discoveries of Columbus and Vasco da Gama, of Magellan and Cook, of Yermak and his successors across Siberia, spread Western ideas and methods over the earth. In sparsely inhabited continents white populations multiplied; to established civilisations Europeans brought order and exploitation, and the tempo of economic and social life was changed. Then, in the twentieth century, Europe, as the political centre of the world, lost its lead. Great world wars destroyed her hegemony and left two competing centres of political and economic power based on the land masses of Eurasia and North America, while in China and all Asia the Eastern peoples flung off their dependence upon the West and in Africa the native populations established their own states.

It was mainly through obsession with national sovereignty that the Europeans, who had created this world-wide transformation and opened up such wide horizons for themselves and their dependent peoples, lost a position which had long appeared unchallengeable. They thought in terms of European power politics, at most, of their own empires, and the vast majority remained unaware of the culture and the history of the great and ancient peoples of the rest of the

Introduction

world. When these dependents won their freedom the bitterness they felt was due too often to the blank misunderstanding they had suffered.

This European parochialism reflected a limited outlook upon history. Yet, in the circumstances of our time, there is bound to be interest in the history of the whole world; hence the wide popularity of H. G. Wells' pioneer work and the public commanded by Toynbee. And this popular interest is realistic. The Elizabethans could afford to be indifferent to the policy of Ivan the Terrible, but it is impossible today to ignore the policy of the Kremlin; Texas and the Middle West no longer stand aloof from events in Europe, the Middle East or China and its periphery. And politics apart, modern travel and television can offer a new enrichment of mind which can only be appreciated by those with some knowlege of the world's past. An understanding of hitherto alien peoples is now a necessity.

The landmarks of such knowledge this new outline attempts to supply. It has been designed to set in perspective the entire history of mankind. Omissions have been inevitable, but most of the essentials are here. The geographical background has been particularly emphasised: maps follow a consistent design from which the permanent setting of the drama is apparent, for it is not the shifting political frontiers which are significant in the long run, but the unchanging mountains, the strategic passes, the rivers and harbours, the forest and the steppe, the desert and the sown. Only through a grasp of the structural features of the continents can military, economic and cultural movements become intelligible and memorable. Each chapter has therefore been provided with a map closely co-ordinated with the text.

As well as a common background mankind has a common ancestry. The earliest human origins have therefore been described and considerable space given to that cardinal and gradual event, the Neolithic revolution, which substituted an agricultural for a gathering and hunting economy. Anthropology and archaeology, which have made such advances in the last half century, are now essential to the understanding both of prehistory and of the structure of societies in historic times, while fresh discoveries—the invention of radio-carbon dating and the recent excavation at Jericho—have thrown new light upon problems of a common past.

The outlines of the history of Mesopotamia and Egypt are comparatively familiar; they have therefore not been treated in detail, so that more space can be devoted to the origins of China—the most populous and the most enduring of all civilisations—of India, and of the native cultures of the Americas. Chinese, Indian, Near Eastern and European history have been periodically convulsed by the incursions of mysterious peoples from the Central Asian steppes: here a chapter has been devoted to the nomad empires, so destructive to the cultures they assailed.

Of the history of medieval Africa most readers are ignorant, and experts have long been in little better case. Today much is coming to light, and some account has been given of the expansion of the Bantu, of the Kingdoms of Ashanti and the Emirates of Nigeria, of the dim background of the ruins of Zimbabwe. One of the stranger episodes of cultural expansion has been the spread of the Moslem faith into Malaya and Indonesia, where it has competed with the Buddhism which there achieved such wonderful artistic expression. The landmarks of both these movements have been charted, as well as those of the extraordinary migrations which peopled the Pacific islands and which reached New Zealand about the twelfth century, when in the west Henry II was attempting to rule the Angevin Empire.

Attention has also been focused on the Mohammedan culture which radiated from the Middle East, west into North Africa and Spain, eastward into Iran and India, which challenged and ultimately, in its Turkish manifestation, overcame the Byzantines, overran the Balkans, and threatened Vienna just at the time that Europeans were first colonising the Americas and outflanking the Arab economy in the Indian ocean round the Cape. The four main phases of this empire are delineated as they shifted from Damascus to Baghdad, to Cairo, and to Istanbul, the conquered capital of Rum.

But the main thread of the story is still the rise of the classical civilisation of Greece and Rome, which owed much to Egypt and Asia Minor yet whose contribution was dynamic and original. With its Western medieval and Byzantine sequel, it formed the background to the expansion of Europe which first made a world culture possible. While, therefore, attention has been directed to extra-European events unfamiliar to many Western readers, European history has been more closely out-lined, with emphasis not only upon Athens but upon Knossos and Mycenae, not merely on Rome but upon the Carthaginians, a people neglected and perhaps maligned, because they suffered defeat. The fascinating transition from paganism to Christianity has been investigated in the light of the mentality of pagans and of Jews, while the extraordinary achievement of the Western missionaries in taming the barbarians of Northern Europe has not been neglected, and the importance of Byzantium for Muscovy and also for the West brought out.

From the Renaissance to the French Revolution the intellectual initiative of Europe determined the future of the world. Decisive inventions in science, technology and medicine transcended racial boundaries. Besides giving Europeans an unprecedented mobility and power, they were exportable anywhere. When in the nineteenth century the Japanese decided to exploit this Western knowledge, they were pioneers of a swiftly expanding movement, while Western settlers in vast new territories had new scope for the application of European technology. The relatively short span of four centuries in which these decisive inventions and discoveries were made has universal significance, and the political events of the period have been strictly compressed, so that scientific, technical and cultural achievements may be in dicated. Familiar in the West, they will be less familiar, though equally important, to Eastern readers. The Industrial and Technological revolutions also are world-wide phenomena, and have been described not so much in terms of their local origins and social background as in those of their universal achievement, running from the first crude devices which harnessed steam, through the internal combustion engine and electricity, to nuclear power.

II

History is mainly studied through the printed word: it is revealed most vividly through the eye. In the Palais de Chaillot in Paris there is a famous exhibition—*Le Musée de l'Homme*. It presents a panorama of mankind. It is the finest ethnological display in Europe and it ranges from Paleolithic man until today; from the harsh hunting cultures of the Eskimo to the easy-going islanders of the Pacific; from the kraals of tropical Africa and the Dayak long houses of Borneo and Sarawak to the desert nomads of Arabia and the Tartar horsemen of Central Asia. It moves from the convolutions of Hindu sculpture and the glitter of Burmese pagodas to the masks of Aztec ritual cults, from the solid and traditional arts of China to the flimsy hunting cultures of the Indians of North America. Nowhere can one obtain a better impression of the overwhelming interest and variety of the cultures of mankind, reflecting the contrasts of environment imposed by structure and climate. It is a panorama which can enrich the mind; and it counteracts, in a most practical way, the limitations even of a great traditional nation. The spectator becomes for a time literally cosmopolitan, part of his own culture, but part also of mankind—a world citizen—for robes and head-dresses, weapons and hunting gear, strike home to most minds more directly than the most vivid printed page.

Modern civilisation, though precarious, has unprecedented range.

But the lives of the majority of mankind are still circumscribed; there are few who can escape routine and take full advantage of modern travel. But knowledge and imagination can enrich experience, and, particularly among younger readers, prepare the mind to seize any opportunity.

Today, moreover, history has come to play a greater part in education than ever before, both as a substitute for the old classical discipline, and as a counterweight to over-specialisation among those who study technology and science. It ranges from an investigation of the past of village and county, through the achievements of the national cultures into which men are born, to a study of far-flung events and foreign peoples. While few can be expert in any but a limited field, anyone with interest and imagination can grasp some aspect of the broad results of modern research and the main outline of decisive events. It may even be that some day the film and television will come into their own through accurate and untravestied versions of history, in which the mentality as well as the dress and surroundings of the participants are projected. Certain it is that today, although the peoples are sundered by monstrous 'ideologies' which have come down from the nineteenth century, the force of economic and technical change and the spread of scientific method are driving mankind to a wider view and to a recognition that the realities of the modern world transcend racial and national and even 'ideological' boundaries. It is the fate of this and the coming generations in all countries to learn to live together or perish, and in no way can this object be better promoted than by an understanding of the history of the world.

John Bowle

I THE DAWN OF MIND

by J. S. Weiner

Varieties of human species have existed for at least half a million years. This fact has been established by geological and chemical dating of their dwelling sites and of their remains. Throughout those five or six thousand centuries, groups of men of varied kinds lived as food-gatherers and hunters, thinly scattered over a wide extent of the world's surface. This first immensely long period in an untamed nature, known as the Paleolithic, was indeed the primordial Eden of Mankind, for it was only some six or eight thousand years ago that some men at last abandoned the life of savagery and took to the toilsome farming that made possible the first settled villages in the Middle East. The beginnings of our urban civilisation are to be seen in the earliest Neolithic sites at Jericho c. 6000 B.C. and at Jarmo c. 4500 B.C. in Iraq, to be described in the next chapter.

II

How did man come to be on the Earth? For centuries no other answer could be given but to ascribe this phenomenon, seemingly as cataclysmic and incomprehensible as the Cosmos itself, to supernatural agencies whose workings could be expressed only in the dramatic and awe-inspiring images of mythology by peoples the world over. But as a result of the biological science of the last two hundred years, a determinist and rational explanation of man's 'creation' is provided in the modern doctrine of organic evolution. According to this doctrine, man has finally emerged by a long and complicated but entirely natural process of biological transformation from earlier and more primitive creatures. As the Darwinian sees and understands it, mankind has acquired its distinctive features in the course of the incessant, inescapable struggle for survival of its ancestral stock against the difficulties of harsh and changing environments and in constant competition with other, sometimes closely related, animal species.

The emergence of man is but a particular case of the pervasive evolutionary processes that have brought about the diversity we find in the whole animal kingdom, indeed in all living matter, for evolutionary change has been at work in different ways and with varying tempi from the time, perhaps three or four thousand million years ago, when conditions on the earth first made possible the existence and propagation of life. For about the last 1,000 million years, abundant fossil and geological evidence is available, testifying to this succession of life. This evidence exhibits clearly the replacement of simpler forms by, on the whole, increasingly complicated organisms evincing new modes of survival and adaptation, often so efficient as to allow them to spread extensively and achieve the appearance of yet more novel forms. Most of the ancestral forms became extinct. Some survived for varying periods, even to the present day, like the coelacanth fish which first appeared some 300 million years ago. The whole process explains, of course, why existing species of animals,

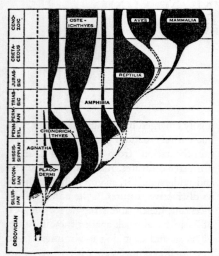

Vertebrate evolution: a family tree showing the times of appearance and relative abundance at various eras of the vertebrate classes. Agnatha are jawless vertebrates; Placodermi are archaic-jawed fishes; Chondrichthyes are shark-like fishes; Osteichthyes are higher bony fishes. (*Reproduced from 'Man and the Vertebrates', A. S. Romer, University of Chicago Press, 1933, and Penguin Books, 1954*)

despite their special characteristics, display such remarkable resemblances and inter-gradation of structure, function and behaviour, and why they can be arranged in a large-scale 'family' scheme. The animal kingdom, past and present, truly comprises a gigantic network of radiating lines of evolution. The chart seen above illustrates, in a simplified way, how the great classes have emerged and flowered; from single to many-celled; from the first vertebrates through to the great animal sequence—fishes, amphibia, reptiles, birds and mammals.

Some 200 million years ago the mammals began to supplant the reptiles, from amongst whom they had evolved as the dominant land-living vertebrates. Amongst the mammals there appeared that tree-living group, or Order, the Primates, which ultimately, after some sixty million years, gave rise to the stock leading to men. But before this ancestral stock emerged, the Primates had undergone a long period of evolutionary preparation.

One may distinguish a first stage, the Prosimian, of simpler Primates. They are represented today by lemurs, lorises, and tarsier; the most primitive, the tree-shrew, retains clear connections with other mammalian orders. The Prosimian stage leads quite naturally to the next, the Anthropoid, which comprises the animals most closely related to man—the monkeys and the apes.

Now the Prosimian and Anthropoid Primates as a group display a consistent pattern of evolutionary change. They have developed all those faculties making for more efficient adaptation to a tree life, as is to be expected from the workings of natural selection. They have tended to improve in dexterity and co-ordination by achieving a greater mobility of the fore-limbs and especially of the hands, which become free for exploration and the grasping of objects. Along with this manual dexterity, touch and vision have become more acute. These develop at the expense of the sense of smell, so much more useful to ground-living animals. All this is reflected in the structure of the brain, which becomes bigger and more complex as we pass from Prosimian to Anthropoid, and which exhibits enlargements of those parts of the brain necessary for collecting information and executing complicated and skilled movements.

It is amongst the great apes and man that these changes in the brain reach their height, marked in man by the appearance of powers of conceptual thought, of memory and speech. While mankind still retain strong traces of this ancient tree heritage, a special impetus was given to further development when tree-life was abandoned.

In the two-footed posture and gait (only a semi- or occasional upright posture is displayed by apes); the hands, entirely free of any locomotor function, could now be employed for the handling and later the making of tools, so necessary for food-gathering and defence. The ground-living mode of life, indeed, brought about large alterations not only in physique, but also in powers of communication and in the brain, as necessary adaptations for survival in the new ecological setting.

The higher *Anthropoidea* thus displays a fundamental divergence. One line remained arboreal and became highly specialised for 'brachiation', that is, progression by swinging through the trees by the arms. These are the *Pongidae*, which include fossil apes and the present-day large apes of Africa and South East Asia including the gibbon and orang-outang which are noted for their exceptionally long and powerful arms. They are distinctive, among other things, in the great elongation of the upper limbs in relation to the trunk and legs. The other line of *Anthropoidea* which adopted a ground-living existence, dependent on an erect posture and bipedal locomotion, are termed the *Hominidae*.

After their long history of divergence the modern representatives of these two zoological families are very different. The limb-structure shows striking contrasts and the brain in man is larger; the tooth structure of apes is different, for example in the strong tusk-like eye teeth; the jaw lacks a chin and has a V-shaped contour; the cranium is small in relation to the muzzle-like projecting face and carries well developed eyebrow ridges. Apes eat fruit and insects; man is meat-eating. Modern man could not conceivably have

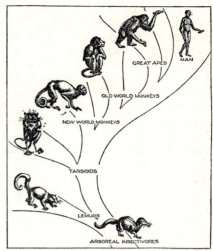

Photo: Penguin Books

The Primates: a simplified family tree. *(Reproduced from 'Man and the Vertebrates', A. S. Romer, University of Chicago Press, 1933, and Penguin Books, 1954)*

evolved from any form at all closely approximating modern apes. But man and ape share a very distant common ancestry, so that it still remains true, as T. H. Huxley first clearly demonstrated, that man physically resembles the chimpanzee more closely than any other living Primate. Moreover, amongst present-day great apes unmistakable, though slight, indications of mental and social behaviour akin to the human are discernible. Chimpanzees can deliberately use sticks and other objects; some have been successfully taught to use a few sounds as 'names'; they can display a measure of planning and forethought and work co-operatively to obtain desired ends. In short, they have the rudiments of the ability to 'conceptualise' a situation, and this also confirms, on the psychological plane, a remote evolutionary link with man. Even the various types of social groupings amongst

3

apes provide indications of how social evolution may have begun. The intermittent mating pattern, based on the restricted and entirely endocrine-determined period of sexual attraction of the lower Primates and other mammals, and leading to the 'harem' system of baboons, has been entirely transformed in apes and man. In the gibbon, for example, the single 'monogamous' family unit is based on a continuing sexual attraction of the same female for the same male, a relationship which is preserved by driving out the offspring as they grow at maturity into possible competitors.

At the stage before the divergence between *Pongidae* and *Hominidae* set in, we would expect, on general evolutionary theory, to find generalised types not particularly specialised for living among the branches or on the ground. Indications of this long-vanished ancestor are not lacking in the fossil record. They occur amongst the dryopithecine apes—a widely distributed family of extinct early *Pongidae*, found in Pliocene and Miocene deposits in India, China and East Africa. The Miocene *Proconsul* from Kenya had a generalised limb structure which could have led to the Hominid type; moreover, the face and jaws have in some important ways escaped the specialisations typical of later apes. The lightly wooded grassland is a suitable environment in which life on the ground could with advantage complement, and in due course supersede, tree-life.

It follows also that if we go back sufficiently along the Hominid line, we should find that Pongid-like features become more obvious; we should expect a stage when the two-footed posture had already been achieved by a creature still bearing many marks similar to the Pongids. Traces of a more ape-like condition are indeed to be found all along the evolutionary succession of *Homo* in the Neanderthal category

of man and the more primitive genus *Pithecanthropus*. As for a creature representing the very beginning of the Hominid line, there is just such a stage in the *Australopithecinae* of South Africa.

III

Australopithecus is the first of the primitive Hominids. These creatures are known from a number of sites in the Transvaal in South Africa and nearby, and the remains

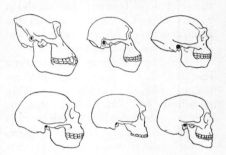

Lateral views of the skull to show the morphological changes during Hominid evolution (by comparison with the ape): Female gorilla; *Australopithecus; Pithecanthropus pekinensis; Homo neanderthalensis;* Steinheim Man; *Homo sapiens. (Courtesy of author)*

of several dozen individuals have come to light. They were small, light, bipedal, ground-living and cave-dwelling; their pelvic bones are remarkably similar to those of man and are very different from that of any Pongid. The heads of these creatures (above), reveal a combination of Pongid and Hominid features. In essentials the jaws and teeth are Hominid, the front teeth strikingly so, as also the contour of palate and mandible; yet Pongid affinities are not to be denied—particularly the combination of a small cranium or brain case with a heavy ape-like face—and in some of these creatures the brain case bears a bony crest somewhat like that of a gorilla. The brain size, too, is small, about 700 cubic centimetres, which falls short of the smallest brain size of fossil men. Even so, closer inspection reveals many significant Hominid features in the architecture of face and cranium. As a 'missing-link', *Australopithecus* fulfils most expectations of the earliest Hominid stages; it reveals clearly what can be deduced from other evidence—that the erect posture preceded the enlargement of the brain. The successful development of a way of life based on handwork, on the use of tools and on transmitting technical knowledge, was possible only for creatures of superior brain size and intelligence. It has been much debated whether these South African Hominids fashioned even the most crude implements, breaking stone on stone and putting these to use. There is some suggestive evidence that they used ready-to-hand objects in their hunting; they seem to have hunted animals as large as baboons, if the fractures on the baboon skull are indeed made deliberately, as they may well have been.

There is no evidence of any knowledge of fire. Very recently, stone artifacts of the oldest recognised types have come to light in strata which also contained australopithecine remains. Their stone tools are of material foreign to the neighbourhood, and though it is likely that they were made by Hominids of more advanced type, it is just possible that *Australopithecus* was in fact a tool-maker. *Homo habilis* (East Africa) *Telanthropus* (Transvaal) are claimed as advanced toolmaking *Australopithecines*. How far back they go is still unclear—the earliest seem to date from the beginning of the Pleistocene period, perhaps two million years ago; the creatures from the latest sites were contemporary with the first undoubted human beings. We must think of the South African Hominids as survivors of a lineage which could certainly have given rise to the line leading to modern man.

IV

The first human being was *Pithecanthropus*. His remains have been found in Java, and he made tools. The last 600,000 years is the age of tool-making men. The history of these men of the 'Old Stone Age' unfolds against a background of world-wide climatic fluctuation. These climatic oscillations accompanied the successive advances and recessions of the northern ice-sheets of America, Europe and Asia. At its maximum, the ice covered more than double the present area, including some expansion in the southern hemisphere; the snow-line of the northern mountain ranges of Europe and Asia descended considerably. As a simplified chronological background to the Paleolithic world (p. 6), the four main glacial periods must be considered separated by three warm inter-glacials; all of these were interrupted by milder or colder phases. The last glaciation, ending with the Paleolithic, went through three phases with warm 'interstadials' and each cold phase was less intense than the preceding one: after the third, the ice-recession has continued, with some pauses, over a period of some 10,000 years to the present day. The cultures of the Mesolithic followed the ending of the last cold phase and lasted till the introduction of agriculture and with it the Neolithic period. They varied greatly in duration in different regions.

The influence of these climatic alterations extended well beyond the periglacial zones. During the glacial phases, the wide, uninhabitable Eurasiatic tundra covered areas which, in the interglacial periods, would, as today, have had a temperate climate with forest. The southern outer tundra passed into a belt of dry and cold steppe, and this region of loess-sand wind

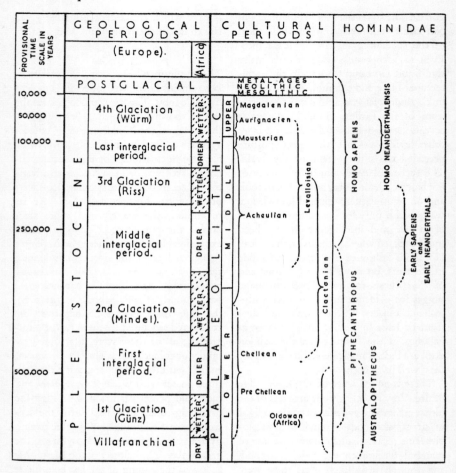

Table showing the probable chronological sequence of paleolithic cultures and of different forms of *Hominidae*, related to the climatic succession of the Pleistocene period. (The Villafranchian, it should be noted, may have lasted as long as the rest of the Pleistocene period). *(Courtesy of author)*

blown deposit, largely grassland, merged gradually into a zone of temperate forest which stretched well into the present Mediterranean region. The climate of the loess was continental, but even the warmest month was probably not more than 50° F.; the prevailing winds were predominantly dry glacial winds from the north-east. But these lands were of great economic importance for early man, probably in the third, and certainly in the fourth, glacial periods, for they provided ample grazing for great herds and their prey.

The extension of ice-cover and of the periglacial zones of the northern hemisphere shifted the whole system of climatic belts southwards and changed their character. The tropical and equatorial zones seem to have had greater rainfall than at present. In Africa, a chronological background is provided by these alternating wetter and drier periods. The four main pluvials are roughly in step with the major glaciations, though differing in duration from them. In these pluvials the dry belts, too, enjoyed a much increased rainfall and much of the Sahara would have carried a cover of scrub vegetation.

The interglacial periods, on the other hand, offered man hot and temperate regions of much greater extent than they are now. Exposed to these large changes of habitat, human populations underwent a marked physical and cultural transformation. Within half a million years the primitive varieties had been replaced by men of the modern kind. The Pleistocene fauna, even more at the mercy of changing conditions, altered considerably in distribution and in character; during much of the period man lived on many animals that have become extinct at the present day. European fauna which underwent marked evolutionary change include, for example, hyenas, cave and brown bears, voles, deer, elephants, mammoths and rhinoceros.

The pattern of human evolution in this vital period is indicated on page 6. It comprises a series of overlapping stages, each developing from the last, the whole forming a 'matrix' or genetic 'pool'. The fossil record displays a continuity and progression in the appearance of true men. We can apply this term equally to the varieties of the genus *Pithecanthropus* and to different species and sub-species of the genus *Homo*. The test is the manufacture of tools, for, together with the use of fire and other activities, this implies conceptual thought and the communication of com-

plex notions. The term 'human' on this definition can now, on our present information, be applied to some of the australo-pithecine Hominids.

Pithecanthropus is known to us from substantial finds in Java, from an impressive number of skeletons from China (so-called *Sinanthropus*), and a few jaws recently uncovered in Algiers (Ternifine man). Though a 'true' man, *Pithecanthropus* displays ape-like features. But his posture and gait were entirely human, and the bones of the leg differ from those of *Homo sapiens* in only a few minor particulars. Yet the balance of the head on the vertebral column is not quite as in modern man; the relatively large face juts forward and the jaws are massive (p. 4). The extensive ridges of bone over the forehead and the back of the head are somewhat ape-like, as are the orbits and the nose. The lower jaw is chinless, and in certain details intermediate between that of modern apes and modern man. The Chinese variant, however, does show a faint chin eminence. Though the jaw and palate are large, their contour is Hominid: in the teeth certain ape-like traits can be recognised.

The brain capacity affords a good index of the status of *Pithecanthropus*. The range extends from about 900 c.c. for the Javanese to as much as 1300 c.c. in some of the Chinese specimens which even overlap the modern value. These figures show the advance made by *Pithecanthropus* over the *Australopithecinae*.

The genus *Pithecanthropus* is thus regarded as the ancestral stage from which the ultimately distinct forms of mankind, *Homo neanderthalensis* and *Homo sapiens*, developed. These species emerge from within an intervening, rather complex, phase. It can best be described as consisting of a mixture, in different degrees and in different regions, of *sapiens* and Neander-thal; these have sometimes been called

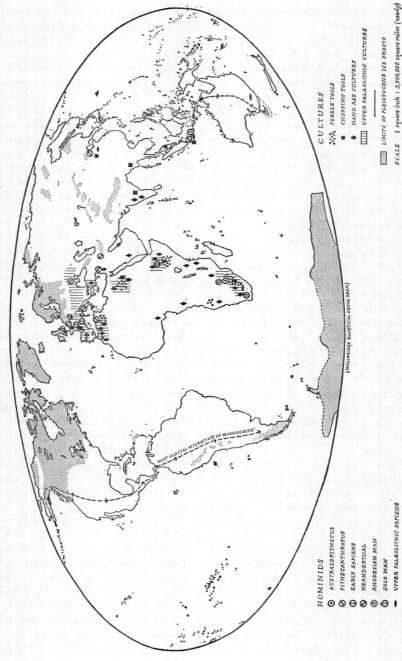

FINDS OF FOSSIL (PLEISTOCENE) HOMINIDS AND PALÆOLITHIC TOOLS

HOMINIDS

◉ AUSTRALOPITHECUS
⊘ PITHECANTHROPUS
⊕ EARLY SAPIENS
◍ NEANDERTHAL
◎ RHODESIAN MAN
◉ SOLO MAN
▮ UPPER PALÆOLITHIC SAPIENS

CULTURES

∴ PEBBLE TOOLS
■ CHOPPING TOOLS
◆ HAND AXE CULTURES
▥ UPPER PALÆOLITHIC CULTURES
░ LIMITS OF PLEISTOCENE ICE SHEETS

SCALE   1 square inch : 2,000,000 square miles (nearly)

(MOLLWEIDE ELLIPTICAL EQUAL AREA)

POST GLACIAL MIGRATION OF MONGOLOIDS

'early *sapiens*' and sometimes 'early Neanderthal'. They are represented by forms such as those found at Steinheim and Swanscombe of the second interglacial period; Ehringsdorf and Krapina in the third, and they persisted in the Mount Carmel population. As a connection between, say, Pekin man (*Sinanthropus*) and *Homo*, Steinheim man (p. 4) fits quite well both in time and in structure, with its relatively small cranium, its still prominent eye-brow ridges and lack of a chin eminence.

Pithecanthropus may well have persisted for some time after these early populations of *Homo* began to appear. It is also likely that the other varieties (some would call them species) of *Homo*—Rhodesian man and Solo (or Ngandong) man—from Java—represent regional end products of the *Pithecanthropus* stage. These forms have much in common with both Neanderthal and *sapiens* varieties, both early and late.

The 'classical' or fully-fledged Neanderthalers lived in western and Southern Europe during the first, severest, cold phase of the last glaciation. They were the first men to withstand such extremely cold conditions. But as a group they display a number of characteristics marking them off quite distinctly from modern man. These 'fully-fledged' Neanderthalers are known particularly from fossils in Western Europe; from Gibraltar, from La Chapelle-aux-Saints and Le Moustier in France and Sacco Pastore and Monte Circeo in Italy.

In these specimens the brain capacity on the average is large, varying from a figure similar to that of the largest *Pithecanthropus* (the Gibraltar skull is 1300 c.c.) to one well beyond the average for modern man (La Chapelle is 1600 c.c.). The skulls (p. 4) are in their length and breadth measurements as great as or even greater than modern man. But, as in *Pithecanthropus*, the forehead is receding and the vault is much lower; the back of the skull presents a rather characteristic flattened appearance, reminiscent in profile of the early Javanese and Chinese Hominids. Like these again, the skull bones tend to be very thick with a well-developed brow ridge, though with not so marked a buttressing on the occipital bone. The jaw is chinless and shows a number of other ape-like features; the teeth, when X-rayed, are often of that specialised kind called 'taurodont'—they are stumpy with short roots. The jaw socket, in its construction and its position relative to the ear hole, is in some respects reminiscent of the apes. The head is thrown forward to allow room for the movement of the massive lower jaw. Thus the contour of the occipital region is also reminiscent of that of *Pithecanthropus* and the Anthropoid apes. The limb bones of Neanderthal man, although similar to those of modern man and *Pithecanthropus*, also show some peculiarities. The bones are thick and clumsy; they are bowed and are shorter than those of modern man. But though Neanderthal man presents a brutish appearance in his carriage and posture, he was nevertheless responsible for a distinctive Paleolithic culture. The stone workmanship is characteristic, Mousterian or its derivatives, and at a number of sites there is evidence of fire-using and of a burial rite.

V

It was about 50,000 years ago that *Homo sapiens*, the present-day type of man, appeared everywhere. He supplanted all other non-*sapiens* varieties—Western Neanderthalers, the mixed Mount Carmel population, Solo man and Rhodesian man, who had reached the vicinity of The Cape of South Africa. With this decisive dispersion, some of the regional or 'racial' differences begin to appear. The Upper

Paleolithic populations in Europe are already much like modern groups—'nordic' and 'mediterranean'. They include the Aurignacian populations from the French sites of Combe-Capelle, Grimaldi and Cromagnon; the Magdalenian from Chancelade and Laugerie-Basse, also in France, and the east European Aurignacian from Predmost and Veronice. *Sapiens* men of the Upper Paleolithic from North and East Africa are also physically much like present-day inhabitants: in North Africa, the Mechta type; in the Sahara, the Asselar; in Kenya, the Oldoway type. In South Africa, the early *sapiens* have left a distinctive skull from Boskop showing some affinities with Hottentots and Negro, but it is only later that unmistakable representatives of the latter appear. In the Far East, few remains from the end of the Pleistocene period have come to light, but some authorities believe that Mongoloid features are noticeable in the Upper Paleolithic populations from the upper cave at Chou-kou-tien. The Wadjak skulls from Java and those from Talgai and Keilor in Australia, appear to be late Pleistocene forerunners of the Australoid division of mankind. By the time Europe entered the Mesolithic period, man's migration across Asia had reached the Behring Straits, and before about 6000 B.C., Mongoloid peoples had made their way into America and down to the tip of the South American continent (*see* Chapter 13).

These true men of the Paleolithic were capable of survival in harsh and varied conditions. The first Hominids, millennia before, undoubtedly began as sub-tropical or equatorial animals and they became uniquely equipped for life in hot conditions, if we can judge by the type and density of the sweat glands in present-day apes and man. The earliest undoubted tools, the split pebble tools in Africa, also come from warm regions, and those of Europe occur only in warm interglacial times. As we have seen, tropical Java was the homeland of the most primitive group of the *Pithecanthropus* genus; it seems that at the *Pithecanthropus* stage, for cultural and perhaps biological reasons, man was not yet equipped to endure the really severe conditions of the periglacial steppe. Only in the third glacial period, and for a limited time, do undoubted tools appear in these areas; their makers remain uncertain—they were probably men of the Steinheim-Swanscombe variety. But Neanderthal populations persisted successfully from the last interglacial into the first cold phase of the last glaciation. Some have supposed that their failure to survive beyond that time in Europe was an outcome of this period of isolation in periglacial regions and of ultimate unfitness for these conditions, though yet other Neanderthal-like non-*sapiens* populations in more equable climates disappeared at about this time or somewhat later. Destruction at the hands of *sapiens* men seems as likely a cause as extinction through climatic rigour. *Homo sapiens* alone passed successfully through the greatly contrasting environments of the last glaciation to become the sole survivor of the Hominid line some 50,000 years ago.

The extended range of *Homo sapiens* over such vast areas of the world is based primarily on a highly responsive and adaptable body, an efficient and flexible heat-regulating system, the ability to digest and metabolise diets of the most varied foodstuffs, and the capacity for sustained muscular activity. But the increasing mastery of a world environment was, of course, made possible by the development of his mental abilities, by his inventiveness, powers of learning and communication and his capacity for co-operative action.

Technologically, the first men could have made shift with a simple set of quite crude tools, as testified by the practice of food-gatherers of our own day. A pebble, or better still, a piece of flint, deliberately or even accidentally broken, can yield a cutting edge sharp enough to enable digging sticks and spears to be shaped. With these, edible roots can be dug out and small animals killed; on a technology as simple as this some Australian tribes still manage a precarious survival. While no woodwork has survived, split pebble tools and crudely worked flints are known from the early Pleistocene from many parts of the world—as we have seen, Oldowan pebble tools occur in the australopithecine strata.

To take advantage of large game demands more complex implements. For the stripping and cutting up of the carcase so as to transport and share it out, well-made flint knives are necessary; such knives will also serve for the shaping of spears and staves and the digging of pit traps for the hunting itself. Long before, *Pithecanthropus* in China had achieved just such a hunting technique. The cave of Chou-kou-tien is full of the broken bones of a large and varied collection of animals, including deer. The stone tools comprise crudely shaped choppers, useful for smashing bones, and large, roughly trimmed flakes serviceable enough as knives. These stone tools are in the tradition of the pebble-tool industries of Africa, where the next step was the implement called the hand-axe. This is a pear-shaped, symmetrical, and quite standardised tool, shaped from the core of a piece of flint. Hand-axes persisted for a long time practically everywhere, going through a number of stages of improvement. Those of early Acheulian design are found in Europe during the first interglacial period. Ternifine man in Algeria (allied to *Pithecanthropus*), made these Acheulian hand-axes in the second interglacial, as did the early *sapiens* man of Swanscombe. Ternifine man's hunting included hippopotamus, sabre-tooth tiger and elephant; like Pekin man he was obviously able to hunt in large teams.

Accompanying hand-axes are to be found tools made from flakes; they could be made deliberately or from the pieces detached in the course of shaping a core tool. Like hand-axes, flakes of simple or advanced types are found over a wide area of Europe, Africa and Asia, and likewise, men of different species made and used similar flake tools. In the second interglacial period, a more reliable and less wasteful method of striking off the flakes came into use. The core was first prepared to give a flattish upper surface, the nodule trimmed round to block out the desired shape and the flake was then detached. By this technique the nodule can be made to yield a whole series of fairly uniform sharp flakes. This 'prepared platform' method was widely adopted in Europe, Asia and Africa. It is an important ingredient in the Mousterian culture of Neanderthal man. Flakes produced by these and other methods serve many purposes—for cutting up animals, scraping the inside surface of skins, cutting down branches, scraping the shafts of spears or clubs. The flakes could also be hafted as spear points.

A kit of Lower and Middle Paleolithic stone implements might thus include a variety of hammerstones, chopping tools, crude knives, pointed flints and scrapers. Spherical stones tied together by thongs in groups of three or so could be used as hunting missiles known as bolas. With the manifold purposes to which they could be put, rather similar sets of implements would serve for the life in temperate forest, in the grassland steppe and in the warmer savannah. With variants and improvements, these were the tools which ensured human survival from the first to the third glaciation in Europe and for an even longer period in Africa.

The control over environment attained by early man rested on one other major acquisition—fire. Fire conferred great power. With it man could keep dangerous beasts out of caves and away from rock-shelters. With it he could drive game into pits or staked traps or over cliffs in organised hunts. The warming (and dim lighting) of caves opened the way to more northerly migrations. *Pithecanthropus* in China had learnt the uses of fire, obtaining it from some natural conflagration and carefully tending it, as did the Neanderthalers after him and the Andaman Islanders in recent times. Whether Pekin man cooked his food is not certain. But the charred bones found in many early Paleolithic hearths show that cooking was practised long before *sapiens* men came on the scene. Eating this far more easily and rapidly digested food—and meat with raw green-stuffs, berries and insects was the source of practically the whole energy supply in the hunter's diet—must have produced quite profound effects, not only on health, but on the jaw, the teeth and the cranium as a whole.

But the technical superiority of the Upper Paleolithic cultures of the now dominant *sapiens* man is clearly evident. Knowledge of fire-making was one mark of this. The first certain evidence of *sapiens* fire-making comes from a Magdalenian site. The technique was percussion. By striking a nodule of iron pyrites, sparks were obtained that would kindle dry tinder—a method still in vogue among Greenland Eskimos. The insufficiently hot flames produced by striking ordinary flint must have been observed for thousands of years before that. Fire-making by friction, as by the fire-drill, came much later, probably with the Neolithic, when it had become common practice to work a variety of materials by grinding, polishing and boring.

VI

The two final cold phases of the last glacial offered a challenge which was successfully overcome by the hunters of the great European grasslands. Caves and rock-shelters were extensively occupied, mostly in the winter; in summer, huts and tents could be constructed in the open. In central Europe, in the late Upper Paleolithic underground winter houses were built with supports and rafters of mammoth-bones and logs. Clothing gave warmth, and the success of the mammoth hunters rested on a much improved and expanded technology, not only in flints, but also in bone, horn and ivory. The needles and awls of bone for piercing skin testify to their skill. Instead of hand-axes, which persisted in many areas, particularly outside Europe, the basic tool of the cultures of Europe, the Mediterranean basin, Western Asia, North and East Africa, was the burin or stone chisel with an edge sharp enough to cut wood; with this precision-tool, awls, spearheads and harpoons of bone and antler were made on a large scale. In Magdalenian times, seals were harpooned and, by the Mesolithic, whales. The wooden spear was the main hunting weapon, and the spear-thrower was also used. Well-made spears could be tipped with bone points. Other common and highly serviceable tools were the backed stone blades, large and small, which could be used as knives for skinning and cutting up animals and for working wood.

The burin was the main tool of the engraver, for it was from the Aurignacian to the Magdalenian period that cave art flowered. Incised-line engravings were made on walls of caves and rock-shelters, on pieces of stone, bone or antler, and on weapons of these materials. The carvings of the period are important not merely for the skill displayed, but because they include objects such as the 'Venuses' or 'Mother Goddesses'. These are generally regarded as votive offerings of fertility cults. All this artistic activity, whether engraving, drawing, colour-painting, sculpture or modelling, underwent remarkable and complex changes of style, composition and expression. It demanded not only high artistic ability but great devotion and effort; the pigments (carbon black and various oxides of iron and manganese) had to be obtained from a variety of sources and then carefully prepared and mixed. The physical effort involved in the painting itself was often astonishing, for almost inaccessible rock surfaces were frequently used, and, indeed, most of the paintings are deep in the interior of the caves, so that lamps of hollowed out stones or animal skulls, with a wick of moss in animal fat, must have provided light.

While the Aurignacian and Magdalenian cultures were impressive European achievements, parallel developments went on in the stone and flint industry and in primitive art in areas of quite different climates and vegetation. The burin and the backed-blade are important tool types in North Africa, in Kenya, South Africa, the Middle East and India, though there are many traces of older traditions. Some art of the Upper Paleolithic age is to be found in East and North Africa, though most of the art there and in South Africa is later. The specialist can recognise much local variety in the technology of all these areas; but there is also much diffusion of ideas. The Aurignacian of the Middle East appears to have provided the stimulus for similar cultures to the west; while East Africa seems an important centre for developments which spread north and south.

With the great changes in climate and forest cover as the ice receded in northern Europe, the cultures naturally changed, and the Mesolithic has its own traditions of flint working; the hunting and fishing and the wood-working techniques are based on an extremely skilful 'microlithic' culture. There was a great use of bone, and cave-art in Spain and in Africa is largely based on the Mesolithic. The bow is thought to have been introduced from North Africa at this time. The polishing and grinding of materials from the end of the Upper Paleolithic onwards led in due course to its application to flint, and so to the highly efficient stone axes and adzes of the Neolithic farmers. Domestication of the dog in Mesolithic times, or earlier still, presages the domestication of other animals in the Neolithic.

VII

The species of man which emerged from the Paleolithic world was single and highly adaptable. Although, as a result of its evolutionary past, its world-wide dispersal and its exposure to the vicissitudes of late Pleistocene times, it had acquired considerable variation, it remained a single biological species—a network of inter-related populations. Biological continuance did not demand, as with many other far-ranging species, a sacrifice of this unity, for environmental pressure did not lead to the splitting up into separate, specialised, and hence reproductively incompatible, varieties or secondary species. To be sure, *Homo sapiens* did not wholly escape the influence of ecological selection, and this is displayed in the regional variation of some bodily characters for example, in physique, in hair form and in pigmentation. But these are modifications only of degree, so that adjacent populations invariably intergrade and overlap. In spite of the racialist myths politically popular, there never have been 'pure' or homogeneous races, and racial distinctions remain genetically only partial. By the end of the Pleistocene, *Homo sapiens* was to a large extent the 'polytypic' species of today, with constituent populations bearing the marks of the main 'racial' groups recognisable today.

Biological unity and resistance to break up as a single species are due to a variety of causes. First, whatever his geographical or 'racial' origins, man possesses the general quality of adapting himself physically to new conditions. He is not utterly dependent on special genes to enable him to withstand changes of habitat, although, as we have seen, some localised geographical variation in certain characters has evolved. As far as our evidence goes, much, perhaps most, of the tolerance, for example, to the extreme heat or extreme cold displayed by indigenous peoples living in a stone-age culture, such as the primitive people of Tierra del Fuego at the extreme tip of South America or the Australian aborigines, especially where their material resources are poor, is an acquired and not an inborn quality.

The relative freedom from locally 'fixed' genotypes rests partly on this physiological responsiveness, but even more on cultural adaptability—equally a general human character since it rises from the mental attributes common to mankind. Hence, the changes of technique and style in tools for food getting, for making shelters and clothing. Nothing is more striking about Pleistocene man, dispersed as he was, than the repeated diffusion of new techniques from different centres of invention and from continent to continent. This technical knowledge made man less dependent on purely biological qualities than he had been. It implies also that communities did not become permanently isolated and that some inter-breeding always occurred. Hybridisation was much intensified, of course, in the Neolithic period and onwards, as populations grew denser and migrations became larger and more frequent.

Even in the Paleolithic, within the limits set by hunting economies, man's growing reliance on control of his surroundings is apparent. Such power as he could command derived not only from the manipulation of material objects, but from the organisation and ordering of the community. Soon there appeared the complex behaviour so characteristic of man's subsequent history. Thus, in technology there was not a continuous development, but an intermingling of stages of stagnation and of innovation. Long periods when industries remained unchanged, or even regressed, were followed by periods of advance when tool types multiplied, became specialised and attained greater precision. The rate at which tradition gives way to change varies, but their intermingling is a universal feature. As a social being, Paleolithic man displayed only too clearly the contradictory attitudes of co-operation and conflict. Successful hunting of bison, mammoth or horses demands closer collaboration than the trapping of small animals and gathering of simple food. But co-operative activity existed side by side with violence and aggression. Pleistocene man, armed with his weapons of the hunt, could and did prey upon his fellow-man. Cannibalism was practised by *Pithecanthropus*, by Neanderthalers and by *sapiens* man.

The manipulation of things and persons, on which primitive society depended for survival, had far-reaching effects on man as an intellectual being. For it led, no doubt insidiously, to some degree of self-awareness; to a growing realisation, felt rather than formulated, of the 'separateness' of mankind from the natural world. This appreciation of an order of things, implicit only in the *Pithecanthropus* stage, flares up in the cave art 300,000 years later. The cave art is in essence an achievement which springs from some awareness of a 'humankind' opposed to, yet dependent on, 'nature'. For here is an accurate record of the hunter's world, intensely observed and experienced. The supreme importance to the life of the community of the game animals depicted cannot be doubted. More than that, it has been strongly argued from the content of the paintings and by analogy with the practices of still surviving savage societies, that the paintings, so often superimposed in profusion on the same rock-surfaces, were accompaniments of magico-religious ceremonies for ensuring the success of the hunter and the abundance of game. The famous painting of the masked 'sorcerer' of Trois Frères, set as a tableau behind a raised platform or 'pulpit' deep in the recesses of the cave, strongly supports this interpretation. The 'Venus' figurines of the Aurignacian are additional evidence of fertility cults. Whether as decoration or as 'documentary' record, or as sympathetic magic or even as self-expression, in the cave art man puts a projection of his own interests and values on his surroundings. Like primitive peoples surviving today, Upper Paleolithic communities found the power of their technology too limited for the difficulties and mysteries of the world; they had resort to the special techniques or cults of magic and religion. Hence the treatment of the dead, who were given careful burial even by Neanderthal man and who, by Upper Paleolithic peoples, were often coated with red ochre, presumably as life-giving material, and provided with implements and food.

The total culture of Upper Paleolithic peoples leaves no doubt of their capacity for conceptual thought, their imaginative power, their ordering and transmission of ideas. Their culture clearly demands well-developed language, and both their abstract and representational art shows their facility for the symbolism and the conventions of spoken language. We cannot be surprised at the amazing proliferation of myth and ceremonial or at the elaborate social and kinship rules which primitive societies display; for it is in the realm of language and of notions about behaviour and social relationships that primitive man finds a relative freedom of action. In this way, a materially poor society comes into possession of a highly complicated social code, much of which is non-rational accretion, though much is, of course, practically useful or even vital to the survival of the community.

It is in the material world that primitive man remains severely constrained. The hunting economies, even at their most successful, can attain only an uneasy and insecure equilibrium; this is expressed in the meagre population of Paleolithic times and of all savage societies today. The hunting culture is a precarious subsistence economy which supports only the family group over a large territory; there is no surplus to support non-producers; the growth of population is limited by the poverty of resources, by disease and the hazards of the life. Most of these hunters were dead by thirty.

The stalemate of the Paleolithic and Mesolithic way of life was broken at last by the invention of agriculture. The promise of Upper Paleolithic man now obtains a greatly enlarged scope. Technology advances; communities work together in larger and more complicated units; food production, now more dependable and predictable, allows a surplus for craftsmen who are not mainly engaged in farming. The increase in population means an aggregation of more brain-power and the survival of many more able or gifted individuals. As the Neolithic settlements grow into villages and towns, as farming becomes dependent on elaborate systems of irrigation; as trade develops and metal-making begins, the time comes when the unaided human brain proves inadequate for recording and storing the mass of social data, and the invention of writing is forced upon mankind.

2 THE NEOLITHIC REVOLUTION AND THE FOUNDATION OF CITIES: MESOPOTAMIA, EGYPT, THE INDUS VALLEY, CHINA

by John Davies Evans

We now have to consider a crucial phase in human history. The catch-phrase 'Neolithic Revolution' with which V. Gordon Childe summed up the effects of these changes and developments, has now passed into general archaeological use; it contains no exaggeration in its implied comparison with the changes of the Industrial Revolution of the later eighteenth and nineteenth centuries. A series of interrelated developments determined all the later achievements of human societies for which they were the indispensable prerequisite. Had it not been for these changes, it seems unlikely that any human societies more complex than the small groups, which are all that a purely hunting and gathering economy can generally permit, would ever have come into being at all. Indeed, there is no other economic movement in human history with which they can be compared in their revolutionary and far-reaching effects. On the other hand, the term 'revolution' must not be taken too literally in its suggestion of a sudden, violent change. The period of time during which the Neolithic Revolution was carried to completion in its original area was indeed relatively short in relation to the span of human history as a whole, but it must be reckoned in millennia, and the individuals who lived during

those centuries were probably all quite unconscious of any sharp change in their way of life.

A period so pregnant with consequences for humanity obviously deserves the most careful study. Since no system of writing was known anywhere in the world at that time (for writing was one of the indirect consequences of the revolution itself), the evidence must be sought in the material remains, and the task falls chiefly to the prehistoric archaeologist, assisted more and more by zoologists, climatologists and other experts in natural science. Over the past twenty years particularly, archaeologists have investigated the problems of this phase of human history; new data have piled up very rapidly, and are still doing so. It is thus now even more difficult than before to give a connected account of the period without doing violence to some of the facts. The results of the many excavations are as yet not fully published, the evidence is, or appears, contradictory, and experts are sharply divided in their opinions on many points. Moreover, new facts which may alter the picture considerably are pouring in almost daily, and it seems unlikely that the flow will stop for a long time. We can, therefore, merely set out the results so far obtained, and the provisional conclusions which can be drawn from them. At the same time, the recent discoveries are not only exciting in themselves, but they have already shed a flood of new light on the processes at work, and have provided vivid glimpses of human life and activity during a crucial period.

The momentous significance of this phase was only gradually forced upon the attention of archaeologists. They first recognised it as a distinct period because the kinds of objects which they found on Neolithic sites differed markedly from those to be found in the earlier Paleolithic, or Old Stone Age, context. In the latter period, tools were made entirely with *chipped* stone, whereas on the more recent sites implements of *polished* stone were found. Hence the name Neolithic (Greek *neos*, new, *lithos*, a stone) or New Stone Age, with which it was baptised. This minor technological distinction has long ceased to be essential for distinguishing the new age; it remains merely one diagnostic trait among others, though one not entirely to be trusted, since polished stone objects have been found in assemblages which are not in any other sense Neolithic. However, the name remains firmly established by custom, and, though in some ways misleading, is still a convenient label. But for the prehistorian today the fundamental difference between the Paleolithic and the Neolithic is economic, not a mere contrast in implements. Throughout the long ages of the Paleolithic, man was dependent for food on what he could catch or gather, but in the new period he succeeded in discovering how to produce it. That is to say, he contrived to domesticate certain animals and he began to sow the seeds of various grasses and reap the harvests.

This is the really important achievement that divides these men off from all who went before them—of which the greater variety of materials found on their sites is merely a reflection. The abundance of polished stone axes and adzes, the widespread development of the arts of pottery and weaving, the construction of more permanent houses, and the rest were all consequent on this achievement, but were in no way essentially connected with it. For these things do not necessarily appear in communities which demonstrably had some knowledge of agriculture and herding, or not until after a long interval, whilst some of them do appear now and then among food-gathering communities who certainly had no such knowledge. But it was undoubtedly the greater security of life consequent upon a more certain food supply which paved the way for the full development of these and many other arts in the Neolithic and later periods, and which alone made the ultimate achievement of civilisation possible.

There have indeed been remarkable flowerings of culture among communities of food-gatherers where the environment has been exceptionally favourable; for instance among the Upper Paleolithic hunters of South-West Europe who produced the remarkable cave art of France and Spain, or the Haida Indians of the north-west coast of America with their remarkable stylised art. But such achievements last only as long as the circumstances which produce them. When conditions alter, they vanish without trace, as did the culture of the cave artists. With the advent of food producing, on the other hand, men took a crucial step towards emancipating themselves from the thraldom of absolute dependence on their environment, and so made the continuity of cultural tradition less liable to sudden interruption.

Whilst it is still rather uncertain whether

the invention of agriculture and herding took place only once or several times in the history of mankind, there is now relatively little doubt where it first happened. All the available evidence points unequivocally to Western Asia. It was here that communities based on stock-breeding and primitive agriculture first emerged. This is an area long regarded by Western man as the cradle of civilisation, but it has only recently been possible to show why this was so. A long history of settled life in peasant villages underlies and leads up to the first flowerings of civilisation. Peasant farming was the soil out of which civilisation was ultimately to grow.

The change-over to food production is the result of the domestication of animals and the realisation that food plants could be deliberately grown. To some extent these two developments run parallel and even react on each other, but animal domestication undoubtedly began first, though it was less important than agriculture in bringing about a change to settled life. The domestication of certain animals may, of course, take place without changing the habits of food-gathering groups in any essential way. This is so with scavengers, such as the dog, which would first of all become tolerated in the camp and later be found useful. The dog was soon found to be a good auxiliary in hunting, and it does in fact seem to be the earliest domestic animal. Bones of dogs are well known among the remains on sites belonging to the later Mesolithic food-gathering groups. Nomadic animals, like sheep and goats, for which the settled life of Neolithic communities would have been less suitable, seem to have been domesticated before the end of the Mesolithic, or Middle Stone Age. There is in fact a growing amount of archaeological evidence for this. Reindeer also come into this category, and groups whose economy is based on reindeer breeding have tended to remain nomadic. Other animals, however, such as cattle, need more settled conditions for domestication to be possible, at any rate in the early stages, and their remains tend first to appear along with the earliest traces of agriculture in settled villages.

Agriculture, on the other hand, is not really compatible with nomadic life. It is true that some Bedouin tribes are known who sow a crop on suitable land and either wait for it to come up or return in time for the harvest, but this practice remains purely incidental to their economy, whereas dependence on agriculture demands a more or less settled existence. Thus whilst mobile hunting groups may have reaped wild grasses, or even have sown on the off-chance of reaping a crop, their increasing dependence on the harvest for a livelihood led inevitably to loss of mobility because of the constant attention necessary to ensure it, and so to the growth of more permanent settlements.

II

At the end of the last Ice Age, which we can put at roughly about 10,000 B.C., the regions of the Near East which have been mentioned as the home of the first food-producing communities were still inhabited, like Europe and the rest of the world, by small groups of hunters with a purely gathering economy. The gradual retreat of the ice sheets around the pole and of the ice-caps of the big mountain ranges was accompanied by corresponding changes in climate, which varied from region to region, but tended generally towards amelioration. The Near Eastern lands were never actually under ice themselves. But the cyclones which now pass across Central Europe were deflected southwards across the Mediterranean and brought more rain to the now desiccated lands of North Africa, Mesopotamia, Persia and Arabia. Many areas which are now barren were then covered with vegetation and supported abundant animal and plant life.

Present evidence seems to suggest that climatic change in Postglacial times was very gradual in Western Asia as a whole, and that human activity there since the beginning of Neolithic times, particularly deforestation and overgrazing of grasslands, has had more to do with the production of the present conditions than any climatic factor. Thus the old idea that desiccation due to changed climatic conditions forced men to take to protecting and breeding plants and animals, and thus to become food producers, is not now favoured. It seems much more likely that mixed farming communities developed out of very gradual changes in habits due to a complex of factors which produced a gradual drift, or trend, in this direction. The development of farming must represent the gradual exploitation of new possibilities of the environment rather than resulting from any failure of resources for pursuing a nomadic hunting and gathering existence of the old type.

Whatever the explanation may be, the facts remain, and it is not solely archaeological evidence on which we have to rely. It can be shown that only in the Near East at the end of the Pleistocene could all the wild ancestors of the main domesticated species of plants and animals be found together. This has been demonstrated not only from finds of archaeological sites, but also from the present day distribution of the wild species. North Africa, which on other grounds (climatically, for instance) would seem to be an equally suitable area for the origins of food-production, lacks some of these wild ancestors of our domes-

ticated animals. In particular, it has no wild sheep, whilst the Near East possesses three which have all given rise to domesticated species.

When we come to consider the archaeological evidence itself, the balance is still heavily in favour of the Near East as opposed to North Africa, and whilst we cannot as yet completely rule out Egypt as a possible independent centre of food production, no site has yet been found there showing evidence of farming as old as some of those now known in Western Asia. We shall therefore concentrate mainly on the Asiatic evidence, taking into account the Egyptian only as it becomes relevant.

Professor R. J. Braidwood has distinguished three phases in the change-over from food gathering to food production: first a terminal period of the food gathering stage when hunting groups did not range as widely as before in pursuit of game, but concentrated on exploiting more fully the resources of a limited area; secondly a period of incipient, experimental agriculture and animal domestication; and finally arising out of the more successful experiments, the rise of stable village communities based on relatively efficient mixed farming. Though some of the most recent evidence seems at first to be inconsistent with this classification, I think that it is still basically valid, and may serve us as a rough guide in grouping our material, though, as Braidwood himself admits, it cannot be absolutely foolproof. Its greatest advantage is that it is based purely on economic criteria, and therefore allows us to dispense with terms like Mesolithic and Neolithic, which, with their strictly technological implications, are now irrelevant to the main issues. Like them, however, it is a classification of stages, and has no chronological implications. Chronology, for this period, depends on radio-carbon dating.* There are now enough radiocarbon dates to provide us with a rough framework of absolute chronology, but we need many more before we can begin to pretend to any real exactitude.

The materials available to illustrate Braidwood's first phase are not at present very extensive. But there is some evidence in the caves of Turkey, Palestine, Syria and Iraq of the activities of groups of hunters with a flint industry of basically late Upper Paleolithic type, but including also numbers of the very small flints known as microliths. These were used in conjunction with wood or bone to make compound implements of various kinds, and are considered typical of the Mesolithic technological stage. At the caves of Palegawra and Shanidar (the latter dated by Carbon 14 to c. 10,000 B.C.) in northern Iraq the animal bones associated with these flints included those of sheep, goat, pig, horse, deer and gazelle—all presumably wild, but the first four at any rate tamable.

The next stage is of more importance. It is the most vital, and, at the moment, it presents us with the biggest problems. Many of these are insoluble on our present evidence, and we are probably just at the beginning of an era of fresh discoveries. Already we know that it occupied a long time, and probably included many diverse experiments, some of which became incorporated in the main stream, whilst

* The radio-carbon (or Carbon 14) method of dating is an extremely complex process. It relies on measuring the amount of the radioactive isotope of carbon present in samples of organic matter collected from sites. Since this amount is fixed during life, and decays at a known rate afterwards, it is theoretically possible to calculate the period which has elapsed since death occurred. There are still a great many difficulties, but archaeologists are coming to rely more and more on this method of dating, especially for the periods for which no written records exist.

others died out, and left no trace. The area covered by these beginnings, too, may be a good deal larger than that in which the process finally reached its culmination. It may, in fact, extend from the Caspian Sea to North-West Africa. In North Africa there are indications of this phase in cave and midden sites, and equivalent sites are known in Egypt and the Sudan. In the Near East also a number of sites are known which give us glimpses of it. It is nevertheless difficult to recognise and evaluate the traces of the beginnings of food-production, since, as V. Gordon Childe said, 'cultivators can hardly be recognised unless they had standardised implements of durable material for tilling the soil, reaping and processing the crop', whilst 'to identify stock-breeders on acid soils where bones dissolve or within the natural habitat of domesticable animals is almost hopeless'.

At a higher level in the deposits of the Shanidar cave there was found a most interesting assemblage. The flint industry was poorer than before, but a whole set of new pecked and ground objects had appeared, which included querns for grinding up seeds, pestles and mortars, pounders, hammer stones, etc. Probably contemporary with this stratum at Shanidar was an open village site, Zawi Chemi, which was found nearby in the valley of the Great Zab. This consisted of remains of circular stone huts made of river boulders, and it may represent the summer quarters of the people who were living in the Shanidar cave. The material found includes querns, mortars and pounders, but also bone sickle shafts. Red deer, sheep and goat were hunted, and by the latest stage of the occupation sheep had perhaps been domesticated. A number of burials, chiefly of women and children, were found at the Shanidar cave belonging to this period of occupation. Some were accompanied by grave-goods and they were associated with stone platforms suggestive of a funerary cult. A date of about 9000 B.C. is suggested for this stage by radiocarbon determinations from both the village and the cave. Some other early settlements are known in northern Iraq which seem slightly later than Zawi Chemi. They include Karim Shahir, M'lefaat and Gird Chai. These do something to link it with later developments in this area, but it seems possible that the sequence may still not be complete. A similar early stage on the road to food production is now known from the southern Zagros in western Iran, where the site of Ali Kosh had produced evidence of goat herding, and also of the cultivation of emmer wheat and two-row barley, as well as of the systematic collection of seeds and wild legumes and a considerable amount of hunting. According to the Carbon 14 dates, however, the Ali Kosh site would have been inhabited about two millennia later than Zawi Chemi and Shanidar.

Far to the south, in Palestine, materials which appear to belong to an early part of the transitional phase have also been known for some time from the caves of Mount Carmel. They constitute what is known as the Natufian culture. Their originators were hunters whose chief game was deer, and who fished with bone hooks and harpoons. These people paid great attention to personal adornment, as is shown by their elaborate necklaces of bone and shell, and they also embellished objects of daily use with naturalistic animal carvings. They apparently lived in relatively easy conditions and had leisure to think of other things than merely getting enough to eat. Though their economy was basically a gathering one, some of the finds suggested activities which could have led on to the development of agriculture. For instance, deer-ribs were found which had been

grooved along one side to hold a series of flint blades. The gloss on the edges of these flints showed that they had been used for cutting some sort of grass. Moreover, some circular basins hammered out of the rock in front of one of the caves might have been intended for pounding grass seeds, and pestles were also a part of the Natufian equipment. Palestine is a likely home for wild barley and emmer wheat.

The Natufian culture gave rise at a very early date to some remarkable developments, the most striking of which took place around the copious perennial spring at Jericho in the Jordan valley. Here a shrine had been established by Natufian hunters in the tenth millennium B.C. Eventually this was burnt, but occupation continued on the site. At first this was perhaps only seasonal, but eventually there developed a permanent settlement. Gradually, a low mound was formed by the debris of houses, which seem to have been rather flimsy structures, so that it has not been possible to make out the plans, though it seems certain that they had clay walls. This first permanent settlement at Jericho must represent the beginnings of a real food-producing economy, and though as yet there is no direct evidence available to document this, subsequent developments at Jericho leave little doubt that it was so. A most interesting feature of this basal tell was the occurrence in the settlement debris of pieces of obsidian, a black volcanic glass produced by volcanic eruptions which was much prized in early times for making cutting tools. This is of relatively rare occurrence, and the nearest sources to Jericho are in Turkey. It also occurs at Zawi Chemi, and presumably must represent some kind of early 'trade', though it is not possible at the moment to say how far this may have been organised.

About 8000 B.C. a kind of 'population explosion' seems to have occurred at

Jericho. There was no break in the cultural development, but there was a rapid and spectacular development in size and social organisation. This was presumably due to the introduction of a full food-producing economy; emmer wheat and barley have been found in these levels. This settlement of the 'Pre-Pottery A' culture, as it is called, covered about ten acres, and had houses built of plano-convex mud bricks which have been christened 'hog-backed' bricks, and having near-circular rooms sunk beneath ground level and entered either by sloping ramps or steps with wooden treads. These rooms may have been domed, with a roofing of plastered branches, and the floors were of beaten mud. This settlement was defended by a large wall of rough stones, which still survives to a height of over eleven feet. At one point in it was found a massive stone tower twenty-five feet high at present and thirty feet across. A stairway leading down through the centre of this tower may have been designed either for manning the tower or for obtaining water from the spring. At all events, it is a remarkable architectural and engineering feat which must have demanded considerable social organisation. These defences were renewed at least twice, and were finally strengthened by the cutting of a ditch twenty-seven feet wide and eight feet deep in the rock fronting the wall. This feat is sufficiently impressive at so early a period as this appears to be, and there may of course be other towers in the full circuit of the walls.

The people who succeeded these first settlers at Jericho were a new folk with different traditions. Perhaps they conquered the older inhabitants, as some burials of the latter high up in the silt of the tower staircase might suggest. Certainly they built quite different houses, with several rectangular rooms. The building was of cigar-shaped bricks, and the walls and floors were covered with highly polished plaster. They still knew nothing of pottery, but the stone bowls which they used instead and the flint implements they made were of quite new types. Their settlement also had a stone wall around it. Considerable traces of their religious cults have been found. In one room a small column of volcanic rock had been set on a pedestal as a cult object, and small female figurines were found of a type which is normally taken to indicate a fertility cult. But perhaps the most startling finds of this kind were a series of skulls with the features restored in plaster. In Polynesia, skulls of enemies or ancestors were until recently treated in this way; the skulls at Jericho seem most likely to be ancestors, since they were derived from headless burials beneath the floors of the houses in which they were found. This phase seems to occupy the seventh millennium B.C.

A gap of at least a few hundred years follows the end of the Pre-Pottery B settlement at Jericho, during which the site lay unoccupied, though eventually it was reoccupied by people who were making primitive pottery, but whose social organisation and general culture seem to have been at a considerably lower level.

When first excavated in the 1950s, Jericho was the only site of its kind known in Palestine, and it is still the most remarkable in size and complexity. Its special development in the pre-pottery phases may have been partly due to its spring and to an environment rich in other opportunities, but partly also to the command of natural resources such as the salt, bitumen and sulphur of the Dead Sea. Some of its prosperity may have come from trading in these materials; obsidian, nephrite, cowrie shells and other exotic materials which were found in the remains strengthen this impression that trading activities were an important part of the life of pre-pottery Jericho. But the Jericho tell is no longer the sole representative of this stage in Palestine. A number of other sites, some of them perhaps more typical of the average settlement of the period, are now known. They include Nahal Oren, a settlement on Mount Carmel, where circular houses with stone foundations have been identified. They are between two and five metres in diameter, and each contained a central stone fireplace. At Beidha, near Petra, a settlement site covering about two acres has been found and excavated. This has sub-rectangular houses with plaster floors. The flint industry of these sites, and, in the case of Beidha, the house types also, link them rather closely with the Pre-Pottery B occupation at Jericho.

Evidence of other remarkable developments resulting from experiments in food production has come in recent years from Turkey. Here little is still known of the Mesolithic background out of which they developed. On the south coast of Turkey the two caves of Belbasi and Beldibi show an interesting development from a Mesolithic (or terminal food-gathering) stage to a rudimentary Neolithic (or incipient food-producing) stage, though the material was not rich enough to document the process very fully. Of prime importance in the early food-producing stage, however, is the enormous site of Çatal Hüyük, on the Konya plain, which represents the remains of a settlement covering thirty-two acres, and which was occupied from *c.* 6500 to *c.* 5600 B.C. It has some striking similarities to Jericho Pre-Pottery Neolithic B, with which it is probably partly contemporary, but the cultural remains are in many ways much more spectacular. The rooms were rectangular in plan and each house consisted of a number of such rooms; the walls

were of mud brick on a brick foundation. The buildings consisted of only a single storey, and were so crowded together that movement within the settlement had to be across the roofs. There was no defensive wall, as at Jericho, but a continuous frontage of windowless house walls served the same defensive purpose. Benches served for sitting in the houses, and the dead were buried below the floors. About forty of the rooms excavated seem to have been shrines, and a remarkable picture of the religion of the Çatal Hüyük people was obtained from the contents of these rooms and the elaborate paintings on the walls, which were usually preserved to a considerable height. The paintings represent scenes of life and death, sometimes set contrastingly on different walls of the room. Sexual symbols, breasts and bulls (including sculptured bulls' heads fitted with real horns) are prominent among the recurring motifs; in some scenes vultures appear, which seem to be symbolic of death, and on occasion are actually seen devouring human carcasses. The stone and clay statues which were found in great variety also emphasise the sexual emphasis; they include both female and male figures of different ages, sometimes associated with animals (leopards are favourites), while in a few cases the figures are grouped.

The basis of the economic life of the Çatal Hüyük settlement was agriculture, and the crops grown included wheat of various kinds, barley, peas, vetches, etc. Wild cattle were hunted and there were domesticated cattle also in the later phases at any rate, and perhaps domesticated sheep also. Deer were hunted and nuts and wild berries collected for various purposes.

Technologically, the Çatal Hüyük people were remarkably skilful. Their work in flint and obsidian was of the highest standard, and they also worked various hard stones to make fine ornaments. Copper and lead were also employed in small quantities for this purpose. Containers were made chiefly of wood or basketry; pottery was also known, though they did not develop this medium much, presumably finding the other materials adequate for most purposes. There is also evidence that the Çatal Hüyük people, like those of pre-pottery Jericho, benefited from a fairly highly developed system of 'trade'. They probably controlled the important sources of obsidian deposited by the volcanoes of Karaca Dag and Hasan Dag (both probably still active at that time), which lie at the eastern end of the Konya plain. In return for this, they received fine flint from Syria, sea shells from the Mediterranean, and various kinds of exotic stones from different places.

Çatal Hüyük is an amazing site, only comparable with Jericho as yet as an example of precocious social development resulting from the first successful attempts at exploiting the resources of a rich environment in a new way. Like that of pre-pottery Jericho, however, its culture vanished, and seems to have had little direct effect on succeeding developments in Anatolia. In the story of the development of civilisation, both these sites seem like brilliant comets which appear and disappear with equal abruptness. So far as we can see at the moment, they were dead ends which led to nothing, and played no real part in the definitive development of civilisation in the two great river valleys. More important for later developments in Anatolia are the much smaller sixth millennium villages of Can Hasan and Hacilar, the one in the Konya plain, the other in the Burdur region of South-west Anatolia, whose culture, based on a fully developed mixed farming economy, was characterised by a beautiful painted pottery.

III

After the rather heady speculations to which the Jericho and Çatal Hüyük discoveries have given rise, the evidence of relatively poor and meagre beginnings which confronts us elsewhere is something of an anti-climax. Nevertheless, some of these will lead us on to greater achievements than any attained by the early Jerichoans. Whilst Palestine and Anatolia remain areas in which fully-literate city life was attained relatively late, Mesopotamia and Egypt reached this stage surprisingly quickly from less promising beginnings. After Zawi Cherni, Karim Shahir and the others mentioned earlier, the next stage in Mesopotamia is represented by the settlement of Jarmo, a small mound of habitation debris, again lying on the flanks of the hilly zone, which covers about three acres and reaches a height of about twenty-five feet. The debris had accumulated since the settlement was rebuilt about a dozen times. The buildings were rectangular, with walls made of packed mud and sometimes set on stone foundations. Objects of flint and stone were found, including querns and flint sickles, and the study of grain-impressions on the mud walls and oven floors made it possible to recognise two types of wheat and barley in an early stage of domestication. Ninety-five per cent of the animal bones were those of sheep, goat, pig and ox. A study of the sheep and goat remains indicated that a very high proportion of the animals killed were immature, and therefore probably domesticated. Trade is indicated by the occurrence of objects of obsidian, which must have come from Turkey. Pottery, however, is found only in the upper third of the deposit, though clay-lined ovens, baked in place, were known from the beginning. Clay female figurines attest a fertility cult.

At Jarmo we thus have a settled village

which must have persisted over a considerable period. It belongs to the beginning of Braidwood's third phase of efficient village farming. Some advance on this primitive community is seen in the mounds of Hassuna and Matarrah, and in the earliest deposits at Nineveh. These sites, all in northern Iraq, show us the peasant economy of Jarmo well dug-in and almost monotonously set in its ways. There are several varieties of pottery, and there are simple tools made of baked clay, as well as the usual stone, flint and bone industries. The houses are well-built, mud-walled affairs, with curved rooms, in the lower levels, and, later, rectangular rooms but otherwise not particularly exciting. The only artistic outlet seems to have been in the decoration of pottery, which is painted or incised. Obsidian from Turkey and shells from the Persian Gulf attest the continuance and widening of trade relations.

It seems now to be fairly generally accepted that the Jarmo materials fall in the earlier part of the seventh millennium (c. 6750) B.C., a date indicated by radio-carbon tests. This would lead us to think that the beginning of the Hassuna phase should be dated in the end of that millennium, which seems reasonable. By 6000 B.C. peasant farming villages are well established over a wide area of the Near East, and quite a number of sites, or levels in sites, outside Iraq can be assigned to this phase. Among these would be the earliest settlements at Ras Shamra, in Syria, Byblos in the Lebanon and Mersin in southern Turkey. There are also sites in Egypt which illustrate an equivalent stage. Some of these have been found on the old shoreline of a now much-reduced lake in the Fayum in Lower Egypt. These people cultivated wheat, barley and flax and kept pigs, cattle, sheep and goats. They reaped their grain with sickles set with flint teeth and stored it in silos dug in the ground

and lined with straw matting. Grain was ground on the usual querns. Fishing was also practised with bone harpoons and hunting with bows and arrows. Potting was well-developed, though the pots remained simple, and polished stone axes and mace-heads were common. Radio-carbon tests have been made on some of this material and the results indicate a date in the second half of the fifth millennium B.C., though this may well turn out to be too low. A slightly later stage is illustrated by the site of Merimde on the western edge of the Delta, whilst in Upper Egypt the so-called Badarian culture is the earliest known, though it has not yet been possible to date it by the radio-carbon method.

There is, then, abundant evidence that by the sixth millennium B.C. the peasant farming economy was well established over the whole Near East, and more particularly in northern Mesopotamia, though apparently not till considerably later in the Nile Valley. Mesopotamia and Egypt are the two traditional centres of the earliest civilisations, and if by this we understand the first literate societies, living in cities, and having a complex social and political structure and division of labour among many kinds of specialists, archaeology has abundantly confirmed this assumption. We must now see how those civilisations arose out of the general level of the peasant farming economy with its village organisation, and why these two areas were most favourable to this development. Since the process itself, the reasons for it, and the type of civilisation evolved were very different, it will be most convenient to follow the story separately in each area. We will begin with Mesopotamia.

IV

The Hassuna phase in Iraq was followed by a series of later phases each showing a greater mastery of techniques and an increasing complexity of material and spiritual culture. The phase which immediately succeeds that of Hassuna, known as the Halafian, is characterised by a very finely made and elaborately decorated painted pottery, baked in a kiln. It is found, with some local variations, over a considerable area which extends well outside the frontiers of modern Iraq. Its home, however, seems to be in the northern parts of Syria and Iraq, where its development can be followed out. Evidence of agriculture is abundant on the Halafian sites, and rough clay models of female human beings and animals attest the continuance of the fertility cult. Trade is also well attested by the exotic materials found at the sites, and metal, in the shape of small copper ornaments, begins to appear. There is unfortunately, less evidence concerning the extent and organisation of the villages, but we know that houses with rectangular rooms continued in use, though at the site of Arpachiyah several examples of a circular domed structure, entered by a covered passage, were found.

The Halaf culture must fall in time in the later part of the sixth millennium (*c.* 5000) B.C. and beginning of the fifth. At this time southern Mesopotamia, and the later home of the Sumerian civilisation, was still uninhabited, and it was only in the next phase, called the Ubaidian, that it was finally colonised. For some reason this area had previously been unattractive to settlers. Why this was so is not entirely clear. Perhaps it was all new land, recently emerged from the floor of the Persian Gulf, but the actual explanation may possibly not be so drastic, though more significant. The flat alluvial plain of South Mesopotamia had immense possibilities for the development of agriculture, but for these to be realised, great problems had to

be overcome. Habitation on any scale would not have been possible without a system of irrigation, and this would require a relatively high degree of social organisation and technical skill, both to build and to maintain. The Ubaid phase may have been the first in which a sufficient level was reached in either respect. On the other hand, once it was fairly launched, these very natural conditions helped to cement the bonds of society even more firmly, and to put a premium on technological development. The lack of natural materials was a stimulus to invention, and to keep the irrigation canals open demanded unremitting toil and vigilance, since they would quickly silt up if not regularly cleaned.

The earliest colonisers of the alluvial plain seem to have come from the hilly zone to the east, and their pottery links up with the Iranian equivalents of the Halaf type. Pots with a decoration even more closely allied to Halaf have now been found on one site. But in general the decoration of the Ubaid pottery is much rougher and more loosely organised than that of the Halaf, so much so as to seem almost decadent beside it. But the Ubaid potters could do many things which were beyond the Halafians. The Ubaid culture, in fact, is progressive in every way, and represents an almost perfect adaptation to conditions in southern Mesopotamia. The local materials were fully exploited. Since no stone could be procured locally, axes, sickle-blades and even nails were made from baked clay. The huge reeds of the marshes were used to construct dwellings and byres, which seem, from the pictures we have of them, to be much like those used by the Marsh Arabs of the same area at the present day. The lack of stone also prompted the use of mud brick, which Ubaid people seem to have been the first to mould in wooden forms. In this phase, too, we first find copper being used to make tools, having first, of course, to be imported. The Ubaid culture was evidently one of great vitality, and it is no surprise to find it expanding into northern Mesopotamia and superseding the Halaf culture there.

But however great the efforts made by man, natural forces were peculiarly liable to bring catastrophe in southern Mesopotamia. Any one of many causes might swell the volume of water in the great rivers until they burst their banks and drowned the land. It is not surprising that we find later that the Mesopotamian cities had all put themselves under the protection of a god, who, in theory at any rate, was the ruler of the city. This kind of theocracy naturally gave a great importance to the temple of the god and the priests who manned it. It became in fact the focus of life. And we can trace the beginnings of this state of things back to the Ubaid phase, for it is there that we find the first simple temples. At Eridu the sanctuary built by the first settlers was succeeded on the same site by a whole series of later edifices on a rising scale of magnificence, and presumably all dedicated to the same god. The temple is the real key to the development of literate civilisation in Mesopotamia. It is in the temples that writing was first developed, evolved for a very down-to-earth, practical reason to meet a pressing need. For in the Mesopotamian theocracy both the people and the land belonged to the god. The land was the god's estate, the people his slaves. Now in practice this led to a kind of state socialism administered by the temple staff, headed by the priest, or *sangu*, as the god's bailiff, and his *nubanda*, or steward, who supervised labour and administration. This situation made the keeping of exact accounts and records a necessity if the temple was to function efficiently, and so

led to the devising of a system of conventional signs for this object. Eventually this produced a real system of writing which could be used also for a great variety of other purposes.

V

The Ubaidian colonisation of the marshlands of southern Mesopotamia set the stage for the complex developments of the succeeding phases. The most important of these is now known as the Proto-literate, which is separated from the Ubaid phase by a probably short period which has been termed the Warka, but which is as yet relatively little known. The Ubaid and Warka periods saw the establishment of temples, and of what we may call market-towns, but it is in the Proto-literate phase that the social and political developments implied really crystallise and produce the incipient city. Though no city of the Proto-literate period has as yet been completely excavated, enough is known to assert that many cover a relatively large area, and, furthermore, a good number of them seem to be new foundations, built on virgin soil. This would imply a rapid expansion of the population, probably due to the success of the new agricultural techniques earlier developed. These Proto-literate cities, like the earlier towns, centre round their temples, which were often, as at Eridu and Erech, on the same site as those of earlier times. These temples differ from the earlier ones in their much greater size, and in the development of the great artificial mound, or *ziggurat*, on which the temple was set. These mounds, though not found in all the temples of this phase, were to become a standard feature of the Mesopotamian temple, and persisted down to the latest times. The *ziggurat* clearly symbolised a mountain, and this is also implied in the names of many temples, the temple of Enlil at Nippur, for example, which was called the 'House of the Mountain, Mountain of the Storm, Bond between Heaven and Earth'. To the Mesopotamians, mountains stood for all that was divine, for the power and fertility of the earth, and even their gods themselves are sometimes represented with their bodies growing out of one.

These Proto-literate temples were richly adorned, often with brightly painted frescoes, or, as in one at Erech, with a colonnade in which each column, measuring some nine feet in diameter, was covered with a skin of tens of thousands of coloured clay cones, each one separately made and baked, and forming patterns of lozenges, zig-zags, or triangles. The scale of these temples and the labour problems involved can be judged from the estimate of the excavator of the so-called 'White Temple' at Erech that its construction would have taken 1500 men, each working a ten-hour day, five years to complete. In these circumstances it is no wonder that a system of writing became a necessity, and it is in fact in the temples of this phase that the earliest traces of writing have been found. From the first these are impressed with a reed on clay tablets. There are of course as yet no literary texts; writing is still purely a device for keeping accounts and making memoranda. Some examples are simply tallies with a few numerals, but in others the object of the transaction is indicated by a drawing of it following the numerals, and indicating that they refer to so many sheep or cattle. In one case there is a wage list, with personal names and rations for the day. Others again are impressed with seals to indicate the parties to a transaction or the witnesses to it. Seals had of course been known earlier in the Warka and Ubaid phases, and were used for identification, but they were stamp seals, whereas the Proto-literate seals were small stone cylinders which

were rolled on to the clay to produce an impression. The stamp seal may be very ancient indeed, if the clay object decorated on the base with a swastika pattern which was found recently in the pre-pottery levels of Jericho really is one, and it is a very widespread type, whereas the cylinder seal remained always a characteristically Mesopotamian object.

In the Proto-literate phase southern Mesopotamia first surpasses the surrounding areas in cultural achievement. An astonishing vigour and vitality manifests itself in every department of life, and we cannot doubt that this *élan* was chiefly due to the way in which the challenge of difficult natural conditions had been so successfully met and overcome. The energy elicited was by no means exhausted in coping with it and went on to produce achievements which greatly exceeded anything that the nature of the country rendered essential. The wheel was now available to the potter, who had become a specialist craftsman, and to the wagon builder. Oxen and asses were used as a means of transport, being made to draw wheeled carts and sledges, and ships had already been designed. Metallurgy had also made great strides, and metal vessels could be made, at any rate for cult purposes. Art also had advanced, though its subject matter remained largely religious. Apart from the often exquisite seal-carvings, we now find fresco painting and even monumental sculpture in stone. On a smaller scale, stone carvers were able to make vases with decoration carved in relief, and imitated complicated ceramic forms in stone, whilst small animal and other figures were carved in stone or cast in metal to serve as amulets or weights.

But the social, religious and political organisation of the Proto-literate period can only be described by projecting back the evidence from the written documents of later times to supplement the archaeological evidence and leaving out features that are obviously later. This is a fair procedure, since there was complete continuity. The political units of early Mesopotamia were independent city states, whose government was by a kind of 'primitive democracy', an assembly of all free men and a council of elders. On the religious plane, however, the land and people still belonged to the gods. Perhaps at one time each city formed the estate of one god only and had but one temple, but by the time written records are available each city has several temples, though only one of these belonged to the 'city god'. Each citizen belonged to one of the temples and worked on the temple land. Part of this land was divided into allotments and rented to members of the community; the rest was common, and was cultivated by the society as a whole, its produce being stored in the magazines which formed a part of each temple. The magazines stood inside the oval enclosure wall and surrounding the platform on which the temple stood. From these stores came not only such things as the seedcorn for the next year, but the rations supplied to the priests and to various specialist craftsmen, as well as the supplies needed for sacrifices. Some of the produce also returned to the generality of citizens, in the form of rations of barley and wool, and extra rations distributed on feast days. But even the specialists, the priests, merchants (who traded on behalf of the community) and craftsmen were farmers in their own right, in that they all worked their own allotments, as were many of the town dwellers in Europe in the Middle Ages. Hence it is misleading to think of the division of labour as absolute, or to regard the specialists as a separate class subsisting on a surplus of food produced by the farmers whom they kept in subjection. This is an anachronism from a later period, and Childe's use of the term 'Urban Revolution' with its suggestion of a complete separation between farmers and townsmen, is less happy than his 'Neolithic Revolution' for the beginnings of settled life. Labour in the field was largely a seasonal matter, in which all, or nearly all, took part.

Nevertheless, there were gradual but far-reaching social changes in these early city-states, and ultimately there emerged some sort of class structure. We have, also, from this same Proto-literate period, the first evidence of organised warfare. Some of the seal-impressions show battle scenes with chariots and a character who appears to be a war-leader or king. It seems likely that these early kings were temporary dignitaries, elected to deal with a particular emergency, whose term of office expired with the situation which produced it. But as has often happened afterwards, the possessors of this temporary power sooner or later found means to make it permanent. The frequent wars between the independent cities of southern Mesopotamia, as one tried to extend the territory of its god by conquering another, must have materially aided this process. At any rate, it is certain that by a little before 3000 B.C., when Sumerian civilisation emerges into the full light of literacy, the old balance had been upset, and we find hereditary kings reigning everywhere, though the old theocentric organisation goes on parallel with them.

This is the beginning of the period known as Early Dynastic, which covers the greater part of the third millennium B.C., and leads on to the age of the early empires, which began with that built up by Sargon of Akkad in the latter part of the third millennium. Perhaps the most striking finds illustrating the character of the Early Dynastic phase are the famous

Royal Tombs at Ur of the Chaldees, with their magnificent furniture and the barbarous rite by which a whole court was sacrificed to accompany its royal master in death as in life. It is a far cry from the first poor villages of the Ubaidian colonists of the southern Mesopotamian marshes.

The empire which Sargon (or Sharrukin) of the Semitic-speaking city of Akkad created was formidable for its time. After reducing the Sumerian cities one by one, he finally extended his power westward as far as the coasts of the Mediterranean. The inscription, found by the French excavators at Susa, in which he recounts his victories, mentions the Mediterranean, and also the Lebanon mountains and the Taurus range of south-eastern Turkey. Sargon became the first semi-legendary figure of a mighty conqueror. Today we are apt to attach more significance to a Mesopotamian king of a slightly later period. This great man, Hammurabi, a king of a dynasty established at Babylon, who reigned at about the beginning of the second millennium, *c.* 1950 B.C., is generally thought to be the orginator of a code of laws inscribed on a stele which was found at Susa. This code, however, is chiefly a compilation of ancient Sumerian laws, and has little originality, though it gives a most interesting picture of the administration of justice at the time. Hammurabi's greatness really consists of his outstanding organising and administrative capacity, of which we see much in his letters, many of which have been preserved since fortunately they were written on baked clay tablets. The lasting result of his work was to make Babylon the centre of the Mesopotamian world throughout the rest of ancient times.

VI

In Egypt natural conditions differed much from those existing in Mesopotamia. Despite certain transient influences exerted on it from the latter area, early Egyptian society differs greatly from Mesopotamian, not only in its outward and material aspect, but in its whole orientation and ethos. In Egypt conditions were more favourable to the enterprises of man. The yearly inundation of the Nile was regular and its effects beneficent, not destructive. Each inundation brought its deposit of rich, fertile silt which guaranteed a full harvest. Indeed the present-day practices of the Hadendoa, a nomadic tribe living high up on the Blue Nile in Nubia, suggests that the earliest cultivation in the Nile Valley might have occurred without irrigation of any kind. The Hadendoa simply sow their seed in the mud left by the inundation and wait for it to germinate and ripen of itself, when they reap the crop and return to their pastoral occupations. In prehistoric times the whole of the Nile Valley was a land of marshes through which the river wandered at will, frequently changing course as it silted up one bed and sought another, but leaving the banks of the abandoned bed rising out of the plain as a favourable spot for human settlement. The old beds themselves became papyrus swamps, teeming with game and fish. This situation survived in part even as late as the Middle Kingdom, about 2000 B.C. But the early settlement sites in the valley have long since been washed away, and we depend for our evidence of the first phases on remains from the edge of the valley and on spurs at the foot of the cliffs.

We have seen how a number of sites have been found, in Egypt, which appear to illustrate very primitive phases of settled agricultural life. For the story of the subsequent development of these groups we are largely dependent on remains from Upper Egypt, since the Lower Egyptian settlements are buried deep under the mud of the Delta. Apart from actual material progress, the story is largely one of political unification rather than urbanisation. Towns and cities appear, but they are less important than in Mesopotamia. Egyptian civilisation remained essentially rural; her towns were market-towns, and in times of confusion the leaders who emerge are the rulers of extensive regions of the Nile Valley rather than heads of cities.

The natural conditions of the Nile Valley made political unification logical, and in the end it was Upper Egypt which imposed unification on the rest of the country. The culture of Upper Egypt was the lineal successor of that Badarian culture which we saw to be flourishing there in the late fifth millennium, *c.* 4250 B.C. Now the affinities of the Badarian culture are strongly African, rather than Asiatic, and it is this strain in Egypt which forms the African substratum of the later Dynastic civilisation. It is recognisable again in the Hamitic affinities of the Egyptian language and even today appears in resemblances in physique and modes of thought to the Hamitic peoples. These Hamitic peoples are widely spread in Africa, north of the equator and are represented today by, for instance, the Gallas and Somalis.

The Badarians in Upper Egypt were succeeded by the Amratians who must have begun really systematic cultivation of the Nile Valley itself, although they still relied partly on hunting, and the distribution of their rock drawings reflects the range of their hunting expeditions. It seems likely that the Amratian villages were organised as clans following a particular totem. This would explain representations of crocodiles, scorpions and other animals on their vases, some of which creatures later appear as the emblems of provinces in Upper Egypt. The degree of social organisation arrived at by the Amratians is apparent from their mining for flint,

hammering native copper into small tools and pins (but not smelting or casting it), collecting malachite and gold, and manufacturing vases of hard stones like alabaster or basalt. These things imply a certain degree of specialisation, and presumably of trade. Imports now include obsidian, juniper berries and coniferous wood. Efficient boats made of papyrus bundles had also been designed.

But it is in the succeeding, or Gerzean, period that the greatest transformation takes place, and the country is prepared for the emergence of the literate Pharaonic civilisation. These changes seem to be at any rate in part the result of the penetration of Upper Egypt by people with Asiatic affinities, perhaps coming from Lower Egypt, though this influence was not enough to change the general character of Egyptian culture. There was again an increase in the population, perhaps this time as a result of a change-over from the Amratian mixed hunting and farming to a basically farming economy. This may have been accompanied by, or have resulted from, the first attempts at irrigating and draining the marshes in the valley itself. Copper was more than ever in use, and simple cast tools occur regularly, though rarely. This increasing reliance on trade is reflected in Egypt at this time by objects of Asiatic type, in particular by cylinder seals, and by Mesopotamian motifs in art.

Despite the evidence pointing to collective enterprises such as the draining of the marshes, it is not until the end of the period that we get traces of large political units, and among the thousands of graves known there is not one which can be attributed to a great chief. By the end of this 'Late Predynastic' period, however, such organisations and chiefs had appeared, for it is then that the event which sets the pattern for later Egyptian history took place. It was the unification of the country by the legendary Menes, the first Pharaoh of the first Dynasty. We know of two candidates for the role of 'Menes', predynastic kings called 'The Scorpion' and 'Narmer' respectively. But 'Menes' might be an amalgamation of these, or even of these and others as yet unknown. And this important event gave rise to a theory of kingship which was the foundation of the Egyptian State. The Pharaoh was now a divine absolute king, an incarnate god to whom the whole realm and people of Egypt belonged as of right. This is far removed from the Mesopotamian city state with its rulers who are, after all, merely human, with the gods above all. The Mesopotamian ruler was one among many, but Pharaoh was alone in his exaltation, and his position necessarily implied a unified realm.

The structure of Egyptian society, with its basically rural character, also reflected this difference, as did many other aspects of culture. Art, for instance, though temporarily affected by some Mesopotamian conventions, soon dropped these and returned to a naturalistic bent. Instead of being devoted entirely to the service of the gods, it is employed to record scenes from daily life or historical events in the tombs of Pharaoh and his great ones, for their benefit in a future life. Significantly, these are often scenes of rural occupations and pleasures. With writing, too, it is the same. This appears in Egypt at the beginning of the Dynastic times already well developed, and it is possible that the Egyptian system may owe more than a little to Mesopotamian influence. Nevertheless, its signs are quite individual from the beginning, and quite a different use is made of it. Egyptian writing is first used not for administrative purposes (though it was so used later), but to record historical

events, and as an element in monumental art.

For more than a thousand years after the foundation of the First Dynasty, Egyptian civilisation pursued its own way with little or no interruption from the outside world. At one point there was indeed a complete breakdown of the central government, but it was restored with little interruption of tradition. The period of confusion is known as the First Intermediate Period, and the dynasties immediately preceding and following it are known as the Old (*c.* 3000 B.C.–2500 B.C.) and Middle Kingdoms (*c.* 2000 B.C.–1800 B.C.). But early in the second millennium (*c.* 1850 B.C.), the central government again became weak, and this time Egypt fell a prey to Asiatic conquerors, who were probably using the horse-drawn chariot, a new weapon of war. The foreign conquest of this Second Intermediate Period was a bitter blow to Egyptain self-esteem, but in the sixteenth century B.C. they succeeded in driving out the foreigners under a series of leaders, of whom the last was Aames I, the founder of the Eighteenth Dynasty and of the New Kingdom.

This victory ushered in what is in many ways the most splendid period of Egyptian history, signalised by massive building and fine sculpture. Thothmes III founded an Egyptian Empire in Palestine and Syria. Egypt was in close contact with all the kingdoms of Western Asia, and even the inhabitants of Crete and the Aegean islands sent presents to Pharaoh. Minoan art influenced that of Egypt, giving it a lightness and movement never known before. Thought was stimulated also, as evinced by the tragic attempt of Akhenaten, the 'heretic' Pharaoh, to introduce a monotheistic religion in place of the old cults. The New Kingdom is, however, the last manifestation of the creative power of

33

Egyptian civilisation, which later, in the first millennium B.C., fell into formalism and rigidity, though the agricultural wealth of the country remained unimpaired, and Egypt was the richest granary of the Roman Empire.

VII

From the sixth millennium onwards more or less settled village-farming economy had spread widely in Asia and in Europe, and it was in this period that the basis of the populations of historic times was laid, but it was only in one other area, and then only towards the end of the third millennium, that the second stage was reached—the emergence of cities with a large population, many specialist craftsmen, a distinct political organisation, and some measure of literacy. This was that part of north-western India centring upon the Indus valley. Hence the civilisation which arose here is generally known as the Indus civilisation, since we do not know what name the originators of it applied to themselves. Our knowledge of the civilisation of the Indus cities only dates back to the early 1920s, when excavations were undertaken at two of them, Harappa and Mohenjo-daro. A large number of settlements of this period are now known, but only three have been extensively explored, the two just mentioned, and a smaller town called Chanhu-daro. From these, considerable knowledge of this remarkable culture has been acquired, though many gaps remain. In particular, we still know little about the processes which led up to this efflorescence of civilisation, and can only guess at the nature of the drive behind it. Recently it has been shown that both Harappa and Mohenjo-daro were dominated by a citadel with massive defences of baked brick which included or controlled large granaries. But whether these citadels were temples for a god or palaces for a king we do not yet know, since it has not so far been possible to examine the interior of one thoroughly.

The Indus civilisation was preceded in Sind, the province in which its sites are mainly concentrated, by a culture of peasant villages, whose inhabitants had some knowledge of the metallurgy of copper, to which the name of the Amri culture has been given. This culture is one among a number of very varied and localised societies with the same status which covered the whole of Baluchistan at about the same period. The varied material aspect displayed by these cultures leads one to suppose the absence of any central control or arbitrarily imposed standards. The local traditions, reflected in the archaeological evidence, presumably imply a similar political decentralisation. These metal-using peasant communities must already have a long history behind them, of which we still know very little, though traces of a pre-pottery stage seem to have been found on one site in Baluchistan. It seems unlikely, in view of the much earlier evidence from Mesopotamia, that agriculture and herding could have been independently invented in India, but the knowledge may have been diffused to this area in relatively remote times.

Towards the end of the third millennium B.C. the emergence of the Indus civilisation presents us with a new situation. Material equipment now takes on a surprising and monotonous uniformity over a very large area. Mohenjo-daro and Harappa are 400 miles apart, but they exhibit complete agreement in every detail of architecture, town-planning and equipment. This implies something more than parallel development, or loose cultural connections. We have here a large political unit with an efficient central government—in fact, as in Egypt, an empire.

At present the two cities of Harappa and Mohenjo-daro far outstrip the other known sites in the size and magnificence of their remains. The walled area of Harappa extended for at least half a mile on all sides, according to old accounts, and the area of Mohenjo-daro must have been similar. The other known sites cover only between one and a half and fifteen and a half acres, and must presumably represent the market-towns, villages, and in some cases, frontier posts of the realm governed from one or both of the great cities. In the society of the cities themselves it is possible to discern traces of a certain social stratification. Apart from the citadels of the rulers, two-roomed houses appear to have accommodated an artisan class, whilst large buildings with courtyards, bathrooms, and often a private well, would have been the dwellings of the more well-to-do. The fact that even in the latter the ground-floor rooms were used as shops or stores indicates that this upper class was probably an aristocracy of commerce.

The economy of the Indus people seems to have been based on agriculture, and it is known that bread-wheat, barley, sesame, and peas were cultivated. For agriculture to support such a population, there must have been an irrigation system, though no traces of one remain. Cattle, both humped (like modern Indian cattle) and humpless, elephant, buffalo, goat, sheep and fowl were domesticated. Wheeled carts were used for transport on land, and were drawn by oxen, and boats were known. The industries were similar to, and at about the same stage of development as, those of the civilisations of Egypt and Mesopotamia. Seals were used, as in those areas, and it is from inscriptions on these that we know that a system of writing was in use, though the signs have not yet been deciphered. We also get a good deal of information about the fauna from

engravings of animals on these same seals. The kinds of animal which appear imply that the climate was tropical in Sind when the Indus cities flourished, though today the whole area is desert. Professor Stuart Piggott favours the view that the tip of the south-west monsoon area has shifted eastwards and that the monsoon rains reached further west at that time than they do now to account for this. Trade flourished in the Indus civilisation, but contacts between it and the civilised lands of the Near East are scanty. Evidence for contact with Egypt is still lacking altogether; Mesopotamia has yielded a very few imports in contexts belonging to the later third millennium B.C.; and seals and stone vases from some as yet unknown intermediate area have been found in both India and Mesopotamia. Yet these contacts do at least show that the Indus cities persisted until some time after 2000 B.C. Their final destruction was brought about presumably by the invading Aryans, of whom we know very little, but whose arrival is generally placed somewhere about 1500 B.C.

The Indus civilisation vanished utterly in its material achievements, for the Aryans were illiterate barbarians. We have in fact a similar situation as occurred at the end of the occupation of Roman Britain, when a literate civilisation was superseded by an invasion of illiterate tribesmen, the result being several centuries of obscurity and confusion. Nevertheless, it has been possible to show that a good deal actually survived of the religion and ways of thought of these pre-Aryan Indians and was incorporated into the original nucleus of the Vedic religion which the Aryans brought with them to India (*see* chapter 4). Representations identifiable as the god Shiva, and of goddesses and tree-spirits on Indus seals show clearly that it was from this source that the non-Vedic elements of

Hinduism were drawn. The smooth development of Indian civilisation was rudely broken by the Aryan invasions, but the earlier traditions were nevertheless not entirely blotted out.

VIII

One other Asian country, China, has traditions which claim for its civilisation an immense antiquity. But archaeology has not entirely confirmed these claims. Since 1920 a fair amount of work has been done on the prehistory of China, and the results so far, though only provisional, seem to indicate that literate civilisation cannot be traced farther back than the middle of the second millennium (*c.* 1500 B.C.). But the peasant farming economy is very much older in these regions, though it is still uncertain how far its introduction was due to contact with or movement from the West. This problem, along with many others, is unlikely to be solved until more materials are available for the study of the period over the whole of the Far East.

The earliest Neolithic culture so far discovered in China is characterised by coarse, hand-made pottery, and represents small communities of primitive farmers whose only cultivated cereal was millet, and whose only domesticated animals were dog, pig and fowl. They seem to have used beehive-shaped earth-houses in winter, and to have built houses for summer use which were at times raised on stilts. The unpainted pottery of this apparently indigenous Chinese Neolithic has also been found on some sites mixed with other types of pottery which are characteristic of the more advanced cultures called Yangshao and Lungshan. The former is characterised by painted pottery which seems to be related in some way to the early painted pottery of South-West Asia, and it seems possible that this

may have spread eastwards via Turkestan. The first evidence of rice cultivation, in the form of imprints of rice-husks on a sherd of pottery, belongs to this culture in China. The Yangshao culture probably started not much before 2000 B.C. on recent estimates. Related to it is the Lungshan culture, which has wheel-made pottery, and in which the domestication of cattle and horses is attested. Regular towns, defended by beaten earth walls, are also first found in the Lungshan culture, but the first remains of literate civilisation so far known in China come from the ruins of an ancient city situated near Anyang, in the north of Honan.

The citizens of Anyang were literate, had a calendar, and were fine craftsmen and artists. They made fine bronze vessels and weapons, and excellent carvings in bone, stone and ivory. Attention was first drawn to the site by peasants finding pieces of bone, inscribed with characters, in their fields. These have been identified as oracle-bones. We have, then, in this city, which is generally thought to have flourished in the middle of the second millennium B.C., all the elements of historic Chinese civilisation. It has even been possible to establish a direct link with that civilisation by the identification of the site as the capital of the legendary Shang Dynasty, long known from Chinese records

IX

There is thus nothing in the evidence from India or China to challenge the priority of the Near East in the evolution of the peasant-farming economy, or of Mesopotamia and Egypt in the establishment of the first civilisations. The importance of these areas for this phase of world history remains supreme, and the sharing of their achievements with most other parts of the globe was due to a complicated process of diffusion of ideas. A possible exception can be found in the civilisations of Central and South America, which may be of independent growth, but are certainly much later than those which we have been discussing.

By the time the Anyang civilisation was flourishing in China, a literate civilisation, that of Crete and Mycenae, was already established in one corner of Europe. The fortunes of this civilisation and its successors will be discussed in the succeeding chapters.

3 MEDITERRANEAN CULTURE: CRETE, MYCENAE, ATHENS

by W. G. Forrest

As the influence of Egyptian and Mesopotamian culture spread into Asia Minor and across the Eastern Mediterranean, there appeared, in this area, a number of new civilised or semi-civilised powers; the Hittites, Mitanni, Arzawa and others. One of these was the Minoan Empire of Crete.

As early as 2500 B.C. the prosperous but primitive Neolithic settlements in and around the fertile valleys of the mountainous island of Crete had given way to more substantial towns and villages of stone and brick, but it was not until about 2000 B.C. that its history as a Mediterranean power began. Then the first great palaces were built at Mallia, Phaestos, Hagia Triada and, most important of all, at Knossos, in the centre of the northern coast, the capital of the Minoan world.

Of the exact relationship between Knossos and the other Cretan cities we know little. At first, though perhaps nominally subject, they seem to have enjoyed a considerable degree of independence. But later they were brought, peacefully but effectively, under firm central control; a network of roads was built radiating from Knossos, the most important running across the island to the southern sea; local administration was gradually transferred; towards the end, some of the larger settlements began to decline and were replaced by clusters of smaller villages. This shift of power did not, however, mean any falling-off in the prosperity even of the outlying districts.

Far from it; almost the most important fact we know of Cretan history in the six hundred years before the final destruction of Knossos is the ever-increasing wealth of the island as a whole. The increase was interrupted from time to time by disasters of various kinds, mainly earthquakes, but such were its resources and resilience that each disaster led only to a more brilliant reconstruction. The palace of Knossos was rebuilt no less than four times before 1400 B.C.

The basis of this prosperity was not agricultural, as in the Mesopotamian kingdoms, nor did it depend on military conquest through the development of new military weapons and techniques, as with the Hittites; it rested rather on something entirely new in the history of the world, the first systematic exploitation of the sea. 'Minos (King of Knossos), according to tradition, was the first to build a fleet and set up an empire in the Aegean Sea,' says Thucydides. Although the Pharaohs had organised a navy many years before, it had played a comparatively unimportant part in the development of Egypt's economy. Now under the protection of Minos' fleet, which is said on one occasion to have sailed as far west as Sicily, Cretan merchants developed their trade throughout the Mediterranean, westwards to Sicily and perhaps beyond, eastwards along the southern coast of Asia Minor to Cyprus and the Syrian port of Ras Shamra, north to the west coast of Asia Minor, to the

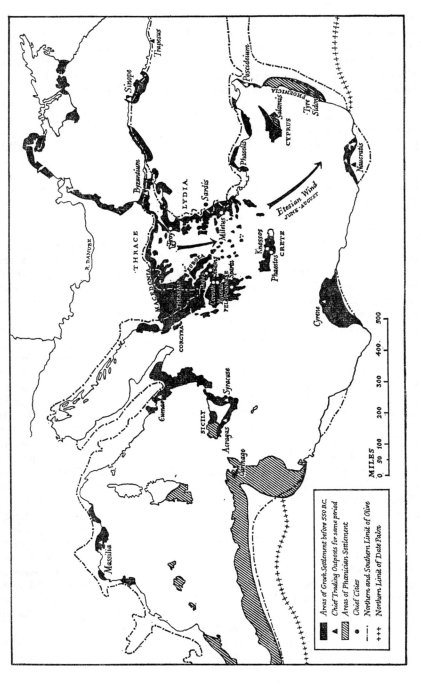

PHŒNICIAN AND GREEK SETTLEMENT   7th — 5th Centuries B.C.

Trapesus

Sinope

Poseideium

PHŒNICIA

Salamis

Tyre

Sidon

CYPRUS

Phaselis

Naucratis

Byzantium

THRACE

LYDIA

Sardis

R. DANUBE

Troy

Miletus

Etesian Wind

JUNE-AUGUST

MACEDONIA

EUBŒA

Knossos

CRETE

THESSALY

Phaestos

Thebes

Corinth

Mycenae

Sparta

PELOPONNESE

CORCYRA

Cyrene

Cumae

Syracuse

SICILY

Acragas

Carthage

MILES
0 50 100   200   300   400   500

Massilia

Areas of Greek Settlement before 550 B.C.
▲ Chief Trading Outposts for same period
Areas of Phœnician Settlement
• Chief Cities
─ · ─ Northern and Southern Limit of Olive
+++ Northern Limit of Date Palm.

mainland of Greece and the islands of the Aegean. (It was only here, apparently, that any kind of political control was established: 'Minos installed his sons as viceroys of the subject islands' (Thucydides), and tribute was imposed on Athens and perhaps on other cities of the Greek mainland.) Most important of all, close and continuous contact was maintained with Egypt. It was under the impetus of new intercourse with Egypt in the Early Dynastic period that the first great advances in Cretan culture were made. From then on there was a constant flow of trade between the Delta and the Cretan ports. At one point there was even an Egyptian official, an ambassador or trade attaché, permanently resident at Knossos.

Geographically, Crete was ideally situated to be the centre of a maritime commercial empire. Favourable and reliable winds and currents made access to North Africa and the Levant safe and easy, her long northern coastline dominated the Aegean —as Aristotle says, 'Nature seems to have designed it to rule over Greece.' Politically, too, she was fortunate. The disintegration of the Egyptian Empire soon after 1800 B.C. gave Crete a clear field in the Eastern Mediterranean. There was, as yet, no other rival.

In what the trade consisted we do not know; olive oil and wine, perhaps, and other perishable goods, as well as the distinctive painted pottery and exquisitely engraved seal-stones from which the archaeologist can still measure the extent but tell little of the nature of her influence. For archaeology is essentially a supplementary study, it can describe the background to events but not the events themselves. Without a reliable literary tradition, real history cannot be written, and since it is on the archaeologist that we largely depend for our whole picture of Cretan civilisation, that picture remains tantalis-

ingly incomplete. Later Greeks remembered little but vague legends of an early Cretan empire and although some Cretans, at least, were literate, no historical records or works of literature have been found among the surviving documents.

These documents, clay tablets which have been unearthed in hundreds in various sites throughout the island, are inscribed in two different forms of syllabic script; the earlier, a development of a hieroglyphic script, known as Linear A, remains undeciphered, but a sufficient number of tablets in the later script, Linear B, have now been translated and these show that they are no more than palace inventories, business records and the like. In their limited field, they throw a great deal of light on the organisation of the Minoan kingdom: these are the documents of a rigid hierarchical society, where everyone from the priest-king to the slave had his appointed duties and privileges; a highly organised bureaucratic system, controlled in almost every aspect from the palace itself, in the offices of which every labourer, slave or free, every bushel of wheat, every chariot wheel was carefully registered and filed. So much is clear. But of the political life which went on and the personalities who operated the system or lived under it we still know nothing.

We can see the same bureaucratic mind at work in the planning of the palaces themselves, where row upon row of almost identical storerooms, each with its orderly complement of giant jars for oil or wine, open on to long straight corridors —less striking than the splendid royal suites, the great courtyards and stairways, but, in their way, no less remarkable. But, in general, the Minoans carried their bureaucracy lightly. The impression that we get from the other remains is one of luxury, sophistication and gaiety, the last, at least, not limited to the royal court. For, although little or nothing is known of the state or even the standing of the lower classes, the noble ladies on the Knossan frescoes, for all their elegance, are certainly no gayer than the riotous peasants of the Harvester Vase. There is a similar spirit in the work of the artisans, not perhaps of the engineers and architects, for it is difficult to be light-hearted about plumbing—there we can only admire the technical efficiency of the roads, viaducts and drainage systems, the last more advanced than any in the ancient world. But the potters, painters, sculptors and engravers combined with this same technical ability a flair for colour and design, an imagination sometimes bordering on fantasy, liveliness, sensitivity and lightness of touch which in their own line have never been surpassed. Their subjects varied; the potters concentrated on patterns of plants, flowers, fishes, shells and the like; on the seal-stones we find exquisite studies of animal life; the frescoes show athletic contests, religious ceremonies, human figures, singly or in groups. All have in common a sensitive appreciation of nature unparalleled in ancient art.

Historically more significant, perhaps, is the complete absence from their work of any scenes of war or of anything suggesting war; and this is not simply the result of artistic convention. There are very few traces of arms or armour among the surviving remains before the last palace period. It is even more remarkable that the palaces and towns of Minoan Crete were entirely unfortified. We must not imagine that the kings of Knossos were men of peace, but it is clear that, behind the protection of their powerful navy, the people of Crete enjoyed a life in which war and thoughts of war played little part.

But towards the end all this was changed. One political event of the greatest importance does emerge from the remains alone.

About 1500 B.C. a new dynasty came to power in Knossos and these new rulers were Greeks. From what part of the mainland they came, how they seized power, what changes they made, we do not know. It seems likely that they simply took over much of the existing administration as it was, as they certainly took over the existing Minoan script and adapted it to fit their own language: it is now that Linear B begins and it is the decipherment of Linear B as Greek that proves their nationality. But the whole atmosphere of Cretan life was changed. These 'warrior-kings' had established themselves by force and had to maintain themselves by force; the tablets record large stores of chariots, arms and armour of a kind unparalleled before. At first their authority was limited to the region of Knossos itself; the rest of Crete was undisturbed. But about 1450 B.C. the palaces at Phaestos, Hagia Triada and Mallia were destroyed and it is tempting to see here again the hand of the Greeks, extending their rule throughout the island.

Their reign was brief. About 1400 B.C. a great fire destroyed the palace of Knossos for the last time. It is unlikely that this was caused by accident or by yet another earthquake, though the last is possible. More probably it was the result of violent attack, either by the native population rising against the Greeks or by a new wave of Greek invaders.

Whatever the reason, the catastrophe marked the end of the Cretan Empire; the palace site was never more than partially re-occupied, the imperial city of Knossos dwindled to a small provincial town. The centre of power in the Aegean shifted to mainland Greece.

II

The first Greeks entered Greece in the earliest days of Cretan power. Conquering

41

the earlier, non-Indo-European population, they established themselves in a series of cities throughout the peninsula, Mycenae, Tiryns, Athens, Orchomenos, Pylos and others. They did not at first come into contact with Minoan culture, but by the second quarter of the second millennium, their vases begin to show signs of Cretan influence and soon it takes an expert eye to distinguish mainland from island products. Whether the kings of Mycenae were politically subject to Knossos or not, it is clear that Crete dominated the mainland from 1600 to 1400 B.C. Cretan art in many forms—and even a Cretan type of administration were largely taken over by the mainland princes. Again the Linear B tablets appear with their evidence of a bureaucratic and quasi-feudal organisation. But the Mycenaeans were Greeks, the Cretans were not; as yet they were scarcely civilised, while the Cretans had almost a thousand years of civilisation behind them, and as a result, for all their debt, artistic and technical, to Cretan models, the impression we get is one of semi-barbaric splendour, not sophisticated refinement. Moreover there always remained the threat of further invasion from the north; naval defence was not enough and so their cities were ringed with great defensive walls. There was no need in Crete for the massive structure of the Lion Gate at Mycenae or the vaulted galleries of Tiryns.

Before 1400 B.C. Mycenaean trade was already extensive, but with the fall of Knossos it inherited the former Cretan markets and with them Crete's political influence in the Eastern Mediterranean; Mycenaean pottery and other artifacts now broke away from the earlier tradition and human figures appeared on the vases in place of the former marine designs. Mycenae's direct control was limited to the Argive plain in the north-west Peloponnese but there is reason to believe

that she also had some kind of hold over the other mainland cities and, at the head of this powerful federation, the kings of Mycenae were on equal terms with the Pharaohs and the Hittite kings of Asia Minor. There are frequent mentions in the Hittite documents of the 'Achaians' (the early name for Greeks) as a more or less united kingdom, friendly but suspicious references which show each of the two great powers waiting to take advantage of the other's weakness.

Mycenae's opportunity came when the weakening of the Egyptian and Hittite Empires in the thirteenth century led to a wholesale disruption of Near-Eastern peace. Invaders from the north harassed Asia Minor, and others (among them some Greeks) sailed south against Egypt (1221 B.C.). It may well have been this confusion that tempted the Greeks to sail against Troy, the powerful city which guarded the entrance to the Black Sea and had previously been under the protection of the Hittite kings. Homer wrote his magnificent epic of the Trojan War five centuries later in a different world; few genuine details can have survived the retouching and rehandling of the theme by the generations of nameless bards who came between. But that Troy was sacked by invading Greeks in the mid-thirteenth century seems fairly certain. It was a sad mistake; for while the Mycenaean Greeks exhausted themselves in plundering expeditions overseas, another tribe of Greeks, the Dorians, were pressing down into the peninsula from the north.

III

About 1200 B.C. the defences broke, and much of the Peloponnese was overrun. The citadel at Mycenae held out for another hundred years but houses were destroyed within a stone's throw of the walls; Athens and some other centres were never captured but the Mycenaean world collapsed. For three hundred years or more, Greek history becomes a confused story of shifting populations and petty tribal squabbles set against a background of primitive social, political and economic conditions of which we can catch only occasional glimpses from the inadequate evidence that has survived. The Dorians, like the 'Achaians', were Greek; they did not introduce much that was entirely new, except the use of iron in place of bronze, and we can often trace a gradual evolution in the artifacts from the Late Bronze Age down into the Early Iron Age and the later geometric period. At the same time such were the effects of the invasion that the social and economic structure, which Mycenae had in part inherited from Crete and ultimately from the great Near-Eastern kingdoms, could not survive even in a modified form. With it went much of the culture—even the art of writing was apparently forgotten. The society which the Greeks were now beginning to construct was something utterly different from anything that had gone before.

It is impossible to give a coherent account of these dark centuries. Gradually the Dorians occupied the greater part of the Peloponnese and began to settle down in stable communities at Sparta, Argos and elsewhere, rather later at Megara and Corinth. Some of the earlier population was enslaved, some assimilated, some displaced. Those who could, settled in other parts of Greece, many more fled overseas to occupy the Aegean islands or found new cities on the coast of Asia Minor, the Aeolians from central Greece to the north, the Ionians from Attica further south. Still further south, the Dorians spread out from the Peloponnese to Crete and the other southern islands. And so the pattern of later Greek life began to emerge, the same for Dorian,

Ionian, Aeolian alike; small towns and villages, each cooped up in its valley or plain, some few inland, most grouped around the long irregular coastlines of the Aegean, divided from their neighbours by the rocky hills which occupy some four-fifths of the total area of Greece. Each was an independent city-state and the history of Greece down to the time of the Macedonian invasion is the history of these tiny independent states, of their individual constitutional and economic development, of the occasional merging of one with another or annexation of one by another, of the temporary coalitions and even empires which were established as they learnt to use the one element which could unite most of them—the sea.

But before these first moves towards unification could have any real effect, the Greek world was overrun again by outside invaders. The Greeks were conscious of their common blood; they celebrated their unity in various pan-hellenic festivals, among them the great Olympic Games where inter-state quarrels were temporarily set aside; they could at times unite against a 'barbarian' (i.e. non-Greek) threat—but they never managed to create a single sovereign state, or anything approaching it, which could be called 'Greece'. For this they have been rightly condemned, though their critics should remember that the city-state was for its day no more outmoded than the nation-state today. For our purpose it is more important to notice that, for all their narrow-minded parochialism, they evolved within the limits of the city-state a kind of political life which represents the most important advance in the history of civilisation that has ever been made.

We see our clearest picture of the early days in the Homeric epics, the *Iliad* and the *Odyssey*. Homer's heroes were Mycenaeans, but the world in which they moved, the battles they fought, their manners and morals were those of the far more primitive society, the 'heroic age' of the tenth and ninth centuries which was fast disappearing, indeed, had almost disappeared, when Homer wrote. It was an aristocratic world with a rigid aristocratic code. The state's economy depended in large measure on the products of the nobleman's estate, however scanty they might be when compared with the resources of Mycenae; just as its safety depended on the skill in war which he alone had the leisure, and the equipment, to acquire. With the *demos*, the people, beneath him (the smaller independent landowners, the artisans, the hired labourers, even the bards from whose lays the Homeric poems were evolved), the only possible relationships were those of employer and employee, patron and client. The political influence of the *demos* was hardly greater than that of the slaves. It is true that there seems to have been some rudimentary form of popular assembly, but it was an assembly without rights or powers, convened to let it admire and approve its leaders' wisdom, to boost its morale and nothing more. For failure to approve, a loss of confidence, would have meant perhaps a defeat in war but not a change of government.

Above the nobles stood the king, in principle a hereditary king. But his position was precarious. There was no feudal tie between him and them, as there had been of a kind at Mycenae. The noble held his estates outright, not on any conditional tenure, and if he gave his allegiance to the king it was because the king was even wealthier and more skilled in war than he was. In such a constitution, where the king's position rested largely on his personal power to impose his authority, the most stable element was the aristocratic council, and gradually, as accident produced an inefficient or unpopular king,

they were able to usurp the royal powers. The process differed from state to state. At Corinth one exclusive aristocratic clan, the Bacchiads, overthrew the monarchy altogether and members of the clan took it in turns to hold the royal office for a year at a time; at Athens only the name of king was retained to describe one of the aristocratic magistrates who administered the state under the guidance of an aristocratic council, the Areopagus; at Argos, which had inherited the position of neighbouring Mycenae as the most powerful state in the Peloponnese, the hereditary kingship survived, but with its powers much curtailed. By about 750 B.C. effective power almost everywhere was in the hands of the nobles. Theirs were the administration of justice, the political decisions, and above all the wealth which made their position secure.

Not long before 700 B.C. a Boeotian farmer, Hesiod, composed a didactic poem on agriculture. Among his gloomy instructions to his fellow-farmers for grubbing a precarious living from their few infertile acres, we get an occasional glimpse of this nobility seen from the outside. To Homer they are divinely-favoured heroes, proud, brave, generous and (to each other) courteous, who would squash with a well-earned beating any upstart Hesiod who presumed to question their authority. To Hesiod, they were corrupt administrators of justice with a cruel disregard for the common man. But even Hesiod, miserable as he was, could not conceive of any change. It was possible to hope that they might become better, kinder men; to challenge their supremacy was unthinkable.

But Boeotia was one of the richer parts of Greece. There, as in Attica and Thessaly, the poor farmer could still survive. Elsewhere the narrow valleys and coastal plains ruined by inefficient farming and desperate overcropping, were soon wholly inadequate to support an increasing population. By the early eighth century the crisis had become acute and the only possible solution was emigration. Yet the openings for private emigration were few, though some Greeks took service as mercenaries in the Near East, in Syria and later in Egypt, and only large-scale expeditions to settle the undeveloped areas of the Mediterranean could be effective. Towards the middle of the century, overcoming their mistrust of the sea and their natural reluctance to leave home, Greeks again set out to found new cities abroad. From then on a constant stream of 'colonies' went out from Corinth and Megara, from the Euboean cities of Chalcis and Eretria, from Miletus in Ionia and many others, at first no farther afield than to the coastline of Thrace, but soon into the Black Sea, to Syria, and even more important, westwards to Sicily and southern Italy.

The effects of this sudden expansion of the Greek world were enormous. The new foundations were politically independent city-states, but they kept strong religious and sentimental ties with their mother-cities; more important, though the main purpose of their foundation was agricultural, they found in the mainland a ready market for their surplus produce and soon trade became a regular and highly organised business, at least by contrast with the occasional, haphazard and slightly disreputable ventures of earlier years.

The economic revolution created the conditions for political change. Land was no longer the only source of wealth; while many of the nobles themselves took an active part in the development of commerce, new wealthy families emerged, anxious for the political recognition to which their economic strength entitled them. Beneath them again there gradually appeared a prosperous middle class, not yet politically ambitious or even conscious, but united with the newly-rich by common interests and a common hatred for the existing régime. Suddenly they found themselves with the means to effect the necessary changes. Colonial expansion did not go on without its quarrels, and towards the end of the eighth century a war broke out between two large groups of allied powers, a war that was totally unlike the border squabbles and random raids of earlier centuries. In its closing stages, a new type of fighting began to evolve, based not as before on the individual nobleman but on a number of heavily armed infantrymen, called *hoplites*, in close formation—the non-aristocrats who could now afford to arm themselves. The aristocrats had lost not only their economic stranglehold but also their military monopoly, and the new men had acquired the means to force their way to power. The revolutions that followed during the next hundred years took many different forms but in almost every case the ultimate cause was the new prosperity, and the decisive factor, the *hoplite* army.

Revolution by committee is never easy, and often the people, or rather their leaders, found that the best way to real, if not apparent, power lay in backing a *coup d'état* by a single man, in restoring the semblance of a monarchy in which they would form a new governing class. At Argos the hereditary king, Pheidon, thus found an opportunity to reassert the royal power (about 680 B.C.) and with his *hoplite* army was able for a short time to control most of the northern Peloponnese. In trying to extend his control to Corinth he touched off the troubles which broke the aristocracy there, and a certain Cypselus, though himself a Bacchiad on his mother's side, led the Corinthians against their Bacchiad rulers (657 B.C.). Elsewhere similar autocracies were established by other renegade aristocrats or outsiders and the whole class soon acquired the name 'tyrants'.

In the seventh century, at least, the word tyrant in Greek carried with it no sense of moral reproach. To later Greeks a tyranny was unconstitutional, and therefore wrong, but the seventh century Greek was not yet thinking in terms of constitutions. To him tyranny meant only change and in most cases a change for the better. So long as the tyrant ruled well and in the interests of the men who put him into power, tyranny was popular—Cypselus never had a bodyguard. It was only when the people became politically conscious enough to demand a real share in government, or when the rich began to think that collective leadership was preferable to monarchy, that the tyrannies began to give way to the established constitutions, oligarchic or incipiently democratic, of the later sixth and fifth centuries. Under Periander, Cypselus' son, who ruled from 627 to 585 B.C., Corinth reached the height of her power. Her prosperity at home and influence abroad were unrivalled. But in his later years, at least, Periander could only maintain his position by political persecution and intimidation and, only three years after his death, his successor was expelled.

The new wealth and widening horizons had a tremendous effect on the artistic and intellectual life of Greece. Trade encouraged manufacture, and with the increasing technical accomplishment of the potters and painters went an artistry often inspired, but never enslaved by oriental models. At home the richer states used their surplus revenues to build new temples and public buildings and the first great advances were made in architecture. It is said that the Doric order was first developed at Corinth. Poets, too, found generous patronage at the tyrants' courts but it was not now the kind of patronage that had kept the Homeric bard in the nobleman's household. The poets were more the friends than the servants of their benefactors, their independence a consequence of the wider distribution of wealth and wider opportunities for leisure that the wealth brought with it. Their status in turn affected their work. Epics on the Homeric pattern were still being written but alongside them there grew up a new personal lyric poetry, its subjects the emotions and experiences of the poet. Archilochus of Paros (c. 650 B.C.) writes of his cowardice in battle, Alcaeus of Lesbos (c. 600 B.C.) attacks his political enemies. At the same time new poetic forms were evolved for public festivals, choral lyrics and the so-called dithyramb from which Attic drama was later developed.

Others, again, used their leisure to ask questions about the world they lived in; about its shape, extent and composition; its government, divine and human. Many of the answers they gave were silly, even some of the questions were wrong, but they were the right sort of questions and by asking them the Greeks took the first steps towards one of their most astonishing achievements, the invention of mathematics, science and philosophy. Invention is perhaps an odd word to use in this context, but no other is appropriate. As with much else, the stimulus came from abroad but the achievement was wholly Greek.

This movement began in Miletus, richest of the Ionian cities of Asia Minor. In the middle of the seventh century, the non-Greek state of Lydia in the interior had begun to expand under a new and vigorous dynasty, the Mermnads, who gradually extended their control to the Greek cities on the coast. In return the interior was opened up to Greek influence, and through Lydia, Greeks came into contact with the

Near-Eastern kingdoms. Already the Phoenician alphabet had been imported (*c.* 750 B.C.) perhaps through a Euboean colony on the Syrian coast and, as a healthy trade was developed with Syria and Egypt, a Milesian trading station was set up in the Delta (*c.* 650 B.C.). So the Greeks met with civilisations that were far older, far richer and utterly different from their own. They were impressed by the wealth and antiquity, surprised by the differences and prepared to learn, and it was this surprise and interest that provoked their first inquiries and controlled the direction those inquiries took.

From Babylonian astronomy, Thales of Miletus (*c.* 580 B.C.) moved on to speculate on the physical nature of the universe; his successor, Anaximander, evolved a complicated cosmology and a rudimentary theory of evolution. Pythagoras of Samos (*c.* 525 B.C.), starting from the simple rules of thumb which passed for geometry among the Egyptians, produced for the first time the deductive proofs of real mathematics. Our fragmentary knowledge of these first philosophers hardly allows any clear or sympathetic understanding of their ideas. But we can easily judge the enormous importance of their speculations, however primitive, when we look at the work of their successors. By the end of the fifth century Leucippus and Democritus, in direct line of descent from Thales, had worked out an atomic explanation of the universe which has many startling affinities with that of modern science. This coincidence in itself is of more interest than importance; like most Greek scientific thought, their atomism was not founded on empirical evidence and was unchecked by experiment. Far more remarkable is the logical thinking that produced the theory and the philosophical, theological and, ultimately, ethical conclusions that were drawn from it. Freeing themselves

completely from the influence of conventional religious beliefs, they allowed no room in their determinist and materialist thought for a god, for metaphysics, for any teleological explanation of the universe; nothing existed but the atoms and the void in which they met and moved apart.

The mathematical theories of Pythagoras, on the other hand, gave rise to a still more influential, though in one respect less fruitful, line of thought. To them, of course, can be traced back the brilliant work in pure mathematics of Plato, Eudoxus and the later Alexandrian scholars. More immediately, they provoked a wider philosophical problem. Until quite recently it was thought that mathematical or logical demonstration provided some real information about the world, that the theorems of Euclidean geometry were somehow true of actual space, not simply about the way we see the world or measure space. But the mathematician's circle is far more perfect than any physical example of it, his idea of twoness is purer, more permanent, more reliable than any two apples which may decay or any two rabbits whose multiplication is outside his control. The world of thought, then, is something apart from, and better than, the world of sense. But what is the exact relationship between them? In what sense does the first exist? Does the second exist at all? From this point it is an easy step to some kind of mathematical mysticism. Pythagoras himself came to the belief that all things were numbers (whatever that may mean); his successors, and they include almost all philosophers from Plato to Kant, have been more or less beset with similar worries, their thinking often vitiated by similar conclusions.

The roots of all this fantastic achievement—and it remains fantastic whether their ideas were right or wrong, helpful or misleading—lie in the economic and social revolution of the early seventh century. It created the conditions in which this kind of work could be done. Fortunately there were men, artists, writers and thinkers, with the energy, imagination, curiosity and courage to take advantage of them.

IV

Two states which stood slightly apart from the rest in the early political development of Greece dominate the history of the sixth and fifth centuries, Athens and Sparta.

Some time in the tenth century two Dorian communities in the south-eastern Peloponnese had merged to form the state of Sparta. From this merger came her remarkable institution, the dual kingship, which survived until the third century. A large part of the pre-Dorian population was enslaved and tied to the land which they worked for their Spartan masters. These *helots*, as they were called, were at once freer than their fellows elsewhere in that they belonged to the state and were not subject to the whims of their individual masters, and more constrained in that they could never hope, as could other slaves, for freedom. Hence they were more dangerous. But, apart from these two oddities, early Sparta was in no way distinguished from the rest of Greece: in 750 B.C. she was faced with the same problem of over-population that provoked the colonial movement elsewhere. She solved it, however, in a peculiar way— by the annexation of neighbouring Messenia and the enslavement of the population. This vast increase in her national wealth brought with it the now familiar consequences, the appearance of a *hoplite* class and political agitation, but in wholly different circumstances. Elsewhere it took time for the effects of colonisation to be felt in the mother-cities; in Sparta

trouble could begin as soon as the rich lands of Messenia had been divided (unfairly, we may suppose) among the Spartans. But on the other hand there was no clash of economic interest between the landed gentry and a commercial class. Sparta was and remained an agricultural society. Besides, the menace of the now large *helot* class encouraged agreement among their masters. So it came about that, with the help of two enlightened kings, Theopompus and Polydorus, a compromise solution was reached even before other states had turned to tyranny (*c.* 700 B.C.).

By this compromise the kings and aristocratic council were left in real control, but limited rights of assembly were granted to the whole citizen body, under firm supervision from above. More important, the principle of strict equality among all citizens was laid down and land was redistributed to ensure some kind of equality in fact; it was from his land that the Spartan had to produce that contribution to his common mess which entitled him to citizenship. These messes, a primitive Dorian institution, were now reorganised to form the basis of a new highly trained and efficient army on which Sparta was to depend for the control of the *helots*. But we must not imagine that these changes led at once to that gloomy barrack-like existence for which later philosophers so much admired her. For the rest of the seventh century, Sparta was the most politically advanced and one of the happiest states in Greece. She had acquired a defined constitution at a very early stage and the mere fact of definition is of the greatest importance. It makes far more difficult any usurpation of power by individual magistrates, it puts the law above the magistrate who administers it, and it creates or at least encourages the concept of legal or constitutional rights which in turn makes possible the kind of thinking which leads to alterations and improvements. The idea of the written code had thus been introduced to Greek political thought and many of the principles embodied in Sparta's first constitution were adapted, applied and later developed in the rest of Greece.

In Sparta itself these advances were not made. For a hundred years or more she was the centre of a lively cultural and artistic life—the poems of Alcman (*c.* 630 B.C.) show a very un-Spartan gaiety and love of pleasure. Her new army, at first heavily defeated by Pheidon of Argos in 669 B.C., soon recovered to crush the serious Messenian revolt which followed the defeat. There followed a series of almost entirely successful campaigns against her northern neighbours, the Arcadians, and Argos. By 550 B.C. Sparta was in control of the greater part of the Peloponnese. But now the two peculiar problems she had created for herself by the annexation of Messenia began to have their effect.

She had chosen to ignore the development of trade and manufacture elsewhere and for a time this hardly mattered. But about 610 B.C. coined money was introduced to Greece from Lydia; soon every state with any kind of commerical pretensions began to issue a coinage of its own and the effects on international commerce were enormous. Sparta did not; for internal business the unwieldy iron spits that had served for currency in the past were still enough. Such imports as she had (mainly in luxury goods) were not important enough to justify a change. And so these imports ceased; foreign poets and artists no longer came and, in the end, cut off from outside inspiration, her own art decayed. Sparta was committed to an agricultural future and the resultant seclusion and economic ossification brought political ossification as well.

What had been for its time an advanced and liberal constitution became a harsh and narrow oligarchy. By the end of the fifth century Sparta was a model for all the reactionaries of Greece.

Her other problem was more obvious and more ably solved. If neighbouring states tried to stir up *helot* discontent for their own advantage, her army would be strong enough to deal with them. The Arcadian wars of the early sixth century were prompted as much by fear of such interference as by any desire to extend Spartan territory. But once Arcadia was conquered, the dilemma became clear. Annexation would mean more *helots* and another, wider circle of potentially dangerous neighbours. Each new conquest would simply push the danger farther back and put more strain on her limited military resources. An able Spartan statesman, Chilon (556 B.C.) found the solution. Arcadia was not helotised but was granted an alliance; Sparta began to represent herself not as a Dorian conqueror but as heir to the kings of Mycenae, a pan-Achaean leader of the Peloponnese. The propaganda worked; the alliances were extended, at first by Chilon and then by his ambitious but erratic, young protegé, King Cleomenes (*c.* 520–489 B.C.). The Peloponnesian League, which was thus created, was the first Greek attempt at anything like a federation.

Although there was never any question about the leadership, there was a League assembly, there was a rudimentary form of constitution. Whether such a federation could ever have been extended to cover the whole of Greece is perhaps an idle speculation. In the event Spartan caution and Athenian ambition prevented it, and Sparta's second great contribution to the political development of Greece proved no more profitable (for Sparta) than the first. But the immediate achievements of the League were considerable enough. In its formation, maintenance and extension, Sparta found her way blocked by several states still ruled by tyrants. Whether she was moved, in expelling these, by opposition to tyranny as such, or by disagreement with each tyrant in turn, or whether there was some chain of alliance between them which drew her on from one campaign to the next, it is difficult to say. Whatever the motive, Sparta and her allies put an end to the age of the tyrants in Greece. And it was in part a result of these campaigns that Greece was able to unite as effectively as she did against the threat of Persian invasion. That invasion was repelled by an army and a fleet built up around a nucleus of the forces of the Peloponnesian League, led by Spartan commanders.

But although Sparta provided the organisation and the leadership, the victory over Persia was largely due to Athenian initiative and Athenian naval enterprise, and it was Athens that took the credit and most of the rewards for victory.

At an early date the villages and townships of Attica had combined to form a single state under the leadership of Athens. The comparatively large amount of cultivable land which she thus acquired gave her early prosperity and success; it also robbed her of any incentive to join in the colonial movement and the lead soon passed to Corinth and other commercial-minded states.

By the end of the seventh century, Athenian pottery already shows signs of the mastery of technique and design which in the next fifty years was to put all her rivals out of business, but its distribution is limited to neighbouring states; her surplus corn could not compete in price or quality with the imports that were now coming in from Sicily, Egypt and the Black Sea; the rich silver mines at Laurium,

which supported her later naval development, were not yet being exploited.

Meanwhile Attica was in the grip of an agricultural crisis. Very many, perhaps most, of her small farmers had become formally bound to the rich. How this had happened is unclear—had the early dependence of commoner on aristocrat gradually developed into a more rigid, because anachronistic, system? Had economic distress, the result of typical Greek conditions led to formal submission? But whatever the reason, the poor farmer now worked as a sharecropper, his land effectively in the rich man's control, his person liable to enslavement if he failed to pay his due. By 594 B.C. these miserable men, or at least those of them who retained some semblance of freedom, were ready for revolution, but revolutions cannot be won by a crowd of hungry farmers, however desperate. Fortunately for them there were other, more powerful forces, equally anxious for change. Some members of the nobility and some enterprising commoners, whose estates lay near the coasts or in outlying districts of Attica, had already found that olive production was more profitable than grain on their less fertile land. Experiment showed that there was a ready market for Athenian oil abroad and already these experiments had made them rich. Wealth brought the usual demand for political recognition and they found ready allies in the agricultural poor.

Athens in 594 B.C. might well have had a tyrant; instead she found a mediator. Solon, one of the leaders of the revolutionaries though himself an aristocrat, rejected his more extreme supporters' demand that he should make himself tyrant and had himself appointed chief magistrate for the year with full powers to reform the constitution. His immediate remedy for the social distress was simple and drastic; he restored to the sharecroppers full and unencumbered title to their land; he freed all Athenians who had been enslaved; he made it illegal in the future to contract any loans on the security of the person. So the past was wiped out and some provision made for the future, but the soil of Attica remained the same and only a radical transformation of Athenian economy could effect a permanent cure. Here Solon did what he could—he encouraged the development of manufacture and prohibited outright the export of any agricultural produce except oil.

His constitutional reforms earned for Solon in later years the title of father of democracy, but it is not a title that he would have claimed or even understood. What he did was rather to create the constitutional framework within which democratic ideas later grew. 'I gave to the people such recognition as was necessary', he says in a surviving poem, and by 'necessary' he meant 'necessary to protect them from aristocratic oppression', not 'necessary to control the state'. Right of assembly was guaranteed; more important, right of appeal to the assembly was established against a magistrate's verdict. But that was all.

His immediate concern was not to destroy the governing class but to alter its composition and this he did by making wealth, not birth, the criterion for all the offices of state. From office the new men would pass into the old aristocratic council and slowly the balance of power in it would be altered—too slowly for Solon's taste and so, while it retained much of its former power and prestige, he created alongside it a new council to arrange the assembly's business and, if necessary, check its enthusiasm, this council again being drawn from the higher property classes. The popular courts and democratic council, the corner-stones of fifth-century

democracy, developed directly from Solon's court of appeal and non-aristocratic council. But in neither case did he intend, nor could he have imagined, that they would develop as they did.

Solon had tried to save Athens from tyranny. In fact he postponed it for a generation and perhaps made it milder when it came, but in the end something stronger than a code of laws was needed to break the power of the aristocratic factions. Not that it was only Solon's moderation that opened the way to tyranny; he had turned Athenian attention to trade and the astonishing progress that was made in the next thirty years brought further dislocation and unrest. Through this the ablest of the faction leaders, Peisistratus, intrigued and fought his way to power (546 B.C.). For the next twenty-five years he and his sons, Hippias and Hipparchus, ruled Athens well and with moderation, until, in 510 B.C., a Spartan army under Cleomenes drove them out for good and the old nobles returned to resume their familiar, but now outmoded, quarrels.

Under the tyrants, Athens became the wealthiest state of mainland Greece. There was peace at home and abroad; her trade was encouraged; oil, pottery and coined silver were sent out to pay for the foreign grain on which she was becoming increasingly dependent; her arts were developed, her temples rebuilt, even the struggling farmers were helped by occasional loans. When Peisistratus came to power her black-figure pottery was at its best; when the tyranny fell she was already producing the even finer red-figure ware that was sold all over the Greek trading area. In other arts it was still a period of experiment, but of daring and remarkable experiment. In 535 B.C. Thespis added an actor to the traditional dithyrambic chorus and produced an elementary form

C

of drama; about the same time the sculptor of the 'peplos kore' achieved in stylised archaic form a representation of the human figure in the round, intensely and nervously alive, which points the way directly to the classical period. In all this the tyrants helped by individual patronage and general policy, but their greatest contribution to the advancement of Athens was more accidental. The old aristocratic factions had had local roots and strong local influence. By fostering national cults and festivals Peisistratus helped to create a sense of civic unity which had not existed before. At the same time he established, however illegally, a strong central authority to which the ordinary man, previously bound to individual aristocratic patrons, could now look for guidance and protection.

When the nobles returned in 510 B.C., they tried to resume their interrupted game of family faction politics but the people had already forgotten the rules. One of the faction leaders, Cleisthenes, half realising the nature of the change, was driven in a moment of defeat to make use of the new popular feeling. He proposed radical constitutional change and, as Herodotus says, 'took the people into his faction'. His rivals were overwhelmed and the reforms put through; an entirely new social organisation, based on locality, replaced the old kinship system in every branch of state administration; the village council replaced the 'big-house' as the centre of local government. Cleisthenes had noted and taken advantage of the people's new unity, but he had not reckoned with their independence. He had hoped to establish himself as an old-style patron with the whole people as his clients; instead he had given them a constitution in which they themselves became the only patron. For much of the fifth century the people still chose its leaders from the upper class, but its choice was free and it alone determined the policy they were to put into effect.

V

In 499 B.C. came the first hint of trouble from abroad and for a time domestic politics were forgotten. By the middle of the sixth century most of the Greek cities of Asia Minor were contentedly paying tribute to Croesus, King of Lydia. They retained their political independence (in Greek eyes the city-state's most valued right, autonomy, meant no more than the freedom to order its own political affairs) and Lydian friendship more than compensated for the price they had to pay. But not long before 540 B.C. Cyrus led the armies of his new and rapidly expanding Persian Empire into Western Asia Minor; Lydia was overwhelmed, and the Greeks faced with a different kind of subjection. The Persians were generous conquerors and tolerant rulers, but they were rulers, not just superior friends as Croesus had been. They admired the Greeks and learned much from them but they never understood them. Tyrants, Persian nominees, not popular leaders, were installed in the cities, autonomy had been infringed, and when, in 499 B.C., one of these tyrants, in temporary disfavour with the Persian court, broke away, the whole of Asiatic Greece rose in revolt. The revolt began well; Greek forces even entered Sardis, Croesus' old capital, and it took some time for the Persians to organise a counteroffensive. But when they did, disunity and treachery among the Greeks weakened the resistance. A disastrous defeat at sea was followed by the recapture of Miletus (494 B.C.) and the revolt was over.

Meanwhile Cyrus and his successors, Cambyses and Darius, had pushed the boundaries of their empire north-eastwards to the Caspian and south-west to Libya.

Darius had crossed into Europe (514 B.C.) and, unsuccessfully, tried to annex southern Russia. Greece herself was clearly threatened and for the mainland cities the most urgent question was whether to submit or fight. For Athens the problem was especially acute. Cleisthenes tried to come to terms with Persia and his followers throughout argued for appeasement, but the people's first real act of independence was to refuse to ratify his agreement, and in 499 B.C. a naval force was sent to help the revolt.

It was hardly likely that Darius would ignore this rash, if admirable, gesture, and in 490 B.C. he sent a fleet across the Aegean. It landed at Marathon on the north-east coast of Attica and there the Persian forces were routed by the skill of an Athenian general and the courage of the Athenian *hoplite*. Militarily, Marathon was perhaps of small importance but its effect on the morale of Athens was enormous. 'These men were the first Greeks', says Herodotus, 'who had the courage to face up to Persian dress and the men who wore it, whereas up to that time the very name of the Persians brought terror to a Greek.' When the Persians came again by land in 480 B.C. through Thrace and Thessaly, with vastly greater forces, something like a united Greek army was there to meet them. Many states still held back, others collaborated with the enemy, but Boeotia, Athens, Aegina, Corinth and all the other members of the Peloponnesian League, joined forces under Spartan command, and ridden though it was with jealousies and rivalries between both states and commanders, this new 'Hellenic League' survived. Even more surprisingly, it routed the invaders. Attempts to check them in the north had failed; the Athenians had to abandon their city and watch its destruction from their ships or from the neighbouring island of Salamis where the allied ships were stationed. There the Persian fleet was lured into the narrows and overwhelmed; their army withdrew from Attica, and in the following year (479 B.C.) was decisively defeated at Plataea to the north. Meanwhile, after Salamis, the allied fleet had nervously followed the retreating Persians across the Aegean and after some hesitant manœuvrings among the islands came up with them at Mycale near Miletus. Again the Persians were defeated, a large part of Asiatic Greece set free and admitted to the League.

Though heavily outnumbered on land and sea, the Greeks had repulsed the most formidable military power in the world; however one may stress the inefficiency of Xerxes, the Persian king, his difficulties in supply and communications, even his bad luck, the victory remains a remarkable achievement. The Greeks were not unreasonably proud of what they had done. Moreover they were now more conscious than ever before of their unity as Greeks. This sense of common achievement, with the concrete prospect of future gain by further common effort, made political union possible. But Sparta, the recognised leader, ignored the chance; she withdrew her forces, the coalition on the mainland dissolved, and Athens was left to do what she could with the considerable remnants of the naval arm.

For Sparta, as we have seen, security abroad could help towards security at home but it could never guarantee it. She could not commit her army to foreign campaigns for any length of time without considerable risk. Some were prepared to face the risk, others were not. In 479 B.C. there were enough signs of trouble among the *helots* and in the Peloponnese to justify the isolationists' case and her forces were recalled.

At Athens there was no such caution.

Without argument or hesitation she took over Sparta's lead and organised a new confederacy of the Asiatic Greeks and islanders; its purpose, collective security and further punishment of the Persians for what they had done; its constitution, ostensibly democratic, for each state had a vote in the regular assembly. But from the start Athens provided the executive; Athenian generals commanded the fleets, Athenian officials controlled the tribute which came from those states too small or too idle to furnish ships, using it to build yet more Athenian ships. As the early enthusiasm waned, a few states tried to secede—they were at once reduced; many contracted to pay money instead of ships, glad to let others do their fighting for them. So Athens' hold grew tighter, and by 450 B.C. the League had become an empire.

At Athens, political argument was not on the question of leadership but on what direction the lead should take. For some, the future held no more than a long succession of campaigns against the Persians in the Salamis tradition, with a sentimental collaboration with Sparta for old times' sake, a glamorous but ultimately empty programme. But Themistocles, the man who had built the fleet and laid the plans for Salamis, saw that there was now another more immediate danger than Persia. Should the expansionist party ever come to power in Sparta, their first objective would be Athens which had usurped their place as leader of the Greeks. At the moment Spartan caution had been interpreted as weakness and she was struggling desperately to maintain herself against restless *helots* and disaffected allies. One quick campaign and Athens' rival might be removed for good, the way would be opened to control of mainland Greece, perhaps even for expansion to the west, to Sicily and Italy. Domestic issues

were also involved. For Cimon, the brilliant young naval commander who led the anti-Persian party, political life still centred round the Areopagus, the aristocratic council which Cleisthenes (naturally) had left undisturbed. But for Themistocles and his lieutenants, Ephialtes and the young Pericles, who accepted, indeed passionately believed in the democracy that had come from Cleisthenes' miscalculation, the Areopagus was an anomaly whose judicial powers and natural prestige made it a dangerous centre of aristocratic reaction.

For thirty years, the people followed now one, now the other, but in the end Themistocles' policy won, though he himself had already died in exile.

The profitless war with Persia was ended (449 B.C.) on not unfavourable terms but, to the shocked surprise of many of the allies, the League was not disbanded; at home there was full democracy, for in 462 B.C. the Areopagus' powers had been made over to the popular courts, the democratic council and the assembly; and already diplomatic interest was being shown in the west. Even where Themistocles' policy had apparently failed, its principles were accepted; war had begun with Sparta in 460 B.C. and during the indecisive fighting of the next decade, Athens gained, and then lost, control of much of central Greece. In 445 B.C., however, peace was made and by it Athens appeared to abandon her claims to mainland empire, but every Athenian knew by now that Sparta was her real opponent.

The man who brought all this about and controlled Athenian affairs without a rival until his death in 429 B.C., was Pericles, wonderful orator, brilliant politician and able general, a man who has won more admiration than any statesman of any time and has given his name to the most remarkable years in the history of the world—the Periclean Age. It is an unfortunate name. For many historians these are years of odd contrasts and inconsistencies: the policies of the man they so much admire led directly to a war which ruined Athens and much of Greece; with enlightened government at home went (so it is often thought) a harsh and savage tyranny over the subject-allies; the Parthenon, most glorious of the temples and public buildings which made Athens a city of unparalleled beauty, was built with the tribute from these allies; the astonishing intellectual and artistic development is marred from time to time by vicious attacks on poets, artists and philosophers, by prosecutions and even executions. Some see the answer to all this in a sharp dichotomy between the educated élite and the Athenian mob, or between the gross world of politics and the secluded life of the intellectual, which Pericles, in some mysterious way, is made to share.

But Athenian society was too small and too simple to allow distinctions of this kind. All played a part in public life. Euripides (480–406 B.C.), last of the three great tragedians, was seen by his contemporaries as an intellectual recluse, but even he joined ardently in the propaganda campaign of the early Peloponnesian War; the first and greatest of the three, Aeschylus (525–456 B.C.), saw in contemporary politics the same moral issues that inspired his plays; Thucydides (471–401 B.C.), whose detached narrative of the war is one of the most remarkable pieces of historical and political analysis ever written, and Sophocles (495–406 B.C.), the other tragedian, were both Athenian generals. The Athenian people could be cruel, but no more cruel than the oligarchs of the late fifth century whose leaders were the favourite pupils and intimate friends of the 'enlightened' philosophers; they could at times be stupid and narrow-minded but they were the audience who

listened to, approved and presumably understood the 'lofty idealism' of a Periclean speech and they were the judges who gave the first prize to Aeschylus and Sophocles and, with admirable perception, the second so often to Euripides.

This is not to say that the average Athenian was a poet or a philosopher, far less that he was endowed with some mysterious genius of his own, but only that he shared to the full the optimism, enthusiasm, curiosity, the sense of adventure and love of experiment of the artists and thinkers of the time; that he was responsible for the development of the constitution in which they flourished, and the administration of the city from which they got their livelihood and their inspiration. The sculpture of Phidias was not created for a private patron or for his own pleasure but for Athens.

This constitution was a direct democracy; policy was decided by a regular assembly of all adult male citizens; which elected and controlled the most important officers of state; its members were eligible for service as jurors in the lawcourts which since 462 B.C. conducted all important judicial business; they were also eligible for election by lot to the annual council which directed day-to-day administration and prepared the assembly's business. To ensure that all could spare the time to fulfil these public duties, state-pay was introduced. To criticise this democracy on the grounds that slaves and women were excluded is beside the point. That the Athenian economy, like that of every Greek state, depended on its slaves (about one-third of the total population) is an important historical fact—it explains, perhaps, why the Greeks were no technologists. It is also important to remember that the average Greek did not recognise equality of sex, race or colour. But neither criticism is relevant here. We must compare Athenian democracy with the contemporary constitutions of other states, where, outside the Athenian Empire, oligarchies of varying degree of narrowness were still the rule, and not with present-day systems or, even worse, Utopias. We must judge it not by what it failed to do but by what it did. It introduced into human society for the first time the ideas of individual freedom and individual responsibility and, moreover, it showed that these ideas could work.

In Athenian democracy, as in any other working constitution, there was room for corruption, stupidity, injustice and mismanagement. All these existed. They became more obvious in the political rivalries which followed Pericles' death. Able men outside the nobility, who had believed Pericles when he said that all could serve Athens according to their ability, began to take part in politics. The ablest of them, Cleon, was for a time Athens' most influential politician. On the other hand many of the upper classes who had accepted Periclean democracy because Pericles was one of themselves, were shocked by the emergence of these 'demagogues' into open opposition to democracy itself.

At the same time young men to whom the issues or the 460s meant nothing, who had neither the passionate attachment to, nor the violent hatred of, democracy of the earlier generation, were ready to toy with ideas of change; these young men had been educated by a new class of professional teachers, the so-called sophists —philosophers, scientists and rhetoricians who were now applying the inquiring rationalism of the early Ionians to wider fields, among them to ethics and politics. For the sophists themselves, at least for the best of them, the exposure of the fallacies and absurdities of conventional beliefs was only a preliminary to the establishment of

a real logical foundation for social organisation and moral principles, but it was their facile destructive logic, not the tedious and speculative job of reconstruction, that appealed to their less able pupils and inspired these young men to see in politics no more than an easy way to self-advancement or a field for theoretical experiment according to self-made rules. The tensions thus produced between old and young, oligarch and democrat, sophistically educated and simple minded, were exacerbated by the terrible stress of the last years of the Peloponnesian War; for two brief interludes (in 411 and 404 B.C.) oligarchs were able to recapture political power, only to show themselves more corrupt and more incapable than the people they despised. But with these exceptions democracy provided Athens for more than a hundred years with a stable, well-ordered and efficient government, and for sixty years it administered an empire with fairness, good sense and considerable profit both for the rulers and the ruled.

This empire is often described as a savage and selfish tyranny. A tyranny it may have been but it was neither savage nor entirely selfish; the tribute, with which Athens built her temples and fought her wars, was a small price to pay for the external security which she guaranteed. In general, political, military, judicial and economic interference in her subjects' internal affairs was no more than was needed for an efficient ordering of the whole (nominally, of course, the subjects remained entirely free) though sometimes, it is true, Athenian enthusiasm led her to encourage or even impose democracy where it was not wholly necessary; there were cases of brutality, oppression and extortion, but they were few; there was resentment among the subjects and even disaffection but it was mainly limited to the wealthy who paid the tribute and had lost political power. Through all the anti-Athenian propaganda circulated by these oligarchs, and echoed by their sympathisers ever since, four facts stand out: that the allies remained remarkably loyal to Athens until the very end of the Peloponnesian War; that when they did revolt it was almost always the work of dissident oligarchs, while the people were often prepared actively to support the return of the Athenians; that many of the ordinary citizens of the subject-states looked on the Athenian assembly not as an oppressor but as their defender against the oppression of their own oligarchic compatriots; that the Athenian assembly itself thought not only of the profits but also of the responsibilities of empire. A large part of this book is taken up with the stories of nations' attempts to dominate one another. Among all these attempts the Athenian is one of those least worthy of condemnation.

And yet Athens failed. But it was not a failure of democracy as such but of her character. That complete self-confidence, which is one of the most remarkable features of her art and thought in the mid-fifth century, led in politics to a deliberate policy of expansion. To the outsider this was aggressive ambition—as a frightened Corinthian said in 432 B.C., 'Success spurs them on, defeat does not discourage them. If they do not take what they have planned to take, they feel cheated of what is theirs by right; if they do, they treat it as no more than a step to further expansion.' To the Athenian it was a conscious attempt to impose the Athenian ideal—'Our whole city,' said Pericles, 'is a model for the rest of Greece.' But the Athenians tried to do too much and the opposition was too strong.

War broke out in 431 B.C. as the direct result of a small quarrel between Corinth and her powerful Adriatic colony, Corcyra. Corcyra appealed to Athens, who at once took her side. Urged on by a frightened Corinth, Sparta chose to fight a preventive war rather than see her empire crumble before Athens' peaceful, but none the less destructive, expansion by carefully chosen alliance and vigorous economic pressure. Almost the whole Greek world was involved by alliance, subjection or sympathy and even the internal peace of many states was broken as the war became more and more an ideological struggle, the oligarchs looking to Sparta for aid, the democrats turning to Athens. Fighting dragged on expensively but indecisively for ten years; the Spartan army could ravage Attica every year but could not break the long walls which joined Athens to the sea and secured her supplies; the Athenians, sadly weakened by the great plague of 430–428 B.C., could only use their naval superiority to blockade Corinth and make random raids on the coast of the Peloponnese. Neither had gained a clear advantage when peace was made in 421 B.C. and it was perhaps in part the despair of ever reaching a final decision in mainland Greece which encouraged the renewal of Athens' old ambitions in the west, and led her to answer an appeal for help which came in 416 B.C. from one small Sicilian state.

The early western colonies, surviving the occasional threat of Carthaginian expansion from Africa, had developed on much the same lines as the mainland states; they had played their part (an important part) in art, literature and philosophy; above all, they had prospered, many were now richer than their mother-cities. This was a tempting prospect and in 415 B.C. a huge armada sailed from the Piraeus for Syracuse, the richest and most notable of all. Two years later it and all the later reinforcements had been wiped out. In this one reckless adventure of sickening stupidity, Athens had lost about half of her forces, her fleet and almost all her financial reserves. Sparta had already reopened hostilities; some of the allies were ready to revolt; Persia, always waiting to take advantage of Greek weakness, was prepared to interfere. And though Athens survived the moment of despair and built another fleet which doggedly held its own for eight years more, when that fleet in turn was destroyed at Aegospotami (405 B.C.) by the new Spartan navy backed by Persian gold, she could do no more. The Spartans entered the Piraeus and the long walls were torn down.

So the two great leagues and the two leading cities destroyed each other. Nominally, the victory was Sparta's, and for a time she cherished the illusion that she could order Greece to her liking. But random brutality without a clear policy or the means to carry it out was useless, and as she now posed as champion of the Greeks against the Persians, and intrigued for Persian aid in the subjection of Greece, her prestige quickly waned. Another mainland state, Thebes, who had suffered less than most in the Peloponnesian War, though firmly on the Spartan side throughout, used her new position of comparative strength to build up an army which inflicted on the Spartans at Leuctra (371 B.C.) the first clear military defeat for two hundred years. But it needed more than new military tactics and two able leaders, Pelopidas and Epaminondas, to impose order among the quarrelling cities, and the short-lived Theban hegemony dissolved into a chaos of shifting alliances and minor wars which opened the way for Macedonian conquest.

VI

The Peloponnesian War exhausted Greece, materially and morally. The shoddiness of later Greek art is due as much to lack of money as to lack of skill, but art lost more than its financial backing after 400 B.C. The inspiration had failed. Philosophy, too, was affected, and though the two greatest Greek philosophers, Plato and Aristotle, both belonged to the fourth century, Plato, at least, could never escape from the effects of 404 B.C.

Plato (born 427 B.C.) grew up among that group of dissatisfied aristocrats who had tried to apply their sophistic training to practical politics in the later years of the war with such disastrous results. Though too young to play an active part and able, therefore, to appreciate the faults of these oligarchs in action, he shared with them their pride in Athens and their mistrust of the Athenian people. In 399 B.C. the pride was shattered and the mistrust deepened into hatred when the restored democracy condemned Socrates to death, the man whom (rightly or wrongly) it saw as the inspirer of the oligarchic reaction. Socrates was a sophist, albeit an amateur, to whom many of these young men had listened with an excited lack of comprehension and in whom Plato had found inspiration. Plato inherited from his teacher his peculiar development of sophistic logic, the dialectic, his overriding interest in ethics and, with it, the Pythagorean mysticism which more than anything else distinguished his thinking from the uncompromising rationalism of the other sophists.

Plato wanted stability; he found it politically in the rigid Spartan oligarchy which had survived superficially unchanged for three hundred years and in the end had crushed the brilliant but short-lived Athenian experiment; and he found it philosophically in the certain truths of mathematics. For him there was no reality in the unsteady material world, but he created another 'real' world in its place, the world of the 'forms', apprehended by the mind and understood only by the philosopher-mathematician. Only here was there real beauty (the 'form' of beauty), real goodness, or a real table, and only in contemplation of these realities were real knowledge and real happiness to be found. This was not of course a mere dream-world; it was conceived as an explanation of, not as an escape from, the distressing logical problems of perception, an explanation which itself raised problems which Plato was the first to realise and which he was never satisfied that he had solved. What was the nature and the number of the forms? What was their exact relationship to the world of sense? Nor could the philosopher shut himself off from the world and spend his days in a contented orgy of contemplation. It was his duty to return and apply his knowledge in the miserable darkness of everyday life by administering the only good kind of government there could be, a strict authoritarian régime.

This brief, and, it must be admitted, hostile account does little justice to Plato's achievements. The problem of knowledge with which he was ultimately concerned is a real one. Philosophers ever since have been worried by the questions he asked and many of them have done no more than re-state, modify or develop his answers; many who disagreed have been prepared to argue in the terms which he laid down. But we must not let his philosophical genius, his passionate sincerity, or for that matter, his incomparable style obscure the fundamental weakness of his idealist philosophy or the horror of his authoritarian republic. For, to the writer at least, they are weak, as is any philosophy which dismisses the world it is trying to explain, and horrible, as is any political theory which claims for its author privileged access to the truth.

His pupil, Aristotle (384–322 B.C.), a native of Stagira in Thrace, did not follow him in his outright rejection of the world of sense. For him, the field of knowledge was not limited to mathematics or an ideal world but included the whole of human experience; he was by nature a collector, a rationaliser, not a mystic, and it is all too easy to dismiss his works as 'glorified common sense'. But they are far from that; his *Ethics* and *Politics*, for all their crudities of style and sometimes tedious statements of the obvious, are brilliant accounts of human behaviour and human society, based not on any private vision of what ought to be, but on a meticulous analysis of actual behaviour and real societies. Elsewhere he produced the first real system of deductive logic and one which was only superseded less than a hundred years ago. So great was his influence that 'throughout modern times', as Bertrand Russell says, 'practically every advance in science, logic or in philosophy has had to be made in the teeth of opposition from Aristotle's disciples.' But this is hardly Aristotle's fault, unless it is a fault to achieve too much at once. Aristotle himself would have been the first to condemn the blind acceptance of his views by his successors.

VII

In 343 B.C., Aristotle was called to the court of King Philip at Pella to act as tutor to his son, Alexander. Here, in the rough hills of northern Greece, the small kingdom of Macedon had for long played an insignificant but troublesome part on the outskirts of the Greek world. Now, a weakened Greece could no longer keep in check the semi-Hellenic or semi-Hellenised powers around its borders, and with the accession of Philip in 360 B.C. a new phase began. By a series of tough and masterly campaigns he established order on his unruly northern frontiers and then by a mixture of bluff, deceit and military force extended his control over the rest of northern Greece. Meanwhile, Greek politicians kept up their domestic squabbles and inter-state disputes; of those who recognised the importance of Macedonian expansion some, like the Athenian Demosthenes, called hysterically for unity in defence of freedom; others, like the scholar Isocrates, dreamed of a pan-Hellenic crusade under Macedonian leadership against the Persians; others again welcomed the appearance of a potential patron. While they argued and intrigued, Philip moved further south until, after years of desultory and disconnected fighting and intermittent peace, the

brilliant oratory of Demosthenes had its effect and some sort of Greek alliance was formed. But its troops were no match for the superb Macedonian army and an overwhelming victory at Chaeronaea (338 B.C.) brought Philip into southern Greece. How he would have used his victory we do not know, for he was assassinated only two years later. He left to his son Alexander a restless northern frontier, a divided kingdom and a broken but unsettled Greece; he also left him with the finest army in the world and an opportunity to establish for the first time a real Hellenic kingdom and a Hellenic empire.

4   EASTERN EMPIRES: IRAN, INDIA AND CHINA

While the brilliant but miniature civilisation of the Hellenes had been flourishing in the Eastern Mediterranean and colonising westward to Sicily, Italy and southern France, and north to the Black Sea, much larger societies had long been established across the great land mass of Asia from the Levant to India and the Far East. The Persian Empire bordered not only upon the Greeks but upon northern India, while the Sassanian and Parthian Empires which succeeded it created perennial problems for Rome. In India, Aryan-speaking invaders from the north had already carved out kingdoms by the seventh century B.C. when the Greeks were emerging into history, and the great Maurya Empire reached its widest extent under Asoka, less than a century after Alexander's incursion into northern India in 327 B.C. In China, meanwhile, the Chou Dynasty in the area of the Yellow River was established by the time of the Trojan War and of the rise of the Hebrew kingdom in Palestine. The period of the warring states had lasted from the early fifth to the later third centuries, to be concluded with the establishment of the Ch'in Empire.

Iran

by R. H. Pinder Wilson

At the outset of the first millennium before Christ, hegemony of the civilised world west of China lay with the peoples of Western Asia: it was only at the close that it had passed to those of the Central and Eastern Mediterranean. In this process the people of Iran played a decisive part. In considering the struggle between Greece and Persia, we are inclined to draw too sharp antitheses—Greek and Barbarian, liberty and oriental despotism. Greece emerged victorious from that struggle but did not stem the tide which the Achaemenians had set in motion; the founders of the Achaemenian Empire refashioned the political state of the ancient East in accordance with a new concept of empire. Nor was the influence of the Achaemenian Empire limited to its span of two centuries.

Alexander the Great proclaimed himself the lineal heir of the Great King; and four centuries later the Sassanian monarchs set out to restore the empire of their ancestors dividing the civilised world with the Emperors of Rome. Sassanian Persia in its turn influenced the later concept and practice of universal autocracy at the Roman imperial court.

II

The country from which the Persians set out to conquer an empire larger than any previous one is a land of physical contrasts. These created widely different ways of life among its inhabitants and had hitherto defied unified control. Essentially it consists of a high plateau surrounded on all sides by mountain barriers. Geologically, these are extensions of the Armenian Knot in the north-west and the Pamirs in the east. In the west, the mountains of Kurdistan and the Zagros range divide the Iranian plateau from the Mesopotamian plain and provide a defensive bulwark whose only practicable route is the pass that runs through Kirmanshah to Hamadan where the road debouches into the plain below. Through the 'gateway of Asia' marched the armies of Darius I (fifth century B.C.), of Alexander (fourth century B.C.) and the Arab conquerors of the seventh century A.D.

In the south-west, the Karun river flows through the mountains and forms the plain of Khuzistan which is an extension of the Mesopotamian plain. Here, with its centre at Susa, arose the kingdom of Elam, the earliest urban civilisation in

Persia. The mountain chains continue in a south-easterly direction and then turn east along the Persian Gulf and the Sea of Oman, forming the province of Fars, Persis of the ancient world and home of the two dynasties which brought Persia into the orbit of world history, the Achaemenians and Sassanians. This is a region of upland valleys supporting a sparse population and divided from the sea by a narrow coastal strip. The climate was unfavourable to the development of a maritime community and this partly explains why Persia never emerged as a sea power in ancient times. The province, too, was cut off from the north by uninhabitable desert so that communications had to take a north-westerly direction along the mountain chains to Babylon and Susa and to Ecbatana. Remote from the more accessible

IRANIAN EMPIRES

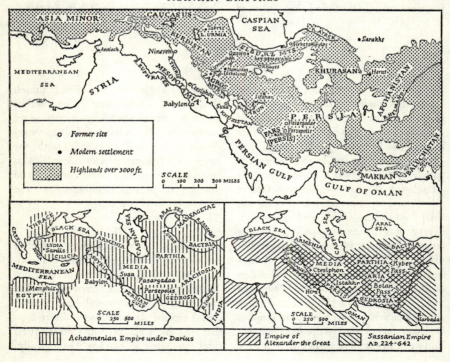

and more populous provinces of the north, Persis was ill-fitted to play the central role in the Empire and its cities of Persepolis and Istakhr never possessed the importance of Babylon, Susa and Ctesiphon.

In the north-west of Iran a mountain range extends from Armenia to the shore of the Caspian Sea and protects the province of Azerbaijan, the most fertile and populous region of the whole country. The great trade routes which today converge on the city of Tabriz made the province an important centre of communications from earliest times. But easy access in the north laid this region open to invasion by peoples from across the Caucasus. It was through these weak points that Aryan tribes, the ancestors of the Medes and Persians, entered Persia at the beginning of the first millennium B.C.

Directly north, the Elburz range, running parallel to the southern shore of the Caspian Sea, acts as a formidable defence, culminating in Mount Demavand, an extinct volcano 19,000 feet high. Further east, the high mountains and plains of Khurasan are vulnerable at two points—along the valley of the Atrek and across the plain of Gurgan and further to the east through the wide gap in the mountains, west of the city of Sarakhs.

In the east, the mountains turn south and skirt the uninhabitable desert that covers the greater part of central Iran. The only inhabitable settlement in this inhospitable region is around the basin fed by the waters of the river Helmand.

Such are the boundaries of Iran: settlement was possible along the periphery of the highland belt in those areas which caught the rains from the mountains or from the mountain stream, and were suitable for the cultivation of wheat and crops. The upland valleys with their rich pastures were better adapted to a pastoral economy, and in ancient times the plain of Kirmanshah was famous as a breeding ground of the finest horses. The country was also rich in iron, copper, tin and lead. When iron came into general use at the beginning of the first millennium B.C., these iron deposits enriched Iran. The marble and alabaster of the Iranian quarries were sought by the Sumerians, and precious stones, such as turquoise and lapis lazuli, were being exploited even in Neolithic times.

Iran, moreover, forms a land bridge between Europe and Asia and in history acted as intermediary between these two continents. Along the strategic and mercantile routes which skirt the mountains arose great cities; in the north, Qazvin, Rhages, Hekatompylos and Herat; in the south, Isfahan, Pasargadae, Istakhr, Persepolis and Shiraz.

III

The name Iran has been applied to the country since Islamic times. It is the modern Persian derivative of the old Persian genitive *Aryanam*, '(the land) of the Aryans'—a reminder that it was the coming of the Iranians that changed the whole course of the history of the country.

The earliest inhabitants of Iran were an Asiatic people who established settlements on the plateau as early as the fifth millennium B.C. The first large urban community arose in the plain of Susiana as early as the beginning of the third millennium. This kingdom of Elam played an important part in the history of Mesopotamia constantly coming into conflict with Babylonia; it disappeared about 1200 B.C. but revived in the eighth century until it was destroyed by the Assyrian king Assurbanipal. It left behind its language which enjoyed equality with Babylonian and old Persian in the Achaemenian Empire.

In the course of the second millennium,

the first wave of Aryans entered Western Asia at about the same time as another branch invaded India. Among these were the Hittites who founded a powerful empire in Asia Minor and Syria, and the Mitanni who established themselves in Upper Mesopotamia. Others attached themselves as a tribunal aristocracy to the indigenous Asiatic inhabitants; the Kassites, for example, conquered and ruled Babylonia for nearly six hundred years.

About a thousand years later, a second wave brought the Iranians in from the Caucasus and Transoxiana. Unlike the earlier Aryans, who became assimilated to the indigenous population, the Iranians retained their identity and by slow stages succeeded in gaining control of the whole country. In the middle of the ninth century two great Iranian tribes, the Medes and the Persians, were dwelling in the area between Lake Urmia and the plain of Hamadan. About 700 B.C. Phraortes, son of Deioces—founder of the Median royal line—united the Median chieftains into a confederation which his son Cyaxares succeeded in building into a formidable military power. He established his capital at Ecbatana, guarding the road against the Assyrian invader. Turning his attention to the west, he captured Nineveh in 612 B.C. and destroyed Assyria as a world power.

The Persians had moved south in the course of the eighth century and settled in the land of Parsumash, north-east of Susa. Teispes, son of Achaemenes, while submitting as vassal to the Median king Phraortes, was able to add the country of Persis to his dominions. The young Persian kingdom avoided becoming embroiled in Assyrian politics as the Medes had done, and so was able to conserve its energy for the coming struggle with the Medes. A descendant of Teispes, Cambyses I, married the daughter of the Median king, Astyages, and the son of this marriage,

Cyrus, threw off the yoke of his Median overlord whom he defeated and captured in 549 B.C.

Cyrus the Great is the true founder of the immense and elaborately organised Persian Empire, which set standards imitated by Alexander and by Rome. His territorial expansion was dictated by two objectives; to capture the rich commerce of the eastern littoral of the Mediterranean —the natural terminus of the Asiatic caravan route—and to secure the eastern frontier of his empire. The rich kingdom of Lydia and the Greek maritime cities of Ionia in Asia Minor were conquered in 546 B.C.; for the next seven years Cyrus was engaged in extending his eastern frontiers to the Aral Sea and the Jaxartes and to the eastern limits of Afghanistan and Baluchistan. He was then able to deal with his one remaining rival in the west by enforcing the submission of Babylonia and its dependencies, Syria, Palestine and Elam. Towards the close of his reign he put his son Cambyses in charge of the plans to conquer Egypt, while he himself was called away to deal with affairs in the east where he was killed in battle in 530 B.C.

The success of Cyrus in founding and maintaining his empire was due partly to his genius as a general and strategist, and partly to the policy that he adopted towards the people of his conquered territories. The Assyrians and Babylonians in their relations with their subject races had resorted to the most savage repression, destroying their religious and social institutions, and enslaving and sometimes deporting whole communities. Cyrus, on the contrary, respected the institutions and customs of his subjects, who differed widely in race, religion and civilisation. They received him as a liberator and gave him the title 'the just King' and 'the Anointed of the Lord'. He legitimised his succession to the throne of Babylon by divine investiture from the Babylonian god, Marduk; and allowed the Jews, after their forty years' captivity in Babylon, to return to their land and rebuild the temple at Jerusalem. He retained his capital at Susa, spending the winter at Babylon and the summer months at Ecbatana. In the province of Fars, where tradition has it that he defeated Astyages, he founded the city of Pasargadae, where his body was buried beneath a stone tomb in the form of a gabled house raised on a plinth of six steps. Resembling the Nordic house, it reminds us of the kinship between the Iranians and the Indo-European tribes.

Cambyses, in accordance with his father's intentions, annexed Egypt, thus succeeding where the Assyrian kings had failed. He died in Syria before reaching Persia, where a pretender to the throne was endangering the whole fabric of the Empire, for the Medes were trying to restore their supremacy in Persia and the Babylonians aimed at recovering their independence. The situation was saved by Darius, a young Persian noble claiming descent from Achaemenes. He secured his ascendancy in nineteen battles in which he defeated nine rebel leaders.

These events are commemorated in a relief sculptured in the cliff face of Mount Bisitun guarding the 'Gateway of Asia'. It represents Darius crushing beneath his foot the false pretender to the throne and the nine rebel princes led before him in chains. With right hand upraised, the King offers his victims to Ahuramazda, the supreme god of the Persians, symbolised by the winged sun disc and human profile. In and around this relief is inscribed in Babylonian, Elamite and Old Persian, the greatest of all Iranian inscriptions beginning with the words: 'I am Darius the Great King, King of Kings, King in Persia, King of countries, son of Hystaspes, grandson of Arsames, an Achaemenian.'

Then follows the list of the victories which Darius won over his enemies 'by the help of Ahuramazda and the other gods', thereby vindicating his claim to the throne.

Darius' campaigns outside Persia added more territories to the Empire. Thrace and Macedonia were annexed and converted into provinces, thus providing a foothold in Europe. But the attempt to conquer the continental Greeks failed with the disaster at Marathon in 490 B.C. By securing possession of islands in the Mediterranean, however, Darius consolidated his hold on the commerce of the Levant. In the east the conquest of western India as far as the Indus provided the Empire with further riches.

Building on the foundations already laid by Cyrus, Darius welded these diverse components into a unified empire. At the same time each region and race retained its own religion, institutions, officials and, in certain cases, its king. The Great King was a despot ruling by divine right and was the source of all law. He nominated his successors from among his sons; and his nomination was confirmed by Ahuramazda and the gods of Babylon and Egypt.

After the conquest of India, the huge Empire was divided into twenty provinces, each governed by a satrap, who was appointed by the King from among the royal princes or nobles. The satrap was responsible for maintaining security within his province and for collecting and despatching the taxes to the royal treasury at Susa. In order to maintain central control, the satrap was assisted by a royal secretary who carried on the royal correspondence between the imperial administration and the province. As a further precaution, royal inspectors, or 'King's Eyes', were sent with commissions into the provinces in order to supervise execution of imperial policy.

Tribute was in the form of silver and

gold or natural produce, or both. Precious metals were despatched to the royal treasury, where a part was converted into coin—the gold darikos and the silver siglos —on which the King is represented for the first time in any oriental coinage. Money was reserved for the King and for this reason was scarce in the provinces. The revenue was used to maintain the imperial armies and the administration.

Darius realised the need for a common language that could be understood throughout the Empire. Babylonian was already archaic, Elamite was spoken in a limited area, and Persian, having no tradition, was not suited for the purposes of administration. Moreover, all three languages were written in the unwieldy cuneiform character. Darius chose Aramaic which had long been the language of commerce in Mesopotamia. The Semitic Aramaeans had penetrated Syria and Mesopotamia at the beginning of the first millennium B.C. bringing with them their language, the writing of which was based on the Phoenician alphabet and therefore suitable for the new writing materials, papyrus and leather.

For strategic, administrative and commercial purposes so vast an empire required an efficient system of communications. A part of the imperial revenue was used to develop and maintain the royal roads. Along these great highways a postal system for imperial correspondence was organised which for speed was only equalled by that of the Mongols in the later Middle Ages. By means of relays, an imperial letter could travel from Sardis in Asia Minor to Susa in seven days—a distance of 1500 miles which the normal caravan took up to ninety days to cover.

The religion which the Aryans brought with them from their original home was based on worship of the forces of nature and involved the sacrifice of animals. In the course of centuries it was elaborated by the Magi, a priestly class acting as intermediaries between gods and worshippers. Fire worship played an important part in the religious observances. The religion of the Magi was reformed by Zoroaster, who probably lived about the seventh century B.C., and in its new guise spread throughout the Achaemenian Empire, although it was not formally adopted as the state religion until the Sassanian period. It is not known whether Darius was an adherent of Zoroastrianism. In his inscriptions he asserts the supremacy of Ahuramazda over the other gods; but under the later Achaemenians several of the latter were given official recognition, including Mithras, the sun god, whose cult acquired wide influence in the Roman Empire during the first three centuries of the Christian era.

The King and his court were patrons of art. Lacking a strong tradition of its own, Achaemenian art was composite, reflecting the styles current among the subject peoples who were employed in the building projects of the Great King. The most impressive example of Achaemenian architecture is the ruined city of Persepolis which Darius founded near Pasargadae. Here he and his successors were buried in tombs cut in the rock face of the cliffs. The royal palaces are laid out on a stone terrace, a system derived from Sumero-Babylonian tradition. The royal audience hall of Darius consisted of a cedar wood ceiling supported on seventy-two fluted columns; this trabeate form of architecture was inspired by Egyptian prototypes. Walls were decorated with bas reliefs reminiscent of those of the Assyrians and Babylonians. The façades of the great stairways formed of double ramps, are decorated with reliefs depicting an endless line of tribute bearers, or the royal guards known as 'Immortals'. Elsewhere the King is shown in single combat with a lion or fantastic beast. The overriding intention of Achaemenian art was to glorify the greatness and majesty of the King. Often monotonous and ostentatious, it seldom fails to achieve a certain grandeur.

With Darius' death in 486 B.C. the decline of the Achaemenian Empire set in. None of his eight successors possessed either his generalship or political perspicacity. Military intervention in the affairs of Greece and serious rebellions in the provinces, in some of which the satraps set themselves up as independent rulers, strained the resources of the Empire and imposed a heavy burden of taxation on the subject races. The toleration which Darius displayed towards the latter was discarded in favour of conformity brutally enforced. In the reign of Darius III the Empire still retained the appearance of power, but the forces of disintegration left it unable to withstand the determined onslaught of Alexander of Macedon. One after another of the provinces fell to the conqueror and the victory of Gaugamela in 331 B.C. sealed the fate of the Achaemenian Empire.

Alexander had set out on his Persian adventure to avenge the 'Medic wars'. But after the liberation of the Greeks of Asia Minor, he began to conceive the idea of a political union between the Greek and Iranian worlds. His early death in 323 B.C. prevented the fulfilment of his ambition; and his empire was divided among his generals, Syria and Iran going to Seleucus. (*See* Chapter 5.)

IV

The Hellenic Seleucids held Iran for only a short period. Soon after 250 B.C. the Parthians under Arsaces, and then under his brother Tiridates, established themselves in north-eastern Persia and achieved independence. The Parthians were a nomadic people of Aryan origin and newcomers to the Iranian plateau from the Asiatic steppes. Within a century they had torn from Seleucid control the whole of Iran, as well as Babylonia where they established their capital at Ctesiphon on the Tigris. In the west they were brought into contact with the Romans, who successively conquered Asia Minor, Syria and Egypt, but in spite of ephemeral Roman victories, the Euphrates remained the dividing line between the two empires.

The Parthian monarchs claimed to be the restorers of the Achaemenian Empire. From the time of Mithridates I, the real founder of the Parthian Empire, they assumed the title Great King. The structure of their empire was feudal, with the dangers inherent in such a society. An aristocracy of warriors and horsemen, they never possessed the ability to weld their subjects into a closely knit state. The Seleucids had introduced a new element into the social and economic life of Iran by their policy of extensive urbanisation. New cities were created in which Greek colonists and a Hellenised Iranian bourgeoisie formed a community based on Greek principles. Possibly it was with the object of conciliating this important element that the earlier Parthians styled themselves Philhellene on their coins.

Opposition to the Romans seems to have contributed to the revival of the dormant spirit of Iranian patriotism. About the first century A.D., the social and cultural life of the Iranians underwent a 're-orientalising' process. Greek was gradually replaced by Persian written in the 'Arsacid' script; according to one tradition, the Zoroastrian writings known as the Avesta were collected at the order of the Great King in the first century A.D. This process is also reflected in the art of the period. In architecture, the decorative use of wall painting and carved stucco belongs to the Assyrian rather than the Hellenistic tradition. Two features also occur for the first time in Iranian architecture; the 'ivan' or great vaulted niche having the function of an audience hall, and the squinch used to support a dome on a square ground plan. Both features were to be widely used in Iranian architecture of the Sassanian and Islamic periods. In the few surviving reliefs the human form is always depicted full-face rather than side-face and seems to derive from a tradition earlier than the Achaemenian period.

V

This national revival was fully realised under the Sassanians. The Parthians belonged to outer Iran and never elicited the same response from the Iranian people as did the Sassanians, who originated in Persis, where the memory of the Achaemenian past was kept alive during the centuries of Greek and Parthian rule. Persis was ruled by a king who acknowledged the overlordship of the Arsacid Great King. Sassan, the ancestor of the future kings of Iran, held a high religious office at Istakhr, capital of the kingdom: and his son Papak founded the fortunes of the house by putting the King to death and placing himself on the throne. But it was Papak's second son, Ardashir, who was destined to raise the family to the throne of Iran. He defeated the last Parthian king Artabanus V in A.D. 224 and two years later was crowned King of Kings. Like the Arsacids, he fixed his capital at Ctesiphon.

The empire founded by Ardashir survived more or less intact for four centuries. Unlike the Parthian Empire, it was a unified state. The feudal organisation was retained but the danger of rebellious vassals was met by the creation of a formidable mercenary army the core of which was the body of heavy-armed cavalry directly dependent on the King. Like the Achaemenians, the Sassanian monarch was invested by Ahuramazda with the divine right to rule and his person was sacred and hedged about by means of an elaborate court etiquette. Zoroastrianism became the state religion and a national Church under the direction of the Magi was established. The clergy became powerful in the state and few kings survived without their support. In the reign of Shapur I, Mani, a Persian of noble birth, preached a syncretic religion combining Christian, Jewish and Buddhist elements with Zoroastrianism. He and his followers were favourably regarded by the King; but his successor, Bahram I, had Mani executed (*c.* A.D. 273) at the instigation of the Magi. Persecuted in Persia and in the Roman Empire, Manichaeism eventually found a refuge in Central Asia. Christianity, too, was at first tolerated, but after Constantine made it an official religion of the Roman Empire, the Christians were persecuted where they were regarded as the subjects of an enemy power. Religious unity was the necessary outcome of political unity and was also dictated by external circumstances. On their western frontier the Sassanians had the Christian empire of Rome, while Buddhism was the state religion in the Kushan kingdom of Bactria and northern India, Persia's eastern neighbour. Religion, too, could be used as a weapon in the political struggle with Rome. Thus, in the sixth century, the Nestorians, officially banned in the Roman Empire, were given an asylum in Persia.

The wars with Rome continued, with sporadic truces. Spectacular, if short-lived, successes were gained by the Persians: in A.D. 260 Shapur defeated the Romans at Edessa and captured the Emperor Valerian. In the sixth century Chosroes I inaugurated a great resurgence of Sassanian power, and carrying the war into Syria, captured Antioch. Almost on the eve of the Arab conquest, Chosroes II penetrated Egypt and pillaged the cities of Syria, removing the relic of the True Cross from Jerusalem.

But the Sassanians had also to face threats on their eastern marches. The White Huns maintained their pressure during the fifth century and were finally held on the Oxus by Khusrau I. This danger was followed by the threat of invasion by the Turkish tribes whose full force was to be felt in the Islamic period.

By the seventh century both Persia and Byzantium were exhausted by their constant wars. They were powerless to resist the onslaught of the desert Arabs inspired with the fervour of a new religion, and a desire for conquest of rich territories. Byzantium lost the eastern provinces of Syria and Egypt. Persia fared worse, Iraq passed to the Arabs after the Persian defeat at Qadisiya in A.D. 637. Three years later, they had crossed the mountain barriers of Persia, broke the final resistance of the Persians at the battle of Nihavand and the last of the Sassanian rulers, Yazderjird III, was murdered by his own people in A.D. 651.

VI

The Sassanian Empire is notable for its artistic achievements. Sassanian art liberated itself from Hellenistic forms and reasserted Iranian elements. It is more than a restatement of Achaemenian forms, by which it was no doubt inspired, since it evolved its own particular manner of expression, its own style. Sassanian architecture dispensed with the trabeate form of the Achaemenians. The Sassanian palace is a massive structure of walls and bastions and vaulted rooms. The column is discarded in favour of the pier. These forms were dictated partly by the use of bricks, baked or sun-dried. The royal audience hall becomes a square or oblong chamber surmounted by a dome. The most impressive architectural monument is the ruined palace at Ctesiphon where a façade is built on either side of a vast vaulted niche. This was the royal audience hall, where the Great King was seen by his subjects behind a veil and above him a golden crown suspended from the roof.

The most important monuments of Sassanian art are some thirty rock sculptures. With the exception of a group near Kirmanshah, these are all in Fars. All serve to glorify the King and his exploits. A number represents the symbolical investiture of the Great King by Ahuramazda. God and king mounted on horses face each other in an almost heraldic composition, and with his right hand the King receives the crown from his divine protector. Another series portrays Shapur's victory over Valerian; in one version the Roman emperor kneels as a suppliant before the Sassanian majesty and in another they combat together as in some medieval tourney. Stylistically, some of the sculptures reveal a Roman influence, while others are rendered in a wholly Iranian idiom, but the significant difference between the Roman and Persian commemorative sculpture is in the handling of the subject. Where the Roman sculptor depicted the actual course of the event, the Iranian sculptor represented it by a symbolic encounter between the main protagonists.

Fine metalwork, both silver and bronze, was produced in the Sassanian period; and Persian silk weaves even found their way to Europe. In this way Sassanian decorative motives were introduced into the Byzantine and Western repertory.

Sassanian art did not come to an abrupt end with the fall of the dynasty. With the advent of the Abbasid caliphate in A.D.

750, the Persians became the dominant force in the Islamic world. Sassanian court etiquette and methods of administrative procedure were adopted by the Caliph. Persian architecture and art developing out of the forms evolved in the Sassanian period had an immense influence on what was to become Islamic art.

Thus the original massive empire of Darius created a tradition which was exploited by the Parthians and given a new and vigorous interpretation by the Sassanians. Through Alexander's successors, Persian methods of administration, the cult of the Divine Ruler, and the concept of empire on a great scale descended to Rome. With the decline of Rome, they greatly affected the whole future of the West, while after the defeat of Byzantine power in Syria, the influence of the Persians became decisive in the new empire of Islam.

India and China
by G. F. Hudson

The Persian Empire of Cyrus and Darius was in direct contact with the ancient Greeks and Hebrews. It was thus closely connected with the origins of the civilisation of Europe. But away to the east, beyond the horizon of the Mediterranean peoples of those days, were other countries with their own forms of civilisation, which, although they arose later than the early cultures of Egypt and Sumer, were almost entirely independent in their origin. With these countries Europeans had very little contact or communication before Vasco da Gama's voyage opening the Indian Ocean to European shipping in 1498. Yet fully half the population of the world today belong by its tradition to the cultural sphere of either India or China, and even if the ancient history of Further Asia has little relevance to that of Europe, the West no longer possesses the ascendancy of a generation ago.

During the two centuries after the death of Alexander the Great, empires comparable in extent to that which he had conquered were created both in India and in China. In the generation after Alexander, Chandragupta extended his sway from Bengal to Kabul, and his grandson Asoka, who reigned from 269 to 232 B.C., when

Rome was a struggling city state, ruled over the whole of the Indian sub-continent except for the extreme south. In China the empire of the Ch'in Dynasty, established in 221 B.C., covered the whole territory from the Great Wall down to Tongking, though not the lands to the north and west included in the China of today. Both in India and in China, these great empires arose from the forcible amalgamation of a number of kingdoms and tribes which had been almost continually at war with one another, and each represented the climax of a long process of ethnic development which shaped a society with a common culture over a wide area. In each case the original homeland of the civilisation was only a small part of the territory covered later on by the Empire.

The Indian civilisation began in the basin of the Indus, the Chinese in that of the Yellow River. In both areas, recent archaeological discoveries have revealed ages of history going back far beyond the boundaries of knowledge of fifty years ago. In India the excavation of the sites of Mohenjo-daro and Harappa from 1912 onward disclosed a flourishing culture of city-dwellers datable as early as 2500 B.C. or a millennium before the time of the oldest hymns of the Rigveda which had previously been regarded as belonging to the dawn of Indian history (*see* Chapter 2); in China, digging on the site of Yin Hsu near Anyang, carried on intermittently from 1910, gradually provided a body of direct evidence about the legendary period of the Shang Dynasty of the second millennium B.C. But there was one great difference between these two extensions of historical knowledge by the spade of the archaeologist. The memory of the Shang Dynasty and the names of its kings had been preserved in Chinese tradition, so that the

archaeological discoveries merely served to give a vivid picture of an age which had previously had only a shadowy and dubious existence. The civilisation of the Indus cities, on the other hand, the so-called Harappa culture, was totally unknown at the time when material traces of it were first found; all memory of it had been lost. Thus the discovery of the Harappa culture has modified older ideas about the origins of Indian civilisation to a much greater extent than the Anyang excavations have altered the scheme of ancient Chinese history

ANCIENT CENTRES OF CIVILIZATION

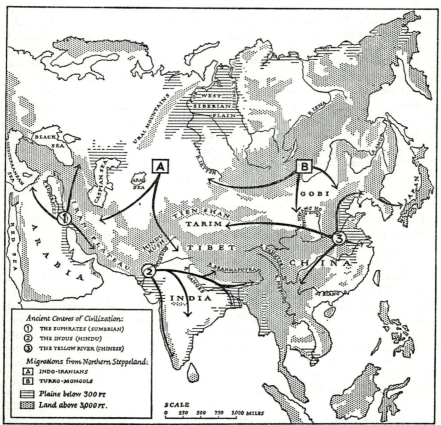

Ancient Centres of Civilization:
① THE EUPHRATES (SUMERIAN)
② THE INDUS (HINDU)
③ THE YELLOW RIVER (CHINESE)

Migrations from Northern Steppeland:
Ⓐ INDO-IRANIANS
Ⓑ TURKO-MONGOLS

▤ Plains below 300 FT
▦ Land above 3,000 FT.

SCALE
0   250   500   750   1,000 MILES

accepted by the scholars of the nineteenth century.

In another way too, there has been a striking difference between the two fields of archaeology. The Anyang finds have included great numbers of inscriptions on bronze vessels and on 'oracle bones' used for divination, which, though often difficult to read, are definitely in archaic forms of the Chinese language and script of later times. There has been thus in the region of the Yellow River a continuous development of the same language and culture from the second millennium B.C. But the Harappa culture, although its brick-built cities have left us far more in the way of architectural remains than Shang China—which appears to have been built entirely in wood—has given us no written evidence that can be read; it had a script, but one which did not survive or link up with any later Indian form of writing, and nobody has yet succeeded in deciphering it. The Indians of the early Vedic age were illiterate, and the Vedic literature was preserved by oral transmission; it was only after a lapse of centuries that an alphabet derived from Western Asia came into use in India. We cannot therefore be certain what language it was that was written in the Harappa script and was spoken by the inhabitants of the Indus cities around 2000 B.C. But we can be fairly sure it was not the Indo-Aryan speech in which the earliest Vedic literature was composed. The Vedic culture is strikingly different from its Harappa predecessor in the same area, and its traditions leave no doubt that the Aryans were an invading people. Their entry into India, which probably brought about the destruction of the cities of the Harappa culture, made a break in the cultural development of India to which the early history of China affords no parallel.

In China today the vast majority of the population speak one or another dialect of the Chinese language, but in the mountains of the west and south there are remnants of people speaking languages akin to Tibetan or Siamese, and these were formerly spread over wide areas where they have in the course of time been absorbed by Chinese expansion. Their languages, however, belong to the same family as Chinese, and their racial type is generally similar. In India and Pakistan, on the other hand, four different linguistic families are represented—the Indo-Aryan prevailing in the plains of the Indus and Ganges and in the western Deccan; the Dravidian in South India and in part of Baluchistan to the west of the Indus; the Austro-Asiatic in the Khasi Hills to the east of Bengal and in the hill tracts of central India; and the Sinitic—which includes Chinese and Tibetan—in the Himalayas. It is probable from this geographic distribution in modern times that Dravidian speech once prevailed in the Indus basin and was used by the Harappa people, and that the domain of the Austro-Asiatic languages originally covered Bihar, Bengal and Orissa. These peoples, in other words, occupied the Indian sub-continent early in the second millennium B.C., when the Indo-Aryans invaded India across the north-western mountains from Central Asia.

II

The Indo-Aryans were a branch of a people which developed a distinctive culture, with the possession of horses and wheeled vehicles, in the wide grasslands between the Carpathians and the Altai; their westward movement into Europe produced the Greek, Italic, Celtic, Teutonic and Slavonic peoples, while the Indo-Aryans, Iranians and Armenians represent their migrations to the south. Wherever they spread, the Aryans absorbed older peoples on whom they imposed branches of their language, but by whose influence their culture was modified and assumed new regional forms. Their immigration into India was no exception, and the European scholars who tried to reconstruct early Indian history in the nineteenth century, after it had been proved that Sanskrit was a cousin of Greek and other European languages, always recognised that there was both racially and culturally, an element in the Indo-Aryan civilisation which was derived from the older inhabitants of the country. But before the discovery of the Harappa culture, it was assumed that the Aryan invaders, barbarous though they might have been, were on a higher level of civilisation than the peoples they encountered.

It has been impossible to retain such a belief since the excavations of Mohenjo-daro and Harappa. The Harappa people dwelt in cities comparable to those of ancient Egypt and Mesopotamia, whereas the Aryans who overran their territory were a mainly pastoral people living in villages and pasturing their cattle and horses over wide areas; their superiority was in warfare, not in the arts of peaceful living. Nor, even though their cities were ruined, was the Harappa culture entirely destroyed; their religion survived. Finds on the sites of their cities indicate the cult of a mother-goddess and of the god who is worshipped as Shiva in modern Hinduism. The earliest Sanskrit literature, consisting of the hymns of the Rigveda, belongs to the religious cults of the Aryan invaders; it celebrates Indra, Varuna and other divinities whom the Aryans regarded as their own, while Shiva—or Rudra as he was anciently called—appears only in the margin of the pantheon, a god of the mountains and forests, feared rather than honoured. But as time goes on, Shiva

becomes more and more prominent, until at last he is rivalled as an object of Hindu worship only by Vishnu—who is by origin an Aryan deity, though his myths also have been modified by pre-Aryan traditions. It is now clear that the growth of the cult of Shiva and of his 'wife', the mother-goddess Parvati or Kali of later times, was not a new development, but a revival of a religion already established in its essential features in the third millennium B.C. Shivaism indeed may claim to be the oldest religion widely followed today by civilised people, for whereas the ancient gods of Egypt, Babylonia and Greece have been superseded by Christianity or Islam and survive only in literature or archaeology, the cult of Shiva has persisted in India with little change for more than four thousand years.

The Harappa culture was virtually confined to the zone of Sind and the Punjab which has less than twenty inches of average annual rainfall—an arid environment similar to Egypt and Mesopotamia in which agriculture depended on irrigation. With the breakdown of the original irrigation system, presumably as a result of the Aryan invasions, this zone came to be scantily inhabited and relatively unimportant; the Aryans concentrated on the more rainy, though still almost treeless, part of the Punjab, where there was plenty of pasture for their herds, and it is there that we find them in the age of the Rigveda. In these poems the rivers of the Punjab are in the centre of the picture; the Jumna also is known, but the Ganges is only once mentioned. Gradually, however, the Aryans began to spread into the basin of the Ganges, then a region of vast forests, and at the same time their economy became less pastoral and more agricultural. The pre-Aryan inhabitants of the Ganges plains seem to have been quite primitive; there is no evidence that the Harappa culture ever extended to that region, though it did have outposts to the south along the west coast of India. The eastward expansion of the Aryans shifted the ethnic centre of gravity; in the end, the bulk of the population came to be located in the basin of the Ganges, and the Punjab lost its primacy.

The Aryans differed from the native inhabitants of India, whom they called Dasas, not only in language but also in racial type; they felt a strong sense of racial superiority to them, and strove not only to dominate them but also to preserve their own race free from admixture with them. In the early days relations with the Dasas were nearly always hostile, and those of them who were not killed or driven out were reduced to serfdom. To give a permanent form to the society thus created, the Aryans evolved a system of four hereditary 'castes'; their own occupational classes, the priests (brahmans), warrior nobles (kshatriyas) and farmers (vaishyas) formed the first three of these and were admitted to religious ceremonies by which they became 'twice-born'; the fourth caste, of the sudras, was reserved for the subjected Dasas, who were excluded from the social rights reserved for the conquerors. But as time went on, this scheme, while retaining the rigidity induced by the conditions of a bi-racial society, ceased to correspond to any racial reality. It happened more and more often that Aryan tribes made alliances with Dasa tribes in warfare against other Aryan tribes or that Aryan settlers came to terms with the local inhabitants, who adopted Aryan speech and customs; in such cases the Dasas' priests became brahmans, and their chiefs, kshatriyas. It was the infiltration of the brahman caste by Dasa elements which brought about, as already mentioned, the revival of the pre-Aryan Shiva cult under brahmanical patronage and in other ways modified the Aryan

religion, as revealed in the Rigveda, in the direction of the complex of beliefs and practices characteristic of later Hinduism.

The most striking feature of the society thus formed was the great prestige of the brahman priesthood and its sharp differentiation from the lay nobility of the kshatriyas. The brahmans secluded themselves from the rest of society, often in separate settlements, and transmitted their sacred learning through special schools within their own order. They performed sacrifices and other rituals for the kings and chiefs and as their chaplains, might perform the functions of political advisers and administrators, but they remained as a class independent of royal control; their status was hereditary and they managed to impose the belief that to kill one of their order was the worst of all crimes. The kings frequently opposed the pretensions of the brahmans to social supremacy, but were unable to deprive them of the power and influence they had acquired.

By about 800 B.C. when the first rudimentary Greek civilisation was emerging in the Levant from the dark age that followed the break-up of the Mycenean culture, Aryan speech prevailed throughout the greater part of India north of the Vindhya mountains, the east-west range which shuts off the plains of the Indus and Ganges from the great peninsula to the south. During the following centuries, Aryan settlement reached South India also, but here the tide of ethnic conquest was stayed; except in the Maratha country, Orissa and Ceylon, the Dravidian speech of the older inhabitants survived, and today the Dravidian languages—Tamil, Telugu, Malayalam and Kanarese—are spoken over the greater part of the area south of the Vindhyas. But the Dravidian peoples of South India submitted to the influence of the more highly developed culture of North India—a culture which, as we have seen, already included elements which were probably of Dravidian origin. Colonies of brahmans were established in the south, and Sanskrit became even in the Dravidian-speaking zone the language of religious learning. Thus India had attained by the beginning of the Christian era a high degree of cultural unity from the Himalayas southward to Cape Comorin and Ceylon.

Politically, there was no approach to unity before the fourth century B.C., on the eve of the incursion of Alexander, but there was a gradual process of formation of larger and larger political units. The early Aryans were divided into numerous tribes under chiefs who led them into battle, but had little administrative authority. As time went on, however, the old 'frontier' conditions were superseded, the forests were cleared, population became more dense, towns grew up and the primitive agricultural economy was modified by increases of commercial exchange and division of labour. Along with these changes, went developments in the art of war. It became possible to put larger forces into the field and their handling involved greater organisation and discipline; bodies of cavalry were added to the chariots in which the chiefs of the Vedic age, like those of Homer, went to war, and elephants also began to be used on the battlefield. With the enlarged scale of war the smaller chiefries were more and more absorbed by the larger, and kingdoms of considerable size came into existence. In the seventh century B.C. there were sixteen kingdoms covering most of North India. There were in addition some minor independent principalities and a number of republican tribes governed not by kings but by councils of the noble families; these republics tended to disappear in the turmoil of dynastic rivalries, but some of them held their own as either independent or subordinate political entities for many centuries. One of the republican tribes was that of the Sakyas into which Gautama the Buddha was born; they lived in the plain close to the foothills of the Himalayas.

The dating of the Buddha's life is uncertain, but he probably lived from 563 to 483 B.C. At his birth, according to legend, the soothsayers prophesied that he would become a universal monarch, with the exception of one who prophesied that he would renounce the world and become a universal teacher. To promote the fulfilment of the former rather than the latter prediction, his father, who was a Sakya chief, sought to immerse him in the life of a wealthy young noble, but could not prevent him from pondering on human destiny, with the result that one night he rode away from his mansion, sent back his robes and jewellery to his father by the hand of a faithful servant, and became a homeless, wandering ascetic, owning nothing but the single garment he wore. North India at this time swarmed with such people, who either begged their food or lived alone or in small groups in the forests, subsisting on herbs; they practised various kinds of self-mortification (*tapas*) and mental concentration, according to established techniques which were taught by master to disciple. These practices, to judge from the archaeological evidence, go back to the Harappa culture; originally they appear to have been undertaken as a means of acquiring magic powers, but later they were valued as inducing states of ecstatic trance which were felt to bestow a 'liberation' from the conditions of mortal and finite existence. In the seventh and sixth centuries B.C., the followers of this ascetic way of life developed systems of philosophy with widely different views of the nature of the universe, but what they had in common was the belief that 'liberation' was the highest end of human endeavour; this idea must be understood as reflecting not so much a despairing revulsion from normal human life—which has never in fact been characteristic of the Indian mind as expressed in its literature and art—but rather the attraction of the transcendental states of consciousness supposed to be attained by the ascetics.

Gautama, after practising austerities and meditation for several years without obtaining real peace of mind, is said to have sat under a pipal tree near the town of Gaya in Bihar and to have vowed that he would not move from the place until he had discovered the secret of salvation. After forty-nine days he became 'enlightened' (buddha) and his difficulties were at an end. He then set out to teach the doctrine which he had found out for himself, and continued to propagate it until his death at the age of eighty. His adherents were divided into an order of monks and a body of lay followers, for each of which a strict ethical code was laid down. The originality of the Buddha did not lie so much in his basic ideas, which he shared with other schools and sects of the age, but in his practical ability as a popular religious teacher and the personal influence he exerted over people in all walks of life.

Socially, the tendency to seek a personal salvation through ascetic self-discipline and meditation threatened the position of the brahman caste, which depended on the brahmans' monopoly of the knowledge of traditional sacred rituals and the right to perform them. Buddhism, and the parallel religion of Jainism which was founded about the same time—it still has some two million adherents in India, but has never, like Buddhism, spread to other countries— were both originated by men of kshatriya, not brahman, birth and offered salvation to all, irrespective of caste. Nevertheless,

in spite of a great expansion of the new 'heretical' faiths, they never superseded the religion of the brahmans in the way that Christianity and Islam superseded the old paganism of Europe and the Middle East. The masses of the population continued to worship traditional gods and goddesses, and the brahmans carried out an effective counter-reformation of their religion by re-interpreting these cults in accordance with a pantheistic philosophy which they had begun to work out even before the time of the Buddha. In the end this revision of the older religion, now known as Hinduism, was triumphant over Buddhism, which disappeared in India in the twelfth century A.D., but not before it had spread to many countries of South-East Asia and the Far East, where it still survives.

In the age of the Buddha, India was still parcelled out among many separate states, but the idea of a universal empire had already been formulated. It was not entirely a dream without any foundation in precedent or example, for in the days before the wider Aryan expansion the Bharata tribe had held a kind of paramountcy over others, and later on, the Persian Empire under Cyrus and Darius provided a model of imperial power on the grand scale to stimulate the ambitions of Indian kings as it also had its effect on the Mediterranean peoples. The Persians annexed the Indus valley and part of the Punjab, so that India was brought into close contact with the Persian system of government. Then, when Alexander the Great overthrew the Persian Empire, he followed up his victories with an invasion of what had been the Persian territory in India, but had by this time (327 B.C.) recovered its independence and was divided among several kingdoms and tribes. Alexander succeeded in subduing these, and wished to advance farther east towards the Ganges, whither the Persians had never penetrated, but on the Beas river in the Punjab his troops mutinied and refused to go any farther. He, therefore, left some garrisons to guard the most easterly territory of his empire and returned to Babylon, where he died in 323.

In the years that followed Alexander's death the Greek garrisons were expelled from the Indus valley and the whole of North India was unified by a great soldier and conqueror called Chandragupta, known to the Greeks as Sandracottos, whose family was related to the reigning house of Magadha, the most powerful of the kingdoms of the Gangetic plain, which had its capital at Pataliputra, the modern Patna in Bihar. Chandragupta—though very little for certain is known of his life— appears to have made his mark as an adventurer in the service of other states, and finally displaced the reigning Nanda Dynasty of Magadha, founding a new dynasty which bore his family name of Maurya. By a combination of military leadership with political and administrative skill which was frequently to be repeated in Indian history, Chandragupta established his imperial power with the aid of a brahman minister named Chanakya, who figures in legend as a model of subtle and prudent statecraft. We have a fragmentary Greek account of Chandragupta's court from Megasthenes, who was sent there as ambassador by Seleucus, the successor to Alexander in the eastern provinces of the Macedonian Empire after its partition. He reached Pataliputra by a royal road made by Chandragupta and running across North India from the upper Indus to the mouth of the Ganges. Pataliputra itself, though built entirely of wood, he describes as a magnificent and populous city; it was surrounded by a wall with 570 watch-towers and a moat 600 feet broad. The King, who had himself

usurped the throne, lived in perpetual fear of assassination, and was surrounded wherever he went by a special body-guard of armed women; on the other hand, he spent most of his time administering justice in open court, and was always accessible to the pleas of his subjects. We get a picture of a mighty monarchy which nevertheless retains a certain patriarchal simplicity and has not yet been encased in the structure of an imperial bureaucracy. The Empire indeed comprised two different forms of control; parts of it were administered by governors appointed from the centre, but other parts were left under the rule of kings who had made their submission and become feudatories of the imperial power.

Chandragupta was followed on the throne by his son Bindusara and by his grandson Asoka (269–232 B.C.), under whom the Mauryan Empire reached its greatest extension, covering not only the whole of North India, but also South India down to a point a little way north of Madras. It was the slaughter involved in his war against the Kalinga kingdom (in the modern Andhra and Orissa) which led to Asoka's conversion to Buddhism and his endeavours, recorded in his edicts inscribed on rocks and pillars all over the territory of the Empire, to base its administration and public life on a universal moral code. In the Kalinga War, declares Asoka in one of his edicts, '150,000 people were carried off captive, 100,000 were killed and many more died. Just after the taking of Kalinga, the Beloved of the Gods [*Devanam Priya,* a title used by Asoka] began to follow righteousness [*dharma*], to love righteousness, and to give instruction in righteousness. . . . If today a hundredth or a thousandth part of those who suffered in the Kalinga war were to be killed or taken captive, it would be very grievous to the Beloved of the Gods.' In Asoka's reign we see the heir to a sovereignty founded on violent conquest trying to stabilise and humanise it by means of a pacific and philanthropic religious teaching. He has left to posterity a glorious name for high-minded aspiration, but he failed to give stability to the Mauryan Empire, for it began to break up immediately after his death, and about 183 B.C. the last ruler of his dynasty was assassinated by his commander-in-chief, who seized the throne. Thereafter, India was again divided among several kingdoms, though they tended to be fewer and internally better organised than those of the pre-Mauryan period. At length, during the fourth century A.D. North India was reunited under the Gupta Empire, but the Guptas, unlike the Mauryas, did not make any permanent conquests in South India. Not until the time of the Moslem conqueror Mohammed bin Tughluq in the fourteenth century did any other Indian monarch control as much of India as Asoka had done.

III

It was while Asoka was trying to consolidate the Mauryan realm that a series of ferocious wars between rival kingdoms in China led to the creation of an empire comparable to the Mauryan in power and extent. About the middle of the first millennium B.C., the area of Chinese culture, like that of the Indian in the same period, was divided between a dozen or so independent states. There was, on the other hand, to a greater extent than in India, a tradition of political unity, for the Shang Dynasty during the later part of the second millennium B.C., and the Chou Dynasty which replaced it about 1100 B.C., had held a paramountcy over the Chinese tribes along the Yellow River, and even after the real power of the Chou had almost disappeared, the various indepen-

dent states which shared a common Chinese culture were still nominally its feudatories. These states had not, however, arisen from a mere dissolution of the original Chou realm; they were for the most part beyond its borders. For centuries a great territorial expansion of the Chinese people had been going on, with the settlement of new lands and absorption of the relatively primitive non-Chinese inhabitants. The original China consisted approximately of the modern provinces of Shensi, Shansi, Honan and Shantung, all within the basin of the Yellow River; from this homeland the Chinese spread out, northward into the region of Peking and round the shores of the Yellow Sea into southern Manchuria, southward into the valley of the Yangtse. The Yangtse basin was destined ultimately to support an even larger population than the Yellow River lands, but until late in the first millennium B.C. it was largely a wilderness of forest and swamp with aboriginal tribes carrying on shifting cultivation on the higher ground. As with the spread of the Aryans from the Punjab into the plain of the Ganges, the immigration of the Chinese from the Yellow River into the Yangtse basin was a movement from a drier to a wetter zone, from a lightly timbered to a heavily forested area. It was also an expansion from a country where wheat and millet were the most suitable cereals into one where rice—the cereal that can feed the greatest number of human beings to the square mile—was the most rewarding crop.

The two centuries and a half from 481 to 221 B.C., broadly co-incident with the most brilliant period of Hellenic civilisation, are known in Chinese history as the Period of the Warring States, for it was an age of almost incessant armed struggles between the various kingdoms. As in India, armies tended to become larger and better organised, and the addition of cavalry to the old-fashioned chariotry gave a new intensity to warfare. The larger states swallowed up the smaller until there were only half a dozen left to contend for supremacy; finally Ch'in, the most westerly of the kingdoms, from which the name of China is derived, eliminated all the others and created a great centralised empire, which included not only all the territory at that time inhabited by Chinese, but also the non-Chinese kingdom of Nan Yueh covering the modern Kwang-tung and Tongking.

The King of Ch'in, who made himself Emperor with the title of Shih Huang Ti, had emerged victorious over his rivals largely because of the system of vigorous militarist rule which he had established in his own state, and he extended the same methods of efficient but ruthless despotism to the whole of his empire. Not only the independence of the rival dynasties, but the local powers of the nobles were wiped out, and all authority vested in centrally appointed officials; varieties of local custom were also disregarded and a completely uniform administration introduced. The whole country enjoyed peace and order for the first time, but there was widespread discontent, fostered by the class of 'scholars', who were the custodians of traditional learning and customary law and had carried on much of the civil administration of the feudal courts. These scholars formed a class which corresponded in some ways to the Indian brahmans, but, unlike them, was not sharply differentiated from the military nobility or detached from the secular authority of the state. The scholars were the residue of an ancient priesthood, but whereas in India the brahmans retained for themselves a monopoly of the major religious rituals, in China the kings and feudal lords themselves performed such rituals and the scholars

acted only as their assistants. The scholars nevertheless jealously preserved as their special field of knowledge a body of tradition concerning the usages and precedents of ancient times, and they had developed schools of moral and political philosophy, the most influential of which was that founded by Confucius.

Confucius (552–479 B.C.), K'ung-fu-tzu, was a minister in the state of Lu, but resigned from office when his good advice to its ruler was disregarded; he then became a teacher of moral and political philosophy and wandered about China, looking, like Plato, but without success, for a monarch who would put into practice his precepts for a just and enlightened administration. He was essentially a traditionalist, and deplored the decay of ancient custom in his time, but in his endeavour to revive it he gave it a new ethical content; he propagated the ideal of the *chun tzu* or 'superior man', educated in the traditions of the past, standing firmly on moral principles, strong in his personal integrity and disinterestedly devoted to the service of the state. The teaching which was handed down by his disciples is generally known in the West as Confucianism, but in China it is commonly called simply Ju Chia, 'the scholars' doctrine'.

The Confucians were not interested in metaphysics, or in a personal salvation, and their religious belief was virtually confined to a recognition of 'Heaven' as an impersonal divine power sustaining the moral law; their concern was with the moral obligations involved in the life of man in society, and particularly with those between members of a family and between a king and his subjects. For their exemplars they looked back to the remote past, when kings were supposed to have governed by 'virtue', and they attached great importance to traditional usages and ceremonies.

The opposition of the scholar class to the

drastic innovations of Shih Huang Ti's new empire caused him to make up his mind to be rid of their traditions once and for all. On the advice of his minister, Li Ssu, he ordered all books in the Empire, except those dealing with medicine, divination and agriculture, to be collected and destroyed. Although many scholars tried to hide their books, and 460 of them were put to death for attempted concealment, the edict was ruthlessly carried out and resulted in a wholesale destruction of literature of the pre-Ch'in period. This famous 'Burning of the Books' did not, however, give permanence to Shih Huang Ti's régime, for his dynasty survived him only three years. The minister Li Ssu and the chief court eunuch Chao Kao brought about the death of the Crown Prince, who was ill-disposed towards them, and put another son of the deceased Emperor on the throne; Chao Kao then murdered both Li Ssu and the new Emperor, and set up yet another puppet monarch, but by this time the whole country was in revolt, and the third Ch'in Emperor perished with his entire family at the hands of the rebels. To the Confucians this swift and bloody end to a régime of unprecedented grandeur seemed a fitting retribution for a lawless tyranny which had insolently set at nought the traditions of antiquity.

But Shih Huang Ti had done his work of unification too thoroughly for it to be undone, and after a brief period of civil war, a new imperial dynasty, that of the Han, was founded and endured, with one brief interruption, for four centuries. The Han emperors maintained the centralised empire of the Ch'in, and even extended its area by conquests in what is now south-western China and Chinese Turkestan, but they paid a greater regard to custom and tradition and sought to consolidate their authority by conciliating, instead of antagonising, the scholar class. In 191 B.C. the prohibition against the ancient literature was formally repealed, and the scholars were encouraged to collect books which had been successfully hidden during the period of persecution or to restore them from the memories of persons still living who had once been familiar with them. In this way the canon of the Confucian 'classics' was formed, and the Confucian school attained a new prestige as the interpreters of a body of literature which, although very little of it was in fact religious, came to be regarded as possessing an almost sacred character. More and more the scholars were employed as civil officials, and thus were laid the foundations of the system to be developed in later times, whereby the imperial civil service was recruited almost exclusively from successful candidates in public competitive examinations based on the Confucian classics. The scholars became a kind of clergy devoted to the service of the state, an educated class possessing a doctrine and unified by it, yet not separately organised as a church or a priestly order. It was this class, with its special outlook on life, which more than anything else was to give Chinese civilisation its peculiar characteristic quality and difference from Europe, India or Islam.

5 ALEXANDER, CARTHAGE AND ROME

by A. R. Burn

The staggering if short-lived success of Alexander, already touched upon, was due both to his genius and his background. He had learned war at his father's side and his intellectual training had been conducted by Aristotle: he was only twenty when his father was murdered. He was at once confronted by rebellion on every side; but those who called him 'a mere boy' soon found out their mistake. In one astonishing campaign (335 B.C.), Alexander drove north to the Danube, where he met red-haired Celts on the move and made a treaty with them; routed the Illyrians of Albania; turned south into Greece, relieved his garrison in the citadel of Thebes, and razed that city to the ground, a terrible and effective warning. Then he renewed Philip's League at Corinth, and with Greek allies to reinforce Philip's army of Macedonians and professional soldiers, he plunged into Asia.

Official propaganda represented this enterprise, planned by Philip, as a Hellenic crusade, a war of revenge for the invasion of Xerxes; but there was also a more pressing reason for it. Philip, for all his victories and his gold mines, died in debt. The splendid army which he had built up was too expensive to maintain, unless conquest could be made to pay for itself. Alexander did not hesitate. In his code, war was the most magnificent of careers. To emulate his boyhood's hero, Homer's Achilles, believed to be his mother's ancestor; to shine in the eyes of that mother, the fierce and beautiful Olympias, perhaps the only woman he ever loved; to outshine his father, with whom he had quarrelled violently when Philip forsook Olympias for another bride—every motive concurred. Philip's generals urged him first, at least, to marry and beget an heir to the throne. Alexander refused. An Oedipus complex, perhaps, had left him sexually cold. All his energy went into war and empire-building, and though he knew well that he might be killed leading a charge, he never made any arrangement for the future of his country. With all his glamour, and with many romantic and generous impulses, Alexander the Great was essentially an egoist.

As he swept into Asia, no army, fortress or natural obstacle could stop him. Everywhere, after directing the battle until that moment, he led the decisive charge. Repeatedly he was wounded. Any specially difficult obstacle he regarded as a challenge. The moral effect was tremendous. In 334 he overran Asia Minor; in 333 he routed the Persian king in Syria. Tyre on its island, Gaza on its high 'tell', supposed impregnable, resisted strongly and were destroyed. In Egypt, he founded Alexandria, the most successful of many cities to bear his name and his most lasting monument, and the oracle of Amon at Siwa saluted him as Son of God, which to the Egyptians, as their Pharaoh, he was.

In 331 he routed a huge Persian army at Gaugamela, east of the Tigris, stalling off its outflanking cavalry and smashing its centre; occupied the Persian homeland, after fighting his way through the mountains in mid-winter, and denied its manpower to the enemy. In 330 the last king, Darius III, was murdered by his own officers. The warlike north-eastern Iranians accustomed to hold the Oxus frontier against the nomads, fought on for two years; but by 327–6 Alexander was conquering India (modern Pakistan). He aspired to march to the eastern ocean, which he believed to be not far away, but his troops, war-weary, homesick, and having won a severe battle against an army including 200 elephants, refused to march against the Ganges kingdoms, which were reported to have 5000. He returned (325) to Babylon, personally leading a column which almost perished in the deserts along the Persian Gulf.

During all these years Alexander had been under great moral as well as physical strain. His ideas had grown with his conquests. He had learned, like many Greeks before him, to admire the courage and ability of Persian officers and soldiers; and, in any case he had not enough Greeks and Macedonians to hold and govern the Persian Empire by force, nor had they sufficient local knowledge to govern alone. From the first, he made use of Persian governors. Before long, transcending Aristotle's advice, to be 'a leader to Greeks but a master to Orientals', he made it a policy to treat both alike. As 'King of Asia' he often wore the comfortable and civilised Median dress of coat and trousers. Persians were among his friends. The Macedonians felt their position threatened; the more so when, being customarily saluted by his Persians with prostration, he tried to exact the same prostration from Europeans. For to Greeks this action was an act of worship. He was more than once threatened by conspiracies; and among

those who consequently perished were his old general, Parmenion, whose son had concealed a plot, and his official historian Callisthenes, Aristotle's nephew. Finally, after the return from India, he began the formation of a new imperial army, one-third Macedonian, two-thirds Persian, serving together in the same regiments. The Macedonians tried to resist this 'dilution' by a strike. Alexander suppressed the mutiny, executing thirteen men, taking the rest at their word and proposing to dismiss them all. His prestige was still tremendous, and the movement collapsed. Soon after, he celebrated the famous 'marriage of East and West', when he took Darius' daughter as his wife (he was already married to Roxane, daughter of a gallant north-eastern lord) and solemnised the unions, it is said, of 9000 Macedonian and Greek soldiers to Eastern women, most of them no doubt the men's *de facto* wives already. Greek seers and Persian Magi together poured the drink-offerings, and Alexander prayed for 'concord and fellowship in the Empire between Macedonians and Persians'.

That this implied Alexander's belief in the Brotherhood of Man does not follow from the evidence, though it has been alleged by some modern scholars. The 'marriage' was rather a practical and necessary measure if his empire was to be stable. He proceeded with the reorganisation of his large new army and with preparations for an expedition to the spice-lands of southern Arabia. Then, in 323, not yet thirty-three years of age, he died.

There was still no heir to the throne, though Roxane bore a son a few months later, nor any instruction laid down in the event of the king's death or disablement. Before long his generals were fighting each other for the Empire, or as much of it as they could get. Roxane, who had murdered Darius' daughter, perished with her son amid these convulsions. Chaos was come again.

II

One only of the great marshals set himself from the first a limited objective. The able and crafty Ptolemy, having noted the wealth of Egypt and its defences of sea and desert, seized that province and kept it. He also captured the embalmed body of Alexander and installed it in a mausoleum at Alexandria. Here he also founded a library, the greatest in the ancient world, and an endowed institute for scholars, the *Museum* (Temple of the Muses), where much of the best literary and, especially, critical and scientific work of the next centuries was done. His dynasty, exploiting the wealth of Egypt through an elaborate Greek bureaucracy, lasted until the death of his descendant, Queen Cleopatra, in 30 B.C.

The bulk of the Empire fell to Seleucus, commander of Alexander's foot-guards. He ceded the Indus provinces to the great Indian conqueror, Chandragupta (*see* page 77), in return for 500 war elephants, which he found very useful in destroying his rivals. The greater part of Asia Minor too, was lost. The Celts whom Alexander had met on the Danube, raided through Macedonia (*c.* 280) far into Greece. Driven out by the Greeks, they then blackmailed the cities on the Sea of Marmara into ferrying them into Asia. The Greeks of Ionia delivered themselves from the invaders under the Greek captain of the fortress of Pergamum, who founded a Kingdom of Pergamum, including Ionia and western Anatolia. Its kings, who bore the names of Eumenes and Attalos, founded a library second only to that of Alexandria, using parchment (pergamene) when the jealous Ptolemies cut off the supply of papyrus; and the great altar which was their war-memorial for the defeat of the

Celts, with its vigorous but florid sculpture, was counted one of the wonders of the civilised world. (It was probably also the 'Satan's Seat' of the Apocalypse.) The Gauls, driven back eastward, founded Galatia, in inland Asia Minor.

Seleucus' line, among whom the four most important kings bore the name Antiochus, kept a trade-route open through the south to Miletus, but the centre of their power was in Syria. Here was their capital, Antioch, greatest of the many Greek colonies bearing the names of Antioch, Seleucia or Apameia (Apame was the Persian bride of Seleucus the Conqueror), with which they supplemented the many Alexandrias in Asia, such as Iskenderun and Herat. Greeks, Macedonians and their descendants, often of mixed blood, staffed their administration and their armies, though occasionally an Iranian officer might rise in the service. This was as far as Alexander's dream of a mixed empire went. The culture of the Seleucid Empire, as of Pergamum and Ptolemaic Egypt, was entirely Greek. In scores of places, the ruins of their ornate and elaborate town-centres and public buildings still tower above the mud-brick houses of Turkish or Arab villages, or stand alone on what has since become the desert-edge; or only their pillars stand, the squared blocks of the walls having been removed by later ages. In these cities sat Greek courts of law, Greek speeches were delivered, Greek literature and philosophy were taught, Greek poetry was read and even written. Some of the most exquisite Greek minor poetry, poems of love and wine and nature, poems about poets, attaches to the names of Antipater of Sidon and Meleager of Gadara—that non-Semitic Gadara of the herd of swine. Meleager's verse especially, full of 'raptures and roses', has a sensuous beauty less like anything in classical Greek poetry than like that other Syrian masterpiece, the Song of Songs.

Outside the cities the Semitic peasants, taxed for the benefit of a culture that was none of theirs, remained aloof. They outlasted the Greeks in the end. But the Seleucid Empire, which followed Alexander, laid the foundations of that hellenised East which lasted in Asia Minor till the coming of the Turks, in Syria till Mohammed, and transmitted the tradition of Plato and Aristotle to Moslem philosophers. Many of the existing Syrian cities received Greek names; Halep was called Beroea, after Beroea in Macedonia, Hamath Epiphaneia, Gerasa became an Antioch, Rabbah of Ammon Philadelphia; but today, as they have been for centuries, they are once more Aleppo, Hamah, Jerash and Amman. By 170 B.C. the Jews, indeed, had already revolted violently against westernisation.

Further east there were fewer Greeks. A great Seleucia on the Tigris was the predecessor of Baghdad, eighteen miles away; and there was a concentration of them in Bactria, where Alexander, keeping his Macedonians with him, had left Greek soldiers to garrison the Oxus frontier. (After his death they tried to march home, but were forcibly prevented by the Successors, as the heirs of Alexander are commonly called.) Their generals set up an independent kingdom which struck some of the most splendid Greek coins ever produced: realistic portraits of forcible soldier-kings, sometimes wearing tropical sun-helmets or a diadem in the form of an elephant's head. A Demetrius (Chaucer's 'great Emetrius, lord of Ind') even reconquered the Punjab after the death of Asoka, and a King Menander actually figures in a Buddhist classic, the Milinda Dialogues, in which 'Milinda the Ionian' questions and is converted by a Buddhist sage. Greek Bactria lasted for about 170

years, and might have lasted longer had not usurping generals brought about its downfall by internecine strife. As it was, power was to pass to an Iranian kingdom, set up first by nomad invaders in the old province of Parthia, which had captured Mesopotamia from the house of Seleucus by 130 B.C.

In the west, Macedonia reverted to being a modest, hellenised, national kingdom, defending its northern marches and dominating, though not directly ruling, Greece through such strategic points as Chalcis and Corinth. Athens made one brave attempt to regain her independence, about 260, hoping for help from Egypt, which let her down; after that, she became increasingly a 'university' town, the resort of philosophers from all over the hellenised world. Her famous drama was now represented by a comedy of manners, known to us from papyri and the Roman version of Plautus and Terence; young men about town win their girls, against the will of peppery but not irreconcilable fathers, by the help of a clever manservant, a Figaro or Jeeves. Another characteristic figure is the Boastful Soldier, home from making his fortune in the wars in Asia. Greece was still important as a source of soldiers and expert advisers to the hellenised world, and was considerably weakened by the number of such emigrants.

Made formidable by Greek techniques, the new giant states now dwarfed Greece. The Greek-city states, the better to survive, experimented with federal union. In western Greece, the Achaian and the Aetolian Leagues overhauled their machinery and enrolled new and not always willing members; but they were too late to save Greece from foreign domination. Once again hostility amongst themselves rendered them helpless.

There was also a widespread feeling of social unrest. The Persian kings, through

200 years, had accumulated a gold-reserve equal to wages for a thousand million skilled-man-days at current Greek rates. The slow exaction of this immense sum, and its withdrawal from circulation, had contributed to depressing farmers to serfdom and generally weakening the Persian Empire. Alexander with his wars and those of the Successors rapidly dispersed these assets, largely into the Greek world. Prices rose steeply. Speculators profited; holding goods for a rise meant easy money. Rich men were able to buy more slaves, always a by-product of ancient warfare. The free workman (we have direct evidence from inscriptions) was degraded. All the evils of the slave economy, perhaps less grave in the classical period than is sometimes thought, were accentuated.

The only actual revolution was in Sparta, in the later half of the third century; precisely in the city which, by Herculean efforts, had avoided constitutional change four hundred years before. Under the 'national socialism' of Sparta, the Spartiate's 'lot' of land could not be sold; but failing heirs male, it could pass in a female line. Hence, since 'Lycurgus' had not succeeded in making Spartans less avaricious than other men (rather the reverse was true), there was competition to marry heiresses; and since heiresses are naturally more likely to appear in rather infertile families, infertility and the concentration of Sparta's landed wealth marched hand in hand. Five thousand Spartan Peers or full citizens had fought against Xerxes; in the time of Aristotle the number sank below 1000, while the landless and discontented multiplied. In these circumstances, two young kings successively tried, in an idealistic spirit, to restore the ancient commonwealth of Lycurgus as they imagined it to have been. Agis IV, refusing to use force, was indicted for treason by the leaders of the rich full citizens and hanged about 240; his successor Cleomenes III, whom they expected to find compliant, took advantage of his position as commander-in-chief during a war and carried through the revolution, at a cost of fourteen lives. He redistributed the land and was able to put an army of 20,000 men into the field; but he disappointed the poor in other states by failing to extend his reforms to these regions. Aratus, the wealthy general of the Achaian League, however, found him so dangerous that he called in the Macedonians, whom he himself had ejected from the fortress of Corinth years before, and the revolution was overwhelmed by superior numbers on the field of Sellasia (222). Cleomenes fled to Egypt, where Ptolemy IV disappointed his hopes of help, and perished in an unsuccessful attempt to raise a revolution among the unwarlike Greeks of Alexandria.

Fifteen years later a much more drastic revolution, of which we have only hostile accounts, broke out under one Nabis, bloody and strong-handed, who went to the length of freeing serfs. Its strength was broken only after intervention by Rome. It was finally crushed by the Achaians, when 3000 of Nabis' supporters refused the offer of being deported to Achaia, and preferred the grim alternative of being sold as slaves.

III

Naturally the new age, its new conditions and its anxieties, had a profound effect upon Greek philosophy. Socrates, Plato, Aristotle and their circles, all had discussed the world and man from the point of view of the city-state. The city, at least if it were Athens, was powerful enough to hold up its head in the world, yet small enough for a man to feel that he counted for something in it. But now, after the changes described, political forces were too great to control. The new cities in Asia were municipalities, dependent on the great kings, and even those of Greece could seldom preserve their existence without compromising their liberty. The giant states themselves, with their mixed populations, inspired no patriotism, though the rulers, often able and hard-working men, tried sometimes with success to produce a *mystique* of personal loyalty. Many were acclaimed by such titles as Saviour or Benefactor (compare Luke 22, v. 25); the Ptolemies and several Seleucids were even honoured as gods; and the flattery was not always cynical. A philosopher named Euhemerus had already suggested that the gods of Olympus had in their time had been kings who established the ways of civilisation.

The problems that beset thinking men were therefore those of how the individual was to conduct himself among the overwhelming forces of such a world. One solution was to keep out of politics and, as Voltaire was to put it, 'cultivate one's garden'. This was the answer propounded by Epicurus, the gentle Athenian (*c.* 340–270), who in his garden at Athens preached to his friends the way of attainment of true pleasure. As his metaphysic, he adopted the materialist atomic theory of Democritus; he did not profess himself an atheist (to do so, contrary to modern popular belief, was quite dangerous in a Greek city), but he taught that the gods exist in space 'between the worlds', and take no interest in men. Pleasure therefore seemed to him the only rational goal; but he did not mean sensuality; on the contrary, he preached that men should cultivate their finer sensibilities, and attain 'freedom from worry'. He himself lived very simply, and the circles of his followers have been described as a 'society of friends'. His teaching remained a source of inspiration far into the Roman age. Horace

professed himself his follower; and his most famous disciple was the Roman Lucretius (d. *c.* 55 B.C.), whose great poem *On the Nature of the Universe* is a tract in favour of a scientific world-view, against superstition and its evil consequences, cruelty and anxiety.

But the Garden of Epicurus made little appeal to many more active spirits. Conspicuous in the late Greek and Roman world, though too drastic in their asceticism to become widely popular, were the Cynics, the 'dog-like' philosophers so-called because of their contempt for conventional decencies. Founded by a disciple of Socrates, the sect first became famous in the person of Diogenes of Sinope, who, pushing Socrates' indifference to comfort to the point of parody, lived in an upturned earthenware storage-barrel at Corinth and would not deign to be civil to Alexander himself. From his time on, philosophy became a profession or vocation, followed by those who felt called to try to deliver their fellow-men from overmuch dependence on material comfort, and from the misery and crime that followed. The drab, voluminous cloak or 'plaid' of homespun wool, often the only garment worn; the philosopher's beard, in a society where the 'polite' were clean-shaven; the crisp and pungent sarcasms of the street-corner *homily* or *sermon* (both words used by the Cynics, meaning a *talk,* a straightforward affair avoiding formality and rhetoric); all these became as familiar as the rough cassock of the Franciscan in a later age. In a world given over to the worship of power and wealth, the Cynics did much to uphold an ideal of non-attachment, and they were by no means without their influence.

To a disciple of Diogenes at Athens, soon after the death of Alexander, came for instruction, a tall dark, gaunt young man named Zeno, son of a merchant of Citium (Chittim, Larnaka) the Phoenician city in Cyprus. In due course, Zeno began to teach on his own; he abandoned some of the Cynic eccentricities, though he too was second to none in following an argument to its logical conclusion, however outrageous. Shy and plain, he impressed by the sheer incisiveness of his reasoning, and also by his integrity. He remained at Athens all his life, and for this hellenised Semite the Athenians recorded in stone a decree of their Assembly, honouring him as one who had taught the young goodness and temperance, by both work and example. Antigonus Gonatas, the tough grandson of two of Philip's generals, who restored Macedonia after the Celtic raid, would have taken him home as his adviser. Zeno refused, but sent a disciple, also from Citium. Having no place of his own, unlike Epicurus, he taught in the colonnade below the market-square, under the great frescoes that recorded the defeat of Persia. It was called the Painted Stoa, and it and Zeno gave the word Stoic to the world.

Stoicism, the philosophy of virtue and reason, was the philosophy, indeed the religion of many educated men of action for seven hundred years. In so long a time it changed and developed in detail, but its central tenet was that the virtuous life, which is also the happy life, is life in accordance with nature and with reason, whose commands are the same, for the world is the self-expression of the fiery god whose home is in the empyrean beyond the stars. The spirits of men also are 'fiery particles', and those who preserve the fire faithfully will return at last purified to heaven that is their home. Looking at nature, Zeno concluded that pleasure is not the goal of all life, as Epicurus had taught, but the preservation of the being in its natural form, plant, animal, man,

society; pleasure is a by-product, which comes when the natural functions are properly performed. The function of man is to be a good member of his society: good son, good spouse, good parent, good citizen and, if destiny lead that way, good ruler. The good man will therefore not shun trouble by keeping out of politics; but when his duty is done, if his situation becomes intolerable, he may escape by suicide. Destiny played a great part in Stoic thought; as with most systems that tend to fatalism and to pantheism, its devotees were not always consistent. The belief in a heaven above the stars, also, was consistent with the assignment of some divine significance to the stars themselves, and the later Stoicism was not untinged by one of the symptoms of intellectual decay in the later antiquity: the revival of Babylonian astrology.

Thus if the Greek *polis* could no longer be self-sufficient, Zeno and his followers—several of whom came, like St Paul, from the Levant, three actually from Tarsus—provided an ethic based on the concept of an ideal world-state, a *cosmopolis* of which all good men are citizens, without distinction of Jew, nomad, barbarian, bond or free. One of the great masters of Stoicism under the Roman Empire was the slave Epictetus; and if Stoics were the spiritual directors of many kings and noblemen, they several times, as in the Sparta of Cleomenes and the Rome of the Gracchi (*see* pages 85, 95) directed them on the paths of revolution.

IV

Greek science did not transform the conditions of transport, labour and society. The disadvantages of a slave economy may have been partly but not entirely the cause. Heron of Alexandria, at a date unknown, produced plans for a steam-engine; it was designed to cause the doors of a temple to swing open without visible agency when a fire was kindled on an altar outside it. But it is doubtful whether, if Heron's steam-engine had been applied to transport or pumping, it could have functioned in the existing conditions of metallurgy. Boilers and cylinders were continually bursting even in the early days of the modern steam-engine, despite the vastly improved metallurgy that had produced Renaissance weapons and armour.

Aristotle was perhaps the last Greek to 'take the whole of knowledge for his province'; but considerable further progress was made in details and in application, even where he had been greatest, in biology and natural history, from the work on botany of his pupil Theophrastus to the great physician of the Roman Empire, Galen (Claudius Galenus, *c.* A.D. 130–210) whose achievement was to become a positive bar to further advance during the centuries in which men revered the authority of classical science and ignored its methods.

But it was the mathematics of the ancient world which proved to be the most fruitful part of its legacy, through the Arabs to modern science. Here, and in the mathematical sciences of astronomy and physics, the men of the 'institute' at Alexandria did much of their best work. The great names are nearly all of the third century B.C. Euclid (Eucleides), the great systematiser, worked under the first Ptolemy (323–283): Eratosthenes (*c.* 276–194) was head of the institute under his successors; he measured the size of the earth, getting a result only some 10 per cent too large, by noticing that the sun at midsummer at Assuan shone to the bottom of a dry well, since it was vertical, and then measuring its angle at Alexandria at the same season. He expressed in a phrase the cosmopolitan feeling of his time, saying that one should consider all good men as

fellow-countrymen and the bad as foreigners. Apollonius of Perga in Asia Minor worked out at Alexandria, as a branch of pure mathematics, the theory of conic sections, which has proved to have applications far beyond his ken both in astronomy and in ballistics. Archimedes, adviser on siege-engines and other branches of engineering to two kings of Syracuse, formulated the principle of specific gravity; as a famous story tells, after noticing the displacement of water by his own body in the public bath, he is said to have run home naked through the streets shouting 'EUREKA!' ('I've got it'). He then applied it to the detection of whether the goldsmith, charged with making a wreath of gold leaves for the king, had or had not adulterated the precious metal. His death in 212, killed unrecognised by a Roman soldier in the sack of the city, symbolises the shadow of Rome which was now falling over the hellenistic world.

Most striking of all is the achievement of Aristarchus of Samos at Alexandria, about 275 B.C., in concluding from observation and mathematics that the sun was the centre of the solar system and the earth revolved round it. But his observations, made with the naked eye, were not sufficient to prove his contention beyond doubt, and a view so revolutionary failed to carry conviction. Cleanthes, successor of Zeno as head of the Stoic school, and an ex-boxer, who supported himself by market-gardening while teaching philosophy, and author of a noble *Hymn to Zeus,* went so far as to say that Aristarchus ought to be prosecuted for impiety. To readers of Gibbon it is perhaps worth while to stress that such a cleavage between science and religion thus long ante-dates the rise of Christianity. The astronomical system which was the direct legacy of the ancient world to the Middle Ages was that of Claudius Ptolemaeus of

Alexandria, Ptolemy, a contemporary of Galen in the best age of the Roman Empire. He succeeded in 'saving the appearances', by his ingenious theory of epicycles (circular orbits whose centres move on a greater circle), and froze astronomical theory until the days of Galileo.

V

In 217 B.C. a peace conference was being held in Greece. It was trying once more to put an end to the incessant wars that weakened Greek society. Agelâus, a delegate of the Aetolian League, pointed to the tremendous struggle then being waged in the west between Rome and Carthage. Whoever won would be a menace to Greece; 'for if the cloud in the west once overspreads Greece, I fear we shall no longer play these childish games of ours together. We shall be praying the gods to give us back the chance of calling even our very quarrels our own.' Everyone applauded, and a peace was made. But within five years there was war again; Macedonia was in alliance with Carthage, and Aetolia with Rome.

What were the origins of this Italian city, which was to dominate not only the hellenistic world, but great areas of Europe hardly known to the Greeks?

Among the peoples affected by the Greek expansion to the west, none had been more influenced than the Etruscans of north-central Italy. They were speakers of a non-Indo-European language, a people among whom at least the aristocracy were believed to have come from Asia Minor. Through them, as conquering overlords, and through the Greeks of Cumae and its colony, the 'New Town' of Naples, Greek art and the elements of eastern civilisation reached the Aryan-speaking peasants of Central Italy, among them the lowland Latin communities south of the Tiber mouth. Among these

was Rome, at the lowest point where the Tiber could be conveniently bridged, and the highest to which small ships could ascend. It was a position like that of London, in virtue of which Rome was from the first an exceptional Latin town, more mercantile and more open to foreign influence than those inland.

About 500 B.C. the Etruscans, defeated by the Greeks of Cumae, lost control of Latium, and Rome ejected the Etruscan dynasty of the Tarquins. Control was now held by a Council of Elders or Senate; its members were called the Fathers, and were drawn from a circle of landed families, those 'qualified to be Fathers', or Patricians. From among them were appointed two annual Generals, the consuls or 'colleagues'. Early Roman internal history consists of the struggle of other classes of the growing city, the Plebeians or populace, for security against patrician magistrates or judges, and of their leading families for a share in the government itself. Several times they threatened to secede or 'walk out' and found their own city a few miles away; always rather than provoke revolt, the patricians had the good sense to make concessions; the struggle remained almost bloodless, and ended with leading plebeians as well as patricians sharing in the consulship itself.

Throughout this struggle Rome's population and military power continued to grow. She destroyed Veii, in southern Etruria, and doubled her territory (399) five years after the defeat of Athens in the Peloponnesian War. From a leading city in the Latin League, she became its mistress, while Latins who migrated to the growing capital could become Roman citizens. A raid by Celts settled on the Po, which sacked the evacuated city in 390 and had to be bought off, harmed Rome no more than her rivals; and in the repulse of later raids she became the champion of Italy.

She protected the lowland peoples of Campania against the Samnites, their highland cousins, and after long fighting, emerged clearly as the strongest Italian power. Finally the campaign and decisive victory of Sentinum (295) against a coalition of Samnites, Etruscans and the Gauls with their Homeric war-chariots, showed that she could not be defeated even by such an alliance. All central Italy, between the Gauls in the north and the Greeks in the south, was now bound to follow her in war and foreign policy, by alliances on various terms which bound each city and canton to Rome, but not to each other; and strategic points were held by colonies of Roman farmer-citizens established in walled towns.

The Greeks of South Italy had already more than once called in help from old Greece against the pressure of Italians, increasingly well organised and well armed. Now they invited Pyrrhus, King of Epirus in north-west Greece, whom Hannibal ranked second only to Alexander among generals. He was a commander trained in the warfare of the Successors, and hopeful to carve out for himself an empire in the West, as Alexander had in the East. Out on personal reconnaissance, in the year 280, the king saw from a hill the square outline of the Roman camp; the ordered lines, the alleys and 'streets' dividing legions and companies; and said to his officers: '*That* is not barbaric. As for action—we will see.' Thus the two worlds met.

Pyrrhus won two 'Pyrrhic victories', but only by using everything he had, especially elephants, which the Roman cavalry horses would not face. The ranks of his professional soldiers were sorely thinned. The Romans lost twice as heavily, but their citizen soldiers were replaceable out of a pool of 750,000 Roman and allied fighting men. Finally Pyrrhus retired

beaten, saying of the West 'What a battle-ground I am leaving for Rome and Carthage!' In 264 Rome and Carthage clashed in Sicily

VI

'The absent are always wrong'; and so, for remote future historians, are most of the defeated. About the Phoenicians, including the Libyan-Phoenicians of North Africa, we hear almost solely from their enemies, the Greeks, who were their superiors in art and thought; from the Jews, their cousins, superior in religion, and from the Romans, superior probably in law and government, and certainly in numbers. In art the Carthaginians certainly were not great; Carthage imported vast quantities of Greek painted pottery, and not the best. The Etruscans were far more discriminating. Nevertheless, for Phoenician art at its best, it would be fair to look, say, at the attractive animal-figures in the Beirut Museum, rather than at the imitation Egyptian 'trade-goods' which their sailors palmed off on the benighted natives of Europe. Of poetry they had some, marked by parallelism of statement, in the Hebrew manner, as in the little lyric on Sidon, preserved in a Greek version:

Did the sea cast thee forth upon the shore
    as a pearl?
Or didst thou come down from heaven
    as the morning star?
The mainland is made bright by thy
    brightness,
And the sea reflects the beauty of thy
    joy.

Their religion was a polytheism which could resort to human sacrifice in a national crisis; and Rome did as much in face of Hannibal's invasion. They were gallant sailors, who had re-opened the sea-ways to the western Tin-lands, after the Mycenaean collapse; honest traders, too, capable of developing the Silent Trade with timid West Africans. They would leave their merchandise on the beach and return to their ships. The natives, seeing the ships, would lay gold beside the goods, and retire to the jungle. The Phoenicians would come again, inspect the gold, and retire with it, if they thought it was enough; if not, then without it, waiting a further 'bid'. 'And neither side cheats', remarks Herodotus.

The only piece of Carthaginian literature that we have, saved by translation for the Greek Polybius, is a thrilling account of the voyage of Hanno (one of the commonest Carthaginian names), as far, probably, as Macaulay Island, off Sierra Leone, where his men killed three 'hairy women' of a species 'which the interpreters called Gorillas'. We hear also of a work on agriculture by Mago, translated for Cato, the most bitter foe of Carthage. They were not soldiers by choice; for centuries they paid tribute to the Berbers for the site of Carthage itself; but they were stubborn and resourceful when pressed. They had the knack of getting on with other peoples; Etruscans, Sicilians, Spaniards, Libyans allied with them to check the advance of the Greeks; their officers could make a formidable army out of barbarians serving for pay, to supplement their own slender manpower. The Romans call them cruel and treacherous; but some of the treachery seems to have been merely good military deception; and nothing could out-do for blackness some parts of Rome's own record in the Punic (Phoenician) Wars.

The first twenty years of warfare left the Romans masters of Sicily. They had invaded Africa, but here a Spartan condottiere, Xanthippus, used elephants to trample to death the army of Regulus.

After the war, Carthage suffered a savage mutiny of her barbarian mercenaries, left unpaid through economic exhaustion and the Roman indemnity. Rome took advantage of this to seize Sardinia and Corsica too, and increase the indemnity; she thus made a bitter enemy of the great Carthaginian general, Hamilcar, surnamed Barca— Barak, 'the Lightning'. Having at last crushed the rising, he left for Spain, where, with slender resources, he built up an empire to redress the balance of power. With him he took his nine-year-old son, Hannibal.

Rome became alarmed; agreed on a delimitation of spheres of influence at the Ebro, and then offered protection to the city of Saguntum, south of that frontier. In 219 Hannibal, in command at twenty-eight, took Saguntum, and the Second Punic War resulted.

The Senate ordered the consuls for 218 to Spain and Sicily; but Hannibal had other ideas. By a daring march with 26,000 Spanish and African troops, he crossed the Alps into Italy and raised the newly conquered Gauls in revolt. In battle after battle, with his tactical brilliance and superior cavalry, he slaughtered the brave but inexperienced Roman legionaries. At Cannae in the south (216) he lured an army double his own into attacking his centre, routed its cavalry wings, extended his own wings with reserve infantry, and enveloped and slaughtered 80,000 men. But he had not the strength to assault or blockade Rome, or even the greater Roman colonies. The Samnites and some of the Greeks joined him, but the central Italian confederacy stood by Rome. The delaying tactics of the dictator (emergency supreme commander) Fabius checked him; his own government, jealous, perhaps afraid of him, sent troops to Sicily which should have gone to him; and in a war of attrition there could be but one end. The Romans, even during his invasion, with sound strategy maintained an army in Spain, cutting off the hope of reinforcements from there; and when, after eleven years, his brother, Hasdrubal, broke away and marched to join him, Hasdrubal was defeated and killed in Italy before they could meet. A brilliant young general, Scipio (though he let Hasdrubal get past him), cleared the remaining enemy forces from Spain, and despite the fears of Fabius and the party of caution, obtained permission to invade Tunisia. Then and only then was Hannibal with his remnant recalled, undefeated, from Italy, to be beaten at Zama in 202.

On his advice, Carthage at once sued for peace. She saved her small home territory, her walls, and ten ships—enough to chase pirates; surrendered the rest of her navy and all imperial claims; and submitted to paying an indemnity of 10,000 talents (60,000,000 skilled-man day-wages; her population was under a million) over a period of fifty years, and agreed not to wage war without Rome's permission.

During the war, the number of Roman citizens liable to military service had sunk by nearly a quarter (270,000 to 210,000). The Romans remained implacable and the end of the history of Carthage is tragic. There was at first some economic recovery. Hannibal, going into politics, reformed the administration and tried to democratise the merchant oligarchy. Rome grew alarmed, and against the will of Scipio, a cultivated and generous aristocrat, demanded his surrender. He fled to the court of Antiochus III, the last Seleucid to march east to the Oxus, and now turning west. But Rome, having already settled her account with Macedon in a preventive war, in alliance with Pergamum, routed Antiochus (191–90) and drove him out of Asia Minor. Hannibal now fled to the King of Bithynia. In 185 Rome again demanded his extradition, and finding his house surrounded, he took poison, which he had long carried with him. Marcus Cato, a farmer-soldier, took the lead at Rome among those who held that Carthage must be destroyed, and the clause forbidding Carthage to make war without Rome's permission gave them their opportunity. Rome's ally, the King of the Berbers of Numidia, harried the Carthaginians until they made war in despair. Then Rome sent an army to Africa, and demanded that the city be transferred ten miles inland. This, to a city of merchants, meant starvation; they closed their gates, improvised arms, and stood a siege of three years. Only 50,000 of the population survived. Carthage, as Cato had wished, was 'blotted out'.

VII

The defeat of Hannibal had left Rome by far the strongest state in the Mediterranean world. She did not at first realise he power. Italy had been invaded both from east and west, and Rome's aggressions in the East may be explained in part by fear. In the barbarian West, on the other hand, the sole motive was greed. The 'pacification' of Sardinia in 177–75 flooded the slave-market with unskilled labour, fit only for the chain-gangs—and there competing formidably with free peasant agriculture. In Spain guerrilla resistance, punctuated by major wars, became endemic as soon as it was clear that the Romans intended to stay. Here it was easier to dispose of prisoners of war; there was always need for haulage in the mines. Gold as well as slaves poured into Rome, as direct tribute, from rent on confiscated lands, as backsheesh for favours received or expected, as plain spoils of war. After the final conquest of Macedon (168) the Romans were able, amid continuing wars

ROMAN EMPIRE

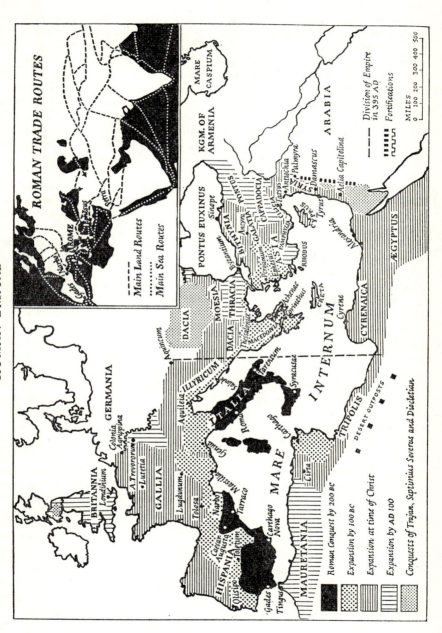

ROMAN TRADE ROUTES

Main Land Routes
Main Sea Routes

Division of Empire
in 395 AD
Fortifications

MILES
0 100 200 300 400 500

Roman Conquest by 200 BC
Expansion by 100 BC
Expansion at time of Christ
Expansion by AD 100
Conquests of Trajan, Septimius Severus and Diocletian

Desert outposts

BRITANNIA
Londinium
GERMANIA
Colonia Agrippina
A. Trevororum
Lutetia
GALLIA
Lugdunum
Tolosa
Narbo
Massilia
Tarruco
Carthago Nova
HISPANIA
Olisipo Toletum
Caesar Augusta
Gades
Tingus

Aquincum
DACIA
ILLYRICUM
Aquileia
ITALIA
Roma
Tarentum
Syracusae
Carthago
Cirta
MAURETANIA
MARE INTERNUM
TRIPOLIS

DACIA
MOESIA
THRACIA
MACEDONIA
Byzantium
Thessalonica
Athenae
Corinthus
CRETA
Cyrene
CYRENAICA

PONTUS EUXINUS
KGM. OF ARMENIA
MARE CASPIUM
BITHYNIA
PONTUS
Sinope
GALATIA
CAPPADOCIA
Nicomedia
Nicaea
Ephesus
ASIA
PAMPHYLIA
LYCIA
Tarsus
CYPRUS
RHODUS
SYRIA
Antiochia
Palmyre
Damascus
Tyrus
Aelia Capitolina
ARABIA

Alexandria
AEGYPTUS

of conquest, to abolish direct taxation of themselves altogether. Great fortunes were made, not merely by triumphing generals but by average senators, governing a conquered land for one year, by the rich non-senators (called 'knights') who 'farmed' provincial taxes, and by the businessmen who lent money back to the provinces to provide the taxes for next year. This did not, however, bring Rome peace and felicity. Prices in the city soared, especially rents. Food prices, in a city now dependent on imported corn, largely tribute from Sicily and Tunisia, rose whenever shipping was delayed by storms or piracy, which became rife after Rome had destroyed the Greek navies and ceased to maintain her own. It was only normal business practice to hold corn-stocks for a further rise. Ex-soldiers and other citizens who had settled in Rome in the expectation of a comfortable retirement, found themselves pinched; and there was no better source of supplementary income than the sale of their votes to senators' sons, competing for election to the offices which might lead to a governorship and a fortune.

There was much that was admirable about the Romans who conquered the Mediterranean world in the second century B.C. Polybius, third among the great Greek historians, son of an Achaian general, and carried off to Rome among 1000 Achaian hostages in 168, learned to admire them. He became a member of the cultivated, Philhellenic circle of the second Scipio 'Africanus' who carried out under orders the destruction of Carthage, and wept over it. Polybius was inclined to blame his own people especially the democratic parties, for the disastrous Achaian War, which led to the destruction of Corinth, like Carthage, in 146. A Roman general, he says, would administer vast public funds honestly on his word of honour alone, whereas in

Greece every transaction required seals and witnesses, and still men cheated. The Roman Republic, says Polybius, was a wonderful blend of monarchy—the strong executive; aristocracy—the Senate, in which the higher ranks were almost monopolised by a circle of patrician and great plebeian families, and democracy—the election to offices, which gave admission to the Senate, by the people. In the next hundred years, under the impact of unexampled wealth and power and ruthless competition for the spoils of office between the great houses which had the prestige and wealth necessary to carry an election, there was a sad decline. Many of the worst Roman deeds of oppression are known to us only because other Romans called for their punishment.

VIII

The Roman world, in that appalling last century B.C., like many civilisations at the height of their power and ostentation, was acutely class-divided, with a gigantic gulf, quite difficult for us to conceive, between the richest and poorest. Cicero, the great barrister and politician, self-made and by no means one of the richest senators, had half-a-dozen country houses, with a separate domestic and home-farm staff at each. He remarks once in a letter that he is delaying arrival until after the slaves' midwinter holiday, the *Saturnalia*, in order not to be a nuisance to them—a pleasant touch of humanity. But there were not just two classes; there were all manner of complications. There were the rich, nongovernmental, trading and financial families, the old cavalry or 'knightly' class; a large but (to the anxiety of social philosophers) diminishing number of citizen farmers, chiefly round the old military colonies; a citizen proletariat in Rome, which could raise a very ugly mob; the non-citizen countrymen and small-town people of Italy, irked by conscription for long overseas wars and garrisons, but voteless, for the poor voters at Rome were not at all anxious to share their lucrative franchise. The slaves themselves were endlessly divided; comfortable senior domestics and farm bailiffs; the indispensable secretaries of great men, friends of their masters and very influential; gladiators, being trained to kill wild animals or each other in the arena on Roman holidays; the chain-gangs, and the freer, mounted cowboys on great ranches in war-depopulated South Italy. Each class was jealous, especially of those nearest to it, and on top of the whole seething mass the few scores of the greater senatorial families long remained in control. The brothers Gracchus, idealistic young aristocrats under Stoic influence, as Tribunes of the People in 133 and 123 respectively, led a movement to resettle citizens on the land. The younger, Gaius, also instituted a state-subsidised bread ration at Rome, such as Alexandria had earlier possessed; a well-meant attempt to iron out fluctuations in the cost of living, afterwards developed by unscrupulous politicians into a demoralising free dole. But when he tried to do something for the Italian allies, the voters turned against him, and he was killed, like his brother before him, in a riot. The Italians revolted in 91, and extorted a wide extension of the franchise. The slaves in Italy rose in 70 under Spartacus, a Thracian gladiator; he was defeated and killed only after three years of horror. Crucifixion, 'the masterpiece of the torturer's art', had been invented as a method of keeping slaves in order, and Crassus the Rich, the victorious general, thus dealt with 6000 prisoners. This was the largest crucifixion on record.

The break ultimately came because of the inadequacy of annually elected magistrates to govern an empire. When a rebellion or frontier war proved serious, the average noblemen elected as consuls repeatedly proved inadequate, and in the end the best general available had to be sent out with powers extended, both in space and time. As there was no standing army at home, for the citizens would not have tolerated it, these great pro-consuls, if they chose to disobey the government, had irresistible military power. Gaius Marius, a soldier risen from the ranks, enlisted the *proletarii* of Rome in view of the lack of farmer-soldiers, and introduced an oath of allegiance to the general personally. The landless citizens thus gained a share in military power; ambitious men exploited this situation, and the sequel was a civil war of frightful slaughter, ending, after Marius' death, in a restoration of the old régime by Sulla, a patrician pro-consul, as dictator in 80. Pompey, one of Sulla's supporters, became the indispensable general of the next generation, clearing the sea of pirates and permanently settling the East, where the Seleucid Empire had finally disintegrated. He chose to serve the republic, though he was constantly breaking its rules; but finally both he and the oligarchy were overthrown by Julius Caesar, a patrician popular leader, at the head of the army trained in the ten years of his great special command in Gaul—the command in which he extended Roman power from Provence to the Rhine and even raided the remote island of Britain.

Caesar, whatever his ambitions, was left no choice but to overthrow the government or be brought to trial by his jealous enemies for earlier illegalities. He determined to make his power permanent. He was elected dictator for life, and over-hauled the administration; he steadfastly refused to massacre his political opponents (Gauls were different); but, for his pains, he was murdered on the 15 March, 45 B.C., by some of his officers headed by a doct-rinaire republican and hard-fisted money-lender, Brutus, the son of his own mistress Servilia.

But hopes of restoring the republic were still-born. The Caesarian soldiers had no intention of letting power fall back from their generals into the hands of the old cliques. An attempt by Cicero, the old champion of civilian rule, to split the Caesarian leaders resulted only in bringing forward Caesar's adopted son, Octavian, his sister's grandson, as a rival to Caesar's right-hand man, Mark Antony. Patching up their differences, these two massacred their opponents, crushed Brutus, and settled their time-expired soldiers on lands ruthlessly seized. Antony left this unpopu-lar task to the young Caesar, while he went off to more spectacular work in the East. But he failed to conquer Parthia, while the young Octavian consolidated his power in Italy, offering an agonised world the hope of peace; and when Antony married the cool-headed and fascinating Queen Cleo-patra, last of the Ptolemies, divorcing his rival's sister, Caesarian propaganda used the fear of an oriental monarchy against him with devastating effect. In 31 B.C., Antony and Cleopatra were defeated at sea and driven to suicide. In 27 the victorious Caesar went through a form of 'restoring the republic' (he remembered his uncle's fate) with himself as its General-issimo (*imperator*), in charge of all frontier provinces, and was acclaimed Augustus, a novel title of honour, meaning something like 'the Holy'.

IX

It was a true revolution. There was no extirpation of the old aristocracy, so long as it was compliant; but it was increasingly mingled with the new men who had risen under the Caesars.

Augustus lived till A.D. 14, and during his long lifetime the Roman world took shape, the memory of which haunts Christendom to this day. His revolutionary monarchy was carefully disguised. He was *imperator* only to his troops; in civil life, he was officially known simply as 'Caesar', his family name, and informally as *princeps*, 'the Chief'. Remnants of the old aristocracy survived, often to grumble against the Caesars more or less academic-ally, sometimes to dine with them, some-times to conspire; but they were increas-ingly mingled with the new men who had risen in Caesar's service to the Senate and to consulships. Hundreds of thousands of Caesarian ex-soldiers, too, many of them of north-Italian Celtic descent, were now owners of land. With their support and that of the serving soldiers, the revolution was secure. Caesars might be murdered; it happened more than once among the successors of Augustus; but talk of restor-ing the old régime remained mere words.

Now at last the administration of the law and of the provinces could be taken out of politics—to the disgust of aristocrats, to the benefit of everyone else. Provincial governors were salaried, and if oppression and corruption did not cease, they were greatly reduced. Court poets—Vergil, son of a north-Italian farmer, Horace, son of a freed slave—hailed Augustus as the restorer of a new and purified Rome; Greeks in the East worshipped him as a god; even in Rome Augustus was con-strained to countenance a cult of 'Rome and the *genius,* [a sort of guardian angel] of Augustus'; while the murdered dictator, Caesar, was officially deified, and a comet (Halley's?) was deemed to be his star.

Above all, there was peace and stability, except on remote frontiers, where August-us' generals, including his stepson Tiberius, pushed forward methodically to the Danube line and, for a time, to the Elbe.

The great roads that already traversed Italy were pushed out across Gaul, Spain, Syria, Asia Minor; and in Provence especially, where the descendants of Julius Caesar's old army of Gaul were settled in a whole constellation of military colonies, most of the great amphitheatres, aqueducts and triumphal arches, which are still among the most famous and impressive of Roman monuments, date from this time.

At Rome there was a great efflorescence of literature. To create a literature that could compare with that of Greece had long been the ambition of cultivated Romans. Orators and writers—Julius Caesar himself, Cicero and their contemporaries, Lucretius (*see* page 86) and the fiery young Catullus, the poet of love and hate—had shown what could be done with the once stiff but always sonorous Latin language; the Augustans continued their work in what has ever since been felt to be the culmination of the golden age of classical Latin. Livy, from North Italy, wrote the history of the republic with such verve that Augustus chaffed him with being a republican at heart; early modern Europeans, from Machiavelli to the men of the French Revolution, found in him an inspiration. Horace was quoted in eighteenth- and nineteenth-century English Parliaments. Vergil, the prophet of Rome's mission 'to impose the way of peace', by force if necessary, was the master of every generation of Roman poets after him. Even Christians, who sometimes felt qualms of conscience about loving the pagan literature, could not resist him. In the end, they persuaded themselves that he had been inspired by God. The famous early poem in which he associated the new Golden Age of peace with the coming birth of a child (it is not certain whose) was thought to be a Messianic prophecy. His name, changed to Virgilius, was thought to signify that he was born of a virgin. He had already

long been established in men's minds as a magician and 'prophet of the gentiles' when Dante, in the *Divine Comedy*, chose him for his guide to a world beyond time.

Hardly less read, though no one could make a Christian forerunner out of him, has been Ovid, who in Augustus' later years delighted a pleasure-loving younger generation with his tales from the mythology and his witty, cynical poem, *The Art of Love*. He became the chief guide to classical mythology of the poets and artists of the Renaissance; there are echoes of him in Shakespeare. But his tone was not favourable to Augustus' earnest desire for moral reform. In the end he was banished, to die, an unhappy exile, on the shores of the Black Sea.

The great reign was ending in bitterness and frustration. Julia, Augustus' only child, was married three times, always for dynastic purposes. She had a large family by Augustus' friend and general, Agrippa; when he died, Tiberius, happily married to Agrippa's daughter by a former wife, was ordered to divorce her in Julia's favour. They had one child, who died; but it is hardly surprising that Julia, at thirty-five, became the centre of the circle whose favourite poet was Ovid, while Tiberius, an embittered man, threw up all his official appointments and retired to the cultivated Greek society of Rhodes. Julia herself was banished, some years before Ovid. Two of her sons died before Augustus; the third was sub-normal. At last Augustus was forced to recall Tiberius and share his powers with him so as to designate, so far as was possible in what was nominally a republic, his chosen successor.

There was disaster in the north too. The newly conquered lands that are now Yugoslavia and western Hungary rose in fierce revolt. Three-fifths of the whole imperial army, under Tiberius himself, were needed to suppress them; and just when the work was almost done, news came that the army in Germany, reduced to three legions, had been ambushed and destroyed in supposedly conquered country ('Varus' disaster': A.D. 9). All the land between the Elbe and the Rhine was lost. Even to replace the lost men was difficult. The civil wars had made havoc of the fighting peoples of Italy; the birth-rate was falling, and the Greek names on many thousands of Italian tombstones show what followed. The old stock in Rome and even in the country towns was increasingly diluted with easterners, largely the descendants of liberated slaves, intelligent but unmilitary. As the generations passed, there was an increasing shortage of really Roman fighting men.

These were the circumstances in which Tiberius, now fifty-six, succeeded his step-father in A.D. 14, to reign till A.D. 37. He tried to rule constitutionally, through the Senate; but the senators were afraid of the Generalissimo, and persisted in fulsome servility, punctuated by silly pinpricks. Informers poisoned Tiberius' mind further with allegations of disloyalty, which were not always baseless. This was the position of all Augustus' line, down to the overthrow of the last descendant of Julia, the 'spoilt boy' Nero, in A.D. 68. A great historian, Tacitus, at the end of the century, told with fine gloom the history of those fifty-four years: the outrageous luxury of state banquets, the sudden execution of a minister or general, the spies, the rumours, the all-pervading suspicion.

But in the provinces there was still peace and the rule of law, protected by an army which became increasingly a frontier garrison. Twenty-five, later thirty, legions, each of 5500 Roman citizen armoured infantry who were also skilled builders and pioneers, lay along the Rhine and Danube and in Syria, Egypt and North Africa; while outlying forts were held by at least an equal number of native cavalry and infantry, serving for twenty-five years to the legionary's twenty, and receiving citizenship on their discharge; their children could thus serve in the legions, and many did. This was one of the chief ways in which the population of the Empire was both mingled and Romanised. It was this highly efficient, long-service, professional army commanded by Roman senators as the Emperor's Legates (lieutenant-generals) which conquered South Britain under the Emperor Claudius, starting in A.D. 43, and, after failing to conquer Scotland, finally came to rest at Hadrian's Wall with outposts up to the Cheviots, from about 190 to 383.

Behind this shield, and under Roman provincial governors, the populations of the Empire administered their own municipal affairs; city-states on the Greek model in the East, cantons based on the old Celtic tribes in Gaul and Britain. Even here, the local Councils met in Roman-style town-centres. The sons of chiefs and townsmen became Roman citizens, wore the awkward toga on state occasions, learned Latin in schools. The basis of government tended to be aristocratic or plutocratic; the imperial government associated democracy with sedition, and made no secret of the fact. All popular associations were suspect (this was part of the case against the Christian Church). Even the strong Emperor Trajan (A.D. 97–117) refused to permit a volunteer fire-brigade in an eastern city, though it was recommended by a trusted governor, for fear lest it might become 'cover' for underground activities. And this leads to a consideration of the weaknesses from which, in the West, the Empire ultimately perished.

These causes were undoubtedly very complex, and it would be a rash man who would claim to know them all. Among them were certainly causes both economic and political. The colossal inequalities of wealth, which developed under the protection of the strong Roman state, meant that there was money to spare for the luxuries of the very rich, and less for those of the free-born working or middle classes. Much of the prodigious Roman activity in ornamental buildings, for example, which, though impressive in ruins, were at no time productive, was due to the vast accumulations of money and the availability of slave labour.

Provincial cities competed with one another to have the smartest temples, theatre, forum or town-centre; rich men, to gain prestige by endowing athletic meetings (mainly professional), or feasts, or schools. Money was thus put into circulation; but it always seems to have found its way back pretty quickly, by way of rents and interest, to the very rich, or in taxes to the government. Much also went abroad: to southern Arabia for spices, to India by sea for pepper, to the Parthian middlemen who handed on the most exotic of luxuries, Chinese silks. The East received nothing in return except gold and silver; and the slow but steady drain of the precious metals eastward, while taxes remained at traditional levels, could not but have a depressing effect, felt first by the middle-class traders in the towns. Already in the second century, the great period of the Roman peace, we hear of such people having to be pressed to accept the honourable post of town-councillor; for the councillors were personally responsible for making good the district's quota of taxation to the central government.

The great political weakness of the Empire was still the theory that the *imperator*, informally known as *princeps*, was only the chief magistrate of the republic. Every successor, therefore, had to be officially appointed by the Senate; in practice, to be accepted by the Emperor's guards and the frontier armies. Intrigue was thus encouraged, though emperors often did their best to secure the succession by associating a son or kinsman with themselves in power. Not one of Tiberius' first six successors died a natural death, and it is doubtful if Tiberius did. Ultimately, too, nothing could prevent the army from feeling its power. A round of emperor-making in A.D. 69, the 'year of four emperors', was indeed followed by the great century of peace; Vespasian, Trajan, Hadrian, Titus Antoninus (of the Antonine Wall), Marcus Aurelius the Stoic, lived laboriously and maintained order. But another round of civil wars in A.D. 192–7 ended in the accession of the African Severus, who increased the pay of the army and relaxed its discipline; and after the murder of the last of his line in A.D. 235, for fifty terrible years the evil became endemic, while inflation by the debasement of the currency raised prices thirtyfold, and barbarians, the Goths, the Franks, the Alemanni, began their devastating raids across the ill-kept frontiers.

Order was restored by a succession of 'Illyrian' (Danubian) soldier-emperors, uncultured but efficient, culminating in Diocletian (A.D. 284–305). He divided and re-grouped the provinces, to make rebellion more difficult; introduced oriental ceremonial from the new Persian Empire to surround the throne with an aura of sanctity; and tried to fix prices by edict, causing goods to disappear into a vast black market. His great successor, Constantine, had better success with the restoration of an honest currency. But from their time the Empire was, it has been said, in a state of permanent crisis. For lack of gold many payments to the state had to be made in kind. To maintain the fabric of society, the peasant was tied by law to his rented field, the tradesman to his father's calling; both not infrequently ran away to join robber gangs, or even preferred the barbarians to the imperial tax-collector. At last in the fifth century, the Empire did not 'fall', as we in the West often say; but it lost the western provinces and even Italy to Germanic chiefs, who, having settled within it, often under treaty, promising to defend the frontiers against other barbarians such as the Huns, ceased gradually to pay attention to puppet emperors in the marsh-bound fortress of Ravenna or to senior emperors at Constantine's new capital of Constantinople. Britain, drained of its garrison by the rebel general Maximus (A.D. 383–8) and by other ephemeral pretenders after him, was taken over by the Saxons, first called in by Romano-British civilians to assist them against increasingly dangerous raids from Ireland and from the north. Here alone among the Western European provinces, even the Latin language perished; but in the Celtic west, especially in the christianised 'Homeric' society of unconquered Ireland, enough of culture survived to have a profound effect in the re-civilising of English Northumbria, and later even of the nearer continent in the days of Charlemagne.

There had been much feeling of frustration in the Roman Empire, even in its flourishing days. The mundane and often bitter competition for social distinction had been fruitful of disappointments, and brought often a sense of futility even to the successful. Great Romans might find satisfaction in Stoicism and hard work; but among the masses, there was an increasing turning to eastern religions, with more of spiritual content than the cults of outworn European polytheism. Mithras, the Persian soldier-god, had a great vogue among the legionaries and

centurions of the second and third centuries; Isis, the Egyptian Sorrowful Mother, gave both to men and women the comfort that Mithras extended only to men. There was a widespread interest in Judaism, especially among many Roman ladies, before it was outshone by the rising sun of Christianity.

The Roman Empire in the West was dead, but its influence has never ceased to haunt Europe. The great buildings still stood, sometimes converted, like the amphitheatre at Arles or the mausoleum of Hadrian at Rome, into dark-age fortresses; the great roads served the movements of barbarian war-bands. But even through this misuse, the prestige of Rome survived, and barbarian princes knew no greater ambition than to be a Roman *imperator* or, as they said, borrowing the Greek word for 'king' from the emperors still reigning at Constantinople, a *basileus*. Christian clerics kept, in Latin, the necessary records for illiterate German rulers, and handled their correspondence; and in Latin were the books of the heroic Celtic or Roman missionaries who brought the promise of eternal life to those who would repent and believe. These influences helped to maintain the prestige of all things Roman, including even the pagan literature and Roman Law, which would perhaps have been hard put to it to survive the early Middle Ages if they had depended only upon the few who appreciated them for their own sake. Much of the ancient literature did perish; that some books have survived was due to Christian scholars like Boethius, who advised the great Goth, Theoderic, in sixth-century Italy, or St Benedict, the organiser of western monasticism (*see* pages 188, 207), or the great Gallic hymn-writers Prudentius in the fourth century and Venantius Fortunatus in the sixth, men who loved the ancient poetry in which they themselves had been schooled, and would not willingly permit more ignorant Christians to cast it away as wholly of the devil. Behind the entire subsequent development of European society there remained the pervading influence of the Mediterranean world, which had its roots in the Hellenistic civilisation of Greece and of the East, and its framework in the military and legal system created by Rome.

6 PALESTINE AND THE MAKING OF CHRISTIANITY

by P. R. L. Brown

At the end of the fourth century A.D., the Christian poet Prudentius could look back on the troubled history of his times with a thrill of pride: the greatest empire, the Roman, had adopted the most perfect religion, Christianity. This is the most important immediate legacy of Rome. In Europe and the Near East, and as far apart as Russia and Ethiopia, a unitary religious society—with one god, one Church and one ruler—was regarded as the highest ideal of civilisation for well over a thousand years. This type of society was the result of a transformation of the ancient world caused by the peculiarities of Judaism, the rise of Christianity and the circumstances of the later Roman Empire.

I

The political history of the Jews is the history of the life-line of the Near East, the 'Fertile Crescent' of sown land between sea and desert, in which the Neolithic Revolution had developed, connecting Egypt with Mesopotamia. Indistinguishable from other nomads, the Jews had wandered along its fringes from the Euphrates to the Delta of the Nile. In Egypt they were pressed into public works, but in about 1200 B.C. they escaped into the Sinai desert, formed a confederacy of twelve Tribes called 'Israel', and invaded Palestine. Lying across the war-paths of great empires, whose temporary decline had enabled them to settle by the sword on fertile land, the tribes survived,

with glimpses of political greatness, until crushed and deported to the Euphrates by the Assyrians in 720 B.C. and the Babylonians in 589 B.C.

The religious evolution of the Jews was unique. It was formed by intense dependence on a national god, whose worship began with the flight from Egypt; Israel had been made into a nation by Moses, a devotee of Yahweh, the awesome mountain-god of Sinai. The laws governing the settlement had been Yahweh's direct commands. He was a god of deliverance, the patron of their escape. Local fertility-gods might suffice to bring in the harvest, but when faced with extermination, the tribesmen turned again to Yahweh, the deliverer from the desert:

I remember thy grace in thy youth,
Thy love as a bride,
How thou followedst me in the waste,
In a land unsown.

They would need such deliverance. Israel had settled in Palestine only to become a vassal of the Philistines—Mycenean settlers on the coast who inherited the high civilisation of the Canaanites (the previous rulers of Palestine), their fertility religion and their walled cities. A revolt was led by the devotees of Yahweh; Samuel, his priest, consecrated Saul, who had lived like a Moslem dervish among the 'prophets', as king. But priest and warrior disagreed.

Haunted by his lapse, Saul died, a tragic hero, on the battlefield of Gilboa (*c.* 1050 B.C.).

But David and his son Solomon (d. 975 B.C.) made the new monarchy a major power stretching from Gaza to the Euphrates. Two generations of grandeur created the memory of a thousand years. Jerusalem, hitherto an alien fortress, was now turned into a sanctuary of Yahweh. The god of Sinai sanctified by his presence the city and the temple with its priestly ritual; they would be as eternal as his laws. Deliverance would come again, not from the desert, but from the Holy City, and the greatest deliverance of all, the final triumph of Israel, by a king of the lineage of David—the 'Messiah'.

The hegemony of Solomon did not last, and the kingdom was divided by his sons. The two states—Isreal in the north and Judah in the hill-country of Jerusalem —were dependent for communications on their neighbours; the exclusive cult of Yahweh became impossible. In the Near East, political alliances and marriages were regarded as the alliance of gods, who would reside in the territories of their partners, but to his devotees, the cult of Yahweh was sullied by the presence of these divine 'in-laws'. In Israel the apostasy of Ahab and Jezebel was expiated in a blood-bath by Jehu and Elijah (? 842 B.C.). In Judah the kings Hezekiah (? 693–685 B.C.) and Josiah (638–609 B.C.) led official reactions. But in the seventh century—the age of the great prophets, Hosea, Amos, Isaiah, Jeremiah and Ezekiel—the religion of Yahweh was fighting a losing battle against dire political necessity.

No amount of tergiversation could save the kingdoms from the smash and grab raids of the Assyrians and the revived Babylonian Empire of Nebuchadnezzar (604–561). By 589, nothing was left; dispersed and transplanted, Israel had suffered the fate of many nations.

But the uprooting of the religion of Yahweh led to a change of vast importance: the Jews had a glimpse of monotheism as a universal religion. As the god of a tribal resistance-movement, Yahweh had shunned his rivals. Polytheism was not so much rejected as ignored; only the émigrés at Aswan in Egypt troubled to make him the monarch of a pantheon. Babylonian myths of the creation and the flooding of the world had been purged of their gods to make Yahweh the sole creator and judge of mankind. His dealings with the nations which had beleaguered and destroyed Israel were obscure. To Ezekiel it seemed as if he had withdrawn from his people. But deliverance would come soon by repentance and a return to the law of holiness: in that 'Day of the Lord', the vultures would be sated with the flesh of his enemies. The poet of the 'Servant Songs' in the book of Isaiah saw differently. Deliverance, he believed, had already come. Israel was already consecrated by the sufferings of the faithful, and all nations should join in its happiness: 'it is too light a thing that thou shouldst be my servant to raise up the tribes of Israel? I will also give thee for a light to the gentiles, that my salvation may be unto the end of the earth.'

Thus the realisation of the unity of God and mankind was an unexpected result of the humiliation of Israel in the maelstrom of the nations.

II

Deliverance came soon, under the Persian Empire of Cyrus (559–529 B.C.). Scrupulous in restoring the religious status quo, he sent the Jews of Babylon back to Jerusalem. The Temple was rebuilt by Zerubabel (520 B.C.), Nehemiah (445 B.C.) and Ezra (? 398 B.C.), acting as Persian officials. The remnant of the nation was ruled by an aristocracy of priests, and the cult of the Temple was reinforced by prayer and the study of the Law in assemblies—the 'synagogues'. Unlike the theocracies of the Near East, the Jewish religious state combined the sacrificial ritual of the Temple with the spiritual life of the synagogue—a development of the circumstances of the Exile. Judaism, as we know it, was a creation of the Persian Empire.

Jewish religion had also been deepened by contact with Persia. Its primitive beliefs were replaced, under Zoroastrian influence by a more sophisticated picture of the supernatural. Religion became the expression of a cosmic drama, whose protagonists were not nations, but good and evil, where the 'Day of the Lord' meant not a national triumph, but the Last Judgment, in which the world is destroyed by fire. History now gained a meaning outside itself. So did man. Primitive views on survival gave way to a belief that the bodies of the just would be resurrected by God in a new creation. Immortality was a reward, not an accident. Such a religion could never be alone; its world was haunted by rival hierarchies of good and evil powers—angels and demons. Quite as important for the future as the glimpses of universal monotheism is this growing Jewish experience of the hopes and fears of another world.

Meanwhile the tide of universalism was flowing away from Judaism; the missionaries of the third century B.C. were not the Jews but the Greek conquerors of Asia, confident propagators of hellenistic culture. The Jews were left high and dry, a quaint and quiet race of 'philosophers' whose alternative to civilisation was a laudable adherence to ancestral custom.

So it was now the misfortune of the Seleucid rulers of Syria to try to 'civilise' Judaea. It had seemed easy. The Jewish aristocracy had settled down as none too scrupulous courtiers of the Greeks; and many non-priestly houses stood to gain by a change. They would outbid each other for the office of High Priest by turning Jerusalem into a Greek city-state and educating their youth in Greek gymnasia. The competition for power began in 169 B.C.; but in 167 Antiochus IV (176–163 B.C.), a zealous Hellene, alarmed by the Roman conquest of Macedonia, resorted to violence. Jerusalem was sacked and the Temple defiled; Jewish observances were prohibited, and the people were forced into the Dionysiac processions.

This was too much for the Jews, fanatically devoted to their national Law. The resistance was led by a priest and his seven sons, headed by Judas called 'Maccabaeus'—'the Hammer'. He waged a savage guerrilla war against collaborators backed by trained armies. The odds were too heavy. By 160 B.C., Judas was rounded up and slain, the Seleucids had learnt their lesson and adopted a conciliatory policy. It seemed as if the Hasidim, the pious fanatics who had faced martyrdom for their traditions, would become a harmless sect of irreconcilables—like the Old Believers in Russia and Judaea, a hellenised Jewish colony, like Alexandria. It might have produced a philosopher such as Philo—not Jesus of Nazareth.

But the claimants of the Seleucid kingdom had to compete for the support of the rebels. In 152 Jonathan, the brother of Judas Maccabaeus, was made military governor of Judaea by Demetrius I; in making him High Priest, Alexander Balas trumped his rival. The leader of the extremists was now sovereign in Judaea. In 143 the country became an independent Jewish state under Jonathan's brother Simon—as king and High Priest. It seemed as if the last great deliverance had come about, but by a Messiah of the priestly house of

Levi, not of David. He was succeeded by his son, John Hyrcanus (135–106 B.C.), who combined the roles of king, priest, and prophet with the pomp and mercenary army of a hellenistic monarch.

The grandeur of the 'Hasmonaean' priest-kings was short-lived. Established as rebel leaders of a religious revival, they ended by crushing or abusing every institution and aspiration of Judaism. The traditional mould was broken; and Christianity is one result of this century of religious turmoil.

The Hasmonaeans had become High Priests by accident. Their combination of royal and priestly powers, which might be justified in leaders of a Messianic deliverance, was blatantly illegal in such rulers as John Hyrcanus and Alexander Jannaeus (105–78 B.C.). The pious were shocked. Alexander Jannaeus was pelted when officiating, and retaliated by a massacre. The Temple had become an instrument to legitimate the rule of the degenerate kings of Judaea. It might still be reverenced as the palladium of independence, but the rabbis had replaced its priests as spiritual leaders of the people in the contemplation of the Law and of the Last Things.

This is the century not of the priests but of the Law and its *avant garde* interpreters, the Pharisees. Their rabbi, Simon ben Schetach, had enjoyed great prestige in the reign of Alexander Jannaeus. Under his wife, Alexandra (78–69 B.C.), the Pharisees were the power behind the throne. In their teaching they sought to deepen the content of Judaism as an established alternative to hellenistic civilisation. The Law was of paramount importance; on its observance depended the survival of Judaea and the salvation of the individual. It was explained by glosses and made applicable to every occasion by casuistry. The national monotheism was widened

to admit pagan proselytes; and the quest for 'righteousness' gained meaning by belief in the resurrection of the dead, the Last Judgment and the working of the 'Spirit of God'. Pharisaism was ambiguous: it combined the ambition for an organised Jewish state with the realisation that Judaism had a universal God whose Law was a means of salvation. Christianity shared with the Pharisees many beliefs rejected by the conservative priestly aristocracy—the Sadducees. St Paul could count on the Pharisees' support in upholding the resurrection of the dead. An ex-Pharisee himself, he inherited the dilemma of a Law which was both the revelation of God's will to an ignorant world and the bulwark of Jewish particularism.

The Law also had devotees more extreme than the Pharisees. A new sect of priests and pietists, led by an anonymous Teacher of Righteousness, was forced by some obscure breach with the official High Priest to retire in protest to the desert—as Israel had from Egypt. The writings of their settlement by the Dead Sea reveal a mentality and imagery of religious dissent not unlike that of the early Christians.

They lived a strictly communal life (compare Acts 2 : 44) under a penitential discipline. In a world rent by the war of Light and Darkness, the remnant of true priests—'the simple ones in Judah, the doers of the Law'—awaited the final deliverance which must surely follow the apostasy of Judaea. They lived on their hope of the Last Things. God would send the Last Priest and the true royal Messiah to lead them in mystical warfare, and to preside over a consecrated banquet which the faithful already celebrated in expectation. As befitted those living in the Last Days, they had the gift of perceiving in the Scriptures prophecies relating to their own time and mission: a commentary on Habbakuk showed how the drama of the Teacher of Righteousness, his enemies and his death, were all foretold by the prophet. So they waited, performing the correct priestly ritual in the 'house of division'.

Yet, in this last ditch of the Law, an attitude was evolved which resembled that of Paul, the abrogator of the Law. By taking the Law seriously as a declaration of God's will, both had to wrestle with the mighty paradox that man's righteousness could only depend on God's. The 'Thanksgiving Psalm' echoes the Jewish penitential liturgy, as Paul does:

> As for me, if I slip, the steadfast love of God is my salvation for ever; and if I stumble in the iniquity of the flesh, my vindication in the righteousness of God will stand to eternity.

The Law more than ever needed a Messiah. Roman rule had by now been established in the Levant by every kind of blackmail and usurpation. Judaea was not spared: the Hasmonaeans were ousted ignominiously by Herod of Idumaea, 37–4 B.C., the henchman of Pompey and Augustus.

The final degradation seemed oppressively close, when the pagans would set up the 'abomination of desolation' in the Holy Places. The Pharisees were only one faction in a country terrorised by brigands and haunted by hopes of a supernatural deliverance. Every festival led to bloodshed and ugly outbursts of religious emotion. The 'multitude', which had been massacred in a Passover riot in 4 B.C. and had lain in protest for five days outside the house of the Roman governor, Pontius Pilate (A.D. 26–36), looked for the last remedy. Elijah the prophet would rise from the dead to herald the 'Kingdom of God'—

the coming of the Messiah whose triumph must mean the end of the world.

John, the son of a priest, seemed such a prophet. Crowds of penitents came in fear of the Last Day to be purified by baptism, and his disciples went as far as Ephesus. A dangerous leader, he was imprisoned and executed by Herod's son (A.D. 31). But his cousin, Jesus, had been baptised by him; and had gained a reputation for miracles throughout Syria. From prison, John had challenged him: 'Art thou He that cometh, or look we for another?' On entering Jerusalem two years later, Jesus was acclaimed as Messiah by the 'multitude' which had followed John and intimidated the authorities.

III

The Judaea in which these events took place was only the centre of Judaism. Since the seventh century B.C. Jewish colonies had been scattered throughout the great empires; and the rise of Rome served to increase their prosperity and cultural importance. Their Judaism was perforce universal. It could appeal to Greeks and Romans as embodying many features dear to the ancients: traditional wisdom preserved in writings of impressive antiquity and guaranteed veracity; intricate observances reflecting the mysteries of the universe; proverbial kings; and an unflinching obedience to saintly laws. Judaea, it seemed, might become the ancestral demesne of monotheism as the 'sacred land' of Egypt was of polytheism.

But this was a shop window. 'Hellenisation' meant attaching the prestige of ancient cults to Greek thought; Judaism could never be hellenised in this way. Jewish universalism proceeded from Jewish premises. The proselyte was a beneficiary of the dispensation of Israel; he never enjoyed full membership of the Jewish community. This might suit pagan habits, but Judaism claimed to be an 'inheritance' for all its members, not a mystery-cult with spectators and the fringe of 'god-fearing' foreigners was a source of weakness when Judaism was faced with the rise of the Christian heresy.

For the appearance of Christianity coincided with the peak of Jewish proselytism. Not only did Judaism appeal to individual Greeks and Romans, but the rhythm of its observances affected the daily life of the eastern cities. Its god was used for exorcisms and its Sabbath widely kept. It was always most successful where Hellenism was weakest—in the Aramaic areas of Mesopotamia. Adiabene, on the Tigris, became a Jewish kingdom.

The Jews were always a problem to the Roman state. There was a large colony in Rome, and the peace of the Greek cities and the eastern frontier depended on their good behaviour. The feud between Jews and Egyptians in Alexandria threatened to stir up communal violence throughout the Levant. Claudius called them the 'plague of the earth', and the Roman colony had to be dispersed in A.D. 19, 41 and 59. The last expulsion was occasioned by the impact of Christianity whose propagation had led to similar incidents in the Aegean. Spiritually and politically, the relations of Judaism and the pagan world had reached a climax.

IV

Christianity began as a Jewish sect awaiting the return of the Messiah. Its gospels are biographies of Jesus of Nazareth designed to show that his life fulfilled in every detail the career of the Messiah foretold in the Scriptures. His disciples had the prophetic gift of perceiving such 'mysteries of the Kingdom of Heaven'. Their master had lived in the last days of Israel, preaching to a nation under the curse of blindness. He had suffered every humiliation Israel

had ever suffered; but he would receive from God the rewards promised to his Anointed One (in Greek, *ho christos*: Christ). In A.D. 33 he was condemned for blasphemy by a Jewish court, and he was disposed of by the Romans as an agitator claiming to be 'King of the Jews'. The holy man was buried in a private tomb to avoid the common grave of criminals. The prophecies were fulfilled. On the third day he rose from the tomb and was taken up into Heaven, to reappear on the Last Day as God's judge.

The disciples would share his triumph. They were to gather in by miracles and baptism all those who would be saved in the Day of Wrath. Their penitential movement in Jerusalem was enthusiastically received by the pilgrims from abroad.

Jesus of Nazareth had been condemned by the religious authorities; now a schism would develop if the enthusiasm of his disciples were not restrained. The priestly aristocracy took the law into its own hands. Stephen was stoned for attacking the Temple, and the community was dispersed. Herod Agrippa (A.D. 37–44) courted popularity by persecuting the heresy. But Paul, a zealous Pharisee, had been converted, and the sect had spread among the Jews of the dispersion and the schismatics of Samaria, between Jerusalem and Antioch.

As already emphasised, the weak link of Judaism was its fringe of proselytes, to whom the Christians could offer full membership in the real Israel and salvation in the Last Judgment. Paul concentrated on these Judaised pagans: he founded communities in the hinterland of Asia Minor and the ports of the Aegean. When he returned to Jerusalem in 59, he was set upon by the Jews and had to be rescued by the Roman authorities. Having made an impression on the governor of Syria, he appealed as a Roman citizen against the condemnation of the Jewish religious court, and ended his life when a prisoner in Rome (A.D. 67) as one of Nero's scapegoats for the burning of the city. Although trained as a Pharisee in Jerusalem, he had lived most of his life as a Christian outside Judaea. His religious enthusiasm, fed by a vision of the Messiah and an ecstatic experience, shook Christianity out of its Jewish mould.

Meanwhile the Christians in Judaea were content to await the Last Day observing God's Law: James, the brother of Christ, was universally revered for his austerities in the Temple courts. Pagans would be admitted, but on the old terms—circumcision and abstention from forbidden foods. But Paul saw in the life and death of Jesus something more than hope for the Last Day. His letters dealing with the problem show a Jewish mind wrestling with the Law on the heroic plane of God's providence and man's nature.

The old drama of God and the Jews, Paul came to believe, had been played out. Christ had founded a new Israel under a new Law. The old Law had shared the bankruptcy of the corrupt nature it had existed to punish. The change must be accepted on faith, as Abraham, the first nomad, had wandered into the unknown at God's command. The new life would be lived by sharing with Christ in the victory of the spirit over the body. The intensity of Paul's experience led him to stress the intimate nature of this dependence and, as a Jew, to extend it to the whole community of the new Israel; the Messiah was close to his community not only because his return was imminent. The mysteries of nature were ransacked to explain this relation. Christ was the 'Head' and his congregation the 'body'—or his 'bride'. Communion with him in the re-enactments of the Messianic banquet resembled the partaking of the magic of the god which the pagans believed to

happen in their sacrificial meals. The great range of Paul's thought had turned the local Messianic hope into an epic of God and man.

In this epic, Jesus was a more than human deliverer. Paul strove to express a belief which could not be expressed in Jewish terms. Yet the early Christians did believe that Christ was God—the one God of the Jews: 'My brothers,' wrote an early devotional writer, 'we must think of Jesus Christ as God.' How to do so was a different problem. The theology of the early Church is an attempt to use the most advanced techniques of Greek thought to provide a statement sufficiently majestic and impregnable to do justice to a new god of Jewish origin.

In the ancient world, indeed, the human qualities of Christ were ignored. He was a superhuman being: the giver of knowledge, the healer of soul and body, the destroyer of demons and the terrible judge of the Last Day. This was a latent revolution. Ultimately, European history happened as it did because Christ was crucified in Jerusalem when Tiberius ruled in Rome.

V

The content of Christianity must be left for the theologians to explain. Unlike a theologian, an historian does not deal with the relations of God and man, but with the relations of men who are limited to the narrow horizon of their generation and moved by pressures which they can never fully understand. To him the rise of Christianity, like any other profound historical change, is a blind revolution. While admitting that it is largely inexplicable, he can only suggest that certain circumstances which affected large bodies of men—such as the fate of Judaism, the crisis of the pagan world and the conversion of Constantine—make it easier to understand.

The political crisis of Judaism reached a horrible climax in the revolt of A.D. 66. Jerusalem was taken over by the extremists, in defiance of the priests, and the Temple became the headquarters of an irreconcilable faction as the Roman army dug itself in around the city. An heroic defence, embittered by atrocities, degenerated into tyranny over a city reduced to cannibalism. Jerusalem had to be stormed and the Temple was burned. The mission of Israel seemed lost: 'the world which was made for us continues. And we, for whom it was made, disappear.'

Yet Judaism overcame this humiliation. God's justice had been shown in his vengeance on the sacrilege of the extremists. The Temple was lamented; but the Law survived. The rabbi Johannen ben Zakkai had been smuggled out of Jerusalem in a coffin to persuade the Emperor Vespasian to found a law-school at Jabneh. Its teaching could not be interrupted to rebuild the Temple, and alms replaced the altar in obtaining the remission of sins. The real losers in the revolt were the nationalists and the sectaries; the Law, scattered by God's will over the earth, was more firmly established.

The strain of Trajan's wars in Mesopotamia proved too much for the stability of Roman rule. In A.D. 117, Jewish demonstrations in Cyrenaica developed into a full-scale war. In 132, the last Messiah, Simon bar Kochebah, led a desperate resistance in the hills of Judaea. The Emperor Hadrian (117–38) settled the Jewish problem. Jerusalem became an Italian colony, and the Jews had to pay for the upkeep of a pagan temple. In return, Judaism became an official religion (135). The 'patriarch' enjoyed complete sovereignty over the religious affairs of his people. His emissaries collected the temple-tax, and orthodoxy was defined by allegiance to him. The Jews were freed from all obligations contrary to their religious duties and Judaism continued to be revered. It developed a religious art—a sure sign of popularity. In the narrative paintings of Dura Europos (third century), which show the epic of the Jews, Moses is an heroic figure of almost god-like proportions.

Judaism, indeed, continued to represent established monotheism until ousted by an established Christianity. Only after A.D. 425 did the patriarchs move to Baghdad, and Judaism withdraw into its Hebrew shell. But Christianity had already hindered its advances in the Roman world. The orthodox became increasingly unwilling to make proselytes only to lose them to heretics; only the Law and nothing but the Law, they insisted, could keep Judaism from being eroded by a penumbra of fantasies.

By 135 there were thus two forms of Jewish monotheism in the Roman Empire, Judaism and Christianity, the one respectable, the other almost indistinguishable in its religious habits and vocabulary—but small and suspect. Like Judaism and unlike paganism, Christianity was an 'inheritance' for all its members. The religious community had exclusive and permanent power over the individual; its observances were for everybody and for every day. The Christian liturgy used the language of hellenised Jews. Christ and his mysteries replaced the Law; but the expressions of gratitude for the gift of the 'knowledge of salvation' were the same. In its concern for the Messiah, Christianity was more Jewish than the liberal Jews; but it had a god of its own.

VI

The Christians lived in a profoundly religious society whose forms were as prolific as the underworld of medieval Catholicism. It is necessary, in order to understand the Christian background, to examine them and take account of the spiritual and intellectual problems of the ancient world. Tribal religions of vast antiquity survived unchanged in backward areas—the Balkans and Asia Minor—or as venerable relics hallowed by culture and success—in Greece and Rome. The temples of individual gods were centres of local devotion, pilgrimages and boisterous propaganda. The temple of Yahweh at Jerusalem and of Diana at Ephesus are well-known examples; but Syria and the 'sacred land' of Egypt were the homes *par excellence* of institutions which combined the prestige of the great Benedictine monasteries with the mystery of Tibet. The craving for the exotic was fed from outside the Empire, where even Persia seemed as remote as Rome and Antioch were close. The philosophical notions of monotheism and contempt of the world had long been popularised by the Stoics (*see* page 87). The great Greek philosophers—especially Pythagoras—were regarded as holy men whose teachings were zealously preserved by their disciples: they loomed, like Jewish patriarchs, behind a haze of awe.

There were times when religiosity had not seemed so intense. But such periods were themselves only turning points in a religious crisis—when the traditional gods seemed incapable of helping men in a world ruled by chance and violence. The veneer of sceptical urbanity was pathetically thin; both the highest and the basest elements in ancient civilisation left man with religion as the only answer to his problems.

Ancient philosophy, in delivering the mind from the tyranny of chance and custom, had left man alone with God. Nothing else mattered. Natural science was only a 'knack' and incapable of certainty; truth was to be found only about man and God and as man's environment

could not be controlled, it was allowed to crumble away, leaving the sage on the edge of an abyss, content that his soul was divine. Such a belief produced saints, pagan and Christian. It was nobly expressed in the life of the crippled slave Epictetus (b. *c.* A.D. 60): 'What else can I do, an old man and lame, but praise God. If I were a nightingale, I would do the part of a nightingale. But as it is, I am a being of reason: I must praise God.'

The flight to God was achieved at a heavy price; the surrender of the world to the irrational. When the philosopher ceased to be a critic and became a saint, man was left as a misfit in an unknown universe, haunted by demons and helpless before iron laws of Fate mirrored in the ineluctable motion of the stars. A new chaos has arisen. Unbounded curiosity and the desire to explain and manipulate the unknown were emotions as powerful in the second century A.D. as they had been in the age of Socrates; but the new attempt to make the world intelligible was made by religion. From this time onwards, every resource of ancient culture was pressed into an attempt to explain the world in religious terms. Christianity was the residual legatee of this momentous revolution.

Curiosity and pessimism dominate the new mentality. The world and the human body were unalterable by-products of a cosmic oversight, suffocating the soul as in a tomb. This fallen element of the divine could escape only by full knowledge of the complicated apparatus of gods and demonic powers which separated the One God of the philosophers from the botched handicraft of his subordinates. The search for ways and means could take the form of ransacking the traditional cults of the Mediterranean, or adopting the new religions such as Christianity and heresies driven out of Persia. Apuleius of Madaura

(b. *c.* 125), the author of the *Golden Ass*, claimed to be such a *type croyant*: 'I . . . learnt worship on worship, rites beyond number and various ceremonies in my zeal for truth and my dutifulness to the gods.'

The ancients loved traditional wisdom—the older and the more obscure the better. The Fathers of the Church only inherited their passion for wresting elaborate allegorical information from the most unpromising materials; and there was no lack of these in the venerable institutions of Greece and Egypt.

Egypt, in particular, enjoyed vast prestige as the Holy Land of polytheism. The curious flocked to the immemorial shrines of the Nile to see the wonders and hear the wisdom which had vanished from more prosaic lands. Egyptian religion had long been hellenised for export; Hadrian copied the temple of Serapis in his Roman villa, as the Russians of the seventeenth century copied the churches of Jerusalem. The Emperor Septimius Severus (A.D. 190–212), fascinated by these mysteries and anxious to gain the support of his African and Egyptian subjects, adopted the hairstyle of Serapis in his monuments and persecuted the Christians as enemies of the gods.

Egyptian religion was active in pressing its services throughout the Empire. The progress of its gods was marked by miracles publicised by medallions and professional raconteurs. These scribes were conscious of a lofty mission: 'And every Greek tongue shall tell the story; and every Greek shall reverence Imouthes son of Ptah.' Such miracle-literature formed a rich humus for popular devotion; St Augustine read a Christian pamphlet produced only forty-eight hours after the event.

For ancestral piety was not enough. The gods had to establish their claim to veneration by ministering frequently to mankind; by the end of the second century, Christian apologetics tended to degenerate into a boasting-match between Christ and Aesculapius the Healer. An unexpected rainstorm which saved the day on one of the campaigns of Marcus Aurelius (161–180) was ascribed by the Christians to Christ, by the Emperor to Jupiter Pluvius, and by the Emperor's biographer to the Emperor.

The luxuriant new devotion was opposed by many, not so much as sceptics, but from the fear that enthusiasm for exotic cults would dissipate loyalty to the traditional gods of the Empire, at a time when plague and the revival of the German threat in the Marcomannic War (167–9) made official piety essential. Lucian, the satirist, (*c.* 145–90) saw the danger of impostors such as Christ, or the ingenious young man described by Lucian in the 'False Prophet' who built up a whole cult in Asia Minor. But devotion was patronised by the dynasty of Septimius Severus, who had married into a Syrian priestly family. In the salon of his remarkable wife, Julia Domna, religious knowledge was a passport to success.

This circle produced a life of the Greek revivalist, Apollonius of Tyana. A Pythagorean philosopher, he had sought and imparted the true worship of the gods all over the world. He had lived among the brahmans of India; but he was particularly concerned with reviving paganism in Greece. The ritual purity of the temples was stressed and their ceremonies explained. His appearance before the tyrant Domitian (81–96) was marked by miracles similar to those of the Christian martyrs. He had risen from the dead and disappeared into heaven. He was the exemplary pagan saint, whose later prestige grew to meet the challenge of Christianity.

The cults offered knowledge of the powers which imprisoned the soul: and so the possibility of release. Their mysteries were based on a magical view of the universe as old as the Egyptian Books of the Dead. Between the soul and the One lay a hierarchy of hostile and benevolent powers to be courted or overcome. Freedom from fate decreed in the stars was one advantage: 'I conquer Fate, and Fate obeys me', was the boast of Isis. Protection from demons was another; the devotees of Mithras had to pacify Ahriman, the baleful monster who guarded the paradise of the Milky Way.

The element of sympathetic magic was strong in their occult formulae; the initiate went through rites—such as death—in this world to avoid doing so in the next. With Mithras, as with Christ, a cosmic drama had already been acted to secure the success of the initiate. But the sacraments of the mystery cults were not like those of Christianity. Their communal sacrificial meals and purifications were as old as paganism itself: and the initiations of the new saviour-gods were reserved for the elect—or the rich. Lucius, the hero of the *Golden Ass*, was initiated three times on the command of the gods, communicated in dreams. Nor were they regarded as fitting man for a good life. They assumed a high degree of ritual purity before they were administered, but their aim was rather to wrench the soul out of its prison. The mystery cults reflect the basic pessimism of pagan religiosity. The devotee lived for the few high-lights, when ecstasy or initiation left him gasping for a fatherland beyond the stars, and crushed by the shame of ever having been born into human flesh.

Such rites established ties of gratitude towards the gods concerned. But this dependence was not exclusive, although it might be as intense as the loyalty of a medieval monastery to its patron saint. Those who denied the ministrations of

many gods were dismissed as 'mean-souled'; there seemed no need to deprive the One God of a well-stocked court of beneficent henchmen, and by the third century, there was a tendency to give expression to this sense of an underlying unity. The Sun was regarded as the supreme manifestation of the incomprehensible One: like Christ, it was a life-giving mediator between God and the universe. Its worship had deep roots in the primitive and widespread cult of Apollo. The Sun-god was adopted by Aurelian (270–3) as most worthy of the Empire; and by the family of Constantine. The 'Prayer to the Sun' of the Emperor Julian is the noblest expression of pagan theology. It seemed quite natural for Christians of the time of Constantine to apply to Christ—'The Sun of Righteousness'—the prestige of a god which had already accustomed pagans to look to a supreme saviour.

The emotions behind the mystery-cults were so powerful that Christianity was almost swamped at the outset. The Christian Gnostic heresy was more than the lunatic fringe of the Church; it had become inevitable as soon as St Paul challenged Judaism. An alternative mythology to that of the Jews had to be worked out and the Gnostic systems are the most vivid evidence of the mainsprings of pagan religiosity as it affected Christianity that have survived.

The systems vary but the underlying themes—pessimism and knowledge—are the same. To Saturninus of Antioch, original man was a pathetic cripple, badly copied by rebellious angels from an image which had flashed across the divine consciousness. To Valentinus, the world was a monstrous misbirth caused by the passion of widsom to catch a glimpse of her unknowable maker. In all cases, the villain of the piece is Yahweh, the god of the Jews, a clumsy and proud subordinate, and Christ is the deliverer. Magic, the rich sediment of ancient religion where all known gods come to rest as 'Names of power' in incantations, is used to people the universe with incongruous demons—Zarathustra, Melchisedek, Rhadamanthus, Anubis and Eresh-ki-gal, Babylonian god of the underworld.

In Manichaeism, this Christian Gnostic cult, grafted on to Persian dualism, became a world religion. Mani, a cripple of royal blood from Upper Mesopotamia, had created a religious system from the welter of faiths in that area. It was almost accepted as the creed of the new Sassanid Empire, but he died in 277, the victim of an orthodox Zoroastrian reaction. The astounding growth of Manichaeism is one of the most revealing phenomena of the end of the ancient world. In Christian guise, it spread through the Roman Empire, attracting such members of a semi-Christian intelligentsia as the young Augustine; and it continued to lurk beneath the surface of medieval Christendom, erupting with the Bogomils in the East (tenth century) and the Cathars of Languedoc (twelfth). It was recognised in China in the eighth century and had been the religion of Central Asia. It was a mystery religion with the advantages of Christian organisation. The élite of austere 'Perfect Ones' was supported by an active laity, and heresy was avoided by strict centralisation and an agreed canon of the writings of the founder. As the twin of the Holy Ghost, Mani was the final teacher; but he had been preceded by messengers—Zoroaster, Buddha and Christ. It is significant that the last and the greatest mystery-religion should have been a Christian heresy.

VII

The success of Gnosticism shows that Christianity could have become another mystery-cult. It did not do so. The 'Great Church' held on, despite alarming fluctuations, to its Jewish tradition. It remained a community for all whose purpose was to live righteously from day to day until their bodies were resurrected for a final reckoning.

Nothing could have been more repulsive to the educated pagan, who preferred a timeless myth of cosmic dimensions, than this theology based on the local history of Judaea and an arbitrary intervention of God in favour of the human body. The reverence displayed by the Christians for the corpses of their martyrs nauseated him. But to many it was a relief from the hopeless monotony expressed in the epitaph: 'I was not. I was. I shall not be. I do not care.' When combined with apocalyptic beliefs in the imminent reign of Christ, Christianity could become a popular movement whose hopes were fed by every ominous creaking of the structure of the Empire. In Phrygia, where Christianity was only a veneer on a savage religiosity which had already produced the Bacchantes, Montanus led such a movement in the 170s.

Elsewhere, Christianity still remained a small sect, resembling the sodalities which are a common feature of ancient and medieval life. It was suspect because its organisation had been founded by a Jewish heretic who had been executed for treason. In law, denunciation as a Christian could mean execution; but it was usually left to the mob to stir up violence against the coterie of 'atheists'. In 177, political disasters led to horrible scenes when the populace of Lyons turned on these helpless scapegoats.

The growth of Christianity had been haphazard. It had enjoyed a short-lived success in Roman society through the households of the Jewish loyalist magnates. Flavius Clemens, the consul for 95, was executed by Domitian; 'atheism' was one of the charges brought against his wife. But Christian austerity and monotheism could appeal to professional intellectuals such as Justin (100–163/7), who continued as a wandering philosopher to popularise his new faith until denounced by a rival. The Christian Church also harboured such strange birds of passage as Peregrinus, the butt of Lucian's 'Death of Peregrinus', who ended by burning himself in a Pythagorean ritual suicide at the Olympic assembly of 167.

On the whole, the Christian communities of the second century were made up of uneducated pietists, clinging to bishops who preserved an oral memory of the teaching of the disciples as the only guarantee against fantastic accretions. Polycarp, Bishop of Smyrna, is an example of this type of saintly patriarch. He had seen St John as a youth, and died at an incredibly old age in 155, refusing to recant before the mob in the public theatre. 'These eighty-six years I have served Him; and He has never done me wrong. He is my King and my Saviour, how could I blaspheme him?'

Like Judaism, Christianity was more at home where classical culture was weakest. It was established in Osrhoene by King Abgar IX (179–214) and produced Bardaisan (b. 154) the great Syriac hymn-writer and philosopher. But in Africa, Cyprian, a notable lawyer in provincial society, became the universally respected bishop of Carthage (248–258); and in the great catechetical school of Alexandria, Greek intellectualism first emerged in orthodox form from the Gnostic swamp. The prodigious learning and balanced judgment of Clement of Alexandria (b. *c.* 150) saved Christianity from the dilemma of becoming an irrational mystery-cult or remaining a Jewish heresy. His school taught that a wise

Christian was a better Christian; and wisdom meant hellenisation. Origen, his successor (*c.* 185–*c.* 254), is a type of the future. A man of inexhaustible enthusiasm, he had thrown himself headlong into every aspect of Christianity: the quest for martyrdom, the absorption of pagan learning, Hebrew translations and a systematic theology expounded in the great book *On First Principles*. His asceticism foreshadows the later Byzantine saints; he had castrated himself in a fit of zeal. His literary output was incredible. He dictated to a staff of stenographers provided by a rich patron, and his collected works filled six thousand rolls. In 218 he was brought under cavalry escort to the salon of Mammaea, the niece of Julia Domna, to explain the faith which he had represented with all the vigour of Apollonius of Tyana. Christianity had become an inescapable challenge.

VIII

If it is an over-simplification to say that Christianity ever defeated paganism, by entering politics it gained the ascendancy in a society which would accept such leadership, and kept it into the Middle Ages. At the end of the second century this development seemed remote. Pagan society was oppressively active and the apologist Tertullian ridiculed the idea of a Christian Roman Empire as a contradiction in terms.

But in the third century the last transformation of the ancient world took place, while in the fourth century, the reorganised Roman state enjoyed a new lease of life and survived in the East for a thousand years. Under the Antonines the Empire had been regarded as the natural and unrivalled expression of Greco-Roman civilisation. In the third century, its very existence was challenged by the political and economic disasters described in chapter five. From then onwards, neither state nor civilisation could be taken for granted; heroic efforts were needed to preserve them.

Loyalty to the Empire now became a spiritual issue. The allegiance which the emperors exacted in their task of preserving the largest political society in the world was tinged with religious awe: they posed as saviour-gods and heroes who strove to save civilised society from chaos. The exaltation of the role of the toiling Emperor reached its climax at the court of Diocletian (285–305), who claimed to be regarded as Jupiter directing the labours of his colleague, Maximian-Hercules. The choice of cults was no longer a matter of personal preference; for Emperor and subject it must be an expression of the destiny of the Empire. Religion had entered politics before Constantine. In this and succeeding centuries, Roman emperors were as filled with a sense of a divine providence ruling their empire as the popes of the Middle Ages.

It was in this crisis that the Christian Church suddenly gained momentum. Origen had made Christianity intellectually respectable in circles eaten up with religious curiosity. The Emperor Alexander Severus (222–35) had included Christ in the pantheon of his private chapel. Now the Church became confident of its historic role. In his *Answer to Celsus* Origen prepared Christianity for its triumph. Christ had defied the Empire for two hundred years; he could no longer be treated as an impostor. Roman history was here regarded as important only in providing the conditions necessary for the spread of the Gospel. By 300 the Christians may not have been more than a tenth of the population of the Empire; but even this advance had been unexpected and alarming in an age which took religious dissent seriously.

Christianity first became a leading religion in the eastern parts of the Empire. Its success was achieved at a crucial time. In 226 the Sassanid Dynasty of Persia revived the imperialism of Cyrus and Xerxes: Roman politics could only be played out on the eastern frontiers. As a result, Philip the Arab, a native of the Christian Syriac kingdom of Osrhoene, became Emperor in 243: he was a nominal Christian. Syria was overrun by the Sassanids after the death of Valerian in 260; the independent Palmyrene kingdom of Zenobia (266–72) made use of the aspirations of the frontier region. Among these was Christianity. Christian writers hated the persecuting emperors from the West and foretold the rise of an Oriental monarchy in their place. Paul, Bishop of Antioch (260–72), became the first political prelate as a leading counsellor of the Queen. The conversion of Armenia by Gregory the Illuminator and King Tiridates (303), a classic example of the establishment of a Christian state before Constantine, was due, in part, to hatred of Sassanid rule. In the Near East Christianity had sprung up under the shadow of Persia. For the emperors, an Eastern policy had come to involve a Christian policy.

Elsewhere the crises of the century— and especially in the relations between towns and villages—led to a new phenomenon, mass conversions. Among the semitised Berber villagers of North Africa, Christianity replaced the old cults as an object for the fierce devotion of an increasingly important class. The same happened in Upper Egypt and in Pontus.

The great persecutions of Decius (248), Valerian (253) and Diocletian (303) are not fortuitous results of an age of military despotism. They were carefully planned attempts to destroy Christianity by confiscating its buildings and sacred literature, cutting off its endowments and separating the clergy from the laity. The Roman state had been alarmed. Neither side could be the same again. The persecutions had an unexpected and enduring aftermath. They greatly strengthened local loyalties at the expense of the unity of the Church—and of the Empire—when Christianity became established. The Donatist schism in North Africa is an example. The brunt of the persecution of 303 had been borne by the Berber peasantry, already exasperated by campaigns and taxation. In the aftermath the extremists triumphed. In one town, a mob locked up the more respectable laity and elected as bishop a deacon who had redeemed his collaboration during the persecution by a raid on an imperial warehouse. The doyen of the Numidian bishops, Purpurius of Limata, owed his position to the violence of his language and an alliance with a bandit chief. Donatus, their leader, could never bring himself to trust an emperor, whether pagan or Christian. Attempts in the fourth century to impose Catholic orthodoxy and law and order only widened a breach which was not healed before the Arab conquest. In such a situation, St Augustine was compelled at the beginning of the fifth century to develop a Christian theory of coercion quite as cruel in its application as the persecution of Diocletian.

The leaders of the Church, the future court-bishops, became convinced by the fate of the persecutors that the prosperity of the Empire depended directly on the piety of the emperors. Everyone was afraid that the Roman Empire would collapse: the Christian answer, stated forcibly by Lactantius (*c.* 260–*c.* 340), was that it would if the emperors did not confess to Christ. In a century, we have come a long way from Tertullian.

IX

Diocletian had divided the Empire between his colleagues, who drifted into civil war when he retired in 305. The rule of Maximian and his son Maxentius at Rome was unpopular and a temptation to their ambitious partners, Constantine in Gaul and Galerius in the East.

Galerius, a superstitious bigot, had been behind the persecution of Diocletian. His invasion of Italy in 310 was a disaster. Suffering from cancer, he turned to the Christians whose god had afflicted him. In 311, he issued an Edict of Toleration: the Christians were asked to pray for the dying Emperor.

Constantine was more formidable. He was a dashing soldier, and pious in that he believed that he bore a peculiar relation to whatever deity guided the Empire. He had lavishly endowed the sun-cult of his family, and had been granted a favourable vision from that god. He had come across Christianity in the court of Diocletian at Nicomedia. Further, before his dangerous campaign against Maxentius, he had a vision of the Cross against the sun; this was followed by a dream, and the adoption of a Christian monogram—the XP 'Labarum'—as his heraldic device. At the decisive battle of the Milvian Bridge (28 October, 312), the Cross proved as effective a talisman against the armies of his rivals as against demons. The Empire which Constantine had set out to save had found a new patron in the proscribed god of the Christians, an embarrassing fact which his entourage tried to disguise by euphemistic references to the 'Highest Divinity'.

The conversion of Constantine turned the withdrawal of Galerius into a rout. The situation was regulated by the Edict of Milan in 313, and Constantine's last war against Licinius in the East was fought with religious fervour on either side (324). Christianity was delivered from a pagan ruler by a crusade.

Constantine was determined to reward

the religion of his new patron in a manner worthy of a Roman Emperor. Privileges and large sums of money were granted to the churches in every municipality. A colossal statue in Rome showed him holding the Cross as the emblem of his victory, and the pagan necropolis on the Vatican Hill was buried to build a basilica of St Peter. Constantine was nothing if not lavish, and as the fulfilment of his ambitions was marred by appalling domestic tragedies, he inclined more and more to the ostentatious piety of his mother, Helena. The Holy Land was endowed with magnificent shrines. The Fathers of the Church were assembled at Nicaea to celebrate his victory over Licinius, and the Emperor devoutly kissed the scars of the Egyptian hermit Paphnutius, a victim of the persecution of Diocletian. He intended to be buried with his peers—the Apostles.

But he had been converted without the intervention of the Church, and was baptised only on his death-bed. 'The Thirteenth Apostle' remained very much a Roman Emperor; he preached long sermons at court, indulged in clumsy theological manifestoes, and acted as master of his Church.

Constantine founded this Byzantine tradition not through any cold-blooded intention of using Christianity as an instrument of government, but because, as absolute lord of the Roman world, he had a right to such obedience. In deciding against the Donatists in Africa, in summoning the council of Nicaea in 325 to define the nature of the new god of the Empire, and in exiling the irreconcilable Athanasius in 327, he hoped to pacify his divine patron by organising the Church as he thought best.

The Emperor was a revolutionary. His city, Constantinople, was founded in 330. It was to be the centre of a new Christian Roman state, supported by the eastern parts of the Empire. Paganism seemed to exist only on sufferance, and at the end of his life some great pagan institutions were suppressed—among them an order of eunuch priests on whom the flooding of the Nile was supposed to depend (331–7). The Emperor's past devotion to the sun survived only in his choice of Sunday and 25 December (the birthday of the sun) as Christian festivals.

But Constantine failed to realise the strength of traditional Christianity in the East, and its hatred of heresy. Alexandria was the storm centre, where Arius, an attractive and intellectually obstinate personality, threatened to explain away the distinction between Father and Son in the Trinity by subordinating the Son. It was a self-confident heresy, which bore an alarming resemblance to the hierarchy of pagan gods, and it was bitterly opposed by Athanasius, later patriarch of Alexandria— a striking figure, who used every device of religious propaganda and the violence of the Egyptian mob to defend the 'tradition of the Fathers'. Bewildered by these feuds, which were the laughing-stock of pagan theatres, Constantine had dropped the decision of the Fathers of Nicaea and insisted on reconciliation.

The policy of Constantine was continued by his son, Constantius II (337–61), a superstitious man warped by the burden of his imperial mission. At one time it seemed as if paganism would be officially abolished; but this rash edict was withdrawn. Rather, his reign reveals the precarious position of the established Church.

X

The later years of Constantius show that Constantine's policy was no longer applicable, and his reign was followed by a pagan reaction. Distracted by Persian wars, the Emperor could control the West only by concessions to the strong pagan sentiment in Rome. He had to send his nephew, Julian, to protect Gaul from a German confederacy. Julian was a conscientious general, and he was known to be a pagan. After brilliant victories, the army proclaimed him Emperor. In 361 he made a lightning march into the Balkans. Constantius died, and Julian 'the Apostate' became sole master of the Empire. In Rome, a solemn pagan purification, celebrated opposite the new basilica of St Peter, 'scattered the darkness of twenty-eight years and brought light again'.

Julian (361–3) was the pagan Constantine; a revolutionary and a *dévot* in his attempt to preserve the Empire. Brought up as a Christian, he had derived no satisfaction from the academic Arianism of the court chaplains. His craving for the mysterious was stimulated by magic séances at Ephesus and the poems of Homer. To the Greek piety of an Apollonius of Tyana, he brought a fanatical devotion to the sun god, a high literary training and an abhorrence of Christianity. For him, Christianity was a matter of mumbo-jumbo—of putting salt on babies and using the Cross to scare demons. It was also a blasphemy against the true gods and an attack on the morality of Roman citizens. The Christian policy of his family had been a national apostasy, which could be expiated only in reviving paganism by every device known to either religion. The temples were to resemble Christian churches in their almsgiving, religious instruction and provincial organisation. A leading Roman pagan, Praetextatus, was made governor of Achaia, the centre of Julian's hopes for an Hellenic revival. The Christians were excluded from education, and given over to pagan mobs and the vengeance of their own schismatics. The pagan empire was to be gloriously re-established by a campaign into Persia with an unbeaten army led by Julian, who believed himself to be the reincarnation of Alexander. The gods failed him. The army was lost beyond the Tigris, and the Emperor was mortally wounded in a skirmish, crying out against the 'Galilaean' (26 June, 363). An ascetic and a philosopher, he was the last of the pagan saints.

Paganism survived in the immensely wealthy Roman aristocracy, whose power had been disguised rather than destroyed by the autocratic constitution of the later Empire. The circle of Praetextatus, Nicomachus Flavianus and Symmachus (d. 384) continued to evolve a pagan theology in terms of the sun-cult. When the Altar of Victory, the talisman of the Roman State, was removed from the Senate house in 382, Symmachus made a classic appeal for toleration: 'More ways than one,' he said, 'must lead to so great a mystery.'

Behind these men were many generals, barbarians who became more pagan than the pagans on being Romanised. In 392, Richomer the Frank set up a rival to Theodosius the Orthodox; Flavianus emerged from retirement to organise a pagan revival in Italy. The collapse of Christianity was prophesied. But his army was betrayed in 394; and this great scholar and theologian committed suicide in the antique manner.

But Paganism lasted as long as the ancient world. It only sank out of politics to continue as tenaciously in whole sections of society and popular belief.

The terrors of the barbarian invasions and the sack of Rome in 410 provoked immediate outbursts of pagan feeling. These were met by St Augustine in his *City of God* (412), a refutation as massive as its adversary. Pagan coteries throve in the intense atmosphere of lay education in Alexandria and the law-schools of Beirut, and the hinterland of Syria and Anatolia provided resorts for sacrifices—a source of frequent scandals in which prominent courtiers, and even bishops, were implicated as late as 579. Rural paganism survived well into the sixth century, to shock ecclesiastics who knew more of what it meant than the ignorant peasants. Witchcraft and divination were endemic. They were rife in their original form in the Byzantine court of the eleventh century.

XI

In 378, the Roman army was destroyed by the Goths at Adrianople. The barbarians were on the move again; and the end of the world seemed near. In the religious crisis which followed, the orthodox Christian Empire was finally established by Theodosius (378–95), a passionate man with a fanatical entourage.

The Christian society of the Middle Ages was by now foreshadowed. Everything that needed to be said on the relations of Church and state, and of lay and ecclesiastical culture, was said in this remarkable generation of the Fathers of the Church.

Yet these men were visionaries in a society still firmly rooted in the forms of the ancient world. They were educated in lay schools, often by the leaders of the pagan revival, and their writings show the high standards of traditional rhetoric. Inspired by a delight in words, their arguments move not from syllogism to conclusion, but from verbal association to association, in an intricate pattern of puns, monumental slogans and allegories. St Augustine's *City of God* is not a systematic statement of Christian thought; it is a prodigious theological symphony. The sermons of St Ambrose are examples of this mysticism based on a proliferation of imagery. In the East, bishops such as John Chrysostom—the 'golden-mouthed'—could whip up enthusiasm for orthodoxy and the practical virtues by oratorical displays which had previously been the

privilege of the imperial court alone. They had arrived at Christianity through many intellectual phases; to them, it represented the 'perfect philosophy'. They did more than confiscate ancient thought; they transformed it to admit a new view of God, the universe and man.

Contemporary religious philosophy was tainted with crass materialism. Good and evil, the body and the soul, were regarded as substances—the one pure and light, the other corrupt and heavy. St Augustine had thought in these terms until he was over thirty. The purer Platonic idea, that the soul was a spirit, and bad a defect of good, came as a revelation to him which dominated his later work. Anyone who thought sanely about the relation of divine and human in Christ had to reconsider Aristotle's definitions of personality, substance and will. Though decided by the violence of the ignorant, the great theological controversies were accompanied, in the peaceful co-operation of Christian and pagan in the schools of Alexandria, by a reassessment of traditional metaphysics as important as that of Thomas Aquinas.

Christian culture also transformed monumental art. In sculpture, man is no longer animated by his soul but immobilised, with raised eyes, in the contemplation of eternity. Roman architecture continued to develop: its greatest achievement is the Hagia Sophia in Constantinople. From the time of Hadrian, Roman architects had tried to build from the interior outwards, to capture space in a dome and in the lightness of arcades—an ideal suited to churches which were both places of assembly and mysterious sanctuaries. The exquisite art of glazed mosaics were perfected to line basilicas as splendid as imperial palaces and as frequented as public baths, with pictures in rainbow colours, whose intricate symbolism and triumphal style popularised the mysteries and heroes of the new faith.

Christianity had become respectable. Christian experience was greatly widened as a result. An educated man could become a Christian without thinking; but when he did, his piety took a more spectacular form. The tone was set by the remarkable ascetics of the Near East. St Jerome (d. 420) led an emigration of pious ladies from Rome, and Paulinus rejected the 'tame credulity' of the Gallic aristocracy to become an obscure parish priest. Conversion had come to mean what it meant throughout the Middle Ages—undertaking the leadership of the world of nominal Christians by a spiritual aristocracy of monks and bishops.

Those who remained laymen were often devout and learned. But lay piety lacked a centre, such as was provided for it by the later medieval Church in a suffering Christ and the sacraments. When Boethius awaited death in prison (524), he turned for consolation not to the Passion, but to the old truths of pagan philosophy.

The Church, meanwhile, had produced a new aristocracy. As almsgiver, judge and protector, the bishop rivalled the Emperor as the benefactor of cities and the tamer of barbarians. He continued to do so when the Western Empire collapsed. The last military commander in Noricum (Austria) returned from a hopeless quest for reinforcements in Italy to meet the Germans as their bishop. The great landowners of Gaul continued as churchmen to live as Romans and rule as Romans for many centuries.

In the East, the bishops were political figures of the greatest importance. The 'Empire' of the patriarch of Alexandria, who could control the corn-fleet of Constantinople, the public services of his city and the hinterland of Egypt, was only the most formidable. Public opinion took theological forms, and the slow growth of a sense of local pride and local loyalties in the Asiatic provinces was aggravated by emperors who as theologians appeared to be flouting the 'faith of the Fathers', and who, as rulers, had to attempt the impossible task of making their wishes felt in provinces that lay a good two months' journey from the court. The Council of Chalcedon (451) clarified the issues. The rallying of Eastern opinion against its decisions began a schism which contributed to the loss of Egypt and Syria to the Arabs. When the Saracen confederacy of Islam defeated the Byzantine army on the Yarmak in 636, the cause of the Empire had already gone by default. 'The Greeks wish to fight on,' said a citizen of Alexandria, 'but I wish to have no dealings with the Greeks in this world or the next. I renounce for ever the tyrant of Byzantium and the orthodox who are his slaves.'

Nonetheless, Christianity had been established in the framework of the ancient world, and the medieval Church continued to reflect some of the stability of Roman rule. To Prudentius, the Empire had existed for this. His god preferred law and order, and seemed out of place among savages. Yet what would happen when the Empire collapsed in the West, and its Eastern provinces preferred Moslem rule to the orthodox emperors of Constantinople?

7 THE ARABS AND THE EXPANSION OF ISLAM

by P. M. Holt

On the eve of the Islamic conquests in the seventh century two great monarchies dominated the Near and Middle East: the Byzantine Empire, which from Constantinople controlled the lands of the Eastern Mediterranean, and the Sassanian Empire, with its capital at Ctesiphon, ruling the Tigris-Euphrates valleys and the Iranian plateau. The hostility between these two states, one Christian, inheriting the culture of Greece and Rome, the other Zoroastrian and the heir of ancient Persian traditions, was passing through an acute phase. Between 611 and 616 the Sassanian ruler, Chosroes II, occupied Syria and Egypt. Byzantine fortunes were saved by the Emperor Heraclius who in 629 drove the Persians from their new conquests.

To both Byzantium and Persia, Arabia was a land of barbarian tribes, yet it was important to their economies and strategy. In southern Arabia a series of sedentary civilisations had flourished from ancient times but by the end of the sixth century much of its prosperity had departed and, nominally at least, it was a Persian province. From the Yemen a trade route ran through western Arabia, the Hijaz, to Syria. In this way spices were brought to the Byzantines by Arab merchants, among whom the most prosperous were those of Mecca. This route had attained a new importance in the sixth century, when the Persian wars and disorders in Egypt had rendered older routes unsafe.

On the desert frontiers of the Byzantine and Sassanian empires were two client-states of Christian Arabs, originally nomads from the Yemen, which shielded the sedentary cultivators and the towns of the Fertile Crescent from the nomads in the interior of Arabia. Ghassan on the Syrian frontier had flourished in the sixth century but in recent years internal troubles, the Persian invasion and the ending of the Byzantine subsidy had weakened it. Its Iraqi counterpart around Hira, near the Euphrates, had been brought under direct Sassanian rule in 602.

Throughout Arabia proper, society was essentially tribal. The chiefs, arbitrators in disputes rather than rulers, were leaders in war, and custodians of the tribal shrines. For the rest, custom governed the activities of the community. The mass of the Arabs were nomads and except in the south, where settled agriculture was possible, even the townsmen were but a few generations removed from nomadism. Among the towns, Mecca was pre-eminent. Situated in a barren valley, it owed its importance to its position on the spice road, to the business ability of its merchants from the tribe of Quraysh, and to its shrine, the Ka'ba, which was a place of pilgrimage for the western Arab tribes. A rudimentary oligarchy governed Quraysh and arranged the business affairs of Mecca. Elsewhere, towns had sprung up in the oases, such as Yathrib.

Arab tradition distinguishes sharply on linguistic and genealogical grounds be-

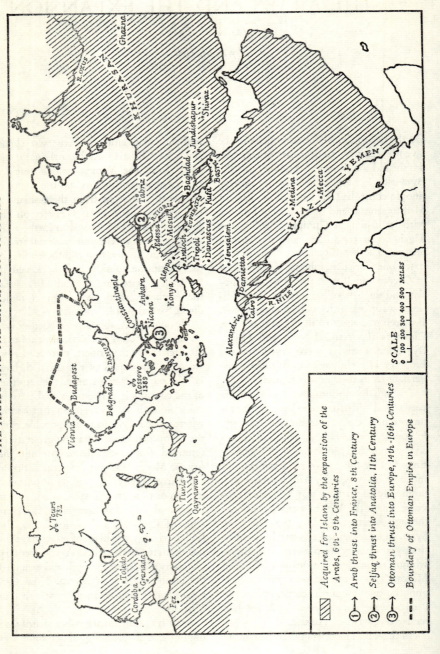

THE ARABS AND THE EXPANSION OF ISLAM

Acquired for Islam by the expansion of the Arabs, 6th–9th Centuries

Arab thrust into France, 8th Century

Seljuq thrust into Anatolia, 11th Century

Ottoman thrust into Europe, 14th–16th Centuries

Boundary of Ottoman Empire in Europe

SCALE
0 100 200 300 400 500 MILES

Toledo
Córdoba
Granada
Fez
Tunis
Qayrawan
Vienna
Budapest
Belgrade
R. DANUBE
Kossovo 1389
Constantinople
Nicaea
Ankara
Konya
Alexandria
Damietta
Cairo
R. NILE
Jerusalem
Damascus
Tripoli
Antioch
Aleppo
Edessa
Mosul
R. TIGRIS
R. EUPHRATES
Kufa
Basra
Baghdad
Jundishapur
Shiraz
Tabriz
Medina
Mecca
HIJAZ
YEMEN
KHURASAN
Ghazna
R. OXUS

Tours 732

tween Arabs of southern (Yamani) and northern (Qaysi) origin. The northern Arabs had evolved a common literary dialect and a highly sophisticated poetical technique. The religion of most of these Arab tribes was pagan, centring in sacred places, trees and stones which were regarded as the dwelling-places of vaguely defined powers. There was also a belief in more personal gods including a high god named Allah. Both Judaism and Christianity had penetrated Arabia. Jews or Judaised Arab tribes formed a relatively advanced minority at Yathrib and elsewhere. Christianity was the religion of the Arabs of the border states as well as of isolated groups and individuals in the peninsula. Discontented with the paganism of their environment, individual Arabs were feeling their way towards an indigenous monotheism.

Thus when the seventh century opened, the way was prepared for the appearance of Islam and the expansion of the Arabs. The Byzantine and Sassanian empires were weakened by disaffection and exhausted by mutual warfare. The Arabs, disunited and backward in the mass, had nevertheless produced in Quraysh an élite of experienced traders in touch with the outside world. The genius of Mohammed was to create in Islam a new bond of union which was to sweep the Arab tribes to conquest and empire.

II

Mohammed was born, traditionally in A.D. 571, into one of the clans of Quraysh. Orphaned as a child, he was brought up first by his grandfather and subsequently by his uncle, Abu Talib. He was a townsman by birth and upbringing, a member of the most advanced and alert community in northern and western Arabia. His early years were obscure and difficult but he acquired a reputation for trustworthiness. At the age of twenty-five he married a wealthy widow, Khadija, whose business manager he had been.

About his fortieth year, Mohammed went through a period of intense spiritual tension culminating in a vision in which he received the first of the revelations which now form the Koran. He was convinced that he had received a divine call to attest the unity and transcendence of Allah, to warn his people of the Day of Judgment and to tell them of the rewards for the faithful in Paradise and the punishment of the wicked in Hell. At first Quraysh paid little attention but Khadija at once believed in his mission and amongst other early followers were his cousin 'Ali, the son of Abu Talib, and a kinsman, Abu Bakr. Later he was joined by a man of outstanding strength of character, 'Umar, who had previously bitterly opposed him, and 'Uthman, a member of the important Umayyad family. But for long the chief response to his preaching came from the poor and the slaves. Mohammed's teaching was known as Islam, the 'Submission' to God, and his adherents were called Moslems.

As Mohammed's followers increased, the Meccan oligarchs began to see in him a potential danger, since an attack on Arab paganism threatened the economic and social hegemony of Quraysh as guardians of the Ka'ba. A persecution of the Moslems began and some of them sought asylum in Abyssinia. Mohammed himself was protected by his clan but his movement was at a standstill. He therefore began to look for allies outside Mecca. A visit to the nearby town of Ta'if was a failure but shortly afterwards he was invited to go to Yathrib, later known as Medina, the oasis town on the spice road, nearly 300 miles north of Mecca.

Here was a mixed population of Arab and Jewish tribes, much disturbed by internal feuds. Mohammed was invited as an arbitrator and those who welcomed him and the Moslems were known as *Ansar*, 'Helpers'. Mohammed's emigration to Medina (the *Hijra*) took place in A.D. 622 and the Moslem calendar is dated from the beginning of the year in which this event occurred. From his arrival in Yathrib, henceforward called *Madinat al-Nabi* (The City of the Prophet) or Medina, Mohammed was a political personage, the head of a community which in time became exclusively Moslem. Within the community, tribal rights and the blood bond were superseded by loyalty to the Prophet, to whom all disputes were brought for settlement. The Koranic revelations of this period are much occupied with legislation and exhortations to obedience to God and His Apostle.

In one respect Mohammed's expectations were disappointed: the Jews, whom he expected to welcome him as the successor of their own prophets, ridiculed his claims. Gradually the Jewish tribes were eliminated and their property seized for the Moslems. The Arab character of Islam became more pronounced and Mecca superseded Jerusalem as the direction to which Moslems turn in prayer. Mohammed's main political activity in these years was the organisation of hostilities against Mecca. Strategically the Moslems were well-placed to threaten Meccan communications with the north, while the acquisition of booty removed the dependence of the Meccan immigrants (*Muhajirun*) on their Medinese hosts. Among the nomad Arabs, from whom these townsmen were not far removed either in space or time, raiding was an accepted economic activity.

A skirmish, the battle of Badr, in 624, with the Meccan caravan was the first of the victories of Islam. Quraysh retaliated in 625 and defeated the Moslems but did not follow up their victory. In 627, however, a Meccan army marched against Medina but was baulked of success by a trench which Mohammed, advised by a Persian follower, had dug around the town.

Mohammed now made a fresh approach to the Meccan oligarchs, who realised that his hostility was more of a danger to their commerce than was his religion. In 628 a ten-year truce was negotiated; Moslems might enter Mecca as pilgrims and leading Quraysh began to accept Islam. But in 630 Mohammed attacked Mecca. There was little resistance and only four persons were put to death after the capture of the city. The Prophet's chief opponent, the wealthy and powerful Abu Sufyan of the Umayyad family, declared his conversion to Islam. The Ka'ba, purged of its pagan associations, became the chief shrine of the new faith. The pilgrimage became an Islamic institution. Thus Mohammed effected a compromise which maintained the essential tenets of the faith yet rooted it in Arab custom and tradition. Events were to show Quraysh maintaining under Islam their hegemony in Arab affairs.

The Prophet lived for only two and a half years after the conquest of Mecca. During this time his influence spread among the tribes, many of which sent delegations to Medina offering submission. This political and personal relationship to Mohammed did not necessarily imply conversion to Islam, which followed only slowly and superficially. When he died on 8 June, 632 after a short illness, the Moslem community was taken unprepared. It possessed a capital in Medina, a rudimentary organisation and the prestige of victory, but with the death of the Prophet its mainspring had gone.

III

The Moslem community had been created by the mission and genius of Mohammed and with his death it seemed likely to break up into its component elements. The question at once arose of the leadership of the community in prayer and war. As Prophet, of course, Mohammed himself could properly have no successor. He had no son and in any case there was no tradition of strict hereditary descent of office among the Arabs. When rivalry seemed likely to break out in Medina between the *Ansar* and *Muhajirun*, decisive action by a small group of the Prophet's closest companions imposed on the community one of their own number, Abu Bakr, who took the title of *khalifa*, 'deputy', from which comes the English form, 'Caliph'. The term 'Orthodox', which is applied to Abu Bakr and his three successors, 'Umar I, 'Uthman and 'Ali, is a translation of the epithet bestowed upon them by Moslem historians, and is used to distinguish this first phase of the Caliphate.

Immediately a challenge came from the remote tribes who felt that their recent contract of loyalty had been cancelled by the Prophet's death. In various parts of Arabia claimants to prophetic status had arisen and gained followers from the tribesmen. The reign of Abu Bakr was chiefly occupied by wars to bring the dissident tribes back under the control of Medina and an outlet for tribal energies was found in expeditions against the Byzantine and Sassarian empires. Although the attacks on Syria and Iraq were foreshadowed under Abu Bakr, the decisive victories were won in the time of 'Umar I.

The Moslem success in Syria was largely due to the general Khalid ibn (i.e. son of) al-Walid who, after fighting on the edge of Iraq, crossed the desert and joined the Moslem expeditionary force in Syria. Damascus was captured in 635 but in the following year the Emperor Heraclius brought a large army against the Moslems. The Arabs concentrated on the Yarmuk and defeated the Byzantines in July 636.

This was virtually the end of Byzantine rule in Syria.

Khalid's first raid in 633 had shown the feebleness of the Persian hold over Iraq. Here his successor won a decisive battle in 637 at Qadisiya, not far from Hira. The Sassanian army was routed and Ctesiphon, the capital, seized. At the end of the year another victory at Jalula' opened the way to the Iranian plateau, which was gradually brought under Moslem control. Rather against 'Umar's will, Khalid's rival, 'Amr ibn al-'As, led an army from Syria across the Sinai peninsula to Egypt. The fortress of Babilyun at the head of the Delta, surrendered in 641 and after a year's siege Alexandria, the capital, was evacuated by the Byzantines in 642.

Various causes contributed to the Moslem victories over the Byzantines and Sassanians. The two empires were exhausted by warfare. The frontier Arabs, disaffected to their suzerains, were natural allies of the Moslems. The Syrian and Egyptian Christians resented Byzantine rule, which repressed their heresies and taxed them heavily. Thus the wars were fought against the imperial armies rather than the provincials, who accepted and even actively assisted the change of masters. The victories of the Arabs in the field were due largely to their mobility and unorthodox tactics, which surprised the heavy, slow-moving armies of their opponents. The nomad tribesmen provided an endless supply of warriors. The devout Moslems were spurred by religious enthusiasm, while the incentive of booty appealed to all. Emerging from the deserts on their camels and asses (horses were comparatively rare), they could pierce the unguarded sectors of the enemy frontiers and return, in time of need, to their remote and inaccessible bases. Raids turned almost imperceptibly into wars of conquest. The most serious obstacles to Arab expansion were not the armies but the walled towns, for the Arabs were inexperienced in siege-warfare, but here they were often assisted to victory by the townsmen themselves, weary of their former rulers.

'Umar, assassinated in 644, was succeeded by 'Uthman, a member of the wealthy and aristocratic Umayyad family. The first phase of conquests was now over and the Arabs were settling down to enjoy the fruits of victory. They formed an army of occupation in the conquered provinces and were concentrated in a number of newly-founded camp-cities such as Kufa and Basra in Iraq. The warriors and their families received pensions, graduated according to their standing in Islam. The revenue of the state came partly from lands confiscated from the Byzantine and Sassanian rulers or from fugitive landowners, partly from taxes, which were levied at a higher rate upon non-Moslems than upon Moslems. Otherwise the non-Moslems were little disturbed. There was no attempt to convert them. Islam was regarded as a perquisite of the Arabs, who formed a warrior-aristocracy maintained by the subject peoples.

Under 'Uthman the tensions inside the Moslem community reappeared. With the cessation of the conquests, the tribesmen had time to feel and resent the claims of the Medinese government. Moreover, the appointment of 'Uthman afforded an opportunity to his kinsmen, the former Meccan oligarchs, to reassert their pre-eminence. The Moslems who had grown old in the faith were dismayed to see post after post falling to these late and opportunist converts.

Events came to a head in 656. There were intrigues in Medina itself, in which a notable part was played by 'Amr, who had been ousted by 'Uthman from the government of Egypt, and 'A'isha, the daughter of Abu Bakr and widow of the Prophet. Revolt broke out among the tribal warriors in the provinces. A party of mutineers from Egypt marched on Medina, broke into the Caliph's house and killed him. The Prophet's cousin and son-in-law, 'Ali, was proclaimed Caliph in Medina. At once opposition broke out on the grounds that 'Ali was associated with the regicides. Mu'awiya, the son of Abu Sufyan and governor of Syria, demanded vengeance for his Umayyad kinsman. 'A'isha and her confederates joined in the outcry against 'Ali and withdrew to Basra to organise resistance. This group of opponents was defeated in December 656, but the more dangerous hostility of Mu'awiya remained. The two opposing armies met in May 657 at Siffin, an engagement which terminated in an agreement to submit the dispute to arbitration. 'Ali's acceptance of arbitration led to a secession among his own followers of a group known as the Kharijites, 'those who go out', who had to be suppressed by force. The result of the arbitration further weakened 'Ali's position and his authority was soon virtually limited to Iraq. He was assassinated by a Kharijite in January 661.

IV

Mu'awiya, who was generally accepted as Caliph on 'Ali's death, had governed Syria since 'Umar's time. His diplomatic finesse concealed a tenacity of purpose which brought him success. Under him the Caliphate became dynastic, although the elective form was preserved. By negotiation, the Arab tribes were persuaded during Mu'awiya's lifetime to take an oath of allegiance to his son Yazid. Thereafter the Caliphate remained in the Umayyad family until the revolution of 750, and this phase is known as the Umayyad Caliphate.

Mu'awiya's strength lay in the support

of the Arabs of Syria. These formed his army and were used to repress rebels and to raid the Byzantine frontiers. Elsewhere his authority was questioned. Kufa, which had been 'Ali's capital, resented the passage of the seat of power to Damascus and opposition in Iraq tended to centre around 'Ali's descendants. The Umayyads were well served by the governor of Basra, Ziyad, a former supporter of 'Ali, whom Mu'awiya had attached to his cause by recognising him as his half-brother. Mu'awiya died in 680.

Under Mu'awiya's successors troubles occurred which showed how shallow were the roots of the dynasty. Hussein, the son of 'Ali, was invited by the Arabs of Kufa to rule over them but failed to find general support in Iraq. In the ensuing hostilities with the Umayyad forces, he was killed at Karbala' (681), an event which stimulated 'Alid opposition to the dynasty. 'The Party of 'Ali' (in Arabic, *Shi'at'Ali*) began as a group of Arab political opponents of the Umayyads. In time it lost its Arab character and developed into an important and permanent religious division of Islam, believing that the head (*imam*) of the Moslem community must be a descendant of 'Ali. Today the Shi'a, as this division is called, is found chiefly in Persia and Iraq. Other Moslems, who form nowadays the great majority, are called Sunnis.

Another source of difficulty to the Umayyads was the hostility between the Arabs of northern and southern descent, the Qaysis and Yamanis. Since at this juncture the dynasty relied largely on the Syrian Yamanis, the Qaysis turned to an anti-Caliph, 'Abdallah ibn al-Zubayr, who had established himself in the Hijaz and was also recognised in Iraq. Umayyad supremacy was restored by Marwan I (684–5) and 'Abd al-Malik (685–705), Marwan crushed the Syrian Qaysis and

appointed his own son as governor of Egypt. Iraq was reconquered for the Umayyads by 691 and 'Abd al-Malik sent a devoted servant of his house, Hajjaj, to reconquer the Hijaz. Mecca was captured in 692 and 'Abdallah died in the fighting. In 694, Hajjaj was transferred to Iraq where he took strong measures to impose Umayyad authority on the turbulent warriors of Kufa and Basra. Between these two garrison-cities, he established a third at Wasit and manned it with Syrian troops. He continued to hold office under the next Caliph, Walid I (705–15).

Iraq was extremely important, not only in itself but also because on it depended the control of the vast and growing empire in Persia and Central Asia. In the reign of Walid I, Moslem expeditions thrust into the Turkish lands beyond the Oxus. Another force even established Moslem power in Sind. Thus the Arabs gained control of the trade routes running by land across Central Asia and were masters of the Persian Gulf, the Red Sea and the Indian Ocean. A similar great extension of Moslem power and trade was taking place in the Mediterranean. Against the Byzantines, hostilities were inconclusive; raids across the Anatolian frontier did not result in permanent conquests, while Constantinople itself defied Arab attacks. The failure of the Arabs to take the city set a limit to their conquests of Byzantine territory. But North Africa was steadily brought under Arab control. The straits of Gibraltar were passed and in 711 the Moslems defeated Roderick, the last Visigothic King of Spain. Soon practically the whole of Spain had fallen under Moslem rule. The conquest was effected by a combination of Arabs with Berber warriors from the recently Islamised parts of North Africa. But between the two groups there was little cordiality and this fact contributed to the failure of the Moslem invasion of France, arrested by Charles Martel at the battle of Tours (732).

Meanwhile a serious social problem was facing the Moslem state. Islam had won many converts, the native populations of the Nile Valley, the Fertile Crescent and Persia. The entry of former Christians, Jews and Zoroastrians into Islam stimulated the development of the faith, rather as Christianity had developed by contact with the Hellenistic world. The position of these converts in the Moslem-Arab social system was anomalous and at first they were assimilated to the freedmen and poorer Arabs whose status depended upon their position as clients (*mawali*) of important tribes. Conversion also posed a fiscal problem since Moslem landowners paid a lower rate of land tax than non-Moslems and the revenues of the state were threatened. In Iraq, where the problem was particularly grave, Hajjaj had levied tax at the higher rate on converts.

The Caliph 'Umar II (717–20) attempted to effect a compromise between the privileged fiscal position of Moslems and the needs of the treasury. All Moslem landowners alike were to pay tax at the lower rate, but land held in 719 by non-Moslems was to be regarded as inalienable state property. If the actual holder of such land was a Moslem, he was to pay tax at the lower rate and also a rent to the treasury which would make up the deficit. Under 'Umar II, also, the *mawali* were given a status closer to that of the Arab Moslems and peaceful conversion was encouraged. These attempts to amalgamate the Arab and the non-Arab peoples into a genuine Islamic Empire averted crisis for a time, but the internal tensions continued. The reign of Hisham (724–43) saw the consolidation of the fiscal system. Henceforward most of the land paid tax at the higher rate, irrespective of the religion of

its holder, while the non-Moslem subjects of the Caliph paid a poll-tax as well.

The strict financial policy of Hisham contributed to the downfall of the Umayyad Dynasty. Opposition naturally assumed a religious form, either that of Kharijism with its appeal to the Book of God against the Caliph, or Shi'ism which sought to replace the Umayyads by rulers descended from 'Ali. There were numerous Shi'ite groups under the Umayyads, rendered ineffective at first by their divisions. But about the year 718, the control of one of these groups, the Hashimiya, was taken over by a descendant of 'Abbas, the Prophet's uncle. Although this man had no claim to 'Alid descent, the propaganda of the Hashimiya made astonishing strides in the next generation. It was particularly successful in Khurasan, the province of eastern Persia where there was a large population of *mawali* and where the Arabs, originating from Iraq, resented Umayyad rule. The final stage of activity began in 743 with the arrival of a Persian agent, Abu Muslim, to organise the movement in Khurasan. In 746 overt rebellion appeared; Khurasan was conquered for the 'Abbasids and Abu Muslim advanced westwards. The last Umayyad Caliph, Marwan II (744–50), saw his armies defeated in Iraq and fled to Egypt, where he was slain. In 750 the head of the Hashimiya movement, Saffah—the Bloodshedder—became the first Caliph of the 'Abbasid Dynasty.

The Umayyads fell because a century of Arab rule had created tensions in the Islamic state which they were unable to resolve. The Arabs had established the state by their conquests and had thereafter formed its warrior-aristocracy. As the wave of conquest spent itself, the Arab aristocracy ceased to fulfil any useful purpose. The *mawali*, on the other hand, had achieved in economic and cultural matters an importance which they were denied in politics. Only a change of régime could bring them to power. Moreover the vast extent of the Empire demanded stricter centralisation, a more autocratic Caliphate and a more elaborate bureaucracy. There had been tentatives towards this under the Umayyads, notably in the reign of Hisham, but they were resented by the Syrian Arabs on whom that dynasty depended. The name which the 'Abbasid government took, *dawla*, implied the beginning of a new era. It was much more than a mere dynastic revolution.

V

The 'Abbasids set about liquidating both their opponents and dangerous or disaffected supporters. Saffah followed up his military victory by a slaughter of Umayyad princes, but consolidation of early 'Abbasid power was largely the work of his brother and successor, Mansur (754–75). The second and all succeeding 'Abbasid Caliphs bore throne-names of pious significance of which Mansur, Ma'mun, etc., are shortened forms. Thus Mansur's full throne-name was *Al-Mansur bi-llahi,* 'He who is made victorious by God.' Only one 'Abbasid Caliph, Harun, is usually referred to by his personal name as well as his throne name, *al-Rashid.*

In 755 Abu Muslim, potentially a dangerous king-maker, was assassinated. His death provoked a series of risings in the Persian provinces. The Shi'a for their part found that the revolution had brought them no nearer to the centre of power and revolts broke out in Medina and Kufa headed by descendants of 'Ali. The risings were suppressed, but henceforward the Shi'ite sects were centres of opposition to the 'Abbasid Caliphs as they had been to the Umayyads. Under Mansur the new dynasty cut itself free from its heterodox origin and supporters.

The 'Abbasids, in contrast to the Syrian Umayyads, made Iraq the seat of their power. In 762 Mansur laid the foundations of a new capital at Baghdad on the Tigris. The choice of site was significant. No city had stood there before, so it was free from associations with earlier Moslem rulers. Lying near to Ctesiphon and Babylon, it indicated, for the first time, the Moslem Caliphate as the heir of the great oriental monarchies. Syria now passed from the centre to the fringe of the Empire: the 'Abbasid state turned its back on the Mediterranean and looked eastwards for administrative traditions and support. The new capital was magnificently placed to command the trade-routes of the Moslem world, linking the Mediterranean with Central Asia and the Persian Gulf. The centre of Mansur's Baghdad was the Round City containing the Caliph's household and officials and the Khurasani guards who formed the physical bulwark of the dynasty. Outside this nucleus grew up the quarters of the merchants and artisans which continued to flourish long after Mansur's Round City had fallen into decay.

The alliance with the Persian *mawali* which had helped to bring the 'Abbasids to the throne was reflected in growing Persian influences on the court and administration. The Caliph himself ceased to be a shaykh of shaykhs, accessible to his subjects and handling the Arab aristocracy by finesse rather than by force. The 'Abbasids developed the autocratic tendencies which had been foreshadowed by Hisham. The new monarchy, which owed much to the Sassanian tradition, was hedged about by an elaborate etiquette, while the executioner beside the throne symbolised the sanction of capricious force. An office perhaps imported from Persian practice was that of the *wazir* (vizier), the head of the government, all-powerful while he enjoyed the Caliph's confidence.

The reign of Harun al-Rashid (786–829) marks the highest point of 'Abbasid power, although the Caliph himself, in spite of his legendary reputation in *The Arabian Nights*, was not the greatest of his line. Before succeeding to the throne, he had commanded the last Arab expedition against Constantinople. He was a contemporary of Charlemagne, and Frankish sources tell of an exchange of embassies between the two monarchs on which the Moslem writers are silent. His government owed much to the administrative ability of a distinguished Iranian family, the Barmecides, converts from Buddhism, who since Mansur's time had held high office under the dynasty. In 803, for reasons which remain obscure, the Barmecides lost Harun's favour and fell from power. They were the most illustrious representatives of the new bureaucratic class, largely drawn from the *mawali*, who had now taken the place of the Arab aristocracy as the administrators of the Empire.

In Harun's reign the first signs of impending decline become apparent. His death was followed by a civil war between his two sons, the younger of whom, Ma'mun, supported by the Persian provinces, succeeded in reuniting the 'Abbasid dominions. Ma'mun (813–33) attempted to win over the Shi'a by designating an 'Alid claimant as heir to the throne but this experiment was soon abandoned and Shi'ite hostility to the dynasty continued.

In general the 'Abbasids put themselves forward as defenders of Islamic orthodoxy. Much respect was paid to the Holy Law of Islam and its exponents. The history of the Umayyad century was rewritten in the interests of 'Abbasid propaganda to depict the earlier dynasty as irreligious tyrants. This stress on the religious character of the state reflects the decline of the former Arab aristocracy. The 'Abbasid revolution had brought the *mawali* to the fore, the old tendency to equate Islamic faith with Arab ancestry was obsolete; henceforward the Faith itself and loyalty to the Caliph as its head constituted the bond of empire. Under Ma'mun and his immediate successors there was indeed an episode when the authority of the Caliph was used to enforce a theology known as Mu'tazilism, which Islamic opinion has since held to be heretical, but this trend was reversed under the Caliph Mutawakkil (847–61). Culturally, Mu'tazilism reflects the influence of Greek philosophical speculation.

The reign of Ma'mun was a significant period in the transmission of Greek learning. Before the Arab conquests, the Aramaic-speaking Christians of the Fertile Crescent had preserved and translated much of Greek philosophy, medicine and science. Within Sassanian territory the academy of Jundishapur had given asylum to Nestorian and Athenian scholars, refugees from Byzantine orthodoxy, and had developed as a centre of Greek studies, especially in medicine. Alexandria had lost its ancient Hellenistic reputation, but here also some philosophical and medical studies continued in the last period of Byzantine rule.

The conquests placed many of the chief centres of Hellenism under Moslem rule and in the later Umayyad period the work of translation had begun. Under the early 'Abbasids it was organised with official support. Ma'mun himself established in Baghdad a library and a school of translation. The best known translator was Hunayn ibn Ishaq (809–77) who made an Arabic version of the works of Galen. Medical, scientific and mathematical works particularly interested Moslem scholars, while Aristotelian philosophy and Neoplatonism had a profound effect on Islamic theological and philosophical speculation. The period of the translators was followed by the golden age of Islamic medicine and science in the tenth and eleventh centuries, when in all parts of the Moslem world scholars produced an impressive body of work in Arabic, the common language of Islamic learning.

VI

The Arab Empire had begun to disintegrate immediately after the 'Abbasid revolution. The western provinces were broken off under dynasties, some of which recognised 'Abbasid suzerainty but nevertheless remained effectively independent of Baghdad. An Umayyad prince, 'Abd al-Rahman I, escaped from the slaughter of his family and reached Spain in 756. Welcomed by his partisans, he succeeded in conquering the country and setting up an independent state. In 929 a later Umayyad ruler, 'Abd al-Rahman III, assumed the title of Caliph. Morocco became independent under an 'Alid who had fled from Medina after a revolt against the 'Abbasids and founded at Fez a dynasty which lasted nearly two centuries.

Other North African states were created, not by opponents of the 'Abbasids but by their governors. The region was remote from the centre of authority and the Mediterranean environment presented special problems and opportunities. The governors became hereditary rulers, owing only a nominal allegiance to the Caliph. Thus Ibrahim ibn al-Aghlab, appointed to Qayrawan, near Tunis, by Harun al-Rashid in 800, founded a dynasty which controlled the waist of the Mediterranean and conquered Sicily. The growing importance of the Turks was already reflected in the history of Egypt, where a dynasty was founded by the Turkish governor, Ahmad ibn Tulun. Although the Tulunids held power only from 868 to 905, they anticipated future developments by gaining control of Syria. After a short interval, another Turkish governor set up the Ikhshidid Dynasty (935–69), which added the Hijaz as well as Syria to the territories ruled from Egypt.

The accession of the 'Abbasids also led to the decline of Arab supremacy as the Caliphate fell more and more under Persian and Turkish influences. The garrison cities of the former warrior-aristocracy turned into centres of commercial and cultural life, dominated by the descendants of the *mawali*. Some Arabs became absorbed into the mass of townspeople and peasants, others reverted to nomadism. In the tenth century a last Arab state was established in northern Iraq and Syria by the Hamdanids; a brief efflorescence of Arab culture which ended in 1003.

The eastern provinces of the Empire were held more securely. Control from Baghdad was easier and the earlier 'Abbasids ruled in tacit alliance with the Persian *mawali* and aristocracy. The first symptoms of unrest came from the depressed peasantry of the Iranian plateau. Their revolts assumed a religious aspect but the traditions they expressed were rather those of the old Iranian heresies than of Zoroastrianism or Islam, the official faiths of the old and new rulers. Abu Muslim, himself a Persian, came to be regarded as a martyr by these movements. A series of these peasant revolts began in the middle of the eighth century. The most serious, that of Babak in Azerbaijan, lasted for twenty-one years before it was crushed in 837.

The establishment of autonomous dynasties in the east followed on the weakening of the Caliphate after Harun al-Rashid. The earlier dynasties were Persian. The first was founded by the Khurasani general Tahir, to whom Ma'mun owed his throne. It ruled over the Iranian plateau and eastwards to the borders of India. The dynasty lasted from 820 to 872 and was followed by two other short-lived states, the Saffarids (867–908) and the Samanids

(874–999), each of which devoured its predecessor's territories. The rise of the Turks was reflected in the Ghaznavid dynasty. Its founder was a Turkish slave, appointed by the Samanid ruler as governor of Khurasan. In 962 he carved out for himself a kingdom with its centre at Ghazni in Afghanistan. Under his successors, notably Mahmud (999–1030), the state was extended across the Iranian plateau and into the Punjab (*see* Chapter 14). But after Mahmud's death the Ghaznavid Empire broke up, although the dynasty continued to exist in Lahore until 1186.

From the mid-ninth century the Turks had acquired increasing importance in the Moslem world. The expansion of the Arabs into Central Asia had brought them into contact with these hardy and warlike nomads. Turkish slaves were imported into the heart-lands of Islam, and the Caliphs from Ma'mun's time onwards relied increasingly on Turkish troops, which supplanted the obsolete Khurasani bodyguard. Under Ma'mun's successor, Mu'tasim (833–42), himself the son of a Turkish mother, the Turks were extensively recruited for the Caliph's service and were placed under officers of their own nationality. A new power was thus established in the capital and soon the Turkish generals became king-makers holding successive Caliphs in tutelage.

The authority of the Caliphate was temporarily restored in the reign of Mu'tamid (870–902), whose energetic brother, Muwaffaq, was the real ruler. In the previous year a revolt had broken out among the East African Negro slaves, called in Arabic *Zanj*, working in the salt deposits near Basra. Headed by a Persian who claimed 'Alid descent, the *Zanj* dominated the swamps of the lower Euphrates, routed their opponents and in 871 sacked Basra. It was not until 883 that they were finally suppressed. Muwaffaq's tenure of power also coincided with the appearance of the Saffarids and Tulunids. Although he could not prevent their rise, he was able to check the growth of their power. On his death, he was succeeded by his son, who in the following year became the Caliph Mu'tadid (892–904).

After the death of Mu'tadid's successor, Muktafi (902–3), the Caliphate again declined and its holders became the puppets of the Turkish soldiery. In 936 the Caliph Radi (934–40) placed the administration in the hands of a military governor to whom the title of *Amir al-Umara'* was given. Nine years later a Shi'ite Persian dynast, Ahmad ibn Buwayh, who already controlled western Persia, entered Baghdad and became the effective ruler of the diminished 'Abbasid state. His descendants, the Buwayhids, succeeded him, ruling from Shiraz for over a century. The eastern frontiers were now open to the migration of Turkish tribes, entering Moslem territory as free nomads. In a great wave of immigration which began about 970, the paramount family was the Seljuqs whose chief, Tughrul Bey, entered Baghdad in 1055, ended Buwayhid rule and was recognised by the puppet-Caliph as regent, with the title of *Sultan* (literally 'power'). The Seljuq sultans inaugurated a new phase of Moslem history: they established their control over the eastern half of the old 'Abbasid Empire and extended their authority to Syria and Anatolia. The seat of their power was in Persia and they were deeply affected by Persian culture. Tughrul's successors, Alp Arslan (1063–72) and Malikshah (1072–92), were served by a very able Persian minister, Nizam al-Mulk, under whom the fiscal system was reorganised.

The early 'Abbasid period had been one of economic progress and prosperity. The Moslem world, sitting athwart international trade routes and containing valuable raw materials and skilled workers, developed from a militant agrarian state into an Empire with a flourishing commerce and industry. But the ninth century saw the beginnings of economic decline. It was hastened by the fragmentation of the Empire, the luxury of the court and the cost of the bureaucracy. An attempt to ensure revenues by appointing provincial governors as tax-farmers aggravated the disease and strengthened the trend towards provincial autonomy. Although the unity and order introduced by the Buwayhids and Seljuqs helped to restore prosperity, Nizam al-Mulk perpetuated and system-atised the abuses which had grown up. Fiefs were granted to officers on condition of furnishing troops and these new quasi-feudal owners were allowed to take the revenues of their estates. By the end of the eleventh century much of the Moslem world had reverted to an agrarian sub-sistence economy.

The economic stresses of these three centuries produced social and religious results. The multifarious resentments of the depressed classes against established authority were harnessed by the Isma'ili movement. Ostensibly this was a sect of the Shi'a, owing its name and origin to a descendant of 'Ali named Isma'il (d. 760). It displayed much of the extremism which in an earlier period had characterised the Hashimiya movement. It had a secret organisation of ascending grades, culmina-ting in an infallible leader, the Imam. The Isma'ili movement appealed both to peasants and artisans, gaining many follow-ers among the urban population. It absorbed ideas from Hellenistic and other non-Islamic sources from which Moslem orthodoxy had turned away.

Its greatest political success was won in North Africa. Here Isma'ili missionaries gained the support of the Berbers, over-threw the Aghlabids and installed the Imam 'Ubaydallah as Caliph in 908. The new dynasty was known as the Fatimids, since it claimed descent from Fatima, the daughter of the Prophet and wife of 'Ali. In 969 Egypt was conquered and became the seat of the dynasty, which made its capital in the newly-founded city of Cairo (Arabic, *al-Qahira*, 'the Victorious'). Fati-mid rule soon extended over Syria and for a time over Sicily and western Arabia as well. Profiting by the decline of the 'Abbasid territories, the Fatimids deflected trade from the Persian Gulf to the Red Sea and fostered commerce with Europe. But the relations of the Fatimids with the movement which had brought them to power were uneasy. Unlike the 'Abbasids, they did not sever their connection with their original supporters, but their policies naturally changed when they passed from opposition to sovereignty. The conquest of Egypt was followed by a clash with a related group known as the Carmathians. Further trouble occurred in the late eleven-th century. By this time the Fatimids, like the 'Abbasids, were controlled by their own soldiery, and a group headed by a Persian, Hasan i Sabbah, broke away and organised a new revolutionary Isma'ilism in the Seljuq territories. This group, known as the Assassins (Arabic, *al-Hashshashun*, since they were said to drug themselves with hashish), endeavoured to overthrow the established authorities by murder and terrorism. Among their victims, in 1092, was Nizam al-Mulk.

VII

After the disintegration of the 'Abbasid Caliphate, the Islamic world of the eleven-th, twelfth and thirteenth centuries was threatened by external enemies—the Chris-tians of Western Europe and the Mongols of Eastern Asia. The Christian pressure appeared in three regions; Sicily and Spain (where territories were reconquered from Islam) and Syria, where the Crusades won only a temporary success. The centre of Islamic power became the Mameluk Sultanate of Egypt and Syria.

Sicily, first an Aghlabid and then a Fatimid possession, had become virtually independent under hereditary governors. The end of this dynasty in 1040 was followed by civil war and in 1060 Messina was captured by Normans from southern Italy. By 1091 the whole island had been conquered and for over a century a mixed Moslem and Christian population was ruled by Norman kings.

The Christian reconquest of Spain was preceded by similar hostility amongst the Moslems. In 1002 the western Umayyads lost by death their great minister and warrior, Al-Mansur ibn Abi 'Amir, of whom a Christian chronicler wrote, 'Almanzor died and was buried in hell', showing the terror which his campaigns had inspired in northern Spain. Less than thirty years later, the last Umayyad Caliph was deposed and Moslem Spain split up into numerous petty states ruled by the 'Party Kings'. The 'parties' or factions, reflected the composite nature of society. The old Arab military aristocracy had been absorbed and had lost its political significance. The Berbers, on the other hand, had steadily grown in numbers and power, being constantly recruited from their African homelands. Settled in the mountain areas, they had preserved their group individuality better than the Arabs. From the middle of the ninth century a new military and political force had appeared, the 'Slavs' or European slaves. These came mostly from Central and Eastern Europe, but not all were Slavs in the modern sense. Employed by the Umayyads as the Turks were by the 'Abbasids, they had, like them, come to dominate their masters. Finally, there were

the descendants of the pre-Moslem inhabitants, assimilated in varying degrees to their Islamic environment. Those who were converted to Islam are known in Spanish as *Muladies*, from the Arabic, *muwalladun*, 'adopted'. Others remained Christian but adopted Arabic speech and Moslem customs. They are known as the Mozarabs, from the Arabic word, *musta-'ribun*, 'arabised'. The Jews formed a wealthy and cultured minority of the population.

The political weakness of Moslem Spain under the Party Kings enabled the Christian states of the north to expand. Alfonso VI of Leon-Castile captured the important city of Toledo in 1085 and became the arbiter of Moslem politics. A Berber invasion from Africa re-united Moslem Spain, defeated the Christians at Zallaqa (1086) and installed a dynasty known as the Almoravids (Arabic, *al-Murabitun*, meaning in effect members of a military-religious order). This dynasty declined rapidly and Christian pressure was resumed. In 1147 another Berber dynasty, the Almohads (Arabic, *al-Muwahhidun*, 'the asserters of God's unity') supplanted the Almoravids in Morocco and Spain. Its power was broken by Alfonso VIII of Castile at Las Navas de Tolosa (1212), after which the Christian reconquest swept steadily forward. By the end of the century Moslem power was limited to the tributary state of Granada, which survived until its destruction by Ferdinand and Isabella in 1492.

Through the Christian reconquest of Sicily and Spain, Moslem learning was transmitted to Western Europe. The tolerant Norman kings of Sicily welcomed Moslems at court, among them the great Arab geographer, Idrisi, who dedicated his work to Roger II. In Spain, Toledo after its capture became a centre to which Christian students flocked. The translations of Arabic works were made largely with the aid of Jewish and Mozarab scholars. The work had the patronage of churchmen and kings, notably Alfonso the Wise of Castile (1252–84). Like the Moslems in early 'Abbasid times, the Christians were avid for medical, mathematical and philosophical works. In this way some of the learning of ancient Greece passed to Western Europe through a series of Syriac, Arabic and Latin translations.

In this transmission the Crusades played a negligible part. Various motives— religious fanaticism, land-hunger, trade— combined to turn the eyes of Western Europeans to the Syrian coastlands. After the death of Malikshah, the Seljuq Empire broke up under different branches of the dynasty and there was no power capable of combining the Moslem East against the invaders.

The age of the Crusades can be divided into two periods; the first covering the establishment of the Frankish principalities, runs from 1095 to 1144; the second saw their decline and elimination from 1145 to the end of the thirteenth century. The warriors of the First Crusade, in uneasy alliance with the Byzantines, defeated the Seljuqs of Rum, the Moslem state in Anatolia, and regained some of the lost Byzantine lands. Their victories in Syria resulted in the establishment of four states, Edessa (1098), Antioch (1098), Jerusalem (1099) and Tripoli (1109), which were organised on the model of Western feudalism and maintained their strength through fresh contingents of crusaders from Europe.

But their existence was a *tour de force*. The ruling classes lacked roots and were never assimilated to their Arab and Moslem subjects. Recruits from Europe arrived sporadically and disturbed the harmony which developed between Christians and Moslems. The crusading states remained

essentially confined to the coastal areas; the only inland state, Edessa, was the first to fall.

Their survival, indeed, depended on the absence of effective Moslem opposition. This was slow in developing. The 'Abbasid and Fatimid caliphates were no longer effective political or military powers. The Seljuq territories were divided and their centre of gravity lay further east. The resistance movement began in territory neighbouring the Crusader-states when Zangi, the ruler of Mosul, nominally a vassal of the Seljuqs, captured Edessa in 1144. Ten years later his successor brought the Moslem buffer-state of Damascus under his rule.

These changes prepared the way for the hero of the Moslem reconquest, Salah al-Din al-Ayyubi, generally known as Saladin. Originally a Kurdish vassal of the Zangids, he became the *de facto* ruler of Egypt and in 1171 suppressed the decadent Fatimid Caliphate. In 1174 he took Moslem Syria from his nominal overlord and thereby encircled the crusading principalities. A victory at Hattin (1187) was followed by the capture of Jerusalem, a gain which the Third Crusade (1189–92) was unable to reverse, although by retaking Acre from the Moslems, Richard I of England secured for the Crusaders a base for their diminished power. When Saladin died in 1193, the decline of the Crusaders had begun, although they were not expelled from their last footholds for another century.

After Saladin's death his realm split up among various members of his family, the Ayyubids, of whom the sultans of Egypt were the most important. This was recognised in Europe, where hopes of regaining the lost territories were not yet extinct. In 1219 and again in 1249 Damietta was occupied by crusading forces but on both occasions the Franks failed to conquer Egypt. The second occupation of Damietta, by Louis IX of France, coincided with the death of the last effective Ayyubid sultan. The control of Egypt now passed into the hands of the standing army formed from Turkish slaves known as the Mameluks.

From 1250 until 1517 the Mameluk sultans ruled Egypt. The early Mameluks achieved the great and dual success of liquidating the remaining bases of the Crusaders and of barring the westward advance of the Mongols. This wave of victorious nomads had been set in motion by Genghiz Khan and had overthrown the Moslem states of Central Asia by 1220 (*see* Chapter 9). A fresh advance under Hulagu, grandson of Genghiz, began about the middle of the century. The Mongols swept across Persia and in 1258 Baghdad itself fell to them, the last 'Abbasid Caliph being put to death. A further advance into Syria was stopped by the Mameluk victory at 'Ayn Jalut (1260). Henceforward Syria formed with Egypt the Mameluk Empire, while Iraq was an outlying portion of the dominion of the Mongol Il-khans of Persia who from 1295 were Moslems. The devastation caused by Mongols and nomad Arabs, and the distance of Iraq from the new centres of government and trade completed its decline.

The Mameluk Sultanate had become the guardian of Islamic traditions. With the abolition of the Fatimid Caliphate, Egypt had returned to orthodox Islam and Cairo became a leading centre of Islamic culture. Baybars (1260–77), the greatest Mameluk sultan, installed an 'Abbasid with the title of Caliph to legitimise his rule. The reality of Mameluk power rested on other grounds. The Crusades had stimulated the trade of the Eastern Mediterranean and to this the Mameluks fell heirs after the disappearance of the Frankish

states. Merchants from Italy thronged the Egyptian and Syrian ports. The goods of the Far East came by way of the Red Sea as the route by the Persian Gulf and Baghdad declined. The fertile land of Egypt was parcelled out in fiefs, the revenue from which maintained a Mameluk warrior-aristocracy, constantly recruited by the importation of fresh slaves. Until 1383 the Mameluk sultans were Turks and some degree of hereditary succession appears. From that date, power passed to men of Circassian origin and the rule was held by the strongest. The elaborate bureaucracy maintained by the Mameluks prevented the disintegration of the state in these recurrent crises, but the fourteenth century saw a decline. This was hastened by unwise attempts to squeeze the utmost revenue out of the transit-trade, a policy which ended the harmonious co-operation of interests with European merchants and stimulated the Portuguese voyages of exploration. When in 1498 Vasco da Gama rounded the Cape of Good Hope and reached India, the doom of Egyptian commerce was sealed. Less than twenty years later the Mameluk state collapsed before the Ottomans.

VIII

The Arab conquest had stopped at the Taurus. Even the 'Abbasids had failed to do more than raid the Byzantine frontier provinces. The expansion of Islam in Anatolia had resulted from a Seljuq Turkish victory. In 1071 Alp Arslan defeated the Byzantine Emperor at Manzikert in Armenia. Although he did not go on to conquer Anatolia, a collapse of the Byzantine frontier followed and during the next four years Moslem bands pushed as far as the western coast. But these were not the state forces of the Seljuqs; they were march-warriors whose predecessors had for centuries struggled with their Byzantine counterparts in the debatable land between Christendom and Islam. The Turkish immigration contributed warriors to these frontier-bands, who were of varied ethnic origins. Living on booty, and devoted to the Holy War, these *ghazis* became deeply imbued with the indigenous culture and traditions of the frontier-districts and, apart from their religion, had much in common with the Byzantine march-warriors. Hence their expansion after Manzikert was not, in eastern Anatolia at least, a conquest of alien and unfamiliar territory. The newly acquired territories were placed under a Seljuq prince and thereby linked to the older Moslem world. Thus had been founded the sultanate of Rum.

Western Anatolia was regained for Byzantium by the Crusaders but the sultanate of Rum, with its capital at Konya, held the interior and east. A new march was formed between Seljuq and Byzantine territory, reproducing the military and social conditions of its predecessor. Another wave of expansion began in the later thirteenth century. The sultanate of Rum was in decline and became a vassal-state of the Mongols. Its hold over the *ghazis* grew weaker, and the *ghazis* themselves were augmented by people displaced by the Mongol conquests. Byzantine powers of resistance, which had been high from 1204 to 1261 while the capital was at Nicaea, were reduced with the return of the emperors to Constantinople. A new thrust was made into the western provinces and by 1300 almost the whole of Anatolia was in Turkish hands. The former Byzantine territories were divided among a number of small and disunited principalities.

One of these in the north-west was the nucleus of the future Ottoman state. It lay between the remaining strip of Byzantine territory and Karaman, which had succee-ded to much of the old Seljuq territory around Konya. The situation of the Ottoman principality meant that there was still war and booty for *ghazis* on its frontier and so it continued to draw warriors from the other Turkish states where the work of conquest was finished. The Byzantines were virtually eliminated from Anatolia by the middle of the fourteenth century. Intervention in their dynastic quarrels followed, and the Ottomans established a foothold on European soil in Gallipoli.

The comparatively slow expansion of the Ottoman principality had enabled the organisation of its territories to be carried out with unusual thoroughness. Its proximity to the old Seljuq lands allowed it to draw on townspeople and jurists to establish its prosperity and administration. Between 1362 and 1402 it expanded on two fronts. Ottoman armies penetrated the Balkans. In 1389 a combination of southern Slavs with other Balkan forces was defeated at Kossovo and seven years later a last crusading army was annihilated at Nicopolis. Meanwhile the Anatolian principalities were losing their independence to the Ottoman sultans through marriage, purchase and conquest.

This phase of Ottoman expansion was completed by Bayezid I (1389–1402), under whom the absorption of neighbouring territories went on at unprecedented speed. The older tradition of a gradual advance, with alliance and vassaldom preceding incorporation in the Ottoman state, was set aside, and the forces which had been developed in the wars against Christendom were turned against the Moslem principalities.

This career of victories was suddenly interrupted. A Turkic conqueror from Central Asia, Timur Leng (lame Timur) had made himself the master of the older Moslem lands and proceeded to invade Anatolia. In a battle near Ankara (1402) the forces of the newly acquired territories deserted. Bayezid was defeated and made prisoner. Timur re-established the Turkish princes in their old possessions and then, having apparently broken Ottoman power for ever, left Anatolia.

But the European possessions remained untouched. During the following ten years a reduced Ottoman state was reconstructed. Under Murad II (1421–51), expansion began again. This time the process was slower and more cautious. Murad's reign saw also an important development concerning the Balkans. Here the rapid advance of the frontier had allowed no time for a gradual assimilation and Islamisation of the subject peoples, such as had occurred in Anatolia. The interior of the peninsula remained Christian and Greek or Slav. A means of incorporating the Balkan peoples into the machinery of the Ottoman state was devised in the *devshirme,* the regular recruitment of Christian boys for the Sultan's service. They were converted to Islam and taught Turkish. The mass of them were drafted into the standing army, where they formed the famous corps of Janissaries (Turkish, *yeni cheri,* 'the new troops'), the courageous and disciplined infantry which gave the Ottomans victory in many battles. The cream of the recruits were trained for the court or the administration. In this way the Ottoman state came to be governed, defended and expanded by men of Balkan Christian origin, who were regarded as slaves of the Sultan. From these fields of public life the free Moslem element was largely excluded.

The next Sultan, Mahmud II (1451–81) achieved the crowning success of the capture of Constantinople in 1453. In some ways its significance has been exaggerated. The idea that it was the cause of the European Renaissance has long been exploded. Politically, Constantinople was no longer the wealthy and powerful met-

ropolis of earlier centuries; the Byzantine Empire had shrunk to the capital and some separated territory in Greece, while the emperors were already satellites of the sultans. The fall of Constantinople, seen from this point of view, is merely an example of the traditional Ottoman policy of absorbing a vassal-state. Nevertheless, the event was not on a level with the incorporation of the Turkish principalities or Balkan states. It acquired a legendary quality to the European mind. The Turks became the masters of one of the great markets and trade-routes of the world. Strategically, the capture of Constantinople welded together the two halves of the Ottoman Empire. The Ottoman ruler, seated in the old imperial capital, supported by his slave army and ruling through his slave administrators, now became a remote autocrat of a type far removed from the warrior-leaders of the *ghazis.* Finally Istanbul as the city was called, succeeded Medina, Damascus, Baghdad and Cairo as the political and cultural heart of the Islamic world, the repository of Moslem traditions of religion, law and government.

The next century was to see further territories added to the original empire of Anatolia and the Balkans. The final phase of major expansion took place in the reigns of Selim I—the Grim—(1512–20) and Suleyman I—the Magnificent or Lawgiver—(1520–66). At Selim's accession, three great powers dominated the Moslem Near East; the Ottomans, the declining Mameluks and the newly founded Persian state of the Safavids, which comprised the Iranian plateau and Iraq. This state was created by a militant Shi'ite movement of which Shah Isma'il (1501–24) was the hereditary head and its strength was drawn chiefly from the Turcoman tribes, nomadic or semi-nomadic groups which had migrated from Central Asia as far west as

Anatolia and formed a reservoir of man-power for Ottomans and Safavids alike. The proximity of this Shi'ite state was a threat to the external and internal security of the Ottoman Sultanate, which had assumed the role of protector of orthodox Islam and feared the attraction of Shi'ite movements for its discontented classes. Frontier troubles led to war and in 1514 Selim invaded Persia and defeated Isma'il at Chaldiran. He entered Tabriz, the Safa-vid capital, but made no permanent conquest. For over two centuries there was frequent war between the Ottomans and Persians.

Isma'il sought the assistance of the Mameluk Sultanate against Selim. Al-though the Mameluk did not intervene actively, the Ottomans had reason to feel uneasy. The Mameluk Empire marched with the Ottomans in south-eastern Anatolia and here, too, frontier disputes arose. In 1516 Selim postponed a fresh attack on Persia in order to remove the Mameluk menace. The Mameluk sultan died in battle north of Aleppo and the conquest of Syria was followed in 1517 by that of Egypt. The Ottoman sultan also became the suzerain of the Holy Cities of Mecca and Medina, thereby acquiring prestige as the leading ruler of the Moslem world.

The reign of Suleyman saw a great extension of Ottoman territory in Europe. Advancing from the Balkans up the Danube valley, the sultan took Belgrade (1521), crushed the Hungarians at Mohacs (1526) and turned Hungary into a puppet-state. In 1529 Vienna itself was besieged but here the Ottomans failed and Austria remained outside their empire. In the East, Suleyman fought against Persia. Baghdad was captured in 1534 and Ottoman rule established over Iraq. In Suleyman's reign also the Ottoman navy rose to supremacy in the Mediterranean, a deve-lopment which was largely due to the freebooter, Khayr al-Din Barbarossa, who had made himself master of Tunis and from 1533 onwards organised the sultan's fleet.

These brilliant conquests brought less strength to the Empire than those of the previous century. The enormously pro-longed lines of communication created problems of defence and administration. A decline in the quality of Ottoman rule becomes noticeable after Suleyman. His successors lacked the abilities of earlier sultans. The bureaucracy and army fell into disorder and the *devshirme* ceased to be applied. The prosperity of the Empire began to contract as the conquests ceased and as world trade opened new channels to the Far East and the Americas. Neverthe-less, the original Ottoman Empire of Anatolia and the Balkans, together with the Arab provinces, held together until the nineteenth century, and even after its disintegration, the original heartland, created by the *ghazis* in Asia Minor, preserved its vitality and political tradition.

Byzantium

by Gervase Mathew

The Byzantine state, which had for so long remained the centre of the highest civilisation in Europe and the bulwark against Moslem attack, had grown directly out of the later Roman Empire. Influences from it were at times to be decisive both in Western Europe and among the Slavs.

On 11 May, in the year 330, the Emperor Constantine I had formally inaugurated a new imperial headquarters at the old Greek colony of Byzantium on the Bosphorus. It was to be re-named Constantinople after him and he was never forgotten as its founder, but during the fourth century it had none of the unique prestige which it possessed in the medieval world.

Fourth-century Byzantium as the centre for the Imperial Administration in the Eastern provinces was the successor to Diocletian's Nicomedia and could be paralleled in the West by Trier and Milan. But the whole Empire stayed undivided even if ruled by associate emperors and it was Rome, not Constantinople, that was The City.

Byzantine or East Roman history and civilisation can first be considered as a separate entity in the reign of Theodosius II (408–50), when Rome had been sacked by Alaric and when the imperial administration of the Western provinces was collapsing under the pressure of the barbarians. All Byzantine history and culture is derived from the crucial fact that the Roman Empire survived in unbroken continuity in the predominantly Greek-speaking provinces of the East while the West sank into anarchy. At first this seems inexplicable, for the causes that led to the catastrophe seem equally common throughout the Empire as a whole. First, there was the diseased economy of the fourth-century Empire with its symptoms of excessive taxation, excessive regulation of trade and industry and an oppressed and dwindling middle class. Secondly, there was the rising pressure of the German peoples against the frontier lines. Thirdly the presence of German mercenaries in the imperial armies, only slightly assimilated by Rome but increasingly holding the highest military commands; it was these *'foederati'*, like Alaric and his mutinous troops, who were so often to paralyse Roman resistance and to provide the barbarian invaders with efficient military leadership.

German *'foederati'* were as prominent in the army of the East as of the West; in fifth-century Constantinople, Aspar combined the roles of Stilicho and Alaric, while the young Theodoric the Ostrogoth was to be more capable and ruthless than either. German pressure was as strong against the line of the lower Danube as of the Rhine; it was the line of the lower Danube that snapped first. There was an added danger from the highly organised military power of Persia. But the Empire possessed in Asia Minor a permanent reserve from which a native army could be recruited, and although the same system of taxation and restriction was enforced, East and West, the East retained a more vital city life as a legacy from its Hellenistic past. By the year 575 it was clear that the Roman Empire would survive in its Eastern provinces. But no one who knew all the facts could have guessed that it would have survived for a further thousand years.

II

Byzantine history seems to fall naturally into five phases. There is the essentially East Roman phase which begins with the accession of the child Theodosius in 408 and ends in 602 with the murder of the Emperor Maurice, the last and perhaps the greatest of the house of Justin and Justinian. It is followed by the period of heroic resistance, reorganisation and reconstruction under the Heraclian and Isaurian emperors from 610 to 820, when the Eastern Empire was first overrun by a suddenly resurgent Sassanian Persia and then by the new dynamic forces of Islam. The essentially Byzantine Empire of the Amorian and the Macedonian dynasties came into being during those two centuries of stress. It was to last from 820 until 1071 as a 'world-state' centring in Constantinople, now indisputably The City and second Rome, strong in the possession of great wealth, of a highly organised civil service and of a professional army, but strongest of all perhaps in the tranquil consciousness of the possession of an immemorial past and in the serene trust in the dominance of mind. But as early as 1042 there are the symptoms of economic maladjustment and decay; there are desperate financial expedients and the beginning of the debasement of the coinage. These coincide with a new pressure on the

Eastern frontiers from the rising power of the Seljuq Turks. After the battle at Manzikert in the summer of 1071 the balance of power in the vital area of Asia Minor swayed finally towards the Seljuqs and it could well have been judged that the Empire would have dissolved by the year 1100.

Yet it survived into a fourth phase, that of the years between 1071 and 1204. Though now apparently mortally injured, it remained poised precariously among the avalanches of the crusades. At one time it might have seemed that the Fourth Crusade had destroyed it; a mixed force of French and Venetians, Flemings and Germans stormed and sacked Constantinople in the late spring of 1204 and then kept possession of it. Within the next few years they conquered Thrace and Thessalonica, Greece and the Aegean islands. Byzantine nobles and officials kept control of Epirus by the Albanian border, of Trebizond on the Black Sea and of Nicaea in north-west Asia Minor. Nicaea under its astute ruler Theodore Lascaris became the chief focus of resistance. After fifty years of slow sporadic reconquest and of elaborate but skilful diplomacy, Constantinople was retaken by the Byzantines led by Michael Palaiologos in 1261.

The fifth and last phase of Byzantine history began at the end of July 1261 when the Emperor Michael VIII Palaiologos made his solemn entry into the church of Hagia Sophia; it closed on 29 May, 1453, when the Emperor Constantine XI Palaiologos was killed fighting by the gate of St Romanos as the Turks stormed The City. During these two centuries the Empire consisted primarily of Constantinople itself and Thessalonica with small fluctuating areas round both and with Mistra in the Peloponnese and Trebizond as appanages. Yet it seems probable that

Constantine XI could still conceive of the Empire as the central power on earth. He was the Roman Emperor.

III

There was thus nothing static in Byzantine history and yet it preserved its continuity to the end. This is equally true of Byzantine civilisation. It had its roots in the imperial Hellenism of the second and third centuries; it seems to preserve an integral unity until the mid-fifteenth century, yet, at least in its first and last two phases, it was vividly creative and it never sank into sterile repetitions.

It is gradually becoming recognised that the first phase of Byzantine civilisation, from 408 to 602, was one of the primary creative periods in human history in architecture and art, and perhaps also in thought and literature. In architecture this is primarily due to the prestige accorded to the engineer and the mathematician and to the fashionable zest for new mechanical contrivance. When the great church of Hagia Sophia was consecrated at Constantinople in 537 it was admired as much for its technical daring as for its mathematically perfect harmony. A contemporary wrote of it that 'the like has never been seen from Adam' and that it was 'marvellous and terrifying'. But Hagia Sophia was only one of many architectural experiments; the creation of the five-domed cruciform church, of the domed church with radiate plan and of the final evolution of the basilica, and of new types of citadels, aqueducts and cisterns. Art was seen primarily as a part of architecture; mosaics, like differing coloured marbles and the carving upon capitals, were functional parts of an architectural whole. The mosaics in San Vitale at Ravenna and the marble columns in Hagia Sophia are characteristic of a fresh art based on a new aesthetic of colour which took into account the play of light on changing tints.

The creative thought of this period is commonly ignored. But no one who has studied them can doubt the speculative strength and originality of vision of St Cyril of Alexandria and of his opponent Theodoret, or the lasting and transforming influence of Proclus and Pseudo-Dionysius. Roman Law, with all the crucial concepts latent or explicit in it, came to the West through two Byzantine syntheses; the fifth-century Theodosian code and the sixth-century Corpus Juris of Justinian. Old literary forms still lived, like the epigram and the epic and the dialogue; new literary forms were created in hymns and liturgy, chronicles and lives of saints. There was nothing sterile in a literature which produced an orator as great as Chrysostom, an historian as great as Procopius, a poet as great as Romanos.

The climax of so many forms of achievement coincided with the long reign of Justinian I (527–65). The personalities of Justinian, of his wife Theodora and of his great general, Belisarius, well illustrate the characteristics of this transitional period in East Rome.

Justinian was very consciously a Roman. Though he was bilingual in Greek and Latin, Latin remained his first language. Old Roman ideals of *gravitas* and *majestas* seem to have influenced even the way he carried himself, with his thick squat body, his heavy powerful face, his steady eyes; yet he was typically Byzantine in his serene belief that he was the Vicegerent upon earth of a transcendent Godhead who was also transcendent Mind. His legislation suggests that with an always impersonal and sometimes ruthless benevolence, he sought the welfare of his subjects even to minute detail. But this was a loveless burden and he was divided from those he ruled by a gulf almost as wide as that between Creator and created. By custom imperial isolation could be tempered by the choice of an associate in the Sacred Majesty. Justinian's choice was Theodora.

An actress, a professional beauty, and an adept in the chess-play of Byzantine court intrigue, she married Justinian when he was already the heir to the Empire, and ruled in partnership with him as *Augusta* until her death in 548. Her direct political influence foreshadowed that of many later Byzantine princesses. She could be pitiless and at times coldly and elaborately cruel. She was as incapable of stupidity as of cowardice. So much of her quality seems conveyed by her reputed saying during the attempted revolution of 532: 'Empire makes a noble winding sheet.' It seems primarily due to Theodora that Justinian's chief subordinates were chosen so rapidly and unerringly, used so efficiently and dismissed with such nonchalance.

The career of Belisarius provides an illustration. He was appointed to the great office of *Magister Militum* when only twenty-five. He defeated Persians and Vandals and Ostrogoths and Huns. He was twice disgraced and died after three years of complete obscurity. In many ways he was an anachronism; the last of those fifth-century Roman leaders who had acquired from the German *foederati* in the imperial service some of the standards of the Heroic Age. Relying on his chosen band of heavily armed horsemen, delighting in his own prowess, deeply emotional and sporadically magnanimous, he seems an oddly Arthurian figure against the still life of the court in that golden age of Byzantine civilisation.

The period from 408 to 602, of which Justinian's reign is in many ways the climax, was the period of Byzantium's greatest wealth. The Empire was never again to command the same revenues for it was never to approach the same extent

From the fifth to the seventh century the Byzantine Empire included Greece and much of the Balkans, Asia Minor, Syria, Palestine, Egypt and Cyrene, as well as areas in the Crimea, the Caucasus and North Mesopotamia. In the sixth century all North Africa was conquered, Sicily and southern Italy and south-east Spain, while the Exarchate of Ravenna was established on the Italian shore of the Adriatic. State ownership of all mines, of many factories and of great domains, as well as an elaborate system of direct and indirect taxation, made the Emperor at Constantinople the richest sovereign in the world. Theoretically he was also the most absolute.

The Emperor was conceived as the sacred Vicegerent of God on earth. His sovereignty reflected the omnipotence of God. But just as the Divine omnipotence was conceived as an act of mind and love —all things were brought into being and kept in being by his knowledge of them— so the imperial sovereignty was an act of mind and love, exercised according to the law of reason and finding its fulfilment in the essential imperial virtue of '*Philanthropia*', the love of man. The Emperor's power was therefore conceived as absolute, not as arbitrary.

In practice much of the power must have rested with the great Ministers of State. The Master of the Offices was in charge of the imperial chancellery and had the functions of a Secretary of State for Foreign Affairs; he also had command of the Bodyguard and as head of the '*Agentes in Rebus*' was Chief of the Secret Police. The Quaestor of the Sacred Palace was President of the State Council and Minister of Justice. The Praetorian Prefect was in control of the internal administration of the Empire and Chief Finance Minister. The Count of the Sacred Largesse had direct control of the Treasury; the Prefect of the Sacred Chamber was dominant in the elaborate court. Each of the great ministers subdelegated parts of his power to subordinate officials. In spite of the presence of a well-trained professional army, Byzantine civilisation was normally to remain an essentially civilian society in which education was highly prized and in which all careers were open to talent. Even the imperial power was considered as elective—the Emperor was conceived as chosen by the Senate and the Army and the People; in practice it had become adoptive. The tendency therefore was that the succession lay within the same family grouping, but though this was increasingly supported by popular sentiment, there was never to be a doctrine of hereditary right. At least until the early eleventh century the Byzantine social structure was neither aristocratic nor plutocratic. Status in it was determined by personal official position or personal education. Sometimes perhaps those two concepts tended to fuse, as in classical China. Even after the early eleventh century, the families of hereditary wealth exercised their political influence rather through the military high command than through the civil service.

The achievement of East Rome from the fifth to the seventh century had been due as much to able ministers like the Prefect Cyrus of Panopolis, the Quaestor Proclus and the ruthless financier John of Cappadocia as to able emperors like Anastasius, Justin, Justinian and Maurice. But the Empire during this phase had two dangerous weaknesses; it was economically insecure and bitterly divided.

Great as was the public revenue, it barely balanced the huge expenditure on public works, subsidies paid to subject allies, the salaries due to so large a civil service and the upkeep of a fleet and army. There are frequent evidences of arrears but none of a reserve.

Taxation was no longer excessive in the towns; in the fifth century the Emperor Anastasius had given fresh incentive to the merchants by abolishing the Chrysargyron, the profit tax. But the coincidence of land tax and capitation tax was sapping agriculture, and the custom of extorting contributions in kind and forced labour from the peasants and town proletariat, must have made many of them welcome any alternative to the imperial tax gatherer.

There was no religious unity. The Empire had become officially Christian under Theodosius I in 378, but there is evidence that the worship of the old gods survived as a vital force until the seventh century, both among crypto-pagans in the civil service and in the popular paganism of the country districts. Fifth-century controversies as to the nature of the Incarnation had divided the Christians into Chalcedonians, Nestorians and Monophysites. These divisions had become associated with rivalry between the two main political parties, 'The Blues' and 'The Greens', and gradually they were becoming linked with linguistic and racial divisions. By the end of the sixth century the native-speaking population in Egypt, Syria and Armenia were all vehemently opposed to the religious policy of Constantinople.

It might have seemed that the Empire would collapse in the first crisis brought about by serious external pressure. It almost did so. In the year 602 the Emperor Maurice was killed by his mutinous troops as he was attempting to check the hordes of Slavs and Avars pressing south across the Danube. The Persians under Chosroes II broke the eastern frontier, conquered Syria and Palestine, ravaged Asia Minor and threatened Constantinople. When at last they had been defeated by the Emperor Heraclius in 629, there was a new threat from the south. The Arabs had been united by the preaching of Islam. Mohammed had died in 632 but by 635 his followers had conquered Syria, by 638 Palestine and by 642 Egypt. By 670 the Arabs were overrunning North Africa, by 673 they were besieging Constantinople. They were checked there and driven from Asia Minor. But they returned, and Constantinople nearly fell to them in the siege of 717. The crisis was probably over by 750: it was not till the accession of Michael II in 820 that the Empire could be judged to be secure.

IV

This second phase in Byzantine history is one of survival and of reorganisation. The powers of the great ministers were curtailed; there was no longer a Master of the Offices, and three officials shared the authority once held by the Prefect of the Sacred Chamber. The ancient provinces, the *Dioceses*, were re-grouped and normally subdivided into *Themes*, each under the effective military control of a *Strategos*. Imperial estates were divided among peasant holders who were obliged to perform military service. The imperial government developed a consistent policy of fostering a free peasantry. The Guilds were still more closely organised in the towns and prices strictly controlled. There is little evidence of anything creative in either literature or the arts; the most distinguished philosopher and theologian of this period, St John Damascene, studied and wrote under Arab rule outside the Empire, and the dispute between Iconoclasts and Iconodules—'image destroyers' and 'image worshippers'—led to the destruction of much church decoration. Yet, here again continuity was somehow maintained.

The Byzantine Empire of the Amorian and Macedonian dynasties from 820 to 1071 was in many ways very different from the Empire of Justinian. It was far

smaller in extent. It essentially consisted of Greece, part of the Balkans and Asia Minor with footholds in Italy and in the Caucasus, though it was gradually to expand into northern Mesopotamia and northern Syria, while the new Slavonic peoples to the north and the north-east were to come increasingly into its sphere. It had become culturally and linguistically homogeneous. Latin, which was still the official language of Justinian, had vanished, leaving a mass of loan words. The Coptic Syriac-speaking peasants and traders were now under Arab rule. Armenia had become normally a border state. The Byzantines still called themselves Romans, 'Romaioi', but Greek, in either its literary or popular forms, was the universal language of the Empire. It had also become homogeneous in religion. Secret paganism seems to have faded into an occasional literary tendency and popular paganism to have been absorbed into popular beliefs among a Christian peasantry. The disputes as to the use of religious images was ending in the victory of the moderate Iconodules. The dispute as to the nature of the incarnation had closed with the final victory of the Chalcedonians. All men accepted a single orthodoxy of a Universal Church.

In becoming homogeneous the Empire had become far more effectively a corporate state. But the ideals that governed it were still those of sixth-century East Rome. These pre-supposed a conception of the intelligibility of nature, a conviction of the causality of law and a world-view of hierarchic order. The underlying serenity of that self-concentrated Byzantine culture came from its recognition of the dominance of the Idea and of the necessary rule of Intellect.

It is becoming customary to speak of a Byzantine renaissance in the ninth and tenth centuries. It is true that there is some evidence of a wider knowledge of some literary classics, certainly of Homer, possibly of Euripides, and that late classical models were more frequently used in art, notably in manuscript illumination. But Greco-Roman civilisation was conceived of as immortal; it was no more thought possible that it could be re-born than that it could die.

It was customary to speak of Byzantine Caesaro-Papism, but that, too, is an anachronism—perhaps the result of reading back into a Byzantine past the half Lutheran church-and-state practice of the later Tsars. The Sacred Emperor might be conceived as the Moses of his people; the Patriarch of Constantinople was their Aaron; the doctrines and the moral teaching of the Church could no more be changed by either than could geometry. Spiritual and secular administration were distinct as two functions in a single organism. The prestige of the Apostolic See of St Peter at Rome was very high, and on occasion its authority was appealed to; a brief uneasy quarrel between Rome and Constantinople when Photios was Patriarch was followed by a long uneasy peace. But as a whole the Byzantines of this period tended to be oblivious of the Barbarian West. Theirs was a civilisation and an empire that turned inwards on itself. To them Constantinople was the centre of the world.

The loss of Egypt and Syria to the Arabs had made Constantinople the successor city to Alexandria and Antioch as well as to Rome. It was also in some fashion the predecessor of Venice as the chief *entrepôt* for Eastern trade. It was never to be so wealthy or so thickly peopled as in the ninth and tenth centuries. It has been calculated that the annual state revenue exceeded, perhaps greatly exceeded, a hundred million gold francs. The Purse had become part of the imperial insignia and the Emperor Nicephorus Phocas

threatened that with his gold he could break the 'empire' of the West like an earthen vessel.

The length of the reigns of successful emperors must have deepened the sense of security. There were no greater rulers, different as each was from the other, than Basil I, Leo VI and Constantine Porphyrogenitos; together they cover the years from 867 to 959. The great Basil II Bulgaroctonos was to reign from 963 to 1025. Even now it is hard to understand how the Empire came so close to collapse in 1071. The only serious external menace, that from Bulgaria, had been successfully countered. It is the economic and social structure that seems so oddly and rapidly undermined.

A rise in agricultural prices and the prohibition of usury had made land the most profitable investment for capital; in consequence the number of great landowners had much increased by the beginning of the eleventh century. There had been a steady development of monasticism—Mount Athos is a characteristically tenth-century creation—and this had led to the development of great monastic estates normally exempt from taxation. Both these factors diminished the strength of the free peasantry and the first was a threat to the power of the civil service. The weak administration of Romanus III (1028–1043) relieved the great landowners of the heaviest of their financial obligations. The extravagance of his successors exhausted the reserve in the Treasury and their financial expedients proved disastrous. Successive debasements between 1050 and 1078 reduced the value of the gold 'nomisma' from twenty-four to twelve carats. The right to farm taxes were sold either to firms of contractors or to individual landowners. When the Emperor Romanus IV was defeated and captured by Seljuq Turks at the battle of Manzikert in 1071 the Empire almost disintegrated.

Looking back on this phase in Byzantine history there is an odd contrast between the achievements in literature and art. The literature is barren, partly because of the value placed on an encyclopedic approach to the Greek classics, as in the case of Photius, partly because of a standard of impeccable but frozen good taste that can be illustrated by the poem on spring by John Geometres—'the gracious gold-flowered crocus, the anemone, the narcissus gleaming whiter than the snow'. There was no original speculation, primarily because earlier Greek Christian philosophers and theologians had been elected to form a canon of 'Fathers', and it had become the primary duty of the scholar to select and arrange the truths they had enunciated. It was an age of anthologists. The Palatine Anthology of Greek epigrams has been its characteristic legacy to European literature. But it was also the age in which Basil I built the church of the 'Nea' at Constantinople and Leo VI redecorated Hagia Sophia with mosaics. The Nea with its many domes, diminishing vaults and decorated façade, was to be the forerunner of a new type of Byzantine architecture of which St Mark's at Venice is the most familiar example. The greatest of all Byzantine mosaics are those in Hagia Sophia. The textiles, ivories and manuscript illumination of the age were never to be equalled. Perhaps the contrast may be explained since literature was the work of scholars, while architecture and the arts subordinate to it was ranked far lower as the work of anonymous technicians. Inventiveness which would make a scholar suspect was valued in technical skill. In the sixth century Agathias had defined architecture as 'the inventions of engineers who apply geometry to solid matter' and this would

seem to hold good until the end of the Empire.

The sense of rhythm and balance, sight and touch, seems to have been abnormally well developed in Byzantine connoisseurs. Perhaps a study of Chinese procelain is the best introduction to that of the Byzantine minor arts.

V

Byzantine civilisation had reached its definitive form by 1025; the next four centuries are an epilogue but one that is vital for the history of Western civilisation.

The Empire was saved from disintegration primarily by the astuteness and tenacity of Alexius I Comnenus (1081–1118). Much of Asia Minor had been overrun by the Seljuq Turks, the troops were mutinous, the great landowners were formed into factions, but the chief danger came from the West. The Normans had conquered Byzantine southern Italy and attacked Greece. Venice, once a small commercial and cultural outpost of Constantinople, was now becoming its trade rival. Hordes of Crusaders swarmed across the Empire from the north.

The Byzantine state attempted to cope with these new dangers from the Franks by an elaborate, traditional and perhaps too sophisticated diplomacy, which led to a new relationship with the West and North. This reached its climax during the reign of Manuel I Comnenus from 1143 to 1180. The Norman court at Palermo; Venice; and the royal palace at Buda (in Hungary), became the three outlets for a Byzantine influence that transformed the intellectual life of the West. At each of the three there then existed a bilingual milieu in which Greek treatises could be translated and sent north or west, to satisfy the new desire to know which was leading to the creation of the universities. Thus the *Mechanics* of Heron of Alexandria, part of

Euclid, part of Ptolemy and treatises on optics and on meteors came to France or England from Constantinople by the Sicilian route during the reign of Manuel I. So also did the *Phaedo*, and the *Physics* with the *Anima* of Aristotle. The writings of John Damascene, which were to affect Western theology so deeply, came both by way of Venice and of Hungary.

The *Metaphysics*, *Ethics* and *Politics* of Aristotle were to follow from Constantinople, often with contemporary Byzantine commentaries, like that on the *Ethics* by Eustratios of Nicaea, and contemporary treatises like the *Kirannides*. The impact of this new learning on the West was to create a conception of the material world that followed natural laws and was ordered and real and therefore ultimately intelligible. But all twelfth- and thirteenth-century Western philosophy, theology and mysticism were transformed by the influences of texts that came from Constantinople. It was an influence that stretched far beyond the young universities. The Hellenistic love-romances had been revived in twelfth-century Byzantium with *Rhodanthe and Dosicles, Drosilla and Charicles, Hysminias and Hysmine*. There are the obvious sources for the Old French 'roman courtois' and therefore for all later novels.

Yet Byzantine and West European civilisation still stayed sharply contrasted. There was nothing in common between the Great Hall of some baronial household and the imperial palace, with its small rooms with their floors strewn with rosemary and myrtle and their walls mosaiced with flowers, the golden 'pineapples' and the enamelled birds in their trees of gilded bronze. The Byzantine court still maintained the liturgy of its ceremonial and an unchanging decor—the blue silk robes, tight girdled, the scented tapering beards and the use of harsh cosmetic and the great officials holding in their hands the red enamelled apples of their rank.

For the twelfth-century Byzantines were still the conscious inheritors of an Hellenic tradition frozen and formalised. It was this heritage which inevitably coloured their conception of any possible relation to the Western Barbarians, 'men tall as palm trees who spat better than they spoke'. The *Alexiad* of Anna Comnena describes a conflict with the Normans: 'but the Caesar's bow was indeed the very bow of Apollo', or, again, 'but the Queen stayed in the palace for she was anxious about the fair-haired Menelaus as the Poet says'. Education in the classics had never been more prized both among women and men. The Empress Irene could write a commentary upon Homer, and Anna Comnena could state: 'I perused the works of Aristotle and the dialogues of Plato and enriched my mind with the whole of learning'. It still provided an open road to advancement, as a satire of Theodore Prodromos stresses: 'when he was studying he did not know the entrance to the Baths but now he takes the Baths three times a week. Once he possessed fleas as great as almonds but now gold pieces with Manuel's effigy upon them.' The civil service had come to terms with the great landowners but it was still a career open to conventional talent. Its highest ideals are perhaps best conveyed by the panegyric on Constantine Leichudes by Michael Psellos—'he was accurately versed in affairs of state'; 'he had moreover something harmonious and distinctive about him especially when he was proclaiming the Imperial Decrees as from on high'; 'he acted always philosopherwise'.

The study of philosophy was closely linked with that of good letters, a consciousness of past Greek thought conceived as corporate rather than as individual. Some scepticism and a certain irony led easily to a serene but light acceptance of philosophical conclusions that were apparently divergent.

The eternity of a transcendent truth seemed best expressed by remote formulae that were imperfectly revealing. Perhaps no phrase is more characteristic of eleventh-century Byzantium than that of Michael Psellos 'when you have stolen from intelligence the incorporeal quality in things and have realised the light within the body of the sun then you will turn with keenest vision to the incorporeal itself'.

Politically the Empire was surviving only precariously until 1204, but by the twelfth century some of its economic stability had been restored through careful administration. It is probable that the agricultural system never recovered. The attempt to reconquer all Asia Minor failed disastrously when Manuel I was defeated at Myriokephalon in 1176. But Constantinople itself benefited by the rapid increase in world trade, since it was the point of juncture where the trade routes from east to west crossed those from south to north. The Jewish traveller, Benjamin of Tudela, records that Manuel I received 20,000 gold ducats daily from customs dues and market dues in Constantinople. So much portable wealth was a temptation to Western adventurers and a stimulus to Venetian trade rivalry. As a result, Crusaders stormed and sacked Constantinople in 1204. It is perhaps only surprising that this had not happened earlier.

Yet since Justinian, Byzantine civilisation had never been more creative than in the eleventh and twelfth centuries. The phase of disintegration had coincided with the writings of the philosopher and court historian Michael Psellos and the creation of the *Akritas Cycle*, the greatest of Byzantine epics. It had been followed by the histories of Anna Comnena and Zonaras and by the re-emergence of the satire and

of the love romance and at least one example of the drama. It is true that all these except the epic were from a classical mould—the drama begins: 'Now in the fashion of Euripides: I tell the Passion that has saved the world'. But no one who has studied them can doubt the essential originality of each or their individuality of talent.

Art forms in this period differed widely. Reminiscences of the antique were still fashionable, as they had been under the Macedonian emperors, for the antique was equated with the classical and gained prestige from association with literary classics. Perhaps, also, to the Byzantine patron, as to those of the Italian renaissance, the antique had an up-to-date appeal. But it was no longer the fashion to render such reminiscences only monumentally. The eleventh-century scenes from the life of the Virgin at Daphni foreshadow the small scenes in the mosaics of the church of the Chora in their humanism and in their naturalist detail and their too-obvious elegance. The same tendency led to the development of the naturalistic portraiture of the individual, so marked in the mosaics of the Empress Zoe, the Empress Irene and the young Alexius discovered in Hagia Sophia.

In contrast there was also an influence from contemporary Islamic art, perhaps prized as novel and bizarre. This would explain the use of Kufic script in decoration, the adoption of Islamic forms in ivory work and fresh combinations of pattern and colour.

Most significantly for the future, there are now attempts to express dramatically moments of searing emotional tension. This had perhaps begun in an Asia Minor peasant art of which we have relics in the paintings of the Cappadocian rock churches, but it reaches the highest level of artistic achievement in the mosaics of Nea

Moni in Chios and in the twelfth-century wall paintings at Nerez in Macedonia and at Hagios Chrysostomos in Cyprus.

In the twelfth century, as Byzantine influences came flooding into an unknown world, all these tendencies in Byzantine art came with them, passing north-west to Winchester by way of Monreale and Cefalu in Sicily, penetrating across the Alps by way of Venice or Torcello or reaching north-eastward through Kiev and Vladimir to the Neredetzi monastery near Novgorod.

Only the strength of the intellectual and artistic movements in twelfth-century Constantinople can explain their survival into the fifteenth century past the gap of the Frankish occupation of the city. Poets and scholars were fostered at the exiled imperial court at Nicaea. When Constantinople was re-taken in 1261 continuity seems to be still unbroken; movements that can be traced to the eleventh century culminate in the fifteenth.

VI

During the last phase of Byzantine history from 1261 to 1453, the area controlled from Constantinople was so small that it was only nominally an empire. Politically it was obviously doomed. The army, now mainly mercenary, was negligible, the fleet barely existed, the fortifications were becoming outmoded and would be rendered useless by the development of artillery. The civil service and the imperial ceremonial went on unaltered. The eleven emperors who reigned during this phase form a relatively undistinguished series, though Michael VIII Palaeologus and John VI Cantacuzene were brilliant, if conventional, diplomats and Constantine XI Palaeologus had a quality of greatness. There were some able ministers like the Grand Logothete Theodore Metochites, though circumstances were forcing them

to rely primarily upon subtlety. The Empire was being exploited economically both by Venetians and Genoese but it is becoming clear that it still possessed great wealth. This was due primarily to a development in Central Asia. The Mongol conquests of the thirteenth century had created a 'Pax Mongolica' that stretched from the Caffa in the Crimea to Pekin. Much of this new Far Eastern trade had to pass through Constantinople, as also did the increasing trade from Persia and the Caspian which reached the Black Sea at Trebizond. Westward and to the north, Genoese merchants had now linked the East Mediterranean trade not only with Spain but with Bruges and Southampton and London—the malmsey wine of fifteenth-century England was a Byzantine import. At Bruges and London, the Genoese met the northern traffic of the Hansa league. Another route passed from Flanders and so down the Rhineland to Milan, then to Venice, then by sea to Ragusa and so overland to Constantinople.

All this world traffic brought prosperity not only to fourteenth- and early fifteenth-century Constantinople but to its subordinate cities, Trebizond and Thessalonica and Mistra and Monemvasia in Greece. It was wealth that was becoming very unevenly distributed. The great riches of a few individuals suggests that the guild system was in decay and price controls relaxed. The factions at Thessalonica imply that the small traders and the town proletariat were now combining against the officials and the rich. This new grouping of the economically oppressed would naturally be linked with the peasant serfs who had taken the place of the smallholders and who were burdened by the 'Kapnikon', the imperial hearth-tax as well as by the 'Peribole' or forced labour. Both found their leaders among the monks who were so often recruited from their numbers. Leading ascetics could gain some of the authority of Old Testament Prophets. This was an amalgam which seems curiously reminiscent of the faction of the 'Greens' in fifth- and sixth-century Byzantium. As in the case of the feud between 'Greens' and 'Blues', is was further embittered by a difference in religious policy.

It is now clear that the religious schism between East and West had been a far slower and more gradual process than nineteenth-century historians believed. Relations deteriorated sharply after the excommunication of the Patriarch Michael Cerularios in 1054. In the twelfth century they had begun to improve. Greeks considered that there were errors among the Latins, Latins that there were errors among the Greeks; neither side considered the others to be heretics and there is frequent evidence of inter-communion. Towards the end of the century there were violent anti-Latin riots in Constantinople but these seem to be primarily anti-Venetian, provoked by trade rivalry and fear and hatred of foreigners. Relations between Eastern and Western Christians had become envenomed in 1204 by the brutal sack of the city and still more by the consequent appointment of a Latin Patriarch. But after 1261 it seemed a diplomatic necessity to the Byzantine emperors to re-establish a full union with the Christendom of the West, at first in order to ward off further attacks from the French kingdom of Naples, and, later and more urgently, in order to muster full Christian support against the Osmanli Turks in North Anatolia who early in the fourteenth century had become the primary threat to the Empire.

In two general councils at Lyons in 1274 and at Florence in 1439, the official church accepted the full claims of the medieval Papacy and proclaimed a complete religious union with the Latins. Partly at least this was the result of imperial pressure. But quite apart from diplomats and civil servants, the Party of Union numbered convinced adherents; scholars like Manuel Calecas and George Bessarion, great churchmen like the Patriarch John Beccos. It had hardly any following in the great monasteries. For the mass of the monks, as of the people, the Party of Union and such emperors as favoured it were Latinisers and defilers of Orthodoxy. The cleavage grew wider through the Hesychast controversy.

Hesychasm was a school of mysticism that had had its origins in third-century Alexandria and was already recognisable in eleventh-century Constantinople. But in the fourteenth century it became fully articulate in the teaching of Gregory Palamas, a monk on Athos and Bishop of Thessalonica. Some practices in contemplation and the emphasis on the blinding vision of the eternal and uncreated Light of Godhead exposed it to attack from a group of traditional theologians. It was a misfortune that its chief opponents, Gregory Akyndinos and the less reputable Barlaam of Gerace, were closely associated with the Party of Union and that Hesychasm became suspect at the court of the Palaeologan emperors through the political affiliations of some of its leaders with the faction of the Cantacuzenes. The monasteries on Athos remained its stronghold. It became one more factor of disruption. Religious homogeneity which had strengthened Byzantine civilisation for five hundred years, had vanished a century before Constantinople fell to the Turks.

Yet possibly it was the existence of these tensions that made the last phase of Byzantine history also the most fertile. The relation between Byzantine painting and the new schools in fourteenth-century Italy has not yet been studied adequately.

It seems increasingly likely that Giotto and Duccio were influenced by art movements in contemporary Constantinople. The oddly styled 'arte Bizantina' which the school of Giotto slowly ousted was in fact old-fashioned and formalised provincial Italian. There were at least four Byzantine painters of genius between 1312 and 1444: the newly discovered Master of the Chora, the Master of the Peribleptos at Mistra, the two Masters of the Pantanassa. The great tradition in historiography culminated in the fifteenth century with three major historians. There are fresh developments in romances and chronicles, due primarily to the influence of French adventurers in Greece. There is coarser and more realistic satire and a sudden outburst of love lyrics.

But it was the development in the status and individualism of the Byzantine scholar that had most significance for the Italian Renaissance. It is probable that there had always been a secularist element in the court civil service with its sophisticated Hellenism. Towards the end this becomes far more openly expressed when the main force of monasticism under its Hesychast leaders was in sporadic opposition to imperial policy. In the fifteenth century not only pagan sympathies but pagan beliefs could be openly avowed by a court writer like Gemistos Plethon. The name 'Hellene', which had for so long been a synonym for Pagan, was now claimed with pride. The standard of exact classical scholarship remained and also that of exact imitation of the classics. Critobulos of Imbros, who survived to become the court historian of the Turkish conqueror, would seem to have almost identified himself with Thucydides. But in the last century of the Empire, as the civil service dwindled, an increasing number of scholars were forced to live precariously by their learning and their wits.

Many left the capital in search of patrons, at first Mistra and Thessalonica, later for Italy. The presence of Byzantine scholars in the Italian towns between 1400 and 1470 had some of the effects of the presence of Latin translations of Byzantine texts in the twelfth- and thirteenth-century universities. It is not only that they were primarily responsible for the knowledge of Greek classics which distinguished the circle of the Medici from that of Petrarch, but their own tastes and conceptions influenced their patrons, since they had the combined prestige of being both modern and antique. This would be equally true whether they were men of original talent like Bessarion at Rome, of high scholarship like Lascaris at Venice, of enterprise like Argyropoulos at Paris, or members of an academic proletariat suddenly dependent on their wits alone.

That characteristic renaissance quality which is mis-described as Machiavellian may have owed much to these 'Graeculi', with their essentially civilian ideals, their traditional veneration for statecraft and their delight in astute subtlety. Wherever the Italian Renaissance spread there seem to be echoes, however remote, from fifteenth-century Constantinople—in the conception of the Prince or of the Minister, of the Diplomat or in the beginnings of a bureaucracy. Throughout the West the links with the earlier 'feudal' kingships were being broken.

Byzantine civilisation had always been a corporate whole, centred not so much on the person as on the mind of the Roman Emperor conceived as a ray of the Divine Wisdom. It therefore could not survive the destruction of imperial sovereignty. It had lasted for over a millennium, and even after it had been destroyed, stray influences from it remained almost as world wide as had been its claims. The Slavonic peoples were at times to seem polarised towards memories of the Byzantine Empire. The Turkish sultanate, the successor state upon the Golden Horn, preserved great fragments of ceremonial and organisation and much private custom —the Audiences, the Sublime Porte, the Baths—and transmitted much of them as far east as the court of the Grand Mughal at Agra. Though Byzantine civilisation was quickly forgotten in the West and then travestied in Western histories, something of Byzantium remains wherever there is a belief in the dominance of cool and temperate mind.

Rus and Muscovy

by Michael Vyvyan

The Slavs entered history behind the peoples who overran the West Roman Empire and separated it from the continuing Empire of Byzantium. Their western branch moved in the wake of the martial Germans, and by the tenth century had settled the lands which the latter's advance left empty as far west as the Elbe although they were later to be colonised and absorbed by the German backwash from which only the Poles, Czechs and Slovaks survived. As early, perhaps, as the first century they had left the east and south Slavs behind them in the great plain between the upper courses of the Vistula, the Dniester and the Volga; some three or four hundred years later those two branches were themselves to be divided. Of the south Slavs the Serb group spread south-west to the Adriatic and north towards the middle Danube. There they were kept apart from the west Slavs first by the nomad Avars and then by Germans and by the Magyars who settled Hungary and were themselves separated from their Finno-Ugrian kindred on the middle Volga by the east Slavs. The near kin of the Serbs, the Bulgars, took their name from another people with a Volga homeland, a Turkic minority under whose leadership they became a powerful nation which soon absorbed its rulers and pressed upon the northern frontiers of Byzantium.

While this pattern of settlement was forming to the west and south-west of the future Russian state, the east Slavs, who were all to be intermittently included in it, remained in their river valleys. Northwest of them lay Lithuanian tribes, to the north and east Finnic; on the south they were cut off from the Black Sea by a broad belt of steppe which formed the corridor of Asian invasions of Europe from the Huns to the Mongols and which the Russians were not to succeed in dominating until another millennium had gone by. When Russian history begins most of the corridor was in the hands of Turkic nomads, the Pechenegs; to the east of these lay the declining Turkic kingdom of the Khazars.

Like the Bulgars, the Russians were given a political framework by an alien dynasty. The Varangians, known in Russian history as *Varyagy*, were Swedish or possibly Danish vikings who established themselves among the east Slavs in the ninth century, using their rivers and probably also their man-power for forays from the Baltic to the Black Sea and even to the Caspian. In 860 they appeared at Constantinople and it is two years later that tradition places the date for the founding of the first Varangian principality at Novgorod by the semi-historical Ryurik. Other petty states arose about the same time at Kiev and elsewhere, whether or not any of the Vikings were invited by the local tribes as the later chroniclers relate, and in the next generation a Varangian federal empire developed. This became known by the name of Rus, probably a Norse word, but there is authority for its Iranian origin and the cosmopolitan links of the Varangians which this would reflect are being increasingly emphasised by historians. The axis of the Empire lay between Kiev and Novgorod and expanded west and north-eastwards, gradually bringing in all the east Slav tribes—largely by force, as the fame of its slave trade shows—and an increasing number of south-eastern Finns whom the tentacles of Slav settlement at the family and village level were already assimilating.

Ryurik's traditional successor Oleg—a name transformed from the Scandinavian Helgi—established the federation under the primacy of Kiev and reserved it to a single family. The system of succession adopted the Slav custom of dividing the inheritance, so that rulers of the petty states tended to move from one to another by way of promotion instead of founding separate dynasties, and this principle proved tenacious in spite of the practice of violence and usurpation among rivals which was common to Russia and the West. The degree of unity thus maintained in so vast a forest land of river-bank culture depended partly on the mobility of the Viking rulers with their warbands, but also on the pre-existence of Slav townships as potential centres of government. The historical picture, still common in the West, of pre-Varangian Russians living on game, honey and fish has had to yield to archaeology as well as common sense. In fact agriculture was following the clearing of the forests, although the steppe lands remained closed by martial nomads. The very abundance of the trading staples of furs and wax, known to us from Greek and Arab, as well as Russian sources, favoured the growth

of miniature urban communities instead of the centrifugal lordships with subsistence economies which were prevalent during the dark ages in the West. The stockaded villages which were to grow into the towns of Kiev, Novgorod, Chernigov, Pereiaslavl, Smolensk and the rest had their counterparts in the castled settlements of the Slavs of Central Europe, the *castellanea* of the medieval Latin chroniclers, and like these may have housed a princeling and his paid following who exacted tribute from the surrounding countryside rather than lived among the peasantry as their manorial lords. Such a system could well be adapted to the needs of a Norse military aristocracy. The origin of the Slav peasant commune, the *mir*, in tribal or patriarchal society is highly controversial even in Soviet historiography, as is its relation to the early townships and demesne where the latter is identifiable. Documentary references to the commune in the twelfth century imply its long existence whereas the Western alternative, the manor is more notoriously absent and the contrast between these two basic economic and social units would help to explain many differences in the social, legal and constitutional paths of Russia and the West.

The Norse leaven not only created the state of Rus but threw it into relations of war and trade with the Byzantine Empire and this brought Russian membership of the Greek Church. Without the continuance of the Viking tradition unification of the east Slav tribes might have proceeded as that of the west Slavs was doing under indigenous dynasties, but the contact with Byzantium across the hostile nomad territory depended on the same Scandinavian initiative and method as was conquering England and northern France and colonising Greenland. The first Russian chronicle compiled from earlier sources in the twelfth century is the testimony to the

Varangian urge southwards, but it is backed by Greek evidence. We learn that Oleg led an expedition to Constantinople in the first decade of the tenth century and extorted a commercial treaty for the traders of Rus in 911. Then, under Ryurik's son Igor (Ingvar in Scandinavian) the warbands twice threatened Constantinople, besides making temporary conquests as far afield as the southern shores of the Caspian. Igor's widow, Olga (Helga), is praised by the chronicle of imposing the justice of Kiev among the tribes and it was as a Christian convert that she visited Constantinople. But her son Svyatoslav, whose regent she was, showed himself the most typical Viking of them all. His conquests ranged from the upper Volga to the lower Danube where he maintained a second capital among the Bulgars until he was driven out by the Emperor John Zimisces. He broke the Khazar Empire but thereby strengthened the Pechenegs and it was by these nomad enemies that he was defeated and killed in 972. He was the first of the dynasty to bear a Slav name, but neither his Varangian warband nor those of the junior princes seem to have yet become slavicised as *boyars*. The Russian name for the prince's followings, *druzhina*, is an exact translation of *comitatus*, the Latin word used by Tacitus to describe the 'companionage' surrounding a German chief of the first century A.D. But it proved a more lasting and influential institution in its Slav than in its German setting, restricting as it did the development of an ingrained territorial aristocracy until the Mongol and Byzantine examples of despotism were absorbed into Russian life to reinforce the older tendencies towards centralisation.

II

The Viking period of Russian history may be considered to end, and the era of Kievan

civilisation to being, at the end of the tenth century with the conversion of Vladimir to Christianity. He had succeeded Olga and Svyatoslav as senior Varangian prince at Kiev after a comparatively brief dynastic struggle. This event followed his earlier career of conquest within the east Slav homeland among the Poles in the west, the Volga Turks in the east and the Lithuanians in the north. Then Vladimir had lent his spare Viking mercenaries to the Byzantine Emperor and promised to accept baptism in return for marriage to the Emperor's sister. But it needed the siege of an imperial fortress and probably the mediation of the Norwegian royal saint Olav Tryggvason to complete the deal. The Church rejoiced the more over Vladimir since, according to the earliest chronicle, the convert had been a notorious lecher as well as a persecutor of the Christians already established in Russia and two centuries later he was canonised. But the reform was effective; mass baptism took place with little resistance except in the north where mutinies in favour of the old cults were still occurring half a century later. In these, Soviet historians have found an element of class warfare because the chronicle tells us that some of the 'best people' were massacred. Meanwhile the Church was progressively endowed, and Russian literacy, which had stagnated in native runic writing, went forward with the influx of Bulgarian priests. These made prevalent the script devised by the earlier missionaries to the Slavs and Pechenegs, Cyril and Methodius, and they also introduced a south Slav dialect in the historic Russian liturgy. Greek art was at once accepted as well, but Vladimir's religious buildings in Kiev were destroyed by the Mongols and the multidomed *desyatina* church remains a legend.

The prime of Kievan Russia belongs to the eleventh and early twelfth centuries, after which the 'mother of Russian cities' lost its hegemony. Like the chronicles, the vernacular ballads—the *byliny* which indirectly date back to this period and form an important source of Russian history before the ascendancy of Moscow —link the national glory with the favoured rulers: Vladimir, his son Yaroslav the Wise, and his grandson, Vladimir Monomakh, who was was called after his maternal grandfather, the Byzantine Emperor Constantine Monomachos. This reflects the dependence of Russian social organisation upon the protection of the princes. The centres of civilisation and trade on which the political identity of Rus rested lay near the western or southern marches, Kiev in particular being exposed to Polish intervention, as well as the nomad incursions, first of the Pechenegs from the east and then of the more deadly Polovtsy. Kiev was therefore the chief sufferer from the internecine struggles for succession which the extraordinary system of dynastic promotion along the ladder of principalities involved between the major reigns. It was after a comparatively short interregnum of this kind that, under the grand prince Yaroslav (1034–54), Kiev reached its first peak of prosperity and fame and that the whole of federal Rus reached its limits of territorial expansion; in breadth from Murom to Polotsk and Galich, in length from Lake Ilmen to the isolated princedom of Tmutarakan on the Sea of Azov. This was also the most cosmopolitan era in Russian history until the eighteenth century. The reception of Greek religion and culture had been, like all subsequent Russian importations except Mongol rule, voluntary and not exclusive. The grand prince Vladimir had exchanged several embassies with Rome and had encouraged the mission of St Boniface to the heathen. Yaroslav's prestige abroad and the scope of his foreign relations can

be judged from his marriage to a Swedish princess, and that of his sister and daughters to kings of Poland, Hungary, Norway and France. Kiev's hospitality to foreign merchants and its multiple channels of trade are attested by Arab, Greek and European sources, and in the north-west Novgorod was in treaty relations with the great German trading federation, the Hanse.

Whether the cosmopolitanism inferred from this amounted to membership in medieval Europe, a status which lapsed as it were when the Mongol conquest interfered with cultural and commercial exchanges, or then again whether that question itself has any meaning, are matters which have been debated by historians of Russia for a century and a half. Whatever is meant by the entity of Europe, a basis for comparison with it is provided by the first two institutional records in Russian history which belong to Yaroslav's reign and represent the two essential elements, Byzantine and native, in the contemporary society. These are the *Ustav* or statute of ecclesiastical law and the *Russkaya Pravda*, 'Russian justice', a kind of mixed civil and criminal code. The first is of Byzantine complexion and therefore shares an ultimate common origin in the age of Justinian with the canon law of Latin Christendom. Like its Western counterpart it provided an important though indirect agency for Roman jurisprudence in a non-Roman world, but without contributing to the competition of spiritual and temporal authority which was so characteristic and fruitful in European politics. The *Russkaya Pravda* on the other hand, with its provision of compensation (like the Germanic *wergeld*) to the victim or his family as a solution of the gravest felonies, harks back to a legal system which contemporary Europe had, under ecclesiastical suasion, generally abandoned. But being a digest of pre-Varangian and Kievan customary law, the *Pravda* in its different versions tantalises historians by denying them a consistent picture, in spite of its allusiveness, of the grades of personal status or the relationship of communal society to the semi-feudal organisation supposedly taking its place.

Culture in the shape of letters, architecture and art, were of course predominantly Byzantine in the heyday of Kiev, but Greek had none of the status of a literary or even liturgical language that Latin had in the West. Nor were domestic arts, costume, tools or weapons Greek; Russian usage was eclectic. But Marco Polo thought the Russians 'have the manner of Greeks' and as regards the urban scene and life, Adam of Bremen praised Kiev as an 'ornament of Greece', rivalling Constantinople. Indeed it is hard to identify in retrospect a diverging national style in the pictorial art or in the buildings of the period which have survived. Perhaps there is a greater tendency to the perpendicular, but this is paralleled in south Slav countries. It is uncertain whether even the 'onion' dome is a Russian invention. The cathedral of St Sophia at Kiev was begun in 1019 and the frescoes and mosaics there, as conserved and restored, do not differ in manner from the tradition of Constantinople and Ravenna. After Kiev's cathedral came Novgorod's St Sophia, complete in 1052, which eventually bore the same symbolic status as St Mark's in the analogous city-state and trading empire of Venice. Cathedral, church and also convent building then went forward in the junior cities without interruption by the wars of succession until the Mongol conquest, although enterprise shifted north and north-east as Kiev declined. As in building, the Greek example was, of course, also followed in ecclesiastical literature, and a school of copyists and

translators was patronised by Yaroslav the Wise and his contemporary Hilarion, the first native metropolitan of the Russian church and author of a religious work of linguistic rather than historical interest.

The death of Yaroslav gave rise to half a century of internal warfare between competitors for the grand princedom. Gradually Vladimir Monomakh emerged as the most successful warlord and he was finally installed in Kiev at the demand of the townspeople in 1073. He is perhaps the most engaging hero of Russian history, and his *Instruction to My Children*, another vernacular treasure, is rich in autobiographical detail. Tough and elderly, he had already begun to recover the borderlands which fell away during the civil wars to Poles, Circassians from the Caucasus and above all to the Polovtsy, the more formidable tribe of Turkish nomads who had been supplanting the Pechenegs since the crushing defeat of the latter by Yaroslav in 1034. Vladimir's reign was an Indian summer for Kiev, and indeed for a united Rus, since he not only ejected the foreigner but asserted the hegemony of the grand prince by force inside the federation. National consciousness seems to have been well developed in the twelfth century. It is shown not only in the chronicles and the retrospective *byliny* that extol Vladimir, but in the frustration of the author of the *Lay of Igor's host*, which laments the Polovtsian incursions in the following time of troubles. Then there is the account of a pilgrimage to Jerusalem in the beginning of the twelfth century by an obscure abbot Daniel. Daniel tells how the Frankish King Baldwin, 'a good man, very simple and not at all haughty', gave him permission to light a candle on the holy sepulchre 'in respect for the Russian princes' and 'in the name of his whole Russian land'. He adds with satisfaction that the Russian candle burned whereas the Latin ones went out.

III

This was the end of a phase of Russian history, for after Vladimir Monomakh, leadership passed from Kiev to the north-eastern group of princedoms between the upper Oka and the upper Volga; Rostov, Ryazan, Tver, Suzdal and Vladimir, particularly the two last-named, and eventually to a new member of the group, Moscow. Migration went with political change as wars of succession and the menace of the Polovtsy increased the insecurity of Kiev; trade, too, was moving away from the northern to the southern hinterland of the Black Sea. One current of migration flowed north-east; another flowed westwards forming east Slav salients beyond the existing princedom of Galich in the living space of the Poles, and even across the Carpathians, the natural frontier of Hungary. In the north-west Novgorod, with its satellite Pskov, was less affected, developing its own colonial rather than military empire which out-flanked Suzdal on the north, based on an exchange economy and oligarchical government.

The founder of the Suzdal region's power, Andrei Bogoliubskii, sacked Kiev in 1169, and although the old capital's prestige did not at once disappear, there were thereafter two 'grand princedoms'. It is significant that the seat of the rising one was moved to Vladimir because there less popular restraint lay upon despotism than at Suzdal. Such restraint in Russian towns came from the old Slav institution of the *veche*, a generally sporadic popular assembly, sometimes extending to the surrounding country, which, when fully effective, chose the administrative officials, the *posadnik* or mayor and the *tysyachnik*

who was the commander of the militia. The *veche* was long to survive even in the despotic princedoms, but in the most republican state, Novgorod, it was, like the prince, overshadowed by the patrician assembly. This *boyarskaya duma*, which elsewhere became the council of the auto-cratic princes, in Novgorod bound the princes by a contract and after 1276 even chose the archbishops. The *boyars* of Novgorod were less directly than in other states successors of the prince's *druzhina*. Many had their status through wealth in trade or slaves and acquired land by settling empty areas with slaves, usurping it from subject tribes. Novgorod, too, traded in cash products—wax, hides, flax— and could be coerced by cutting off its corn imports, as happened in 1170.

Elsewhere in Russia grants by the prince probably accounted more often for the emergence of landed property, although the transformation of members of the *druzhina*, who had been paid by him, into territorial nobles was gradual, and involved neither the legal and moral subtleties of Western feudalism nor a parallel evolution of tenure. Land-owning also arose, as in Europe, by 'commendation', that is the mortgaging of peasant holdings if not personal liberties for protection or debt, by the settlement of empty lands by slaves, and according to Marxist historians through the survival of the fittest in peasant communities. Land in 'medieval' Russia was, however, relatively abundant compared to labour, and wealth lay in slaves and claims on tillers rather than in territorial extent. But in Russia, as in Europe after the Black Death, the shortage of labour did not yet make serfdom more rigid, rather the reverse. Even the settled slaves began to acquire rights of inheritance which the serfs of Tsarist Russia were not to possess, and the bulk of peasants, the *smerdy*, had freedom of movement and only owed service when settled on land granted to a lord, or in exchange for tools or stock when his tenure was of the share-cropping type. Russian tillers were traditionally nomadic and when they moved on to public lands, the so-called *chernyi* (black) land, they were then 'black' too, and such peasantry owed no service but taxes only to the princes as his subjects. There was no principle as elsewhere in Europe of every man having a lord.

IV

On these political and social developments the Mongol conquest supervened. The first invasion was in 1223 when a reconnoitring army destroyed the forces of the Polovtsy and the South Russian princes on the Kalka. In 1236 Batu the future *kagan* (i.e. supreme khan) of the Empire, returned and stayed in Russia for five years with a devastating excursion into Europe (*see* Chapter 9). All the cities of the Suzdal region were burned and Kiev utterly razed, but Novgorod was untouched. The slaughter and wastage doubtless caused depopulation; but it was not the immediate calamity, it was the future tributary régime which left its mark on Russian history. To call this 'Mongol' is misleading, because almost all the original Mongol element soon returned to its homeland or followed Kublai Khan to China. The whole of Russia, though not Lithuania nor Poland, became subject to the at first subordinate and then successor state of the Mongol Empire called the Golden Horde, with its capital at Sarai on the Volga. This khanate was in fact an outcome of the warlike migrations of the Turks of which the Ottoman Empire was to be the westernmost extension, the Mongols having played for the 'Turco-tatars'—the word *Tatar* being a Mongol one—the same part as the Varangians had for the Slavs.

The effects of the Tartar (properly Tatar) régime were both material and moral. In the first category there was the tribute; basically a tithe on everything, men, goods, money, variously assessed by Tartar officials through the new device of a census. This was exacted first in furs and then generally in silver; it was heavy and erratic enough to provoke occasional useless mutinies. Overlapping it were tillage taxes, post levies on men, animals and labour, the duty of supporting Tartar officials—which later continued in *korm-lenie*, the 'feeding' of their Muscovite successors—and, worst of all, the arbitrary levies of recruits to the Asian armies. The insecurity of subjection struck Russian princes as well, and in nearly two centuries over a hundred of them had to visit Sarai or even the inner Asian capital of Karakorum itself, many of them several times, and some of them dying on their journeys.

In comparison with the whole national experience specific relics of the Tartar régime in language, dress, even administrative custom were negligible, while the racial admixture is indeterminate. More controversial is the moral influence which Russian and Western historians, according to their outlook, have treated as a fatal or fortunate alibi from European cultural history, as a refining tribulation or an irremediable brutalising of the Russian people and government. A compromise judgment would be that the experience of the Turco-tartar khanate contributed as much as the Byzantine tradition to the particular absolutism of the future Muscovy. If this is so, it is significant that the policies of the khans tended to nourish the most despotic of Russian princedoms and furthermore that the Church, as custodian of the Byzantine tradition, received not merely toleration but privileged treatment from the khans even when it might seem to be incorporating

Christian passive resistance against a Moslem suzerain.

Politically, Russia transformed itself in two ways under the Tartar rule, as the old centralising system of succession to the princedoms among the descendants of Ryurik broke down into primogeniture or subdivision. This led on the one hand to competition and war among the greater princedoms, out of which Moscow finally emerged as the nucleus for a new centralisation; and on the other hand to a temporary phase of quasi-feudal independence in Russia, as the divided princedoms multiplied into mere patrimonial estates, freely choosing their allegiance among the greater states. At first the larger competing princedoms depended on the Tartar khanate for favour and even for recognition as the grand princedom; later the declining khanate of the Golden Horde and then its successor states in the Crimea and Kazan were to enter on more equal terms into the power politics with the princedoms, with the republic of Novgorod and also with Lithuania, which at one time looked as if it might play the centralising role in Russia.

At first there was no resistance to the Mongol suzerain. The contemporary Russian hero, Alexander Nevsky of Suzdal, who in 1240 saved Novgorod's northern marches from the Swedes in a battle on the Neva and later fought another western enemy in the shape of the Teutonic knights on Lake Peipus, sacrificed his popularity by submission to the Mongols and died in returning from a journey of intercession with the Great Khan. It was his son Daniel who began the rapid expansion of the obscure village of Moscow, and his grandson Yuryi (1303–25) who, under the patronage of the Golden Horde, began to compete with the neighbouring state of Tver and bought the title of grand prince. Another grandson,

Ivan Kalita, established his power by means of a Tartar army, became tribute-collector for the khan as well as grand prince and continued the policy of territorial expansion by purchase and usurpation.

Symbolic of Muscovite hegemony was the transfer from Vladimir in 1326 of the metropolitan archbishopric, but Moscow was still so primitive that Ivan's cathedral was its first stone building and it had a stockade instead of walls until the second half of the fourteenth century. A setback for Moscow followed during the zenith of Lithuania. This half-Russian state reached the Volga on the north and the Black Sea on the south. It restored the metropolitan see to Kiev, which it annexed and which was lost to Russia proper for three centuries. But the first hero of Russian resistance against the Tartars, Dimitry Donskoi (1359–89), restored the balance against Tver and Lithuania before leading a composite Russian army to defeat the khan Mamai at Kulikovo beyond the Don river in 1380. That victory was justly celebrated in popular epics for it was a moral turning point. But it was not otherwise decisive; the khan Tokhtamysh sacked Moscow two years later, Dimitry continued to pay tribute, and before the end of the century, the Russian states were threatened in the east by a greater than Mamai in the shape of Timur Lenk (Tamerlane) himself, while in the west Lithuania was strengthened by union with Poland. Moscow survived precariously between these greater powers, now in alliance with the Horde, now at war with it, in turn seeking from it recognition of the grand princedom and refusing tribute, provoking invasion and submitting, but meanwhile unobtrusively acquiring territory. The nucleus of Muscovy was now so tough that twenty years of civil wars and intervention from East and West in the middle of the century could not de-compose it. Vasilyi II (1425–62) surnamed the blind when his eyes were put out by enemies who blamed him for his close relations with the Tartars, in fact exploited the rise of factions in the Horde and it was this new development which was to make the final emancipation of Russia from its tributary status possible in the next reign.

V

The consolidation of a sovereign, centra-lised and homogeneous Muscovy by the end of the fifteenth century coincides in time with similar developments in Euro-pean countries. But the causes do not closely correspond. The success of Ivan III (1462–1503), who was called the great, was due first of all to the comparative decline of his external rivals. The Horde had split between Kazan and the Crimea, and Ivan was not only able to refuse tribute to the former from 1480, but to outface it in the field. The Crimean Khan-ate he treated as an ally, but this was in fact to be the future source of the Tartar menace which Moscow suffered for another century. Meanwhile Lithuania ceased to be the power it had been, particularly after the interruption in 1489 of the union with Poland and two wars extended by treaty the frontiers of Mus-covy to include Smolensk.

Linked with the success of Muscovy against Lithuania was a peculiar process in Russian history which Lithuania shared. This was the independence of private lord-ships in their allegiance, which had grown up after the Varangian system of succession in princedoms declined, and the latter had split up into patrimonial estates. Not only these princely 'appanages', as Western historians call them, but the land granted by princes to their *boyars* acquired this allodial, that is sovereign ownership, and on that account the two centuries of the Tartar domination have often been called 'the period of appanages'. The drift of such independent nobles in the marchlands, with their land and serfs, from allegiance to the Lithuanian grand prince to that of Moscow, was the cause of Ivan's wars with his western neighbour and reflected a new rating among the larger powers. Already in the previous century the drift had begun, parts if not the whole of the lesser states falling into the greater states' orbit, particularly Moscow's, where the princes were to be assimilated against their will losing all political status and preserving only, when putative descendants of Ryurik, the higher social rank. Nizhnyi Novgorod had been acquired when its *boyars* came over; later Moscow had gained territory, not only from lesser states, but from Novgorod.

That republic, as is the way with oligar-chies, was weakened by class as well as regional antagonisms; first it was made subject to Ivan by treaty and then, in 1478, annexed. 'The *Veche* bell (the symbol of free government in Russia) is to be removed from Novgorod', so ran Ivan's terms, 'the office of *posadnik* is to be abol-ished and the whole state power will be exercised by us.' Novgorod's envoys were promised that there would be no depor-tations—a device of state-craft appearing in Russia probably under Asian influences —but in fact within the next decade Ivan removed almost all the Novgorod *boyars* and most of the ecclesiastical landowners, replacing them by nominees from Moscow who were to hold the land as service fiefs. It was an important episode in Russian history, presaging the growth of the homo-geneous service state as well as the extinc-tion of particularist liberties. There is further significance for the future in the closing by Ivan of the Novgorod branch of the German trading corporation of the Hanse. The other lesser republic of Pskov was also assimilated by means of wholesale deportations during the next reign, but the states of Tver which Ivan III took, and Ryazan which fell to his successor in 1517, had no republican liberties to surrender.

Another cause of the swift ripening of Muscovy under Ivan the Great was the Russian succession to the myth of the Byzantine Empire. It was not that Moscow accepted the mantle of the Greek caesars on the fall of Constantinople to the Turks in 1453; rather was it that this calamity was held to prove the Byzantine Empire unworthy, and the Russia of St Vladimir—whom Ivan was invoking as his predecessor when he began to call himself 'sovereign of all Russia' and 'Tsar and autocrat by the grace of God', to be the proper vehicle of the orthodox Church's mission. It was in this sense that Moscow was to be the 'third Rome' as the monk Philotheus and the metropolitan Zosimus now claimed. The marriage of Ivan with the niece of the last emperor of Constantinople, therefore, implied no inheritance. Although the use of the imperial device of the double eagle came in and Greek court ceremonial ousted Tartar influences, Zoe Palaiologos was brought up in Rome and sponsored Italian rather than Greek culture. She was the patron of Fioravanti who, besides commanding Ivan's artillery, began an era of eclectic Russian architecture with new cathedrals and new walls for the Kremlin. The rise of this Italianate school at the same time as the activity of Russia's greatest school of ikon painters, that of Rublev with its Sienese influences, is one of those mysterious coincidences which occur when a new state begins to flourish. But there was no renaissance in Russia; there was no memory of the classical world and no nostalgia for it. That is a cardinal fact in Russian history, like the absence of the reformation. Those experiences of contemporary Europe passed Russia by, just as Europe itself, at least west of Hungary knew nothing like the Tartar domination.

The Russian Church, which seconded Ivan's ambitions, had been a powerful expansive and cohesive force during the Tartar régime. Monasticism, like other movements, had been set back by the conquest but in the fourteenth century, in the era of St Sergius, it reached its zenith. The foundations as far afield as Solovetskii on the White Sea had a colonising function. Moreover, since there were no rival orders, the monastic clergy were national and not particularist. The diocesan clergy also served a nationalising role; the unity of the orthodox Church and the liturgical language tending to restrict the dissociation of western and southern lands in the period of Polish-Lithuanian rule, and as the differences between the Great Russian and the other dialects of the east Slavs grew up. Meanwhile, Church land-holding increased by benefactions and purchases, through tax and service immunities and through attracting peasant labour by its prestige, so that the Church led Russia in agrarian prosperity. But before its maximum share of perhaps a third of the tilled area of Russia was reached, the Church had begun to compete with secular interests. Ivan III had expropriated ecclesiastical land in annexed states, but not in Moscow, and the check to acquiring property came partly from taxation, and partly from an ascetic opposition in the Church itself at the end of the fifteenth century. Yet in this first ecclesiastical controversy in Russia the defenders of Church property took, as its scope extended, an extreme view of absolute monarchy. This 'Josephism', so called after the leader of the party made a certain contribution to the course of the tsarist autocracy in the sixteenth century.

Of Ivan the Great's successor, Vasilyi III (1505-33), the imperial ambassador, Herberstein, wrote that his 'power over his subjects far surpasses all other monarchs of the world', and that he had 'completed what his father began in as much as he took away from all princes and magnates their towns and fortresses. He oppresses all equally in cruel subjection.' But after his two trying missions, Herberstein was an unfriendly witness, contrasting Russia with an ideal Europe, like other travellers then and since, when he observed that 'this people had a greater pleasure in servility than in freedom'. In fact the completion of the Muscovite autocracy was achieved in the reign of Ivan the Terrible (1530-84) in successive phases of reform and terror. He was the first grand prince to be crowned Tsar—in 1547—and in the first phase of his reign the national rather than the absolutist element was uppermost. He introduced a new law-book (the *sudebnik*) in 1550 which brought an elective element into local courts, he issued a reform of ecclesiastical law (the *stoglav*), he replaced officials at the lower levels of local administration representative of the communes, he substituted taxation for the Tartar system of authorising officers and officials to 'feed' themselves on the local population; he obliged merchants and artisans to enter guilds with collective responsibility for taxation. Most of his reforms persisted in influence if not in form, including his use of the *Zemskii sobor*. This 'land assembly', as unsystematically composed and convened as an early English parliament, included besides soldiers, clergy and officials, townsmen and on occasion even free peasants. Its role was considerable until it withered into a vestigial institution like its French counterpart, the estates general, at the end of the seventeenth century and it remained important in the Russian historical mem-

ory. The most organic change was the institution of a kind of state feudalism under which a new class of nobles, *pomeshchiki*, which had already been evolving out of officials and military commanders holding non-hereditary fiefs, was formed with obligations to muster men for military service in proportion to the size of their fief; the hereditary land-owners (*votchiniki*) being equally liable to serve in a higher rank, for instance as the *boyar* in charge of a government department in Moscow or as a general officer (*voevoda*) but not to raise troops at the lowest level.

As a military reorganisation this measure completed a process which began during the Tartar régime with its example of conscription. The decline of the towns owing to devastation and loss of trade had made their militias less important than during the Kievan period, when armies were anyhow smaller and peasant manpower was not drawn upon. Now the Tsar could count on an annual muster of over 50,000 men, besides his new household corps of some thousands of arquebusiers (*streltsy*). In the Kazan campaign he was credited with 150,000 men and 150 guns, probably an exaggeration. The Poles thought the Russian army backward but potentially irresistible. Their King Sigismund warned Queen Elizabeth in 1569 that if the Russians were allowed to bring in material and technicians they would be able to 'prepare the subjection of all princes'. They cast their own bronze cannons—some of the largest, like their bells, in the world. But for modern small arms they were largely dependent on imports, until the first Romanov Tsar brought in foreigners to found an up-to-date metallurgical industry. An interest in the Western strategic contribution was certainly the main motive in Ivan the Terrible's reception of English merchants and envoys to which we owe Richard Chancellor's and Giles Fletcher's accounts of the régime, and it continued the chief limitation on the xenophobia of Russian policy remarked on by foreigners until the time of Peter the Great.

Formalising the conscription of all classes had had important consequences on the agrarian side of Russian history. The service fiefs had to be provided for the new *pomeshchik* class and this was done partly by the allotment of new unsettled land, partly out of confiscations, but even more largely by granting 'black' lands held by 'black', that is free, peasants. Side by side, therefore, with the subjection to the autocracy of the nobility went the subjection of the peasantry to the latter. This was intensified by legislation, progressively limiting, and in the seventeenth century eliminating, the right of peasants to leave privately owned land. A belated military and then fiscal feudalism was thus established, although it never produced a territorial aristocracy with local allegiances, interests and independence, for the landlord was to act as the drafting authority for recruits and as a tax collector until the reforms of the 1860s.

Like the autocracy which had created it, the function of the service state was strategic, not conservative, and its first task was to find secure if not natural frontiers. This was never achieved in the era of Muscovy. In the north there were no natural frontiers until the Baltic coast could be won from the Swedes, Poles and Lithuanians; in the south until the Black Sea coast could be won from the Crimean Tartars. Ivan the Terrible strove unsuccessfully for the first objective until the end of his reign; he shirked the second. After the Tartar raid of 1571, when Moscow was burned, and the less successful one of the following year, he built a defence line across the upper Don and Donets, garri-

soned by the military fief holders, but the real defence of Muscovy was developing independently in the Cossack movement. This migration southwards out of the clutch of Russian princely government and Polish catholicism was founding autonomous military colonies on the Dnieper and the Don, even the Ural and the Terek, mixing with the Moslem enemy and opening new lands.

Meanwhile, however, Russian arms were completely successful on their eastern front against the weaker successor khanates to the Golden Horde, cutting off the Crimean Tartars from the Volga basin. Kazan fell in 1552 and Astrakhan in 1556. But a no less important military achievement in the long run came from an unobtrusive raid by a Cossack leader, Yermak, in the pay of a noble land and mine prospecting family, the Stroganovs, across the Urals to overcome the decrepit khanate of Sibir in 1581. Within a few years Cossacks and traders were spreading across Siberia, so that, in the most rapid military and administrative expansion ever seen, the Pacific was reached within fifty years and the whole of Northern Asia occupied on a skeleton basis shortly thereafter. The advance was directed and supervised in astonishing detail by the foreign and treasury departments (*prikazy*) of the now proliferating bureaucracy in Moscow, with the motive of exacting fur tribute from the natives. Its momentum during the Time of Troubles in the beginning of the seventeenth century disproves the common supposition that the central administration was either primitive or unwieldy, and shows, also, how superficial and episodic the period of interregnum was in the organic development of Russia.

The second phase of Ivan's reign reflected a persecution mania with causes in his private as well as his public life, and it is a sinister coincidence that the only school of Russian historiography and drama which has summed up Ivan as a national hero belongs to the *Stalinschina* of the 1930s and 40s, when a vast purge and terror was again applied in Russia at peace and at war with a more presumable though still inexplicable rationality. Ivan's paranoia culminated in the régime of the *Oprichnina* instituted in 1565. This was an expanding police zone supervised ostensibly for the protection of the Tsar, the rest of Muscovy, the *Zemshchina*, and its constitution involved a further mobilisation and transfer of noble lands. The process was intensified by a terror directed by the *oprichniks*, first against the suspect nobility and later, by way of execution and confiscation, against other classes of the population and against selected localities. Novgorod, accused of treasonable relations with the Western enemy, was one victim; the contemporary chronicle puts the number of people killed at a thousand a day for five weeks and most of its surviving nobility lost their lands to swell the pool available for 'serving men'. The Tsar's absolutist frenzy is rationalised in his famous correspondence with Prince Kurbskii, one of his *boyars* who had defected to the West. Why, he asks in one letter, has he 'feared an innocent death which no death is, but gain' at the Tsar's hand and preferred damnation? The polemical exchange between these two men of powerful intellect and wide experience is of neglected significance in the history of political thought.

Ivan the Terrible's murder of one of his sons and the feeble reign of the other combined with the profound political and social disturbances caused by the *Oprichnina* to produce the *Smuta*, that is 'the time of troubles'. Schiller and Pushkin, aided by Musorgsky, have romanticised some of the circumstances for world literature and drama. The reigns of the usurping *boyars*, the able Boris Godunov and the incapable Shuiskii, were followed by the sequence of 'false Dimitris', pretended heirs of Ivan, the interventions of Polish and Swedish forces, even a Polish garrison in the Kremlin, and the ravaging of central Russia by Cossack armies. But these humiliations evoked no concentration of national resistance until Kosma Mninin and Pozharskii emerged as leaders in Nizhni Novgorod and a *Zemskii sobor* elected the undistinguished son of the Patriarch Michael Romanov to found a new dynasty in 1613. This phase of Russian history has been misrepresented as a threatened national dissolution barely overcome. But that is far from the truth. The national core of Russia was solid, its hinterland unlimited and neither foreign intervention nor aristocratic faction was more than episodic. The autocracy resumed the claims of Ivan the Terrible, even if it was at first cautious in enforcing them.

The restored continuity of Russia in the seventeenth century inevitably appears to the historian as a preparation for Peter the Great's transformation of Muscovy, social, administrative, strategic, cultural and economic. A 'rise of the gentry' has been identified in Russia as elsewhere in Europe in the early seventeenth century although a sympathetic cause is impossible, and certainly it was the princely families which suffered most through the *Oprichnina* and the *Smuta* in status and property. A service fief (*pomestie*) was turning effectively into a patrimony (*votchina*) and a *votchina* was tending to incur service obligations before Peter amalgamated all of the nobility into a single class, differentiated only by the bureaucratic and military rank which individuals achieved in their service careers. What the lower nobility of fief holders demanded was still tighter control over their peasants and that they gained in the *Ulozhenie* of 1649, the legal code which enforced among other things the serfdom characteristic of the next two centuries, with peasants on private lands virtually enslaved and those on former free lands approximating to state serfs. It remained for Peter to stamp the organisation with the uniform poll tax on peasants.

Meanwhile the higher nobility had not yet given up the abuse of *Mestnichestvo*, the system whereby their members claimed service rank according to their family precedence, and this was a handicap to Russian military, if not administrative, progress. Indeed, the Russian army had a poor reputation in the seventeenth century in spite of the increasing use of foreign mercenaries as officers and even as self-contained units. The improvement of the western and south-western frontier, the final acquisition of Smolensk and of the ancient capital of Kiev, and the absorption of Cossack communities in the Ukraine was rather due to the comparative decline of the rival Polish state. And yet ambition was unlimited; as Siberia was militarily occupied up to its mid-nineteenth century frontiers, a foreign contemporary could record talk among the bureaucrats of the conquest of China.

There were more jobs for all ranks of the nobility and for new entrants to it as the state expanded and was militarised and bureaucratised. Centralisation led to a system like that of contemporary Bourbon France in which intendants were represented by *voevodas*, the formerly operational military commanders and now the prototypes of the governors of the fifty eighteenth-century provinces, having no local ties. The system worked in Russia as in France towards social as well as political centralisation and the withdrawal of political power from land

owners. It remained for culture to be centralised and Westernised so that the Great Nobility would be further downgraded. But there was no cultural revolution in the seventeenth century. Printing had started in Moscow in the 1560s but there were few secular participators. Learning was clerical; science was not glimpsed.

Under the first two Romanovs (1613–76) direct military needs and direct fiscal interests such as the fur and liquor monopolies and coinage depreciation were the limits of government economic management. Foreigners were brought in to start a metallurgical industry in Tula and lesser industrial operations elsewhere, but there was no faith yet in the utility of general intercourse with the outside world. Both technicians and military experts were confined to specified quarters in the cities, and indeed the Russian commercial and industrial class tended to be similarly confined so as to make tax gathering easier. Yet there does seem to have been industrial progress; so that Soviet historians have recently dared even to impugn Lenin's strict periodisation of Russian economic history and to emphasise the function of trade in capitalist beginnings. Early capitalists were, of course, nobles such as the *boyar* Morozov who produced and exported through Archangel both flax and potash on a large scale even by contemporary Western standards.

To contemporaries the crisis in seventeenth-century Russia must have appeared to be the religious Schism. Tsar Aleksei, like his father Michael, was religiously devout, but he favoured the reform of the Russian rite in accordance with the purer Greek practice propagated from Kiev, and his nominee, as Patriarch Nikon, enforced a liturgical revolution. This had two results: the defection of conservative believers and the temporary build-up of the patriarchate to rival the sovereignty of the Tsar. The belated parody of the medieval Western conflict of Pope and Emperor may be seen as leading to the subjection of the Russian Church to a government department which was one of the lasting reforms of Peter the Great. But the creation of the *raskol*, the enormous underground religious dissent, with eventual political implications among proliferating and often extremist sects, was of greater importance for the next two centuries of Russian history. It may be taken as marking one aspect of the incompatibility of society (*obshchestvo*) and the state (*gosudarstvo*) which was to become a classical theme of political self-criticism in imperial Russia—one which

Rousseau's intuition perceived early on when he observed that Peter the Great had tried to turn his subjects into Englishmen or Germans before he had turned them into Russians. So the era of insurgency in which the Romanov Dynasty began lasted for a century and a half, including the great territorial risings of Stenka Razin (1670) and Pugachev a hundred years later, while in the seventeenth century the many minor popular revolts in Moscow and elsewhere generally had a wide political bearing. Indeed insurgency continued in Russia until the fully developed imperial police state was able to break down social and regional alienation into local agrarian riots and its Soviet successor to purge it by decimation and eventual national success.

9   THE NOMAD EMPIRES OF ASIA

by John Bradford

The impact of the Mongols and their kindred and subject peoples on Muscovy was only one aspect of a movement which radiated from the Central Asian steppe, and covered a vast range of territory and a great tract of time. Their domination was fluctuating, sometimes ephemeral and the word 'empires' has been chosen in this context to include ties of culture, art or language which lasted longer than the rare political unifications. The scope of such a study covers 4500 miles from the China Sea to the Carpathians, and about 4500 years up to the present day. Only a few of the crucial peoples and periods can here be discussed; they need combined analysis by archaeology, history, anthropology and philology. Pastoral nomadism on the steppes was a specialised and distinct economy.

Although we rightly think of the 'corridor' of steppe grassland across Central Asia as the core of nomadic tradition, important contributions were continually added by the Tungus reindeer-herders in the forests northwards, and also by pastoralists who maintained a vigorous nomad culture in mountains or deserts along the southern flank of Central Asia. 'The Steppe and the Sown' have no sharp division between them: the steppe being the level treeless grassland used almost exclusively for grazing; the sown being crop-bearing; the plains of Asia stretch far into Europe, and steppeland comes close to Pekin. Events at the east and west ends of the steppe often call for joint consideration.

The basic nomad unit was the family with its flocks of horses, sheep, cattle or camels. The Kazakh of today can be seen proudly seated on his horse, eagle on wrist, summing up the legacy of past centuries of mobility and endurance. He and his horse are one. The daily life of nomads was 'a continuous rehearsal of campaign conditions'. Men and animals are co-partners, and neither partner can maintain itself separately.

Pastoral nomads have a regular cycle of seasonal movements to tribal grazing lands, unchanging unless pressure from neighbours causes repercussions from one tribe to the next. They hate towns and civilisations, but probably have always been compelled to trade with them and been influenced by them.

Nomadism differs essentially from migration. From the first, one fact is clear, the steppe is no place for weaklings; one must get on, or get out. The ruthlessness of the Asiatic nomad is instinctive, as much a product of his harsh environment as his clothes. Caravan travellers in Mongolia today regard the acute sufferings of man and beast as merely 'the business of the Gobi Desert'. We must not romanticise the vigorous ruffians who would so disconcert us if we were confronted by them.

It seems agreed that nomadism, as a specialised economy, was derived from Neolithic cultivators who had domesticated animals, and had spread across Asia, backed by an older trans-Asian continuum of Mesolithic hunters. A very large area of pasture was needed to support compara-

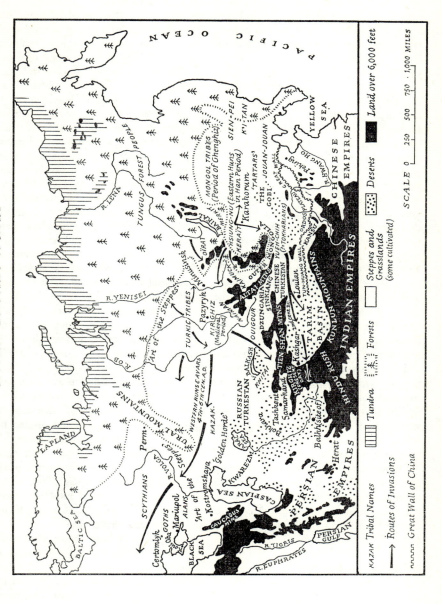

NOMAD EMPIRES OF ASIA

PACIFIC OCEAN

YELLOW SEA

CHINESE EMPIRES

INDIAN EMPIRES

PERSIAN EMPIRES

BALTIC SEA

LAPLAND

SCYTHIANS

BLACK SEA

CASPIAN SEA

PERSIAN GULF

TUNGUS FOREST PEOPLE

R. LENA

R. YENISEI

OB

URAL MOUNTAINS

'Art of the Steppes'

TURKIC TRIBES

OIRAT

KIRGHIZ (Medieval Period)

Pazyryk

'Art of the Steppes'

Perm

R. VOLGA

Kostromskaya

Golden Horde

ALANS

GOTHS

Mariupol

Certomlyk

KAZAK

Oba

HSIUNG-NU (Eastern Huns in Han Period)

MONGOL TRIBES (Period of Ghenghiz)

SIEN-PEI

KY-TAN

MERKIT

Karakorum

'TARTARS'

JOUAN-JOUAN

GOBI

OUTER MONGOLIA

CHINESE MONGOLIA

Peking

R. HWANG HO

ORDOS

KANSU

GREAT WALL

YUEH-CHIH

Loulan

TARIM BASIN

SINKIANG

TIEN SHAN MTNS

Kashgar

Turfan

OUIGOUR

DZUNGARIA

ALTAI MTNS

Irtysh R.

R. OB

Tashkent

Samarkand

Bokhara

RUSSIAN TURKESTAN

Balkash

KWAREZM

Herat

Balkh (Bactra)

HINDU KUSH

KUNLUN MOUNTAINS

CHINESE TURKESTAN (TOKHARIANS)

CAUCASUS MTNS

R. TIGRIS

R. EUPHRATES

WESTERN HUNS & AVARS 4TH-6TH CEN. A.D.

NAZAK Tribal Names

→ Routes of Invasions

ᴧᴧᴧᴧ Great Wall of China

Tundra

Forests

Steppes and Grasslands (some cultivated)

Deserts

Land over 6,000 feet

SCALE 0   250   500   750 · 1,000 MILES

tively few nomads. Any increase in their herds or population would exhaust a steppe region and hunger was probably the spur for the raiding of civilisation, always an essential of nomad economy. Indeed a distinction between the settled Chinese and true Steppe Nomads became clear only during the Chou period (*c.* 1122–255 B.C.). This specialised pastoral economy had a composite origin, in oasis-settlers, in marginal cultivators crowded off the sown on to the steppe, and in tribes from the Siberian forests.

Climatic changes may well have been the key to events. Professor A. J. Toynbee has suggested that periodic three-hundred-year phases were linked with increased desiccation and corresponding nomad activity, which would push them off the steppes; or alternatively that they would be incited by a temporary weakness in the *cordon sanitaire* of surrounding civilisations. The most aggressive nomad tribes came usually from the adjacent 'marginal' areas. Others have argued convincingly that these outbursts can best be explained as the envy of wealth which was both static and obviously vulnerable, combined with the effects of inter-tribal rivalries inherent in nomadic life in spite of the cement of tradition. In marginal regions, such people were in a state of flux, often ruling settlements of cultivators established long before, as in South Russia.

From the start such cultures are only dimly defined and precise dates are still uncertain, for example in the dispersal of the Indo-Europeans of South Asia from Europe to India in the centuries around 2000 B.C. Archaeologists and philologists are still not sure how far pastoralism or agriculture predominated.

II

An early and impressive trans-Asian cultural unity throughout the steppes can be seen from the art and archaeology of the 'Scythic' world, a convenient but generalised label for nomad tribes who had for many centuries shared a similar life and environment. The evidence is shown by an individual art-style, traces of which are found from Hungary to North China. Herodotus, in the fifth century B.C., described the groups of Scyths in South Russia at the peak of a power which had developed some centuries before and continued for some centuries. By combining his narrative with evidence from modern archaeology, we obtain a most interesting picture of 'marginal' tribes on the edge of civilisation. He mentions that these Scyths included tribes of both nomads and cultivators, and gives many details of tribal life and customs—for example the importance of horse-archers, the practice of human sacrifice, and elaborate burial rituals. Round a king's tomb fifty servants and fifty horses would be killed and buried; and, in fact excavation of the Kostromskaya burial-mound (seventh-sixth centuries B.C.), just north of the Caucasus produced a similar sacrificial ring of bodies.

The essence of this art was its intense preoccupation with the animal world, and its style is instinct with life. Some of the gold and bronze objects rank among the best ever made in Asia. The Bronze Age of Central Asia may well have contributed fundamentally to its development but the intrinsic qualities and origin of the 'animal art style' perhaps owed most to hunters and herders in Siberia. Rostovtzeff and other experts have also shown how strongly it was later influenced by the civilisation to the south—from Greece to China.

Among fine examples of this art of the steppes is the stag ornament, hammered out of sheet gold and dating from about the fifth century, which was found on the plains of Hungary, and which is closely paralleled by others found in the distant Altai Mountains in Central Asia. A favourite theme of this bold art is two wild animals in combat, or a hunting scene. One gold ornament of the latter type shows a nomad hunter from Central Asia (*c.* third century B.C.) wearing leather trousers, characteristic of a riding-people; he is aiming at a boar with his bow of specialised type (the 'composite' bow) which combines layers of horn and sinew to give additional tensile strength. Accurate pictures of the Scythian tribesmen on the South Russian steppes are preserved by the electrum and silver vases made for the nomad chiefs in the Greek cities on the Black Sea; and the nomads would have insisted on the life-like details on these 'luxury goods'. One vase shows them as tamers of wild horses. Another vase shows nomads of the same physical type, 'European' not 'Mongoloid'. They have long beards and wavy hair, felt or leather trousers, and specialised cases for their bows. Most of their clothes were decorated with embroidery or gold appliqué. Naturally, most Scythian remains are things which were easily portable, for example the 'pole-tops' which supported the coverings over carts from Hungary to Siberia; clearly these show trans-Asian cultural contacts.

The finest examples of the textiles preserved in the steppe art-style during the last generation have been excavated by Rudenko from Pazyryk in the heart of Central Asia, from burial-mounds of *c.* 500–200 B.C. in the Altai Mountains, where special local conditions of freezing preserved them. The head-dresses of the horses (some with reindeers' antlers), and the richly ornamented harnesses reveal that passionate feeling for bright colours shared by all primitive peoples. Fortunately, even perishable ornaments of felt, leather, and dyed birch-bark were preserved; and elaborate curvi-linear patterns survived tattooed on the human bodies. A magnificent pile carpet, bordered by horses and riders and stags, is an outstanding example of Persian tradition intermixed with nomad art.

Meanwhile, in South Russia, the Scyths faced the eternal problem of nomad conquerors—how to combine the steppe and civilisation without being absorbed. But a new influx of nomads, Sarmatians, settled their fate. Traces of the 'animal art-style' later spread westward across Europe via Celtic and Teutonic peoples, and its influence is recognisable even among the jewellery of the mid-seventh century A.D. from the royal burial at Sutton Hoo in England (in particular the bird of prey on the purse mount).

III

The next major episode in steppe-history centred round the Hsiung-nu, the stock from which the Hun invaders of Europe apparently originated. These powerful nomad tribes had their home in the heartland of Asia. The great Emperor Ch'in Shih Huang Ti (*c.* 221–210 B.C.), one of the strongest tyrants of history, decided on drastic action against the nomads who had long raided Chinese lands from Mongolia (*see* Chapter 4). The 'Great Wall' built by the Ch'in emperors is a vast work of military architecture and planning, even more impressive than the frontier defence lines which the Roman Empire built across Europe to keep out the barbarians.

Earlier, lesser local walls had already been built by Chinese princes against one another. It is said that parts of the Great Wall were based on work by pre-Ch'in states. Certainly, it was kept in repair and strengthened down to the seventeenth century. For about 1600 miles it stretches from the sea north-east of Pekin to the heart of the mountains in Central Asia.

Its construction is a record of much human misery, but also of huge will-power. 'Three hundred thousand soldiers were "rewarded" by being sent to build the Great Wall. In addition criminals were made to do forced labour on it, also civil servants who had fallen short of their duty and scholars who had failed to surrender to the flames any book banned by the Imperial censor' (T'sui Chi). There are many Chinese legends which describe the homesickness of men labouring on the Wall and the yearning of their wives left in distant homes.

The first great Khan of the Hsiung-nu who is known to us by name is T'ou man of the late third century B.C. It was a Chinese historian, Ssu-ma Ch'ien, who described him about a century later. This Kahn gave his son, Mo-dun, as a hostage, hoping he would be killed. But he return-ed, and his father gave him command of 10,000 horsemen whom he taught to obey by the signal of the 'whistling arrow'. Those who disobeyed were killed. First, the son tested their loyalty by shooting at a favourite horse: his followers did the same. Finally, he shot at his father. They did so as well.

It was probably inter-tribal enmity which was responsible for the still little-known, but major, movement westward of the Yueh-Chih to the Oxus region during the second century B.C., a zone in which an amalgam of Greek and other cultures survived. Some authorities believe that they were connected with Tokharian-speaking people (of Indo-European stock), not Turkic or Mongol. Their later mi-grations contributed to the foundation of the Kushan Empire in North-West India, whose greatest ruler was Kanishka (A.D. 120–160).

The Chinese attempted to meet the nomads on equal terms, and even to out-flank them. Ssu-ma Ch'ien tells us that the Chinese Emperor sent a mission to the Oxus region in search of stronger horses. There was hope, too, that allies in the rear of the nomads could be gained. The Han emperors extended the power of Chinese civilisation far more deeply into the heart of Asia in a counter-offensive. On the north side of the Tarim Basin ran the long defence line which Sir Aurel Stein discovered, mapped and named the Tun Huang *limes*. The Han Empire thus took control of Central Asia and the Tarim Basin, establishing the military power of civilisation against the barbarian nomads and protecting the ancient cities. This was a western bridgehead which Chinese power placed right in the middle of the nomad world. Stein, excavating remains of an outpost at Loulan, found Chinese documents; the latest was dated A.D. 330 giving a regnal period that in China had ended fourteen years before, but this little outpost was obviously out of touch and cut off from the central administration.

It seems that the successful offensives of the Chinese Han Empire expelled a branch of the Hsiung-nu westward and it is believed that they nomadised around the Aral Sea from about the end of the first century B.C. for several hundred years. They were long sealed off from contact with the Roman world by the Visigoths and Ostrogoths, supposedly from North-West Europe, who had settled in South Russia several centuries before. To classical writers they were a new people, and their eruption into Europe implies a mass migration and not merely the arrival of 'royal' families.

'In the year A.D. 376 reports reached the Roman officers commanding the Danube garrisons that a new and unusually large movement had begun among the Northern barbarians . . . and then the first refugees appeared on the north bank, begging to be taken into the safety of the Empire . . .

until an immense multitude crowded on the bank of the river.' It is said that 200,000 Goths were allowed to cross the Danube that autumn. As always, it was a fatal error to allow barbarians to enter civilisation, for within two years they defeated the Eastern Roman Emperor at Adrianople, and the Huns moved into the Balkans behind them. The Huns then concentrated on raiding across the Caucasus and into Anatolia and Syria. Goths and Vandals fought their way across Europe moving with great speed, but they were peoples who had long been sedentary and infinitely less primitive than the Huns. They crossed Europe in a generation, forcibly propelled by the Huns, but some Visigoths, collaborating with Roman troops, played a vital part in defeating the Huns in the crucial battle near Troyes in eastern France in 451.

Descriptions of the Huns survive from several contemporary writers. Ammianus Marcellinus declared that they were the crudest of nomads. Followed by their herds, they almost lived, ate and slept on horseback: they never sought the shelter of houses which they looked upon as little better than tombs. Most of them were clothed in animal skins; but some had linen garments, which must have been obtained by barter or plunder, for without a knowledge of agriculture they could not have grown flax. Ammianus in fact mentions that they practised food-gathering to supplement the produce from their herds: 'None of them ever touches a plough-handle'. In battle they relied on the speed of their manœuvres, suddenly dispersing and coming together; Ammianus mentions their arrows 'pointed with sharpened bones skilfully fastened to the shaft'. At close quarters they used swords and nets which they threw over their enemies to entangle them. 'They are so changeable and so easily angered that many times in the day they will quarrel with their comrades on no provocation and be reconciled, having received no satisfaction.'

Naturally, it is difficult to apply archaeology and excavation in studying Hunnic movements, for they travelled light and looted their more permanent possessions or forced captive craftsmen to make them.

The first Hun known by name is a chief named Uldis in the Balkans about A.D. 408. Towards 425 we hear of three brothers as ruling chiefs over the hordes. By about 434 power seems to have passed to two others, Attila and Bleda. Attila later eliminated his brother. After 420 a crisis of power was developing between the Huns and the Roman Empire, and we begin to know more of the individual Hun leaders because the Western nations found out more about them. Their headquarters seems to have been in Hungary, whence they could raid both Eastern and Western Empires, for the great plain of the Alföld forms the end of the steppes in the heart of Europe. Again and again Vienna has been the terminus of Asian invasions. Tribute in gold and skilful diplomacy by the civilised powers managed to preserve an equilibrium. But one very sinister aspect of these semi-hostile relations is the constant demand made by the nomads for the return of fugitives who had taken refuge within the Roman Empire. This was intended to stamp out opponents: Attila insisted very strongly on this point.

Fragments survive of a brilliant account of the barbarian court of Attila written by the historian Priscus who accompanied an embassy in 448 from the Eastern Roman Empire. The ruthless daily brutality, the almost impossible task of reconciling the civilised and barbarian people, are recorded with honest vigour. No one who appreciates history written with insight into human character, and concerned with dramatic events, should fail to read

Priscus. A Byzantine interpreter it appears, Vigilas or Bigilas, had been bribed in advance to assassinate Attila but never succeeded; Priscus mentions that a 'Scythian' spy, acting on Roman orders to obtain information about the Huns, had just been captured and, on Attila's orders, was to be impaled.

There are no coins or portraits of Attila, but Priscus describes him as short, powerfully-built, with a large head, a flat nose and small fierce eyes. It seems that he looked typically Mongol. His headquarters lay in a plain on the far side of the Danube and consisted apparently of wooden huts and tents inside palisades. Seated on a raised couch in his primitive 'hall', he was surrounded by his chiefs who continued drinking from captured vessels of gold and silver all through the night.

Attila died in 453, when he was still aiming to marry the ambitious Honoria, sister of the Western Emperor—and perhaps he even dreamed of setting himself up as Emperor. He was found dead one morning, with a burst artery, beside a bride whom he had married the day before. The tribesmen cut off their hair, gashed their faces, and following their ritual galloped wildly round him. His empire collapsed with his death. A great revolt by subject barbarians decisively defeated the Huns in 454 on the river Nedao in Hungary. 'The Hunnish Empire,' wrote Hodgkin, 'is from this time forward mere driftwood on its way to inevitable oblivion.' In South Russia two hordes of Huns survived for a time, but their hopes of re-uniting another great confederacy were cancelled by a new flood of nomad warriors, the Avars, who were crowding into the Ukraine. We catch only glimpses of these struggles on the steppe. Hun raids had also been felt at many other points on a long 'front'; in attacks on the Sassanian Empire in Persia, and the Gupta

Empire in North India, during the fifth century, but they were either defeated or they disintegrated and were absorbed. But in China nomad pressure eventually triumphed in the fourth century A.D., ending the great and constructive period of the Han Empire.

IV

It is not possible to describe in detail the rise and fall of the many nomadic and semi-nomadic powers in Asia during the next few centuries, but a few of the most important must at least be mentioned and the periods of their greatest influence. For example there were the Hsien Pi in the fourth century in China; in Mongolia the Jouan-Jouan (sixth century), followed by the T'ou-Kiue, and the Ouigour. In China the K'i-tan played a vital part in the tenth century; in Western Asia the Khazar tribes were ruling north of the Caspian in the seventh; Magyars were prominent in South Russia in the ninth; and the Qiptchaq masters of this same region in the twelfth. And by that time, from Persia to Anatolia, the Seljuqs were menacing Islamic power.

The most notorious leader of the medieval Mongols of Eastern Asia, was Genghiz Khan. He was born *c.* 1167, and his tribe, the Mongols proper, dwelt between the Kerulen and Onon rivers near the east border of modern Outer Mongolia. Probably they numbered only a few tens of thousands. Round them was a hard core of other rival pastoral tribes, various mixtures of Turkic, Mongol and Tungus people—to the west the Kerait up to the Altai and beyond, and the Naiman; to the north-west the Merkit and Oïrat, to the south-east the Tartars. Northwards were Tungus-speaking forest-tribes, primitive hunters who bred reindeer and stretched far into Siberia. This heart-land of nomad tribes shaded off in marginal zones into the belt of civilisations with ancient city life which hemmed its southern side—the Khorasmians in Persia, the Kara Khitai on the Oxus and round the Tarim Basin, and the Chinese.

Genghiz's name at birth was Temudjin. His father, a minor Mongol chief, captured his wife from her original husband while hawking. When Temudjin was only twelve years old, his father was poisoned at a feast by the neighbouring Tartar tribe, but his mother, Ho-elun, by strength of character and determination, kept a few servants faithful to them.

For Temudjin there followed a child-hood of misery. Near starvation, he murdered one of his half-brothers in a quarrel about a fish; nomads captured Temudjin in a raid, but he escaped by hitting his guard on the head with the y-shaped wooden cangue which bound his neck and one wrist. Luckily for him, a friend hid him in a pile of wool, which would be thought too hot to live in. By the force of his personality Temudjin now made himself a power on the steppes, becoming the vassal of Toghril, the Khan of the Kerait, who had befriended him. But once again Temudjin's little camp was attacked. An old servant gave the alarm; his young wife was left behind and carried off and given to a Merkit warrior. Later, she was recaptured and Temudjin accepted her again.

Soon after, he broke friendship with the chieftain, Djamouqa, whom he had known since the age of eleven. Then came the next stage in his rise to power when four Mongol chiefs nominated him as a Mongol king or khan: he took the name of Genghiz, which means 'strong', 'inflexible' or 'severe'. He had to maintain a vigorous front against the Tartars: the new Khan gave special attention to the efficient administration of the herds by his trusted friends and his tribesmen. It was primitive but effective; one was in charge of flocks, another of his personal guard, others of food-supply, pastures, or of discipline in meetings or of sending his commands. In spite of reverses Genghiz attracted followers, and, when obstreperous, the Mongol chiefs who had elected him Khan, were destroyed.

In the battles which followed a faithful supporter sucked out the venom from a poisoned arrow-wound and covered his master with his own clothes: this was the low-water mark of Genghiz's career. But he soon recovered and challenged his old patron the Kerait Khan. One by one rival nomad tribes were knocked out. His old friend, Djamouqa, was crushed without mercy, and later executed, and the Kerait Khan was conquered.

Genghiz's success was largely due to his genius for administration; he organised the nomads under commanders of thousands, hundreds, and tens. He had a personal guard of seventy by day and eighty by night, regularly changed. But tribal ritual retained its force: Genghiz made sacrifices to the white flag with nine tails in which lived the spirit of his own group.

Later, in 1205, Genghiz made his first raid on a Chinese people, the Si-Hia in Kansu, and in 1206 he summoned an assembly of his followers. Again he was consecrated Khan, but in more imperial style by the chief *chaman*, Kokotchu. Ninety-three leaders of 'thousands' were created and those who had befriended him in his youth were given vast pasturages, many wives and posts of command. It is said that Genghiz wanted a moral, besides a military, unification of the tribe he ruled; but it is certain that his mind was fixed on personal ambition. For example, his day and night guard was greatly increased, and each one of them took higher rank than the leader of a thousand. A tragic end followed for the *chaman*

Kokotchu. He was the son of an old friend of Genghiz's father, and began to think himself an equal or even a rival; clearly he aimed to take a personal hand in power politics. Genghiz, warned by his wife, organised the murder. The *chaman's* spine was broken by three assassins in a picked quarrel. The body was placed in a tent; on the third day the tent was opened and it was empty.

The elements of Genghiz's empire were still very simple. Before attacking the Kin Empire in China he worshipped the primitive divinity on the mountain of Bourqan Qaldoun; the Turkic secretary of a Naiman chief had to be employed by Genghiz as tutor to his sons. Very severe discipline was enforced among his followers. At first, there were short, sharp raids, but the nomads soon learnt how to conduct siege-warfare. The Mongol and his horse hunted the Chinese, Persians, Russians and Hungarians, as they hunted wild game.

One by one the Mongol armies attacked and devastated the civilised countries. First in 1215, they attacked the Kin Empire in China. The Emperor fled from Pekin, the Governor committed suicide, the Mongols massacred and pillaged in the city for the space of a month. Genghiz now chose a Chinese prince as adviser, impressed by his stature, beard, widsom and voice. A few years later the richly-civilised cities of Persia were destroyed in the most terrible episode of barbarism in the life of Genghiz Khan. In 1220–21 Bokhara, Samarkand, Balkh and Herat were ruthlessly sacked. Genghiz's son, Tuluy, as general, was guilty of every known atrocity. At Nichapur (1221) a pyramid of skulls was built to make sure that no one was pretending to be dead; those of men, women and children were piled separately—even the cats and dogs were killed. Cities destroyed were re-

destroyed, and the second massacre of re-peopled Herat took a whole week. The nomad generals seemed to wish to make an artificial steppe and deliberately to kill the land. In 1222 the Mongol forces defeated the Russians near Mariupol on the Sea of Azov; the Prince of Kiev negotiated an honourable surrender, but nevertheless was slaughtered with all his men.

But this incursion was only a long-distance raid. The career of Genghiz was drawing to its close. He had been injured in 1223 when he fell from his horse while hunting a bear near Tashkent; he died in August, 1227, and in 1229 his successor, Ogotai, made offerings to his father. The forty most beautiful women with their jewellery and their finest horses, were sent to join him, just as the Scythians had sacrificed their dependants 2000 years before. Grousset's judgment of Genghiz, in his *L'Empire des Steppes*, is too sympathetic; he was not he says as wicked as Timur, because the latter was more civilised and should have known better. He excuses mass killings as part of the nomad method of making war, and indeed, pastoral peoples do not like urban life.

Yet it is completely wrong to imagine Genghiz as an Alexander of the steppe. Grousset claimed that he established a *paix gengiskhanide*, but this was the peace of the grave. This very brief interval of authority could not compensate for the destruction, and a barbarian's *yassaq* (peace) never resembled a *pax augusta*. There is no reason to romanticise the stark facts of Genghiz's life.

In Western Europe the thirteenth century invasions of the Asiatic nomads are described by contemporary historians—by Matthew Paris, for example—with horror and disgust. They were, he said, barbarians clothed in ox-hides, short and thickset; wonderful archers with strong horses, sparing no one of whatever age or sex. Their wives were taught to fight like men. So great was the fear of the nomads that people from the Baltic did not dare to come to Yarmouth for the herring-fishing season. In Matthew Paris there is even the scandalous rumour that Emperor Frederick II had brought them into Europe to help him against the Papacy.

From 1236 the nomads renewed major attacks on Russia and Eastern Europe. The marginal peoples—partly cultivators, partly pastoralists—were the first to suffer. Then Kiev was stormed (1240), the Polish knights were routed at Leibnitz (1241), the Hungarians defeated in a terrible battle and the city of Pest burnt. In December, the Mongol chief Batu (*see* Chapter 8), crossed the frozen Danube and was hovering round Vienna, ready to destroy it.

If they had continued, these nomad invasions could have brought vast destruction to Western European civilisation. Chartres, Venice, Antwerp and Hamburg might have been destroyed like Kiev. But at this crucial moment Western Europe was saved by a pure accident of history. Far away in Asia the Khan Ogotai died in December, 1241, and the nomad hordes hurried back to elect a successor, the tribal leaders eager to seize power.

All this destruction had been accomplished by relatively small armies. Recent studies suggest that the numbers of these nomads were smaller than was previously believed. To take a typical example, all the war hosts of Genghiz which invaded Khorasmia perhaps numbered about 200,000; but only one-third of them were Mongols proper. Captives and local conscripts made the majority, and were regularly treated as expendable. Fear often made the civilised peoples exaggerate the numbers of invaders.

V

After their vast conquests, the Mongol rulers enjoyed great wealth, particularly in furs and silver, and lived in barbaric splendour. They developed a rapid system of communications and taxation on the principle of collective responsibility. 'The inscribing of the taxable population,' writes B. H. Sumner, 'the system of taxation by households, a new coinage and the organisation of customs dues and of transport services were distinctive features of the first century of Mongol rule (1240–1340).'

This systematic collection of tribute was the basis of nomad wealth, and Tartar administration had its influence on Muscovy.

There are two admirable accounts of the Asian nomads at the height of their power. They are eye-witness narratives written by two courageous friars who journeyed to Central Asia in the mid-thirteenth century. Their systematic and factual descriptions of tribal life—its habitat, economy, and society—sometimes strangely foreshadow the descriptive methods of modern ethnologists.

The first is by a Franciscan, John de Plano Carpini (*c.* 1182–1252). Soon after the Mongols had invaded Eastern Europe, he was sent East by Pope Innocent IV to protest against their incursions and to find out the extent of their power. Carpini, resolute, heavily-built and about sixty-five years old, was head of this embassy from the West. On Easter Day 1245 he left Lyons, with another friar, on a journey of unimaginable hardships to the heart of Central Asia. He arrived in time to see Kuyuk (son of Ogotai, and a grandson of Genghiz) enthroned as Khan. Only two years later, in 1247, Carpini successfully returned to Lyons to give his intelligence report to the Pope on his experiences at first hand in the vast Mongol Empire.

Europe stood desperately in need of such information.

Carpini's objective style compels admiration. 'The Mongols, or Tartars,' he says, 'are in appearance unlike all other people, for they are broader between the eyes, they have flat, small noses, and their heads are shaven like priests. Their hair is braided into two short locks, one behind each ear; they wear garments of skin, with the fur on the outside, but some wear jackets of woven materials, even brocade. They own vast herds—camels, oxen, sheep and goats. I think they have more horses and mares than all the rest of the world. Their emperors, chiefs and nobles have much silk, gold, silver and precious stones. Their victuals are all things that can be eaten; for we even saw some of them eat lice. Their manners are partly praiseworthy, and partly detestable; for they are more obedient to their lords and masters than any others, either clergy or lay-people in the whole world. . . . Moreover they are disdainful of other people, and beyond all measure deceitful and treacherous towards them. They speak fair in the beginning, but they sting like scorpions in the end. . . . Whatever mischief they plan against a man, they keep it wonderfully secret. They are unmannerly also and unclean in taking their meat and their drink, and in other actions. Drunkenness is honourable among them, and when any of them has taken more drink than his stomach can well bear, he calls it up and falls to drinking again. They are most intolerable exactors, most covetous possessors and most niggardly givers. The slaughter of other people is accounted a matter of nothing with them.'

Details of the religious beliefs of these nomads are elaborated. Presumably, they originated from thousands of years of life on the steppes and the need for economy in hard conditions. Fire and water played an important part in their purification rituals. But much more important and interesting to Europe and us was Carpini's practical advice about their weapons and tactics in war and the counter-measures which should be used against them. Each soldier he advised, much have efficient bows, a good supply of arrows, and, if possible, lances with hooks at the ends to pull the nomads from the saddle. By this period the richer nomads had swords and various kinds of armour for themselves and their horses; river-crossings did not greatly impede them for they had perfected rudimentary boats and floats.

Carpini sums up as follows: 'No one kingdom or province is able to resist the Tartars; because they use soldiers out of every country of their dominions. If the neighbouring province to that which they invade will not aid them, they waste it, and with the inhabitants, whom they take with them, they proceed to fight against the other province. They place their captives in the front of the battle, and if these do not fight bravely they put them to the sword. Therefore if Christians would resist them, it is expedient that the provinces and governors of countries should all agree, and so, by a united force should meet their encounter.'

In addition to his special advice to the forces of Christendom on the choice of suitable weapons, he gives a warning against any long pursuit after the enemy, for this was their favourite method of ambush. 'For the Tartar fights more by cunning than by main force. Also, a long pursuit would tire our horses, for we are not so well supplied with horses as they are.'

Carpini also describes the election of Kuyuk as the Great Khan. 'We saw', he writes, 'a huge tent of fine white cloth so big that more than two thousand men could stand inside it, and round it there was set up a wall of planks, painted with many designs. . . . All the chiefs were assembled, each of them riding up and down with his retinue.' On the first day they wore white, on the second scarlet, on the third blue, and on the fourth rich robes of brocade. In the wall were two great gates; one of these was for the use of the Emperor only and this had no guards, for no one dared go in or come out by it.

The Emperor seemed to be about the age of forty or forty-five years. He was a short man, careful and grave in his demeanour. 'A rare thing it was for a man to see him laugh or behave himself lightly. . . . He had at all times a chapel of Christians near his great tent, where the priests do sing publicly and openly, and ring bells at certain hours. Yet none of their chiefs do likewise.' These 'Christians' were remnants of that early heretical sect of Nestorians who spread across Asia into China. Their maximum influence was in the thirteenth century, followed by a rapid decline. Survivors were being massacred in Kurdistan in the nineteenth century.

Carpini and his embassy were carefully searched for knives when they appeared before the throne. Chingai, Kadac and other chief secretaries of the Emperor interpreted the Pope's messages and the Tartars' replies, in spite of many difficulties in translation. Of course the mission was a failure. Even while it was at his court, Kuyuk erected a flag of defiance against the nations of the West.

The Western Powers still hoped to convert the Mongols, and in 1253 King Louis IX of France sent as his personal envoy another friar, William of Rubruquis, of the Order of the Minor Friars. Sartach, the son of Batu, the commander of the Tartar troops in Russia, had become a Christian. Friar William reached Karakorum, a journey of 5000 miles, to the court of Mangu Khan (a brother of Kublai

Khan). By 1255 he had returned to Palestine and was busily preparing his report to King Louis. Like Carpini he was an honest, brave and most intelligent observer.

He began his journey from the Black Sea, and in South Russia he at once reached Mongol forces. He gives details of the traditional type of Asian nomad's tent, so like the *yurt* used today. 'They base it', he writes, 'upon a round frame of interlaced wicker-work: the roof is of the same material, at the top of which rises a neck like a chimney, which they cover with white felt, and often they lay a white soil and powdered bones on the felt so that it will shine white. Sometimes they cover it with black felt. Over the door they hang a felt curiously painted with vines, birds and beasts. These tents are so large that they are often thirty feet across.' Some of these tents were not dismantled but were transported on carts, and once he saw a team of as many as twenty-two oxen pulling one of them. There were two lines of oxen, eleven in each row. 'The axle tree of the cart was of huge size, like the mast of a ship. A man stood in the door of the tent on the edge of the cart, driving the oxen.' When they took down their tents from the carts they always turned the door towards the south. In addition, there were big wicker-work baskets covered with felt and decorated with paintings or feathers. In these large chests they put their household belongings.

This group of nomads in South Russia had accumulated much wealth. Their tents were becoming movable houses. An encampment at first glance resembled a village but they had not abandoned nomadic pastoralism as their way of life. Friar William describes the active part which women played in tribal life—just as we know they did among other nomadic peoples before and since. He specially mentions to Louis IX the beautiful carts made by the women and that one woman could guide twenty to thirty carts, each bound behind the next in a long line. With his usual eye for realism he adds: 'They go at a slow pace at the speed at which a lamb or ox would walk.' Rich nomads owned as many as 100 or 200 such carts.

Not all the Mongols were nomadic. In the region round the River Volga, it seems, the nomad chiefs owned settlements farther south which supplied them with millet and other cultivated crops. Such an inter-mixture of conquering pastoralists with subjugated cultivators had existed, as far as we know, for centuries past—as far back as Scythian times and probably for centuries before. Parallels occur, and have been studied in lands far distant. For example, in recent centuries, in East Africa the cattle-herding Masai conquered the Wanderobo, a tribe of cultivators, and exacted a share of their produce.

The friar's chapters are thus full of important data for modern anthropologists, and give us similarities with observations made among surviving nomadic communities in Central Asia, showing the continuities in tribal customs throughout many centuries. For example, he noted that inside the tent the bed of the 'master of the house' was fixed by custom, always facing south. The women lay on the left, the men on the right. On the wall above the master's head there always hung a figure made of felt which they called the master's 'brother', and another over the head of the mistress of the house. 'Above and between both figures, was a little lean one—the guardian of the whole household.'

Even the 'division of labour' (i.e. tasks reserved for men or women), which has now become a fundamental topic in anthropological research, was described by this observant medieval friar. It will be enough to quote one of his examples: among these Mongols, he says, it was the women who had the task of milking the cows, and the men the mares. There is also much more information in these accounts which can aid archaeological research when faced with problems of recreating ancient societies out of the débris of daily life as recovered by excavations.

Although the rich nomad chiefs in medieval Asia had accumulated a wealth of booty as ruthless conquerors, and their wives wore an elaborate spiked coiffure on their heads, built up with bark and decorated with feathers and jewels, the vast majority of the nomads lived in poverty, and were persistent in their importunate begging all along the friar's route (as Professor Lattimore has written 'it is the poor nomad who is the pure nomad'). These tribes would not sell any goods for coins, even of gold or silver, but only for cloth and garments; and when they were offered coins, they held them to their noses to test them by smell in order to find out if they were made of copper.

The climax of Friar William's narrative describes the court of Mangu (a grandson of Genghiz) who was ruling as Great Khan over the Mongols. His court was in winter quarters near Karakorum in Outer Mongolia on the borders of China. The Khan was seated on a couch, dressed in very glossy spotted furs like seal-skin. He amused himself by dallying with falcons and other birds which he placed on his wrist. After a long time had passed he gave the embassy from King Louis, a haughty interview.

At what we can truly call a 'Royal Command Performance', the friar was asked to intone a psalm in the Western mode, and to explain illustrations in his

Bible. But only a few days later he found Mangu busy in pagan rites to foretell the future. The Khan was intently studying burnt bones, the shoulder-blades of sheep. If they were still completely intact, he believed that he could carry out his plans, but if he saw the least crack he would take no action.

Mangu Khan's palace is described as resembling the plan of a church, i.e. with the central 'nave' and two side 'aisles' separated from the nave by two rows of pillars. The Khan sat on the north side on a high platform in godlike majesty. On raised seats to the right were his sons and brothers, to the left his wives and daughters. One woman was at his side, on a seat just below his own.

Chinese priests informed the friar that Mangu's Court was only twenty day's journey from China, and that ten days would bring him to very primitive tribes to north and east. Some lived by fishing and hunting, possessing no herds (they were the tribes termed 'forest Mongols' by modern anthropology); and there were others who fastened polished bones to their feet, in order to glide over ice or snow when hunting.

In spite of a crude copying of a few borrowed civilised habits, the life at court was brutal and barbarous. The Queen and priests were often drunk, torture was used, and sorcery added to the tensely morbid atmosphere. The Mongol magicians, the *chamans*, had great power. They foretold the future and war was not declared without their advice. Each year on 9 May they consecrated all the white mares in the herd. They claimed to control the climate; once, when the cold was extreme they accused some people in the camp of causing the low temperature and they were put to death at once. While dancing himself into a frenzy or trance a *chaman* beat furiously on a drum. This use of the drum

has survived to the present day in Mongolia, and it has even been a custom in Lapland thousands of miles away—a relic from an Asian people who had arrived in the far distant past.

Mangu's answer to King Louis was couched in tones of supreme authority: 'Wherever ears can hear, or a horse can travel, you will hear my message.' He gave orders and demanded obedience with thinly-veiled threats, asking if it was to be peace or war. Like Carpini, Friar William had to be content to return with inconclusive results.

Two months and ten days brought him to the camp of Chief Batu in the region of the Lower Volga, and there he was reunited with companions he had left behind; already the nomads were asking them if they knew how to guard cattle and milk mares—'If I had not come back they would have made slaves of them.' Between Karakorum and Batu's camp he had not seen a city or any dwelling, only groups of tombs and a village where he could find no bread to eat. It is good to know that after six more months of dogged travelling, a chronicler of such outstanding integrity and courage, reached safety in Palestine.

VI

The power of the Nomad Empires in Asia reached its peak during the reign of Kublai. In the year 1260, following Mangu's death, he was elected Great Khan of the Mongols. But he also became much more powerful—the first Mongol Emperor of China. He completed the conquest of the Sung Dynasty; the last Chinese nationalist outposts were in the south, as before and since. But Kublai, who had the stark nomad warrior Genghiz as his grandfather, soon developed a taste for a life of luxury and dabbled in the arts. As Tsui Chi writes, 'the Mongols were by nature and inclination fighters rather than administrators' and their political power was ephemeral. Europeans were given high governmental posts, and Marco Polo, a quick-witted Italian adventurer, has left us a well-observed contemporary picture of Kublai's court and of Mongol customs. Kublai developed still further the megalomaniac ambition of Genghiz and sent expeditionary armies, but generally to their doom, in attempts to conquer the ancient kingdoms in Japan, Indo-China, and even Java.

It is interesting to note, as with the descendants of Timur in India, how quickly the hard-headed indigenous nomads became dilettanti and gradually lost their grip of affairs, when they mingled with the unaccustomed complexities and luxuries of a civilised people. After Kublai's death in 1294 the Mongol Dynasty in China fizzled out after about fifty years of dissolute successors.

It was inevitable that the Mongol garrisons were absorbed and ethnically overwhelmed by the upsurge of millions of patriotic farmers; this is a problem which defeats most conquering minorities. During this period, horses kept by the Chinese were liable to confiscation, and in 1337 they were forbidden to keep arms—even bows and arrows—by an imperial law. Scholars, for whom Mongol life had little use except as potential administrators, were degraded; but merchants and business men were raised in status, for the Mongols, like all barbarians, understood the importance of barter, especially with bright novelties. 'Kublai had himself sown the seeds of decay, although they did not mature in his lifetime.' Absolute power had its usual corrupting effect. The last Mongol Emperor, Sun Ti, 'the Docile', is described by Tsui Chi as 'a superstitious, lustful, self-indulgent weakling', and it is not surprising that a popular revolt

captured China for the Ming Dynasty by 1368.

At the other end of their empire, the Mongols in the second half of the thirteenth century had hopes of forming an alliance with the Christians against their mutual enemies, the Mameluk sultans ruling Palestine and Egypt. These diplomatic moves might have led to the crushing of Islam between them; Europe had devoted centuries of effort to liberating the Holy Land by Crusades. The Mongols had a keen eye on the potential loot from the age-old cities of Egypt and may even have thought of extending their power along the North African coast. The appalling massacres and sacking of Baghdad and Aleppo in 1258 and 1260, by Hulagu of the Genghiz family, had temporarily made the Mongols a 'World Power' in the Near East, just as their invasions had in Europe twenty years before. They must have realised that they could destroy an empire but could not keep a big one in running order for long, and there must have been a conscious or unconscious feeling of inferiority beneath the aggressive arrogance so frequent in their letters to the rulers of civilised peoples.

But during the fourteenth century the Mongol princes of Persia were themselves being converted to Islam, and the international situation changed. Yet for several generations, the outcome hung in the balance.

One interesting Mongol initiative was the despatch of a group of Nestorian Christian monks who reached Italy and France in 1287–8 with the support of Arghon, the Tartar ruler of Persia. There is a description by one of them, Sawma, of the medieval courts of the Pope and others as seen by Oriental eyes. Sawma mentions his meeting with the King of England, Edward I, who was then in France.

VII

In the interior of Asia, the Mongol descendants of the Genghiz Dynasty managed to keep some power. But for several centuries there was a bitter struggle with a rival dynasty which claimed leadership of Asian nomadism based on the Turkic tribes of Russian Turkestan in South-Western Asia. Its notorious founder was Timur Lenk (Tamerlane), born *c.* 1336 near Samarkand. His ruthless rise to power resembled that of a gangster chief, and was like that of Genghiz himself. There were early years of obscurity and hardship, of gaining local support, and then the 'elimination' of his former patron and chief. With sustained hypocrisy, this cold-blooded fanatic had an insensate desire for power and loot. While claiming to be the destroyer of the enemies of Islam, he wrecked some of its richest civilised centres in Persia, North India and Syria.

When Timur defeated in 1391 his rival Tokhtamysh, who was one of the Genghiz Dynasty and who was increasing the power of the nomads named the Golden Horde in the plains round the Caspian, he set himself to the wholesale destruction of towns and tribal life (only Moslems were spared)—a death-dealing blow to the ancient trade routes between Europe and Asia. In India, too, he left no monument—except piles of skulls at Delhi. The self-satisfied conqueror had 120 court elephants paraded in front of him while he sat monopolising the ancient throne. In theory he came to fight brahmanism, but in practice his chief damage in India was done to Islam. He was willing, sometimes, to spare the lives of craftsmen to work on his palaces. But there is no doubt that this proud, ignorant boy from a Turkic family which had some degree of nobility (it is doubtful how much) became an insane megalomaniac—and that this unbalanced offshoot of the nomad world massacred hundreds of thousands of civilised men, women and children. Shortly before his death he was even planning an invasion of China for new booty. Few despots have been more destructive, and it is not surprising that when he died in 1405 his ephemeral 'empire' collapsed in family quarrels. Some generations later we find poets and dilettanti who were ruling at Samarkand, descendants of this bloodthirsty product of the Turkic steppes.

An important eye-witness description of the Mongols of the fourteenth century is that the famous Arab explorer Ibn Battuta, who journeyed from the Near East to China in the mid-fourteenth century. It is an impartial record of all he saw. Life was held cheap in Asia, massacres of unspeakable cruelty were frequent, cities were destroyed and others built at a despot's whim, works of art were savagely broken up but others were made quickly to satisfy a new ruler. Ibn Battuta himself, although accustomed to it, was continually sickened by so much senseless violence. 'We crossed the river Oxus,' he writes, 'and after a day and a half's march through a sandy uninhabited waste reached Balkh. It is a ruin but anyone seeing it would think it inhabited because of its solid construction. The accursed Chingiz destroyed it, and demolished one-third of its mosque because he was told that a treasure lay under one of its columns. He pulled down one-third and found nothing.' The huge city-mound of Balkh, one of the oldest and most important ancient sites in Asia, remains deserted to this day—to be a perpetual record of Asian steppe nomads long after they have ceased to exist.

VIII

A counter-offensive against the nomads now developed both from East and West. Towards the end of the fifteenth century,

Russian power was growing and expanding as a national state under Ivan the Great (1462–1505). He twice refused to pay tribute to a khan of the Golden Horde. Their armies met (1480), but the Khan withdrew, more or less confirming Russian independence. Among the marginal peoples in South Russia and South-West Asia, between the 'Steppe and the Sown', new and larger power-blocs of khanates were forming, as often happened in such zones where nomads overlapped with cultivators. Ivan the Terrible (1533–84) besieged Kazan and conquered this khanate and also that of Astrakhan (*see* Chapter 8). The use of firearms by Russians and the Chinese gave decisive superiority in counter-attack, though the Khanate of the Crimea founded in 1430 by a descendant of Batu survived until the end of the eighteenth century, and that of Khiva (south of the Aral Sea) also founded by a chief of the Genghiz Dynasty, lasted until late in the nineteenth.

Firearms and artillery put an end to the power of Asian nomadism as a world force, and to the civilised world's fear of invasion by the horsed archers. The Kalmouk archers which Alexander I was to have sent to fight Napoleon on the battlefield in 1807 would have seemed prehistoric. In three centuries, and for ever, the nomads, and most of the peoples on the margins of the Steppe and the Sown, became relatively powerless.

But while the chiefs of the Genghiz Dynasty were disappearing, various new claimants of the same descent continued to emerge from the obscurity of the more remote steppes and tried to replace them. In the fifteenth century, yet another tribe, the Oïrat of western Mongolia (called the Kalmouk by Turkic neighbours further west) showed ambitions to begin again the great imperial adventures of Genghiz. In 1449 they succeeded in capturing the Chinese Emperor himself, but after a century their power in Central Asia declined. The future centuries are a study of the 'decline and fall' of nomadism.

During the long decline of the Asian nomads as a major power, descendants of Cheïban (a grandson of Genghiz) ruled the zone north of the Aral Sea in the fifteenth–sixteenth centuries. Further east in the tribal homeland of Genghiz, a youth named Dayan made a fresh attempt at founding an empire. In a long reign (1470–1543) he reorganised the Mongol tribesmen on military lines, following the methods of Genghiz. But no world-shaking conquests followed. Conditions were changing. Later an Oïrat chief, Altan Khan carried warfare to the very gates of Pekin, while ruling his tribesmen between 1543–83. After his death family quarrels, as usual, destroyed unanimity. Also in the sixteenth century the nomads of eastern Mongolia were being converted to Tibetan Buddhism, and its effect was to emphasise the winning of souls and passivity instead of military ambition.

But during the sixteenth century the marginal communities produced many intelligent leaders. Far the most distinguished and important founder of a great dynasty, was the great Babur, who became Emperor of India having originated from a Turkic horde in Ferghana, a home of ancient cities in the mountain valleys around Samarkand and Tashkent. This brave ruler and genius had merits and intellectual curiosity which remind us of the Emperor Frederick II in thirteenth-century Europe. His origins were Turkic, but he also honoured the Mongol traditions of Genghiz. Babur's immortal autobiography shows a highly civilised mind at work. This was written in Chagatai Turki, the indigenous dialect of South-West Asia. Haïdamirza, his friend, who ruled in Turkestan, was a perfect example of a prince of Mongol descent who had been entirely transformed by his Persian upbringing. Between 1541–7 he wrote a history of the Mongols.

Another example of sophistication was given by the Manchus who conquered China in the mid-seventeenth century. In origin marginal barbarians north of the Great Wall, they were 'sinified' by contact with Chinese civilisation, and already by the end of the seventeenth century we find their great Emperor, K'ang-Hsi, busy with an offensive against the more primitive Mongols, using cannon and firearms with devastating effect.

At the same time, in the late seventeenth and early eighteenth centuries, Mongol tribes were making a final bid to become a major power. The Dzungar confederacy under Galdan and his successor, Tsewang Rabdan, attempted to form a primitive 'empire' in the Altai mountains in Central Asia, the wildest zone which remained. After many campaigns, a Manchu army occupied the heart of the region in 1757, and the Chinese re-settled the area with other Asian peoples.

Pressure from China and Russia and inter-tribal conflict produced big long-distance movements among the nomads of Central Asia in the seventeenth and eighteenth centuries, which set up ripples far and wide, and recall those in ancient times. For example, the Torghout left Dzungaria in 1616 and moved westward with 50,000 tents, reaching Astrakhan by 1643. But ill-treatment and stupidity by some Russian officials caused their return in another great wave.

On 5 January, 1771, more than 70,000 families set out. Although decimated on the way back, they reached Central Asia again and were re-settled by the Chinese. The Russian and Chinese empires now advanced steadily into the heart of traditional nomad territories, building a regular system of forts and colonies as they conquered. The Trans-Siberian railway, in the nineteenth century, consolidated their firm grip. Mongol nomads were much frightened by the gramophone, on first hearing it. Their role had declined from the world-shaking to the ridiculous.

One of the best accounts of the nomads was written by Huc and Gabet (ed. Pelliot) from their travels in 1844–6. They show the decadent state of Central Asia. There is a memorable description of a Mongol who arrived at their camp and respectfully addressed them as Lamas, i.e. learned men. 'Your country is a fine country.' The Mongol made no reply and shook his head sadly. 'Would it not be better to cultivate? Would not fine crops of corn be preferable to mere grass?' He replied, with a tone of deep and settled conviction: 'We Mongols are accustomed to living in tents, and pasturing cattle. When we kept to that we were rich and happy. When we cultivated the land we became poor. The Chinese took possession of the lands, and the flocks and houses have passed into their hands.'

The Mongols claimed that the Chinese sold them wine and tobacco at double their value, and took their flocks and lands for payment, and that justice could not be obtained from local Chinese courts. The travels of Huc and Gabet are full of examples of the anxieties of life on the steppes and in its rare towns. It was a mixture, as they said, both horrible and charming, and there are innumerable passages describing the ruthlessness of the period, and nomadic contacts with Chinese landgrabbers in the vital marginal areas. In 1870 Prejevalsky found the Mongols conservative, apathetic and lifeless. In the 1920s and 1930s the accounts given by Fleming, Lattimore, Skrine and others have first-hand evidence of the age-old continuity in life in spite of change. Later,

Ivor Montagu described in excellent detail the life of Mongol nomadism as it continues today. The People's Republic of Outer Mongolia is said to be seven times the area of Britain, but almost all is desert. The *yurts* continue, and also the *del* (the long dress buttoning on the right which marks a Mongol whether in Moscow or Peking).

In the middle of the nineteenth century legendary sagas of the Turkic nomads of the Yenisei area were written down by Russian scholars, and in *Gold Khan* we have a remarkable collection of their impressive but barbaric traditional poems which maintained direct continuation from the life of the ancient past. The singing of these sagas was more than an entertainment, it was almost a ritual. It was always at night, round the fire in the *yurts*, the nomad tent:

'At the foot of the white mountain,
At the edge of the white sea,

There Alten Khan of the blue stallion
Had set up his *yurts*
With his wife, Alten Areg.'

Very recently, some nomads have made a trans-Asian migration on the great scale of past movements. *The Times* correspondent (20 November, 1952) described the arrival of remnants of Kazakh Turkic tribes which reached safety in Turkey after a long migration. They left their homes in Turkestan and Sinkiang to escape persecution, but the original 18,000 were reduced to 2000; their leader was killed and they lost their thousands of cattle and all their belongings.

Strangely we see, in conclusion, the nomads achowledged as refugees and not as destroyers among civilisations. The question, as always, is: 'Where does barbarism begin and end?' The answer was given thousands of years ago: in the conscience of the individual.

10   THE WESTERN MIDDLE AGES

by Lionel Butler

While the Moslem civilisation developed, Byzantium carried on the tradition of Antiquity, Muscovy emerged, and the nomad empires were exploiting the periphery of the steppe, Western Christendom created a highly original culture. It was founded upon the ruins of the Western Empire, but its centre soon shifted north of the Alps, and it included areas of Europe never subdued by Rome. It contributed new qualities to Western civilisation and formed the base for European expansion in the fifteenth century.

II

The 'Middle Ages' describes the phase of Western European history which lies between Roman times and the modern era inaugurated by the Renaissance, the voyages of discovery, the Reformation, and the scientific revolution. In the eighteenth century historians regarded European civilisation as having passed through a formative classical epoch and a retrograde barbaric 'dark' interlude to an age of recovery and enlightenment. In recent generations a more sympathetic interest in the Middle Ages and closer study of their history have challenged and modified this interpretation. The roots of modern society have been shown to run much deeper into the medieval past than Gibbon's contemporaries realised. One result of reappraisal has been to make exact chronological boundaries dividing medieval from ancient and modern impossible to draw. The present survey takes 476 and 1492 as the limiting dates. Neither is

entirely satisfactory. But in 476 Western Europeans finally lost the political unity conferred on them by Rome; and in 1492, still disunited, they began the domination and exploitation of the continents across the oceans.

Geographically, the medieval West is easy to define and to distinguish from the Western Roman Empire. North Africa and for a time Spain were taken from it by the Arabs. But it included Scotland and Ireland, Scandinavia, Germany east of the Rhine, Poland, and Bohemia. These countries had never belonged to the Romans, who regarded them as part of the outer barbarian darkness beyond the Rhine-Danube frontier; but in the Middle Ages they shared in varying degrees a common civilisation with France, Italy, England and the other old imperial lands. The Roman economy had been Mediterranean. Outside the regions bordering the inland sea human settlement was still scanty in 476. In Central Europe, the Rhine Basin, northern Gaul, Britain and even Lombardy and northern Spain there were huge tracts of primeval forest, heath, and marsh. The clearing, draining, and reclaiming of this waste land—a task never seriously envisaged by the Romans—was undertaken vigorously, though by no means concluded, in the Middle Ages. The most important medieval contribution to the modern economy of Europe was to have claimed for the cultivator extensive areas of the heavy soils covered by 'damp oak' forest or drowned by the floods of great rivers.

The fall of the Roman Empire presents no mystery. From the third century A.D. its population and prosperity were in decline, its urban upper classes were steadily surrendering leadership to irresponsible military adventurers, its increasingly barbarised administration and army were draining the capital which was its life-blood. The surprise is that the Empire survived in the West until the fifth century and in the East until the fifteenth. The agents of its overthrow in the West were migrant barbarian Germans who had been pressing on the Roman frontier since the time of Marcus Aurelius. In the unkempt expanses of the German hinterland, from the Rhine to the Vistula and the Tisza, there was always as much perpetual movement of tribes as there was permanent settlement. The agrarian skill and sense of the Germans was as yet insufficiently developed to extract a greater yield from the soil, or to create new settlements in forest and swamp if the slender supply of open, dry, and accessible land was exhausted. Consequently each tribe always coveted its neighbour's lands. The Germans thought it dishonourable sloth for a man to work when he could plunder his neighbour. What they valued most were great herds: cattle-rustling was a main motive for all their wars. In the fifth century their craving for land and loot was sharpened by famine, which impelled the Vandals westwards, and by the steppe-nomads called Huns who invaded the settlements of the Goths and drove them towards the Roman frontier (*see* Chapter 9).

The last Roman Emperor of the West was dethroned in 476 by a German soldier of fortune in the imperial service. But this formal extinction of the Western Empire was little more than an event in local Italian politics. The crucial blows had been struck in the previous hundred years by the invading Germans, and Huns. The Rhine-Danube frontier had been broken down, and severe damage done to the communications, internal security, and urban amenities of the Empire. The Vandals from the Oder valley had conquered North Africa, wrecked its flourishing agriculture, and, by using it as a base for piracy, all but severed its links with Europe. In the course of the fifth century the German barbarians wrested other great provinces from the Empire. Roman Britain fell to the seafaring Anglo-Saxons. The Franks, most numerous and ablest of all the invaders, established themselves as the ruling class of northern Gaul, as did the Visigoths in southern Gaul and Spain. Italy itself was subjected to several barbarian descents. Theodoric the Ostrogoth got control of the peninsula in the years 488–93 and, ruling from Verona and Ravenna, made a heroic but blundering effort to preserve Roman methods of government and Roman culture as he understood them. The armies of the Eastern Emperor Justinian recovered Italy in the devastating Gothic war of 536–52, but could not retain it, and by 600 it was decisively in the hands of the savage and backward Lombards. All the lands of the Western Empire had now been parcelled out among the barbarians and their kings.

How much of the Roman heritage had perished by 600? The Roman citizenship and the rule of Roman Law had disappeared along with political unity. The links with the Eastern Empire had become attenuated. But the barbarians varied widely in their attitude to *Romanitas*. The Huns had rejoiced in destruction; and their nomad incapacity to settle was lucky for Europe. The Lombards looked on most things Roman with a surly brutal incomprehension. Yet many of the barbarians shared the outlook of Alaric, King of the Visigoths, whose ambition had been to preserve the Empire and obtain for himself a high military post in it and for his people a territory where they could settle as 'federates' of Rome and live by the labour of the Roman provincials. Even after the liquidation of the Western Empire the Frankish leader Clovis got himself made *consul* by the far-off Eastern Emperor, and strove to employ the old Roman administrative machine in the government of northern Gaul. But it cannot be denied that all the barbarians did appalling damage to urban life and trade by their simple greed for loot and their failure or reluctance to keep town walls, public buildings and baths, street-paving and sewers in repair. In the countryside they caused widespread damage less by their struggles with the Roman provincials than by their blood-feuds with each other. The memory of Rome and the desire to imitate its ways was strong among the barbarians; but their mental image of the classical world was always childish and grew more and more inaccurate with the passing of time. Unlike the Arabs who overthrew the Persian Empire they were too backward to assimilate the culture of the conquered. Trier, once the wealthy administrative capital of Roman Gaul, did not become a Frankish Baghdad.

What was the proportion of barbarians who settled in the Empire to Roman provincials who survived the invasions? The historical evidence is too meagre to give more than an approximate answer. But the picture is not uniform. The barbarians who established themselves as the new ruling nobility of Spain, southern Gaul, and Italy had all come in determined bands, probably a few thousand strong, from as far off as Silesia, the Hungarian Plain, and the Ukraine. But the Franks, who had lived along the lower Rhine for generations, were a populous migrant nation, who did not change their settlements so much as extend them to include the basins of the Scheldt, Meuse, Somme, and Seine. Though the Anglo-Saxon invasion of Britain was sea-borne, it seems to have been powerful enough to sweep the Romano-British provincials clean out of the east of the island. That the barbarians were nearly everywhere a minority, though politically dominant, is perhaps to be inferred from the evidence of language. Spain, Italy, and France were conquered by Germans, and yet the Romance languages spoken in those countries in the Middle Ages derived far more from Latin than they did from the Germanic tongues. The eventual linguistic frontier between French and German ran well west of the Rhine, and it is important to realise that it bisected the Frankish lands: which suggests that Frankish settlements among the Romano-Gaulish provincials were thickest on the ground near the Rhine and thinnest near the Loire. Archaeology confirms this impression. In the Anglo-Saxon parts of Britain a Germanic tongue came to be spoken exclusively, and presumably the intruders there were especially numerous and fierce.

It follows that in the so-called 'Dark Ages' of the West from 476 to 800 there grew up a society in which the immigrating barbarians, in most regions a minority, mingled with the surviving Roman provincial stocks. Each group made its contribution to the new civilisation which emerged. Medieval forest clearance and land reclamation north of the Alps owed much to the vigour of former barbarian peoples who had outgrown their primitive distaste for agriculture. More immediately the invaders maintained some degree of political organisation. Barbarian kingship and lordship and respect for customary law were the foundations of all the medieval states. But the most arresting achievement of the Dark Ages was the preservation of the Christian Church in the West, and for that the Roman provincials must be given much of the credit. Christianity had been the official though not the universal religion of the Empire, and the Pope, the Bishop of Rome, was patriarch over all Western Christians. Once again, there were various barbarian attitudes to the Latin Church. The pagan Anglo-Saxons obliterated Christianity in the parts of Britain they overran. The Franks were pagan too, but waged no kind of heathen holy war against Christians. In the fourth century missionaries from Constantinople had converted the Goths and many of the Lombards to Christianity, but had taught them to follow the Arian heresy, and the invading Arians, while not seeking to crush the Roman Church, nevertheless subjected it to intermittent persecution and despoliation. One sympton of the Church's resilience in the West was that its bishops, when Roman secular government was collapsing, led local resistance to the barbarians and negotiated with them on behalf of their flocks. Pope Leo I persuaded Attila to lead his Huns out of Italy.

By 700 the Church had won great victories. Those over paganism began early, when Clovis brought all the Franks with him into the Catholic Christian fold. As early as the mid-fifth century, St Patrick was converting the Irish; the conversion of the Anglo-Saxons began in 597, that of the Germans east of the Rhine in the seventh century. In Visigothic Spain and Lombard Italy the Arian heresy wilted before intensive Catholic missionary effort. The Church's whole struggle in the Dark Ages is epitomised by Pope Gregory I. Born in 540 into the old Roman senatorial class, Gregory was for a time Rome's prefect, and later (590–604) its bishop. His life, spent 'among the swords of the Lombards', was devoted to nursing the growing monasticism of Italy, protect-

ing and developing the papal estates, upholding the papacy's claims against the patriarchate of Constantinople, bringing the churches of the West into closer touch with Rome, combating Arianism, superintending the conversion of heathen England. His achievements foreshadow those of all the great medieval popes.

The clergy of Gregory's day—and many of them had little or no contact with Rome —consciously strove to carry over classical learning into a new age and to teach the barbarians to abandon their purely oral culture for literacy. Under ecclesiastical guidance the great barbarian law-codes, deriving from a common Germanic past, were written down in a form bearing traces of the humane and sophisticated influences of Christianity and Roman Law.

Until the eleventh century the West remained under pressure from without. In 711 an Arab army entered Spain, overthrew the Visigothic kingdom and established a Moslem state, which embraced the southern olive-growing two-thirds of the Peninsula (*see* Chapter 7). Tolerant of the Christians they ruled and reluctant to acquire the bleak fastnesses of Cantabrian and Pyrenean Spain, where a few Christian princes clung to independence, the Arabs created for themselves the conditions which led to the eventual Christian reconquest of Spain, which had its slow beginnings in the eleventh century. Meanwhile new blood was regularly transfused into Moslem Spain by the migrations of fierce Berber groups from North Africa. The Arabs conquered Sicily in the ninth century, and in the tenth their free-booters were the plague of the Western Mediterranean. One great historian, Pirenne, has contended that Mediterranean trade, which flourished under Roman rule, suffered little damage before the Arab conquests, which he thought caused a sudden total eclipse of urban life and commerce in the West and produced there a subsistence economy, without markets and centred upon great estates. More probably the Arabs were only continuing a process begun by the Germanic invaders in the fifth century.

The West was also intermittently exposed to the marauding of nomadic horsemen, who rode out of the steppes, crossed the Carpathians, and used the Hungarian Alföld as their base and gigantic corral. The Huns, who entered Hungary in 406, melted away into Asia sixty years later. Nor did the Avars, arriving in 568, attempt to settle as cultivators. But they raided Germany, Italy, and Gaul for generations, and opened a path for the settlement of Slavs in the Balkans, Poland, Bohemia and much of Hungary itself. The Franks crushed the decadent remnants of the Avars in 791, but within a century the Magyars had crossed the Carpathians, and after sixty years of raiding Europe, settled, with a feeling for permanency rare in the true nomad, as the dominant class in a partly-Slav Hungary which became a Christian kingdom, under the rule of St Stephen, by 1000, and was to be a Catholic bulwark of Christendom against the Mongols and the Ottoman Turks.

About 780 the Scandinavian pirates called Vikings began their depredations. The Vikings had developed ships, navigational techniques and weapons superior to those of their Christian neighbours. Their fleets were well organised, and they profited from the element of surprise in naval attack. Their demand was for tribute, especially silver. If refused, they replied by looting and burning the monasteries and churches, fair game to them as pagans. Recent research suggests that the monastic chroniclers were prone to exaggerate the scale of the Viking raids and the devastation they caused. Nevertheless, the Vikings inflicted serious damage on church life and town life over wide areas of Western Europe, and they kept up their pressures, intermittently, for three centuries. By 830 they were looking for land as well as plunder, and in the next hundred years Scandinavian colonists—warriors, merchants, farmers, fishers—established themselves in strength in many parts of the British Isles, northern France, as far west as Iceland and Greenland, and as far east as Kiev on the Dnieper. (Possibly, but not certainly, Norse seafarers reached North America.) But every permanent settlement the vikings made was eventually absorbed into an existing state. Normandy, their most significant acquisition (911), was held as a duchy of the French kingdom, and the Normans who set forth from it in the eleventh century to conquer England, South Italy and Sicily, and the crusader principality of Antioch, were Christian by faith and of mixed Frankish-Scandinavian descent. By the close of the Viking era Denmark, Norway and Sweden had been drawn into the family of Christian kingdoms.

Arabs, steppe nomads, and Vikings were either absorbed or in some way stopped short by the society they were attacking. The most important though not the only key to this Western success is probably the history of the Frankish nobility which by the eighth century had established itself as the ruling class all over ancient Roman Gaul and was planting colonies—and, with the aid of Anglo-Saxon and Irish missionaries, churches—in the pagan lands of central and southern Germany. The Franks had already begun the expansion of their arable land and their prosperity was based squarely on agriculture. The axis of Western Europe was being turned away from the Mediterranean towards the north, where Frankish wealth and power were to do much to save the West.

III

In 751, Pepin the Short, head of the great noble house of the Carolingians, whose ancestral estates lay in Brabant and the Ardennes, violently usurped the kingship of all the Franks. His son Charlemagne (768–814), led his Franks to a spectacular series of conquests. He subjected and forcibly converted the pagan Saxons of north-western Germany; overthrew the Lombard kingdom of Italy; and united the entire Christian continental West under his rule. His frontiers marched with those of the Arabs, the Danes, the Slavs, and the Byzantine Empire. In 800 Charlemagne assumed the Roman titles of *imperator* and *augustus*, the Pope 'adoring' him as Emperor at Rome. His close alliance with the clergy, in an age of revival in scholarship and the arts, is the background to this event. But his empire lacked the Roman features of a universal law, a common citizenship, a highly professional bureaucracy, and a regular revenue. Little held together its heterogeneity but the common interest of the Frankish nobility and clergy in exploiting it under Carolingian leadership; and in 843 Charlemagne's three grandsons partitioned it. North of the Alps they carved out three kingdoms: France, Germany, and a rich 'middle kingdom' which had no geographical unity, and was soon to disintegrate. The inadequacy and bitter quarrels of Charlemagne's descendants caused them too often to leave to the nobility the tasks of organising local defence against Vikings, Magyars, and Arabs. By 900 the balance of power in the Frankish world had swung from monarchy to the territorial aristocracy. But Charlemagne had already become a legend and was to be celebrated as the ideal Christian warrior King in the eleventh-century *Song of Roland*, and other poems. Most medieval rulers wanted to be like Charlemagne. In sheer power he was the mightiest of them all; in him can be detected most of the characteristics of successful medieval kingship; and with the origins of feudalism he and his nobles had special connections.

Feudalism grew out of two Frankish institutions: *commendatio*, whereby a man put himself under the protection of a powerful lord and agreed to serve him as his vassal, while keeping his freedom; and the *beneficium*, an estate held of a lord in return for a small rent or no rent at all. In the eighth century many men commended themselves to the Carolingians, who needed large military forces. A high proportion of these vassals received benefices, and of the services they performed in return, military service as an armoured cavalryman—eventually known as *chevalier* or knight—was the most important. Established noblemen and rising military adventurers were alike drawn into the vassal class. Charlemagne required all his high officers, his dukes, marquesses, and counts, to become vassals, and the royal vassals in their turn acquired vassals of their own and granted them benefices. This strengthened the hand of the royal magnates against the Crown, and made rebellion easier; but their own vassalage continued to bind them to the king even though the weakening of monarchy after 843 had allowed them to become almost independent princes.

The feudal contact was established by the ceremonial act of homage and the solemn oath of fealty, which bound the vassal to give his lord his loyalty and counsel; his military service and in some instances that of a fixed number of knights to be provided by him; and a money *aid* when the lord knighted his eldest son, married his eldest daughter, or required to be ransomed from captivity. The lord's duty was to protect the vassal's life, limb, and secure possession of his benefice—

more commonly known as the fief or *feudum*: hence the epithet feudal which lawyers used to connote this form of land tenure. Fiefs, originally granted for life, eventually became hereditary. The heir to a fief, usually the eldest son, did homage, swore fealty, and paid a 'relief' before he could be invested with it. The heritable fief also became alienable, and it could be granted by the vassal to a vassal of his own. In default of male heirs it might be divided among co-heiresses. Consequently the feudal tenement as small as one sixty-fourth of a knight's *feudum* could occur; or it might be a large complex of fiefs, treated as a single *barony* held of the Crown by a great vassal who owed the service of many knights and had been granted high judicial powers. The vassal was justiciable in his lord's court; his recalcitrance was visited by distraint and ultimately forfeit-ure; and his recognised weapons against bad lordship were renunciation of homage and armed resistance.

Feudal institutions eventually spread widely over all the lands Charlemagne had ruled. They were taken into England and Scotland and southern Italy by the Normans, and deep into Spain by the *Reconquista*. Many lesser landowners, des-pairing of royal protection against oppres-sive neighbours or Viking raiders, com-mended themselves to powerful local lords, to whom they would surrender their land, receiving it back in feudal tenure.

Basically feudalism was the same every-where, but its practical working from region to region displayed endless variety. France was the most highly feudalised country. Before 1200, outside the narrow limits of the royal estates, the French king exercised more power as feudal suzerain over his vassals than as sovereign over his subjects. The higher French nobility like-wise relied on their feudal rights to rule

their duchies and counties. The thirteenth-century French kings energetically exploi-ted their feudal suzerainty to reduce the power of these great vassals and bring their lands more directly under royal supervi-sion. In Germany feudalism was a pyramid at the apex of which stood the territorial princes, and despite strenuous efforts in the twelfth century the monarchy never secured firm control of it. In England the Norman kings deliberately developed feudal institutions to strengthen their hold on their barons, forbidding them private wars with each other, restricting their castle-building and their judicial powers, keeping considerable control of the barons' relations with their own vassals, and confiscating the estates of rebels without mercy.

As the Middle Ages wore on, the feudal organisation of society and politics under-went radical transformation. In France after 1300 the king held power more and more as sovereign than as feudal suzerain. In England the royal armies had always been in part mercenary and with Edward I's Welsh wars (1277–95) and Edward III's invasions of France (1338–60) the feudal method of raising troops finally became obsolete. The ties binding lord and man were once more changing in charac-ter. The lord of a late medieval English 'bastard feudal affinity' was looked to by his followers to provide them with the cash annuities and other payments called *livery*, and to give them the special assis-tance in the courts of law known as *maintenance*. The Black Prince's soldiers at Poitiers in 1356, who robbed and held to ransom the richest lords in Europe, had been mustered not by the obligations of feudal tenure, but by the promise of daily wages and a share of the spoils. When Edward of York seized the English throne by force from Henry VI in 1461, it was greed for the profits of political success that had rallied most of his supporters to him. In several parts of Europe after 1200 fortunes made in industry and trade were being invested in land. Venetian merchants who bought estates on the *terra firma* were in no sense entering upon feudal contracts. These are only examples of late medieval changes which historians have yet to reconstruct and explain as fully as they have explained the earlier history of feudalism.

Historically more important than the military purpose of feudalism was its fundamental principle that property was something in which the claims and interests of two persons could be combined—the rights and duties of both lord and tenant. Roman Law had conceived of ownership as an absolute and indivisible right. Medieval custom split it into two rights, each balancing the other. There can be no better instance of the radical changes which had occurred in the nature of law in the West.

From the fifth century two streams of law had run parallel: the Roman Civil Law and barbarian custom. Theodoric, for example, had allowed the conquered populace of Italy to live under Roman Law, while his Ostrogoths observed their own customary law. But by 900 the West had fallen back to a stage of social development far behind that of the Roman world. Roman Law was reduced in practice to its most elementary and easily intelligible precepts, and often forgotten altogether. Medieval customary law, which prevailed everywhere, upheld not the natural equality of man but the stability of rights and duties. Every social group, however lowly, claimed to be ruled not by arbitrary power but by custom, that is, by its own peculiar habits and notions, which it might be called on to state in a law-court. Classes which seemed to be at the mercy of ruthless masters preserved many of their customary rights. The jurist Bracton maintained that whatever the English *villein* possessed was his lord's except his belly. But in practice the *villein's* right to his arable holding and his share of pasture and waste was enshrined in the custom of the manor, which might be infringed, but was generally respected. His *seisin* of his land—the fact of his working it and harvesting it—created a presumption of title which could be overset by proof of a better title, but was *prima facie* protected by the court. The customary doctrine of *seisin* was remote from the idea of ownership in Roman Law.

But medieval society was to recover its lost knowledge of Roman Law, as it recovered other parts of the classical heritage. In the twelfth century jurisconsults at the University of Bologna were enthusiastically studying Justinian's *Corpus Juris* and pouring out commentaries on it. In their eyes the inner harmony and logic of Roman Law, its notion of equity, and its claim to the allegiance of all Christians, made it superior to even the most advanced customary law. The contemporary movement to study and codify the Canon Law of the Church enriched Civil Law studies and was in turn complemented by them. Roman Law flowed from the universities to the courts and everywhere came into conflict with customary law. In France, it stifled the growth of custom in the south, and became in the north an auxiliary law, a reservoir of solutions to problems custom could not deal with, such as the demand for an elaborate law of debt which expanding trade called forth. In England the customary or Common Law was emphatically victorious. Yet in all countries—even Italy and Germany where local separatism was strongest—jurists were learning a new exactitude and courts improving their primitive procedures under the influence of the Civil Law. The codification of feudal custom owed much to Roman Law logic and technique.

IV

Medieval writers often saw society as divided into three groups: the warriors who governed and protected it; the workers by whose labours it was fed; and the clerks, who prayed for the salvation of men's souls. This classification, though it has naïve features, provides a convenient pattern for any brief survey. To begin with, the medieval ruling class was a warrior aristocracy. In the three centuries from Charlemagne to the Crusades the West came to be dominated by the feudal knight: the mounted man clad in steel, living in his private fortress. The knights formed an élite because they were indispensable to every army and ever more expensive to mount and equip and train. The lord of a landed estate was himself a knight, kept knights in his household, and made knights of his principal tenants. In the tenth century his private residence was fortified with a wooden tower on a mound and a wooden stockade crowning an earthen rampart. This primitive 'motte-and-bailey' had changed by 1200 into the stone castle which thereafter developed increasingly costly and elaborate features (the concentric plan, curtain walls, flanking towers and barbicans) to contend with the improved siege techniques of the time. Not every lord lived in a castle, but at least he had a crenellated manor-house to overawe the countryside. The nobility became increasingly hierarchic within itself; its code of chivalric behaviour grew more elaborate and esoteric, its consciousness of pedigree sharper, its *largesse* and passion for extravagence more conspicuous. The Norman barons at Hastings in 1066 wore for armour an iron mesh stitched on leather and had the crudest of primitive devices painted on their shields.

The French nobles at Agincourt in 1415 covered themselves with flexible suits of inlaid steel plate and their shields displayed their ancestry in precise and intelligible symbolism. The nobility in Castile preserved itself as a blue-blooded and rigidly stratified caste, whereas in England prosperous minor landowners and royal officials often rose to be barons and even earls. An extreme example is the De La Pole family, Yorkshire wool merchants in the thirteenth century, moneylenders and knights in the fourteenth, Dukes of Suffolk in the fifteenth. In Germany the *ministeriales* of the Salian kings were professional soldier-administrators, recruited from servile families and treading a rapid path to the highest ranks of feudal society. But in every circumstance the warrior nobility kept control throughout the Middle Ages. The places where its power was broken—Florence, Switzerland—or fundamentally challenged—the Flanders of Peit and Zannequin and the Arteveldes in the fourteenth century—were few and isolated. One source of its control was the steady monopolising of military power. When the long-bow and the cannon began to change the character of war, the nobility hastened to equip itself with these weapons. And it constantly absorbed into its ranks the successful soldier of fortune. The Marshal family were menials of the royal household who rose to be Earls of Pembroke; the Hohenstaufen emperors of Germany were once obscure counts with a couple of castles in Swabia; the first Sforza Duke of Milan was a mercenary captain. All rose by the exercise of outstanding military and administrative gifts. The nobility's main resource was territorial lordship. As a class it retained the great estates of which it had possessed itself in Carolingian times. The nobleman might be a keen exploiter of his estates by direct farming. He might lease out his demesne and live exclusively on rents and feudal dues and services and the profits of justice. The need to administer his landed interests at all times made him businesslike, wary, and litigious. The extravagances of chivalric behaviour need not blind us to the fact that the average medieval baron had a hard head under his fine helmet.

There is always the danger that the predominance of a warrior class will lead to a war of all against all and a general social breakdown. And admittedly private war among the baronage was an intermittent scourge of every medieval land. But ingrained in the feudal classes were an ultimate respect for the customary law already discussed and a belief in monarchy. In the later eleventh century a series of knightly adventurers from northern France were winning glittering conquests by the sword. England fell to William of Normandy; Portugal to Raymond of Burgundy; Sicily to the Norman family of Hauteville; Palestine to the Frankish crusaders. In each, the conquerors established or preserved monarchical government, and by 1200 England and Sicily were Europe's most centralised monarchies.

In the Roman Empire the people had been the acknowledged source of sovereignty, but in the interest and the name of all the Emperor had wielded unlimited power. The medieval monarchies were not strictly successor states of the Empire, for they originated in the tie of loyalty which bound the migrant barbarian nation to its *rex,* and in the early Middle Ages they rested on a foundation of personal fealty. The king was as a judge, interpreting a system of customary rights and duties which he was bound to uphold. The concept of the sovereign state reappeared with the renaissance of Roman Law which coincided with a general strengthening of royal power in the kingdoms of the West. But nowhere was monarchy allowed to become absolute.

By 1200 nearly a score of monarchies had emerged in the West. France, Hungary, Bohemia, Poland, Sweden, Norway, and Denmark had acquired most of the territorial framework of the modern nation-states which have succeeded them. The Angevin kings ruled England and Ireland and were mastering the Celtic element in Wales, though the kingdom of the Scots survived all their attacks. In the Iberian peninsula several Christian monarchies, each with its own culture and customary law, were pushing their frontiers south. The Norman monarchy of South Italy and Sicily reached full stature in 1130. Lastly, Germany, the old 'middle kingdom' of 843, and North Italy formed the territories of the Emperor of the West.

Created in 962, under the Saxon Otto I, the German Empire had some resemblance to that of Charlemagne, though it never included France and none of the German dynasties which ruled it was Frankish. In Germany the emperors were only intermittently able to establish a broad enough domain of royal estates to give their power a solid foundation. At times the presence or proximity of the itinerant Emperor and his household was needed to make imperial authority effective. And since the ablest of the emperors were pre-occupied with Italy, Germany was often neglected. The independent spirit of the rising cities of Lombardy and papal resentment of imperial intrusion frustrated any continuous growth of imperial power in Italy. In Germany, although Frederick Barbarossa (1152–90), among others, achieved much success in disciplining the nobility and developing the royal estates, the forces of localism and the great size of the country hampered the growth of a strong feudal monarchy.

After the death of Frederick II—*stupor mundi*—in 1250 the German Empire was universal only in dreams. Its rulers rarely visited Italy, and in Germany the Emperor was little more than a territorial prince, a Habsburg or Luxemburg, elected by other territorial princes to be the arbiter of their disputes.

The medieval kings ruled much as the emperors ruled, though none of them claimed a universal authority, and none was ever strong enough to upset the general balance of power. The highly centralised and well-armed Sicilian Kingdom never seriously encroached on the rest of Italy. The later Capet kings of France (1180–1328) had a certain predominance in Europe, but their Valois successors could not stop the English nobility from ransacking the country in the Hundred Years' War. Wars of conquest were rarely attempted without at least the pretext of dynastic right, and Charlemagne's continental ascendancy was never repeated. The most important political changes in Europe after the end of the barbarian invasions were the Christian reconquest of Spain and the huge extension of the area of German settlement and government east of the Elbe. The historic problem of German minorities among the Czechs and Poles was created in the twelfth century, but by peaceful infiltration, not conquest.

The king was feudal suzerain in his kingdom. The nobility never conceived of a kingless state. But they were as resentful of 'over-government' as they were fearful of the anarchy produced by 'lack of governance', and strove to keep the king *primus inter pares*. Yet the king was also a political sovereign with rights and duties lying outside the feudal sphere: the duty, for example, of overriding private jurisdiction if the 'utility of the realm' demanded it. Institutions like the chancery, exchequer, and judicature which, to begin with, were domestic departments of the royal household and were connected with the king's feudal rights and revenues, came to be expressions of sovereignty too. But that sovereignty, though increasing its scope of operations in France, Aragon, England, Sicily, and elsewhere after 1200, was nowhere as extensive or effective as modern public authority.

For monarchy was limited, partly because of documents like the English Magna Carta, which sought to define its powers, and by defining, restricted; but chiefly because of certain weaknesses inherent in a dynastic system. The vital principles of primogeniture and the indivisibility of the kingdom took centuries to establish. But disputed successions continued to cause civil upheavals like the English Wars of the Roses. Royal rights were prone to be encroached upon when the king was a boy. The minority of James I saw a serious whittling down of royal resources in Aragon. That some kings, like Louis IX of France, came to the throne as infants and were able in manhood to take up royal power relatively unimpaired says much for the sense of political duty of their subjects. Strong government depended on the king's character and physical stamina far more than at a later era. For no kingdom was a 'police-state' and the personal fear of the king was the beginning of civil peace. To secure general obedience to the law was policy enough to preoccupy the strongest ruler.

In many respects the king's most valuable support came from the clergy, who with their unprotected churches and estates had a special interest in civil peace and a duty to preach it. Working for the unity of Christendom, they naturally desired the unity of the kingdom. The clergy crowned and anointed the king. They staffed his chancery and other offices of state. And he used his influence to procure bishoprics and rich benefices for his clerks. Many bishops and other church dignitaries were royal nominees and devoted upholders of royal power.

Royal relations with the barons were more complex. Political disputes and civil wars never saw the whole nobility united against the Crown. There was always a party of 'king's friends'—royal cadets, barons holding high office in the royal household, noble families with a tradition of friendship to the Crown. The barons rarely wanted the lasting responsibilities of ministerial office, preferring to live on their estates, to hunt, to tourney, and to pursue military adventures abroad. The warrior kings who could lead the chivalry on successful campaigns found them more docile than did the peace-loving kings who stayed at home. But the barons demanded a voice at the king's council, for they were his 'natural counsellors', and resented being ousted by professional lay counsellors, such as the legists of Philip the Fair of France, who were usually recruited from the minor nobility, but blackened as *novissimi* and *vilissimi* if they were too efficient and influential. How to control his council and household, while giving the barons his confidence and keeping theirs, was the king's most awkward problem.

Did the Middle Ages give birth to nationalism or the nation-state? By 1450 Frenchmen had certainly identified the English as their common enemy. But xenophobia, which was rife everywhere in the Middle Ages, is only a part of national sentiment, and the French provinces were still divided by profound social and cultural dissimilarities. The union of Spain in 1474 and the exclusion of Portugal from that union were both dynastic accidents. In 1492 the Inquisition was still Spain's only common institution. England

may legitimately be called a nation by the end of the fifteenth century, but the political division of Great Britain endured until 1707. From 1435 to 1477 the wealthiest European ruler was the Duke of Burgundy who ruled the Low Countries and important territories now in France or Germany. The Burgundian state was the product of dynastic marriages. Lacking a common economic structure and a common political interest, it was held together by a purely personal tie and when Duke Charles the Bold died it was again divided. Yet some of the foundations on which the nation-states arose had been laid by 1500. The deeper linguistic divisions in England, France, Spain, and Italy were being overcome by the use in each of a pre-dominant dialect for commercial, administrative, and many other purposes; and much of the political and institutional heritage of modern Europe was bequeathed by the medieval state: above all the notion of the rule of law, and the practice of monarchy whether limited or despotic. In France the king's formal right to raise taxes and make war without consulting the Estates-General was secured by a late medieval ruler, Louis XI, who thereby foreshadowed Louis XIV. The standing army, as distinct from the feudal host and the mercenary company, made its first appearance in fifteenth-century France.

The modern British Constitution is unique in having grown continuously, without violent breaks, from a medieval forerunner. The distinction between King and Crown, the ability of the royal council to throw off judicial institutions of an equitable kind, such as the Star Chamber, the vitality of English Common Law and the practice of local 'self-government at the king's command' were features of medieval public life which played an essential role in later constitutional development; and the English Parliament had a long medieval history. Originally it was a solemn session of the Crown in Council, afforced by elected representatives of the shire-knights and burgesses, and thus constituting the highest court in the land. The Commons came to be regularly summoned to its meetings because the profits of the royal estates, justice, and feudal lordship, and other traditional revenues were inadequate to finance the monarch's frequent wars, and new taxation might not be levied without the consent of the subject; and so extraordinary supplies had to be raised in Parliament. By the fifteenth century it was only in Parliament that the English Crown could legislate and raise new taxes; Parliament had more than once been the theatre for successful attacks on the king's ministers; and the Commons secured redress of grievance before supply, and even claimed to audit the royal accounts. Elsewhere in Europe the late medieval 'parliamentary experiment' had less fruitful results. The French Estates-General secured no permanent footing in the Constitution. And by 1500 the power of the ruler was hardening against the Territorial Diets in Germany and the *Cortes* in Castile.

V

Exact statistics of population cannot be given for the medieval West, but it is probable that the ratio of population in 1300 to that in 1970 was hardly so much as 1 : 10. Nine-tenths of medieval people lived and worked on the land, where productivity was low. Ignorance of fodder root-crops and cultivated grasses denied beasts adequate grazing in summer and hay and fodder in winter. Nor were there ever enough animals to provide the manure to sustain a high fertility of soil. Farm-animals were lean, rangy, and tough. Those not wanted for breeding were slaughtered in autumn. The most

useful food producer was the pig, which fended for itself at all seasons. The peasant fed on bread, bacon and cabbage; leeks and lentils; rough game and fish. The margin between him and hunger was always narrow. In a lean year he starved.

No safe estimate can be made of the proportions of free peasants to unfree at any given period of the Middle Ages. By 1100 the peasants in France were almost universally unfree. Years of Viking attack and later of baronial warfare had driven them to buy the protection of the powerful at the price of personal and economic serfdom. In Spain, from 1000 to 1300, the reconquest created a large class of peasants who owned the land they farmed, but the violence of the upper classes drove many of them into unfreedom. Yet in some regions, such as Saxony and East Anglia, a free peasantry was strongly rooted; and freemen were numerous where villages were small and scattered, or where human settlement had only begun with the great colonising drive of the twelfth and thirteenth centuries. Most peasant freemen were tenants, paying rents to their lords, owing them various services, and subject to their jurisdiction, but free of compulsory labour services and free to sell their tenancies and depart at will. Freedom meant little more than the reduction or abolition of burdens. It could be bought, and it might be given to all the peasants of an estate or a region as an act of piety or government policy. The unfree peasant or villein probably objected little to the compulsion to stay on his land. What he valued most was the hereditary right to its use: the poorest tenant of land, however unfree, stood on a higher rung of the social and economic ladder than the landless day-labourer and farm-servant.

Two major types of agrarian settlement were widespread in Europe. In the North European plain, the lowland zone of

England, and southern Sweden the 'nucleated' village, compact and large, adapted to an economy centred upon the tilling of the soil, was most common. Scarcity of water-supply and the needs of local defence occasioned much nucleation. The 'dispersed' village—a group of hamlets or single homesteads—was most often found in the more mountainous parts, where the emphasis was on pasture: northern England, Wales, Brittany, the Massif Central, the Pyrenees, the Alps, the mountains of Central Europe and the highlands of Norway and Scotland. Both types of settlement were common in Italy, Spain, and southern France.

The nucleated village usually had two or three arable fields, cultivated in rotation. Where there were three fields, one would grow winter corn, the second spring corn, and the third would lie fallow. Probably all villages had originally used the two-field system, in which each field lay fallow in alternate years. The three-field system seems to have first developed on the estates of the Frankish kings and of the great abbeys of northern France in the eighth century. The two-course rotation gave the soil maximum rest and preserved its moisture. Hence it was the normal Mediterranean rotation until modern times. The three-course rotation, with its two harvests a year, reduced the risk of a poor year's production caused by bad weather, and enabled that risk to be spread more evenly over the year.

The English manor, which might coincide with the village or be only part of it, conveniently illustrates the three-field system. The peasant normally held a *yardland* of thirty acres, distributed in scattered strips in the three open fields. He farmed according to the 'custom', or routine, of the manor. One open field was left fallow all the year, and beasts were grazed on it. The two cultivated fields

were fenced for the year. The peasant had a share of the hay-meadow. In the waste he pastured his beasts and got timber, firewood and peat; reeds, salt, and fish; the rabbit and the wood-pigeon. Mingled with his strips in the open fields were the strips retained by the lord of the manor for himself—the *demesne*. Each unfree peasant household owed regular labour-services to the *demesne*. At mowing-time, reaping-time and other busy seasons, *boonwork* was also required and was exacted not only from the unfree but also from the free peasants, who occupied their lands in return for rent. The unfree peasant was tied to the soil; paid his lord an arbitrarily levied tax, or *tallage,* and a fine called *merchet* on his daughter's marriage; ground his corn at his lord's mill, and paid for the privilege; and after death yielded the lord his best beast as *heriot*. These obligations were fixed, as his hereditary tenure was secured, in the manorial court, which safeguarded the 'custom of the manor', policed the neighbourhood, and dealt with petty misdemeanours.

Numerous variations on the 'typical' manor described above may be traced in England itself, as well as on the Continent. The social structures and field systems of 'dispersed' villages or hamlets were equally diverse. But despite the variety of field-patterns and types of settlement, the medieval European was usually engaged in unspecialised farming, with such important exceptions as the intensive production for an international market of wool in England and Spain, wine in Gascony, and vegetable dye-stuffs in Lombardy.

The basic agricultural implement in the open-field village was a heavy plough which alone would turn over the heavy soils of Northern Europe. Its use dictated the great length of the arable strips and the practice of ploughing in common: for both the plough and its team of four or eight oxen were too expensive for the individual peasant. The use of the wheeled plough (*caruca*), which probably originated in the never-Romanised hinterland of Germany, spread steadily in medieval Europe, though the wheelless Roman *aratrum*, more flexible where the *caruca* was more powerful, was never driven off the lighter soils of the Mediterranean lands, nor altogether supplanted elsewhere. About 1050 the introduction from Asia of the stiff horse-collar made it possible to plough with horse or mule. This innovation became widespread in Europe. Yet the ox, far slower and less efficient than the horse, but healthier, and cheaper to feed and harness, continued to do much of the ploughing—in Italy nearly all of it.

The history of the plough epitomises the technical history of medieval agriculture. Change was usually slow, and often resisted, but it could be radical and it met with a remarkable degree of acceptance. If there was no systematic or controlled breeding of farmstock, the horse, because of its military value, was bred with special care on the great estates. If soil chemistry was little studied or understood, marling was a medieval innovation. Forests, in spite of the heavy dependence of medieval men upon timber, were regarded less as a place for rationalised timber production than as a vast grazing-ground. It was not until the thirteenth century that even the commonest fruit trees were cultivated with care and on a large scale. Yet hops and oats were first brought under cultivation in medieval Europe; irrigation and horticulture were greatly extended and improved; and the windmill, the greenhouse, the coulter, and—most remarkable of all—the three-course rotation were medieval inventions. Agriculture and rural society were often sluggish, but they were nowhere standardised and never static.

The period 1100–1350 saw a great extension of the area of human settlement and cultivation. One striking example of this process was the advance of German conquerors and settlers into the lands of the pagan Slavs between the Elbe and the Oder. The lay nobles who subdued this region attracted to it peasants in large numbers from western Germany and the Low Countries. Lured by the prospect of a house and forty acres of arable at a modest rent, with abundant pasture and a good deal of freedom, the pioneer peasant brought to these eastern lands for the first time the heavy plough with wheels, mould-board, and iron share; the three-course rotation; and the cultivation of wheat—as well as such minor novelties as the vine and the water-mill. A poor region of Europe became relatively rich, even though much of it remained boggy or sandy until modern times. Everywhere else in Europe marshes were being drained, forests cleared, lands devastated by feudal warfare reclaimed. In Spain the progressive reconquest of the Peninsula from the Moslems stimulated colonisation. The long struggle to give fertility to the plain of the Po and inland Tuscany began in the twelfth century. Less spectacular, but no less rewarding, was the steady pressure by many a rustic community in older areas of settlement—Kent, the Ile-de-France, the Mosel valley—to expand its arable, meadow, and pasture. The initiative and leadership in this great colonising movement came above all from the lay nobility and the Church. Between 1112 and 1152 the Cistercian Order of monks founded no less than 328 monasteries 'in the wilderness'. Each foundation meant a victory over marsh, forest, heath, won by monks athirst for the ascetic ideal and peasants hungry for land.

After 1350 expansion was followed by stagnation and contraction. The causes of this recession are still obscure, though they certainly include pestilence, especially the Black Death (bubonic plague), which reached Europe from Asia in 1348; wars such as the Hundred Years' War between England and France, and the Hussite Wars in Bohemia; falling prices; and a general decline in population. Abandoned holdings and depopulated villages appeared, emphasising the loss of the old prosperity. Not until well into the next century did recovery begin. To a modern observer the landscapes of 1500, though considerably tamed by medieval pioneers, would still look wild.

VI

After the fall of the Western Empire, European commerce and industry generally declined. A modest recovery under the Carolingians had been reversed by the Vikings, who did great damage to the towns. But the Vikings were vigorous traders and explorers and later helped to produce a widespread revival after their worst attacks were over.

This revival probably began with improved agricultural conditions. Landlord and peasants needed a safe market where they could sell their produce and buy the many manufactured articles the farmer needed. The towns were thus centres of local trade and local administration; and they supplied the needs of well-to-do consumers living within their walls. Medieval Ghent, for instance, grew up round the castle of the Counts of Flanders and the abbeys of St Peter and St Baaf. West of the Rhine, most of the important towns were on Roman sites, except in Flanders, where the urban population was very large but only Tournai had a Roman past. Medieval towns—including those that grew up east of the Rhine from the overgrown villages which were old tribal capitals—were almost always built near navigable water.

All over twelfth-century Europe the towns were growing more prosperous and populous—in great part because of the immigration of peasants—and they were becoming more self confident: the citizens of many a town were now approaching the king for a royal charter, which had to be paid for, licensing them to unite in a single *commune*, with its own town hall, courts of law, and dependent territory outside the walls; and to regulate their industries and trades, organising them into guilds which controlled manufacturing standards, prices, and working hours. The commune was a monopolistic organisation: all marketing must be carried on under its aegis, all manufacture under that of its guilds. The peasant who came to live in the town was not free to work or trade unless he obtained a property qualification and bought guild-membership.

Although the municipal institutions of communes were similar throughout the West, their relations with their kings, or with the bishops or feudal magnates who might be their overlords, varied widely. Paris and London, the two greatest northern cities, both enjoyed a considerable degree of self-government, but were too firmly under the thumb of monarchy to play an independent role. But when the wealthy cities of northern Italy—Milan, Brescia, Parma, Verona, and many others —were confronted by the Hohenstaufen emperors with demands to pay taxes and accept imperial administration, they truculently formed leagues, raised armies, fought the emperors in pitched battles, and withstood them in exhausting sieges to maintain their liberties. After 1250 Lombardy, though nominally still an imperial province, was in practice a chain of city-states. Fourteenth-century Valencia was less lucky when it defied the King of Aragon. In Germany and the low countries the political history of the communes is too kaleidoscopic to yield an easy generalisation.

Medieval industries were not always urban; for example, mining, metal-working, and the vital salt industry were not. The most highly organised industry was building. Edward I's castle-building in conquered Wales suggests the scale and mobility of its operations, for the King required a force of 3000 skilled building workers for several years, and they had to be drafted from England. In most towns the industrial structure was unspecialised, scores of crafts being pursued in small workshops by individual master-craftsmen and their journeymen. Some towns were famed for important specialities: Venice for glass, Dinant for copperware, Nuremberg for armour, Toledo for blades, Genoa and Barcelona for shipbuilding. But in only two instances did the prosperity of large urban communities stand or fall with a specific industry. Both Florence and the Flemish towns (Ghent,

Ypres, Tournai, Douai) were in vital dependence on the woollen cloth industry. In the Flemish towns it was essentially domestic. All weaving was done by small craftsmen, who usually worked at piece-rates for wealthy entrepreneurs who controlled wool supplies, and marketing. Flemish cloth had two main outlets—the Fairs of Champagne, to which merchants from Venice, Genoa, Pisa, came overland to sell high-priced luxury goods, spices, alum, ivory, indigo, pepper, wax, pearls, ginger, imported from Constantinople, Beirut and Alexandria, and the great market and seaport of Bruges, to which English wool and grain were shipped, and herrings and furs from Hamburg and Lübeck.

Medieval merchants, with isolated exceptions such as the Vikings who colonised Iceland, eschewed the open Atlantic and clung to coastal routes. The North Sea was reached from the Mediterranean overland by using the Alpine passes, especially

ALPINE TRADE ROUTES AND PASSES

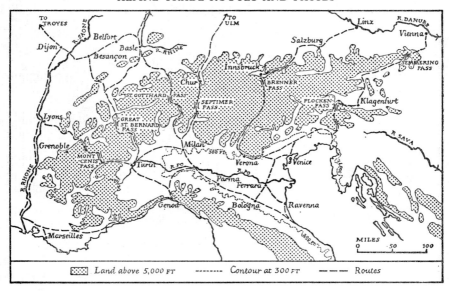

the Brenner, and from the Baltic by avoiding the Skagerrak and crossing Holstein. But in the thirteenth century the Genoese and Venetians made revolutionary improvements to ships. They introduced the axled rudder, the fore-mast and mizzen mast, hulls of greater strength, the magnetic compass and the improved maps of the Jewish cartographers of Majorca. The new ships altered the pattern of long-range trade. The high seas became easier and safer to navigate. Both the long galley with oars and sails and the broad-beamed cog were capable of taking on longer voyages and bigger cargoes, up to 600 tons dead weight. Trade with the Near East, from the Crimea to Alexandria, increased in regularity and volume. A Venetian fleet sailed annually to Bruges to sell oriental merchandise and buy Flemish cloth. The Champagne Fairs declined. Florentine agents took ship with the Venetians to buy English wool at

Bruges, and Florence now began to weave its own cloth as the raw material for the fine products of the Florentine cloth-finishing industry. Cogs of the Hanseatic League, a mercantile confederation of German towns formed to resist Baltic pirates and press for trading privileges in foreign countries, sailed in yearly convoys from Lübeck to Bourgneuf Bay for salt to preserve the Baltic herring catch. In the fifteenth century Bristol developed a flourishing trade with Iceland, and the Portuguese explored the West African coast, rounding the Cape in 1488. The Genoese Columbus, in Castilian service, crossed the Atlantic in 1492.

Benedetto Zaccaria (1240–1307), who made the first recorded sea voyage from Italy to England, acquired in the Near East a monopoly of the production of alum—indispensable in dyeing—and of mastic, a valuable aromatic herb. Importing these rarities to Europe, trading also in spices

THE HANSEATIC LEAGUE

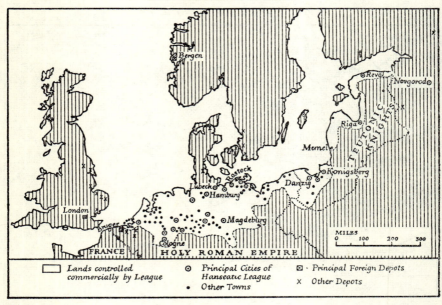

MEDIEVAL TRADE ROUTES OF EUROPE

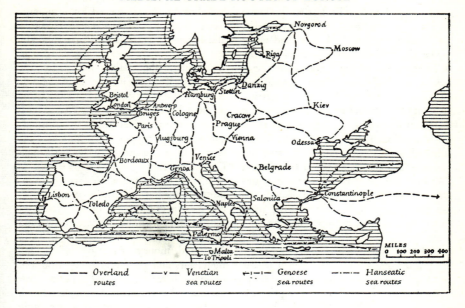

| — — — Overland routes | —v— Venetian sea routes | ←ı—ı→ Genoese sea routes | —ı—ı— Hanseatic sea routes |

and textiles, serving the Castilian Crown with his private war-fleet, he was only one of many late medieval merchants who made large fortunes in international trade. Men like Zaccaria invested their gains in town houses and landed estates, but from about 1200 onwards their profits were also devoted to the development of banking, and they financed the wars of kings, the building programmes of princes and archbishops, and new mercantile and industrial enterprises. Interest rates were high: a reflection of the great risks run. Defaulting debtors could ruin banks, as Edward III ruined the Florentine firms of Bardi and Peruzzi. The Florentine bankers managed the papal finances and controlled Europe's chief money market, and their system depended partly on the depositing of relatively modest sums by thousands of small investors. Developments in the bill of exchange, book-keeping, minting, and the structure of trading companies usually

originated with the Florentines. They practised as the leading business and industrial technicians all over Europe. Even in remote Cornwall there were tin mines under Florentine management.

In the fifteenth century the Medici bank perfected a decentralised type of organisation, with more insurance against failures. The Medici, who ruled Florence from 1434 to 1494, belonged to the patrician class which was dominating European business and urban life by 1400. Outstanding members of this class, such as Jacques Coeur in France and the Fuggers in South Germany, sought to establish a monopolistic grip on industry, trade, and banking alike. In city-states not under monarchical control the patriciate had also acquired a political monopoly. The Florentine patriciate had come victorious out of a long conflict with the weavers and other petty bourgeois craftsmen, who had striven to set up a middle-class democracy. In

Ghent and the other Flemish cities the urban patriciate steadily lost to the Duke of Burgundy the fruits of similar victories. Milan and the Lombard cities had fallen under the rule of tyrant families like the Visconti, who had usually originated with aristocratic soldiers of fortune, interloping into the life of the commune and getting control of its administrative machine with patrician co-operation. Venice was ruled by a sagacious merchant oligarchy which allowed no individual family to grow too strong. With her colonies in the Eastern Mediterranean, state shipyards, state-controlled carrying trade, and professional diplomatic service, Venice was the most 'modern' power of medieval Europe.

VII

To the medieval mind the sword of the warrior and the toil of the worker were in vain without the prayers of the priest. It was an age of faith. Christianity had no serious rivals in the West. Except in the lands of Moslem political supremacy Islam presented no challenge. Judaism was everywhere on the defensive. Paganism evoked on occasion savage hostilities against the Christian missionaries, and in Saxony and Norway it had to be suppressed with gross cruelties. But it never gave battle on intellectual grounds, and since the highest level of its organisation was tribal, it could never launch a universal counter-conversion. In the Middle Ages the Latin Church converted most of Europe from paganism while Byzantine missionaries converted the people of Kievan Russia and the southern Slavs. Once the Franks and the Anglo-Saxons had embraced Christianity they themselves sent out missionaries to the heathen Germans. The Englishman St Boniface (680–753), after studying the Benedictine rule in Italy, founded Fulda, the greatest abbey in Germany, and Mainz, its prime see,

before the Frisian pagans martyred him. Scandinavia was converted by evangelists from England and Germany; Hungary and Poland directly from Rome; and the last great pagan groups—the Prussian, Lithuanian, and Baltic tribes—by the Teutonic Knights in the later Middle Ages. Admittedly, to achieve these successes the Church had to come to terms with many pagan practices and habits of mind; and since the pagans were illiterate, the story has reached us exclusively through Christian writers.

In every land won for Western Christendom the medieval centuries saw the slow but certain crystallising of the system of diocese and parish. Each new cathedral and church could only rise by the gifts in land and money made by nobles and merchants and the humble contributions of unnumbered artisans and peasants. Over the chancel arch or west door of his church the layman could see a painting or carving of the Day of Judgment, which more than any other Christian symbol haunted the medieval mind. If lack of concern with human progress appears to characterise the Middle Ages, that is probably attributable to the prevalent idea, flowing from Augustine of Hippo at the headwaters of medieval thought, that history was near its end and society soon to be as a mantle folded up. To save themselves from the smiling demons at hell's blazing jaws, laymen gladly paid their tithes, took their children to be baptised, and accepted the obligations of confession, penance, and communion. They acknowledged the Church's right to dictate the laws of marriage and pronounce on the validity of wills. Their parish church was the focus of their community life, offering them pictures, music, processions, plays, and tales of saints and Biblical heroes. The Latin liturgy was not designed for lay people nor very suitable for them: and so sermons and readings from vernacular translations of Scripture were the basis of religious instruction.

But the Church also called on laymen to leave society for the monastic life of poverty, chastity, and obedience to a rule, by which they could 'make up for what is lacking in the sufferings of Christ'. Early monasticism was not grouped into separate Orders, though it showed local variations, such as the austere Celtic monasticism, both eremitical and evangelistic. St Benedict (480–543) had laid the foundations of the future Benedictine Order at Monte Cassino where he insisted on a close community life in which the monks' vocation was prayer—the *Opus Dei*—not pastoral work. In the tenth century a new Order grew up in Burgundy under generous lay patronage and the leadership of a line of gifted Abbots of Cluny. The Cluniacs, owing spiritual obedience only to the Pope, spread rapidly over Western Europe, with their elaborate liturgy and zealous pursuit of learning and the arts, and played a leading part in the movement for Church reform which reached its climax with Gregory VII. The twelfth century saw the rise of the Austin Canons, with their special interest in evangelising the laity; St Bruno's Carthusians, who took solitude and silence as their strict rule and foregathered only for the mass; and the fashionable Cistercians, led by a scholar, organiser, and preacher of genius, Bernard of Clairvaux, himself of noble birth like many other members of the Order. The Cistercians strove to follow a rule of extreme austerity in desert places. Consequently they attracted enormous endowments of moorland, forest, and marsh; and by a paradox, with the help of socially humble lay-brethren, they became the leading sheep-farmers and agricultural pioneers of twelfth-century Europe. The preservation of learning and the arts in the West was heavily dependent upon monasticism from 600 to 1200, when the vigour of the nobility was behind the movement. It later lost much of its appeal to laymen, falling in places into lethargy and even corruption. But no brief summary can do justice to monastic history.

The Church was deeply involved in lay affairs. No king could govern without its aid. The cleric's monopoly of writing, which only began to disappear in the later Middle Ages, made him the linch-pin of administration. The royal chancellor was usually a bishop; and he had his counterpart in every nobleman's household. Such men were not mere functionaries but the trusted counsellors of their masters, and helped to shape secular policies. Pious lay endowments concentrated in clerical hands a vast amount of landed property. The papal territories in Italy, the prince-bishoprics of the Rhine, the broad estates of monasteries like San Juan de la Peña and Monte Cassino, Saint-Denis and Glastonbury, illustrate the general rule that every bishop and abbot was set up as a landlord and a judge over many laymen. In England, the bishops did homage and fealty to the king, and owed him knight-service for their lands. Even the parish priest had his tithes to collect. By the eleventh century the more spiritual churchmen like St Peter Damian were entreating their fellows to renounce the corruption of worldly possessions and return to absolute evangelical poverty.

But reforming opinion was even more affronted by the spectacle of lay control in the Church. The bishop was in theory freely elected by the canons of his cathedral. In practice the election often did no more than confirm a royal nomination. The king's view was that since the bishop was *ex officio* a great landowner with political power in the kingdom, he should be chosen by the king. The lay lord who had built and endowed a monastery or a parish church frequently insisted upon the right to select the abbot or rector. Lay patrons did not necessarily choose badly but they were prone to corrupt the Church with simony by selling preferment. In the thirteenth century the kings of England and France were claiming to tax clerical property. The so-called conflict of Church and State arose over these and many similar issues. The Emperor Henry IV and Pope Gregory VII quarrelled over the imperial claim to appoint the bishops in Italy and Germany, Henry II of England and Archbishop Thomas Becket of Canterbury over the claim of clerks to be tried for felony not in the royal courts but in the Church's own courts. Each side fought with sharp weapons, the Church with excommunication and interdict, lay rulers with outlawry and sometimes brute force. Gregory VII declared Henry IV deposed; Henry set up an anti-pope against Gregory. But prudence restrained the worst excesses of a conflict which never rested and which neither side decisively won. The most significant victories were gained by the English and French kings, whose power over their clergy steadily increased.

For centuries the popes exercised only a wavering control over the Church in the West. But between 1046, when the Emperor Henry III broke the Roman nobility's ascendancy over the papacy, and 1230, when Pope Gregory IX issued the *Decretals*, the first official codification of Canon Law, the pope's sovereignty and 'fullness of power' in the Church were established and developed. The papacy made itself the final interpreter of the Canon Law, which was binding on the clergy and the church courts all over Catholic Europe, and built up a supreme appellate jurisdiction in ecclesiastical causes. The organisation of an electoral and advisory college of cardinals and the sending of

papal legates to carry their master's authority into every province and diocese gave coherence and uniformity to the exercise of papal power. The principal stages in this process were marked by two great pontificates. Gregory VII (1073–85) made the resounding claim to supreme temporal as well as supreme spiritual power. Later popes were to wield more effective authority than Gregory but added nothing significant to his statement of the papal claims. Perhaps Gregory's greatest feat was to have aroused by his struggle with the Emperor a new consciousness of community throughout the Church. Innocent III (1198–1216) made secular rulers fear him, punishing two emperors and seven kings with either interdict or excommunication; consolidated the papal lands in Italy into a strong principality; launched the crusade against the Albigensian heretics; strengthened papal supervision of episcopal elections and appointments to benefices; and summoned the oecumenical Fourth Lateran Council, in which he re-stated the faith and re-codified the practice of the Church.

By 1300 the papacy had created the most efficient administration in Europe. But its preoccupation with financial problems, especially during its long residence at Avignon (1308–78), the schism of the rival papacies (1378–1417), and its obesssion with Italian secular politics—the inevitable result of its owning wide territories in Italy—diminished the high reputation it had had under popes of the calibre of Innocent III. The Church's unity had been further undermined by the rise of heretical and mystical sects, and a growing secularism, which called for the surrender of clerical property. From 1414 to 1449 a series of General Councils of the Church, attended by laymen as well as clergy, sought to transfer supreme authority in the Church from the pope to a representative assembly. This Conciliar Movement was a failure; but by striving to introduce representative government into the Church, it widely publicised the idea of checks and balances against absolute power.

The intellectual life of the Church was never stagnant. Its main problem was to reconcile Christian teaching with Greek thought. Before 476 a Christian philosophy had been built up by co-ordinating the teaching of Scripture with that of Greek philosophy, especially Plato. Augustine, Cassiodorus, and Boethius were a bridge from the ancient world to the medieval. In the twelfth century the rediscovery of Aristotle's treatise on logic enabled Peter Abelard (1079–1142) to inspire great advances in logical reasoning and methods of theological proof. The 'wandering scholars' of the age flocked to Paris to hear Abelard, whose stormy career is linked with the development of the cathedral-school of Notre Dame into the University of Paris. At Bologna the Roman Law students were creating their own university. The seventy-seven universities which grew up in Latin Christendom before 1500 were all modelled either on Bologna, where the students governed, or on Paris, ruled by its rector and the masters of its faculties of arts, theology, canon law, and medicine. The main social impact of the universities was to provide the Church with a graduate aristocracy by 1300; and equip Europe after 1400 with a literate and often learned upper class from which sprang the Renaissance humanists.

When Thomas Aquinas (1226–74) taught at Paris the West had finally recovered, through the medium of Arab scholarship, the whole body of Greek philosophical and scientific thought. Aquinas restated the Aristotelian doctrines as an organic philosophy which he attempted to use as a foundation for Catholic theology. For the next two centuries the universities were absorbed in a searching discussion of the work of Aquinas, in which Ockham and others were to carry scepticism to the brink of downright infidelity. Medieval political theorising was usually concerned with Church-state relations: but Marsiglio of Padua (d. 1343), one of the rare thinkers who examined the problem of the best form of government, advanced in his *Defensor Pacis* the ideas of the sovereign people, the 'natural' state, founded by man for temporal happiness, and a clergy completely subject to secular power.

Abelard, Aquinas, Ockham, Marsiglio all on occasion carried speculation beyond the limits of orthodoxy into heresy. Popes and bishops had constantly to guard against heretical questionings of the Church's government and doctrines. But only the obdurate heretics were burnt, and the image of a wholly effective spiritual tyranny must be discarded for one of much practical freedom of thought and criticism. This is borne out by the sheer vitality and ubiquity of heresies—whether Manichaean or Pantheistic, originating in the lecture school or the witches' coven, the mysticism of the Joachites or the masochism of the Flagellants. Yet heresy was often suppressed, sometimes cruelly; and none handled the heretic more cruelly than the layman, as the crusades against Catharists and Hussites show. Nevertheless, the Church preferred to come to terms with its critics, as it did with Francis of Assisi (1182–1226), who, dissatisfied with clerical wealth and clerical lack of learning, founded a movement devoted to prayer, apostolic poverty and healing the sick. So deep was the influence of this all but perfect Christian that he might have wrecked the unity of the Church with his compelling claims on laymen. Yet the papacy was able to 'capture' the Franciscan movement, as it did St Dominic's Friars Preachers and the other Mendicant Orders which arose in the thirteenth century to evangelise Europe's growing towns, improve clerical standards, and dominate university life. In the long run, however, the Church had no answer but persecution to the followers of Waldo of Lyons, who declared that men needed for salvation not the sacraments but the Bible, and of Wycliffe, who denied the Church's final authority in the interpreting of Scriptures. And its greatest danger lay in the sects of devout laymen and women, like the Brethren of the Common Life and the Béguines, who, without incurring persecution, quietly devoted themselves to the study of the Bible and the life of prayer.

VIII

Throughout the Middle Ages the language of theology, philosophy, science, history, administration, and law was predominantly Latin. The Latin Bible, St Jerome's Vulgate with Strabo's interpretative Gloss, held its own for the whole period, though it is often forgotten that the Church did not object to the lay vernacular translations into German, French, English, Sicilian, often for royal patrons, provided the text was not published without the Gloss. The first translation of the whole Bible was by Wycliffe and appeared unglossed. Few written languages have had so wide a range of styles or been written at such varying levels of competence as medieval Latin. In the twelfth century at the cathedral schools of Chartres, Paris, and Orléans, Virgil, Horace, Ovid, Livy, and Cicero were studied as well as Augustine, Boethius, and the grammarians Donatus and Priscian. The writings of Bernard of Chartres and John of Salisbury showed a comprehensive understanding of the Latin classics and an ability to write in their language that was more than mere pastiche. But this 'twelfth-century renaissance' faded when the recovery of Greek learning

in Latin translation diverted attention to theological and dialectical studies.

In fourteenth-century Italy there was a revival of interest in classical Roman civilisation and Latin style under the leadership of Petrarch (1304–75), who discovered some lost works by Cicero and stimulated scholars to search monastic and cathedral libraries for forgotten classics. Though the main source of Petrarch's fame is his writings in the Italian vernacular, he exercised a more immediate influence through his Latin verse and prose, modelled on Virgil and Cicero, and his zeal for the recovery of Greek imaginative literature. Petrarch could not read Greek himself, and his friend Boccaccio, a learned Latinist and great vernacular writer, was the first Western scholar to learn Greek since 900. By 1400 Greek professors had come to teach in Florence, and the intellectual life of Italy began to be transformed by enthusiasm for Greek culture. Pope Nicholas V built up a great library of Greek and Latin literature and hired scholars to translate the Greek classics into Latin, among them Lorenzo Valla, who openly ridiculed the Latin of the Vulgate and contrasted the principles of monasticism unfavourably with those of the Epicureans. Humanism was affecting behaviour as well as style. Wealthy Italian patrons were gathering the humanists at their courts. Pope Pius II—Aeneas Sylvius Piccolomini—was a scholar and a classical archaeologist as well as a patron. The Sforza of Milan, the Gonzaga of Mantua, the Este of Ferrara established academies for the education of their children in Greek and Latin. At the Platonic academy of the Medici Marsilio Ficino and Pico della Mirandola sought not to attack the medieval scholastics but to bring them into a great synthesis with Platonic, Hebrew, Arabic, and Zoroastrian thought, and Christianity was seen less as a dogma than part of a universal religious tradition. From Italy the renaissance of Greek studies was carried far and wide north of the Alps before 1500.

One of the highest medieval achievements was to produce a vernacular literature, the more remarkable since the vernacular in France, Italy, Spain, England, and Germany was nowhere a unified language but in each country a family of growing and changing dialects uncontrolled by lexicographers and grammarians. Between 1300 and 1500, under the influence of courts and governments, merchants and great writers, predominant dialects emerged: in France that of the region around Paris; in Spain Castilian; in England the East Midland dialect. Dante (1265–1321) aspired to write in a courtly *stil nuovo*, meant to combine the best features of several dialects. What he achieved was less a composite Italian than a purified and polished form of his native Tuscan, the tongue of the Florentines.

Long before Dante the vernacular had become a sophisticated and powerful literary medium. Anglo-Saxon verse and prose, flowering in the Dark Ages, withering after the Norman Conquest, had many of the features of subsequent vernacular literature: the epic—*Beowulf*; heroic lays like *Maldon*; religious poems like Caedmon's hymns and *The Dream of the Rood*; chronicles, law-codes, sermons, and translations from Scripture. In Iceland Snorri Sturluson (1179–1241) and others produced in the prose sagas a dramatic and realistic narrative literature which dealt with the heroic age of the vikings. In the later twelfth century the lyric poetry of the troubadours, written in the Langue d'Oc, flourished in southern France. Many of the troubadours were noblemen, and their romantic and subjective art centred upon the expression of courtly love for the learned and cultured feudal lady. 'They

effected a change which has left no corner of our ethics, our imagination, or our daily life untouched, and they erected impassable barriers between us and the classical past'.* The troubadours developed 900 different types of stanza, and this intense medieval interest in technique is to be seen in other lyric poets: the northern French trouvères, writing in the Langue d'Oïl; the Minnesinger of South Germany (1150–1250); the Italian sonneteers, especially Petrarch; and François Villon in fifteenth-century France.

But the most characteristic products of the vernacular writers were romantic legends of adventure in prose and verse. The *Chansons de Geste*, with their simple virile diction and preference for such warlike themes as the deeds of Charlemagne and his paladins, as in the *Chanson de Roland*, reflected the age of unrestricted feudal warfare in France. The Arthurian cycle, springing from the Celtic legends of Arthur and his court, ran a brilliant course through the lays of Chrétien de Troyes and the *Parzival* of Wolfram von Eschenbach to the *Morte d'Arthur* of Malory. This preoccupation with the romanticised heroes of Dark Age history reached its highest point in the South German *Nibelungenlied*, which developed a Homeric theme from the age of the barbarian invasions, celebrated the heroic virtues of courage, loyalty, and implacable vengefulness, and presented women, as well as men, of heroic stature. But the most popular reading of the later Middle Ages was the softer, allegorical, and moralising *Roman de la Rose*. For French was the one vernacular read all over Europe. Medieval vernacular literature was produced essentially by lay writers for a lay public. The fullest expression of

* C. S. Lewis; *The Allegory of Love* (Oxford, 1936), p. 4.

the layman's experience of medieval society may be found in the poetry of Chaucer (1340-1400); and the most inspired vision of medieval man's place in the universe in Dante's *Divine Comedy*. And Chaucer was the principal founding father of modern English poetry as Dante was of the language and literature of modern Italy.

IX

Between 1050 and 1250 Greek and Arab science and medicine reached the West in Latin translations. This body of knowledge was systematised, commented upon, and to a minor extent added to by medieval scholars, but they were slow to criticise it and their theological preconceptions prevented them from developing it significantly. Like the Greeks they possessed neither the mathematical means for describing matter in motion nor such instruments of accurate measurement and observation as the thermometer, barometer, microscope and telescope. Modern science had a certain germination in the medieval universities. At Bologna and Padua the objective study of human anatomy was seriously undertaken. At Oxford, Bacon dimly perceived the importance of mathematics and experimentation in scientific study. At Paris, where the fourteenth century saw much re-examination of Greek scientific ideas, Oresme put forward the theory of the diurnal rotation of the earth. By 1500 modern science was steadily developing. Medieval advances in science had small practical application at the time. Yet modern technological change has deep roots in the Middle Ages. Between 400 and 1000 the stirrup, nailed-on horse-shoe, horse-collar, and tandem harness, all Asian devices, came to be applied in Europe, and made for a more efficient and manageable horse, which could pull far heavier loads than the yoked horse of

antiquity and could work in a team. Burdens which had to be shifted by slaves in Roman times could now be moved by horses. And by 1300 Europeans, often learning from Asia, were making many other things of which the Romans had been ignorant: the wheeled plough, wheelbarrow, spinning-wheel, vertical windmill. Clothing was revolutionised by the functional button, machinery by the crank. Explosives came from Asia, but the first guns were made (possibly in Florence) about 1320. The Arabs brought paper and printing with wooden blocks to the West; but printing from movable metal type was invented at Mainz about 1450. Both these inventions rested on remarkable Western advances in metallurgy; both were applied with zeal. By 1420, no army was strong without guns. By 1500, nine million books had been printed in Europe.

Yet by modern standards the medieval West was technically and economically backward: which makes its achievements in architecture, sculpture, and painting the more impressive. Evolution in those arts was gradual. The enormous output was, until the fourteenth century, largely anonymous. The story is primarily one of the building of churches, and their enrichment with carvings, paintings, glass, gold and silver plate, ivories, illuminated missals, precious vestments. The Romanesque architecture of the earlier medieval centuries was essentially a continuation of ancient types of building. Its common features—cylindrical vaults, massive walls and columns, round arches, small windows—arose from an inability to build large edifices without the support of sheer weight and solidity. Romanesque was an international style, as witness its majestic churches at Verona, Arles, Tournai, Speyer, Santiago, Durham.

In the late twelfth century engineering

discoveries—the ribbed vault, pointed arch, and flying buttress—produced a new style, the Gothic. The thrusts of roof and walls could now be concentrated. Gothic churches appear to rest on pillars and buttresses only. Their walls are mere screens, largely replaced with great windows. The style at its strongest and most gracious is represented by the thirteenth-century cathedrals of northern France, by the façade of Rheims with its sculptured figures, and by the arcaded nave of Amiens. The later variants of Gothic—English Decorated and Perpendicular, French Flamboyant—are characterised by a growing intricacy of decorative feature.

By 1200, painters and sculptors, long under Byzantine influence, had begun to observe and imitate nature more closely. With Giotto (1266–1337) and Claus Sluter (d. 1406) realism grew ever stronger. The development of oil-painting by Jan van Eyck (1380–1440) was a product of the quest for the means to mirror reality in all its details. So were the prodigious discoveries in the sciences of anatomy, light, and perspective made by the fifteenth-century painters and sculptors and architects of Italy—above all the Florentines Masaccio, Brunelleschi, and Donatello and the Venetian Giovanni Bellini. In that century the new techniques, combined with a burning enthusiasm for classical models and the 'renaissance' of the civilisation of antiquity, brought Italy decisively out of the Gothic into a new style in all the visual arts.

The Western Middle Ages did not end abruptly. They merged gradually into Renaissance Europe. But the world of Dante was profoundly different from that of Shakespeare. The medieval environment was more continental than oceanic. The centres of economic power were northern Italy, northern France, the Rhineland, Flanders and the Baltic shore. By 1600 Europe's economic background included not merely the North Sea and the Mediterranean, but the Atlantic and Indian Oceans. The dominant land power was now Spain, her armies financed by the wealth of America and the Indies. French, English and Dutch sea power were far greater.

The horizon of men's minds was also wider. The scholastic discipline was now paralleled by an extrovert humanism, enterprising and practical (*see* Chapter 15). In the Middle Ages, Europeans had made little impact on the outer world: they were now to become the most decisive innovators in world history. The new outlook of the High Renaissance and of the seventeenth century, with its implications for the modern world, will be considered in a succeeding chapter.

11   THE EXPANSION OF EUROPE

by J. A. Williamson

European expansion grew out of reactions between Europe and Asia. In classical times the Greeks were in contact with Western Asia, and the Roman Empire extended, by the second century after Christ, over the whole northern coast of Africa, the whole of Asia Minor and Syria, and into the Caucasus, while Alexander's great military expedition had earlier gained knowledge of lands as far as northern India. There was a luxury trade between Roman Europe and the Far East, by land routes and across the Indian Ocean. This does not imply that Europeans went to China or Malaya, but only that they were in communication with Asiatic middlemen who told them something of Eastern geography. The results may be seen in the second-century atlas of Ptolemy of Alexandria. The Ptolemaic geography shows a world of three continents, Europe almost complete, Africa unknown beyond the Sahara and the sources of the Nile, Asia somewhat distorted in the south, unknown in the far north, and with its eastern coastline yet unmapped.

The rise and expansion of Islam disturbed the early contacts and contracted the European world. The Saracens established their Caliphate in Damascus and Baghdad, invaded Asia Minor, ended Roman rule in North Africa, and crossed the Straits and conquered Spain (*see* Chapter 7). But these southern Mohammedans developed a cultured civilisation, preserving much of Greek and Roman learning; and peaceful contacts as well as frequent wars

prevailed between them and Christian Europe. The Turks, coming later out of the interior of Asia, were more barbarous and less tolerant. They penetrated the Saracen Caliphate, adopted its religion, and became the fighting front of the Mohammedan world against Christendom. The Ottoman Turks, the most vigorous of the race, grew prominent in the thirteenth century, in the fourteenth they established themselves in Balkan Europe, and in the fifteenth they captured Constantinople, a city long past its imperial greatness, but a key position in the Eastern Mediterranean. The Turks, much more than the Saracens, interrupted the contacts between Europe and the East; and it was in their first century of advance that the Christian counter-offensive of the Crusades died out.

Yet another outburst of Asia was important. The thirteenth-century Mongols or Tartars, of the same racial kinship as the Turks, spread their military power far and wide, into China, into Persia and the Middle East, and into Russia, where they took Kiev in 1240. The advancing wave then entered Germany, but soon receded, and the Mongol power satisfied itself with the domination of Asia. The Mongols did not become Mohammedans, and there were some Christian hopes of inciting them to fall upon Turkish Islam from the rear. In the wake of the Mongols withdrawing from Europe two successive papal missions (in 1245 and 1253) penetrated North-Central Asia to reconnoitre the prospects (*see* Chapter 9). They were

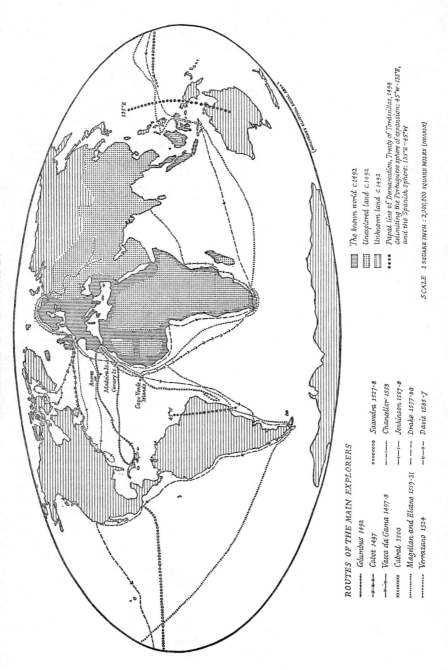

THE EXPANSION OF EUROPE OVERSEAS

ROUTES OF THE MAIN EXPLORERS

+++++ Columbus 1492
-+-+- Cabot 1497
-·-·- Vasco da Gama 1497-8
xxxxxxx Cabral 1500
········· Magellan and Elcano 1519-21
--------- Verrazano 1524

ooooooo Saavedra 1527-8
-··-··- Chancellor 1553
-+-+-+- Jenkinson 1557-8
----- Drake 1577-80
-o-o-o- Davis 1585-7

▦ The known world c.1492
▦ Unexplored land c.1492
▦ Unknown land c.1492
•••• Papal line of Demarcation, Treaty of Tordesillas, 1494
delimiting the Portuguese sphere of expansion: 45°w-135°E,
and the Spanish sphere: 135°E-45°w

SCALE 1 SQUARE INCH : 2,000,000 SQUARE MILES (NEARLY)

kindly received but could achieve no alliance, nor did they go as far as China. That country was becoming the headquarters of the Mongol power, the Empire of the Grand Khan of Cathay.

With the Mongol stabilisation the trade routes between Europe and Asia became more frequented. The so-called silk route was a network of caravan tracks from China through Turkestan to the Caspian, the Black Sea and the Middle East. The silks and other wares passed right through, but not the merchants who handled them. There were many transferences in the intermediate market cities of Asia, and the Chinese with whom the goods originated were never seen by the Europeans who traded in the Levant. The spice route was maritime, the conveyance of costly drugs, perfumes and spices from the islands of Indonesia through the Indian Ocean to the Red Sea and the Persian Gulf. These goods also passed through several hands, and the seaports of southern India were the principal *entrepôts*. From India to the Red Sea the carriage was in Arab shipping. The Arabs dominated the western Indian Ocean, supreme in all the ports from East Africa to western India.

II

Such is the world scene in which the great European advance originated. It could not begin until in the fifteenth century Europe was ready for the task, with improved shipping, maps, navigating instruments and firearms, and also with a new appreciation of geography, an independence of outlook, and the readiness to try great experiments that flowed from the whole late-medieval progress of the European intellect.

Explorers had already played their part in creating these conditions, and the greatest of all was Marco Polo the Vene-

tian. In the late thirteenth century he journeyed from the Levant to China by the continental routes, and returned by the Indian Ocean into the Persian Gulf. He found the Mongol Empire at its zenith under Kublai Khan, and he spent seventeen years in China in the service of the Emperor. The book which he produced on his return told of the civilisation of China, of its wealth, its cities, and its shipping. It described the Indonesian archipelago, and the sea passage thence to the Levant. It exaggerated the riches of Japan, which Marco had heard of but had not visited, so that his 'Cipango' became the goal of later projectors. The book was translated into various languages, copied in hundreds of manuscripts, and printed in the fifteenth century. It became more than any other work the bible of the Renaissance expansionists.

Far back in the Middle Ages there had been a Scandinavian push across the North Atlantic. Norsemen occupied Iceland and went on to Greenland, where they also made a long-lived colony. From Greenland they reached North America, possibly as far south as New England. But the Greenland colony decayed, and the American contact was discontinued. A worsening of climate was probably the cause. Southern Greenland was really green in the tenth century, and supported Norse farmers and their cattle. But the arctic conditions spread southward, and the colony slowly died: there was still a remnant in the late fifteenth century. Scandinavian America yielded an interesting chapter to history, but it had no sequel. Fifteenth-century Portugal began the great advance that has determined the subsequent history of the world. The Portuguese discovered or rediscovered the island groups of the eastern Atlantic, but their main work was in exploring southwards along the coast of Africa and opening the Cape route into the Indian Ocean. Prince Henry, called the Navigator, directed the early stage of the effort. He was in mentality a crusader, extending Christianity, converting the heathen, and perhaps seeking contact with the Christian kingdom of the fabulous Prester John (actually in Abyssinia), which had been cut off from Christendom by the Saracen conquest of Egypt. Henry's expeditions, which he did not lead in person, discovered the great bulge of West Africa, and when he died in 1460 they had turned it and reached as far as Sierra Leone and Cape Palmas. His ships obtained ivory, gums and African pepper, and carried off Negroes to work as slaves in Portugal. This slaving was considered Christian as well as profitable; for by accepted doctrine all infidels were in a state of war with Christians and might be lawfully killed, and to make them prisoners of war was an act of mercy which gave them a chance of salvation by Christian teaching. The advance continued after Henry's death, and the south-facing Gold Coast was opened up. In 1481 the Portuguese founded the fortress of Elmina on this coast and began to gather supplies of alluvial gold from the surrounding peoples.

It was now that speed increased and the outlook widened. Knowledge of geography was expanding in Renaissance Europe, and Marco Polo's book was reaching the height of its influence. The seaway to India came into view as a practicable discovery. A fleet sailing in 1482 discovered the mouth of the Congo. Another, in 1485, reached 22° of south latitude at Cape Cross. Still the long continental shore stretched southward. In 1487-8 Bartholomew Díaz found the end of it, and reached a coast running north-east into the Indian Ocean. He called his turning point the Cape of Storms, but it soon became the Cape of Good Hope.

Ten years later the hope was realised. In 1497 Vasco da Gama sailed round the Cape, northward by East Africa, where he found Arabs holding the seaports, and then across the ocean to southern India at Calicut. In 1499 he came home to announce that India was reached—and also that a maritime war was necessary to conquer Arab power in the Indian Ocean. For the Portuguese were determined to dominate the spice trade with Europe, and the Arabs would fight to retain their hold upon it.

Meanwhile Europeans were looking westward into the Atlantic, colonising the island groups which had been discovered, searching for others which were thought to exist: St Brandan's, said to have been found by an Irish saint, Antilia or the Seven Cities, the Isle of Brasil, thought to lie out west of Ireland. The new geography, more properly the revived ancient geography of Greece and Rome, provided a greater incentive than island-seeking; for the layout of three continents on a spherical earth implied that by sailing west from Europe one would come to the eastern coast of Asia. The idea was obvious to the geographer. The practical question was: how wide was the ocean, and could ships be victualled for the crossing?

Christopher Columbus, a Genoese who made many voyages, was certain that the Atlantic could be crossed. He based his certainty on a geographical error, for he calculated that the distance west to Asia was a matter of no more than three thousand miles, and that was within the range of well-found ships. In 1492 the Spanish sovereigns Ferdinand and Isabella provided three vessels. Columbus sailed to the Canaries, and thence west with the trade-wind. He discovered what we call the West Indies, Hayti, which he identified with Marco Polo's Cipango or Japan, and part of Cuba, which he said was a promontory of the mainland of Asia. In subsequent voyages he discovered the other West Indian islands and coasted parts of the Isthmus of Panama, which he thought was the Malay Peninsula. Columbus never yielded his claim to have made the westward passage to Asia. His Spanish officers soon became incredulous, since the facts did not fit Marco Polo's descriptions: there was no emperor, no cities, no Chinese shipping. A new world had in fact come into view. It was soon to be called America.

There were other projectors of the west. The Englishmen of Bristol traded with Iceland and probably heard of the old Norse discoveries. From 1480 they were looking for the Isle of Brasil. They made several fruitless voyages until in 1494 we have indications that they may have found something, possibly Newfoundland. It would seem that at first they were only island-seekers with no vision of Asia. But in 1497 they certainly had that vision, when John Cabot led a Bristol ship across the ocean and found a continental coast, which he claimed was 'the territory of the Grand Khan'. Subsequent investigation showed that it was not, and the English were disappointed as the Spaniards were. To neither nation was America a welcome discovery. It was a barrier in the way of what they wanted—the short voyage to Asia, spices and wealth. To circumvent the barrier was the next task, and the quest of the North-West Passage round America began. John Cabot's son, Sebastian, tried it in 1509, and for practical purposes James Cook finished it in 1778 by showing that there was no sailing passage feasible at the time. In the interim many voyages were made by many men from all the lands of Western Europe.

The Portuguese proceeded to establish their empire in the Indian Ocean. Their object was not territory but trade, and their method was to place garrisons in the dominating seaports and to base fighting fleets upon them. The coastal cities which they seized were either *entrepôts* for the concentration of valuable goods or strategic points for the war against the Arabs and prevention of the issue of Arab fleets from the Red Sea and the Persian Gulf. Only exceptionally did the Portuguese rule small areas of territory apart from the fortresses. The method was dictated by shortage of man-power. The Portuguese were numerically a little nation, not much over a million strong, and could not maintain armies. Ships needed fewer men, but even so the Empire was a serious drain on the home population, for only a minority of those who sailed east lived to return. The wealth acquired was enormous, and Lisbon became one of the great cities of Europe, but a penalty was paid in the dilution of the vigorous national stock by the African strain brought in as slave-labour to support the economic fabric.

In 1500, the year after Vasco da Gama's return, Portugal sent out her first conquering fleet to the East. Incidentally, it discovered the Brazilian coast of South America on its outward voyage. In the Indian Ocean the Portuguese sought battle with the Arab navies and inflicted severe defeats upon them. In ten years the foundations of the Portuguese dominion were laid. Western India was its basis, convenient for sailing east or west in accordance with the six-monthly change of the monsoon winds. Goa became the capital of the viceroy representing the King of Portugal. Calicut and Diu and Bombay were other occupied ports of western India. In the seats of Arab power the Portuguese took Ormuz, whereby they could bottle the Persian Gulf, while they established themselves also in the chief seaports of the East African coast, of which Delagoa Bay and the colony of

Mozambique represent to this day the remnants of their jurisdiction. Eastwards the Portuguese took Malacca in 1511, in the straits leading through to Indonesia; and thence they reached the true Spice Islands of the Banda Sea, the producers of the then most valuable wares in the world. Foundations followed in northern Java, Celebes and elsewhere in Indonesia. In 1516 Portuguese ships first reached southern China at Macao in the Canton river, and long afterwards, in 1542, they attained Japan, which they found not answerable to the account given by Marco Polo. Portugal organised this wide dominion for trade, the native Asiatic shipping concentrating its cargoes in the Portuguese depots, and the long passage to Europe being made by a new type of great ship, the ocean-going carrack, which was built in sizes exceeding 1000 tons. Great size had advantages for defence and economic carrying, although the carracks appear to have been no more seaworthy than the little ships in which Western Europe had hitherto carried on her commerce. When these results became known in Europe, their impact upon all intelligent minds was great: in a few years the mysteries of tropical Asia were revealed by first-hand knowledge, where previously all had been hearsay and doubt.

Spain in the Atlantic had a period of disillusionment after the falsification of Columbus' claim to have reached Asia. Hayti, called by its new possessors Hispaniola, produced small quantities of gold, soon exhausted, the other Spanish islands none; and the handful of Spanish West Indian colonists devoted themselves mainly to cattle-ranching for the export of hides and to sugar-planting on a small scale. Others established themselves on the north coast of South America, from the Orinoco to the Isthmus, and obtained some pearls and trickles of gold. This coast was known at Tierra Firma—to the English as the Spanish Main. In 1513 Balboa crossed the Isthmus and saw the Pacific, which he named the South Sea. There was still a hope that America might not be an unbroken continent, and that a strait might be found to lead to the ocean on its farther side, and thus to Asia. This hope took Spanish explorers into the Gulf of Mexico, and there they heard a of strong state under an emperor in the interior, with a warlike people rich in gold and silver.

The news opened a period of the utmost energy and achievement, that of the Spanish *conquistadores*, the conquerors. Hernán Cortes, a colonist in Cuba, was the first. In 1519 he landed in Mexico with 500 fighting men, and in three years by valour, diplomacy and a heroic defiance of odds, he took possession of the city of Mexico and the Aztec Empire, not a mere collection of tribesmen, but a well-knit state with a sovereign, a powerful priesthood, civil discipline and a hard-fighting army (*see* Chapter 13). Cortés, with his handful, conquered all that, and set Spain on the path of empire. Soon he was shipping treasure to Seville, to finance the wars of Charles V, while outward from Spain went officials and missionary priests to create a Christian kingdom of New Spain in the new continent.

Increasing knowledge killed the hope of a strait to the Pacific in West Indian latitudes. English and Portuguese were trying in the far north for a passage through to Asia. In 1519–22 Spain found one in the far south. Ferdinand Magellan, a Portuguese officer from India, led the Spanish ships, and in 1520 he passed the strait that bears his name. He crossed the Pacific, and found it infinitely vaster than anyone had expected. With crews at the point of death from hunger and scurvy he reached the Philippine Islands. There he was killed in battle, but his ship *Victoria*, the only survivor of a fleet of five, passed through the great archipelago into the Indian Ocean and made her way home after the first circumnavigation of the earth. On the world map the gap between Europe and Asia was at length filled in, with the new continent and the new ocean. It was a culminating challenge to the expanding mind of Europe, comparable to the scientific discoveries of our time.

The Spanish advance continued into South America. Sebastian Cabot, having transferred to Spanish service, explored the basin of the River Plate in 1526–30. On the other side, Francisco Pizarro sailed south from Panama and landed on the coast of Peru, another treasure-state whose riches exceeded those of Mexico. Pizarro, like Cortés, had very few men, but he found the Incas of Peru less warlike than the Aztecs of Mexico, and overthrew them with ease. Lima, near the coast, became the capital of the Spanish conquest, with Callao its chief seaport; and shipment of treasure began. Peru had much accumulated gold, but produced chiefly silver. Gold came from the coast of Chile, farther south, and also from the interior in the highland of Colombia to the north. This third treasure region, called New Granada, was overrun by the Spaniards by 1540.

The Spanish Empire took shape as a government of the Caribbean, with its seat at Santo Domingo in Hispaniola, ruling the islands and the settlements on the Main; the viceroyalty of New Spain, ruling Mexico and all Central America down to and including Panama; and the viceroyalty of Peru, covering all the west coast south of Panama, and extending inland across the Andes. By the middle of the sixteenth century the great empire was outlined, and thereafter intensified and consolidated within the limits then attained. The Spanish sovereigns concerned, the

Emperor Charles V and his son King Philip II, pursued clear and continuous policies. The native peoples were to be Christianised and humanely treated, left in subordinate possession of their land, and not enslaved. This was the consistent royal doctrine, not always translated into practice; for there was almost continual conflict between the royal will and the intentions of the Spaniards on the spot, bent on making their fortunes and behaving often with the vilest brutality. The Church was the king's instrument for promoting the humane course, and many of its colonial leaders were men of fine character; but many were not. On the whole, by common standards of conquest, the Indians were well treated, and their descendants form the major element to this day in the populations of Mexico and South America. The greatest product of the Empire was treasure, although many other goods were important. Two annual convoys or plate fleets conveyed the cargoes to Spain, one sailing direct from the Gulf of Mexico, the other from Nombre de Dios on the Atlantic side of the Isthmus. At Nombre de Dios were collected the products of the Main, sent along in local shipping, and to it the treasure from Peru and Chile was brought across the Isthmus on muleback, having been shipped up the west coast to Panama. Although Spain had discovered the Strait of Magellan she never used it as a trade route from the Pacific to Europe. Transhipment across the Isthmus was quicker and safer. Slave labour, although not of Indian slaves, was encouraged, and a regular supply of Negroes was obtained from the Portuguese in West Africa. The Negroes were common in all the Spanish territories, and they remained in perpetual slavery, they and their children after them. Finally, it was a strict Spanish policy that no ships from any foreign country were to trade with the American Empire. Foreign merchants were tolerated, if Catholics, but they had to lade their goods at Seville and sail under the Spanish flag.

The hope of penetrating the North-West Passage to trade with Asia revived at frequent intervals in English minds. Under Henry VIII there was at least one expedition, and under Elizabeth several. Martin Frobisher made three voyages in 1576–8 and discovered Baffin Land and the entrance to Hudson Strait. Sir Humphrey Gilbert wrote an elaborate *Discourse* to prove the existence of the passage. John Davis led three expeditions in 1585–7, ending, for lack of money, with high hopes but without actual success. An alternative plan was that of the North-East Passage along the coast of Siberia. A company formed in 1553 sent out ships for this purpose, and the result was the discovery of the White Sea and access to Russia, then an almost unknown state without a sea coast on the Baltic. The company became the Muscovy or Russia Company, a permanent trading body, but it never completed the passage to the Pacific. The northern passages were attractive to the English because of the need to sell cloth, the country's principal manufacture; and it was thought that the explorers would find cloth-markets on the way to Asia, as they actually did in Russia. The tropical Portuguese route to the East offered no great demand for the heavy English cloth.

The sixteenth-century French also grew active. From an early date they took a greater part than the English in the Newfoundland fishery discovered by John Cabot. In the 1530s, under Jacques Cartier, they ascended the St Lawrence and reached Quebec and Montreal. They also were intent on the western passage to Asia. They soon found that the St Lawrence did not provide it, but the name of the

La Chine (China) rapids on that river shows what was in their minds. They did establish a fur trade with the Indians, which led in time to the colonisation of Canada.

In West Africa and in Brazil the French and the English of that century trespassed on the Portuguese monopoly. For some fifty years the Portuguese used their discovery of Brazil simply as a trading coast, producing the valuable dye-stuff called Brazil wood. From 1530 William Hawkins and other English adventurers, and a number of Frenchmen, went to Brazil for dye-wood; and the outward track took them past the West African coast in the neighbourhood of Liberia and Sierra Leone, where they obtained ivory and Guinea pepper. After 1550 both English and French extended their operations to the Gold Coast, and for twenty years there was a vigorous irregular war between them and the Portuguese. European competition became too keen and the supplies of gold diminished, but West Africa remained permanently on the map of Anglo-French ambitions. In Brazil, on the other hand, the Portuguese strengthened their hold into genuine coastal colonies and succeeded in beating off the intruders.

Magellan's crossing of the Pacific aroused the ambition of an Englishman, Robert Thorne, a merchant of Bristol who carried on much of his business at Seville. He believed that there were great undiscovered lands in the tropical region of the Pacific—a conception later to be embodied in the unknown southern continent, *Terra Australis Incognita*, a dream of explorers until the days of Captain Cook. In 1527 Thorne wrote about this to the English Ambassador in Spain, and in 1530 he composed his *Declaration of the Indies* for the eyes of Henry VIII. He came to London to advocate the project, but died in 1532 before action had been taken. Thorne's *Declaration*, however, remained in the minds of projectors until Richard Hakluyt printed it in 1582. The Elizabethans of that time were the first English entrants into the Pacific. Drake, sailing in 1577, was instructed to discover and report upon the unknown continent. He did not do so, but raided the treasure coast of Peru instead. Then, in his *Golden Hind*, the first English ship to sail the Pacific and the Indian Ocean, he returned round the world as Magellan's men had done. He came home with great Spanish treasure and the promise of a spice trade with the Indonesian sultans whom he had visited. Thomas Cavendish made a somewhat similar voyage in 1586–8; and the Pacific, with its two attractions of Peruvian treasure and Indonesian spices, was firmly embedded in English ambitions. The East India Company was founded in 1600 to realise the second of these hopes.

Meanwhile the Dutch, having made good their independence against Spanish overlordship, had become a mercantile oceanic power; and the Dutch East India Company was more vigorous than the English in seizing the trade of the Spice Islands from the grasp of the declining Portuguese Empire.

III

At the opening of the seventeenth century we have thus the following world-position. The two original oceanic empires of Spain and Portugal had staked a huge claim, sanctioned by the Pope's bulls of partition in 1493, and were trying to make it good against increasing pressure from three hungry newcomers, the English, the French and the Dutch. Spain and Portugal were united by common interest and also by the fact that from 1580 to 1640 the King of Spain was also King of Portugal, although the colonial administrations were kept apart.

There had already been small-scale attempts at North American colonisation, by the French in the St Lawrence, and by the English under Raleigh's captains in Virginia, but these had failed; and the long Anglo-Spanish war from 1585 to 1604 deflected effort into commerce-raiding in the Atlantic and the Caribbean. With the peace and the new century colonisation began in earnest. The English made a permanent settlement in Virginia in 1607, and the French at Quebec in 1608. The English also took possession of Bermuda in 1609. Both nations were active in the West Indies, and by 1640 the English had established themselves in Barbados, St Kitts, Nevis, Montserrat and Antigua, while the French had Guadeloupe and Martinique, both larger than any of the English islands. On the northern border of Virginia the English, under Lord Baltimore, founded the new colony of Maryland in 1634, while twenty years earlier the Dutch had also entered North America with their colony of New Amsterdam at the mouth of the Hudson River. An entirely different stream of English emigrants, the Puritans, who were opposed to the early Stuart kings, peopled the colonies of New England, beginning with the Plymouth of the Pilgrim Fathers in 1620, and continuing with Massachusetts, Connecticut, Rhode Island, New Haven, and later Maine and New Hampshire. Newfoundland received its first handful of English settlers in 1610, with Frenchmen following on a different part of the coast. In South America all three interloping nations were active on the coast of Guiana, which then extended from the Orinoco to the Amazon and included the delta and lower course of that river. Little colonies rose and fell, and only a few were permanent, with the Dutch and French in possession. The English found the Amazon delta more attractive, but were beaten out after much fighting by the Portuguese of Brazil. In eastern Brazil, fronting the South Atlantic, the Dutch made a determined effort between 1620 and 1640 to evict the Portuguese. The fighting was on a greater scale than in Guiana. Ultimately the Portuguese prevailed and the Dutch withdrew. It was then that Portugal took her Brazilian Empire more seriously and was rewarded towards the end of the century by the discovery of rich gold mines in the São Paulo region of the south.

The mere enumeration of these ventures (and there were others) has occupied considerable space. Their natures and purposes have now to be considered. One motive, although not the most important, was military. Although France signed peace with Spain in 1598, and England in 1604, irregular fighting went on in the tropics. The treaties were inconclusive, and Spain and Portugal had not formally conceded the right of others to sail in American or East Indian waters. Every foreign sail there was viewed as that of a pirate, and a good deal of freebooting naturally resulted. The Dutch never made a definitive treaty with Spain until 1648, and Spanish-Dutch sea fighting was on a regular basis. The only entire Spanish treasure-fleet captured in all these long wars was that taken by the Dutch Admiral Piet Hein, off the coast of Cuba in 1628. But Atlantic treasure-raiding was in general unproductive, and practical men realised that the best way to oceanic wealth was to found plantations for the growing of wares not producible in Europe. Until about 1640 all the newcomers' plantations south of Canada and New England began on a tobacco-planting basis. Maryland and Virginia, Bermuda and the Caribbean islands, the Guiana coast and Amazon settlements all made tobacco their chief export crop until over-production resulted, and the Euro-

pean market was glutted. After that date Maryland and Virginia continued in tobacco, but the West Indies turned to sugar, which long produced enormous profit since the demand was never satisfied. By the middle of the seventeenth century Atlantic plantations were a first-class economic interest with all five of the ocean-going powers. In the north the codfish of the Newfoundland banks and the furs and beaver skins of the St Lawrence and Hudson river valleys formed parallel types of enterprise, with all concerned striving after monopolies and the depression of rivals. Militant commerce was pursued and thought of as a kind of warfare, and actual appeal to arms was never remote.

Of all the nations engaged in this competition, England alone had a surplus of home population willing to emigrate. In the other countries the traders, adventurers and well-born men seeking careers were plentiful; but working colonists in the requisite numbers were hard to come by. Hence came the phenomenal growth of the Atlantic slave trade, moderate in extent when initiated by Spain and Portugal at the outset, but multiplied many times by the plantation demand of the seventeenth century. With the early Portuguese explorers and Spanish empire-builders there had been a profession of altruistic motive in enslaving Negroes, that of spreading Christianity and saving souls; and the Spanish Government had encouraged the transportation of Negroes to the West with the conscious object of removing the temptation of the colonists to enslave the Indians, whom Spain recognised as her subjects with human rights. In the seventeenth century there was a general deterioration of ethics, and ruthless mercantilists treated the unfortunate African solely as merchandise. The early slavers captured their own slaves by raiding the African peoples of the Guinea coastline. The later development was to employ these peoples as agents for the more wholesale collection of slaves in the unknown interior. European trading forts dotted the coast, and Africans brought droves of fellow-Africans for sale in them. However much European expansion has in general brought material benefit to the world—and there is not the least doubt that it has—West Africa, where during three centuries it wrought little but horror, is a black blot upon its record.

England at the beginning of the seventeenth century was, or was thought to be, over-populated. The country was growing richer, yet there was much unemployment and distress, and this was a principal incentive to colonisation. In the reign of Elizabeth I, before the Spanish war, a group of public men, Gilbert, Raleigh, Hakluyt and others, had been concerned at the conditions of the poor and had sought to find the remedy by settling them in the empty lands of North America. In this aspect, land for subsistence rather than trade goods for sale was the primary object, although the promoters did not omit to point out that mutual trade would play its part; the unemployed of England would be employed in America and, when prosperous, would form a new market for English goods and so increase employment at home. The Spanish war frustrated the Elizabethan schemes by diverting energy to fighting. When it was over, the colonial plans were revived, and the reigns of James I and Charles I witnessed 'the great exodus' which justified the Elizabethan projectors. The merchants ventured the money, the gentry provided the leaders, and the poorer people in their tens of thousands came forward as the working colonists, encouraged by the promise of acquiring land and becoming economically free as they could never be at home. The poor man went as an indentured servant, contracted to work for a term of years for a richer employer in return for his passage out and the necessaries of life while in service. At the expiration of his indentures he was to receive a grant of land for himself and to become in his turn an employer of indentured servants. So long as there was unoccupied land within reach of shipping, and so long as there was a brisk demand for tobacco, whose culture needed little capital equipment, the system worked. It planted the English stock in all the tobacco colonies. Several coincidental changes of circumstances put an end to it by the middle of the century. The tobacco glut came first, reducing the smaller planters to distress while richer men consolidated the holdings and worked them more efficiently. This took place in Virginia, while the islands went in for sugar. This crop could only be worked on large estates with high expenditure on machinery and draught animals, and here the ex-indentured servant had no chance of being a planter himself. The sugar planters preferred the gang-labour of Negro slaves, and after 1650, while the Negroes came in ever larger numbers, the white population of the British West Indies decreased. Another cause of the decline of the indentured service system was that nearly everywhere the lands near 'tide water' were all taken up, and from no other lands could crops be exported. When these conditions became known in England voluntary emigration fell off. Involuntary emigration continued by the transportation of criminals, the kidnapping of unwary people (mostly children) in the English seaports, and the disposal of the prisoners taken in the civil wars. But the persons who went out under these headings were really slaves with little chance of prosperity or freedom, and as slaves they were bought and sold.

The New England emigration was

distinct from that to the plantations, and peculiarly English. Its leaders were mostly Puritan squires and gentlemen who disagreed with the religious views of Charles I and Archbishop Laud. Their motive was to found Calvinist communities in which the elders of the Church were also the rulers of the State. In the main they succeeded, and in the seventeenth century the Puritan colonies, Rhode Island excepted, were not the scene of any popular liberties or democratic politics. They were, however, attractive to the ordinary emigrant because they were economically prosperous. Hard work would bring success and the ownership of a freehold, and the New England colonies as a whole grew rich by exporting their surplus foodstuffs to the plantations. New England merchants came into being, selling their colonies' grain and butter and salted meat, and carrying fish from Newfoundland, sugar from Barbados, and slaves from Africa. In a generation Boston became a little metropolis of Atlantic trade and a rival of whom London uttered complaints.

IV

During the busy half-century which saw the Atlantic colonies founded, the original incentive to European expansion, the quest of Asiatic trade, was not forgotten; and, though the French were not at first active, the English and Dutch ventured more capital in it than in all their western undertakings. In the first stage both nations went for the same object, the spice trade of Indonesia, of which the rich focus lay in the small island group of the Moluccas, the true Spice Islands. No monopoly of these tiny specks was possible without maritime control of the whole South-East Asian archipelago and the approaches to it. Although both Drake and Cavendish had sailed through the archipelago, it was the Dutch who first began regular business

with a series of voyages from 1595 onwards. In 1602 the competing Dutch syndicates were amalgamated into the Dutch East India Company, which had from the outset the aspect of a department of the State, closely linked with it in finance and administration, and exercising monopoly powers which were ruthlessly used to crush interlopers. In the 1590s there were two independent English expeditions to the East by the Cape route, both ending disastrously, and then in 1600 the merchants of London combined to secure a charter as the East India Company. This London Company had also a monopoly as against its English fellow-subjects, but it had not the same measure of State support as the Dutch enjoyed. The early Stuart governments gave it little assistance, sometimes filched its profits, and connived at and even promoted the voyages of interlopers who interfered seriously with the Company's business in the East. The idea of monopoly was unpopular in England, as the domestic proceedings of Elizabeth's later years had shown. The East India merchants were also vulnerable to the economic argument which condemned them for exporting silver coin—in other words, solid wealth—in order to bring home luxuries. This so-called 'bullionist' doctrine carried much weight until it was gradually realised that re-export of the goods brought in more wealth than was originally expended, whereupon the 'mercantilist' view superseded the bullionist.

The Dutch were mercantilist from the outset. They consciously worked their East India Company as an aid to the State in financing its war of independence against Spain, as a contributor to the creation of sea power, and as a wealth-producer for the enrichment of the nation at large; and for more than half a century they were highly successful. They ousted the Portuguese from all the controlling points of Indonesia; and by superior energy and weightier investment they prevented the English from stepping in with them to share the victory. Dutch ships in the archipelago became four times as numerous as English, and the naval bases, notably the new foundations of Batavia in Java, were in Dutch hands. The end of this competition came in 1623 when the twelve English factors at Amboyna in the Moluccas were executed by the Dutch on a charge of conspiring with the natives against them. The Dutch thereafter nearly monopolised the spice trade. In the long run it proved a barren victory. For the value of the spices depended on their rarity, and the monopolists found that when they increased the volume of their business the European demand was over-satisfied and prices fell. The West Indian tobacco-glut was illustrating the same principles at the same time. The Dutch continued to dominate Indonesia, but meanwhile other fields of Asiatic commerce were developing all round them until relatively the Dutch were left with a stagnant possession. This situation began to grow evident in the second half of the seventeenth century and was established in the eighteenth.

Long before the control of the Spice Islands was decided, the importance of these other trades began to be evident. The English early recognised the value of India itself, and especially of northern India, in which the Mughal emperors were firmly established. The trade of northern India had two main exits to the ocean, on the east through the Ganges delta to the Bay of Bengal, on the west through the port of Surat, which the Portuguese had not captured, as they had Bombay, Goa and Calicut. From 1607 the English established themselves at Surat, not as in a possession, which it was not, but as in a merchant factory existing under the juris-

diction of the Mughal Emperor. A long and intermittent war with the Portuguese of western India ended with an English victory which in 1635 achieved a local treaty, opening the Portuguese seaports to English ships. India presented the elements of a trade more expansive than that of the spices—three products at least for which the European demand was unlimited. These were the cotton fabrics produced by Indian hand-weavers; indigo, a dye-stuff much desired by European cloth-makers; and saltpetre, indispensable for the gunpowder of European warfare. In addition, India provided a limited but growing demand for certain English manufacturers, and so enabled the Company to diminish its unpopular exportation of silver coin.

In half a century the London Company established itself at several points on the Indian coastlines, with factories at Balasore and Masulipatam on the eastern side of the Mughal Empire, an outright possession at Madras, which it fortified in 1639, and a river-factory on the Hughli in the rich Mughal province of Bengal. In addition it still retained on the edge of Indonesia its pepper-factory at Achin in Sumatra, and a foothold at Bantam in Java, where Chinese shipping arrived to use the place as a small-scale Anglo-Chinese *entrepôt*. The Chinese kept their own coasts closed against Europeans, except at Macao in the Canton river, where the Portuguese had entry; and Macao was opened to English trade by the treaty of 1635. The English did not at first do much there, but they had at least found the way to China. Some of them learned to drink tea; in 1640 the Dutch brought a few chests to Europe, and in 1660 Pepys mentioned tea in his diary as a novel drink in England. From these small beginnings a mighty trade, far transcending the spices, was to grow in the following century. In western India the

English obtained a possession in full sovereignty in 1660 by the Portuguese cession of Bombay on the marriage of Catherine of Braganza to Charles II. At this stage the English were stronger in western India than anywhere else, and from that coast they had already developed a coffee trade with the Arab ports to the eastward: coffee was about a generation earlier than tea in its real entry into English social life.

By the mid-seventeenth century three European powers were competing in the eastern seas, Portugal declining, England and the Netherlands advancing. Their goal was mercantile wealth, and their methods were those of war. Their field was maritime, and sea-power was showing itself, as never before, a determinant of world-power. A few dozen armed ships, mostly small, and a few thousand seamen, suffering a dreadful death-rate from scurvy, were creating the aspect and the problems of the world to follow.

After the mid-century another competitor appeared. Earlier French entries into the Indian Ocean had been ineffective, although Richelieu's company of 1642 had maintained for a few years a precarious foothold in Madagascar. The permanent French East India Company was founded by Colbert in 1664, to be conducted in complete subordination to the king's government; for Colbert was an ultra-planner who believed in regimenting all commerce, as he explained in a famous document that has often been quoted. The French acted with vigour on the eastern side of India, where they founded in 1674 the fortified stronghold of Pondicherry, not far from Madras on the Coromandel coast. It was now being recognised that Bengal was the richest trading province. The French soon opened business there, and by the end of the century they had established themselves at Chandernagore, which the Nawab allowed them to fortify.

In Bengal the English at Hughli were at a disadvantage, having only a mercantile factory under Indian jurisdiction and often subject to arbitrary exactions. In 1686 Job Charnock, the head merchant, chose an unoccupied site lower down the river at Calcutta, and there established a fortified headquarters for the Bengal trade. Early Calcutta was terribly unhealthy and remote from the populous centres of the province. But Charnock's move was strategically brilliant. Calcutta, unlike the river-ports above it, was accessible to sea-going ships; and the security of its position quickly attracted Indian traders whose settlement provided the nucleus of a great city.

V

The Atlantic colonies developed no less powerfully than the Eastern trades in the second half of the seventeenth century. Spain organised and consolidated the Western Empire which her *conquistadores* had so rapidly grasped. Treasure was still her greatest interest, silver from Mexico, very much more silver from Peru, where the mine of Potosí seemed inexhaustible, and a little gold from scattered sources. But the commodity output of the Spanish Caribbean coasts increased—hides, dye-stuffs, tobacco, sugar; and Spain was also conducting a regular, if restricted, trade with China across the Pacific. Her galleons did not enter Chinese ports, but met the Chinese merchants at Manila in the Philippines, which had become a Spanish possession by reason of Magellan's discovery. All this Pacific trade crossed the Isthmus of Panama and came through the Caribbean to Europe. Portuguese Brazil grew also more important. The coastal settlements were sugar and tobacco plantations, drawing slave labour from Africa.

The gold mines in the southern interior yielded rich results for more than eighty years.

England drew her chief Atlantic wealth from her share of the West Indies, Barbados, Jamaica (taken from Spain in 1655), and the Leeward Islands. Sugar was everywhere the principal plantation crop, but there were others; indigo in competition with the Eastern traders, cotton and cocoa. Cotton was not yet a textile material of prime importance, although soon to become one, but it had various uses for quilting and padding and its yarn was being mixed with wool and flax. But sugar was the maker of fortunes in the Caribbean, and in Charles II's time little Barbados, the size of the Isle of Wight, was rated 'the principal pearl in His Majesty's crown'. Tobacco, which had left the West Indies, was settling down in Virginia and Maryland to steady progress keeping pace with the increase of Europe's purchasing power. New England in this half-century became economically independent of England, and politically very nearly independent. Its growing population was soundly based on an agriculture of English type and thus not tied to shipping facilities for its living. Where the planter farther south concentrated all on producing his plantation crop, and imported foodstuffs for his slaves and luxuries for himself, clothes, wines and furniture, and lumber for all the purposes of his estate, the New Englander lived on his own abundance of corn and flesh, dressed with Puritan plainness in his homespun cloth, wore New England shoes, and was beginning to make his tools and knives and ploughshares of New England iron. And this was only one side of the picture. The New England seaports, Boston more than any, provided the other; for they were dealing as though they were a 'mother country' in the plantation trades, their

ships carrying all the rich wares for New England profit, as freely as if they hailed from London or Bristol. English mercantilists did not like it, and began to regret that England had allowed this questionable offspring to come into being.

Mercantilism valued a colony as a source of supply of goods not producible in the mother country. It valued the colonists also as a market for the sale of home-produced commodities. Both considerations dictated that there must be no direct commerce between the colony and any foreign nation: if the plantation products did ultimately pass to the foreigner, they must do so through the hands of the mother country's merchants, who would make their profit by the transaction. Hence the closed empire, closed to foreign traders both ways, was a policy dictated by mercantilism. At the same time national defence (including national aggression) demanded the maximum of sea-power, and so foreign ships were not allowed to 'carry' goods between the mother country and the colonies. By the English system every ship in the colonial trade had to be English built (unless a prize captured in war), English owned, and three-quarters of the seamen had to be of British nationality. The Scots were legally debarred, but in practice accepted, as contributing to the 75 per cent of English nationals, but Scottish ships were excluded from the colonial trade until the Union of 1707. The word 'English', as used in the Acts, included the colonists, so that colonial shipping enjoyed all the privileges. The English system of Navigation Acts, embodying these principles elaborated in great detail, was built up between 1650 and the end of the century. France under Colbert's economic inspiration was equally committed to these mercantile principles, and more rigid in enforcing them. Spain and Portugal had from the age of discovery sought to exclude foreign ships from their colonial possessions, and this to the discoverers had seemed a natural right. It was reinforced by the religious sanction of the papal donation, and afterwards by the necessity for preserving the overseas populations from Protestant contamination. The Dutch also were hard mercantilists, although by no means doctrinaires, for they perceived that in certain conditions a free colonial port, open to foreign ships, might be to their advantage; and such a port they made of New Amsterdam in North America, although they never showed any sign of such liberality in the East Indies.

The French greatly developed their sugar plantations in the late seventeenth century. Martinique and Guadeloupe were highly productive, and French planters established themselves in the western half of Hispaniola, the largest of the Spanish islands. Under the name of Hayti (formerly the Indian word for the whole island) this French colony became the greatest of all the sugar producers as the eighteenth century advanced.

English mercantilists meanwhile achieved two new advances in North America. In 1663 Charles II chartered a syndicate of prominent men to colonise Carolina, the region lying south of Virginia. The object was to produce silk and wines, for which the climate was thought to be suitable, and to relieve England of the disadvantage of buying these things from European rivals. Carolina ultimately developed as two colonies, North and South, neither of which actually produced the planned products. South Carolina, the more important, found a new plantation crop in rice, grown from seed brought round the world from China. Farther north at New Amsterdam the Dutch used their holding less as a settlement colony (they had only 7000 people there) than as a trading post.

They collected beaver skins from the Indians up the Hudson River, and they also made the port free to the ships of New England and the other English colonies of the American coast. By this means the Dutch were able to ship to Europe plantation wares that by English law should have been sent exclusively to England, and to disseminate among the English colonies manufactured goods from the continent of Europe. This use of New Amsterdam appeared outrageous to the English mercantilists, and in 1664 without declaring war Charles II's Government sent a naval expedition which captured the colony and renamed it New York.

Late in Charles II's reign occurred the last example of the religious-exile type of colony. The society of Friends or Quakers, founded by George Fox, were bitterly persecuted in Restoration England. William Penn, one of their leaders, was a creditor of the Government. Instead of his money he accepted a large grant of land on the Delaware River, and there founded the Quaker colony of Pennsylvania. England thus completed her occupation of the American coast from New England south to Carolina.

The valley of the Hudson leads northwards in the direction of the valley of the St Lawrence, where the French had been in occupation since the beginning of the century. A French officer, on hearing of the English conquest of New York, exclaimed: 'The King of England grasps at all America!' It was indeed a prophecy, for the British on the Hudson and the French on the St Lawrence became inevitably involved in a contest for the control of the unsubdued Indian trading country between them. That contest, in regular or irregular form, was to endure for almost exactly a hundred years until the Peace of Paris in 1763 evicted the French Government, although not the French people, from North America (*see* Chapter 17). For the time, however, New France prospered. It contained agricultural colonists on the banks of the St Lawrence, although never in numbers as large as the country could have supported; and a fringe of hardy pioneers pressing into the forests to the west and south, as traders to collect furs from the Indians, as missionary priests to convert them to Christianity and French civilisation. In both capacities the French suffered heavy casualties, for the Indians of the Six Nations were cruel and bloodthirsty, and many a priest and trader met with death by torture. In some respects the French colonisation differed from the English, and notably it refused to allow scope to the religious exile. The Huguenots were persecuted in Louis XIV's France as the Quakers in Charles II's England. But the Huguenots were not allowed to seek peace in Canada, where many would gladly have gone. Instead they were compelled to renounce their nationality by settling in England and the Netherlands, and France lost good citizens to the gain of her neighbours. A handful of Huguenots even went to far South Africa, where the Dutch had made a settlement at Cape Town for the victualling of their ships voyaging to Asia.

VI

No sooner were the shores of the Atlantic parcelled out among the great oceanic powers than wars for colonial conquests began. These wars were occasioned not only by rivalry in the true colonies of the American side of the ocean but also in West Africa, which had become primarily a slave-catchment area, and in the Far East, where the great trading companies competed. It is not easy to date the beginning of the colonial wars, for at first they were a by-product of and subordinate to the great wars of Continental Europe with which

this chapter is not concerned (*see* Chapter 15). But the colonial interest grew important in the English Elizabethan period. It became the dictating cause in the East when the Dutch evicted first the Portuguese and then the English from the Spice Islands, and in the Atlantic perhaps from 1654–5, when Oliver Cromwell attacked Spain for the primary purpose of making West Indian conquests. The Anglo-Dutch war of 1664–7 was another predominantly colonial contest, involving New York, Guiana and West African slaving, and the oceanic trades in general. Thereafter for a time colonial ambitions were subsidiary to the internal high politics of Europe, although in the great war of the Spanish Succession they filled an almost equal place. The British and Dutch resisted the claim of the Bourbons to the throne of Spain because they dreaded the results of French control of the Spanish Empire in America, a clear instance of the balance-of-power motive applied to colonies, treasure output and oceanic trade. The war ended in the Peace of Utrecht, 1713, a satisfactory compromise in its oceanic aspects, obtained by British naval superiority as much as by Marlborough's victories in Europe.

The Utrecht settlement set the stage for the essential eighteenth-century period that followed. The Spanish Empire remained separately Spanish, although under a Bourbon sovereign who was never to be identical with the Bourbon King of France: there was in practice a Bourbon alliance but not a unity. There followed twenty-five years of comparative peace, chequered by alarms of war but by no great oceanic conflict. During this period Great Britain, with Scotland admitted to participation in the Empire by the Union of 1707, developed and consolidated her oceanic interests. The British West Indies still yielded more wealth to the mother country than any other region, but the value of the Asiatic trades was rapidly coming forward, to surpass the West Indian interest in the second half of the century. The North American trade increased less markedly, and not in proportion to the phenomenal growth of the British-American population, which almost doubled its numbers every twenty years. The Americans were still loyal to the Crown and accepted their membership of the British Empire, within which they were free and prosperous. But they thought of themselves as equal fellow-subjects with those in Great Britain, having carried with them overseas all 'the rights of Englishmen' in the formative period. The British at home, on the contrary, thought of the Americans as their subordinates— '*our* subjects in the colonies'—since Parliament, elected solely by Great Britain, had legal jurisdiction over every subject of the King. These opposing conceptions remained instinctive and unformulated until at a later stage some concrete disputes forced them into definition.

France made a remarkable recovery from her losses in the war, which had seen her shipping almost driven off the seas. Her East India Company revived and made steady progress, with Pondicherry rivalling Madras, and Chandernagore more than rivalling Calcutta. The French sugar islands increased their output, sending to Europe a greater volume of produce than that of the British colonies; and the French took a greater share than the British in the exploitation of the previously untouched islands of the Windward group. French frontiersmen in Canada pushed south-west towards the headwaters of the Ohio and thence towards the Mississippi, up which river other Frenchmen were advancing from its mouth in the Gulf of Mexico, having founded New Orleans in 1717. Although at Utrecht she acknow-

ledged British sovereignty of Newfoundland, France still shared its fishery, the famous 'nursery' of seamen and sea-power jealously tended by the admiralties of both nations.* Altogether, France, twenty years after Utrecht, seemed and was more powerful than she had ever been. It is difficult for us, with our knowledge that Bourbon France was to end in the Revolutionary crash, to realise this: but it was patent to all at the time. Mid-century France was not decadent, but a living, muscular, ambitious oceanic power, intent on wiping out past defeat at the expense of the victors.

Bourbon Spain also recovered and progressed. Her American Empire settled down to a well-disciplined increase in trade and population, with the output of commodities growing more important than that of treasure. Spain also built up a combatant navy in the generation after Utrecht, second to that of France, but the two combined exceeding in tonnage that of Great Britain. In the late seventeenth century Spain had been the most decrepit of the European powers. In the early eighteenth she had to be reckoned with. Portugal as an oceanic empire had long been in peaceful decline. After the first rude Dutch and English assaults in the East, after 1660 let us say, she had lost no more possessions, while in Brazil she had foiled Dutch aggression in a war fought out to the end. But as a world-power she was dying. The reason was that as a mother country she was too small and ill equipped for the changing conditions. These were now making oceanic trade not

---

* It has been pointed out that, on statistics of tonnage and men employed, the prosaic coal trade between Newcastle and London was an even greater nursery of seamen than the fishery. But since it involved no international rivalry the coal trade never received the same publicity in this respect. One of its seamen was Captain Cook.

an isolated objective in itself but a feeder of home industry, and Portugal had no industrial basis on which to grow. Her population was too small, too ignorant and primitive. Lisbon indeed was a great counting-house of world trade, but the trade was nominally Portuguese. In the eighteenth century it was for the most part really British, worked by British firms, feeding British industrial development, and protected by British sea-power. This was the main reason why Portugal suffered no more territorial losses in her decline.

The Dutch Netherlands also experienced relative but less notable decline. Holland, to use the convenient name for the whole combination of provinces, remained a fair civilised country, good to live in, with a vigorous sea trade, plenty of employment, and no desperate poverty. But the population was relatively small, the great wars had whittled away the maritime predominance, the land frontier was naturally weak and the state in dread of the great armies of France, the East Indian monopoly stationary or regressive, the country lacking the coal and iron for the oncoming new industrial conditions. The greatest asset of the Dutch was their traditional financial ability, rendering Amsterdam still second only to London, but it was not enough to maintain them as a great oceanic power.

In 1739 the aggression inherent in the mercantilist conception of European enterprise in the outer world broke down the temporary peace and commenced the last and greatest period of the oceanic wars. They were complicated with internal European disputes, but no longer subordinate to them: the sea powers were consciously fighting out the question of mercantile supremacy. These wars, Jenkins' Ear, the Austrian Succession, the Seven Years', American Independence and the Maritime War growing out of it,

are part of the well-known canon of British and European history, and their details are too extensive for this survey. Their outline is as follows. From 1739 to the Peace of Paris that ended the Seven Years' War in 1763, Great Britain fought the Bourbons for control of North America, the West Indies and India, and of these three objects she achieved the first and the last. No sooner had the known half of North America become completely British than the growing nationhood of the British colonists found passionate expression in the demand for full exemption from the jurisdiction of Parliament. It was a claim that we today now recognise as right and natural in any mature colonial community, but only a few minds recognised it then. It had no chance of being coolly considered, for internal British politics were bristling with angry questions and the focus of interest in the Empire was shifting to the East. The result was the American revolt and the independence of the United States. Out of the War of Independence grew the last general oceanic war. The Bourbon powers struck in for revenge, Spain for the recovery of lost possessions such as Gibraltar and Jamaica, France for the supremacy in world trade that had passed to Great Britain. While the Americans succeeded, the Bourbons failed substantially. In their plans the Caribbean was to become a Bourbon lake, the Mediterranean of America, but in fact the British West Indies emerged unscathed. In India British power was to be ended completely, but in fact, although by a very narrow escape, it survived and grew greater; and India was more than ever as Vasco da Gama had seen it at the outset, the base for the pushing of all interests to the eastward, and especially the China trade, now attaining a stature that bade fair to dwarf the rest. In the last great conflict of the old imperial powers

Great Britain had retained what was essential and even improved her position in it, while she had lost domination of the American colonies, from the mercantile view not valuable, from the moral, incapable in any case of forcible retention.

VII

Three centuries of oceanic effort had thus produced great effects on Europe and the world. In all the Americas the native peoples, some primitive, some civilised in strange isolated forms, had been overrun and their future lives utterly changed. In West Africa native barbarism had been wedded to European criminality and directed without mercy or conscience to the enslavement of men. Throughout Southern Asia old-established though static or decaying civilisations had received great shocks but not an overthrow, and had the possibility of ultimate benefit from a period of subjection to new disciplines. On Europe itself the effects were stupendous. Beneath the courtly glitter and the mental brilliance of the Renaissance age had lain a vast underworld of poverty so ghastly, of physical and moral degradation so usual and untended, as to be almost incredible today. So it had been through all the centuries, the fifteenth no less than the first. The better regions were those with some industrial employment, North Italy, the Rhineland, the Netherlands, England, but even they were terribly

bad. Europe was waiting for something which she could not herself provide. Oceanic trade based on empire-building was the catalyst. New supplies and new demands strengthened industry. The treasure was fluid capital to give life to enterprise. The mental stimulus of world contacts was, if one may make bold to claim it, as great as that of the new learning. An expanding economy provided for rising population, in itself a sign of betterment, for rising population meant not a rising birth-rate but a falling death-rate. East India companies with capital counted in millions taught rulers how to handle finance as business men and not as the spendthrift children they had been. Long-term mercantilist policies trained statesmen to view law-making as something more than mere prohibition and retribution. The trader's desire to sell an increasing range of products begot ultimately the idea that the better the social condition of his customers the more they would buy. All this was inter-acting and cumulative, until the nineteenth century became what would have seemed a material paradise to sixteenth-century men.

And then Europe began to repay her debt to Africa and Asia, where states and nations which the past could not have dreamed of have emerged under European guidance and will develop under their own. But this, while noted to round off one chapter, is the beginning of a trespass into another.

12 THE NATIVE CULTURES OF AFRICA

by Godfrey Lienhardt

Apart from the ancient and medieval connection of the Levant with Egypt and the Sudanese and Ethiopian hinterland, and the Roman domination of North Africa the contacts of Europeans with Africa had been confined to the outer fringes of the enormous continent.

The central theme of a study of Africa's native cultures should be their great diversity—diversity in the racial affinities of those who have created them, in their beliefs and institutions, in the extent and nature of foreign influences upon them, and in the scope and quality of their cultural achievements. The modern political boundaries of Africa were drawn out with little or no regard for these deep indigenous differences, and the early travellers sometimes obscured them. The experienced but irascible Sir Samuel Baker (1821–93), dismissed equally, as the 'obtuseness of savage hordes', both the recalcitrance of his detribalised porters, and the prudence of African rulers whose statecraft interfered with his plans.

In the last half-century, a more discriminating study of the modern native cultures of Africa has become firmly established, but the systematic search for evidence of their pre-nineteenth century history is only now seriously beginning. Evidence of historical continuity between ancient and modern cultures is still very incomplete, and, outside North Africa and Ethiopia, there are no written records by Africans to bridge the gap between the limits of oral tradition, and the more distant past to which archaeological ex-

cavation, and the earliest foreign records, bear testimony. Whole cities, their architecture, their culture, and arts have apparently become lost to the memory of those who now dwell near their sites.

While the record of distant events is uncertain, in much of Africa customs and beliefs which in Europe are known only in the perspective of history still remain part of living cultures. Although it is obvious that even the simplest cultures of Africa have been created by long processes of invention and change, it remains true that some peoples have preserved into the present century ways of life which have probably not greatly changed for many hundreds of years. Values and customs and social institutions reminiscent of ancient Egypt and the ancient World, or of the Hebrews of the Old Testament, or of medieval and pre-industrial Europe, all enter into the modern life of Africa. Thus, even though Africa's own history is largely as yet unwritten, its peoples have a share in ancient cultural traditions through their own living experience. A study of native African cultures can therefore only begin in the present or in the recent past.

II

It is convenient to distinguish broadly between major ethnic groupings in Africa by a combination of physical, linguistic, and cultural tests. In this way, the peoples of Africa may be divided into the Semites, the Hamites, the 'true' Negroes, the Nilotes and Nilo-Hamites, the Bantu-speaking peoples, the Khoisan peoples—the Bush-

AFRICA – ENVIRONMENT AND TRIBES

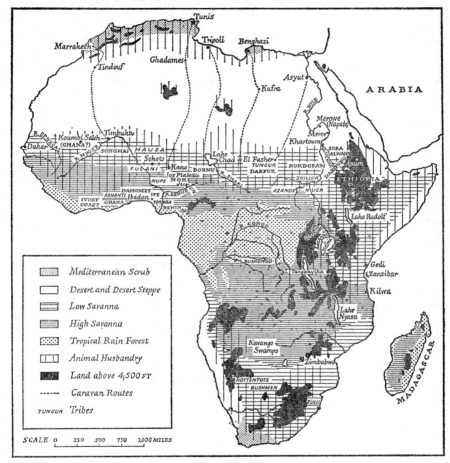

men and Hottentots—and the Negrillos or Pygmies.

The Semites are represented mainly by the Arabs and some of the peoples of Ethiopia. The influence of the Arabs upon Africa south of the Sahara desert is described later, inevitably, in a very brief form, but the literate civilisation of Ethiopia can scarcely be adequately treated in a summary fashion at the side of the many non-literate cultures here considered. However, and hence, despite its historical importance, it is only possible to mention it in passing.

Relating to the Semites, and far longer established in southern Africa, are the Hamites. The origin and even the precise nature of what is known as the 'Hamitic' element in ancient and modern African populations is likely for long to be a matter of controversy among some ethnologists. The purest Hamitic stock is represented in the ancient and modern Egyptians, in some Ethiopians, in the

Galla and Somali of Ethiopia and the Horn of Africa, and in the Berbers of North Africa and the Touareg of the Sahara, among other African peoples. Professor Seligman has written that 'the civilisations of Africa are the civilisations of the Hamites', an indication of a general tendency in African anthropology and archaeology to identify superior cultural achievements, particularly in the arts of government, with 'Hamitic' influence. This may perhaps be in part because the pure Hamites, like Europeans, are racially Caucasian, having typically straight faces, narrow noses, lips which are not everted and other features which are not characteristic of the 'true' Negro. Some of such Hamitic characteristics are found in many of the Negro populations of Africa. What is known as the 'Hamitic theory', in its various forms, attempts to account for the presence of these and other characteristics by positing an original conjunction—or interbreeding—of two quite different stocks, one Hamitic and one truly Negroid. Whatever may be the value of this theory for accounting for observable differences in modern African populations, it must be said that 'Hamitic' physical features are so widely diffused over Negro populations, and so deeply infused into them, that it is often difficult (except by the strictly linguistic definition of the term 'Hamitic') to establish where the 'truly Negro' and 'Hamitic' components can be rightly separated from each other.

Most of the peoples of Africa south of the Sahara are generally and popularly termed 'Negroes'; but the 'true Negro' is considered to be typical especially of West Africa, on the Guinea Coast and in Nigeria, the Sudan Republic, Cameroon and Congo (Kinshasa). To this type belong some of the Bantu-speakers as well as the Sudanic-speakers of West Africa. The 'true Negro' characteristics include, beside black skin, a broad and rather flat nose, everted lips, spirally hair and often a marked prominence of the lower jaw, with medium stature and sturdy build. Such characteristics in whole or in part are found in populations which contain Negroes of more Hamitic type, while some of the physical attributes of the Hamites occur in 'true Negro' populations.

It has been held that the Hamitic strain in Africa is older than the truly Negroid. The earliest skull with 'true Negro' characteristics was found in a Mesolithic site near Khartoum, while Hamitic remains are associated in East Africa with the earlier prehistoric cultures of the Upper Paleolithic. Unfortunately, the equatorial forest region which is the principal home of the 'true Negro' is an environment in which archaeological evidence is less well-preserved than in the drier areas of the Sudan and East Africa.

A blend of Hamitic and Negro characteristics is found particularly among several peoples of East-Central Africa, subdivided primarily on a linguistic basis into Nilotes and Nilo-Hamites. The Nilotes are, typically, tall and slender, and include such peoples as the Nuer and the Dinka, and the various Lwoo-speaking peoples of the Republic of the Sudan, Uganda and Kenya. The Nilo-Hamites are so called because their languages were thought to contain definite Hamitic elements as well as Nilotic, but the extent to which they do so is now a matter of dispute. They are found chiefly in the Sudan, Kenya and northern Tanganyika. Their best known representatives are possibly the pastoral Masai, but they include also the Bari and Lotuko of the Sudan, the Nandi-speaking peoples of Kenya and others.

The Bantu-speakers are the largest group of people in Africa whose languages belong to a common family. They occupy the greater part of the southern half of the continent below a line drawn from the coast of Cameroon and across the Central African Republic and the Congo, through the region of Lake Victoria to the hinterland of northern Kenya. They include very many different tribes and groups of tribes, living in different environments and differing in their basic economies, from the agricultural Negro civilisations of the Congo, with their lavish plastic art, to the semi-pastoral warriors such as the Nguni peoples of South Africa, whose best known representatives are the Zulu. Among Bantu, as might be expected, there are also great variations of physical type between the 'Hamitic' and the 'true Negro'.

The Pygmies or Negrillos, now confined to the forests of the Congo, form another group. They consist of several tribes all of whom have borrowed so extensively from the languages of their Bantu neighbours as to raise doubts about the nature of any indigenous language they may have had. Finally, there are the Bushmen and Hottentots who together are the Khoisan peoples of South Africa. The short yellow Bushmen, with their 'peppercorn' hair, often prominent buttocks, and mongoloid eyes, are sharply distinguished from all the Negro peoples. They are certainly one of the most ancient indigenous peoples of Africa, where they were widely spread in prehistoric times. Like the related Hottentots, the Bushmen have been unable to hold their own against Bantu and European enemies, and their remnants are now confined to the desert and semi-desert of South-West Africa. The pastoral Hottentots exist only in a state of cultural degeneration, in South-West Africa north of the Orange River, though their blood has survived in some of the Cape-Coloured and other mixtures of European, Hottentot and Bantu stocks.

The ethnology of Africa is complex, but the geography of the continent is simple as compared with Europe and Asia. The larger part of it consists of a stable plateau, with few mountain barriers to the movement of populations. The largest natural obstacle is the Sahara desert. Further south, the swamps of the Nile Basin, which even now can present problems to navigation, prevented the penetration of the heart of Africa from the north until the well-equipped expeditions of the nineteenth century. In the west, tropical forest, unsuitable for pastoral peoples, set a limit beyond which such peoples could not expand, discouraged Arab penetration from the north, and helped to cut off the interior from the coastal fringe. The Ethiopian escarpment and plateau kept those who were accustomed to its air and climate from settling in the steamy plains of the south-eastern Sudan.

Yet many of the obstacles to African discovery which delayed foreign exploration of the interior for so long cannot over the centuries have been equally effective in preventing the movements of African peoples themselves. The Sahara desert was less extensive in prehistoric times than it is today, and hand-axes of Chellean and Acheulian type found there indicate that much of the desert was habitable in the middle Pleistocene (*see* Chapter 2). Across the old-established caravan routes, northern influences from the Mediterranean world have constantly filtered into the western and central Sudan, and Negroes, voluntarily or as domestic slaves, have reached North Africa and beyond. In the west, the tropical forest belt has not prevented contact between the peoples of the forest and those of the savannah which encircles it. In most of the continent, in fact, there are traditions of movements of populations, which may, however, have been slow and small in scale. The wide admixture of different stocks also suggests that the present populations of Africa have been produced by long and slow processes of migration and miscegenation, with occasional more dramatic eruptions of conquering peoples who have then been slowly absorbed into the populations they have subdued. The diversity of Africa's native cultures thus cannot be attributed simply to the geographical isolation of many different groups of peoples from each other.

III

These cultures may be related to three principal environmental backgrounds. In the north of Negro Africa towards the Sahara, in the Horn, and in South-West Africa, are desert and semi-desert, the home of pastoral nomads and, in South-West Africa, of the hunting and collecting Bushmen. In the equatorial west is tropical rain-forest, stretching inland from the Gulf of Guinea, across southern Cameroon into Gabon, the Central African Republic, and both the Congo republics as far as the equator. Here, and in the moist savannah which surrounds the central forest, live the primarily agricultural peoples of Africa, broadly divided into those whose staple crops are root-crops and plantains, and those who depend primarily upon different kinds of grains. The rest of Africa south of the Sahara consists in the main of several types of tropical grasslands, with patches of highland forest and high grassland plateau. In the tropical grasslands, various kinds of mixed farming form the basis of the economy.

Even the simplest of African societies—those of the Bushmen and the Pygmies—knew some form of trade and barter, and foreign trade has for several centuries contributed to the wealth of the Negro civilisation of West Africa; but the exploi-

tation of natural resources on a large scale has of course awaited the introduction of a money economy and the extensive specialisation of wage-labour which has accompanied it. The native cultures of Africa have been always basically cultures of subsistence farmers and stockbreeders, in some cases enriched by trade, especially in slaves and gold.

The simple hunting and collecting cultures of the Bushmen and Pygmies therefore occupy only a small part of the picture. Technologically, they are truly 'primitive' in any sense of the word, and though some admiration may be felt for their cleverness in adapting themselves to difficult environments, they represent something of a quite different scale of achievement from the more characteristic cultures of Africa, in which adaptation to environment is combined with a measure of control. The Bushmen have produced notable works of art, but the Pygmies are rather defined by what they lack materially than by what they possess. Possessions would merely hinder them in the nomadic forest existence which, despite contact with 'higher' cultures, they freely prefer, and for which they require little more than their bows and arrows, scanty clothing of bark-cloth, skins and leaves, and leaf-shelters. Their economy of wandering hunters and collectors narrowly limits the size of Pygmy bands, and prevents any elaboration of political institutions.

Yet, with this simple technology, the Pygmies are reported to have great talents which are for the most part not widely appreciated. Their dancing and choral song, their acting, mimicry, and their art of story-telling, recommended the 'dancing dwarfs' to the courts of the Pharoahs, fascinated the nineteenth-century travellers Schweinfurth and Junker, and compelled the admiration of Fr. Schebesta, the foremost serious student of Pygmy life.

This discrepancy between material and mental accomplishments often applies to the rich Negro kingdoms which offer more than the Pygmies for foreign observation and appreciation. In all these non-literate societies, we have as yet only hints of the development of the arts of song, dance and poetry, and no very thorough understanding of the real meaning of their myths and conceptions. Such an understanding depends upon an intimacy with languages and environments which was rarely achieved before the last thirty-five years. Without it, to write of the cultures of Africa is as if to appraise the cultures of Europe without more than an aside about their literature and theology.

The Bushmen are better known than the Pygmies, in that the rock-paintings of their ancestors are a conspicuous achievement. The scarcity of water in the Bushmen's present desert home makes agriculture impossible, and prevents the settlement of any large aggregations of people. Their principal weapons are the bow and ingeniously constructed arrows which, since they are too weak to kill by penetration alone, are often tipped with poisons. Some tribes have hunting spears and throwing sticks, and there are stone-weighted digging sticks, sometimes pointed with iron which is obtained by barter from the Bantu neighbours of the Bushmen. Traps and snares, clothing of skins worked by the men, fire-sticks, and ostrich egg shell beads and incised ostrich egg shells for water storage may be listed as the rest of Bushman material culture.

In their present state, the Bushmen have ceased to produce, and even most of them to understand, the rock-paintings and engravings by which they are best known. Bushman-type pictures of animals, hunting and battle-scenes, dancing and ceremonial activities are widely distributed over southern Africa, and extend into North Africa and parts of Southern Europe. Along with microlithic tools and weapons discovered at many prehistoric sites in Africa, these pictures provide evidence for the early presence of Bushman-like cultures far outside their present home.

The paintings and engravings are of many styles and periods, and some were probably produced until the end of the nineteenth century. The colours of the paintings are earth pigments, mostly reds, browns, yellows and blacks, with occasional blues and greys. These colours were ground in stone mortars and mixed with animal fat, and seem to have been applied either with a feather or pliant spatula to outlines already traced upon the rock face. Like that of the Paleolithic hunters in Europe, this art as Professor Schapera says shows 'a definite attempt to portray objects and scenes as they actually appear at the moment, and not as what they may be conceived ideally.' The artists emphasise 'the unity of the representations rather than the details'. Some of the paintings show an ability to produce perspective by foreshortening. The natural and easy rhythmical lines, creating an impression of a quick coordination of hand and eye, are among the qualities which have strongly recommended Bushman art to European artists and critics. The purpose of the pictures is unknown.

Though racially akin to the Bushmen, the Hottentots have not produced any remarkable art. They are said to have excelled in song and dance, and their original form of social organisation, with its chiefs and tribal councils, was more complex than that of the Bushmen. The Hottentot tribes were pastoralists, practised the smelting of iron, and made pottery and wooden vessels, mats and baskets. Before they completely lost their tribal integrity, they had a way of life comparable in its essentials to that of other pastoral peoples of Africa of different racial stock.

IV

In sharp contrast to the cultures so far mentioned are the elaborate and highly organised kingdoms of West Africa. There are broad differences between the states of the forest Negroes, and those of the Negroes of the savannahs and semi-desert whose lands look northwards across the Sahara to the Arab and Berber cultures of North Africa. The southern kingdoms include those of the Akan-speaking peoples of modern Ghana (ancient Ghana was much further north) and the peoples of Dahomey and south-western Nigeria. Seligman has considered the 'true' Negro peoples to be the numerous 'Kwa-speaking' peoples of the Guinea coast, a group which consists of speakers of many related but very different languages, including the Twi, Ewe and Yoruba linguistic groups. He thus summarises the general material culture of these peoples:

They build gable-roofed huts; their traditional weapons include bows tapering at both ends, with bowstrings of vegetable products, swords and plaited shields but no clubs or slings; among musical instruments are wooden drums and a peculiar form of guitar—the so-called 'West African harp'—in which each string has its own support; clothing is of bark cloth and palm fibre, not of skins. Secret societies, masks and woodcarvings of the human figure are characteristic, while coiled basketry and headrests do not occur. Cattle and horses are rare, the domestic animals being the dog, goat, pig and hen; the plants originally cultivated were beans, gourds, bananas and perhaps earth nuts, though yams, manioc, cassava and maize are now also well-established.

A high level of material and technological achievement was characteristic of these Negro kingdoms, which were well established when they were discovered in the late Middle Ages by Europeans; and their wealthy rulers negotiated as equals, and sometimes as superiors, with European emissaries and traders from the fifteenth until the later nineteenth century. To the last, they vigilantly resisted encroachments upon their territories and prerogatives. The African historian Dike, in his *Trade and Politics in the Niger Delta, 1830–85*, reports a speech made by the King of Bonny who, in 1824, was outraged by an unauthorised British survey of the coast of his territories. The King firmly admonished King George IV:

If brother George commands his battleships to attack the slave-ships of foreign nations that is no concern of mine. But he has no right whatever to send his men-of-war at will into my dominions . . .

and he concluded with a sentence very typical of the philosophy of similar native rulers:

What would be my excuse if my father or grandfather were to rise from their graves and demand to know the reason for presence of English warships in the territories they had entrusted to my charge?

Among these rulers, thus conscious of their status and responsibility, dynastic traditions were carefully conserved. There were court chroniclers, bards and minstrels, reciters of panegyrics and sagas of the kings. There were extensive pantheons, and priesthoods, guilds and cult-groups in the service of the kings and the gods. The work of the professional artists and craftsmen, whose carving is now so highly prized outside Africa, was linked to the court, the shrine, and the secret or semi-secret associations and societies.

The number and variety of examples and styles of West African carving and sculpture defy any brief classification. Not only is it possible to recognise regional styles, but also in some cases to distinguish between works from different villages and different individual craftsmen. Wood, ivory, brass, bronze, gold, terracotta and stone have all been used in West African societies to produce works of art varying from the well-known naturalistic or realistic portrait heads of the ancient rulers of Ife, to widely-distributed anthropo-morphic and zoomorphic masks which since the early years of this century have exercised a very strong influence on the art of Europe. The spirit of sacred carni-val, which these deliberately grotesque masks evoke, reflects the ceremonies of the cult-groups and associations in which they were often used. They have been the subject of much European aesthetic appraisal. André Malraux, for example, writes:

An African mask is not a fixation of a human expression; it is an apparition. Its carver does not impose a geometrical pattern upon a phantom of which he knows nothing, but conjures up one by his geometry. . . .

We know, however, that life-likeness was sometimes considered important, and that there is no reason to attribute all 'naturalism' in African art to the influence of European models, as was at one time the tendency of art-critics and historians. W. B. Fagg thus describes some features of a 'second burial' ceremony among the Owo, who are some of the finest wood-carvers of Nigeria:

. . . as perfect a likeness of the deceased as possible is carved, clothed in the garments of the deceased, and cere-moniously interred some months or even years after his or her death. . . . I saw a life-size effigy of the present Olowo's mother which had been carved by the well-known artist Akeredolu and rejected as an insufficiently close likeness in favour of one by Ogunleye.

Among the richest treasures in ivory-carving and bronze-casting available for study in Europe are those from Benin in south-western Nigeria. They were at one time thought to be of Portuguese inspira-tion, but this theory is generally discarded as more examples of West African bronze-casting, notably the Ife heads, have been discovered. Relations of Benin with Portugal began in the fifteenth century, and like other African kingdoms made wealthy by trade—Ashanti, Dahomey and Oyo, for example—Benin seems to have reached the height of its greatness between the fifteenth and seventeenth centuries. From this period, probably, are derived the collections of masks, plaques, figures, ceremonial staffs, bells and ornaments which were found by a British punitive expedition sent to Benin 1897.

General Pitt-Rivers, who first published a collection of Benin works, helps to light up the background of some of the prob-lems now facing the student of African culture.

In 1896, a party of incautious British traders advanced upon the city of Benin from the coast, against the advice of local chiefs and the express command of the King of Benin, who had none the less signed a treaty which could be interpreted as giving them the right to visit his capital. All except two were killed in an ambush. Five weeks later, the city of Benin was taken by a punitive expedition, which found 'a terrible state of bloodshed and disorder'. General Pitt-Rivers comments:

What may hereafter be the advantages to trade resulting from this expedition it is difficult to say, but the point of chief interest . . . was the discovery, mostly in the king's compound and juju houses, of numerous works of art in brass, bronze and ivory which . . . were mentioned by the Dutchman Van Nyendael as having been made by the people of Benin in 1700. These antiquities were brought away by members of the punitive expedition and sold in London and elsewhere. Little or no account of them could be given by the natives, and as the expedition was as usual unaccompanied by any scientific explorer charged with the duty of making enquiries upon matters of historic and antiquarian interest, no reliable information about them could be obtained. They were found buried and covered with blood, some of them having been used among the apparatus of their juju sacrifices.

It was, ironically, in this way that the first major collection to evoke real admiration and respect for African art became generally known. The Benin bronzes are now said to have been made only at the orders of the Oba, or king, and in some circumstances at least their casting was a rite, in which a new king and his subordinate chiefs in turn poured crucibles of molten bronze into the moulds.

The connections between Benin and the older bronze-casters of Ife further north, or the still older terracotta heads of Nok, are as yet undetermined. The Ife heads, as compared with Benin work, are naturalistic in a 'classical' manner; but it is unlikely that they are directly copied from classical models from Greece or Rome. They are said to bear some resemblance to portrait-heads produced in the first and early second centuries in Egypt under the Roman Empire. These may have been known in the ancient civilisation of Meroe on the Nile, which had vanished by the fourth century A.D. and to which many archaeological tracks have seemed to lead.

Among the artistic achievements of the peoples of modern Ghana are the characteristic gold weights of the Gold and Ivory Coasts, which attest the importance of this trade in pre-European times. The gold weights, associated particularly with the Ashanti are tiny figurines made by one of the *cire-perdue* methods, like the Benin and Ife bronzes and brasses. They are based on a system of weighing known in medieval India, and perhaps introduced into West Africa by the Arabs. The valuable trade in gold, as in slaves, was mainly a chiefly or royal monopoly, and contributed to the wealth and power of ruling dynasties. African rulers, however, without exception are required to be generous, and the royal wealth was undoubtedly widely distributed among the people. Although later European travellers tended to see only the excesses of sacrificial zeal of these West African kings, Sir Richard Burton also observed their standards of magnificence, complaining that some of the official gifts sent from Europe to African rulers were such as they themselves would be ashamed to offer to their slaves.

The general picture we may form of these southern West African cultures is one of numerous kingdoms and city-states held in an uneasy balance of power, and each based upon a prosperous agricultural peasantry further enriched by trade. Around them, and sometimes becoming partly incorporated in their wider polity, were tribes without rulers, or the scattered remnants of tribes broken by slaving and war.

The cultures of these established kingdoms are cultures of the royal stool, the palace and the shrine. Something of the same pattern stretches into the Congo and the Sudan, among the Azande for example; but there (as among other African peoples later described) we find that a more secular aristocracy welded different ethnic elements into a military state. More like the kingdoms of the Guinea coast are those of the Congo, with their great wealth of plastic art which has made such peoples as the Bushongo, the Baluba and Bakuba famous as craftsmen. The old Kingdom of the Congo was ruled with a certain grandeur when first visited by the Portuguese in the fifteenth century (*see* Chapter 11), and under Portuguese influence its first Christian kings are said to have imported luxury goods from Europe, and workmen for the public buildings of the capital. All these kingdoms have their profusion of court officials, and their chroniclers and bards and spokesmen. Indeed, if one characteristic of all African peoples were to be singled out for special comment, it might be the immense prestige attaching everywhere to those who excel in the arts of song and speech, the respect for language and high regard for poetry and rhetoric.

V

Both the Guinea coast and the Congo have looked primarily to the sea and to Europe for trade and influence. Farther north, between the forest belt and the Sahara, in an area stretching from Senegal to Lake Chad and into the Republic of the Sudan, are those peoples who looked, centuries before Europeans appeared there, across the desert, to the civilisations of the North African littoral. In that sub-Saharan region lie numerous states and kingdoms;

emirates of the Hausa, sultanates like ancient Bornu, and pagan or partly pagan tribes who have for long felt the impact of Moorish, Berber and Arab civilisation, as well as that of the Negro states to the south.

One example of the Islamised cultures of West Africa serves to indicate something of their general characteristics. The Nupe of Nigeria, originally a Negro kingdom of people related to the Yoruba-speakers of the Guinea coast, were influenced by the Hausa states which arose to the north of them in the Middle Ages, and conquered and finally ruled by the Hamitic Moslem Fulani in the early nineteenth century. They live in a transitional area between the southern forest belt and the northern savannah and semi-desert, where they have taken full advantage of the economic potentialities of both environments, in a way which shows a high degree of technical control. The result of this, and of shrewd trading, has been to produce a 'Black Byzantium', as Nadel called his standard work on the Nupe. There was an ancient dynasty with its regalia—notably trumpets and drums—and a town capital at Bida with the metropolitan characteristics of the northern cultures of West Africa, which are naturally still more marked in Timbuktu, Kano and Sokoto further north at the termini of trading routes across the Sahara. It seems that while the policy of the rulers of the southern West African kingdoms was to keep foreigners in coastal settlements, discouraging entry into their capital towns which retained their traditional culture more or less intact, the town capitals of the north were long before laid open, by trade or conquest, to foreign influence. For them, it was the influence of Islam.

In such a state as Nupe, great specialisation of skills and in the crafts and useful arts has created well-organised guilds of blacksmiths and ironworkers, weavers, beadworkers, glassworkers and brass- and silversmiths. Such guilds are a marked feature of West African town cultures. Among the Nupe are also professional barbers and doctors, secular dancers and entertainers, and Moslem scholars. A complex system of ranks and age-grades is connected with a political hierarchy of rulers and titles. Though masks and carvings exist, they seem to give way in importance to the non-representational and useful arts, as might be expected under the protracted influence of Islam.

In general, as the ninth parallel in West Africa is crossed from south to north, and the Negro societies are more and more permeated by Islamic culture, the aristocracy becomes military, and traditionally pastoral, rather than religious and agricultural. Urban centres are the strong-points of little secular military and commercial empires, and there are elements introduced from the culture of horsed warriors—chain mail, metal greaves, swords and throwing knives. If the cultures of southern West Africa are somewhat over-simply regarded as centred upon the royal stool, the palace, and the shrine, those of the north are cultures of the fort and the mosque, with a concentration upon the practical arts, and a religion of teachers, preachers and minor seers, losing in part the strongly sacramental view of life represented by the art and culture of the forest Negroes. It was in this northern region that there arose, in the Middle Ages or before, the states or empires of Ghana, Songhai and Melle.

VI

To pass from either northern or southern West African states to the typically pastoral cultures of the eastern Nilotes and Nilo-Hamites is to move to quite a different African world. In these cultures, formed by the nomadic or transhumant life of the savannahs of the Southern Sudan and East Africa, there is little development of representational or religious art, and only a modest concern with the practical arts. An indifference to trade and its potential luxuries is to be expected, since these peoples do not enslave each other and have little to sell.

Some of the Nilotes and Nilo-Hamites are now predominantly settled agricultural peoples growing grain-crops, but they have deep traditions of pastoralism, and although many combine some agriculture with stock-rearing, it is to cattle that they are most deeply attached. In many parts of their country, agriculture is, for climatic reasons, less rewarding than cattle-breeding. Possessions are few, compared with those of the West African peasants. Simple well-constructed circular huts of mud, wattle and thatch are built in the permanent villages, though the herdsmen must spend much of their time abroad with the cattle, seeking the best pastures and living in temporary shelters and windbreaks. The few furnishings of the homestead and cattle camp—cooking pots, milk and food gourds, sleeping-skins and headrests—show an indifference to comfort which amounts almost to contempt. These Nilotes who live primarily by agriculture have a somewhat richer material culture than the pastoralists, but there is nowhere any significant artistic work, unless it be in the little clay models, especially of bulls and oxen, which some of these peoples make as children's toys.

But material and moral refinement are not necessarily linked. Many Nilotes, in any case, live in a harsh environment which even modern technologists may find difficult to control, and their adaptation to these conditions is rather to be admired for its resourcefulness than despised for its lack of enterprise. Egalitarianism is a marked feature of Nilotic and Nilo-Hamitic philosophy. Slavery, even in a simple domestic form, is scarcely known, and human blood sacrifice is unthinkable. In some tribes, notably among the Shilluk of the White Nile, there is a form of kingship, with a court ceremonial and royal emblems; but for the most part rule among Nilotes and Nilo-Hamites is exercised informally, either by minor chiefs and councils of elders, or without even this measure of central control. Then, as among the Nilotic Nuer, the structure of society, like that of some Bedouin tribes, is based upon a system of clan and lineage loyalties sometimes leading to feud. The dignity, independence and courage displayed by such Nilotes as the Nuer of the Sudan, and such Nilo-Hamites as the Masai, have earned the respect of European travellers. Professor Evans-Pritchard wrote of the Nuer, for example, that

> . . . courage, generosity, patience, pride, loyalty, stubbornness, and independence, are the virtues the Nuer themselves extol, and these virtues can be shown to be very appropriate to their simple mode of life and to the simple set of social relations it engenders.

The institution of 'divine' kingship found among the Shilluk, in which the king is at the centre of a complex of ideas about the fertility and prosperity of the whole realm, has for long interested scholars since it recalls features of ancient Egyptian philosophy. These ideas have their parallels in West Africa, notably among the Jukun of Nigeria. It is likely, too, that people of Nilotic origin have had some historical connection with the pastoral aristocracy of the Bantu kingdom of the Banyoro of the Lakes region of Uganda, and some of the names of the early Nyoro

kings are undoubtedly Nilotic and not Bantu.

The Hamitic Galla of Ethiopia and Kenya are quite different from any African peoples so far discussed, though it has been held that peoples resembling them have played a part in the formation of various Negro African aristocracies. The Galla were originally nomadic warriors, but many have for long been settled agriculturists, and alone of the pagan peoples of Africa had adopted plough cultivation long before the coming of Europeans to Africa. Under the influence of Islam, and as a result of expansion and conquest, kingdoms and hereditary rulers were formed, but the traditional system of government appears to have been one of elected tribal rulers, whose position was closely linked with an elaborate age-set system. In some ways, the culture of the Galla is reminiscent of features of the cultures of Northern Nigeria influenced by the Hamitic Fulani, and deriving in part from pastoral warriors who by conquest have created kingdoms in which there has been a considerable development of the useful arts—cotton-weaving, metal- and leather-work—and trade in slaves, ivory and agricultural produce.

The Galla and many other peoples contribute to the complex ethnic and linguistic pattern of Ethiopia, whose culture offers a vast field for specialised research. With their ancient Coptic Christianity, their sacred language Ge'ez (already a dead language by the tenth century) and their long history of royal and imperial rule under kings who look back to David and Solomon, the Ethiopians link Africa to Palestine, Egypt and Byzantium and, as has already been suggested, it is only in the context of those antique civilisations that we can form a just estimate of Ethiopia's past and present greatness.

VII

The Bantu-speaking tribes who cover the greater part of southern Africa, are too numerous to name. They are very heterogeneous in culture and social organisation. Some, like the kingdoms of the Congo, belong culturally to the groups of forest-dwelling West African Negro states. Others are mixed farmers and stock-breeders over whom minor chiefs and councils of elders exercise a limited authority. Among others, such as the South African Zulu and Rhodesian Lunda, centralised states or nations have developed either as a result of conquest or through the influence of a powerful leader and his successors.

Until the late eighteenth century, what became the Zulu nation consisted of more than a hundred separate tribes which acknowledged no supreme authority. They were welded into a single nation by the military and political genius of the ruthless Shaka, who created a highly efficient military organisation at the disposal of the kingship, and even gave a military bias to the older tribal religious rites. As is usual in the kingly and chiefly societies of Africa, the importance of the ruler was emphasised by the use of praise-names—'lion, great wild beast, lord of the soil, beautiful one, devourer of the people'. There were also insignia of rank, especially certain old beads, and the leopard-skins which are widely associated with royalty in Africa.

The Zulus were mixed farmers, with a high regard for cattle, but they were not nomadic like some of the Nilotes and Nilo-Hamites, and their settled way of life made the establishment of a national administration easier than among a nomadic people. The principal weapon was the spear, with various kinds of hide shields for defence. Clothing was of skins, and glass beads were used extensively for decoration. Compared with the West African kingdoms, the practical arts were simple, and fine or religious art negligible. There was little trade, though English traders settled in Natal during Shaka's lifetime and were apparently welcome, and there was scarcely any specialisation of labour, the only specialists being the smiths. It was the Zulu military organisation which created the nation.

Among the Zulu, as among many African peoples, arose individuals with gifts of prophecy and religious leadership, often in opposition to foreign invasion. Their quality is suggested by an account of the prophet, Makanna,

> ... who led the attack against the British headquarters in Grahamstown in 1818, had previously been in the habit of visiting the garrison on friendly terms, and had shown an insatiable curiosity and an acute intellect in discussing matters of war and mechanics with the officers, and theology with the chaplain. (Quoted from H. M. and N. K. Chadwick, *The Growth of Literature,* Vol. III.)

More recently, among the South African Bantu generally, have arisen numerous native leaders of separatist Christian sects, some exercising considerable religious and political influence.

VIII

Some common features of Africa's native cultures can be described in general terms. Like all societies, those of Africa are based upon marriage and the family, but more particularly on the polygynous family. It is partly the conflicting interests of the sons of different wives which have produced the widespread dynastic struggles in African ruling houses. In marriage, the husband's right to his wife and children, and the children's legitimacy, are established by payments in cattle or other commodities made from the people of the bridegroom to those of the bride. These payments have often been misunderstood as involving the purchase of wives, but it is now clearly established that this is a mistaken interpretation of the African custom.

Most African societies count descent and inheritance in the male line; but in some, descent is counted through the females, as among the Babemba of Rhodesia, and the Ashanti of West Africa and related peoples, where the rulers receive their title through their mothers. Though primogeniture is often assumed, it is rarely strictly enforced.

Everywhere in Africa some wider extension of family loyalty is of political, moral and religious importance. Filial piety, and some regard for genealogy and ancestry, are universal among Africans, and are seen at their most highly developed in the cults of the ancestors of kings, and the careful conservation of their traditions.

There are great variations in the extent of any form of central rule. Kingdoms have figured largely in this account because their culture is more easily characterised than that of tribes without ruling dynasties. There yet remain very many African societies in which government is in the hands of advisory councils of elders, or in which, without even this degree of centralisation of authority, groups of kin act together to defend their mutual interests. That such a system does not produce anarchy and disintegration is apparent since tribes without rulers often have more members than those with a greater measure of central control.

The religions of Africa have been too numerous and varied to discuss. We have noted a general feature of Negro African culture, a devotion to the family and to ancestors, in which are rooted many details of political, and of artistic, develop-

ment. As a deeper knowledge of African languages and traditions becomes available, it is increasingly apparent that the pagan philosophies and theologies of Africa, often conveyed in language of great symbolic force, contain such notions as those of sin, atonement, and sacrifice, and in general are strongly sacramental. It is on the whole typical of African pagan religion to attach little meaning to conceptions of personal immortality.

European travellers of the nineteenth century, anxious for the commercial development of Africa, often complained of the lack of ambition of her peoples. But the traditional values of Africa allowed for no such emphasis upon individual acquisitiveness. Where the necessities of life are few and hard-won, and the fortunes of the chase, the herd and the harvest may often reduce individuals to extreme want, men cannot hope to survive misfortune by competitive self-interest. So it is that in Africa generosity and the sharing of possessions, particularly by rulers, were traditionally strong obligations, for they formed the only insurance against individual disaster, and were the pillars of royal prestige. Further, such evidence as is available confirms how wrong the Victorians were to assume that all southern Africa lay inert for centuries before its partition among the European powers.

It has become a commonplace to say that the present state of historical research in Africa can be compared to the state of geographical research before the systematic explorations of the later nineteenth century. Lacking detailed knowledge, as Swift wrote, the eighteenth century and pre-eighteenth century geographers:

> . . . in Africa Maps
> With Savage Pictures fill their Gaps
> And o'er unhabitable Downs
> Place Elephants for want of Towns.

When Africa's geography became known, but solid information about her cultures was wanting, many other 'savage pictures' —of political anarchy, hideous rites, fear and superstition, wife-purchase and so on —were similarly placed before the public. In the study of African history there has also been a temptation to extensive speculation where substantial evidence has been difficult to find. The 'Hamitic theory', and others which would derive all civilisation in Africa from the ancient Egyptians, or even Hebrews, and attempts to establish different circles or layers of African culture—'paleo-nigritic', 'neo-sudanese' and so on—are still speculative reconstructions of the pre-European past. They serve a useful purpose in guiding more detailed researches, and have of course drawn attention to many real parallels. The 'divine kingship' of such people as the Shilluk, with its dual division of the kingdom, and of the Jukun, the artificial deformation of the horns of cattle among some of the Nilotes, and certain features of the royal customs of the Bantu kings of the Lakes region of Uganda, reasonably raise the question of ancient Egyptian influence. But it is still undecided whether such similarities spring from past contact, or whether the Egyptians, in their particular environment, developed to a higher degree of elaboration features already present in Negro-African culture patterns. Such questions may be seen in a new light when the greater knowledge and higher standards of historical criticism now being introduced into the study of African history are fully established.

IX

African political, cultural and economic contacts with Europe and Central Asia go back a long way. Moreover, the stone-age cultures of Africa are, in general, sufficiently similar to those of Europe (though they may be older) for us to suppose that for long periods African and European developments, except in specialised details, were not dissimilar.

The known history of African states south of the Sahara begins, to our present knowledge, with contacts with other civilisations in the region, in the Republic of the Sudan and in Ethiopia. For 2000 years before Christ, the history of the northern Sudan was closely linked with that of Egypt, and as far south as modern Merowe, north of Khartoum, the Sudan was effectively an uneasily-held Egyptian province. In the eighth century B.C., the first King of Kush made his capital at Napata, where modern Merowe stands, and thereafter the rulers of Kush became for a time the rulers of Egypt of the twenty-fifth dynasty. By 500 B.C., the Napatan rulers, or a branch of the family, had moved south to ancient Meroë (not to be confused with modern Merowe farther north). By the beginning of the first century of the Christian era, the Egyptian language had died out in the Sudan, which then had its own hieroglyphic and demotic script. The independent Meroitic civilisation was established.

The wealth of Meroë, with its sphere of influence stretching at least as far south as Sennar and later west into Kordofan, was based partly upon iron-working, and indeed a knowledge of iron-working may have spread from Meroë to the Lake Chad region and thence into West Africa. Egyptian influence is found in the achitecture of Meroë, and Greek and Roman work found in tombs indicate the presence deep into Africa of classical influence from the Mediterranean. There were temples, reservoirs, and pyramid tombs. It was perhaps from Meroë that there came to Jerusalem the eunuch converted by St Philip, who was

. . . a courtier of Candace, queen of Ethiopia, and had charge of all her wealth; he had been to worship at Jerusalem, and was now on his way home, driving along in his chariot and reading the prophet Isaias. . . .

Meroitic influence also spread as far as Darfur, where Meroitic royal property marks are still used as tribal brands, and where there are the remains of stone buildings of the same style as a late Meroitic palace. For reasons which are unknown, this first Sudanese civilisation had come to an end by the middle of the fourth century A.D., when an envoy from Ethiopia, according to an inscription at Axum, found the town of Meroë in ruins. The art of writing had by this time been lost.

Between the sixth and sixteenth centuries, there were Christian kingdoms in the northern Sudan. Orthodox missions were sent by Justinian in the sixth century. The Empress Theodora sent a Monophysite mission, which eventually was more successful. There were two Christian kingdoms. The Northern Kingdom had its capital at Old Dongola, and the Southern Kingdom at Soba south of Khartoum. The Northern Kingdom was called Nobatia, and the Southern, Alwah. There, until medieval times, Byzantine Greek and Coptic influences entered Africa. There were brick churches, and in the tenth century, monasteries, churches adorned with gold, and fine gardens, were reported from the Southern Kingdom, though excavations have not revealed such a lavish culture. It is clear that the early Christian civilisation of Nubia was at the height of its power in the tenth and eleventh centuries, when the ruler of Nubia was regarded as the protector of the patriarch of Alexandria. Nubian became a written language, though few very revealing texts have been found; the Coptic form of Greek was used, with some Meroitic letters. After the Arab conquest of Egypt in A.D. 640, there was frequent warfare in the north of the Nubian kingdom, and links with Byzantium and the south were difficult to maintain. The latest Greek inscription on a tomb found in the Sudan dates from 1181. By the ninth century the presence of mosques already indicates Moslem penetration. The last Christian king of Nubia was defeated by the Arabs in the fourteenth century, and the country became a cultural province of Islam. By 1523, the capital of the Southern Kingdom at Soba was reported to be in ruins, and its inhabitants primitively housed. The extent of Christian influence in the northern Sudan until the end of the Middle Ages is shown by the fact that some sixty churches, some with wall-paintings Byzantine in style, have been found between the Egyptian frontier and Sennar. The influence of Meroë, and later Nubia, upon the peoples to the south and west remains to be established. The most westerly Nubian inscription so far found comes from a site in Kordofan, but various details, some already mentioned, point to earlier connections between Meroë and Darfur.

The first rulers of Darfur were traditionally the Daju (whose descendants still survive) and Darfur was in their hands by A.D. 1200. They were replaced in the fourteenth century by the Tungur, who by tradition came from Dongola to the north. Arab influence spread during their rule, by 1500 Islam was the official religion, and Arabic was spoken at court. Nevertheless the stone architecture of the Tungur capital at Orrei was substantially African in inspiration, with circular huts surrounded by protective walls. This culture was based upon slavery, and may be seen in some ways perhaps to resemble the northern Nigerian states, where an Islamic and

Arabised military aristocracy, of pastoral origins, forms the core of small empires, and becomes progressively assimilated to pagan Negro tribesmen who are first enemies, then slaves, and finally, neighbours and kinsmen. Basically the same situation is found farther west in Bornu, the rulers of which conquered the Tungur kingdom. They were again mounted warriors, whose chain-mail and armoured horses were introduced from the time of the Crusades.

Still further west, in the region of the Niger bend and northern Senegal, are the sites of other ancient kingdoms, also basically Islamic in culture, at least after the tenth century. Arab and other historiographers have given some indication of the impression made upon travellers by the wealth of the states of Ghana, Songhai and Melle already touched upon, and these have been collated by Bovill in his *Caravans of the Old Sahara* to create a picture of an early flowering of civilisation in this northern region of West Africa. Ghana was known primarily for its gold and slaves, in which there was a rich trade with the Maghreb. We hear of a 'silent trade', in which gold was exchanged for imported goods without direct contact between the merchants and the producers. El Bekri, writing in the eleventh century and basing his account of Ghana on the information of Barbary merchants, describes Ghana as a city of luxury and splendour with a court of great wealth and ostentation, a Moslem township with numerous mosques, and a pagan township with sacred groves which recall the sacred groves found in parts of West Africa today. It is also of interest in view of some modern African practice, to note the burial custom for the kings. They are said to have been placed under a wooden dome with some of their servants, and upon this tomb mats and cloths were

placed, over which everyone threw earth until a mound with a ditch round it had been formed. Until a few years ago, a comparable ceremony was performed at the burial of the priests of the Nilotic Dinka, who were sometimes placed in the tomb at their own request as death approached, and the whole is reminiscent of the funeral ceremonies of other Nilotic 'divine kings'. The site of Koumbi Saleh, which is thought to be that of the ancient city of Ghana, has been under excavation, but only a Moslem town has as yet been found, and the reports of its early magnificence still await detailed archaeological confirmation.

In Senegal and the Sudan Republic, and in the original land of the Mandingo peoples of today, there also arose to fame in the Middle Ages the states or empires of Melle, or Mali, and Songhai. The Mali state, which had previously attacked and subdued Ghana, seems also to have prospered by trade in gold and slaves, and under its rulers Sundiata and Mansa (who made a pilgrimage to Mecca in great state), it became the largest of native African states. Contacts with Spanish and Moorish culture had also been made, and marble blocks of twelfth-century Spanish origin have been found at Gao, a town of the Songhai kingdom which was at one time part of the Mali Empire. The wars and rivalries of Mali and Songhai, the attacks of raiding Touareg and later of conquering Moroccan armies which overran these empires, hostilities with such powerful and unsubdued pagan tribes as the Mossi, the dynastic struggles in ruling houses, the trade in gold and slaves, the steady influence and finally the triumph of Islam, all seem to be linked in a pattern which, from medieval and pre-medieval times until the nineteenth century, must have persisted in these sub-Saharan territories of Negro Africa.

In terms of external influence, the coastal kingdoms and tribes of West Africa have a different background. Their chief trading contacts were by sea, and any maritime contact with the north until the Middle Ages would seem unlikely as the prevailing trade-winds in West Africa require a westward sweep for the return journey, and this was possible only with medieval navigation techniques. In any case, the first European traders with coastal West Africa were sojourners who did not (as did the Arabs and Berbers in the north) become largely integrated into local African populations.

As already observed, the forest regions of West Africa are not suitable for the preservation of rich archaeological deposits. Great numbers of Neolithic stone axes in modern Ghana show that there was a considerable early population, but on the whole it seems difficult to piece together much of the history of the coast and its immediate hinterland before the sixteenth century. Some indication of the nature of the historic culture of the coastal kingdoms after that time has been given earlier. Their civilisation seems to have reached its peak by the seventeenth century.

The cultural contacts of Africa outside West Africa, the Sudan, and Ethiopia, are only now, and more slowly, being pieced together. Excavations and research carried out by James Kirkman, Gervase Mathew, Freeman-Grenville and others on the coast and islands of East Africa show the presence there in the fourteenth century of 'Islamic merchant cities, grown wealthy through trade in ivory, gold and iron and with contacts throughout the Middle and Far East'. The relationship of these Islamic and predominantly Arabic coastal cultures with the native cultures of the interior, and the part played in them by indigenous African elements, are still to be determined.

The earlier levels of the city of Gedi, which from the ninth to seventeenth centuries was the site of an Arab-African culture near the Kenya coast between Malindi and Mombasa, yield potsherds possibly related to some discovered at Zimbabwe in western Rhodesia. These coastal cities and island sultanates imported celadon and blue and white Chinese porcelain, Portuguese majolica and glazed Islamic wares and other trade goods. It is possible that Gervase Mathew's discovery of a pre-Islamic culture on Sanje-ya-Kato, south of Kilwa, may give a clue to the earlier history of the African coast. The earliest inscription yet found comes from Zanzibar Island and dates from the early twelfth century.

X

The cultural history and contacts of the area bounded by the Indian Ocean and the South Atlantic are extremely obscure. In East and South Africa, there are remains of stone constructions of various kinds. In Ethiopia and the Horn there are (besides town sites) dolmens, cairns, menhirs, stone circles, and earthworks, some of which may date from the time of Axum, and G. W. B. Huntingford has suggested that in some cases a 'hagiolithic culture' with a cult of sacred stone may be traced to Indonesia. The most celebrated stone remains, however, are those of Zimbabwe in western Rhodesia. These ruins, which are spread over several different sites, consist in the main of walled huts and enclosures, sometimes containing elliptical or conical towers and more massive fortifications. There are also some indications of mine-working. The stonework consists of naturally flaked granite, trimmed roughly if at all, and is of a type constructed until recently by some of the Shona peoples. It is now generally held that in this Rhodesian architecture there is no sign of European or Oriental influence. Zimbabwe, the most celebrated site, seems to have been first constructed not earlier than the ninth century, and not later than the fourteenth.

Reference to 'Zimbaoe' or 'Simbaoe' in Portuguese records of the sixteenth century seems to mean only 'building of stone', understood to be the residences of chiefs. The ruin distinguished as 'Great' Zimbabwe consists of three groups of buildings, of which the most prominent has been called 'the Elliptical Temple', and which have been ascribed to various periods between the fourteenth and eighteenth centuries. At Great Zimbabwe were found four soapstone beams carved with the heads of birds, perhaps totemic emblems, and among other finds have been fragments of medieval Persian faience, Chinese procelain and Arab silver. Other finds have been ornaments of gold, copper and enamelled bronze. The uses to which the buildings were put are not finally known. The Great Zimbabwe ruins contain a platform, with monoliths and a private approach through a stone passage, suggesting some place of public assembly, whether for religious or other purposes, in which a chief or priest might have officiated before his people. The Zimbabwe people probably conducted an *entrepôt* trade in gold for Sofala, but little evidence for a large-scale local gold industry has been found. The archaeological evidence thus does not support earlier legends, based upon Portuguese reports, of a medieval empire rich in native gold in this part of Africa. That there was a late medieval African state in this region, the State (or Empire) of Monomopata, cannot be doubted. It was probably founded by people of Shona stock; and what is inferred about its history strikes a familiar note to anyone acquainted with the better substantiated and more recent history of

the creation of the Zulu nation. In Monomopata, as among the Zulu and in other Bantu kingdoms, dynastic rivalries and the self-assertion of only partially dominated minor chiefs constantly threatened the tenuous hold upon power of any single ruler at the centre.

The present inhabitants of the area of the Monomopatan kingdom have little or no living tradition of the Monomopatan period, nor do the ruins of Zimbabwe convey any meaning to those Africans who live around them. It has been suggested that the founders of Zimbabwe culture were immigrant 'Hamites', related to the aristocracies of the Inter-Lacustrine Bantu of Uganda, and that both these and the peoples of Zimbabwe may have yet older connections with Ethiopia. Excavations are now revealing extensive earthworks in Uganda, which from the air are seen to be elliptical in form. There are also some indications of mining, possibly dating, like Zimbabwe, from medieval times. A stamped pottery, coinciding with a type found in Miss Caton-Thompson's Zimbabwe excavations, has been found in Uganda, but the distribution of pottery alone is notoriously a most uncertain clue to actual relationships between African peoples. Parts of pottery figures found buried in Luzira Hill near Lake Victoria are unique in the discoveries so far made, and their affinities may be rather with the west than with the east. Further light may be thrown upon it if more is discovered about an ancient civilised people the Bachwezi, who according to tradition lived in Uganda, and are regarded as early kings.

Such, without much of the detail in which alone clues to the truth about Africa's past will eventually be discovered, is the racial and cultural history of Africa, the fringe of which by the fifteenth century Europeans were beginning to explore. Far more work will have to be done before the numerous and varied native cultures of the continent can be certainly related to each other, to the Mediterranean and Arabia, and still further to Indonesia, India and China, with all of which there have been undoubted contacts in the pre-European past. Even now, the deaths of a few old men, whose knowledge may go unregarded and unrecorded, can break the continuity of present and past, re-enacting today the loss of living tradition which separates the ancient cultures and the modern peoples of the continent.

One of the first modern Africans to recognise this was a Tiv of Nigeria, who wrote, in *Akiga's Story*:

So it has been my constant prayer that God would help me to write this book, in order that the new generation of Tiv, which is beginning to learn this New Knowledge, should know the things of the fathers as well as those of the present generation. For everything that belongs to the Tiv is passing away, and the old people who should tell us these things will soon all be dead. It makes me sad to think that our heritage is being lost, and that there will be none to remember it.

In view of the overwhelming impact of modern civilisation on Africa, an understanding of the specific qualities, the variety, and the duration of the African past is more than ever necessary.

13 THE NATIVE CULTURES OF THE AMERICAS

by J. H. Parry

The Europeans who first penetrated Africa were faced with an ancient mystery and an ancient challenge. Columbus, too, did not discover a New World; he established contact between two worlds, both already old. He revealed to Europeans the existence of continents and islands which were already inhabited and had been so for many centuries. Moreover, though Columbus' geographical theories were quickly discredited, he was nearer the truth than his contemporaries knew in fixing the name of Indians upon the native Americans. Few archaeologists now doubt that the Americas were colonised from Asia, most probably by way of Alaska. It is possible, but not very likely, that some pre-historic immigrants may have come by other oceanic routes. The Amerindians include a considerable range of different physical types; by no means all display 'Mongoloid' characteristics. There may have been several waves of immigration involving people of different races, moving perhaps at different periods and possibly by different routes. But the combination of probabilities suggests a long, slow drift from Asia to Alaska across the Behring Strait, at a time, probably between ten and twenty thousand years ago, when the northern ice-cap was more extensive than now, the sea level lower, the islands larger, and the channels between them, for part of the year at least, choked with ice. Later, the ice retreated, the sea channels became too wide for rafts or primitive canoes, and the immigration stopped.

So far as we know, there was no truly aboriginal American man; but there were, and are, American cultures. Man in the New World was cut off from Asia at a primitive stage in his cultural development. The people who drifted across the Behring Strait in small groups century after century were hunters and gatherers. Possibly their slow migration was started by a corresponding migration of game animals, moving north in the wake of the shrinking ice. They took with them no domestic animals except perhaps semi-domesticated dogs; the very few species which the Amerindians later tamed are native American. They carried no agricultural tradition; the food plants with which their descendants fed great agricultural populations are all American; not one was grown in the Old World before Columbus' time. Of their tools and weapons scarcely anything is known. No Paleolithic implements have been found in America; though a few Neolithic tools of a type similar to those found in the Gobi have been discovered in Alaska. Except for a very meagre technical equipment, the Amerindians developed their characteristic cultures in America, in the course of wandering and settlement extending over thousands of years. Considering the immense range of conditions between Alaska and Cape Horn, it is not surprising that these cultures differed widely one from another. They all differed much more radically, however, from any Old World culture. Even where similar artefacts or habits occur in both Old and New Worlds, the presumption of independent

MAYA, AZTEC AND INCA EMPIRES AT SPANISH CONQUEST

origins is strong. We have no ground for supposing a connection between the ancient Mexicans and ancient Egyptians, merely because both built pyramids.

Some Amerindian peoples, living in areas rich in fish and game, found their hunting and gathering economy so satisfactory that they never abandoned it. In California one of the densest populations in the Americas maintained itself into modern historic times without any form of agriculture. Some hunting groups, by means of ingenious techniques and specialised social habits, adapted themselves to their environment with remarkable and lasting success. The Eskimo, in particular, were so situated geographically, that they had to hunt or starve, and adjusted their lives accordingly. The possibilities of further development from these hunting techniques were limited. The American continent contained few animals which could be tamed. The indigenous horse, once hunted for food, early became extinct. The bison is probably untamable, and had its main range in country otherwise unattractive to primitive man who—until he acquired European horses—could not even hunt so strong an animal without great difficulty and danger. Similar generalisations apply to the various species of native wild pig. It is true that dogs, besides helping in the chase, were broken to harness in some areas and kept for food in others; in Peru, the llama became domesticated and guinea-pigs were reared for food; and the Mexicans kept turkeys. But, in general, the primitive Amerindian could develop more complex cultures only by developing his gathering habits; by domesticating native wild plants without significant help from animals.

The higher civilisations of the Americas grew up in areas where a relative scarcity of game and wild fruit made agriculture necessary to a growing population; and

where the combination of soil, climate and suitable plants made agriculture possible by man's unaided effort. Without ploughs and plough beasts, the farmer can make little impression on prairie grassland, savannah, or heavy clay. He is confined to soft soils—to alluvial silts, to semi-arid upland soils, or to leaf-mould on the forest floor; and he must find plants which can be made to yield adequately by means of hoe and digging-stick cultivation.

Among the many native food plants of the Americas the most widespread and important were maize and various kinds of beans. We cannot say with certainty where these essential crops originated; but the most likely origin is in Middle America between the fourteenth and twentieth parallels, in which area were concentrated many early centres of intense cultivation and rapid cultural growth. Maize and beans, supplemented by chilis and by various species of squash and other gourds, formed a crop complex admirably adapted to preserve soil fertility in conditions of hoe-cultivation. Maize was the staple; the squashes gave shade and conserved moisture round the roots of the growing maize; and the beans performed a double function, supplying protein in a diet impoverished by the killing out of game, and fixing nitrogen in the soil. From Middle America maize and beans were diffused in all directions, and by the time of the European conquest were grown in most parts of America where agriculture was practised. In North America east of the mountains they superseded less satisfactory plants such as the sunflower and the giant ragweed, formerly grown for their seed. In South America their spread was less uniform. The Andean highland region—another great area of cultural origination and growth—developed an agriculture based not on grain but on potatoes, and the potato was supplemented, not ousted, by the spread of maize and beans. In Brazil and the West Indies, primitive forest groups lived by growing cassava and accepted the spread of maize and beans slowly and late.

II

The development of agriculture, in America as elsewhere, liberated man from the tyranny of the constant search for food; and naturally the areas which first produced a stable complex of cultivated crops were also the areas which first developed highly organised societies and recognisable cultures. Archaeological research has not yet brought to light the stages by which agricultural societies grew up in these areas; the details can only be inferred from remains elsewhere. Both in Middle America and in the Andean region the earliest cultures so far discovered were those of people living in villages, supporting themselves by agriculture, with hunting only a secondary source of food. They had long progressed from basket-making to weaving. They grew cotton and wove it for clothing. They made pottery for the storage and service of food. They fashioned tools of stone, bone and wood, designed ornaments, and decorated their utensils. They achieved a tribal government and evolved a religion centred on the natural forces which control the growth of plants. To these cultures archaeologists have attached the label 'Archaic', perhaps rashly, in view of the probability that remains of still more ancient societies will some day be discovered in the same areas. In the Andean region and in Middle America this stage of development was reached in the centuries immediately before and immediately after the birth of Christ. Archaic-type cultures developed later in other parts of the Americas. Something of their nature can be deduced from the living-fossil societies of the south-

western United States. These Pueblo peoples reached the archaic stage of culture about the eleventh century and have remained in it—except for certain European influences—almost to this day.

Long before the Pueblos reached this stage, the people of Middle America, or some of them, had surpassed it. The higher civilisations of that area were produced not by innovating conquerors or immigrants, but by gradual evolution, a progressive sophistication of archaic forms and habits. The process of development took place in a number of different centres, independent of, but undoubtedly influencing, one another. In Guatemala the Maya evolved a ceremonial civilisation centred in great temple cities. In the Mexican State of Oaxaca the Zapotecs created a rich civilisation, of which the ruins of Monte Albán form the chief remaining monument. In the forests of Tabasco and coastal Vera Cruz there are evidences of other high civilisations which archaeologists are only now beginning to distinguish by the names of Olmec and Totonac. Just north of modern Mexico City, on the fringe of the area of high civilisation, another little-known people built the huge pyramids of Teotihuacán and the complex of sacerdotal building surrounding them. These were all powerful city-building peoples; but their cities—though some of them, notably Teotihuacán, were very extensive and housed large populations—were not primarily fortresses, administrative capitals or centres of industry; they were ceremonial centres. The demands of a forest agriculture did not permit the occupation of large permanent towns. To clear forest land for planting maize, trees had to be girdled, and, when they were dead, burned. Land cleared in this way yielded good crops, from its thin surface of leaf mould, for two or three years, and then became exhausted. Whole villages had then to be moved; or else each family had to be allowed enough land to move its fields every two or three years, allowing the exhausted patches to fallow and revert to bush.

Throughout ancient Middle America, therefore, most settled peoples lived in scattered villages, in flimsy and impermanent dwellings; but they expressed their social unity by building temples, which rose above the forest villages much as the abbeys of medieval Europe towered above the fields and hovels of a devout and patient peasantry. The cities of Middle America were devoted chiefly to religious observance, and secondarily to the social gatherings and market meetings of an intensely religious people.

Of all the city-building cultures, that of the Maya, though not necessarily the earliest, was the most widespread, the most influential, and the most impressive in its religious, scientific and artistic achievements. The Maya area includes three distinct regions; a southern region, in highland Guatemala; a central region in Petén and British Honduras; and a northern region, the Yucatán peninsula. The highland region is physically the most rewarding. Its temperate climate and friable volcanic soil make primitive agriculture easy, and in ancient times it yielded many of the most valuable commodities of Maya society: obsidian for knives and spear-heads, volcanic stone for grinding-stones, iron pyrites for mirrors, specular haematite for ceremonial red paint, feathers of trogons and other brightly-coloured birds used for tapestry and for the mantles of chiefs, and jade. All these articles were traded throughout Middle America and beyond; and the beans of the cacao tree, which grew on the Pacific slope, were used as currency by all the settled peoples. Despite these material advantages, however, the highland region

lagged behind the other two in science and the arts, and today retains little evidence of an early high civilisation. The heartland of Maya culture in its best, its 'classical' period, was Petén, an undulating, low-lying limestone area, with scanty soil and heavy rainfall, and high dense forest. Yucatán is also limestone country, but arid and covered with scrub forest, with little surface water except where the limestone crust has broken through to form *cenotes* or natural wells. There is no evidence that either climate or wild flora have changed significantly since Maya 'classical' times. It is a mystery of human ecology that these unpromising regions should have supported a large, civilised, industrious population. Today, Petén is almost uninhabited, but the ruins of ancient cities, half hidden by the forest, are scattered throughout the region.

The principal buildings in all these Maya centres are temple-pyramids and massive, many-chambered community houses or 'palaces' which probably housed priests and novices during religious fasts and feasts. These characteristics are general throughout Middle America, but the Maya buildings have peculiar features of their own. In decoration, the richness and inventiveness of Maya sculpture—executed entirely with stone tools—is unsurpassed in the Americas and holds a high place throughout the world. In construction, the Maya, alone among Amerindian peoples, supported roofs by means of corbelled vaulting, in which the two legs of the vault draw together until the space between can be bridged with capstones. No American people discovered the true arch. Most characteristic of all was the custom of erecting series of commemorative *stelae* or calendar stones in connection with public buildings. These monolithic shafts, covered with glyphs and sculptured figures in relief, occur only in the Maya lowlands, but there they are widespread. A preoccupation with time was characteristic of Maya religion. Astronomy, or astrology, was studied as an aid in measuring time, in predicting the future, and in fixing the propitious dates for sacrifices and major undertakings. The astronomical knowledge collected, through long observation, by a numerous and highly trained priesthood, was very extensive, and the calendar based upon it was complex and remarkably accurate. All the developed civilisations of Middle America practised this science in some degree, and all possessed sacred calendars; but none equalled the Maya either in the fullness of their knowledge or in the effectiveness of their means of recording it. Since the Maya also—alone among Amerindian peoples—possessed an embryonic form of writing, using glyphs or symbols and not mere pictograms, they were able to record on their stelae astronomical and calendric information and, it may be presumed, historical data also—a form of annals carved in stone. This last point is presumption only, because only the calendric glyphs can as yet be deciphered with any confidence; but at least the stelae enable archaeologists to date ancient Maya sites fairly accurately. According to the most generally accepted interpretation, the earliest surviving dated stelae, at Uaxactún, was erected in A.D. 328. The latest, near La Muñeca in Campeche, may be as late as A.D. 928, but it is a much battered and degenerate example. Most of the Maya cities ceased to erect stelae in the ninth century. Five or five and a half centuries was the span of the 'classical' period of Maya civilisation; roughly the span, in Europe, from Constantine to Charlemagne.

In the central Maya region the ninth century saw both the end of the stele cult and the total cessation of building activity in ceremonial centres. One by one the temple cities were abandoned to decay, and in some at least the abandonment was sudden, for buildings were left half-finished. Many causes have been suggested. Soil exhaustion would not have caused a sudden desertion. Epidemic disease might have done so; but the main killing diseases of the area—yellow fever, hookworm, malaria—are Old World importations, and there is no evidence that the countryside was depopulated. Petén was certainly populous when the Spaniards arrived. Nor does the evidence suggest foreign invasion and destruction due to war. The most plausible explanation, perhaps, is revolution—a peasant revolution spreading from city to city. Possibly the burden of building temples and supporting a priestly hierarchy grew intolerable. Possibly the priesthood, by devotion to astronomy and to sky-gods, and by the neglect of the homely gods of earth and rain and fertility, lost the confidence of a farming peasantry. Whatever the cause, the Maya cities of lowland Guatemala were swallowed up by the forest, and never recovered.

The cities of Yucatán survived to meet a different fate: foreign infiltration and eventually conquest. The Maya never founded any large-scale political unit. Their cities differed considerably in language or dialect and in architectural style, and politically were independent one of another. Although the Maya temperament was, and is, gentle and peaceful as a rule, cities sometimes made war. The Itzá clan, who towards the end of the tenth century possessed themselves of the Yucatec city of Chichén, may have entered the Maya area as mercenaries. Certainly they were better armed and better organised for war than any Maya group. They were of Mexican origin; their own traditions, and similarities in art and customs link them with the Toltec centre of Tula on the

Mexican plateau. They introduced new gods—a sun-god, a war-god, and (most famous of all, because of his later impact on the imagination of Spanish friars) Quetzalcoatl or Kukulcan, 'feathered serpent', god of learning and of priesthood and introducer of maize. The Mexicans believed that these gods required to be nourished constantly with blood, preferably human blood. The sun-god, for example, passed through the underworld each night and arose weary and thirsty for blood each morning. The Toltecs—indeed most Mexican peoples, practised human sacrifice on a scale far greater than was usual with the Maya, and this practice in turn intensified the Mexican pre-occupation with war, as a means of acquiring captives for sacrifice. The Toltecs were great builders; and the Itzás at Chichén and elsewhere introduced new building styles, supplementing the Maya corbelled vault with more spacious but less durable constructions, with roofs supported on columns and wooden beams. In sculpture they lacked the inventiveness and the serenity of the Maya. A monotonous repetition of restless feathered serpents is the principal characteristic of their decorative styles.

The Itzás were few in number. Outside the neighbourhood of Chichén Itzá their influence was at first indirect and even there they adopted many Maya habits and devices. But in the thirteenth century they were reinforced by other more numerous Mexican groups, who succeeded, after much fighting among themselves, in establishing a league of cities, of which Chichén Itzá and Mayapán were the chief. This alliance controlled the whole of northern Yucatán and could, by a slight stretch, be described as an 'Empire'. The decline of art and architecture, especially religious architecture, is obvious at Mayapán. Mayapán was not a ceremonial centre at all, but a fortified city, built to be inhabited by a race of warriors who lived by the labour of a conquered and tributary people. The military dominion of Mayapán lasted until the fifteenth century. Its Mexican rulers, however, gradually became absorbed by the Maya majority and lost not only their identity but their ability to rule. In the fifteenth century their 'Empire' broke into warring fragments. The last hundred years before the arrival of the Spaniards in Yucatán were a period of disorder and progressive barbarisation.

III

A somewhat similar sequence of events occurred in Mexico. The great centres of early civilisation—Monte Albán of the Zapotecs, for example, and Teotihuacán—were ceremonial centres similar in purpose to the 'classical' Maya cities, which were roughly contemporary; though neither in art nor in science did they equal the Maya achievement. Teotihuacán, the largest and most impressive of ruined sites in Mexico, must have been famous over a wide area in its day. Traces of its influence have been found at Cholula, at Monte Albán, and at Kaminaljuyu in the Guatemala highlands. Even long after it had ceased to be inhabited, it retained its sacred character. Like the central Maya cities, Teotihuacán, after at least one rebuilding to meet new religious requirements, it appears was abandoned suddenly in the tenth century, in the full tide of achievement. Ixtlilxochitl, the Christianised Aztec annalist, attributed its downfall to crop failure, religious conflict and revolt. All are possible explanations. To reshape the immense buildings of Teotihuacán in the interests of religious change, vast quantities of lime were used. To reduce limestone on primitive open kilns whole forests must have been destroyed. The consequent desiccation and erosion may well have caused crop failure, and the combinations of labour exactions and food shortages may have led to revolt. Attacks from outside may also have hastened the desertion of the site; there is some evidence of deliberate destruction.

Teotihuacán stood on the northern frontier of civilised Middle America, exposed to recurrent pressure from groups of nomadic barbarians from the arid North who moved in to the fertile land, settled, and in time built up independent cultures of their own. Such a group, the Toltecs, whose relatives were the Itzás who seized Maya Chichén, were engaged in the tenth century in building up a formidable power at Tula, in the modern state of Hidalgo. Possibly the rise of Tula caused the political fall of Teotihuacán. Certainly the Toltecs greatly surpassed the people of Teotihuacán, as they surpassed the Maya, in military skill and organisation. They used the spear-thrower (*atl-atl*) and a sheaf of javelins instead of a single long spear; they possessed highly organised and respected military orders, the Eagles and the Jaguars; they introduced to Mexico, as they did later to Yucatán, a society in which the warrior shared the privileged position of the priest. The Toltecs in Mexican traditional history were described as the Master Builders. Tula—still only partially excavated—lacks the massive ordered bulk of Teotihuacán, but is architecturally splendid, with beautifully proportioned buildings. Unlike Teotihuacán, the site includes extensive refuse heaps; like Chichén in its later period, it marks a transition from purely ceremonial centres to cities lived in and defended by dominant warrior tribes.

The breakdown of highly developed societies and their capture by immigrant barbarians, who in turn took over and adapted their ways of life, was a recurrent feature of Mexican history. When in time Toltec society disintegrated and Tula was abandoned after a long period of confusion and desultory war, fresh centres of power grew up in the Puebla-Mixteca area and in Anáhuac, the central valley of Mexico. The last group of settlers in the valley were the celebrated Aztecs, who were in possession when the first Spanish expedition entered Mexico. Far more is known about the Aztecs than about any other native American people. Their cities, their language, their social habits were described by *conquistadores* and observant missionaries; their history was recorded in writing and in pictograms by Indian and Spanish annalists; more than any other American people they caught the imagination of Europe. Nevertheless, the Aztecs added little to the achievements of Middle American culture; their distinction was military and political. They made notable improvements in the art of war and in organisation for war, accompanied by a great extension of the sacrificial cults, so that their festivals sometimes took on the wholesale aspect of ritual massacre; they achieved, by war, a semblance of political unity in Central Mexico which led European chroniclers to describe their dominion as an empire and Montezuma, the last war-chief of Tenochtitlán, as an emperor.

The Aztecs first emerged as a separate people, or group of peoples, with a recognisable culture of their own, in the late thirteenth century. They occupied a number of villages dotted round the shores of the lake which then filled much of the valley floor of Anáhuac. The villages were independent one of another; throughout the whole of Mexican history before the coming of the Spaniards, the village-tribe, living upon the produce of its own fields, was the unit of political organisation. This remained true even when a tribe grew to many thousands of members and the village became a city-state. When, therefore, a city became too large to be supported by its own productive labour, it had either to split up, some of its members departing to found new colonies elsewhere; or else to prey upon other cities or villages in the neighbourhood. This became the Aztec solution; and the Tenochcas, a small but warlike group living on islands in the lake of Texcoco, ultimately became the most successful of a number of competing predatory tribes. Tenochtitlán, their island stronghold, was settled, probably as a refuge from stronger peoples, about 1325. The population grew, and as the islands became built over, the Tenochcas added to their arable land by making *chinampas*, floating islands of matted weeds, covered with mud dredged from the bottom of the lake, and anchored to the bottom by growing weeds. *Chinampa* agriculture can be seen to this day at Xochimilco, south of Mexico City. Early in the fifteenth century the Tenochcas, by means of an alliance with two of the other lake towns, Texcoco and Tlacopán, secured their first foothold on the lake shore, and for a century their power grew, at the expense both of their allies and of other settlements. Raiding expeditions went out regularly and the city drew tribute in kind, services, and captives for sacrifice, from conquered and terrorised peoples throughout the Valley of Mexico, throughout the Puebla-Mixteca area, as far south as Guatemala and as far east as Vera Cruz. With the tribute, the Tenochcas acquired the arts and crafts of the conquered. Tenochtitlán became a great city, whose temples, community houses and markets provoked the startled admiration of Spanish soldiers. It was linked to the shore by causeways, and drew its water by aqueduct from the hills of Chapúltepec. It was at the height of its power and splendour when, in 1519, Cortés landed at Vera Cruz and began his march inland.

The Tenochcas had become an aristocracy of predators, not of rulers. They performed no duties in return for the tributes they exacted. Their vassal states remained separate, internally self-governing, bound to Tenochtitlán only by fear of punitive expeditions if tribute were withheld. Neither the Aztecs, nor any other North or Central American people, had any conception of a political unit wider than a single city-state.

IV

Such a conception did, however, develop in South America. Like central and southern Mexico and Guatemala, the northern Andean region, both coast and mountain, produced a series of highly developed societies extending over a long period of time. The cultural history of the area shows a marked similarity to that of Middle America, though the nature of the cultures themselves was very different. As in Middle America, areas of growing civilisation began to emerge from the general level of 'archaic' culture in the first centuries of the Christian era. The most striking of these nascent high cultures were the Tiahuanaco culture of the highlands, and in the coastal plain the Nazca culture of southern, the Chimu culture of northern, Peru. Both these coastal peoples developed valley economies, irrigating their arid fields from the rivers, using adobe bricks to build their towns, and erecting great pyramidal adobe mounds as temples and as fortresses. Both peoples—the Chimu especially—are famous for the vigour and realism of their pottery and for the beauty and quality of their cotton textiles. The highland culture, which grew up in the bleak wind-swept basin of Lake Titicaca, derives its name from its principal site, the great ruins of Tiahuanaco just south of the lake, in modern Bolivia. Its most striking characteristics were its immense buildings, of massive cut stone masonry, and its equally massive and very vigorous relief sculpture. There is some evidence for thinking that this area was a political as well as a cultural unity, and that Tiahuanaco, about the sixth and seventh centuries A.D., exercised considerable intellectual, if not political, influence on the coastal societies. Possibly Tiahuanaco imperialism overreached itself; between A.D. 900 and about 1200 there was a sharp decline, amounting in the highlands to a political collapse and a reversion to 'archaic' conditions. On the coast the decline was less sharp; after a period of two centuries or so of cultural poverty—very evident from the archaeological finds of the period—and possibly of economic poverty also—the Chimu and Nazca cultures recovered their autonomy and—freed from the cramping highland influence—their economic and cultural vigour. The continuity between 'early' and 'late' Chimu and Nazca, though not complete, is clear enough to show that the same peoples, and essentially the same cultures, occupied their respective areas for at least a thousand years.

The history of the Andean cultures in the last three centuries before the arrival of the Spaniards is concerned with the rise to power of a small but warlike tribe, the celebrated Incas, who in that space of time, coincident with the later Middle Ages in Europe, by conquest and mutual assimilation, welded all the earlier cultures together into a vast land empire ruled from Cuzco. The Incas originally were pastoralists, one of hundreds of groups of llama-tending, potato-growing mountaineers, of Quechua stock and language. They established themselves in the Cuzco valley in the twelfth century, and within a few decades their own pugnacity and the astuteness of their

chiefs enabled them to subjugate their immediate neighbours in the valley. It was during this early part of their career that the war-chiefs of the Inca tribe—the *Sinchis*—succeeded in establishing themselves as a dynasty; and the tribe as a whole became an aristocracy among other tribes. The Incas—alone among the Amerindian peoples—thus early possessed two essential instruments of empire: a hereditary monarchy and a hereditary ruling class. The ability of their rulers, generation after generation, and the characteristic docility of the Peruvian character, enabled them to govern and not merely to prey upon the peoples whom they conquered. Early in the thirteenth century the Inca army crossed the Desaguadero into the country of the Colla peoples—sometimes miscalled Aymará—and occupied ancient Tiahuanaco. There they learned the art of ashlar masonry, that is, hewn stone, an immense improvement on the *pirca* walling—rough stones set in mud—which they had used until that time. Towards the end of the century they had pushed down the Apurimac valley into the country of the coastal Nazca culture. The piecemeal conquest of the coast, and the assimilation by the Incas of coastal skill and art, took nearly two hundred years. Not until the middle of the fifteenth century were the Chimu people fully subjugated. Some of the mountain tribes held out even longer: the great highland area of Quito, modern Ecuador, was added to the Empire only a few decades before the Spaniards arrived. These relatively recent acquisitions were a source of weakness to the Inca State. It was from the Chimu area that rumours of Inca wealth reached the Spaniards in Darien. Both in Chimu and Quito the inhabitants, still resentful of Inca rule, received the European invaders with acquiescence, if not with enthusiasm.

The society over which the Incas ruled differed in many important respects from the high civilisations of Central and North America. It was a genuine empire, administered by a hierarchy of officials whose effective head was the *Sapa Inca*, with his capital at Cuzco. Throughout the Empire, all but minor local officials were Incas, and the highest officers—those whom the Spaniards later described as 'governors' or 'viceroys'—were normally members of the imperial family, close relatives of the *Sapa Inca* himself. Nothing in Inca history is more remarkable than the sustained ability and vigour of this great dynasty. Its authority was maintained by all possible physical and psychological means. Garrisons of loyal subjects were stationed in strategic places, and sometimes whole towns were moved to hasten the incorporation of newly conquered provinces. Alone among the ancient Amerindians, the Peruvians built roads, or rather footways, of beaten adobe on the coast, paved or stepped in the mountains, to facilitate the passage of armies or of officials. The main Inca routes can still be traced for hundreds of miles. Rivers were crossed by means of bridges, either 'monkey-bridges' with cables of plaited aloe fibre, or floating bridges supported on pontoons of buoyant reeds. Communications were maintained by an elaborately organised system of post-stations and relays of runners all over the Empire; and service as messengers was one of the forms of tribute commonly exacted by the ruling clan. The combination of roads, runners and garrisons enabled revolts to be detected and suppressed as rapidly as the weapons of the time allowed; but in any event revolts were rare. The sanctity of the *Sapa Inca* was maintained by a court ritual of great complexity. The Hispanicised Inca historian, Garcilaso, describes in detail the ceremonial abasement—the symbolic burden,

the bare feet and the downcast eyes—of all who approached the ruler; and the splendour of his ceremonial appearances, whether on civil occasions, or in rites designed to ensure the fertility of crops or the abundance of animals. The Inca Empire, moreover, had a State religion, which supplemented, though it never entirely supplanted, the animistic beliefs and fertility cults. Its object of worship was the sun, of which the *Sapa Inca* was held to be a descendant, and in whose ceremonial worship he played a central and indispensable part.

The existence of a State religion of this kind illustrates the profound difference between Incaic civilisation, and Middle American cultures such as that of the Mayas. The sun-worship of the Incas served, or at least upheld, the interests of empire. To generalise broadly, the Andean peoples directed their energies towards the material technique of supporting life and organising large-scale societies, rather than to the cultivation of supernatural knowledge and power. The Incas held their captives ruthlessly to forced labour; they never sacrificed them wholesale, as did the Aztecs, to appease implacable gods. Their great ruins—buildings, roads, irrigation systems—are secular in character. Their cities were not ceremonial centres, inhabited by a dedicated priesthood, but real cities to be lived in and defended. They erected no *stelae*. Their temples never equalled the magnificent and lavish sculptured pyramids and corbelled shrines of the Maya. Inca masonry, in general, though it is massive, durable and finely dressed, demanded neatness and laboriousness, rather than architectural genius and spiritual drive. The specialised priestly arts did not flourish greatly in the Inca State. There was no highly developed astronomical and calendric science, and no writing. The nearest Andean approach to writing was the *quipu*, a kind of abacus of knotted strings, used for calculating tribute. On the other hand, some of the secular arts flourished exceedingly. Ancient Peruvian pottery in excellence of construction and richness of design had no peer in the Americas; the more remarkable since the potter's wheel was unknown. Surviving examples of jewellery and ornaments in soft metals—gold, silver and copper—are among the great treasures of their kind. Above all, weaving was developed to a point perhaps unequalled by man in the whole course of human history. For this last purpose the Peruvians possessed a remarkable range of raw materials. They had, it is true, no silk or linen; but in addition to many of the coarser vegetable fibres, the coastal peoples grew several species of cotton, of which the best and most important was—and is—the perennial shrub *Gossypium peruvianum* or 'Peruvian Full Rough'. The highlanders had four species of wool-bearing animals—llama, alpaca, guanaco and vicuña—whose fleeces offered a great variety of textures and natural colours. The exchange of lowland cotton for highland wool was probably the most important trade of the Empire, and, characteristically, it was organised by the State, high-grade wool being a State monopoly. The numerous types of loom employed in Peru have been the subject of much detailed study; many of them are still in use. Knowledge of dye-stuffs and mordants has been less fully investigated, though rich and fast colouring and intricate geometrical design are outstanding features of most early Andean textiles. It should be added that in textile manufacture, as in ceramics, the Incas were not innovators; they inherited their genius from the older cultures which they absorbed.

The word 'monolithic' has often been used to describe the Inca State. The *Sapa Inca* certainly inspired a veneration more complete, and wielded a power more absolute than most Old-World monarchs. Inca rule succeeded in imposing a remarkable uniformity upon its subjects regulating in great detail the labour-tribute demanded from each class and age group, regimenting their religious, political and economic activities in the interests of the Empire as a whole, but in return protecting them from war or violence, and to a considerable extent also from want. A high degree of conformity—the willing submergence of the individual in the corporate personality of the tribe—was characteristic of most Amerindian societies. Their technical deficiences were such that without the closest social co-operation they could hardly have supported life, much less built up impressive civilisations. Co-operation was particularly necessary in the Andean region, because of the aridity of the coastal areas and the consequent dependence on irrigation. In most societies —in the East as well as in Peru—where agriculture has depended on large-scale irrigation, an authoritarian central control has emerged, in order to mobilise and direct the population for the labour required. The Incas, accordingly, found means of extending Amerindian conformity, with its intense corporate feeling, from the scale of a single village to that of a large empire. Their state, nevertheless, might more aptly be described as multi-cellular than as monolithic. The *ayllu*—the village clan—remained, and remains to this day, the fundamental unit of social organisation. The Incas themselves, before their rise to power, were only a highland *ayllu* led by a temporary war-chief. They built upon a foundation which they understood, retaining the ancient *ayllus* and their chiefs under the supervision of the hierarchy of imperial officials. The *ayllus* themselves were in most respects self-sufficient and self-contained. In spite of their common subjection to Inca discipline, and the uniformity which discipline entailed, they had little contact one with another; indeed, one of the most characteristic features of Peruvian society was its immobility. Except when the Government, for its own purposes, caused whole tribes to move their homes, ordinary people travelled very little. Incaic highways were for the use of officials and imperial runners. Even trade was local and limited for the most part, confined either to rarities for the use of the nobility or to objects of State monopoly such as vicuña wool. There was relatively little lively long-range commerce, such as the Middle-Americans enjoyed; a curious circumstance, considering that the Peruvians, alone among the Amerindian peoples, possessed a beast of burden, though an inefficient one. The self-sufficiency of the *ayllus* and the immobility of their members were important factors in the Inca rise to power. The villages could be conquered one by one and ruled uniformly but separately. Such a system of rule naturally tended to encourage passive docility rather than active loyalty, except among the ruling caste. The effective geographical extension of the system, also, was limited, for the strain of maintaining garrisons and communications increased disproportionately with every increase in area; and by the sixteenth century the effective limits had been reached and probably overreached. Finally, the system was bound to break down when, as eventually happened, a serious split occurred in the ruling dynasty. The same characteristics, however, which had made the *ayllus* the docile instruments of Inca rule enabled them to survive when the Inca power collapsed.

V

The native cultures of the Americas thus displayed a great variety of attainment, and ranged from the naked savages of some of the West Indian islands to the sophisticated nobilities of Middle America or the Andes. The most developed societies differed greatly one from another; but they all had one characteristic in common. In all of them, remarkable levels of attainment—religious, social, political, artistic—were reached with very limited technical equipment. They had no hard metal tools, no wheeled vehicles, no boats except flimsy canoes or primitive balsas, few and inferior domestic animals. They lacked even that most fundamental of agricultural implements, the plough. Nevertheless, their achievements were such as to astonish the first Europeans who saw them. Their combination of wealth and weakness was their undoing. No *conquistador* could resist the temptations offered by a civilised but infidel people, possessing land and gold, but armed only with weapons of stone.

The events of the Spanish irruption into the New World, and the seizure by the *conquistadores* of the chief centres of Amerindian civilisation, are well known. The first permanent settlement was established in Hispaniola in 1493. By 1512 all the larger West Indian islands had been seized and settled—though sparsely—and the elements of temporal and spiritual government had been set up. The Arawak natives of the islands, too primitive to adjust themselves to new ways, vulnerable to new diseases, physically and mentally unsuited to regular compulsory labour, died off rapidly. Shortage of native labour as well as hope of gold drove Spanish soldiers of fortune to seek fresh fields to conquer. Men from Hispaniola settled in the Isthmus of Darien. Balboa's exploration of 1513 revealed how narrow a strip of land separated the two oceans and encouraged the search for a strait to the Pacific and the East. Expeditions coasted the Western Caribbean and entered the

Gulf of Mexico, and at various points on the coast the explorers heard rumours of powerful cities inland, beyond the mountains. In 1519, the expedition from Cuba led by Hernán Cortés landed at Vera Cruz and made its way through the mountains, by way of Cholula and Tlaxcala, to the captial city of Tenochtitlán. Many Indian *pueblos*, either unwilling tributaries of the Aztecs, or, like Tlaxcala, still unsubdued enemies, assisted the Spanish invaders; and once ensconced in the capital, the Spaniards sought to govern it by kidnapping the head war-chief, Montezuma, whom they wrongly regarded as a ruler in the European sense. The Tenochcas promptly elected another war-chief in Montezuma's place, and drove the Spaniards out, with heavy loss of life. Cortés was then obliged to lay formal siege to the city; his army—a thousand or so Spaniards and several thousand Indian auxiliaries—re-took Tenochtitlán, or all that was left of it after a long and destructive siege, in 1521. With the fall of the city Aztec resistance collapsed. The Maya centres fared no better. Pedro de Alvarado, one of Cortés' ablest lieutenants, profiting by the enmity between the two principal peoples, Cakchiquel and Quiché, mastered the highland area of Guatemala in a ruthless campaign and founded the Spanish city of Guatemala in 1524. The chief cities of Yucatán—though already, as observed, in decline—resisted fiercely under their Mexican chiefs; but they were all subdued, with great brutality, by the Montejos, father and son, between 1527 and 1546.

Alvarado's conquest of Guatemala and that of the ill-fated Olid in Honduras, brought the 'men of Mexico' to the edge of territory already explored by Spaniards from Darien, so that by 1530 all the chief centres of Indian civilisation from Panama to the northern frontier of Aztec influence were in Spanish hands.

The conquest of Peru, in its initial stages, followed somewhat similar lines. After five years of coastal exploration southward from Panama, Francisco Pizarro with 180 men landed at Túmbez on the northern coast of Peru in 1530. His arrival coincided with the final stage of a succession war in which the reigning Inca, Huáscar, was defeated and dethroned by his usurping half-brother Atahualpa, who established himself temporarily at Cajamarca. Reports of this conflict encouraged Pizarro, after establishing himself in the Túmbez region and founding the 'city' of San Miguel, to march inland to Cajamarca. Here, by means of a surprise attack under cover of a formal conference, the Spaniards succeeded in killing most of Atahualpa's immediate retinue and capturing the ruler himself. Aided by surprise, by a favourable political situation, and by a breath-taking boldness which frightened the conquerors themselves, Pizarro and his men decided the fate of the Inca Empire in a single afternoon. His partner Almagro, with 200 men, arrived shortly afterwards. The Inca forces, deprived of the authority of their ruler were unable effectively to resist the conquerors' march on Cuzco. It was taken and sacked by about 600 men in November 1533. The gold looted from Cuzco, together with the roomful of gold vessels which Atahualpa collected in the vain hope of buying his freedom, was melted down, the royal fifth subtracted, and the rest distributed; enough to make every man in the army rich for life, though few lived long to enjoy it.

By the middle of the sixteenth century all the chief centres of American civilisation were in Spanish hands. That is not to say that all the territories subject to those centres had been effectively occupied; there were thousands of square miles in

'Spanish' America which were never penetrated, much less occupied, by Europeans. The *conquistadores*, with unerring instinct and audacity, struck directly at the great cities and captured them all. No other military outcome was possible. Against peoples armed with Neolithic weapons, and brought up in a tradition of ceremonial warfare whose chief object was the taking of prisoners, the Spaniards employed steel swords and lances, steel armour, cross-bows, muskets, mounted cavalry, and ships armed with guns. Even the small numbers of the invaders often proved to their advantage, for they could live off the country and move about it at will, while the vastly larger Indian armies had to carry their supplies with them and could keep the field only for a few days at a time. Over and over again the Spaniards escaped annihilation, as Cortés did after his first retreat from Mexico, by withdrawing out of his enemies' reach. Both in Mexico and in Peru, moreover, the political circumstances were favourable, and the Spaniards secured the support, or at least the passive acquiescence, of discontented Indian groups. The invaders had moral advantages also. They never doubted that they were fighting mortal men; but Montezuma, and some at least of his followers, confronted with men and beasts entirely outside their experience, could not ignore the possibility that Cortés might be a reincarnation of Quetzalcoatl, come to reclaim his earthly kingdom. Finally, the Spaniards had the advantage of their truculent missionary faith; the conviction that, however unsanctified their own lives might be, the saints fought on their side. Every *entrada* produced its crop of miracle stories. The Indian's religion required him to fight and, if need be, to die bravely. The Spaniard believed that his religion enabled him to win.

VI

The remarkable thing was not the military fact of conquest, but the relative ease with which the Spaniards established a permanent, organised, and—despite the efforts of the Crown—often brutal dominion. There was still plenty of resistance after the conquest, especially in Peru, where civil strife between Spanish factions encouraged it. Manco, the last reigning Inca, maintained an independent court in the mountain fastnesses of Vilcabamba for many years. The viceroyalty of Peru was not reduced to general order and obedience until the time of Francisco de Toledo in the fifteen-seventies, and then only by means of an extensive resettlement of disaffected Indians. Resistance, however, was rarely effective over a wide area. It was paralysed by apathy, by treachery, by lack of co-ordination. Only remote and primitive peoples such as the Araucanians of Chile and the Chichimecas of the northern frontier maintained themselves in real independence over a long period. Elsewhere, having seized the great ceremonial centres, the *conquistadores* successfully converted the tributary villages into fiefs or *encomiendas*. They assumed the privileges of the chiefs and priests whom they had killed or deposed; and the villagers, with sullen obedience, rendered to their new masters the services and tributes which they had formerly paid to their Indian overlords. The explanation of this apathy, this collapse of resistance, is to be found not so much in the physical power of the Spaniards—who, after all, were only a handful—as in the nature of the allies which followed in their wake: disease and domestic animals. Smallpox had come into Mexico with Cortés' army, and together with typhoid—contracted through drinking the lake water after the aqueducts had been cut—had sapped the resistance of the defenders of Tenochtitlán. Thereafter

European diseases, from which the Indians had no immunity, reduced the native population at appalling speed. Major epidemics occurred in the fifteen-twenties, immediately after the conquest, in the fifteen-forties, and again in the fifteen-seventies. A recent and well-documented study gives the following approximate population figures for Central Mexico: 1519—11,000,000; 1540—6,427,466; 1565—4,409,180; 1597—2,500,000. Other writers differ in their estimates of numbers, but there is general agreement on the downward trend; and depopulation caused by disease was hastened by the increasing threat to Indian food supplies caused by the increase in grazing animals. In the arid uplands of Castile from which most of the *conquistadores* came, pastoral pursuits, the grazing of semi-nomadic flocks and herds, had long been preferred to arable farming. Naturally, Spanish immigrants brought their beasts with them, and in the fifteen-thirties, in most parts of the Indies, cattle and sheep raising had become the principal occupation of the wealthier Spaniards. Every chronicler of New Spain mentioned, usually with astonishment and delight, the prodigious number of beasts which the country supported. Mendoza, the first Spanish viceroy of Mexico, introduced the merino sheep, the basis of an incipient woollen industry—which, incidentally, earned a sinister reputation for coercion and ill-treatment of Indian labourers in its *obrajes*. Grazing grants were loosely defined, initially in terms of radius from a fixed spot, and little attempt was made to fix boundaries. The beasts invaded the unfenced *milpas* of the Indian villages, despite repeated legislation, and despite the efforts of colonial courts to protect Indian property. The spread of stock ranching was undoubtedly a major cause of depopulation in Central Mexico, and over-grazing the principal cause of the soil erosion which has plagued the country ever since. In Peru, horned cattle were less important, but sheep, and pigs rooting in the potato patches, created similar conditions in many parts of the highlands. In both areas stock ranching, often combined with abuses of the *encomienda* system, tended to the destruction of Indian communal farming, and to the establishment of European-owned *latifundia*.

First *encomiendas* and then stock ranches produced the accumulations of capital which made possible the large-scale mining of precious metals. Mining and ranching were complementary, since the miners needed steady supplies of beef, leather and tallow candles, and often the same people were concerned in both. Mining, like ranching, bore hardly on the Indian population, but in a different way. It created a great demand for pick-and-shovel labour; some of this demand was met by the import of Negro slaves, but most of the work was done by Indians. The Spanish Government insisted that Indian labourers should be paid a fixed wage; but Indians did not—and do not—take kindly to wage-earning labour, so they had to be coerced. Under the *repartimiento* system, a fixed proportion of the male population of each village had to present themselves for work in rotation throughout the year. *Repartimiento* labourers were distributed either for public works, or to Spanish employers. Forced labour, whether within the *encomiendas* in the early days, or through the *repartimiento* system, or by means of peonage—debt slavery—has been a constant feature of Indian life from the conquest down to very recent times. Over-work and under-feeding, as well as the epidemics which spread in crowded conditions, took a heavy toll of Indians in the mines; and epidemic disease was carried by the mine-workers back to their villages. Those Indians who accepted

European ways, who acquired European crafts, or plied Indian crafts near European centres, were effectively protected against ill-treatment (though not, of course, against disease) and could become modestly rich; so could the headmen who organised the labour supply; but Indians who stayed in their villages and tried to carry on in the old way had the worst of both worlds. In general, as the Indian provinces grew rich and prosperous, so they grew less populous. Communal agriculture in many places broke down. Ancient irrigation works were abandoned, and many areas, particularly in the coastal plain of Peru, reverted to desert. The decline of population went on for a hundred and fifty years; not until the second half of the seventeenth century was there any clear sign of recovery.

The conquest of the Indies was not only a military and economic conquest, but a spiritual one also. The essential complement to the rule of swordsmen, whether miners or ranchers, was supplied by the soldiers of the Church—the friars of the missionary Orders. The Franciscans were the first in the field in Mexico, as the result of a request made to the Emperor by Cortés himself. The first Franciscans sent out in 1524—the famous Twelve under the leadership of Fray Martín de Valencia —and many of their successors, were strict Observants, carefully trained for their task. The same is true of the first Dominicans who, under Fray Domingo de Betanzos, went to Mexico in 1525. They were daring religious radicals, picked products of Church reform in Spain, representing both the radical churchmanship of Cisneros and the humanism and learning of Erasmus. Their leadership in the spiritual conquest ensured its efficiency and speed, and their impact on Indian society, despite the smallness of their numbers, was of explosive force.

The conversion which the missionaries sought to achieve was more than a mere outward conformity. Baptism was to be preceded by careful instruction in the Faith, by preaching, by catechism, and by the establishment of schools in which the sons of leading Indians might be educated in Christian doctrine and European ways. The teaching, catechising and baptism of many hundreds of thousands could be achieved, by the small number of friars available, only by the concentration of Indians in urban communities close to the nucleus of church and convent from which the missionaries directed their enterprise. Naturally the friars settled in places where the urban communities already existed; but such concentrations of population were rare. Outside capitals such as Tenochtitlán, Mayapán and Cuzco, the great majority of settled Indians lived in scattered hamlets among their potato patches or their *milpas* of maize and beans. Much of the energy of the missionaries was devoted, therefore, to persuading or compelling the Indians to move into new towns built around church and convent. By these means, they argued, new converts could have the moral and social advantages of urban life on European lines, and at the same time could be kept under ecclesiastical supervision.

In Mexico, the success of the friars in establishing their ascendancy over the Indians was extraordinary, and can be explained only in terms of Indian psychology. The Indians were accustomed to living in accordance with an intricate and continuous ritual which governed all their communal activities, including the all-important processes of agriculture. The Spanish conquest with its destruction of temples, its prohibitions of pagan dances, its forceful proselytising, weakened and in some places destroyed the old ritual organisation. Work—whether forced labour for an *encomendero* or wage labour, or even subsistence farming—ceased to be part of a socio-religious ceremonial system and became a mere profane necessity. A void was created in the spiritual and social life of the Indian which could be filled, though partially and often superficially, by the ritual of the Church and the activities of church-building.

The friars understood this necessity; and the very numerous and very large churches which were built with Indian labour, especially in New Spain, though they owed their massive strength to considerations of defence, also owed their magnificence to a desire to replace the lost splendour of the pagan temples. Similarly the splendour of ecclesiastical ritual—far more elaborate than was common in Europe—was an attempt to meet the Indians' longing for the old ceremonial life which they had largely lost. At the same time, the friars, apart from a few overworked royal judges and officials, were the Indians' only defenders against abuses of *encomienda* and *repartimiento* systems; and in many of them the Indians found a devotion and a humanity which compelled their respect. As a result, in Mexico those Indians who were in close contact with missionaries acquired a new theocracy, a new priesthood, and a hybrid religion. The cult of the Blessed Virgin was superimposed on, and confused with, the cults of earth-mother and corn-goddess. The war-gods were forgotten, because they had proved so patently powerless against Spanish steel. Pagan fertility rites were christianised, by the inclusion of a preliminary mass and a procession through the village with the images of saints, or of local gods—for the difference was often little understood. The outward signs of this intermingling of cults can be seen to this day in sixteenth-century churches decorated by Indian craftsmen. Angels are carved wearing feather bonnets, and the Madonna is depicted with the swarthy skin and lank black hair of an Indian.

VII

The results of Spanish attempts, lay and ecclesiastical, to Europeanise the Indian population, varied greatly from province to province. The most obvious and immediate successes were achieved in Mexico. Cortés decided, immediately after the capture of Tenochtitlán, to rebuild the city and make it the capital of the kingdom of New Spain. He was wise enough to appreciate the prestige of the place, its 'renown and importance', as he expressed it. Christianity has often sought to identify itself with the ruins of preceding civilisations in the relationship of new spirit occupying old forms. By re-occupying Tenochtitlán, by building churches and dwellings upon its temple sites, rather than leaving the ruins as a monument to Aztec grandeur, the Spaniards not only destroyed the pre-conquest appearance of the city; they also identified themselves with its traditions as a religious and political centre. It became a mixed city, in which Spaniards and Indians lived side by side in their respective *barrios*. The rebuilding began that fruitful intermingling of Spanish and Indian ways which has remained characteristic of Spanish North America ever since. Similar mingling took place in smaller centres, even in villages. Both lay Spaniards and missionaries played a part in the process of Hispanicisation. Many Spaniards took Indian wives or mistresess. Today, Mexico is a predominantly *mestizo* country, a country where the majority of the people are of mixed blood and mixed traditions, and—when they think about such things—take pride in both strains of their ancestry (*see* Chapter 17). Its many civil commotions have had political or agrarian rather than racial origins.

Pizarro, unlike Cortés, did not establish the centre of his power in the ancient capital of the kingdom, but founded in 1535 an entirely new and entirely Spanish capital— Lima, the City of the Kings, close to the sea in the Rimac valley. The choice was natural on military grounds, for Cuzco was remote from the harbours on which Spanish Peru depended for reinforcements and supplies from the outside world, and its mountainous surroundings made the use of cavalry, the chief Spanish arm, difficult if not impossible; but by this decision Pizarro emphasised the division between Spanish coast and Indian mountain, and lost one means of attaching the Peruvians to a new allegiance. Cuzco fell into decay. Peru never experienced the rapid interaction of European and Indian ways which was characteristic of the early history of Mexico. The Indians were more resistant, the Hispanicising process less intense. *Encomiendas* were granted in Peru as in New Spain, but there was less opportunity for peaceful organisation. Constant fighting, in civil wars and revolts, took a far heavier toll of Indian lives and property than in New Spain, and the mitigating influence of the missionary orders was less effective. By the time that Peru was conquered, Erasmian radicalism within the Spanish Church had lost much of its vigour. Peru received no picked band of zealots comparable with the Twelve. Christianity, in so far as it was accepted at all, was accepted as a second and separate religion, while the traditional worship was carried on as well, sometimes secretly and sometimes in the open. For two hundred years after the conquest the ecclesiastical authorities found it necessary to send out periodical *visitadores de idolatría*, in a vain attempt to suppress pagan rites. Apart from these occasional persecutions, the Indians, so long as they paid their tributes and performed the labour demanded of them, were left to themselves. They lived their old village life, tilled their fields and tended their looms in the old way, but without the unified purpose and confident serenity which their old priests and rulers had given them. They lost much of what was best in their old culture, without acquiring much of the culture of Spain.

Among the survivors of the Inca aristocracy, it is true that some adopted Spanish ways and lived in comparative wealth and comfort as landlords, even as *encomenderos* of the European type. They never forgot their Inca ancestry, however, and frequently became implicated in Indian risings. In the eighteenth century, when New Spain was enjoying, on the whole, remarkable order and prosperity, Peru experienced a widespread revival of Inca nationalism and a series of dangerous revolts against Spanish government. Most of these revolts were led by prominent and, from the point of view of government, apparently respectable Indians. One, the famous rebellion of the Inca Túpac Amaru— who renounced his Spanish name and resumed a name of a reputed ancestor— placed the whole viceroyalty in danger for a time. The Hispanicised Inca aristocrat, like the Spanish missionary, failed to bridge the gap between Spaniard and Indian in Peru. Peru remained, and remains to this day, a country with a Spanish, vociferously Catholic ruling class, and an Indian, largely pagan peasantry.

Spanish imperial government was paternal, conscientious, meticulous; it was no more oppressive, nor more corrupt, than most contemporary European governments; it strove by legislation and administrative action to protect the native Amerindians against exploitation and brutality, and to safeguard them in possession of their land and personal liberty. Some of its officials and many missionaries were the devoted friends, according to their lights, of the conquered race. Even where legislation could be made effective, however, it could only protect the Indians as individuals, as subjects of the Spanish Crown; and most Indians scarcely thought of themselves as individuals. The warm, close-knit structure of Indian communal life could not be preserved by Spanish legislation; where it survived—as it did on a small and humble scale in thousands of remote villages—it survived by means of stubborn passive resistance to all change, however well meant, sponsored by the conquerors.

VIII

The Spanish invasion of the New World was thus far more than a mere military conquest; it was a relentless attack upon ancient cultures whose values were unacceptable—indeed incomprehensible—to most Spaniards. The attack was at once spiritual, political, social and economic. Their rulers were killed or deposed, or else rendered harmless, Europeanised and pensioned off. Their religions were proscribed, and a new religion, half-understood, offered in their place. The shrines were destroyed and desecrated and Christian churches built on the temple mounds. The old rituals were forbidden, and disappeared except on a purely local scale, in villages where they might pass unnoticed. The pictogrammic writings were destroyed—very few now survive—and the songs and poems lingered only in an uncertain folk memory. The Indian arts of architecture, sculpture and metalwork were largely supplanted—for a time at least—by totally different European arts. The communal agriculture, though it survived in many places, was weakened by the invasion of a pastoral economy, by European notions of the individual ownership of land, and by progressive alienation, over the centuries, of Indian lands—sometimes by seizure, but often by simple sale—so that in many parts of the Americas the poorer Indians survived only as landless *peones* on estates owned by Europeans, *mestizos* or Europeanised chiefs. No culture could survive, intact, so powerful an attack on so many different fronts; certainly no culture with the technical deficiencies of the native American societies. Probably, moreover, the American cultures, had already reached before the conquest, the highest point of development of which they were capable without outside stimulus. Some of them—indeed notably that of the Maya—were already in decline; and so the destruction of their more splendid manifestations—their cities and their state religions—was accomplished with deadly effectiveness.

The world as a whole was made vastly richer by the European discovery of America; and the American articles which have most enriched the Old World are the food crops discovered and domesticated by the 'archaic' cultivators of the New. The Peruvian potato is eaten daily by most Europeans today. Maize, the staple diet of ancient Middle America, is now grown all over the world as food both for animals and human beings. Cassava, once confined to tropical America, is now the staple diet of millions of people in West Africa, whose methods of growing and preparing it are much the same as those which the Amerindians used. West Africa, too, relies heavily for its income on the export of cacao—an American plant, from which the highland Mayas and the Mexicans made the *chocolatl* which so delighted the *conquistadores*. And what of tobacco? Tobacco is an American plant; the Amerindians used it in all the forms known today—in pipes, in cigars, in cigarettes (though rolled in corn-husks) and as snuff. Tobacco is probably the most universal vegetable product known to man. It has made more fortunes than all the silver of the Indies, and full knowledge of the harm it could do came only in the mid-twentieth century.

These valuable products, gifts of the New World to the Old, once formed in the New World the economic basis of a series of remarkable and highly developed societies. The Spanish conquest beheaded those societies. The ideas, the ceremonial, the art, the political organisation which had been developed or encouraged by ruling priests or chieftains, disappeared when the ruling groups disappeared or were absorbed into European society. On the other hand, since the peasants were less affected by conquest than their former rulers, the social organisation of villages and the workaday crafts of villagers—their farming methods, their weaving, their pottery—had more chance of survival. They may all be seen today, by anyone who leaves the towns and the main roads. The revival, in modern times, of interest and pride in Indian art and thought owes much, it is true, to archaeology; but it is more than mere antiquarianism. It reflects a continuing tradition. The Amerindian is by nature intensely tenacious of his traditions and loyal to his past. Especially is this true among the highlanders of the Andes. That vast, wild and unhappy region may yet experience an Indian renascence, as unforeseen and as dramatic as the sixteenth-century destruction.

14 THE CIVILISATIONS OF INDIA AND THE FAR EAST: INDONESIA AND THE PACIFIC

by G. F. Hudson

The Spanish conquerors of the Americas had discovered elaborate but technically primitive societies. The Portuguese voyagers—the vanguard of the oceanic expansion of Europe at the beginning of the sixteenth century, who reached the southern and eastern coasts of Asia after sailing round Africa—came into contact with highly civilised peoples with whom Europeans had previously had no direct intercourse. Although a number of medieval travellers from Europe had reached India and China, and Marco Polo had even reported the existence of Japan, the lands of Islam were interposed between Christendom and the indigenous civilisations of the Further East, and the Arabs and Persians were the intermediaries in whatever traffic there was in commodities, techniques or ideas from one end to the other of the Eurasian land mass.

With the opening of the continuous sea-routes from Lisbon to Malabar, Ceylon and Bengal, Malacca and Ternate, Canton and Nagasaki, a new world was attained, not indeed one hitherto unknown as the Americas had been, but one which it only now became possible to know in any detail. The navigational advance also rendered it possible for Asian shipping of the Indian and Pacific Oceans to sail to Europe and for the civilisations brought nearer by improved communications to interact closely on one another with fruitful results. That this did not happen to any great extent during the three cen-

turies which followed the initial voyage of Vasco da Gama was due partly to the nature of the Eastern civilisations themselves and partly to the attitudes of the new intruders. The civilisations of Asia had reached a point at which their energies were concentrated more on the conservation of their established values than on progress or experiment; they lacked a dynamic of innovation comparable to that which had been developed by the capitalism of the European city-republics and they tended to withdraw into themselves when confronted with strange new ways of life and thought. On the side of the Europeans the early combination of navally supported monopolistic commerce with the desire to propagate an exclusive religion was adverse to the growth of an uninhibited cultural intercourse and aggravated Asian dispositions to regard the representatives of the restless alien civilisation with suspicion and reserve.

II

Two great civilisations had grown up in Asia to the east of the Indus—the Indian and the Chinese. Each of these had its sphere of influence in adjacent countries with cultural characters of their own, but not to the point of basically original creation. By the time of Vasco da Gama's arrival the greater part of India had become subject to Moslem rulers and a substantial minority of its inhabitants had been converted to Islam—which was also the

ASIA *circa* A.D. 750

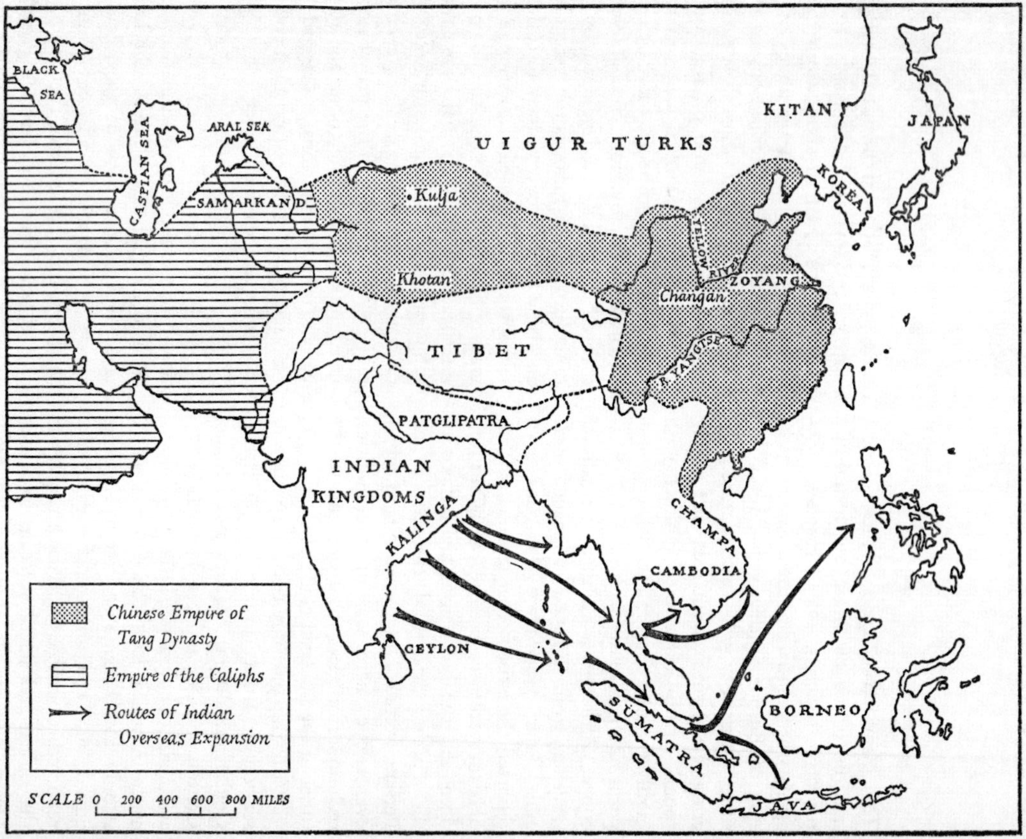

KITAN

JAPAN

KOREA

UIGUR TURKS

YELLOW R.
LOYANG
Changan
YANG.

Kuja

Khotan

TIBET

ARAL SEA

SAMARKAND

CASPIAN SEA

BLACK SEA

PATGLIPATRA

INDIAN
KINGDOMS

KALINGA

CEYLON

CHAMPA

CAMBODIA

BORNEO

SUMATRA

JAVA

Chinese Empire of
Tang Dynasty

Empire of the Caliphs

Routes of Indian
Overseas Expansion

SCALE 0   200   400   600   800 MILES

dominant religion of Asia between the Indus and the Mediterranean—but the native religion and culture of India remained massively established even where the Moslems were the political conquerors, and during the first half of the sixteenth century the powerful Hindu kingdom of Vijayanagar still controlled nearly all India south of the river Kistna. To the east from an earlier period Indian religious and cultural influences had been diffused as far as the Lesser Sunda Islands to the south-east and Japan to the north-east. The more southerly expansion associated with sea-borne trade and emigration across the Bay of Bengal and through the straits and inner seas of the Malay Archipelago, had resulted in the rise, particularly in Java and Cambodia, of kingdoms in which Indian civilisation was modified by the local genius to produce a magnificent art with special variations on Indian themes. In higher latitudes the influence of India had also spread, but without ethnic settlement and in contest with another civilisation of comparable strength—that of China; Buddhism, propagated from India, reached China, Korea and Japan and gained a hold on all three countries, but did not in the long run displace Confucianism as the state religion of China or the stronger influence conveyed by Chinese literary culture to Korea and Japan. Only in Tibet did Buddhism become the decisively dominant cultural element. China's own cultural sphere may be identified with the countries which adopted the Chinese ideographic script and used Chinese as a learned language; this did not correspond to the political range of the Chinese Empire, which never included Japan, but did take in at various times Central Asian peoples whose culture was essentially Indian or Islamic. Geographically the huge barrier of the Himalayas and the mountains

enfolding Burma always kept apart the imperial powers ruling in India and China respectively, but the cultural frontiers were harder to draw, and the whole of the Far East shows the interpenetration of the two civilisations.

The old Indian civilisation reached its zenith in the days of the Gupta Empire which flourished between A.D. 320 and 500. It never covered the whole of India, and was indeed less extensive than the Maurya Empire had been under Asoka, chiefly because of the greater strength of the kingdoms which had in the meantime grown up in the south as the latter became more settled and civilised. But the Gupta monarchs controlled most of North India and the age coincided with the finest flowering of Sanskrit literature; the great poet and dramatist Kalidasa belonged to this period, and the vast epic of the *Mahabharata* and the mythical stories known as *Puranas* received their final literary form about the same time. It was also the most fruitful epoch of Indian science and mathematics, and was highly productive in philosophical thought, though what was to become the most influential school of Indian philosophy— the Vedanta—did not receive its classic formulation until a later date. In architecture and sculpture the art of the Gupta period had a serene and noble quality which tends to be lacking in the more richly imaginative and varied art of later times. The rules of caste had not yet become as rigid as they did later, and women appear to have had greater freedom than in subsequent Hindu society. Hinduism— the complex of cults recognising the authority of the Vedic religious texts and the sanctity of the Brahman caste— underwent a revival at the expense of Buddhism during this period, but the two religions continued to flourish side by side, and Buddhism continued to be important in India almost until the time of the Moslem conquests.

Contemporary with the Guptas in North India, there were in South India several independent kingdoms, the most important of which was that of the Pallavas, holding the east side of the Deccan with the Golconda coast and the Coromandel coast down to Madras. South India still remained in many ways a world apart, for the Vindhya range was still an effective barrier shutting off the peninsula from the Indo-Gangetic plain, and the population of South India, except in Maharashtra, continued to speak Dravidian languages—Tamil, Telugu and Kanarese—in contrast to the Indo-Aryan speech of the North. But the South had accepted Hindu or Buddhist religion and social custom and used Sanskrit as its language of scripture and learning, so that a single civilisation bound together diverse peoples and political units from the Himalayas to Cape Comorin.

India from early times had important commercial connections both to west and east, and its position made it also an intermediary for long-distance trade between West Asia and the Mediterranean on the one hand and the Far East on the other. The main traffic was by sea and the most important commodities were spices, of which pepper, ginger and cinnamon could be obtained in Malabar while cloves and nutmegs came from Indonesia. In the days of the Roman Empire shipping from the Red Sea ports of Egypt went to India, using the monsoons for navigation of the Indian Ocean and making either for a port near the mouth of the Indus or for the Gulf of Cambay whence an overland route ran by Ujjain to Mathura on the Jumna, or for the Malabar coast, which lay south of east by an open sea voyage from the Gulf of Aden. From Malabar 'Roman' merchants—they were

in fact usually Greeks of Syria—could go on to Malaya and Indonesia by crossing the peninsula to the Coromandel coast on the east side and waiting for the next monsoon; the attempt to make a continuous voyage round the south of India and Ceylon seems to have been very rare. But the great bulk of the trade to the east of India was in the hands of the Indians themselves; originally this seafaring was carried on mainly from the ancient kingdom of Kalinga on the Golconda coast, whence all Indians in Indonesia are still commonly known as Klings. By the second century A.D. Indian ships were sailing to Java and Borneo and the coasts of Indo-China. This extensive commerce produced the knowledge of the coasts of Asia reflected in the work of the Greek geographer Ptolemy, who, however, fell into the major error of regarding the Indian Ocean as a closed sea with continuous land to the east and south. The source for such an idea was presumably a knowledge of the existence of large land masses to the east of the South China Sea and perhaps a still vaguer knowledge of the existence of Australia to the south-east. The belief shows that in Ptolemy's time—the second century A.D.—shipping did not sail from India to the east coast of China; but there was an overland route north-eastward into China from a port equivalent to the modern Haiphong, which was the terminus of coasting voyages northward from Malaya. A little later direct sailing between India and China became common.

To the north, in the interior of Asia, caravan routes ran from the ports of the Eastern Mediterranean and Black Sea across the plateau of Iran to India via the Khyber, Bolan and other passes, and to China across the Pamirs. The route to China served the trade in silk, of the production of which China had a complete monopoly until the sixth century A.D.;

the way was to the north of India, and not through India, because of the formidable barriers to trade formed by the Himalayas and the mountains round Assam. Overland contact between India and China was thus through Kashmir and Afghanistan rather than by more direct routes; Tibet was still a barbarous country until after A.D. 600 and the Nagas, Mishmis, Abors and other hill tribes to the north-east of India have remained primitive to the present day, so that very little traffic ever passed that way until American aircraft flew supplies over the 'hump' from Assam to Chungking during the Second World War.

With the growth of a far-ranging commerce in the early centuries of the Christian era Indian merchants travelled far afield to the north and west—to Samarkand, Seleucia and Alexandria—and Indian religious influences spread too; there was widespread conversion to Buddhism in what are now Afghanistan and Uzbekistan, and further west there were traces of Indian thought in certain religious systems that developed during the period—Manichaeism and the Gnostic Christian heresies. But there could not be any significant Indian settlement in these regions, where the fertile areas were seats of long established civilisation. It was different in South-East Asia, where there were great possibilities of agricultural development, but only a scanty and primitive population; there Indian traders were followed by brahmans and soldiers of fortune, who became the founders and organisers of powerful kingdoms. The Indian colonists were numerically small minorities among the natives, who multiplied rapidly with the introduction of intensive rice cultivation and continued to speak their own Austronesian or Austro-Asiatic languages. But the institutions of religion, government and administration became predominantly Indian. Of one of

these South-East Asian kingdoms a contemporary Chinese source states: 'More than a thousand brahmans from India reside there; the people follow their teachings and give them their daughters in marriage.' The most important of the states thus created was Cambodia in the fertile alluvial plain of the lower Mekong, where a dynasty of kings of Indian descent reigned over a population speaking Khmer, a language of the Austro-Asiatic family. The Cambodian kingdom and its culture go back to the age of the Guptas, but were at their zenith from the ninth to the twelfth century; in that period a style of architecture and sculpture derived from India attained a height of beauty and magnificence of which the ruins of the city of Angkor Thom and the great temple of Angkor Wat are the enduring monuments.

To the south, where ships from Kalinga, Andhra and the Tamil lands sailed through the Straits of Malacca into the waters of the Malay Archipelago, substantial Indian settlements were made in Sumatra and Java. In the former island a powerful state emerged under the name of Sri-Vishaya; it had its capital on the Palembang river and among its dependencies was the island of Singapore where shipping between India and the South China Sea passed round the end of the Malay Peninsula. The empire of Sri-Vishaya, which was Buddhist by religion, also extended over the western half of Java, but the states of eastern Java resisted the Sri-Vishayan expansion and created a rival power which finally overthrew the Sri-Vishayan Empire in the latter part of the fourteenth century. The surviving architectural remains of Sri-Vishaya are scanty, but a great temple-building activity in eastern Java from the seventh century onwards has left a large number of ruins, of which those of Boro Budur are the most famous.

The states founded by Indian colonisation in South-East Asia maintained diplomatic and cultural, as well as commercial, contacts with India, but were politically independent of any power based on Indian territory. The exception to this rule was the temporary extension of the Chola Empire of South India to Malaya in the eleventh century. The Cholas were a Tamil Dynasty, who fought a long war against the Sailendra kings of Sri-Vishaya, sending armies across the Bay of Bengal to Malaya and Sumatra. But the Sailendras were victorious in the end and there was no further domination by any Indian state.

III

The history of India from the break-up of the Gupta Empire early in the sixth century to the Moslem conquest of North India at the end of the twelfth is a confused story of rival dynasties often ruling over large areas but never strong enough to unite the whole sub-continent under a single sway. But the cultural unity of India remained and was even emphasised by the process of development which on the eve of the Moslem invasions had virtually effaced Buddhism as a separate religion and made all India Hindu. The reaction against Buddhism took place at the levels both of popular cult and of philosophical doctrine, and in both there was a Hindu counter-reformation that borrowed much from the Buddhism with which it contended. The Vedic gods had now almost disappeared, and the compassionate man-saving incarnations of Vishnu and the benign form of Siva, which became the object of such intense religious devotion in South India, owed much to the projection of the Buddha and the Buddhist saints (bodhisattvas) as teachers and saviours of mankind. Similarly the teaching of the great religious philosopher Sankara, who

in the eighth century reconciled all the myths of Hinduism as configurations of a negatively conceived absolute, took over so much from Buddhist thought that it was denounced by the more conservative brahmans as Buddhism in disguise. Buddhism itself in this period likewise absorbed so much of Hindu myth and practice that it gradually lost its identity as the movement of secession from traditional religion that it had originally been. By the twelfth century it survived only to the south in Ceylon and in the north-east of India, where it still enjoyed the patronage of the Pala kings of Bengal and Bihar; the Moslem invasions, with their new strains and stresses, led to its final disappearance from the Gangetic plain, but it had in the meantime become the faith of Tibet, and there created a highly individual national culture which has endured to the present day.

Indian society around A.D. 1000 was socially well organised and prosperous, apparently stable and secure against external attack, and free from internal conflicts more serious than the frequent, but not too devastating, wars of rivalry between the various dynastic kingdoms. It centred on the royal courts and the temples, the latter tending to become larger and more complex until they quite overshadowed the palaces and castles of the secular rulers. They were places of pilgrimage and of commerce, they often had teaching colleges attached to them and maintained large numbers of priestly attendants, musicians, dancers, sculptors and all kinds of artisans; they were sometimes provided with walls and towers by which they could be converted into fortresses. They were usually—especially in the south—covered with carvings representing every aspect of Indian mythology, legend and everyday life, including erotic scenes which Europeans have always considered inappropriate to a religious edifice, but do not offend against the pantheistic outlook of Hinduism. Today it is difficult to make an adequate comparison between the artistic achievements of North and South in pre-Moslem India because of the great destruction of temples during the early days of the Moslem conquests and again under Aurangzab in North India, but even before the Moslem invasions there seems to have been a certain displacement of the cultural centre of gravity towards the south, and most of the finest architectural monuments of Indian civilisation are now to be found in Orissa, the Deccan and the Tamil country south of Madras.

IV

The onset of Islam against India in the eleventh century came from Afghanistan, which had been a Moslem country since the early days of the Arab expansion carrying the religion of Mohammed westward to Spain and eastward to the Pamirs. Sind had also been overrun in the initial drive but it was geographically isolated from the rest of India by the Thar desert, and the alien occupation was successfully sealed off, so that it had hardly any effect beyond the area of the lower Indus. Hindu kings continued to hold the Punjab and the mountain passes to the west. But at the end of the tenth century the rise of the powerful and vigorous Ghaznavid Dynasty —a line of Turkish origin—in Afghanistan coincided with dissensions among the kings of North India, and the way was open for a series of invasions which involved no mere dynastic warfare but a far-reaching disruption of Indian society. Sultan Mahmud of Ghazni commanded an army of Afghan tribesmen and adventurers from Central Asia in whom impulses of predatory barbarism were concentrated and disciplined by fanatical religious faith. He ranged far and wide over the Indo-Gangetic plain and southward to Gujerat;

he sacked and destroyed many famous cities—Thanesvar, Kanauj, Mathura, Somnath—and burned temples everywhere; he annexed the Punjab to his empire, but elsewhere his forces merely plundered and ravaged. After Mahmud's death there was no further advance for a long time, but Moslem power was now established within the natural frontiers of India, and when in 1192 Mohammed Ghori, who had displaced the Ghaznavid Dynasty in its homeland, overthrew a confederacy of Indian rulers headed by Prithviraj of Ajmer, Hindu resistance rapidly collapsed; within seven years the Ghori army had reached the Bay of Bengal and all North India was under Moslem domination, though subordinate Hindu monarchs often continued to rule.

Mohammed Ghori died in 1206, and his principal general, Kutubuddin, was proclaimed Sultan in Delhi by the army; he founded the line of 'Slave Kings' so-called because the ruler elected by the troops, like the Mameluk Sultans of Egypt, had normally started his career as a slave. The Moslem power was primarily military, based on conquest of a population diverse in language, religion, law and culture from the conquerors, but in some areas the alien Moslem element was reinforced by large-scale conversions. The highest offices under the Moslem rulers were open to converts, who often found advancement much easier under the new dispensation than in the rigidly stratified Hindu society. Mass conversions took place principally in the West Punjab, where earlier invasions from Central Asia had left an ethnic mixture never entirely assimilated to Hindu society, and in East Bengal, where the population consisted largely of aborigines still only on the fringe of the Hindu system. These were the areas which were in our time to form the separate Moslem State of Pakistan.

Elsewhere the Moslems, even when numerous, continued to be in a minority. The two communities lived side by side with hardly any social communication or intercourse; not only were their beliefs and customs sharply separated but their languages were different at the higher levels, for the Moslem rulers and nobles used Persian as the language of administration, diplomacy and higher literature, where the Hindu governments had used Sanskrit. Some cultural overlapping did, however, take place owing to the need of the Moslem rulers for civil administrators, which led them to employ many unconverted Hindus as officials; these had to learn Persian and there was thus a certain exchange of cultural influences. Later a form of Hindu full of Persian words and turns of speech was developed by the Moslems of North India; it was called Urdu, the 'camp language', and eventually became a distinct language with its own literature.

The Moslem conquest encountered strong resistance in the region of Rajasthan (Rajputana), where desert tracts gave a certain protection to relatively small kingdoms holding semi-isolated areas of fertility. The Rajput aristocracy, distinguished by a chivalric code not unlike that of medieval Europe, fought stubbornly for their local independence and there was very little conversion to Islam. But the main Hindu resistance was in South India. After some preliminary raids a serious Moslem effort to subdue the south was made under Mohammed bin Tughluq (1325–51) who for a while ruled over the whole of India from the Himalayas to a point south of Madras. He even had the idea of moving his capital to the Deccan and ordered the entire population of Delhi to move to Daulatabad (Deogir) almost due east of Bombay. In spite of his abilities as a conqueror, his capricious

tyranny ruined his empire, which fell to pieces after his death; Moslem rule continued in the northern Deccan under the Bahmani Sultans, while to the south of them a formidable Hindu power arose in the shape of the kingdom of Vijayanagar, which was still flourishing when the Portuguese reached India at the beginning of the sixteenth century. Under a great king, Krishnadeva Raya (1509–50), Vijayanagar took the offensive against Moslem India and made substantial gains of territory, but its power was broken by a confederacy of Moslem rulers at the battle of Talikota in 1565, and later the Deccan was brought under the rule of the Mughals.

The dynasty which became so famous in Europe because of Western contacts with it during the sixteenth and seventeenth centuries was only the last of a series of Moslem royal houses which reigned in Delhi and held a more or less effective supremacy over North India. At the end of the first quarter of the sixteenth century the Lodi Afghan Dynasty held Delhi, but was threatened by a Rajput confederacy under Rana Sanga of Mewar and Bengal was independent under a separate Moslem house. At this point in Indian history Babur descended from Kabul into the plains of the Punjab and defeated the Lodi Sultan in the battle of Panipat (1526), thus founding the Mughal Empire. A descendant of Timur (Tamerlane) in the paternal line, and of Genghiz Khan, the great Mongol conqueror, on his mother's side, Babur brought yet another influx of Moslem warriors from Afghanistan and Central Asia into the Indian sub-continent. For a long time this new empire was confined to North India; only in the final stage of its expansion did it become really dominant in the south, and then the conquest was thwarted by the endless Maratha wars which led to the disintegration of the Mughal power.

V

Parallel to the Moslem ascendancy by land in India went a Moslem ascendancy—not Turko-Afghan but Arab—in the Indian Ocean. Hindu shipping virtually disappeared from the seas and its place was taken by the Arab merchants who carried spices from Malabar and Malacca to the ports of the Red Sea. This commerce went hand in hand with religious propaganda and conquest. In Sumatra and Malaya, where the empire of Sri-Vishaya had fallen to pieces in the latter half of the fourteenth century, Islam became the prevailing religion; meanwhile in Java the Indian civilisation which had been transplanted to the Malay Archipelago had its last great efflorescence in the empire of Madjapahit, which at the height of its power dominated the coastal areas over much of what is now Indonesia and had outposts in the Philippines. Madjapahit was Hindu by religion and for some time there was a conflict between Hinduism and Islam in the Archipelago comparable to that which was going on in India itself. But in Indonesia, where Indian civilisation had no such deep roots as it had in its homeland, Islam was decisively victorious; the city of Madjapahit itself was captured by Moslem invaders in 1478 and Java became Moslem. Hinduism survived only in the island of Bali to the east of Java. The spread of Islam reached eastward to the Moluccas, the Spice Islands commercially important as the source of cloves and nutmegs for the Indian Ocean trade, and north-eastward to Mindanao, where the Spaniards, finding Moslems after crossing the Pacific westward from America, called them Moros (Moors), a name which they still bear.

In the jungle-covered interiors of Sumatra, Borneo, Celebes and other islands relatively primitive peoples survived who remained, unincorporated in either Hindu-Buddhist or Moslem spheres of civilisation. The Dyaks of Borneo are typical of this continuing 'pagan' culture in Indonesia. Further east there was an entire world of islands which was never touched by the higher civilising influences emanating from Asia, whether from India, China or Arabia, but nevertheless had a remarkable development of its own before the arrival of Europeans. Ethnographically there were two zones of insular population in the Pacific to the east of the Moluccas and the Philippines. The smaller, comprising New Guinea, the Solomons, the New Hebrides and Fiji, was inhabited by Papuans and Melanesians, peoples of negroid racial type, some of whom were skilful navigators, but much inferior in this respect to the people of 'Nesiot' racial type who populated the larger region known as Polynesia. The latter occupied widely scattered island groups from Hawaii in the north to New Zealand in the south and as far east as Easter Island, which is three quarters of the way from Australia to South America. The Polynesians had no written language—except for an obscure script peculiar to Easter Island—but their legendary traditions preserved by oral transmission throw light on the voyages by which the islands of the Pacific were settled. There seems no doubt that the Polynesians originally came from Indonesia; their speech is related to the languages of the Malayan family and the name of Hawaii is etymologically identical with that of Java. In their outrigger canoes the Polynesians made immensely long voyages into the Pacific Ocean and when new islands had been settled generally maintained communication for several generations with the islands from which the colonising expeditions had set forth. The absence of distinctively Indian features in Polynesian culture indicates that the original migrations took place before Indian influence was well established in the Malay Archipelago; on the other hand, some of the most important voyages probably took place much later. The settlement of the Maoris in New Zealand is attributed to the twelfth century, and the migration to Hawaii is believed to have occurred about the same time. It was a 'heroic' tribal society, with small numbers of people and no towns, perhaps comparable to the world of our Celtic and Teutonic ancestors in the time of Caesar.

Other theories have indeed been formulated to explain the vast geographical range of Polynesian culture, and also the exceptional features to be found in the local native culture of Easter Island. The Norwegian anthropologist Heyerdahl advanced the view that the Polynesians had really come from America and sought to prove it by sailing a balsa raft from Peru to the Tuamotus. But this exploit hardly rebuts the overwhelming evidence in favour of an Indonesian origin. Nor have the theories of a lost continent in the Pacific much to recommend them beyond the romantic fascination which such hypotheses always have. It is argued that the remarkable colossal stone images of Easter Island can only be explained as a residue of a vanished higher civilisation, since no such sculptures are to be found elsewhere in Polynesia. But the speech, customs and traditions of Easter Island— as known from the time before it acquired its present mixed population—are typically Polynesian, and the peculiarities of its culture may reasonably be attributed to the prolonged isolation of a small but vigorous community. Easter Island is lacking in large timber and hence could not, after the first settlement, produce the large canoes on which the Polynesians depended for keeping in contact with other branches of their race; on the other hand, the island

abounded in soft volcanic rock which was an invitation to translate wood carving into stone, thus creating the famous statues which have impressed so many travellers.

The sparseness of the island groups of the Pacific and, as it were, the unsubstantiality of the Polynesian world were demonstrated when Magellan in his great voyage across the unknown ocean in 1520 did not see any land except for two uninhabited atolls until he reached Guam. Arriving from there in the eastern Philippines he was convinced that he had arrived in Far Eastern waters—with which he was already acquainted—because he found Chinese merchandise being traded in the islands.

VI

Having followed the Indian and Arab voyagers to Indonesia, traced the Polynesians from Indonesia to Easter Island and turned back across the Pacific to Cebu with Magellan, we must now consider the great civilisation of the Far East which we have bypassed to the south by heading into the Pacific along a line close to the Equator.

Approached early in the sixteenth century by the Portuguese on the furthest stretch of their voyages round Africa and Malaya, and by the Spaniards sailing over the Pacific from Mexico, China was the country—except for Japan—most secluded from the European expansion. It presented one striking contrast to India in that it was entirely under the government of a single ruler. In 1516—when the Portuguese first reached China—the Ming Emperor of China held authority from the Mongolian steppe beyond the Great Wall to the Gulf of Tongking, and there could be no question of dealing, as in India, with a plurality of powers at variance with one another. The Ming Empire was similar in extent to, though rather smaller than, the Han Empire at the beginning of the Christian era, and had fundamentally the same cultural and administrative character.

But China's history had not been without its vicissitudes in the intervening centuries. Two main themes may be traced through the time from the end of the Han Dynasty to the arrival of the Portuguese. The first is that of invasions of China by the nomadic peoples of the northern steppes, and, closely connected with this, the alternating division and reunification of the country. The partition of China between different dynasties was not indeed entirely due to invasions from the north, for after the collapse of the Han Dynasty, China was divided for a time between three states—the famous 'Three Kingdoms' of Chinese legendary tales—with purely Chinese rulers. But in the succeeding period dynasties were set up in North China by invaders from Mongolia, while native Chinese rule continued in the south. China was then again unified under the Sui and T'ang dynasties from before A.D. 600 to after 900. The T'ang Dynasty was followed by a period of confusion; next came the Sung Dynasty (960–1280), which began by ruling over all China, but soon had to yield a large part of the north to the Khitan tribes of south-east Mongolia and then an even larger part to the Juchens from Manchuria. The latter—who gave China the name of Cathay by which it was known to Marco Polo—set up the Ch'in Dynasty, with its capital at Peking, while the Sung emperors continued to govern the south with their capital first at Nanking and then at Hangchow. Then Genghiz Khan founded the Mongol Empire, and after prolonged warfare the Mongols subdued both the Ch'in and Sung states, thus reunifying China and incorporating it in a loose

political unity which at its greatest extent reached westward to the Carpathians and south-westward to the Euphrates. But the Mongol domination (the Yuan Dynasty) was overthrown by a Chinese revolt which, after struggles between its leaders, resulted in the establishment of the Ming Dynasty (1368–1644). One more barbarian invasion from the north was still to come; in the seventeenth century the Manchus, who had created a powerful kingdom to the north-east of China beyond the Great Wall, took advantage of a rebellion in China to make themselves masters of the whole country and set up their own imperial dynasty, the Ching which reigned in Peking until 1912.

From the completion of the Mongol conquest of China in 1280 to the end of the monarchy in 1912, China was united under a single political authority except for short periods of confusion at the changes of dynasty. The trend towards political unity in China thus proved in the long run stronger than the factors making for disruption. The main reason for this successful unification, in spite of the difficulties of communication due to the mountainous terrain of a great part of the country, was certainly the system of selection for the civil service by competitive public examinations. The beginnings of this system go back to the second century B.C., when the emperors of the Han Dynasty were trying to consolidate their centralised rule by linking it with a revival of ancient learning; under the T'ang Dynasty, in the seventh century A.D., the examinations were organised as a regular governmental institution, to be held periodically both in the provinces and at the capital. With the expulsion of the Mongol conquerors of China in 1368 and the establishment of the native Ming Dynasty, the system was further overhauled and assumed the shape which it retained with only minor modifications until its final abolition in 1905.

In its fully developed form it provided for the award of three degrees roughly comparable to those of bachelor, master and doctor in Western education. The holders of these degrees formed the class of 'scholar-gentry', and as such enjoyed the social status of an *élite* and various legal privileges even when they did not receive appointments to salaried administrative posts. The number of candidates for these degrees was always much larger than the number of those who obtained them, and the examinations, which were uniform in their requirements for all parts of the country, became the main objective for all Chinese education. In principle the examinations were open to all, with the exception of certain minor categories of the population, but as candidature involved a prolonged whole-time training, only well-to-do families could normally afford to enable their sons to enter—though promising boys of poorer families were often given the opportunity to study by village, clan or guild endowments available for the purpose. The basis of the education required was a knowledge of the classical literature comprising philosophy, history and poetry together with a capacity to write essays in an approved style; calligraphy was also important, for the Chinese script was written with the brush and beautiful handwriting was the most valued of polite accomplishments. When the candidate had reached the stage at which he considered himself—or was considered by his teacher—ready to attempt the first public examination, he first presented himself before the county magistrate for a preliminary test and then sat for the examination itself, in which he was locked up in a cell for a night and a day and required to compose two essays and a poem on given subjects. Those who

were successful—there might be 50,000 each year in the whole of China—obtained the degree of *hsiu-ts'ai*, which carried with it not only a status recognised everywhere in the Empire, but also exemption from certain taxes and from the ordinary jurisdiction of local magistrates. An unambitious man might rest content with this rank, but most *hsiu-ts'ai* went on to compete for the higher degree of *chu-jen* at the examination held once in every three years in each provincial capital. This was a much more lengthy and severe ordeal, and only a relatively small number got through. The successful ones might then enter for the highest degree of all, that of *chin-shih*, which was awarded after an examination held at the imperial palace. Only a few scholars reached this eminence.

Appointments to the civil service, the central and provincial bureaucracy by which the Empire was governed, were made almost entirely from the scholar-gentry as certified by the public examinations. In earlier times there were also appointments by nomination outside the examination system, but these became increasingly rare, and the holders of offices so conferred lacked the prestige which belonged to the genuine *literati*; so also did those who, when the Government was in need of funds, were allowed to purchase degrees without having to sit for the examinations. Despite these exceptions, the principle was maintained throughout the later centuries of Chinese imperial history that civil administration should be entrusted primarily to men who had all received a special kind of education and had shown their fitness by tests which paid no regard to birth or wealth. The same principle was extended, with suitable modifications, to military service. Candidates for army commissions were likewise to submit to testing through competitive examinations, which were held, as were those for the civil degrees, in three stages, at county, provincial and imperial levels. Skill in archery and in exercises involving great physical strength was the main qualification required. The military examinations tended to produce a brave, but unintelligent, type of fighting officer, who corresponded to the Chinese idea of a soldier as a man far inferior to the civilian scholar in the scale of human values. This downgrading in esteem of the military function in society goes back to the early days of Confucianism, which sought rational and humane principles of government in the midst of the militarism of the age of the 'warring states'; with the acceptance of Confucianism as the religion of the State it entered deeply into the Chinese outlook on life and became more and more marked with the centuries. It did not imply pacifism or any renunciation of force, whether for internal order or defence, nor did it involve a humanitarian aversion to the shedding of blood. The penal law was harsh and rebellions were often crushed with the most drastic severity, but the Confucian ideology was definitely adverse to the social ascendancy of a *noblesse d'épée*, it discouraged glorification of war and martial qualities, and it facilitated control of a vast country with a minimum of force because of the prestige accruing to the scholar-officials who represented the socially approved ideal of human aspiration. It should be added, however, that there was always in China among the masses an undercurrent of martial romanticism, which found expression in the popular novel and drama— forms of writing disdained by the scholars as 'small literature', but strongly rooted in the affections of the Chinese people.

It was the rule that every official was posted outside the province where he was born so that he might not be able to use his position to build up a local family power; officials were also continually moved from one province to another. But wherever they went they found a number of people with the same education, outlook and beliefs as their own, and even when their speech was strange—for the spoken dialects in different parts of China varied so much as to be often mutually unintelligible—they shared a common written language. Only a minority of the scholar-gentry actually held office in the bureaucracy; the rest either lived on rents, if they were owners of land, or earned a living as schoolmasters, secretaries or archivists. The body of scholars who remained outside the governing bureaucracy had no formal political rights as against the imperial authority—there were no parliaments of 'estates' in China—but their collective opinion in matters of custom and tradition was a factor of which the Government had to take account. In China today this social and political order of the *ancien régime*, which survived to the beginning of the twentieth century, is classified as 'feudal', but it bore little resemblance to the conditions of medieval Europe beyond the fact that both belonged to an economic stage prior to the emergence of modern industrialism. In China there was no socially dominant hereditary nobility or any local fragmentation of monarchy by semi-sovereign baronial rulers, nor did the ownership of land by itself, apart from membership of the scholar class, confer any particular social distinction. The scholar-gentry might be compared in some respects to the clergy in medieval Europe, but their social functions were essentially secular, and there was in the Confucian order no division between Church and State.

The examination system was the most important factor ensuring the continuity and permanence of Chinese culture and the massive stability of the Empire as it existed under the Ming and Manchu dynasties. A price, however, had to be paid for this remarkable achievement. The system by putting a premium on conformity to a single recognised norm and glorifying an ancient tradition produced an intolerant orthodoxy and an arrogant self-sufficiency of mind adverse to all originality and especially to any introduction of new ideas from outside. During the first millennium A.D. Chinese civilisation, in spite of the strength and pride of its own tradition, was receptive of influences from abroad, and Buddhism spreading from India through Central Asia was propagated in China to such effect that a majority of the population became adherents of it. Buddhist sacred texts composed in Sanskrit were translated into Chinese and Buddhist doctrine underwent new developments on Chinese soil; art forms of Indian origin were introduced in association with the new religion and had an important influence on Chinese architecture, sculpture and painting.

Buddhism, nevertheless, failed to supersede Confucianism as the religion of the State; divided between a number of sects, and lacking any central organisation, it never attained a position comparable to that of the Catholic and Orthodox Churches in Europe. It reached the zenith of its influences in the fifth and sixth centuries A.D.; under the T'ang Dynasty (616–907) it was still a great cultural force, but under the Sung (960–1280) there was a strong reaction against it, led by a philosophical school which for the first time provided Confucianism with a complete equipment of logical and metaphysical teaching. It was this so-called neo-Confucianism which from the fourteenth century onwards became the established orthodoxy for the purposes of the academic examinations; no other inter-

pretations of the classics were recognised and officially approved: thinking was thus confined within narrow limits. Buddhism and the native Chinese cults grouped under the name of Taoism continued to be tolerated, but except for a few eccentric individuals in the scholar class they became religions of the uneducated, regarded with disdain by the Confucian bureaucrats. The Confucian orthodoxy, with its literary and ethical preoccupations, was also adverse to interest in the natural sciences in which, as recent studies of old Chinese sources have shown, great progress had been made in earlier centuries, so that Chinese scientific knowledge was comparable to European until the sixteenth century. Above all, the established doctrine bred a contempt for all non-Chinese cultures as 'barbarian' and an almost complete indifference to the world outside China. China for the Confucian 'mandarins' was the 'Middle Kingdom', the central country, its culture was only the real civilisation and its Heaven-appointed ruler the only rightful monarch on earth. The only proper political relations between the emperor of China and foreign governments were those between suzerain and vassals; theoretically all other countries should pay tribute to China, the importance of the tribute lying not in its economic value, which might be negligible, but in the ceremonial recognition of Chinese imperial supremacy.

The Chinese official outlook was incompatible with any code of international law applicable as between equal sovereign states; if the imperial government permitted foreigners to visit China for purposes of trade, it was by favour and not as a right. Chinese policy was not directed towards any expansion of foreign trade, but rather towards its restriction, partly indeed with the aim of facilitating taxation of it, but mainly in order to keep foreigners out of the country and avoid their disturbing, and possibly subversive, influence. The attempts of Catholic missionaries to propagate Christianity in China were important in creating a suspicious and unfriendly attitude towards the West, for the Confucians disliked the new religion as incompatible with Chinese tradition and the intervention of the Papacy in the so-called 'Rites Controversy'—provoked by the willingness of the Jesuits to compromise with Chinese ancestor-worship—led to a withdrawal of the toleration initially accorded to the missionaries. Some of the latter were allowed to remain in Peking because their astronomical knowledge was useful for the determination of the calendar—a matter of great importance in Chinese statecraft and ceremonial—but they were forbidden to make converts; they provided a certain minimum of contact with the outside world, but their influence was very limited and never sufficient to make any serious impression on Confucian intellectual self-sufficiency. The visits of European traders to Chinese ports—from 1761 they were confined to the single port of Canton—were even less productive of cultural intercourse; the foreign merchants were forbidden to travel outside the small areas allotted to them for their warehouses or to have any contact with the population except for officially licensed Chinese merchants and their interpreters. These conditions continued until the outbreak of the First Anglo-Chinese war in 1839. China was a self-contained society, indifferent to economic expansion, conserving its own traditional values and excluding all possible factors of disruption and change.

In spite of its fundamentally unprogressive character, the Chinese Empire of the eighteenth century was a magnificent structure which greatly impressed contemporary Europeans. In 1644 the Ming Dynasty, after reigning for nearly three centuries, was replaced in Peking by the new house of Ching set up by the Manchus, who took advantage of a civil war in China to pass the Great Wall and seize the capital. The Manchus, a primitive non-Chinese people, less nomadic than the Mongols but great breeders of horses, had previously created a kingdom in the north-eastern territory known in modern times as Manchuria, and had included in it the Chinese population settled in the basin of the Liao river, so that they were already partly 'sinified' before they entered China proper. Their conquest of China met with prolonged resistance south of the Yangtse and in the island of Formosa, where Ming partisans held out for two decades after being driven from the mainland, and the Manchus remained to the end an alien element in China against which Chinese national feeling could be aroused, but the Ching Government became so Chinese in custom, ceremonial and administrative procedure that the conquest made very little difference to the internal order and culture of China. In order to win over the Chinese scholar-gentry the new masters went even further than the Ming in confirming its privileges and in upholding Neo-Confucian doctrine as the orthodox creed. Externally, however, the Manchu conquest of China resulted in a great extension of the boundaries of the Empire, for the combination of Manchu military vigour with the resources of China created a new political power which carried its arms westward to the Pamirs and north-westward to the Altai. The Khalka and Kalmuk Mongol khanates were subdued, Kulja, Kashgar and Khotan were captured, and Tibet was reduced to obedience; the last-named had previously been conquered by the Mongols at the time of their rule in China, but had not been subject to the Empire of the

Ming. These Manchu conquests more than doubled the area of China as it had been under the Ming, though the additional territories, which included vast tracts of high mountain and desert land, were only thinly peopled and added little to the wealth of the Empire. Perhaps their greatest significance was in creating the impression beyond China's frontiers that the Empire was not only an effective administrative authority, but also a formidable military power—as indeed it was by the standards of its time when in 1791 a Manchu-Chinese army crossed the Himalayas and inflicted a defeat on the warlike Gurkhas of Nepal in their own homeland. But the martial vigour of the Manchus rapidly degenerated, China made no advance in armaments or tactics in a period when the West was striding ahead, and in particular, nothing was done to create a fighting navy; thus it came about that in 1839 China was found to be quite helpless in an armed conflict with a Western maritime power operating with small forces across thousands of miles of ocean, and the Empire became as notorious for its weakness and incapacity as it had been formerly admired for its efficiency and strength.

VII

Outside the boundaries of the Chinese Empire there were three countries which had derived the main elements of their civilisation from China, had been deeply influenced by Confucianism, and followed policies of self-seclusion and static traditionalism on the Chinese model. These were Annam (Vietnam) to the south of China and Korea and Japan to the east. Annam and Korea were both in tributary relations to the Chinese court, but insular Japan refused to acknowledge any Chinese political supremacy—except for a brief period—and evolved a political system

and a culture with strongly marked features of their own. The Japanese, who at the beginning of our era were divided among a number of petty kingdoms, were unified in the fourth century under the sway of the dynasty which still reigns in Tokyo. This monarchy was consolidated as a central governing authority by the introduction of Chinese bureaucratic institutions eliminating the power of local chiefs. But the Chinese examination system never took root in Japan—partly because it was Buddhism, also introduced from China, which became the prevalent religion rather than Confucianism, which had no native roots in Japan. Power remained in the hands of a ring of aristocratic families who contended among themselves for primacy, and finally reduced the monarchy itself to impotence, though they never formally displaced it, but retained it in nominal sovereignty on account of its traditionally sacred character. From the twelfth to the sixteenth century Japan was broken up by a series of civil wars with intervals of peace and unity under some family which had emerged as victor for the time being and obtained a commission to govern—usually with the title of *shogun* or commander-in-chief—from the helpless emperor. Finally in the last quarter of the sixteenth century, Japan was unified under Hideyoshi, a military dictator of peasant origin, whose unlimited ambition led him to undertake the conquest of China; he died in 1598 after his armies had been engaged for several years in indecisive warfare in Korea. During this period the Portuguese, Dutch and English opened up trade with Japan, a considerable number of Japanese were converted to Christianity by Catholic missionaries, and a rapid internal growth of commercial economy took place. These trends, however, were reversed by the Tokugawa family which captured supreme power after Hideyoshi's death and held it until 1867. Under the Tokugawa a genuinely feudal order was preserved, for the territory of Japan was parcelled out into a large number of fiefs under hereditary lords, but the Tokugawa *shoguns* maintained an effective central control. Chinese history was repeated in that Buddhism declined and Confucianism prevailed as the basic ideology of the State. In connection with this, seclusion was adopted as the national policy to an even more extreme degree than in China. Foreign trade was confined to the one port of Nagasaki and to a single Western nation, the Dutch; it was subjected to such severe restrictions that the Dutch more than once thought of renouncing their privilege. No foreigner was allowed to travel in Japan and no Japanese was allowed to go abroad on pain of death if he returned. Christianity, which had spread so rapidly in the later years of the sixteenth century was prohibited, violently persecuted and virtually wiped out. No ships might be constructed capable of anything more than coastal voyages in Japanese waters. Although some intellectually curious Japanese managed, sometimes with disastrous results to themselves, to learn Dutch and read books on geography and natural science smuggled in through Nagasaki, Japan became in the seventeenth and eighteenth centuries, an almost completely closed world, at a time when all the oceans had been opened up to European navigation and all natural obstacles to the world-wide intercommunication of peoples were being broken down.

VIII

In contrast to the seclusion of the Far Eastern countries, India in the eighteenth century lay open not only to European commerce but also to European political intervention. At the beginning of the century the Mughal Empire under Aurangzab, covering the whole of India except the extreme south, was a political edifice outwardly comparable to the contemporary Manchu Empire of China. But the death of Aurangzab revealed the inner weakness of the Mughal imperial system; within a few years it had fallen to pieces and India became a prey to an anarchic rivalry of old and new local dynasties into which the British and French trading companies in India were eventually drawn through their efforts to use alliances with Indian rulers against each other. The failure of the Mughals was primarily their failure to solve the problem set by the cleavage between Moslem and Hindu. A Moslem Empire embracing these two separate and mutually exclusive communities could not attain real stability unless it could either complete the conversion of India to Islam or find a *modus vivendi* of tolerance and reconciliation. Akbar tried the path of reconciliation and sought to give Hindus equality with Moslems in public affairs, but when he went on to invent and propagate a new religion supposed to combine the best features of both Hinduism and Islam he satisfied nobody and the new faith did not survive his death. Aurangzab on the other hand tried to revive the militant spirit of Islam and to crush Hinduism by prohibiting its rites and destroying its temples. But it was too late to win India by such methods. The persecuting zeal of Aurangzab brought about a great revolt of the Hindu Marathas of the western Deccan, and in a series of campaigns Aurangzab, for all his military vigour, failed to break their resistance. In the north-west of India, the Sikhs, a sect aimed at a reform of Hinduism, were organised into a military order by their leader Guru Govind Singh, and became a violently disruptive element in the

Mughal Empire. In other ways also the Empire was crumbling. It had been a centralised bureaucratic structure with firm control over the provinces from the capital and promotion and dismissal of the highest officials by the arbitrary will of the emperor, but it lacked the checks imposed by the Chinese examination system on the growth of hereditary privilege, and after the iron hand of Aurangzab had been removed several provincial governors succeeded in founding hereditary dynasties still nominally subordinate to, but in practice independent of, the central government.

The collapse of the Mughal ruling house would not have destroyed the political unity of India if some other dynasty, sprung either from Hindu or Moslem rebellion within India or from some new invasion through the passes from Iran or Central Asia, had been strong enough to restore a central authority. But this did not happen; the disintegration, aggravated by the conflicts of religion, had gone too far. The Marathas spread out all over Central India, but failed to create a stable, unified empire. The Persian Nadir Shah and the Afghan Ahmad Shah Abdali both invaded India and sacked Delhi (in 1739 and 1757 respectively), but made no permanent conquests, though the north-western provinces were greatly impoverished by the huge tributes they imposed. In every part of India military adventurers carved out new kingdoms for themselves, while some of the ancient dynasties of Rajasthan, long vassals to Agra or Delhi, reasserted a precarious local independence. A century of anarchy followed the demise of Aurangzab, and when imperial unity was restored (and extended) in India, it was neither by a Hindu nor a Moslem ruler, but by the British Raj from beyond the seas.

IX

Over most of India for several centuries Hindu civilisation had been politically submerged under governments of alien faith and culture, and as a result Hindu society had become an organism separated from the State and to an extreme degree independent of politics. It found its structural stability in the rules of caste and its inspiration in the various mystical cults of saviour-gods who were conceived theologically as manifestations of the formless absolute of the Vendanta philosophy. Such a society might have its kings and royal courts, but it could survive and retain a great resilient strength even when political authority had passed into the hands of conquerors adhering to a radically different and hostile creed. That Hinduism could persist in this way was due to the other-worldly character it had already before the Moslem conquests; because of the Hindu outlook on life it mattered relatively little if the earthly ruler belonged to the Hindu community or not. This situation afforded the most striking contrast with China, where Confucianism was so much bound up with the State and its teaching so concentrated on the ends of secular government that a breakdown of the political system must mean the dissolution of the entire civilisation. This was not seriously threatened by the invasions of the nomadic peoples of Mongolia and Manchuria because these conquerors had no developed religion of their own and could be assimilated without great difficulty to Chinese institutions and ways of life. But the abolition of the Chinese classical examination system in 1905 and of the 'heavenly' monarchy in 1912 destroyed Confucian China as no Moslem sultans nor British governors-general nor Nehru's republic have ever destroyed Hindu India. Gandhi and Vinova Bhave are representative figures of modern

India, but they have no parallels in modern China. For two thousand years Chinese civilisation has been uniquely successful in creating a stable large-scale political order, but at the cost of so great a commitment to that order that its collapse under the stress of new conditions inevitably left a great spiritual vacuum; that vacuum has been filled in our time by the ideology of totalitarian communism imported from Europe.

15 THE EUROPEAN NATION-STATE, RATIONALISM AND SCIENCE

by John Bowle

When in October 1492 Columbus sighted one of the Bahamas, the ancient civilisations of the East were still only on the fringe of Portuguese expansion, nearly all Africa was unexplored by Europeans, and the existence of Australasia was unknown. By 1789, the year of the French Revolution, Europe had begun to dominate the world. It was not only a material mastery; it was an intellectual conquest which is only today being challenged.

How did the Western States of a peninsula of the Eurasian Continent come to such predominance in less than three hundred years? A survey of the main development of Europe over the decisive centuries from the waning of the Middle Ages to the rise of the bourgeoisie may provide some explanation.

During these years a new type of polity had come into being and an economic revolution got under way. Even more important was the rise of a rationalist and scientific outlook original in the history of mankind. The ideas of Copernicus and Bacon, of Descartes and Locke, of Harvey and Newton, of Diderot and Montesquieu, are not merely of European but of world importance. Here is a dynamic culture backed by expanding economic power and superior technology. In the eighteenth century it was already set to spread about the whole planet; in the nineteenth and twentieth centuries it did so.

The laborious medieval intrigues of a Rudolf of Habsburg or a Louis XI are a long way from the great Habsburg and French monarchies which they founded, which formed the two main centres of political power in Europe during this period, and whose wars, and those of their allies, decided the fate of vast territories overseas. It is a far cry, even, from the acute but limited observation of Machiavelli to the sweeping world outlook of the Enlightenment. But the same theme runs through all—discipline, method, order. Gradually it became inspired by the idea of improvement through knowledge. The 'Enlightened' Despots claimed Enlightenment: for the mercantile oligarchies of England and Holland 'Progress' seemed natural. Within this new framework of political power, shifting with the chances of politics and war, but never disrupted, a great age of literary, artistic, musical, and, in particular, of scientific achievement came to maturity. It laid the foundations of the immense material advances of the nineteenth century.

The new political framework was the nation state. A form of political association now almost universal, it originated in the monarchies of late medieval Europe. It depended on artillery and cold steel and money; it was built up and administered by a new kind of bureaucrat, and its original impulse was dynastic. Later it was taken over by merchants and capitalists in England and Holland, who pitted their wits against Bourbons, Habsburgs, Vasas

CULTURAL MAP OF EUROPE

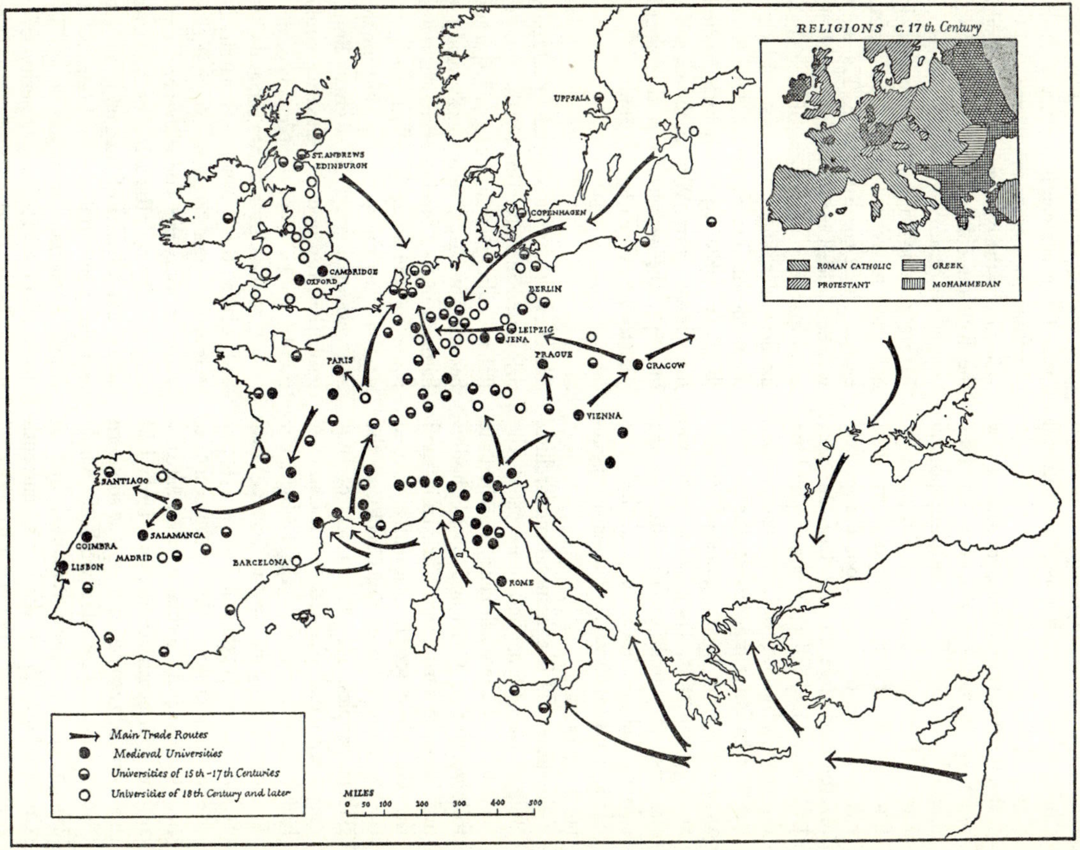

RELIGIONS c.17th Century

ROMAN CATHOLIC   GREEK
PROTESTANT   MOHAMMEDAN

UPPSALA

COPENHAGEN

BERLIN
LEIPZIG
VIENNA
PRAGUE
CRACOW
VIENNA

ROME

ST ANDREWS
EDINBURGH
CAMBRIDGE
OXFORD
PARIS

BARCELONA

SALAMANCA
SANTIAGO   MADRID
COIMBRA
LISBON

MILES
0 50 100   200   300   400   500

Main Trade Routes
Medieval Universities
Universities of 15th -17th Centuries
Universities of 18th Century and later

and Hohenzollerns. While the scale of the kind of state administered by Philip II or built up by Richelieu was comparable only to the governments of Antiquity and far surpassed anything in medieval Christendom, its basis was more national than cosmopolitan.

But if the new great states marked a new order within their borders, externally they marked a decline from the cosmopolitan European standards set by Augustus or Innocent III. Further, through the first two centuries of this period, Europe was on the defensive in the East. In 1453 Byzantium had fallen, a catastrophe long threatened; by 1526 the Turks had crushed the Hungarian Kingdom at Mohacs; in 1529 they were at the gates of Vienna, and again in 1683. They had overrun the Balkans, an area prolific in Roman soldiers and administrators and the scene of vigorous medieval Serbian and Bulgarian kingdoms.

For powerful if ephemeral monarchies, Bulgar and Serb, had dominated the Balkans since the ninth century, when the followers of St Cyril and St Methodius had brought Orthodox Christianity and the Glagolitic script, originally devised for the conversion of the Czechs, to the Balkan peoples. The Asen rulers of Bulgaria, who had plagued the Byzantines, had been overcome by the Serbs under St Sava, and again by the Serbian Tsar Stefan Dusšan (1331–55). But in 1389, at the battle of Kossovo, the Ottoman armies had destroyed the Serbian power. Already by the fourteenth century the Turks had been on their way to turning the southern flank of the Empire. Meanwhile, the whole North African shore remained lost to Christendom. Up to the late seventeenth century the Grand Turk was still considered far the most formidable menace by the West. The Russians, indeed, were colonising Siberia; by 1640 they had reached the

Pacific; on the Baltic, too, the Swedes and the Danes had built up very formidable states, but the overall picture shows Central and Eastern Europe on the defensive. The main initiative which made the seventeenth century a century of genius came from the West.

Such was the background against which the brilliant culture of seventeenth- and eighteenth-century Europe developed. Before turning to this achievement, it is necessary to record the major political events which conditioned it. The survey will be divided into two parts, with their accompanying accounts of social and intellectual change. The first will extend from the decline of the Middle Ages to the Treaty of Westphalia which concluded the Thirty Years' War in the Germanies in 1648; the second from that decisive year to the French Revolution.

II

The new techniques of political power originated in Italy. But by the time that Italian cultural influence was spreading beyond the Alps, Italy was already the battleground of foreign armies in the first round of the struggle of the new great states against the sprawling, still medieval and cosmopolitan, Holy Roman Empire, galvanised through its Habsburg connection by the riches of the New World.

In 1479 the Union of Aragon and Castile had given the Spanish monarchy the mastery of the Western Mediterranean, while by 1485 the Tudor monarchy ruled England. By 1477 the defeat of the formidable Duke Charles of Burgundy at Nancy and the astute policies of Louis XI had consolidated the foundation of the Kingdom of France. The prosperity of the north Italian cities, too, was already matched by the wealth of the great towns of the Low Countries, though the economic initiative had not yet passed from the

Mediterranean to the Atlantic. In the West, already, certain great political facts had already emerged—the Spanish, French and English monarchies (*see* Chapter 10). The other main centre of political power was also dynastic, but it had gathered to itself that ancient European institution, the Holy Roman Empire. By the end of the fifteenth century, the Habsburgs, based on the Danube and the Tyrol, had already laid the foundation for a last attempt to make this institution a reality. But while the Habsburgs could compete with the Western monarchies, in Eastern Europe the Bohemian Kingdom of the Middle Ages had faded by a series of dynastic changes into decline, while in 1505, the Jagellon Kings of Poland and Lithuania had been forced by the Polish gentry to acquiesce in a *liberum veto*, which paralysed the authority of government, and the formidable Hungary of Mathias Corvinus was already disintegrating.

Thus the political scene was set. In the West the great dynastic monarchies; in Central Europe the Habsburgs, who towered above the declining monarchies of Bohemia, Poland-Lithuania and Hungary.

As already emphasised, the constant theme of European politics up to the Treaty of Westphalia and beyond is the conflict between the vast, and later divided, Habsburg Empire and the more concentrated Kingdom of France. Both were attempting the domination of Europe; the one to reassert a medieval universal dominion, the other the domination of a new nation state. The Emperor Charles V (1519–58) ruled not only the Habsburg lands in the Tyrol and on the Danube; he was sovereign of Flanders and Burgundy, of Milan, of Naples and Spain and of the Spanish possessions in America. He conducted a great war on two fronts, against Francis I (1515–1547) over North

Italy and the Burgundian inheritances, and against the Turks in Hungary and North Africa. In 1559 the peace of Cateau Cambrésis recognised the imperial supremacy south of the Alps and confirmed the Habsburg domination of Italy, but the tenacious Emperor was worn out with incessant toil and travel. He had abdicated, and he divided the Habsburg inheritance. Austria and the Central European lands went to his brother, the Emperor Ferdinand I (1556–64); Spain and her American Empire, with the Netherlands, to Philip II (1556–98), Charles' son. The Habsburgs continued their manœuvres from Vienna and Madrid, the main offensive coming from Spain, with the weight of immense American wealth and consequent military and maritime force behind it.

The contest had now become complicated by violent ideological warfare which sometimes cut across and sometimes emphasised the old rivalries. The Protestant revolt, led by Luther and Calvin, had disrupted Christendom, and provoked the Counter Reformation. Europe was divided in religion as never before. Spain and the Empire, representing the old universal order, combined their fleets and armies to destroy the heresy. The new oceanic states, England and Holland, first asserted themselves as great powers in the subsequent conflict; by the defeat of the Armada in 1588 in the triumphant reign of Elizabeth I and by the Union of Utrecht (1579) of which William of Orange was the main architect.

The French monarchy was torn between its Catholic inclinations and political interests. France was long harried by the Huguenot wars, and only with the accession of Henry IV (1589–1610), the founder of the Bourbon House, was the traditional anti-Habsburg policy reaffirmed. It was carried on by Richelieu, the greatest minister of the French Crown and his successor, Mazarin. They secured the eastern frontiers, helped to keep Germany divided, added fuel to the flames of German and Swedish religious conflict. Actually when Richelieu died in 1642 the compact area of France was the strongest power in Europe and the Empire and Spain in decline.

By the sixteen-twenties, indeed, Spain was verging on exhaustion, and in 1618 the Austrian Habsburgs had been confronted with a new challenge. The ancient conflict between the Czechs and the Germans had flared up in Prague, and the Czechs had offered the Bohemian throne to the Protestant Elector Palatine. The rebellion was soon put down, but the war was kept alive for thirty years, in part by Danish and Swedish intervention, encouraged by France. The spectacular career of Gustavus Adolphus Vasa of Sweden had ended at Lützen in 1632, but most of the Rhineland princes were in revolt against the Empire and Scandinavian intervention was backed by the Dutch. By 1648, when the Treaty of Westphalia was signed beneath the thirteenth-century candelabrum in the Rathaus at Munster, the Germanies were devastated and the Habsburg aspect of the Counter-Reformation in Central Europe had failed, as had the great Spanish offensive launched against England and the Netherlands. France was now the dominant Western State, and the English and Dutch were well established: the imperial power, though still formidable, was confined to the Danubian lands, to Tyrol and Bohemia, to parts of Italy and the Austrian Netherlands. The combined efforts of the Protestant maritime powers, England, Holland, Denmark and Sweden, intermittently but decisively aided by France, had wrested from the Spanish and Austrian Habsburgs their traditional and cosmopolitan leadership of Europe, inherited from Charles V. Only in Poland-

Lithuania under Stephen Bathory had the Catholic cause triumphed. The Poles, led by Catholic kings of the House of Vasa, even launched an offensive against Sweden and Russia in the early seventeenth century. The Turks, meanwhile, remained in possession of great areas of Eastern Europe and of all the Balkans, and they were still to launch their final and dangerous attack.

By the end of the first political phase of the three centuries under review, the ancient Holy Roman Empire—which, none the less, represented an ideal of European order against the sovereignty of the nation state—had broken down, the domination of Spain was over, and the North Atlantic Powers were consolidated at the expense of the Spaniards and the Portuguese, and the Baltic States at the expense of Poland. After the failure of the Counter-Reformation in the north, the Papacy became increasingly Italian rather than European, and Italy was no longer an important focus of power politics.

III

The economic initiative, too, passed from the Italians to the west. Medieval Europe had looked south, to the Mediterranean, to the Empire, to Rome. By 1648 great sovereign states were already in being beyond the Alps. Economic power had shifted to the north and west and the stage was set for the momentous conflicts of the eighteenth century.

It was an original society which was beginning to emerge. Its leaders in deed and thought were something new; their background was urban, not feudal, their objectives mainly practical, not religious or romantic. Before surveying their outstanding contributions to European civilisation and its heirs, one must take account of the economic and social changes which formed as important a background to their lives as the political events already recorded.

The new sovereign states had been built by kings, backed by urban wealth. In northern Italy and the Low Countries, north-eastern France and the Lower Rhine and along the Baltic, there were already wealthy cities by the later Middle Ages (*see* Chapter 10). Valois and Habsburg fought to control them. Civic wealth financed the monarchs' successful wars against their own feudatories and their ruinous wars against each other. It was based on the ancient network of European commerce—on the Brenner route which linked the Levant with the Low Countries, the Baltic and the Rhine; on the routes through Switzerland and Burgundy to the great plains around Rheims; on the wine trade of Bordeaux and Southampton, the wool trade of Ghent and Bruges. Though the cloth industry had accumulated considerable capital, this wealth was mainly mercantile rather than industrial. But by the early sixteenth century a rudimentary banking system had been devised. There was more precious metal from the mines of Bohemia and Austria, while in the later sixteenth century Europe would be flooded by the silver from the mines of Peru. The Strozzi of Florence and the Fuggers of Augsburg financed, respectively, the French wars in Italy and the Habsburg backing for the Counter-Reformation. The monstrous scale of the Habsburg enterprises, ineffective taxes, the inflation caused by the metals from the New World, rendered most governments insolvent, but the volume of trade increased. Capital began to accumulate. It financed new joint stock enterprises, to India and Muscovy and the Americas. There arose a powerful upper middle class, emancipated from the control of Church and Guild, methodical, individualist, enterprising. They were very different from the rustic feudatories and

peasantry of the Middle Ages. There was employment, too, in the great towns; the old peasant economy began to be disrupted and a new proletariat came into being. Hence, in part, the wave of peasant revolts and urban unrest in the early sixteenth century, particularly in Flanders and along the Rhine. And the period saw not only unprecedented mercantile wealth but the rise of new methods of production, later to be described (*see* Chapter 19).

This new European prosperity and initiative was something original in the history of the West. The greatest medieval kings and feudatories lived mainly off the produce of their estates and on contributions in kind. A money economy had long been superseding the old order, and with the rise of a new class, living off commerce and investment and saving to invest, a new mentality grew up. Security was their objective, not glory; comfort, continuity, family life. Foresight, routine and accuracy were their weapons. There was a very different way of life in one of the great mercantile houses on the quays of Amsterdam from that long habitual in the castles of the Rhine or the stern keeps of Anjou or the Welsh border. By the mid-seventeenth century an urban rather than a feudal mentality was becoming predominant in the West in those centres of power where policy was being shaped.

IV

The cult of uninhibited thought, of man rather than of revealed religion, came from the Italians of the fifteenth century. But the bias of Renaissance humanism was antiquarian, often pedantic. The more original initiative came from the northern philosophers who made the seventeenth, not the sixteenth, century the decisive epoch. It was their contribution, made after the Renaissance influence had been assimilated, that was most important in world history. Meanwhile, the Italians had set new European standards in art, architecture, music and letters.

Already in the later Middle Ages, Giotto, Botticelli and Donatello had created masterpieces comparable with the great art of Antiquity and with the best Chinese and Indian painting and sculpture. The Florentines, Leonardo da Vinci and Michelangelo, were geniuses of more universal range—typically Renaissance in combining contemplative insight with insatiable curiosity. In the first half of the sixteenth century Raphael, Titian, Tintoretto, Veronese, wrought paintings the like of which had never before been seen. The Flemish achievement was comparable; Van Eyck, Memlinc, later the Breughels, all combined detailed realism with an astonishing power of colour and design. In Germany Dürer, in Spain, El Greco, plumbed new depths of spiritual experience. All these sixteenth-century artists were surpassed in influence and fame by Rubens (1577–1640), the great baroque Flemish painter, whose swirling compositions caught a new splendour of colour and light. The Netherlands produced an even greater master in Rembrandt (1607–1669), and a new kind of painting suited to their broad pastures and towering cloudscapes. The Spaniard Velázquez and the French painters Poussin and Claude Lorrain are of the first order. These are only the outstanding European artists in the first half of the period under review.

Architecture, also, had its revolution. Alberti and Palladio changed the face of Europe; the commanding buildings of the new secular style represented a southern culture, well established in the world, in contrast to the angular fantasy of the Gothic north. By the early seventeenth century the Renaissance style was becoming Baroque, and Bernini embellished the

gigantic forecourt of St Peter's in Rome with its superb colonnade. This kind of architecture, like the Gothic, was a continental, not a national, affair. In England Inigo Jones prepared the way for Wren; the new style spread to Poland and Bohemia, to the Baltic and Russia. It symbolised the spacious horizons of a regal and aristocratic society; in its tamer domestic aspects, the comfort and routine of a long-established middle class.

This sense of order is also apparent in the new Italian music. But here was no revival of Antiquity; the violins and harpsichords of the Renaissance, its elaborate singing, had medieval origins, and gave scope to the lucid genius of Palestrina (1525–94), the first great master of modern European music, the spiritual ancestor of Bach. By the early seventeenth century Monteverdi was producing opera in Venice, and by the mid-century Lully flourished at the court of Louis XIV. The new music had grown out of its ecclesiastical origins into the full confidence of secular achievement.

In literature the variety and brilliance of the Age of the Renaissance and the Baroque are unsurpassed. Printing by movable letters instead of blocks was practised at Mainz by 1450. Sixteen years later there was a printing press at Rome, and by the end of the century Aldo Manutio in Venice had devised the clear 'italic' type. Paper increasingly took the place of parchment. These inventions were decisive: writers obtained a vast new audience, a lay public.

The first books printed were Bibles and elaborate editions of the classics. But printing also opened the way for new vernacular literatures. Beyond the Alps, at the beginning of this period, these were still rudimentary; in less than a century and a half the greatest masterpieces were written: the works of Shakespeare, the greatest writer in the English tongue, by whom, should all else founder, English civilisation would be remembered; of Cervántes; of Milton; the epics of Camoens and Ariosto; the plays of Molière and Corneille. Erasmus early won a European reputation not only as a scholar but a pamphleteer, comparable to that later achieved by Voltaire. The roaring gusto of Rabelais, the mellow wisdom of Montaigne, the genial descriptive power and satire of Vondel, the lyric grace of the Jacobean poets, all express a deep-seated national response to the Italian influence. And while the learned world produced thick tomes in Latin and laid the foundations of modern scholarship, there also grew up a solid tradition of native prose—Luther's Bible, the French version of Calvin's Institutes, Cranmer's book of Common Prayer; in 1612, the authorised version of the English Bible.

The European universities—so distinctive a contribution of medieval civilisation—continued to flourish and expand. They had grown up in close relation to local and continental trade routes; Bologna and Padua in North Italy; Paris, Vienna, Rome; Oxford and Cambridge. They multiplied in the Rhineland and the Palatinate; later along the loess belt of northern Germany (*see* map). There were famous universities at Prague and Cracow by the mid-fourteenth century; in the Iberian peninsula, Salamanca, Santiago, Lisbon, Coimbra. In eastern Scotland they were related to the trade with Flanders, as were the Scandinavian centres at Uppsala and Copenhagen to the Hansa routes. The medieval tradition carried on unbroken and enriched into the new age.

But the creative brilliance of the time gives a false impression of optimism. The sixteenth century was an age not only of intellectual enterprise but of fear. The loss of medieval landmarks, the prolifera-

tion of religious heresies, the obsession with Hell, with astrology and the occult, form the dark side of a time of ferocious ideological conflict. The appeal to conscience and Bible was not particularly new; the Middle Ages saw constant revolts and reforms. On the whole, they had been contained. Now, in part for the political and economic reasons touched upon, the authority of the universal Church was in decline. The merchants and lawyers and civil servants of the new great states went their own way. The Church counterattacked with the highly organised Jesuit Order. Life had become more efficient, more competitive, harsher. The characteristic European concern with practical results is now asserted against the conservatism prevalent in medieval Europe, as in traditional China, India and the Middle East. Many Calvinists, in particular, reviving Hebraic phantasies of a chosen people, cut their way through life with dour self-satisfied efficiency. Incompetence and compassion were alike uncongenial to these urban forebears of the professional classes of the nineteenth century. And if the Renaissance Italians had looked back to Antiquity while the Calvinists were concerned with predestination, both were preoccupied with self-assertion or salvation. Already in the words of the English poet, Dryden, the 'diapason' was 'closing full in man.'

V

This anthropocentric outlook was shared by the great philosophers of the seventeenth century who created the intellectual idiom of the modern world. By 1637 Descartes *Discours sur la Méthode* had set philosophy on a new road. It narrowed the problem of knowledge to the problem of consciousness. He would believe nothing that he could not prove by assembling all the evidence for exhaustive analysis. 'I think,' wrote Descartes, 'therefore I am'. Later philosophers discarded even that certainty, but the main stream of European philosophy through Locke and Hume until today was thus determined. The structure of medieval metaphysics, already undermined by William of Ockham in the early fourteenth century, was now further discredited.

Descartes wished to establish useful knowledge; Francis Bacon was more directly influential in acclimatising the new idea that society could be deliberately improved. He refused to accept the traditional assumption that nothing could be done, and propounded a plan for the 'betterment of man's estate'. His writings reflect upon the muddle and avoidable suffering of society and point towards a humane social order in which efficient technology would transform the human condition. Bacon first related political philosophy to applied science. When one considers the technologically static condition of all other societies over the whole planet at that time, Descartes and Bacon appear as figures of world significance. They were destined to promote the climate of opinion which dominates modern civilisation.

These two men of genius already had behind them more than a century of discovery. In spite of the prevalent concern with astrology and alchemy, which long persisted, the facts were being brought to light. Copernicus, the Polish astronomer, reviving Greek speculations, revolutionised cosmology. The earth, he argued, in 1543, was not the centre of the universe, but moved with the other planets round the sun. The Dane, Tycho Brähe, the German, Kepler, collected supporting evidence. The Neapolitan pantheist, Giordano Bruno, burnt in 1600 by the Inquisition, declared that beyond the solar system lay boundless space, that the whole

universe was informed by Deity. Finally, Galileo of Padua, using a rudimentary telescope, proved that the Copernican hypothesis was correct. His dialogue *On The Two Systems of the World* appeared in 1630. He also discovered sound waves and established the basic principles of mechanics. It took many years before these facts were assimilated, but assimilated they were.

Scientific knowledge was greatly enhanced by better methods of calculation. Arabic numerals were in use by the later Middle Ages: now decimals were invented by a Dutchman and logarithms by a Scot. The use of thermometers and microscopes (1590) led to long needed advances in medicine. Vesalius, a Fleming, and, like Galileo, a Professor at Padua, physician to Charles V, was the founder of modern anatomy. Paracelsus (Theophrastus Bombastus von Hohenheim) an eccentric Swiss, discarding the ancient precepts of Galen, made important discoveries in the use of drugs. William Harvey, an Englishman who had also studied at Padua, published in 1628 his discovery of the circulation of the blood. The Dutch van Helmont, and the German von Gesner, were pioneers in chemistry and botany. All these are but the outstanding figures of this great age, which laid the foundations of modern science in nearly all its fields.

These discoveries were made when Europeans were first pushing out across the oceans; they coincided with new interests and new standards in geography. 'Mercator' (Gerhardt Kremer of Louvain) whose 'projection' still makes so many maps misleading, none the less broke away from the cramped medieval cartography, while Haklyut chronicled the voyages of the Elizabethan and Jacobean sailors, and the Spaniard, Las Casas, wrote his great *History of the Indies*. These fresh horizons and their discoverers have already been described (*see* Chapter 11). They formed a background to the new outlook more spacious than the close cosmology of the Middle Ages and far more interesting. Clearly the world held more authentic marvels than the men of Antiquity and the Middle Ages had imagined. The discoveries intimately concerned not only the few who took part in them but an increasing number of investors, merchants and settlers in all the Atlantic and European lands. The economies of Portugal, Spain, the Netherlands, England and France were all profoundly affected.

The day of the ocean-going sailing ship was only dawning when Columbus set out from Cadiz Bay. By the time of Richelieu and Cromwell the ships had a gun-power, size and manœuvrability not much surpassed in the time of Nelson. The red Turkish galleys which fought Charles V off Tunis, manned by shaven galley slaves, belonged to a different world from the great ships of the line with their crowded canvases and bristling gunports, which could face the tides and storms of the Channel, the North Sea and the Atlantic. On land the lobster-like and individual armament of late medieval magnates had been superseded by disciplined infantry, and by the mixed phalanx of pikemen and arquebusiers, with their train of sappers and siege artillery. The clang of steel on armour, the hiss of the arrow storm, had been drowned in the roar of guns. This progress in armament, though it brought about a dreary and static form of warfare, to which movement was only restored by the cavalry leaders of the Thirty Years' War, gave Europeans a terrible advantage not only in the New World but all over the East. Chinese junks and Arab dhows were smashed to matchwood by the Portuguese and Dutch artillery. Soon tiny well-drilled European forces in India were to be put to rout huge armies of native swordsmen, expert in warfare with horses and elephants, but helpless before organised fire-power.

All these weapons, and the riches they brought to the victors, were at the disposal of governments whose administrative efficiency, though slow and sketchy by modern standards, was very much higher than anything achieved since the greatest days of the Roman Empire. The sheer concentration of wealth and power in the limited area of the new great states was something new. Political philosophers defined it: *Majestas*, Bodin called it, Sovereignty. Rulers were responsible to no one but God. Machiavelli in his concern with security had quietly by-passed the high cosmopolitan political ideas of duty and order defined by Dante and St Thomas. Hobbes, whose *Leviathan* was to appear in 1651, had already in his *De Cive* furnished a utilitarian and absolute theory of the state. Both the prevalent theory of patriarchal authority by Divine Right, and the constitutional theory of government by consent under the rule of law, assumed the existence of the sovereign national state. When Grotius in his famous Treatise *Of War and Peace* laid the foundations of International Law, he reinforced his argument not by an appeal to revelation, but by an appeal to common sense. Within the political framework of these new states the idea of belonging to a national tradition penetrated far deeper into the lower levels of society than it could have in the more cosmopolitan and horizontally divided social system of the Middle Ages. The great mass of the peasantry, even in the West, remained little affected by the civilisation of privileged minorities, as was inevitable before the Industrial Revolution, but the foundations of a national consciousness were already there. What Europe had lost in unity she had gained in variety and vigour. There is a significant contrast between the haunted faces of the medieval aristocracy—violence always lurking beneath their stylised lives —and the casual distinction and well-being of the portraits of so many of the mid-seventeenth century great. Western man by 1648 had become more at home in an apparently intelligible world.

VI

Within the framework of European power politics in which these social and cultural changes took place, the centre of political gravity had shifted by the mid-seventeenth century from Spain to France. By 1648 France had become the strongest European State; it was to remain so until the fall of Napoleon. The Habsburgs long continued their traditional enmity, but France's toughest adversaries were now the new maritime powers that had emerged in the struggle which had crippled Spain. The Dutch and English had their commercial rivalries, but both were Protestant, and they combined with the Habsburgs to prevent a French domination of the Continent. Louis XIV never attained a Franco-Spanish Empire, or overran the Low Countries which commanded the sea routes into London, Antwerp, and Rotterdam.

The political pattern in Central and Eastern Europe also changed. In North Germany Prussia became the dominant power; Poland-Lithuania, after a final flare-up, went into decline and eventually into liquidation, while the Imperial Russia of Peter the Great now became a great European power at the expense of the Swedes and the Turks. If by the early eighteenth century the Habsburgs could discount the Ottoman threat, they had soon to beware of St Petersburg and Berlin.

The decisions of eighteenth-century international politics were momentous for the whole world and set the pattern of the nineteenth and twentieth centuries. In the time of Mazarin it looked as though France would add a great empire overseas to her European predominance; the brilliant achievements of her explorers and empire-builders in both North America and India seemed likely to fulfil this promise, but they seldom had enough backing from their home governments, who set continental victories higher than expansion overseas, and it was not until the nineteenth century that France attained a large Empire in Africa and Indo-China. The Scandinavians, meanwhile, remained preoccupied with their Baltic rivalries, the Germans were in no condition to grasp opportunities outside Europe, and Spain and Portugal, while they retained their cultural domination of Central and South America, were no longer expanding powers but in political decline. The Dutch retained rich dominions in Indonesia, yet won no adequate foothold in India or in the Americas; they had not the resources for such competition. New Amsterdam became New York. It was Great Britain that acquired vast territories in North America, most fully exploited the West Indies with their lucrative sugar trade, and whose East India Company laid the foundations of an Indian Empire. Before surveying the cultural history of the time, it is necessary to chart the political landmarks which determined these events.

The tide of French expansion reached its climax in the reign of Louis XIV (1643–1715). In 1659 he married the Infanta of Spain; in 1660 the Stuart Dynasty regained the British throne and, hampered by the financial control of his Parliaments, Charles II became the pensioner of France. The French King could now concentrate apparently overwhelming forces against the Dutch. But the common interest of the Dutch and English and Habsburgs still proved too much for him. With the

English revolution in 1688, when James II, who had attempted to restore Catholicism, was ousted by his daughter Mary and her Dutch Consort, William of Orange, England was brought back into the Protestant alliance. The gruelling wars of William III and the brilliant campaigns of Marlborough decided the issue in the War of the Spanish Succession. A French invasion threatened; it was prevented at the battle of La Hogue (1692) which made the Dutch and English supreme in the Channel: Marlborough's resounding victories at Blenheim (1704) and at Ramillies, saved Vienna and won the Low Countries, while the capture of Gibraltar gave the British command of the Western Mediterranean. In 1713 the Treaty of Utrecht recognised that the more grandiose ambitions of Louis XIV had failed.

In Central Europe the tide was at last setting against the Turks. The relief of Vienna in 1683 by the Polish King, John Sobieski was the decisive stroke, and Hungary and Transylvania were soon liberated. But eighteenth-century politics were at the mercy of dynastic chance: the death of Charles VI without a male heir provoked the last bout of the old Habsburg-Bourbon contest in which the French now found a new ally. In 1701 the Elector Frederick I had proclaimed himself King of Prussia, and his son, a ferocious martinet, had created an efficient Prussian army. Frederick II (1740–86), that neurotic military genius, succeeded him in the same year that the Habsburg Queen, Maria-Theresa took up her inheritance. All the old Emperor's schemes collapsed. In the War of the Austrian Succession the Habsburgs sustained a combined French and Prussian attack, and Hungarian loyalty and English subsidies barely saved the Queen. For Frederick had at once fallen on Silesia and, four years later, he had taken Prague. By the Treaty of Dresden in 1748, Prussia gained the entire rich Silesian province.

This was too much for the two old-established dynastic powers. Bourbons and Habsburgs, after a struggle lasting from the days of Charles V, now combined in a 'diplomatic revolution' against the Hohenzollerns. But England always regarded France—still the strongest Continental power—as the main enemy; when, in 1756, Frederick II invaded Saxony and began the Seven Years' War, she switched her support from Vienna to Berlin. This contest was the most decisive and far flung of all. Russian armies, collaborating with the Habsburgs, took Berlin, but Prussia survived; England won Bengal at Plassey, Canada at Quebec. At the Peace of Paris (1763) she obtained the vast territories of the first British Empire which extended from the Gulf of Mexico to the Arctic ice. Soon much of it was lost, for the revolt of the American Colonies occasioned a European coalition against the British, and American independence was recognised in 1783 at the Peace of Versailles. The British Empire was greatly diminished but British sea power was never broken, and Canada, and most of the West Indies and India remained.

Such were the principal decisions made by the complex wars of the eighteenth century in Central and Western Europe and overseas. In Eastern Europe, meanwhile, Muscovy had been transformed.

In 1613 the *Zemski Sobor* had elected Michael Romanov Tsar of Muscovy. The new dynasty, backed by most of the *boyars* and the higher clergy, had survived, but at the cost of increasing absolutism (*see* Chapter 8). The Tsar Alexis (1645–1676) had riveted serfdom on the peasants and asserted his power over the Church. The dissident Patriarch Nikon had been deposed in 1666: peasant and Cossack revolts—Stenka Razin's is the most notorious—had been put down. Backed by its foreign-drilled regiments, the Muscovite Government had moved heavily forward on its immense task. Then a Tsar of genius had attained the throne. 'The impact of Peter the Great upon Muscovy', writes Sumner, 'was like that of a peasant hitting his horse with his fist. Muscovy bore many of the marks permanently, and henceforward she became known as Russia'* Peter I (1682–1725) was always determined to win an outlet on the Baltic, and when, in 1709, he defeated the Swedes at Poltava, he got control of Riga. Already by 1711 he had proclaimed himself Emperor and was pushing out across the southern steppe against the Turks; so strong were the Russian armies by the mid-century that the Empress Elizabeth nearly broke Prussia, which was saved only by the chance that her short-lived and crazy successor, Peter III, reversed her policy. But Catherine the Great (1762–96) soon came to terms with Frederick II and together they set about the dismemberment of Poland. By 1772 the Russians had absorbed the eastern provinces; piecemeal, the Austrians and Prussians were gradually to absorb the rest, and the Russians expanded to the Black Sea and took the Crimea.

The scene in Eastern Europe, had thus profoundly changed. While in the early seventeenth century the Poles had invaded Muscovy and the Turks threatened Vienna, now Prussia and Russia were the dominant powers, competing with the Habsburg Empire, still astride the Danube and the Alps, while only the Balkans continued under Turkish rule. But where, in the West, the successful resistance by the maritime powers to the French marked a social

as well as a political shift of power, and the rising bourgeoisie canvassed ideas of constitutional government even within France itself, in the East the peasantries had only exchanged one master for another, a powerful middle class failed to develop, the constitutions devised by the Polish and Hungarian gentry ceased to be viable, and centralised military autocracy remained intact.

VII

Against this political background the social revolution which had begun in the fifteenth century with the rise of rudimentary capitalism slowly worked itself out. The years from 1648 to 1789 saw a climax of a privileged European civilisation. The traditions of the ancient feudal order still made society aristocratic and picturesque, but it was enriched, and ultimately superseded, by mercantile and industrial wealth. All along the Atlantic seaboard new joint stock companies exploited the luxury trade with the West Indies, the Americas, India and the Far East. Chinese silks and porcelain, Indian muslims and jewellery, Persian carpets, coloured servants who had escaped the fate of the majority of their kind on the plantations, elaborate furniture and wall papers, exotic snuff and tobacco, tea and coffee, diversified the classical décor of the seventeenth century. Where the city fathers of Rembrandt's Amsterdam are painted in the Spanish austerity of black broadcloth and white linen, their Frenchified eighteenth-century descendants are depicted in lilac velvet, brocaded waistcoats and powdered wigs.

The prevalent economic doctrine of the seventeenth century was mercantilism. The hoarding of bullion, the imposition of elaborate tariffs, the monopoly of colonial trade, and the expansion of joint stock enterprise with government support, together with new methods of

* B. H. Summer. *Survey of Russian History*, p. 102.

banking and exchange, had greatly enriched the ruling classes. The growing urban proleteriat, on the other hand, divorced from the soil, had little better standards of life and less security than the medieval peasants. But the new capital could be applied to agriculture: in Holland and England, later in France, the rotation of root and clover crops and better methods of breeding greatly improved yield and stock. Canals and roads were developed, though it was not until towards the end of this period that the ghastly *pavé* and broad muddy tracks, over which clumsy seventeenth-century coaches had trundled, began to be replaced by better roads, and communication became again comparable to those of the Roman Empire. A more convenient domestic architecture replaced the gabled houses of the sixteenth century. It was upon the accumulated wealth of seventeenth-century commerce and agriculture that the Industrial Revolution was to expand.

The technical course of this change, comparable in importance only with the Neolithic Revolution or the coming of automation and nuclear power, will be seen elsewhere. (*See* Chapter 19.) But the new methods of production already coincided with the rise of new economic policies. In the France of Louis XV the *Physiocrats* insisted that the economy should be allowed to follow its own laws. This doctrine of *laissez-faire* was supported, with qualifications, by the great Scots economist, Adam Smith. His *The Wealth of Nations* appeared in 1776. His theory of the division of labour, his original analysis, made him the father of political economy. Henceforth, until far into the nineteenth century, the mercantilist theory was at a discount. Industry and commerce were, to a growing extent, freed from the control of governments. They were becoming cosmopolitan—a law unto themselves.

This accumulated wealth, not merely in land but in companies and banks, was now widespread in the more advanced states. The harshness of medieval life had persisted into the time of Erasmus: by the day of Gibbon a tolerable degree of comfort, if not of hygiene or medicine, could be taken for granted. The richer classes of the West had a standard of security, of accepted routine. The decisive wars of the eighteenth century were fought by small professional armies with far less devastation than in previous conflicts, and often outside Europe or on the High Seas. Within a conservative framework, men were probably less callous than in previous ages.

The new security and routine created a new, more 'polite' learning. Latin was increasingly superseded by French as a cosmopolitan language; the wit of the salon replaced the disputation of the lecture hall. There was much coming and going, even during the bouts of war, between the capitals of Europe. In the West political assassination became much less frequent. The decline of fanaticism after the religious wars, and the relatively better discipline and payment of the armies, rendered society less vulnerable. While pestilence and violence still lurked beneath the elegant manners of the eighteenth century, Western civilisation had already acquired a more solid structure and greater momentum than it had possessed when the new monarchies had fought their way out of the later Middle Ages. But there still remained the great contrast between Eastern and Western Europe. Where the weight of political power in Prussia and Russia had increased, and while Vienna became the musical capital of the Continent, and the elegance, as well as the military prowess, of the later Habsburg Court could rival Versailles, social as well as economic and political change was tardy. The contrast between

L

the despots of Berlin and St Petersburg, or the landowners of Eastern and Central Europe, ruling over their peasants, and the urban oligarchies of the West remained profound.

VIII

The comparatively secure life of the ruling classes was reflected in a luxurious and sophisticated art, in elaborate baroque and rococo architecture, and in an unsurpassed range of music. There is, indeed, some affinity between the culture of the European eighteenth century and Chinese civilisation at its zenith. Both had the highest standards of craftsmanship, encouraged by patrons of exquisite taste; both produced literature of extreme sensibility with a strong feeling for landscape; both were rooted in a calm tradition.

The most representative painters were French. The art of Watteau and Chardin, of Boucher and Fragonard, is intimate and gay. The age was a great one of portraits. In England Reynolds and Gainsborough depicted an aristocracy at once homely and cultivated; Hogarth and Rowlandson the brutal underworld of their time. Morland and Richard Wilson created a tradition of landscape, later transformed and enriched by Constable and Turner. The Spanish painter, Goya (1746–1828), was probably the greatest European artist of his time, though much of his achievement belongs to the age of Napoleon. Eighteenth-century sculptors can compare with the masters of Antiquity. Roubiliac (1702–62) a Huguenot who settled in England, had a great mastery of character and form, while the Italian, Canova (1757–1822) introduced an austere, neo-classical style. Architects developed the baroque style of the seventeenth century into rococo and neo-classical forms; elaborate ceilings and mirrors formed a spacious setting for fine furniture, porce-

lain and silver. Savonnerie carpets could compare with the Eastern rugs long fashionable. Like Bernini, de Vries designed splendid fountains and a new art of landscape gardening took the place of the formal designs of the age of Louis XIV.

The patrons of the eighteenth century were as much concerned with field sports as with art and furniture. The standard of blood-stock was further improved, and, if the gigantic formal battues, in which the German princes particularly specialised and in which the Spanish and Neopolitan Bourbons excelled, combined the maximum slaughter with the minimum skill, the eighteenth century glorified and elaborated the ancient European habit of the chase.

But the most magnificent European cultural achievement of the age was in music. Never before in the world had such a range and power of composition been manifest. The Italian tradition was assimilated and developed by German genius. Alessandro Scarlatti founded the brilliant Neopolitan school of opera; his son Domenico, set new standards of keyboard music. Both provided the technical basis for the more elaborate compositions of Haydn, Bach, and Mozart. Johann Sebastian Bach (1685–1750), a Thuringian, for many years organist at Weimar and Leipzig, wrote music in which a deep spirituality was combined with a superb mastery of detail and form. His contemporary, Handel, came from Saxony and made his reputation in England. He immortalised the grandeur of eighteenth-century civilisation; he evoked pomp without vulgarity. After the mid-century, the Austrian Haydn and the Bohemian Glück enriched their formal compositions by the folk melodies of their peoples. But it was in Salzburg that the greatest musical genius of the later eighteenth century was born. Mozart (1756–91) in his short career, put all humanity in his debt. His astonishing productivity, technique and gift of sheer melody have never been surpassed.

This European musical contribution to the cultural wealth of mankind is unparalleled. Antiquity knew nothing like it; medieval music, though subtle and complex, was thin and melancholy in comparison. None of the other great civilisations had attained the musical range, virtuosity and *élan* with which seventeenth- and eighteenth-century composers expressed their feeling for the beauty, the sadness and the order of the world.

IX

This sense of order informs the literature, philosophy and science that reaped the harvest of Renaissance learning and seventeenth-century initiative and charted the fields of modern knowledge. The ponderous apparatus of baroque learning gave place to lucid prose and elegant popularisation. French writers were predominant, but their ideas often came from England. The reign of Louis XIV had seen the climax of classical drama in Corneille and Racine. The establishment of the French Academy by Richelieu crystallised the language; learning was secularised and widespread. The sceptic Bayle produced his Dictionary in 1697. Diderot, in his French *Encyclopédie* (1751), marshalled the greatest writers of his day. He intended, he wrote, acknowledging his debt to Bacon, to expound 'l'ordre et l'enchaînement' of knowledge. Voltaire (1694–1778), whose satire *Candide* appeared in 1749, in the brief interval between the War of the Austrian Succession and the Seven Years' War, won European celebrity and swayed important opinion. Like Diderot, he believed in reason and tolerance and attacked what he held to be the superstitions of the Church. Montesquieu's

Ésprit des Lois surveyed the manners and customs of mankind and related them to their setting.

In Great Britain, after Dryden had acclimatised modern prose, Swift brought it to an unsurpassed and pointed clarity. While the hectic drama of the Restoration gave place to the more staid social comedy of Goldsmith and Sheridan, Defoe's sharp observation made him an originator of the novel, which was developed by Richardson and Fielding, who, in *Tom Jones* (1749), created one of the immortal characters of fiction. As the century advanced, prose became more florid and poetry more romantic. Gibbon's great set piece on the *Decline and Fall of the Roman Empire*, Johnson's sonorous prose and crushing apophthegms, express a culture which thought of itself as classical and had reached a peak of confidence and maturity.

The Romantic movement, of which Gray, whose *Elegy* appeared at the mid-century, and Macpherson, whose Ossian had European influence, were forerunners, took deepest root in Germany. Herder was steeped in the folk-lore of his own people as well as of Scandinavia; the piercing genius of Goethe (1749–1832), whose *The Sorrows of Werther* was, oddly enough, one of Napoleon's favourite books, combined romantic insight and classical discipline in *Faust*.

X

The philosophers carried further the method originated by Descartes. John Locke, who was immensely influential, explored the limitations of mind, casting out many metaphysical devils from philosophy. His analysis was deepened by Berkeley and by David Hume, who urbanely pointed out, in admirable prose, that empirical 'certainty' is only probable and that reason is in fact subordinate to feeling. Convenience, not revelation, he held to be the basis of society and was sceptical even of Deism. But this scepticism did not undermine the belief of eighteenth-century philosophers in progress—something very unusual in the history of ideas.

Orthodox Christianity had always assumed the bald fact of original sin. The eighteenth-century rationalists believed that wickedness and folly could be cured by education and changed institutions. They refused to take confusion, cruelty and hardship for granted, and were determined, with a fine disregard of the difficulties, to master both the social and the natural environment of man. Sceptical of metaphysics and revelation, they displayed the humanitarianism of a privileged minority. This determination, this optimism, was to influence subsequent humanists and revolutionaries.

This belief in progress certainly seemed justified by the advances of eighteenth-century science. Newton in his *Principia* (1687) discovered the laws of the Copernican universe and revolutionised physics. Boyle had rescued chemistry from the alchemists; Cavendish discovered hydrogen, Priestley oxygen; Lavoisier ordered the whole science. In biology Leeuwenhoek's microscope at last revealed the facts of bacteria and the facts of life. The Swede Linnaeus, in his *System of Nature*, made the first great classification of the animal kingdom, and Buffon's *Natural History of Animals* foreshadowed some of the conclusions of Darwin. Hutton, the geologist, began to undermine the belief in a sudden creation; Hunter in Edinburgh made salutary advances in surgery.

The rational and tolerant atmosphere in which these discoveries were made had been hard won. The seventeenth century had seen a climax of religious warfare and persecution. The Deists and Humanitarians shuddered at the memory of enthusiasms which they held to be barbarous. But religion was never stifled. Among the Protestants there arose an Evangelical cult of Christian conduct, which derived from the saner sects who had claimed Revelation during the religious wars. In England, the Quakers listened not to authority but to conscience; John Wesley's Methodist eloquence could convert the masses, and the Nonconformist Isaac Watts became the greatest of English hymn writers. In France the learned Pascal combined mathematics with mysticism. If the predominant tone of both the Catholic and the Protestant establishments was either obscurantist or sceptical, it never destroyed an inspiration which often reinforced the rationalist campaign for betterment.

The cult of sensibility and introspection natural in an increasingly wealthy and secure civilisation, in which the civilian way of life was superseding the clerical and the military, affected political thought. Hobbes had been concerned with security, not honour; Locke with the protection of property and toleration, not with saving souls. Both were strictly practical and thought the state a necessary insurance. Bentham, the first Utilitarian, thought happiness the objective of society; enlightened self-interest, he believed, could be harnessed to reform.

This predominant view was challenged by the Romantics. Burke, an Irishman whose eloquence transfigured the hoary mysteries of the British Constitution analysed by Blackstone, saw the state not as a night watchman or as an improver, but as a great moral being in time as well as space. He stressed the instinctive bonds of society as against calculated self-interest, and declared that 'in every patent of office the duty' was 'included'. Government was the trustee of generations, society the embodiment of a moral law. His cult of the community was eagerly assimilated in Germany, and strengthened the British Conservative tradition.

The Swiss publicist Jean-Jacques Rousseau (1712–79) was even more influential. He declared that the 'General Will' of the people, not force or Divine Right or Natural Law, was the basis of authority. This revolutionary concept, derived apparently from his experience of the meetings of Swiss peasants, was in various interpretations and misinterpretations to have remarkable results and to contribute to the political ideas of democracy. Rousseau, an introspective literary genius, infected the beliefs of Renaissance and seventeenth-century humanism with a romantic cult of the 'noble savage' and the common man. In the name of the individual, he challenged the whole structure of society. His *Contrat Social*, which appeared two years after *Candide*, was to provide democrats with slogans which have spread round the world. He also demanded a new freedom in education. Like St Augustine, Rousseau was an introvert and genius of untiring eloquence, but where St Augustine projected a great cosmic discipline which centred on God and Revelation, Rousseau depicted a scene of cosmic chaos which centred on human impulse.

So by the later eighteenth century the Romantic movement had challenged the classic Catholic and Humanist belief in order and authority, which had inspired the most characteristic achievements of the Age. An hierarchical society was giving place to something still predominantly new.

XI

The Europe in which the old order was to be challenged by the French Revolution was thus a vastly richer, more civilised, more humane, and more far-flung civilisation than the medieval society which had slowly assimilated the classical ideas reinterpreted by the Italians of the Early Renaissance. Politically it was now organised in great national states, backed in the West by massive popular support, if still in Central and Eastern Europe mainly dynastic. The cosmopolitan Empire and the cosmopolitan Papacy had made their last attempt to dominate the Continent and failed. The balance of power had been altered. The Turks had been thrust back into the Balkans, Poland-Lithuania was being broken up; the Austrian Empire still dominated Central Europe, but the Prussian Kingdom and the Russian Empire had emerged as great political facts, and the Russians were spreading across Siberia and into Central Asia.

France was still very formidable, and since economic preponderance had shifted from the Mediterranean to the Atlantic, British sea power had won huge territories overseas, greater than the Spanish Empire of the sixteenth century. In the Americas whose fringe Columbus had discovered there were now well-established communities of European descent. They were predominantly Protestant and spoke English in the north; they were Catholic and spoke Spanish and Portuguese in the centre and the south. In India the long struggle between French and British had been decided and most of the sub-continent was already directly or indirectly under British sway. If Africa remained mysterious, the East and West Indies had been exploited, the Pacific explored, Australasia discovered.

Europe had thus become the dominant political fact for most of the world. And Europeans differed from the conquerors who had imposed themselves on other civilisations before. They brought with them, as well as dynamic ideas, original, powerful and universal gifts—the rudiments of modern industry and administration and the method of modern science.

16 THE FRENCH REVOLUTION, NAPOLEONIC EUROPE AND THE NINETEENTH CENTURY

by F. M. H. Markham

'Bliss was it in that dawn to be alive', wrote Wordsworth when he visited France in the early days of the Revolution. 'How much the greatest event it is that has ever happened in the world, and how much the best!' exclaimed Charles James Fox at the news of the fall of the Bastille. Everywhere men felt themselves to be in the presence of an event of cosmic, universal import. They were not deceived, for the French Revolution unleashed the forces of democracy, nationalism, and ultimately socialism, which shaped the Europe of the nineteenth century with profound effect upon the rest of the world. The reaction between feudal and dynastic Europe and Revolutionary France lit the spark of militant nationalism which, in the turmoil of the Napoleonic wars, spread throughout Europe. By 1815 France, the most compact, unified, prosperous and modernised state on the Continent, had made and lost under Napoleon her attempt to dominate Europe; Great Britain had established her undisputed command of the seas which was to last for a hundred years; Austria had precariously reasserted her hegemony of Central Europe, and Russia had emerged as the dominant Eastern power. In the realm of ideas the changes were no less profound, for the Romantic Movement popularised by Jean-Jacques Rousseau had transformed every aspect of art, literature, and thought. Romanticism, and the reaction against it, following the immense advances in scientific and industrial knowledge and the hardening of the international situation brought about by *realpolitik*, are probably the most characteristic movements of the nineteenth century.

II

It was no accident that the Revolution broke out in France rather than elsewhere. For it was there that the contrast between existing political and social institutions and the mental attitude of all classes towards them was most glaring. The *ancien régime* in France was a tangle of anomalous, unjust and irritating institutions from which there seemed to be no escape except by violent upheaval. The *cahiers mémoriaux* of grievances, drawn up for the Estates-General of 1789, show to what an extent the radical ideas of the eighteenth-century philosophers had penetrated the *noblesse* and the middle class. The philosophers had for half a century attacked these anomalies and contrasted with them the conception of an equal, free and natural order of society. The enlightened nobles such as Lafayette, stimulated by their contacts with the American War of Independence, were ready to exploit the weakness of the Crown and demand a parliamentary constitution in place of arbitrary rule. The commercial middle class, strengthened by the rising prosperity of overseas trade, bitterly resented the privileges of the *noblesse* and the chronic disorder of government finance. The peasants, many of whom now owned land, found that their property was burdened with all sorts of feudal dues and restrictions, and they had to bear the main burden of taxation in the form of the *taille*, from which the upper classes were largely exempted. The *noblesse* were even trying to increase the yield from their feudal rights in order to keep pace with the rising wealth of the middle class. Commercial prosperity had brought inflation, and wages had not kept pace with prices. The distress of the urban and rural proletariat was brought to a head by the bad harvests of 1787 and 1788, provoking the mob-violence of 1789.

It is doubtful whether even the monarchy of Louis XIV would have had the strength to abolish the ancient régime by reform from above. When the weak Louis XVI, dominated by his Austrian wife Marie Antoinette, who was imbued with Habsburg authoritarianism and obstinacy, succeeded the idle and cynical Louis XV in 1774, it soon became clear that the monarchy was unequal to the task. The load of debt added by France's intervention in the American war brought the chronic bankruptcy of the Government to a crisis. In vain Calonne the Finance Minister urged that the only solution was to abolish the exemption of the privileged orders from taxation. An Assembly of Notables in 1787 rejected Calonne's proposals and the King gave way. No alternative was left but the summoning of the Estates-General for 1789. It had last met in 1614.

In accordance with precedent the three Estates of Nobles, Clergy and Commons were represented separately, but the Government conceded that the Commons should have double the number of representatives accorded to the two other orders. When they met in May, 1789 the Commons ignored the Government's demand for supplies, and proposed that the three orders should unite to form a National Assembly with constituent powers. At the end of June, the Government tried to check this dangerous movement by holding a *séance royale* of the Estates-General. The Crown proposed some inadequate reforms, but the rights of the privileged orders were not to be discussed, and the three Orders were forbidden to unite. The Commons, now joined by some of the Clergy, defied the orders of the Government in the oath of the Tennis Court, in which they swore not to separate until France had been given a Constitution. The Government now began to concentrate troops round Versailles and Paris for a military *coup d'état*, but it was forestalled by the rising of Paris and the storming of the Bastille (14 July, 1789). The Court gave way and recognised the National Assembly. The political revolution had been won, and Bourbon absolutism destroyed. At the beginning of October 1789 the women of Paris, inflamed by hunger, marched on Versailles and forced the King to move from Versailles to the Tuileries where he was henceforth the prisoner of the Paris democracy. The political revolution opened the floodgates to the social revolution. In July the peasants sacked the châteaux of the nobles and burnt the manorial records. Alarmed by this agrarian revolution, the Assembly decreed on 4 August the abolition of the feudal régime.

In the new Constitution, which was not completed till 1791, the Assembly reduced the Crown to a limited monarchy, with feeble executive power. The royal intendants in the provinces were abolished, and the provinces replaced by departments with wide powers of self-government. The legislative power was to be entirely independent of the executive; deputies were forbidden to hold office under the Crown, and the King had no more than a suspensory veto on legislation.

In reforming the Church, the Assembly embarked on a policy which was to lead to national bankruptcy and a religious schism. The property of the Church was confiscated and a paper money issued on this security. The uncontrolled issue of a paper currency, the *assignats* soon led to inflation and the abandonment of any attempt to meet expenditure from the taxes. By imposing popular election of Bishops and Clergy the Assembly provoked a breach with the Pope, which split the French Church and the nation and deeply troubled the King's conscience.

Only two men saw clearly, as early as 1790, that the Revolution was heading inevitably to anarchy, terror and tyranny. Burke made this prediction in his *Reflections on the French Revolution*. The Comte de Mirabeau, the only realist statesman of the National Assembly, foresaw this danger from the start. He was foremost in destroying royal absolutism, but he was a firm believer in constitutional monarchy. He was convinced that the monarchy could not only be saved but strengthened through the Revolution if only the King would be true to the historic policy of Richelieu and Louis XIV by allying with the middle class and sacrificing the privileged orders. Debarred as a deputy from becoming a Minister, he offered himself as a secret adviser to the Court, and implored the King and Queen to accept the Revolution, and exploit the situation to regain the influence of the Crown. But he was too untrustworthy in reputation to gain a hearing, and died early in 1791 knowing that the monarchy was doomed. Before he died he was even prepared to provoke civil war and counter-revolution to avert the worse evil of anarchy. Shortly after his death the King and the Queen attempted the disastrous gamble of a flight to the frontier which was stopped at Varennes (June 1791). The republican demonstrations after their return to the capital alarmed the right wing of the Assembly, the Feuillants, and the King was reinstated; but France had learned the lesson that the King was not indispensable, and the last credit of the monarchy was exhausted.

When the new Legislative Assembly met in September, 1793, the princes and the *noblesse*, including the majority of the army officers, had emigrated in a mass strike against the Revolution. From the Rhineland they openly threatened invasion and counter-revolution. The left wing of the Assembly, the faction called the Brissotins or Girondins, thought that they could seize power and establish the Revolution by provoking a war. They were intoxicated by the dream of an ideological crusade which would rally the peoples of Europe to their side. They would occupy Belgium and exploit its wealth to prop up the French finances. By whipping up popular hatred against the *émigrés* and against Austria, with its memories of the humiliations of the Seven Years' War brought on France by the Austrian Alliance, they forced the Assembly and the King to declare war on Austria (April, 1792). The Queen was not averse to war, since she saw the only salvation for the monarchy in Austrian bayonets, and had been secretly imploring her brother the Emperor Leopold to intervene. None of the Powers at first saw any need to interfere: far from regarding the Revolution as an international menace, they complacently assumed that it would nullify France as a Great Power for many years. Austria and Prussia feared that intervention in France would allow Russia to grab the remnants of Poland for herself. But it soon seemed that the war would be a military walkover, as the French armies broke in confusion and flight. The Prussian army approached Paris and the Prussian Commander, the Duke of Brunswick, issued a manifesto threatening the city of Paris with destruction if the Royal Family were harmed. The reaction in Paris to the Brunswick Manifesto was the storming of the Tuileries on August 10th, the deposition and imprisonment of the King, and the September massacres of the political prisoners.

Danton emerged from the revolution of August 10th as the man of the hour. He organised the resistance which stemmed the tide of invasion at Valmy. The French victory at Jemappes led to the occupation of Belgium, which brought England into the war in January, 1793. Under the anvil of war revolutionary France must either succumb or organise herself as a nation in arms, and give to the world the first example of total mobilisation. The Girondins were unable to face this necessity and paid for their failure in their liquidation in June, 1793. The Montagnard faction led by Danton and Robespierre were more realist and practical, and they had the all-important support of Paris. Danton was the chief architect of the emergency war government. He created the Committee of Public Safety and the Revolutionary Tribunal, but his attempt to dissolve the coalition against France by diplomatic negotiations failed and in the reorganisation of the Committee of Public Safety in July, 1793, he gave way to Robespierre and Carnot.

Unlike Danton who, apart from his patriotism, cared little for political principles, Robespierre was a fanatic who owed his influence to his sincerity and incorruptibility. He had predicted the failure of the Girondin war policy, and voiced the needs of the people of Paris.

Mirabeau, hearing one of Robespierre's early speeches in the Constituent Assembly, remarked 'That man will go far: he believes all he says'. Rousseau's *Contrat Social* was Robespierre's Bible; the official cult which he was to introduce in 1794 was a literal application of Rousseau's chapter on 'Civil Religion'. He was also to push to extreme limits Rousseau's distinction between the general will and the will of all. If the majority were unenlightened or corrupt, the general will resided in the minority, who therefore had the right to coerce the rest, in Rousseau's words 'to force them to be free'. Robespierre had thus no difficulty in reconciling his democratic principles with unlimited dictatorship and terror, and he was the natural exponent of Jacobinism and the spokesman of the Committee of Public Safety. He defended the dictatorship of the Committee, explaining that: 'if the basis of popular government in the time of peace is virtue, the basis of popular government in time of war is both virtue and terror.'

Robespierre took office at the most dangerous crisis of the Revolution. The Girondin faction, overthrown in Paris, had raised the provinces in revolt and joining with the royalists, had delivered Toulon to the British Fleet. The Committee barely survived a rising by the extremist faction of the Hebertists who wanted to purge the army of all regular officers, kill all counter-revolutionaries and dechristianise France. With the recapture of Toulon and the victory of Wattignies in the north, the Committee weathered the storm and obtained from the convention dictatorial powers. It was this Committee of twelve men, working with ferocious energy, that saved revolutionary France and created the formidable military power which was to overwhelm Europe under Napoleon. By the end of 1793 Carnot had made conscription a reality, and had equipped and put into the field armies totalling 800,000 men—forces of a size never yet seen in Europe. And already the man who was to lead them with incomparable genius, and then to end the revolution, had appeared. For it was at the siege of Toulon that the young Captain Bonaparte first made his mark.

No sooner had the crisis of invasion and civil war been overcome than the unity of the Government fell to pieces. While Robespierre was fanatically determined to continue the Terror until the ideal Republic of virtue emerged by the purging of all elements of corruption and opposition, the moderate members of the Committee, the majority of the Convention and the mass of Frenchmen, were only prepared to tolerate the Terror at the height of the crisis. At the beginning of 1794 Danton had already declared for a policy of relaxing the Terror, and had paid with his head for challenging the Committee's policy. The daily toll of the guillotine continued to mount even after the victory of Fleurus (June, 1794) which ended the threat of invasion. When Robespierre demanded before the Convention a purge of the Committee itself, of the Convention, and in fact of all who disagreed with him, the Convention rebelled and sent Robespierre to the guillotine. With him fell also the independent Commune of Paris—that formidable Parisian democracy which had terrorised successive governments since 1789.

With the fall of Robespierre the revolution reached the furthest limit of its political and social effort. The middle class regained their control which had been threatened by radical forces since 10 August, 1792, and a tide of reaction against Jacobinism set in. A proletarian and socialist movement could never seriously threaten middle-class liberalism

in the first French Revolution when France was yet only on the verge of an industrial revolution. Yet Robespierre had come dangerously near to a socialist policy by his laws of Ventôse in 1794 which proposed to distribute the property of traitors to poor patriots. And Babeuf, a follower of Robespierre, in his *Conspiracy of the Equals* in 1797, heralded the beginning of a genuine socialist programme.

III

When in 1795 the rule of the Committee of Public Safety came to an end, France returned to moderate constitutional government with a division between an executive directory and a bicameral legislature. The introduction of this constitution produced the last serious rising in Paris in 1795 which was quelled by General Bonaparte's 'whiff of grapeshot'. As his reward for saving the Government, Bonaparte received the command of the Army in Italy, and Europe was to be stunned by the astonishing series of victories—Lodi, Castiglione, Rivoli, Arcola—which by the end of 1797 forced Austria to make peace. Prussia had already dropped out of the coalition in 1795: Great Britain fought on alone. By the time he left Italy, Napoleon's ambition already aimed at supreme power in France, but he felt that 'the pear was not yet ripe'. In the meantime he preferred an attack on Egypt to an impracticable attempt at invading England. The destruction of the French fleet by Nelson at the Battle of the Nile (1798) wrecked Napoleon's eastern ambitions, and revived the European coalition against France. But it also gave Napoleon his supreme opportunity to bid for power and he returned from Egypt at the psychological moment, having regained prestige by defeating the Turks at Abukir. In his absence the loss of Italy and a renewed threat of invasion had finally ruined the credit of the Directory, and Sieyès and Talleyrand were planning a *coup d'état* to alter the constitution. Napoleon was received with public acclaim as the symbol of victory, and was courted by the rival political factions. In the *coup d'état* of Brumaire (1799), Napoleon had only to turn to his own advantage a plot prepared by the politicians. Sieyès realised too late that in calling on Napoleon he had found not a servant but a master. Napoleon tore up Sieyès' complicated plans for a parliamentary constitution, and insisted that the new constitution of the Consulate should confer all effective power on himself as First Consul. It was not, however, till the Consulate had proved itself to be overwhelmingly successful by the victory of Marengo (1800), and the peace of Amiens (1802), that Napoleon was able to muzzle all opposition.

The rapid recovery of France under the Consulate was made possible because, for the first time since the rule of the Committee of Public Safety, France had a strong centralised executive. The Directory had been fatally handicapped by executive weakness, by friction between the executive and the legislature which had to be restored by repeated purges and *coups d'état*, and by the ghastly aftermath of monetary inflation. The creation of Prefects of the Departments (strongly reminiscent of the intendants of the *ancien régime*) enabled Napoleon to organise an effective machinery for the assessment and collection of taxes. 'It is not as a General' he claimed, 'that I am governing France; it is because the nation believes that I possess the civil qualities of a ruler.' His genius shone as dazzlingly in politics and administration as in war, and he succeeded in recruiting to his Government the ablest survivors both from the Revolution and the monarchy. The administrative institutions which Napoleon gave to France, the legal Codes, the Concordat, the Legion of Honour, proved to be durable and survived the changes of régime in the nineteenth century. Napoleon saw that the French people were now prepared to forgo the aim of self-government, if they could secure the equally important social and administrative aims of the Revolution. But he refused to be bound by the revolutionary ideology and declared that 'while conserving every useful innovation produced by the Revolution, he would not reject the good institutions which it wrongly destroyed.' The reforms of the Consulate and the Empire mingle both revolutionary and reactionary elements. If they are in the main a practical realisation of reforms conceived in the Revolution, they are also, in some respects, a surreptitious return to the institutions of the Bourbon monarchy. The Legion of Honour and later the creation of hereditary imperial titles of nobility were a distinct shock to the revolutionaries' principles of equality.

In concluding his Concordat with the Pope, Napoleon resisted the clamour from anti-clerical politicians and generals, knowing that by the religious settlement he would earn the gratitude of millions of Frenchmen, pacify La Vendée and win over to his side from the exiled Bourbons a great moral force. When the Life-Consulate of 1802 was converted into the hereditary Empire (1804), Napoleon was satisfying not only his own ambition but also the needs of the French people. The middle-class and the peasantry who had gained from the Revolution wanted, above all, security, especially the material gains they had acquired in the lands of the Church and the nobility. No guarantee of the Revolution settlement could yet be expected from the exiled Bourbons, and the logical alternative to a Bourbon restoration was a Bonaparte Dynasty. The stability of the régime could not be left to the hazard of Napoleon's own life, as was shown by the dangerous assassination plot of Cadoudal in 1804. Mirabeau's contention that monarchy and the Revolution were not incompatible was to be realised in Napoleon. The new 'fourth dynasty of France' was to carry out the task of modernising the French State which the Bourbon Dynasty had forfeited by their incompetence.

IV

The power and energy of a revitalised France led by such a man as Napoleon inevitably overflowed into Europe. For a brief moment in 1802 when Austria and then Great Britain signed peace treaties with France at Lunéville and Amiens, it looked as if Napoleon might succeed in pacifying not only France but Europe. But the French historian Vandal concisely comments: 'It is impossible to say if the task was beyond the capacity of his genius: it was certainly beyond the capacity of his character.' The crumbling of the old order in Europe seemed to invite French intervention everywhere—in Germany, Switzerland, Italy, and Holland, and to presage the revival of the Empire of Charlemagne.

As in 1914 and 1939, Great Britain could not afford to see the Continent dominated by one power, which might then outbuild Britain's fleet and threaten her existence. The conflict between British and French imperialism for maritime supremacy and world power had to be fought to a finish. By retaining Malta as 'compensation' for France's encroachment in Europe, Great Britain ended the disadvantageous peace of Amiens (1803). In 1805 Austria was goaded into war by Napoleon's assumption of the crown of Italy, and was joined in the Third coalition by Tsar Alexander

I, who had rival pretensions to Napoleon as the arbiter of Europe.

In the great naval campaign of 1805 the threat of invasion was first foiled, and Great Britain's command of the seas was decisively confirmed by Nelson's victory at Trafalgar. With Nelson, naval power of the era of wind and sail reached its peak, while Napoleon, baffled by the intricacies of sea warfare, reluctantly faced the fact that the French navy could never recover in time from the loss of its experienced officers in the Revolution. Three months before the final lesson of Trafalgar, Napoleon had abandoned the scheme of invasion, and switched the *Grande Armée* from Boulogne to the Danube, to launch the ten years' struggle to conquer the sea by land victories.

In the victories of Ulm, Austerlitz, Jena and Friedland, which successively knocked out Austria, Prussia, and Russia, Napoleonic warfare also reached its peak. Military genius defies analysis, for as Napoleon himself said 'Everything is in the execution.' But the obvious basis of Napoleon's strategy is mobility. In the *Grande Armée* of 1805 he had an instrument of incomparable quality: it has probably never been equalled for battle experience, training, and dash. As a young officer before the Revolution, Napoleon had absorbed the new ideas of mobile, offensive warfare and the massing of weight and fire-power at the decisive point, which was being taught by the French staff. The armies of the third Coalition were still professional armies of the era of Frederick the Great, in which the soldier was treated as an automaton. As they could not be trusted to forage for themselves without deserting, such armies were slowed down by their supply-trains. The Revolution, on the other hand, had produced an army of intelligent citizens which could move fast by living off the country, and in which courage and initiative were rewarded by promotion. National conscription enabled a high rate of wastage and casualties to be sustained.

The alliance with Russia at Tilsit (1807) after the victory of Friedland enabled Napoleon to apply the Continental System against Great Britain; its aim was to exclude British exports from the whole of the Continent, and so reduce her to bankruptcy by ruining her balance of trade. In pursuit of this policy, Napoleon was led into the Peninsular War, a quarrel with the Pope, and ultimately the invasion of Russia. The peoples of Europe were exasperated by the hardships imposed by the Continental System, and did not respond to Napoleon's argument that Europe must endure temporary distress in order 'to shake off the economic domination of England.' Austria, encouraged by the Spanish rising to take up arms again, was crushed at Wagram (1809), but only after a stiff resistance which impressed and dismayed Napoleon. Russia broke away from the Continental System in 1810. The Russian nobility was being ruined by the effects of the System, and Russian hopes of exploiting the Tilsit alliance to gain Constantinople were frustrated by Napoleon. The invasion of Russia in 1812 was intended by Napoleon to force Alexander back into the Continental System, so that the final turn of the screw could be applied to Great Britain. The indecisive battle of Borodino failed to avert the consequences of the Russian strategy of withdrawal and 'scorched earth', and in the final catastrophe of the winter retreat from Moscow, only 40,000 returned out of 400,000 men who entered Russia six months before.

In 1813 it became apparent that Napoleon had overspent his capital of manpower. Too many veterans of the *Grande Armée* had been lost in Spain and Russia, and the young conscripts of 1813 had not

the stamina or training to carry out the Napoleonic strategy. Napoleon, too, had temporarily lost his grip. The Napoleon of 1805 would have made the bold decision to cut his losses in Spain and concentrate every man for a quick, decisive blow in Germany. He failed to follow up his initial victories and then, by agreeing to an armistice and peace-talks, allowed Austria to enter the war and the balance of numbers to tilt irretrievably against him at the decisive battle of Leipzig—a verdict which could not be altered by Napoleon's brilliant but hopeless *tours de force* of the campaigns of 1814 and 1815.

V

The stress and turmoil of the Revolutionary and Napoleonic Wars accelerated not only the Industrial Revolution in Great Britain, but also the movement of thought throughout Europe. By 1815 the new ideas in politics, art, and philosophy which were to distinguish the nineteenth century from the eighteenth were already taking shape. The rationalism and cosmopolitanism of the eighteenth century, which reached their zenith in the Declaration of the Rights of Man, the foundation of the Institut and the École Polytechnique and the galaxy of great scientists—Lavoisier, Laplace, Lamarck, Monge—gave way at the turn of the century to new ideas of romanticism and nationalism. The Romantic Movement showed its effects first in literature and art and later in politics (*see* Chapter 15). In music it is foreshadowed by Mozart's later works such as 'The Magic Flute', and burst into full flood with Beethoven, Schubert and Weber. In literature the same note can be heard from Wordsworth, Coleridge and Scott; in Chateaubriand, in Goethe and in Schiller.

The new romantic interest in the past not only opened the way to the great development of historical studies in the nineteenth century, but transformed political thought. The shallow contempt of the Enlightenment for the Middle Ages as 'ages of barbarism and superstition', was replaced by an interest and enthusiasm which has left tangible evidence in the architecture of the Gothic Revival. This new attitude to the past stimulated both a religious revival and the spirit of nationalism. Chateaubriand's *Génie du Christianisme* (1802) heralded a Catholic revival, allied with counter-revolutionary philosophy. Maistre and Bonald used the dogmas of Catholicism as powerful weapons to attack the principles of the revolution. Further, Kant's *Critiques* in philosophy seemed to set bounds to the validity of scientific method in the ethical and political sphere.

Romantic interest in the customs and traditions of the past awakened a sense of the individuality and the value of differing peoples, of the *Volksgeist*. A cultural nationalism everywhere precedes and merges into political nationalism. While Goethe remained indifferent to German national feeling and an admirer of Napoleon to the end, and Schiller declared in 1802 that 'the greatness of Germany consists in its culture and the character of the nation, which is independent of its political fate'; the younger generation—Fichte, Arndt, Schlegel, Hormayr—began to preach patriotic resistance to Napoleon. In Italy Alfieri and Foscolo revived the consciousness of Italy's greatness, and turned against Napoleon when he disappointed their hopes of unity.

Yet the German nationalists of the nineteenth century who christened Leipzig the 'Battle of the Nations', greatly exaggerated the part played by national consciousness in the downfall of Napoleon. Popular guerrilla resistance, as in Spain and in the Tyrol under Andreas Hofer, was excep-

tional and had little in common with the middle-class nationalism of the nineteenth century. Hofer's rising in the Tyrol was a religious protest against Bavarian anti-clerical innovations. Spanish resistance was a spontaneous reaction of monks and peasants against French influence. Napoleon brought it on himself by his brutal disregard of Spanish pride: 'The Spaniards', he wrote, 'are like other peoples, and are not a class apart: they will be happy to accept the imperial institutions.' In Germany and Austria at that time nationalist aspirations were confined to a minority of intellectuals, who were treated with hostility and suspicion by the governments. Francis I and Metternich made peace with Napoleon in 1809 rather than encourage the popular war advocated by Stadion and Hormayr. The dismissal of Stein, the German nationalist statesman, was greeted with relief by the Prussian Junkers, and the reform of the Prussian State after Jena was limited to the practical necessity of modernising the army.

Napoleon's disregard of national sentiment was not therefore as unaccountable as it seemed to the historians of the nineteenth century. In creating the Grand Empire, he assumed that the collapse of the old order in Europe would pave the way for a cosmopolitan united Europe, in which the peoples everywhere would be satisfied with the enlightened administration and the Code Napoleon. He did not realise until too late that his own action in clearing away the lumber of the medieval past would, on the contrary, allow the latent seeds of popular nationalism to flourish. Actually many officers and civil servants of the Napoleonic Empire became the Carbonari nationalists of the period after 1815. It was only at St Helena that Napoleon was able to see the new trend of nationalism, oppressed by the reactionary Holy Alliance, and he cleverly reinterpreted his own career as a crusade on behalf of the peoples against the dynasties. Napoleon's own personality displays the opposing traits of nationalism and romanticism. The romantic side, evident in his soaring imagination and unlimited ambition, appealed to the romantic generation after Waterloo. But in his intellectual and political outlook, Napoleon was the heir of the cosmopolitan Enlightenment and may be truly described as the last and greatest of the Enlightened Despots.

VI

The settlement of Europe made at the Vienna Congress of 1815 was a bitter disappointment to liberals and nationalists. Germany was given an impotent federal organisation which fortified the particularism of the Princes and ensured Austria's domination. Poland was handed over to Russia, and Italy to Austria; Belgium and Holland were forcibly united. It was a settlement based on the traditional principles of the balance of power and legitimacy and the paramount need of guarantees against French aggression. The statesmen of Vienna could hardly have been expected to apply the principle of nationality which seemed to them to be connected with the aggressive Jacobinism which had devastated Europe for twenty years. Harsher, but hardly vindictive terms, including a period of occupation and an indemnity, were imposed on France after Napoleon's disastrous adventure of the Hundred Days and the defeat at Waterloo. The alliance against France was renewed for twenty years, and the Allies announced their intention of holding periodic reunions to supervise the peace-settlement. Alexander also induced the sovereigns of Europe to sign his Holy Alliance, contemptuously described by Castlereagh as 'a sublime piece of mysticism and nonsense', but yet an expression of the general desire to escape from international anarchy. At the congress of Aix-la-Chapelle (1818), the occupation forces were withdrawn from France, and she was admitted to the Congress of Powers. But the Congress System, a premature experiment in international government, soon broke down through the growing divergence of principle and interests between Great Britain and the three eastern autocracies, with whom the name of the Holy Alliance became associated.

Metternich, Chancellor of Austria 1809–48, was the main prop of the European Conservative reaction. He was determined to use the Congress System to fight the contagion of revolution, and in the Troppau Protocol of 1820 it was declared that the alliance would intervene to suppress revolutions against legitimate rulers. Alexander had at first posed as the patron of liberalism, but a mutiny of his palace guards at St Petersburg in 1819, dangerously reminiscent of the palace revolution which had deposed and assassinated his father Tsar Paul, and coinciding with military revolts in Spain and Italy, drove him into the arms of Metternich. Meanwhile isolationist sentiment was growing in Great Britain, and Castlereagh was forced to recognise the new South American Republics in order to retain British trade and influence in that area. He denounced the Troppau Protocol, and his successors, Canning and Palmerston, successfully exploited the policy of countering the eastern block of autocracies by British patronage of liberal movements in Europe.

The huge size of Russia's peace-time army, and the prestige won by her victory over Napoleon, caused exaggerated fears of Russian aggression which were not dispelled till the Crimean War. Ever since Napoleon's Egyptian expedition, Great

EUROPE AFTER CONGRESS OF VIENNA, 1815

Britain was sensitive to any threat to her route to India, and feared a Russian drive to break up Turkey and seize Constantinople. But both Alexander and his successor Nicholas I (1825–55) remained loyal to the principle of European solidarity. Alexander resisted the temptation to exploit the Greek War of Independence (1821–7) and after the Russo-Turkish War of 1828, Nicholas decided that a Russian protectorate of Turkey would be preferable to its dissolution. He was even prepared to accept neutralisation of the straits in the Straits Convention of 1841, renouncing the treaty of Unkiar-Skelessi of 1833 which virtually gave him an exclusive protectorate of Turkey. The Decembrist revolt in St Petersburg at his accession and the Polish revolt of 1830 were warnings which bound him to Metternich's system.

Metternich's interminable platitudes about the principles of legitimacy and conservatism were a cloak of respectability behind which he concealed his acute but cynical and fatalistic perception of the forces at work in Europe. He realised that the forces of liberalism and nationalism would prevail in the end, and privately he bemoaned the fact that his life was spent in propping up a mouldering edifice. If an intelligent conservative in Great Britain, a Peel or Disraeli, could face up to the democratic era and meet it half-way, it was far more difficult on the Continent where liberalism was complicated by nationalism. The emergence of nationalism would expel Austria from Germany and disrupt the multi-national Austrian state. Metternich himself believed that the maintenance of Austria was also a European interest, because he foresaw, and rightly, that nationalism would usher in an era of the most frightful wars. He felt that he had no choice but to combat and postpone the evil as long as possible. His seemingly petty persecution of the German student movement after 1815 and his attempt to muzzle the universities and the Press by the Carlsbad Decrees of 1819, were logical consequences of his outlook: for it was clearly in the universities that the poison of liberalism and nationalism was being germinated. So also he discouraged the development of trade and industry since it would raise up a liberal middle class; and he did not see till too late that the spread of the Prussian customs-union, the *Zollverein*, was slowly shifting the centre of gravity in Germany from Vienna to Berlin.

VII

The first serious cracks in Metternich's system came in 1830 with the July Revolution in Paris, the Belgian revolt against Holland, and the Polish rising. The July Revolution proved that the task of replanting the principle of legitimacy in a France irrevocably altered by the vast changes of the Revolution and the Empire was impossible. Maistre, the Bourbon propagandist, himself said 'Louis XVIII has not been restored to the throne of his ancestors; he has simply ascended the throne of Bonaparte'. The circumstances of the second restoration in 1815 were even more unfavourable than those of the first restoration in 1814. Louis XVIII had returned in the 'baggage-train of the Allies'. The White Terror and the execution of Marshal Ney inflamed hatreds. After dismissing the ultra-royalist Parliament of 1815, Louis XVIII and his favourite minister, Decazes, made a genuine effort to 'royalise the nation and nationalise royalty'. But the murder of the Duc de Berri in 1820 and the accession of the Comte D'Artois as Charles X in 1824, led to ten years of ultra royalist reaction. Artois completely shared the outlook of the ultra-royalists and declared that 'he would rather chop wood than reign like the King of England'. The aggressive counter-revolutionary propaganda of the ultra-royalists, based on Maistre's, Bonald's and Lamennais' doctrines of the alliance of 'throne and altar', placed liberalism on the defensive and appeared to threaten the revolutionary settlement. The huge indemnity paid to the *émigrés* for the loss of their lands in the Revolution particularly angered the middle class, since it was financed by the lowering of interest on Government funds. In 1829 Charles X, faced with a liberal victory at the polls, flung caution to the winds, and appointed a government headed by Polignac, a notorious *émigré* ultra-royalist, and resorted to rule by emergency Ordinances. The Government failed to prepare for the violent reaction in Paris and three days of street fighting sufficed to topple the monarchy. The middle class who had provoked the rising in Paris succeeded in checking it before it ended in a proclamation of the Republic, and persuaded Lafayette to accept Louis Philippe, Duke of Orléans, as 'King of the French'.

The triumph of the middle class in Paris had a decisive effect on public opinion in Great Britain. The result of the first French Revolution had been to halt reform for thirty years. The execution of the King, the September massacres, the Terror, and the war with France, associated agitation for reform with anarchy and Jacobin fifth-column subversion. The British aristocracy, unlike the French *noblesse*, were a vigorous and self-confident governing class, constantly recruited from below, and they were strong enough to survive the stress of the Napoleonic wars, the industrial revolution and the scandalous disrepute of the monarchy under George IV. But the July Revolution dispelled the bogy of the Terror, at the moment when the long Tory domination was crumbling after the death of Canning in 1827. It encouraged the middle class to join forces with the working class and to press for Parliamentary reform even to the point of revolution. The Reform Act of 1832 opened the way to profound social and administrative change, and the predominance of the middle class was confirmed by Peel's abandonment of the Corn Laws in 1846. This shift of power was decisive both for Great Britain and for her vast dependencies overseas.

The Orléans Monarchy represented no principle, only the interest of the middle class. Guizot, the theorist and spokesman of the régime and Prime Minister (1840–8), resisted all demands for widening the electorate. After slight concessions in 1830, it still numbered only a quarter of a million. Parliamentary life was unreal and corrupt, and dominated by an artificial government majority of office-holders. Guizot had great parliamentary and intellectual gifts, but his arrogant, doctrinaire mentality left him in blinkers. As a Professor of History before he entered politics, he had proved to his own satisfaction in his *Histoire de la Civilisation en Europe* that the triumph of the middle class was the culminating point of European history. No further fundamental change or revolution was therefore possible or necessary after 1830. Guizot regarded all further manifestations of unrest as a mere backwash of the Revolution of 1789. He was unable to see that the revolutionary principles had moved from the political to the social sphere, and that a new social revolution was boiling up. In vain de Tocqueville pointed out to Parliament in January 1848: 'Do you not see that the passions of the working class have ceased to be political and become social'? Blanqui, the follower of Babeuf, was organising working-class conspiracies. Saint-Simon and Fourier, writing under the Empire and the Revolution, had provided the critique of capitalism and a complete doctrine of socialism which not only anticipated and influenced the later system of Karl Marx, but was being popularised after 1830 by Louis Blanc and Proudhon. The Industrial Revolution, though later and less extreme than in Great Britain, was exposing the workers to the miseries of the capitalist system in its most extreme *laissez-faire* form and they eagerly drank in the new socialist ideas.

The Orléans Monarchy was also unable to conceal the drabness and sterility of its domestic policy by a bold and glorious policy abroad. Louis Philippe dared not embark on a revolutionary war on behalf of the nationalities, and he had to pay a stiff price for the support and co-operation of Great Britain. He had to decline the throne of Belgium for his son and accept the British candidate, Leopold of Coburg. When he tried to take an independent line by supporting Mohammed Ali of Egypt against Great Britain in 1840, and again over the marriage of Queen Isabella of Spain in 1846, he sacrificed the Anglo-French *entente* and was left humiliated and isolated. The sudden collapse of the Orléans Monarchy in February 1848 was due as much to its own hollowness and fragility as to the innocuous campaign for parliamentary reform which provoked it.

VIII

In the vacuum of power caused by the flight of Louis Philippe, the social revolution, strong in the Paris Clubs and working class, made its first bid for power in Europe; in doing so it killed the Second Republic and opened the way for the Second Empire. The middle class and peasant proprietors of the provinces were so alarmed by the socialist menace that they returned a strongly Conservative National Assembly (April 1848). By June 1848 the Assembly had organised its forces for a showdown with the Paris workers, and the abrupt cancellation of unemployment relief, the *Ateliers Nationaux*, provoked a bloody week's fighting in Paris.

In contrast with the situation in 1789 and 1830, the Government had the support of the provinces against Paris, and, as was once more to be demonstrated in the Paris Commune of 1871, Paris was never again to make and unmake governments. In December 1848 Louis Napoleon, nephew of the great Emperor, was elected President of the Second Republic by an overwhelming vote. He had the votes, not only of the propertied classes who longed for order and security against the 'red peril', but also of many of the workers who detested the republican candidate, General Cavaignac, as the butcher of the June days, and had noted Louis Napoleon's progressive ideas.

In Central Europe the revolutions in Germany, Austria and Italy, touched off by the potentially important February revolution in Paris, were likewise doomed to frustration. The temporary panic instilled into the German Princes by the street fighting in Vienna and Berlin of March 1848, gave a short-lived opportunity to the National Parliament which met in Frankfurt. Their one chance of survival and of overcoming the forces of particularism and reaction lay in combining and encouraging all revolutionaries in order to keep the dynastic rulers on the run. But they were far too respectable a body of lawyers and professors to embark on such a policy. They spent their time in drawing up paper-constitutions and sending futile invitations to the Princes to accept them. They were so frightened of radical movements that they even called in the Prussian troops to suppress them. Their nationalistic prejudices were blatantly revealed when they applauded the Prussian suppression of the Poles, and the Austrian suppression of the Czechs. In little more than a year the dynasties had re-established their position.

The recovery of the Habsburg power in turn doomed to failure the Italian movement for independence. As long as Austrian military power, firmly based on the quadrilateral of fortresses guarding Venetia, and commanded by Marshal Radetzky, an active veteran of the Napoleonic Wars, remained intact, there was little hope that Charles Albert's policy of 'going it alone' could succeed. Ten years later even the flower of the French army could not break the Austrian resistance. Moreover the Italian *Risorgimento* at this stage was weakened by divided aims. Gioberti, with the Neo-Guelph ideal of a liberal Pope launching a national crusade, had raised hopes which were inevitably disappointed when Pope Pius IX refused to take part in war against Austria (April 1848). Mazzini, with his republican movement of Young Italy, despised a 'war of princes' led by Piedmont and aroused the fears of moderates. It was only after the failure of 1848 in spite of the support of Garibaldi who had returned from South America to fight for the republic that the ground was cleared for a concentration of effort behind the progressive Piedmont of Cavour.

So everywhere in Europe the crisis year of 1848 ended in frustration. Liberal ideas of freedom and self-government were poisoned by class-hatred and racial antagonism, and it was left for Bismarck to point the moral. 'The great questions of the day', he said in 1862, 'will not be settled by speeches and resolutions of majorities but by blood and iron.'

IX

Bismarck was to reap where Napoleon III had sown. Louis Napoleon inherited from his uncle not only the name but the legend created at St Helena, and he was convinced that the fortunes of his dynasty and of France depended on the triumph of the principle of nationality. He dreamed of overthrowing the Vienna Settlement, redrawing the map of Europe on the lines of nationality, and regaining for France not only her moral and diplomatic leadership in Europe but also some of her territories lost in 1815. Even one of his opponents admitted that 'if Louis Napoleon succeeds in regaining the Rhine frontier, France will give him anything he wishes'. The Crimean War was a golden opportunity for Louis Napoleon as it split the guarantors of the Vienna Settlement by setting Great Britain against Russia and leaving Austria in uneasy neutrality. The isolation of Austria after the Peace of Paris (1856) opened the way to the next step in Napoleon's programme —the independence of Italy. But the plan concerted with Cavour at Plombières went awry. Napoleon forfeited Italian gratitude by stopping the war short with Austria still in possession of Venetia (1859); he roused fear and suspicion in Great Britain by annexing Savoy and Nice; and he lost Catholic support in France by allowing Cavour to invade the Papal States. In 1863 he offended Russia by diplomatic intervention on behalf of the Poles in the Second Polish Revolt.

When Bismarck took office in 1863 he was able to exploit the general disintegration of alliances brought about by Napoleon III. He was able to avert any Great Power intervention in the invasion of Denmark and the seizure of the Schleswig-Holstein duchies in 1864. In 1865 he met Napoleon III, and came away with the conviction that France would not intervene to stop an Austro-Prussian war. Further, the crisis of German unification caught Napoleon III with his army tied up in the ill-starred Mexican adventure.

A Prussian unification of North Germany was in accord with his principles, and he hoped for compensation on the Rhine. He did not reckon on a lightning Prussian victory (Königgratz 1866) which gave him no time to intervene or mediate.

The reaction of public opinion in France to Königgratz was so violent that it did not allow Napoleon III to accept the unification of Germany under Prussia as a *fait accompli*. The prospect of a united Germany completely altered the balance of power in Europe, and spelt the end of the French ascendancy. The setbacks to French foreign policy since 1860 had weakened the autocracy; the Government and the dynasty badly needed a diplomatic success. So it was that the proposal to put a Hohenzollern Prince on the throne of Spain in 1870 inflamed French public opinion to the point of treating it as a *casus belli*. Under this pressure the French Government refused to be content with a diplomatic success in forcing the Prussian King to withdraw the candidature; they went on to demand guarantees that it would not be renewed. The refusal of this demand led to war. The sudden, overwhelming defeat of France at Sedan (1870) was principally due to the staff work developed by Roon and Moltke, which made the Prussian mobilisation by railways far more rapid than that of the French. In comparison the French army was an outmoded, professional, almost a colonial army. It had not had time since 1866 to catch up with the Prussian military innovations. The Krupp breach-loading field artillery decisively outranged the French muzzle-loaders, and neutralised the effect of the superior French infantry-rifle. The centuries-old French military supremacy was over.

X

Bismarck's ambition was limited to the unification of Germany. With the procla-mation of the German Empire at Versailles in 1871 he regarded Germany as a satiated power, and his aim was now simply to retain and insure what he had won. But the cession of Alsace-Lorraine had made France irreconcilable, and he had to reckon on her enduring hostility. He therefore favoured the Third French Republic, which emerged from the wreck of the Second Empire, rather than a royalist or Bonapartist restoration, because it was weak and unlikely to attract allies. He encouraged France to look to colonial expansion, as in Tunisia in 1878, to distract her attention from the Rhine. The form-ation of the *Dreikaiserbund* of Germany, Russia and Austria in 1873 seemed to make Germany's position secure, but this grouping was constantly liable to disinte-grate through the conflicting aims of Austria and Russia in the Balkans. The exclusion of the Habsburgs from Germany and Italy forced them to look southwards for compensation. At the same time Russian imperialism assumed the form of a Panslav movement and of exploiting Russian patronage of the awakening Slav nationalism in the Balkans. At the Con-gress of Berlin (1878) arising out of the Russo-Turkish war of 1877, Bismarck had to side with Austria against Russia, and sign the Austro-German alliance of 1879. The maintenance of Austria-Hungary was essential to the predominance of the German over the Slav element in Central Europe. Moreover the alternative to the Habsburg monarchy would be a Greater Germany in which Prussia would be swamped.

Despite the tension in the Balkans, Bismarck succeeded in keeping Russia precariously in the German orbit until his retirement in 1890. In spite of the far-reaching reforms of the liberator Tsar Alexander II—emancipation of the serfs, reform of the universities and local government, and finally the promise of a consultative assembly—he was assassinated by revolutionary terrorists in 1881, and his successor, Alexander III, turned to repression and the solidarity of the conservative monarchies. But Bismarck's Reinsurance Treaty of 1887 with Russia was not renewed in 1890, and by 1894 a Franco-Russian *entente* had come into being. The forces which broke up the *Dreikaiserbund* were ultimately to produce the First World War. Bismarck was well aware of the dangerous situation that would arise if Austria became Germany's only effective ally. He wrote in his Memoirs that 'the security of our relations with Austria depends always on the possibility of our coming to terms with Russia'. Once Austria was sure that Germany had no alternative ally, she could blackmail Germany into supporting her at all costs. And her Balkan policy was bound to be increasingly hazardous under the increasing pressure of nationalism. The creation of the Dual Monarchy of Austria-Hungary in 1867 meant in effect that the German and Magyar races in the monarchy were given a free hand to repress the other racial groups, who were therefore forced to look outside the Empire for freedom. The attraction of an independent Serbia for the southern Slavs of the Empire eventually goaded Vienna into an attempt to crush Serbia at the cost of a European war.

Bismarck's attempt to preserve the status quo of 1871 was also frustrated by the internal development of Germany. The rapid industrialisation of the country after 1870 generated forces of expansion and of class struggle in the form of Social Democracy. The era of *Weltpolitik,* erratically guided by the unstable William II, began in the 1890s, and found natural expression in the creation of a great navy, in which the rapidly expanding steel output of the Ruhr could find an outlet.

XI

In the period 1890–1905 the international tensions in Europe were temporarily relaxed by the shift to colonial expansion, made possible by the opening up of Africa and China to European exploitation (*see* Chapter 18). Great Britain as the leading naval and colonial power was pressed hard by her rivals. Until 1865 Great Britain could afford a policy of isolation and freedom from Continental entanglements, strong in her position as the workshop of the world and the arbiter of the seas. But the complete powerlessness of Gladstone to mediate in the wars of German unification and the Franco-Prussian War was humiliating, and Disraeli's strong action against Russia over Turkey in 1878 was designed to restore Great Britain's influence on the Continent by splitting up the powerful bloc of the *Dreikaiserbund*. Disraeli taught the British people to turn to the Empire, and the trade depression of the eighteen-eighties, the rise of competing industrial countries, and the scramble for African territories stimulated imperialist feeling, especially when Joseph Chamberlain became Colonial Secretary in 1895.

There was friction with France over Egypt, and with Russia over China. German public opinion was in a mood of grievance and urgency born of the feeling that her belated unification had handicapped her in the race for colonies and world-power, and this feeling turned to jealousy and hatred of Great Britain. The appearance of a great German fleet, added to the hostile French and Russian fleets, forced the British Government to the conclusion at the turn of the century that Great Britain might be unable to stand the strain of an isolation guaranteed only by overwhelming naval supremacy. An attempt to come to terms with Germany failed, and Great Britain turned to France. The Russo-Japanese War (1904) hastened an Anglo-French *rapprochement*, as France needed an alternative ally while Russia was entangled in the Far East, and Great Britain, as the ally of Japan, had no wish to be embroiled with France, the ally of Russia.

The Anglo-French agreement was a shock to the German Government, as their diplomatic and naval policy had been based on the assumption that Great Britain could never be reconciled to France or Russia, and that she would eventually be forced to come to terms with Germany. William II failed to detach Russia from France by the still-born Treaty of Björko (1905), and the German Government resorted to the unwise tactics of trying to detach France from Great Britain by diplomatic bullying at the Algeciras Conference on Morocco, which had the opposite effect of converting the Anglo-French colonial agreement into a virtual military alliance. By 1907 Great Britain, France and Russia had come together to form the Triple Entente. The crisis caused by Austria-Hungary's annexation of Bosnia in 1908 had to be resolved by a German ultimatum to Russia, in support of Austria. Russia yielded to the threat, but it was certain that she would not yield in the next Balkan crisis. The second Moroccan incident over Agadir in 1911 led to the Anglo-French naval agreement by which the French fleet concentrated in the Mediterranean and the British fleet assumed responsibility for France's northern coast.

Great Britain was now committed to intervention on the Continent, to standing by France in the event of a European war. That event was immediately occasioned by the rottenness of the ancient Habsburg Empire. Germany was faced with the choice of abandoning Austria to collapse and subjecting herself to the diplomatic preponderance of the Triple Entente, or an appeal to arms while the balance of military strength was still on the side of the Central Powers. There could be little doubt about her choice when the murder of the Austrian heir to the throne touched off the next and fatal crisis.

Neither Germany nor any of the other Powers was deterred on the brink of war by a realisation of the kind of conflict on which they were embarking—a four-years' war of utter attrition which was to grind into dust the three great eastern empires and end the era of European predominance. Statesmen and soldiers were thinking in terms of the rapid, decisive wars of 1866 and 1870. Not even the soldiers had woken up to the fact that the development of quick-firing artillery and machine-guns would reduce a mobile war of manœuvre to a seige-warfare of trenches. In 1914 the forces unleashed by the Enlightenment and the French Revolution were turned to destruction. Science had provided weapons of incredible power, and nationalism had produced mass armies who were to slaughter each other by the million in the name of patriotism. Already, in seeking mastery over Nature and over his own destiny, within the traditional framework of competing power, man ran the risk of destroying himself.

XII

Such are the essentials of European power politics from the French Revolution to the First World War. These decisions were fateful for the world. Even more decisive had been the immense advances in knowledge which marked an age as creative as that of Descartes and Newton. For the first time, research became organised on a great professional scale; this network cut across political barriers, and not only did the nineteenth century professionalise its seventeenth and eighteenth century inheritance, but it showed original genius in many entirely new fields.

Its immense industrial achievement, and

the demographic changes that went with it, are described later (*see* Chapter 19). Nineteenth-century Europe was also rich in literature, music and the arts; in philosophy, in economic and political thought, it set the pattern of the modern world. The French writers of the Enlightenment had been deists when they were not atheists. The trend of thought since the Renaissance had increasingly given man the centre of the stage. Now he was placed firmly in his biological context. Lamarck had foreshadowed the modern idea of evolution, but it was Darwin's *Origin of Species* (1859) and his *Descent of Man* (1871) that marshalled the evidence. Man now appeared not as a special creation but as the most successful of the animals. Copernicus and Newton had opened up a new cosmology; Darwin and his collaborators revealed a new explanation in a new setting. This setting was vast in time and space. The geologists had systematised their science and revealed the antiquity of the earth; the geographers and climatologists had discovered the great alternating changes of continents and climates. Fundamental concepts in physics, biology and medicine were defined. By 1865 Lister was practising aseptic surgery and the use of anaesthetics had become common. Pasteur revolutionised pathology when he discovered the microbic causes of disease; by the seventies the bacteriologists were able to attack accepted scourges by elaborating methods of inoculation earlier hit upon by Jenner. When Röntgen discovered X-rays he gave medicine another formidable weapon, while Ross discovered that malaria was carried by mosquitoes. All these and other vital discoveries were the work of men of various nationalities and their achievements gave science an unprecedented prestige. Against its grim nationalist political background, the nineteenth century saw a profound alteration in the climate of

opinion which is still working itself out.

This scientific outlook was contrary to the Romantic movement which had dominated the early decades of the century. Literature and philosophy were conditioned by this tension. In general, as the decades wore on, writers became less romantic and more realistic. The novel was at its greatest. Tolstoy is probably the finest of all masters of this medium, while Dostoievsky, Turgeniev and Chekhov contributed to make Russian literature a world influence. Balzac, Stendhal and Flaubert, in their contrasting idioms, depicted the rich panorama of nineteenth-century society. Great Romantic poets—Byron, Tennyson, Victor Hugo and later poets of introspection and despair, expressed the Romantic climate and its decline. In music the inheritance of the romantics became more complex in Brahms; it culminated and coarsened in Wagner. In painting, the genius of Constable, Turner and Delacroix gave rise to the brilliant impressionist movement and its sequel. In architecture the neo-Gothic fashion did little to mitigate the ugliness of the great industrial towns. It is unlikely that any century had achieved more hideous architecture than the nineteenth. The old traditions of ordered design were swamped, architects catered more for the parvenu middle classes and the governments they dominated than for the kings, aristocrats and clergy, who had often been men of taste. Mass production, too, meant a degradation of craftsmanship and widespread vulgarity and imitation, the price of the astonishing rise in the standards of living of the mass of the Western peoples unprecedented in world history.

On the other hand, the neo-Gothic cult symbolised a new interest and understanding of the past. There had been brilliant historians in the eighteenth century, but the scholarship of a Ranke surpassed that of Gibbon since he had a new range of facts at his disposal. Systematically archives were ransacked, chronicles edited, multifarious sources set in order. Pitt-Rivers invented the techniques of modern archaeology; Bastian's *Man in History* and Tylor's *Primitive Culture* opened up new fields in anthropology; Maine and Maitland investigated the origins of Law in a new historical context. The contrast between the amateurish generalities of Maistre and Hegel in the earlier years of the century, and the professionalised knowledge of Durkheim's sociological method in the 'nineties show the change from romance to realism which can be traced through the whole century.

This change is also apparent in political thought, though the romantic impulse persisted much longer and in baser forms. It was a time of great systematisers and prophets, of men who thought they could discern the entire pattern of human history in a scientific 'explanation' of politics and economics, comparable, as Marx claimed for his revelation, to the work of Darwin. Hegel had devised a mysterious pattern of history in which world-historic peoples successively and inevitably came to predominance in accordance with a 'dialectic' law; Mazzini, on the other hand, equally a prophet of nationalism, proclaimed the self-determination of peoples, the ascent of humanity and the 'Law' of Progress. Together they expressed the gigantic myths of later nineteenth-century nationalism, militant, as in Treitschke; humanitarian and liberal, as expressed by President Wilson and briefly institutionalised by the League of Nations.

The other great nineteenth-century political myth derived from the French Revolution, but with Marx and Engels, political revolution became social and economic. The *Communist Manifesto* appeared in 1848, and *Das Kapital* in 1867. The first, a masterpiece of political warfare, called upon the proletarians of the world to unite in a ferocious attack on property; the second, together with Marx's other works, provided a pseudo-scientific doctrine whereby history could be explained and political action 'correctly' carried out. Here was a militant political creed, at once romantic and realist, and it was to shake the world, seizing its opportunity after the established order had brought itself to disaster in 1914 and winning power in Russia in the October Revolution of 1917. In the wake of the First World War the proto-Fascist ideas of Sorel and Pareto also contributed to the mass revolt against bourgeois society which culminated in Mussolini and Hitler, and marked a reversion to a barbaric social pattern unthinkable to the liberals of the early nineteenth century and to the original idealists of the Revolution.

Paradoxically, it was in the slow-moving constitutional states, which had avoided political revolution—in Great Britain, the Dominions and the United States; in the Scandinavian democracies, the Low Countries and Switzerland—that ideas of ordered liberty made better and more lasting headway. Here a steady but unspectacular campaign developed to meet the demand for social and economic change by constitutional procedures and governments responsive to public opinion. And it was the United States, whose War of Independence had brought about the final bankruptcy of the French Government which had been the immediate occasion of the Revolution, that was to throw a decisive weight into the two World Wars in which the old European system perished, and despite the establishment of totalitarian régimes, most significantly in the U.S.S.R. and in China, to secure great areas of the world for a continuation of the liberal and social-democratic experiment which the French Revolution had initiated.

During the nineteenth century Europe was the focus of world politics and economic enterprise; the foundation and swift expansion of new nations of European descent in vast territories overseas was perhaps, ultimately, more important. In North America there grew up in the United States the richest and most dynamic civilisation which the world has ever seen and in Canada the greatest member of the British Commonwealth. In Central and South America the tradition was Spanish and Portuguese; whereas in the north the original inhabitants had been overwhelmed, here the Europeans became racially mixed with the Indians and a different, though a rich and far-flung, society emerged. Meanwhile, away in the South Pacific, a whole new continent had been settled by people of British stock in Australia and an outpost of Western settlement established in New Zealand. Most of the islands of the South Seas became subject to European domination.

The United States

by M. A. Jones

In 1763 the American colonies had long enjoyed a substantial measure of political and economic freedom: they had owed it to their remoteness from Britain and to the neglect of successive British Governments. But the colonists had come to regard their immunity from imperial control not as a privilege born of circumstance but as a right lacking only formal acknowledgment (*see* Chapter 11). When the British Government attempted to recover its lost authority, the colonists protested at what they regarded as a tyrannical attempt to deprive them of their liberties.

The origin of the new British colonial policy adopted after 1763 was the need to reorganise an empire which had doubled in extent as a result of the Seven Years' War. The acquisition of the vast French possessions in North America presented Britain with a host of new problems relating to the West, not to speak of the difficulties she faced in administering Canada. And it became essential to make fresh provision for colonial defence since renewed French and Indian attacks were expected, while experience had seemed to show that provincial jealousies were too strong for defence to be left to the colonists.

The first measure of the new British programme to provoke colonial opposition was the Proclamation of 1763 which attempted to solve the Western problem by restricting settlement beyond the Alleghenies, an area the colonists had long coveted. But far more unpopular was the British decision to station a standing army

NORTH AMERICA

The Thirteen Colonies
Hudson Bay Co. Lands in mid-19th Century
Transcontinental Railways
Stages of Expansion
State Boundaries
International Frontiers

SCALE
0 200 400 600 800 1000 MILES

French
English c.1650
Land over 1,200 FT

SCALE
0 100 200 300 MILES

in America, and to require the colonists to contribute towards its support. To this end the mercantilist laws regulating colonial trade were more strictly enforced than before and, beginning with the Stamp Act of 1765, efforts were made to tax the colonists. These measures produced not only vehement colonial protest but open resistance in the form of commercial boycott and mob action. For almost a decade the British Government showed itself ready to temporise in the face of colonial intransigence, but in 1774, confronted with Boston's celebrated defiance of the Tea Act, it resolved on coercion.

This decision did much to overcome the internal divisions which until then had seriously hampered colonial unity. And once hostilities had begun, as they did at Lexington in April, 1775, American sentiment in favour of independence mounted steadily. Nevertheless, the more conservative colonists, apprehensive lest independence should be followed by social revolution, remained reluctant to abandon the imperial connection. Not until 4 July, 1776, when fighting had been in progress for more than a year and all hopes of accommodation within the Empire had clearly vanished, did the Continental Congress adopt the Declaration of Independence.

Even without external help the colonists might conceivably have made good their claim to independence. The British Navy had been allowed to decay, British generalship proved feeble and fumbling, and the task of subjugating permanently so vast an area was probably insuperable. Yet it was French intervention that proved decisive. After a Franco-American alliance had been signed in 1778, French military and naval assistance was afforded on such a scale that Washington could force Cornwallis' surrender at Yorktown in October, 1781. This defeat revealed to the British Government the futility of further coercive efforts,

and led to the opening of peace negotiations.

The signing of the Peace of Versailles in 1783 marked the end of the first successful colonial rebellion in modern history. Yet the American Revolution was much more than this. The Declaration of Independence brought into existence not merely a new nation, but one whose institutions and ideals were at once distinctive, experimental and challenging. By proclaiming a republic and designing a federal government for it, the founders of the United States rejected the accumulated political experience of Europe. Moreover, by proclaiming their belief in the equality of men, the founders not only prescribed a standard whereby American achievement could be measured, but laid down a principle which was to influence the whole of the Western world.

During the course of the Revolution great strides were made towards securing the rights on which Americans had rested their claim to independence. New state constitutions introduced broader principles of representation, specifically limited the powers of government and embodied Bills of Rights guaranteeing certain basic freedoms. Relics of feudalism like laws of primogeniture and entail were swept away; the separation of Church and State was decreed; criminal codes and prisons were reformed and, in the northern states, Negro slavery was abolished. Nevertheless there was more of promise than of performance in the youthful United States. Much remained to be done if Americans were to fulfil what they now conceived to be their peculiar destiny, to set an example to the rest of the world. American endeavour continued to be directed toward three main ends—the consolidation of independence, the strengthening of the federal union and the promotion of political and social democracy.

The need to combine for defence against Britain had made some form of union essential to the former colonies. But such had been their attachment to the principle of local liberty that the colonists had been unwilling to surrender to federal authority what they had just denied to an imperial Parliament. Hence the powers accorded the Federal Government by the Articles of Confederation of 1777 were extremely limited, and the Continental Congress proved in consequence incapable either of sustaining public credit, suppressing domestic insurrection or defending American rights against foreign encroachment. But although the defects of the Articles became increasingly apparent during the 1780s, the unanimous assent required for amendment was not forthcoming. Whereupon a Federal Convention, meeting at Philadelphia in 1787, took the unauthorised step of framing a new Constitution embodying a fresh distribution of powers between state and federal governments. Though not attempting either to establish a national government or to determine exactly where ultimate sovereignty lay, the Convention framed a document that went far to remedy the defects of the Articles. The Federal Government was given power over taxation and trade, a federal executive and judiciary were created and, most important of all, sanctions were provided for the enforcement of federal laws.

Despite the spirited opposition of those who saw in state rights the only true safeguard of American liberty, the Federal Constitution eventually won the approval of the states and went into force in 1789, the year of the French Revolution. And for the next twelve years control of the Federal Government remained with the Federalists, as the advocates of the new constitution were known. In their hands the Union was largely freed from the weaknesses that had threatened its existence under the Confederation. The success of Hamilton's financial measures restored public credit; the promptness with which the Whisky Rebellion of 1794 was suppressed proved the new Government's ability to deal with internal disorder; and treaties with Britain and Spain not only brought commercial advantages but rid American soil of the foreign troops who had stayed there ever since 1783. These and other Federalist achievements owed much to Washington who, though politically outshone by his brilliant lieutenants Hamilton and Jefferson, brought to the presidency a vision, a practical good sense and an authority none of his contemporaries could match. But after Washington's retirement in 1796 the Federalist decline was rapid. Factional quarrels and an ill-advised attempt in 1798 to proscribe their political opponents by the Alien and Sedition Acts, completely discredited the Federalists and led to their defeat in the presidential election of 1800.

The new president, Thomas Jefferson, came to office sworn to restore simplicity and frugality to the administration, and to reverse the tendency which had developed under Federalism for the central government to gain in power at the expense of the states. These aims he proved unable to attain, and the two events for which his administrations are best remembered afford an ironical commentary on Jefferson's professions whilst in opposition. It is doubtful if the purchase in 1803 of the huge Louisiana Territory from France—with British funds—which extended American boundaries to the Rockies, was a constitutional act, as even Jefferson himself acknowledged. Again, the policy of peaceable coercion, designed by Jefferson to compel the European belligerents to respect American rights at sea, involved a further extension of federal power to enforce the embargo.

The persistence of controversy over maritime rights, coupled with the eagerness of American frontiersmen to annex Canada, led in 1812 to renewed hostilities with Britain. An unsuccessful American invasion of Canada was followed by inconclusive fighting on the Great Lakes, and after a succession of British raids on American coastal cities, the war ended in January, 1815, with General Andrew Jackson's overwhelming defeat of the British at New Orleans. This engagement, with its rout of Peninsular veterans by an American militia force, together with some striking American successes at sea, gave to the war the character of a second war of independence. While no territorial gains resulted and the question of maritime rights remained unsettled, the conflict proved to Americans their ability to withstand the might of Britain single-handed and thus gave American nationalism an immense stimulus. The war of 1812, moreover, marked the end of American preoccupation with Europe. Henceforth, its security no longer menaced by European rivalries, the United States could afford to turn its back on the Old World.

II

American energies now turned to the peopling of the gigantic and empty West. Ever since 1763 the line of settlement had been advancing steadily westward beyond the Alleghenies, but now, in the generation after 1815, the frontier was carried to the Mississippi and then to the Pacific. The pressure of population, the attraction of virgin land, the defeat and removal of the Indians, the improvement of transport facilities and the lure of Californian gold—these were among the forces that now imparted to the westward movement an unprecedented momentum.

This swift westward rush proved to be decisive for American development during the next half century. It soon gave a significant shift in the Union's political centre of gravity. The admission of new Western communities swelled the number of states embraced by the Union to twenty-two by 1820, and to thirty-three by 1860. This could not fail to increase Western influence in the Union at the expense of that of the original thirteen states. It was the West which took the lead in demanding war with Britain in 1812, and sixteen years later the outstanding military hero of that conflict, Andrew Jackson, became the first Westerner to be elected president.

Yet Jackson was the idol not only of Westerners but of the common man everywhere, and his election symbolised the rise of a new and vigorous democratic movement which was to carry the United States appreciably nearer the goals envisaged by its founders. Jacksonian democracy brought with it universal white manhood suffrage and a phenomenal increase of the electorate. It led also to the growth of modern party organisation, the introduction of the nominating convention, and the popular election of delegates to the electoral college, all of which tended to make governmental machinery more responsive to the popular will. And as well as being a period of rapid political change, the age of Jackson was one also of social and intellectual ferment which gave birth to a host of humanitarian movements, advocating, for example, women's suffrage, temperance reform and the abolition of Negro slavery.

Jacksonian democracy also engendered the widespread belief in the 'manifest destiny' of the United States to extend its institutions over the whole of the North American continent. Out of this belief sprang an aggressive expansionist urge which in the 1840s led first to controversy with Britain over Oregon and then to war with Mexico over the Texan boundary. The Mexican War of 1846-8 brought the United States swift military victory and enormous territorial gains, among them California, New Mexico and Utah. But these successes were won only at the cost of rekindling the long-smouldering antipathy between the free and slave states of the Union. The Mexican War, indeed, ushered in a decade of acute sectional controversy which ultimately ended in Civil War.

Sectionalism, implying a narrow devotion to local interests, was a force which ever since the founding of the republic had threatened its stability and permanence. The Federal Constitution itself was largely a 'bundle of compromises' made necessary by the strength of competing sectional interests. And although between 1789 and 1861 the delicate plant of American nationalism took firmer root, there was never a time when the secession of one section or another did not seem possible. Under the Federalists sectionalism had been most marked in the West, largely owing to frontier dissatisfaction at the failure of the Federal Government to secure the free navigation of the Mississippi. And although, under the Jeffersonian Republicans, the discontent of the West was assuaged by the Louisiana Purchase, it then became the turn of New England to think of separation. Convinced that the injuries sustained by her commerce from 1807 onwards had been deliberately planned by the agrarian South and West, New England was half ready by the end of the war of 1812 to consider forming a separate confederation.

It was, however, Southern sectionalism that ultimately proved the greatest danger to the Union. After 1815 the South became increasingly a minority section. Untouched both by the great tide of European immigration and by the industrial develop-

ments which together were transforming the rest of the country, the South remained predominantly rural, falling ever further behind in the race for population and wealth. For its relative decline the South found a ready explanation in the operation of the Federal Government, and especially in Federal laws respecting tariffs, shipping, public works and the disposal of public lands. All these measures were alleged by Southerners to confer unfair advantages on the North, and in these circumstances the South fell back, as had other minority sections before it, upon the concept of state rights as a constitutional shield for its interests. By 1832 one Southern state, South Carolina, had so completely embraced the state rights philosophy that it passed an ordinance of nullification against a Federal tariff act, succeeding thereby in securing a modification of its provisions.

But the South was set apart from the rest of the nation not so much by its rural character and interests, as by its vast numbers of Negro slaves. And the desire to preserve the 'peculiar institution' of Negro slavery proved much more powerful than did a mere concern for economic interests. After 1830, owing to the rapid spread of cotton cultivation based on slave labour, Southern opinion increasingly asserted that slavery was a 'positive good' besides providing the essential basis of Southern society. Since, in the Northern states, the same period saw the rise of a militant Abolitionist movement, a bitter sectional controversy over slavery now developed. Most Northerners, however, remained unsympathetic to Abolitionism, and even as late as the Civil War were prepared to abide by those provisions of the Constitution which forbade Federal interference with slavery in the states. The real clash of sectional opinion arose over the status of slavery, not in the states, but in those partly settled regions of the West known as territories.

The question of slavery in the territories had become a burning issue as early as 1819. Missouri, a part of the Louisiana Purchase, had sought admission to the Union as a slave state. A compromise had then been devised, prohibiting slavery in the rest of the Louisiana Purchase north of the line 36° 30′, but permitting it to the south. The Missouri Compromise stilled for a time the controversy over slavery in the territories, but the acquisition of vast new areas as a result of the Mexican War reopened the question. And by the 1840s sectional attitudes had become much more extreme than before. The South was now unanimous that slavery had to expand in order to survive; the North was coming increasingly to feel that to allow slavery to expand beyond its existing limits, would be to make a mockery of American democratic ideals. Nevertheless in 1850 a compromise was achieved by applying to the Mexican cession the principle of 'popular sovereignty', which allowed the actual settlers of the new territories to settle the question of slavery for themselves. But after a lull of only four years the whole controversy was revived in aggravated form. A measure was passed which applied 'popular sovereignty' to the northern half of the Louisiana Purchase, and appeared to open to slavery an area hitherto believed to be free soil. Out of the agitation produced by the Kansas-Nebraska Act of 1854 was born the Republican party, sworn to oppose the further spread of slavery. And when in 1860 the new party's candidate, Abraham Lincoln, was elected to the presidency, eleven Southern states thought their 'peculiar institution' so menaced that they seceded from the Union.

The epic struggle that followed was, except for the Napoleonic Wars, the most sanguinary of nineteenth-century conflicts, for it was to result in the death or wounding of more than a million men. For much of the Civil War, the newly-formed Southern Confederacy seemed invincible. Its armies, although outnumbered, were magnificently commanded and were able to inflict on its Federal adversaries a long succession of appalling defeats. But the gallantry and determination of the South were matched by the North's steadfast devotion to the Union, and at the last the superior material resources of the Northern States prevailed. In April, 1865, after four years of grim, unrelenting war, the South's bid for independence ended with Lee's surrender to Grant at Appomattox.

Lincoln's Emancipation Proclamation, issued as a war measure in January, 1863, had dealt slavery a mortal blow, and the ratification of the Thirteenth Amendment to the Constitution in 1865 removed the last vestiges of an institution which had long been a reproach to American aspirations. Yet the abolition of slavery had never been allowed to become the primary purpose of the struggle. The American Civil War remained throughout what Lincoln had proclaimed it to be, a war for the Union. And the preservation of American unity was its greatest and most far-reaching result. But sectional reconciliation was not to follow. The assassination of Lincoln removed the only influence capable of solving the thorny problems of Reconstruction. Lincoln's successor, Andrew Johnson, was anxious that the Southern States should return to the Union as quickly as possible, but his political maladroitness and his apparent lack of concern for the welfare of the freed Negroes lost him the support of his party and led to his impeachment. The Reconstruction policy actually followed was that of the Congressional Radicals, a heterogeneous group in whom a genuine concern for Negro advancement was mixed with a determination to resist any settlement that would threaten Republican dominance of national affairs. As the price of Southern re-admission to the Union, they insisted upon Negro suffrage and the proscription of ex-Confederates. Upon the Southern States, moreover, they imposed political régimes based upon Negro votes and upheld by Federal military power. Most of these 'carpetbag' governments were dominated, not by Negroes, but by white men but they were strenuously resisted by the majority of Southern whites who saw them as the instruments of Africanisation and misrule. They were, indeed, characterised by extravagance and corruption but they made a real effort to promote Negro welfare and they carried out many much-needed reforms, particularly in the sphere of education. Such governments could survive, however, only so long as Northern opinion was prepared to support a policy of coercion. But from 1870 onward the North grew increasingly disillusioned with the experiment of Radical Reconstruction. It was finally abandoned in 1877, when the last Federal troops were withdrawn. Their departure marked the end, for almost a century, of Federal attempts to break the pattern of white supremacy in the South.

With the end of Reconstruction, American politics lapsed into a torpor which was not shaken off for twenty years. The final settlement of issues arising from the Civil War left no difference of principle between the parties, and national elections became in consequence mere struggles for power. But the drabness of politics was due chiefly to the fact that American energies were absorbed elsewhere.

These were the decisive years when Americans devoted themselves wholeheartedly to the development of a country as lavishly endowed by Nature as any in the world. Industry, which had received a great impetus from the Civil War, made giant strides in the generation that followed. Protected by the mass of tariff, banking and railroad legislation enacted by a sympathetic Congress, sustained by the decisions of the Supreme Court, and directed by individuals as ruthless as they were efficient, iron and steel, mining, oil, flour-milling and meat-packing industries enjoyed an unparalleled expansion. So rapid was their growth, indeed, that by the end of the century the United States had outstripped the rest of the world in a colossal industrial achievement. At the same time the construction of a transcontinental railroad network opened up for settlement the last unpeopled region of the immense country. The Great Plains, invaded first by miners and then by cattlemen, were finally reclaimed for agriculture when more scientific farming techniques were devised and when industry provided improved farm machinery. By 1890 the settled area of the United States had doubled within a generation and the frontier had disappeared.

The passing of the frontier, and industry's growth to maturity, contributed to produce in the 'nineties a revival of American interest in the outside world. For a generation Americans had been too preoccupied with domestic concerns to pay much attention to foreign affairs. But now, with the exploitation of the continent well in hand, and with a growing consciousness of America's new-found and gigantic strength, there arose a demand that the United States should play a more active part in world affairs. An outlet was found for these ambitions in Cuba's efforts to win her independence from Spain, and in 1898, in response to overwhelming popular pressure, the United States intervened.

From the Spanish-American War Americans gained a colonial empire. Despite the protests of those who thought imperialism incompatible with democracy, the Philippines, Puerto Rico and Guam were acquired from Spain; the Hawaiian Islands were annexed and a protectorate was established over part of Samoa. And as a further consequence of this expansionist mood, the United States began to pursue a more aggressive foreign policy in the Far East and Central America, the climax being Theodore Roosevelt's acquisition of the Panama Canal Zone in 1903. It was Roosevelt's mediation that ended the Russo-Japanese War of 1905, while in the following year he sent an American representative to the Algeciras conference. Yet all this activity in foreign affairs did not mean that the United States was prepared to abandon her traditional isolationism. The neutrality she proclaimed at the outbreak of the First World War was supported by nearly every American, and it was only when the Germans began unrestricted submarine warfare that the United States was drawn in.

The First World War brought to an end the efforts of the preceding generation to reform the manifold evils that had accompanied the industrial age. The growth of city slums, the prevalence of unemployment and child labour, the widening gulf between rich and poor, and the increasing power of corporate wealth over the life of the community—this was only part of the price that America had had to pay to become the world's greatest manufacturing nation. The first attempt at reform came in the 1890s from the farmers who blamed their declining prosperity on the undue favour shown to big business by the Federal Government. The agrarians seized on bi-metallism as the panacea for their ills, and the Populist party was formed to demand the free and unlimited coinage of silver. Yet despite the enthusiasm of the rural West and South, Populism went down to defeat in the presidential election of 1896, and was never thereafter a serious political force. But the reform impulse lived on in Progressivism, a movement which operated not as a separate party but within the existing political structure. At the municipal level the main Progressive target was political corruption: in the states Progressives aimed at remodelling government to make it more responsive to the popular will: and in national politics their concern was to subject corporate wealth to the restraints of Federal power. These aims first began to be realised in Theodore Roosevelt's administration, but it was under Woodrow Wilson that the greatest gains were made. By 1917 Progressives could claim impressive achievements in tariff revision, banking reform and the regulation of railroads and trusts, as well as in other fields. But many of these gains proved short-lived and the work of reform had to be tackled afresh in the era of the New Deal.

The massive and decisive contribution of the United States to the defeat of the Central powers brought recognition of America's military as well as economic might. The colonies that had revolted from the British Crown had become by 1918 the richest and the strongest power in the world.

Canada

by Jack Simmons

Canada is within the British Commonwealth today, and almost half her population is of British descent. Yet the origins of the state are not British at all: they are Indian and French.

The Indians probably migrated originally from Asia, by way of the Behring Strait and Alaska. They were small in numbers—perhaps 200,000 all told, within the whole of what we now call Canada—when the first Europeans arrived. They made no contact with the outside world, living a tough, self-centred life, dominated at all times by the unending struggle for food in a hard country. Technologically, they were not advanced. They knew nothing of the use of iron, and very little of weaving. Systematic agriculture was practised only by one group of tribes: the 'Five Nations' of the Iroquois, living in what is now south-eastern Ontario and the northern part of the State of New York. Politically, also, the Iroquois were the most advanced of the Indians in Canada. Their Government bore a 'federal' character. It was based on the independent authority of the tribes, co-ordinated in a central council whose members were drawn from each of them in fixed proportions, and cemented by an unusual class-structure, which overrode tribal divisions. The Iroquois proved, in the long run, the most successful opponents of the invading French. It was not that they were more warlike than their neighbours. They were better organised, and better fed.

Though the first Europeans to visit Newfoundland and Labrador were English seamen from Bristol, and though Gilbert took possession of Newfoundland on behalf of Elizabeth I in 1583, it was the French who first developed an interest in the Gulf of St Lawrence and its hinterland.

Their earliest permanent settlement was made in Acadia (Nova Scotia) in 1605. But the French had already penetrated much farther to the west, up the great river, and three years later under Champlain they established a post at Quebec. It was well chosen, at a point where the river narrowed, flowing beneath Cape Diamond, a natural fortress. At once it became the capital of the new French colony on the St Lawrence, with Montreal as its sister, 200 miles upstream, where the rapids on the river began.

The French settlements grew very slowly. Although at first they were run by chartered companies, Louis XIV took them directly under the control of the Crown, establishing an administration in them that was modelled on that of the provinces at home. It was, on paper, a rigid administration—much as Philip II's had been in the Spanish Empire; but it was not entirely rigid in its working. For physical reasons alone, immediate control of the colonies from France was impossible. It was not only that they were separated by the Atlantic. The St Lawrence was ice-bound for half the year. Naturally, therefore, the Government at Quebec dealt with its problems as best it could, as far as possible in agreement with the colonists, who were rough folk to cross.

Yet, though the rigidity of the *ancien régime* in Canada can be exaggerated, it was a closed world, very narrowly confined, contrasting sharply in some ways with the English colonies farther south. The settlements were built up largely by the discontented, the misfits, who had left home because they were political or religious nonconformists. In America, the colonists had scattered themselves in numerous settlements, where they were joined by immigrants from other European countries; and their population was rising fast, to stand by the middle of the eighteenth century at 1,500,000. By that time the colonists in Canada still numbered no more than 65,000. They were Frenchmen and orthodox Roman Catholics—the Governments of Louis XIV and his successor refused to allow Protestants to emigrate to the colonies; and the dominant religious influence on the Canadian Government was exercised by the Society of Jesus.

All in all, then, French Canada was an inward-looking society. After 1713, moreover, when Acadia and Newfoundland passed under British control, it was politically isolated, defended only by French posts in the Gulf of St Lawrence. Nevertheless, the French-Canadians were already developing the fur trade to the north and west of their colony, in rivalry with the British, established on Hudson's Bay, and with the Indians. Most important of all, they were pushing down into the Ohio basin, and that was a cause of alarm to the Thirteen Colonies of Britain. This was a vital struggle. For a long time the advantage lay on the whole with the French. But in the Seven Years' War the British Government, under the elder Pitt, grasped the importance of the issue, whilst the French were concentrating their attention too closely on the war in Europe to spare troops or supplies in adequate quantity for America (*see* Chapter 15). A British expeditionary force was prepared against Quebec, and the city was taken in 1759. Next year Montreal fell too. French Canada was conquered, and kept by Britain at the Peace of Paris in 1763.

To a student of politics, the century that stretches from 1763 to the confederation of Canada in 1867 is of unusual interest. It saw first the establishment of a new administration, whose task it was to learn to live on easy terms with people who were naturally antagonistic to it: different from their conquerors in race, religion, language, laws, and customs. This was achieved, through common sense and forbearance on both sides. The sign of the new Government's success soon appeared. By the Quebec Act of 1774 it restored to the Canadians the French system of civil law under which they had been brought up, and it re-established the Roman Catholic Church. This was a wise and generous gesture, in which Lord North's Government showed itself in advance of popular opinion in Britain—as the fury of the anti-Catholic Gordon Riots in London proved six years later. When the War of American Independence began, the Canadians did not seize the opportunity to join in. They remained passive under British rule, even when France herself entered the war against Britain in 1778. The new Government, in fact, succeeded in its difficult task of ruling the Canadians firmly, yet fairly; and when the test came, they showed their appreciation.

Having dealt successfully with one problem, the Government had to face another almost at once. When French Canada fell into British hands, British traders and settlers began to move into the country, establishing themselves side by side with the French. At the conclusion of the War of Independence their number was greatly increased by the migration of Loyalists from the new United States; men who had fought for the Imperial Government, or at all events sympathised with it, and did not wish to live under the new republic. Some 35,000 of these Loyalists went to Nova Scotia and to a new country that was carved out of it for them, christened New Brunswick. A smaller number—perhaps 6000–7000—went into Canada itself. That produced a fresh political problem. The immigrants had been accustomed to a different government from that established in Canada, they knew nothing of its French civil law, and they were Protestants—militant Protestants, some of them. How could the new settlers and the old be ruled as one?

After prolonged consideration, the British Government decided that the problem could be solved only by partition. Accordingly, in 1791 the country was divided into two provinces, Upper Canada to the west, Lower Canada to the east. Upper Canada, the germ of the modern Province of Ontario, was thought of as a country for British settlers; Lower Canada was the old French colony, including Quebec and Montreal. Each of the two provinces was to have its own government with an elected representative assembly; each was to determine its own system of civil law, which meant that British law was established in the Upper Province, while French law was retained in the Lower.

It was a neat solution, on truly liberal lines. For a time it worked fairly well in practice: well enough, at any rate, to keep both provinces generally loyal during the Anglo-American War of 1812. But it could not be permanently successful. For one thing, a substantial British minority was established in Lower Canada at the time when the division was made. The relations between the two provinces, moreover, were never friendly; and Lower Canada could cut off the Upper Provinces' trade with the St Lawrence and the sea. Within each province, too, there was a sharp struggle between government and assembly. The upshot was a couple of small rebellions in 1837: trifling demonstrations, no more, yet alarming enough to force Britain to give Canada its serious consideration.

The Government sent out Lord Durham

as High Commissioner, to inquire into the causes of the trouble. His stay in the country was unexpectedly brief, lasting only five months in all. Yet on his return home he was able to produce a report (1839) that showed a deep insight into the problems he was dealing with and put forward effective recommendations for solving them. He quickly decided that the partition of 1791 had been a mistake and advised the reunion of the provinces. But on a new political basis: to resolve the continual conflicts he proposed the introduction of a system of 'responsible government', under which the Governor would compose his Executive Council of politicians who enjoyed the confidence of the assembly. Durham recognised that this meant handing over control from the officials to the popularly-elected legislature. He welcomed that, but at the same time he suggested that the Government in London should continue to keep in its hands certain matters of general concern to Great Britain and the whole of the British Empire, such as foreign policy and defence.

Responsible government was not invented by Durham. Its essential principle was no more than the principle of parliamentary government working in Britain at the time. But he did offer a means by which the system could be applied to the government of dependencies, and applied gradually, with flexibility and ease. Although his recommendations on the point were not implemented immediately, they came to be quietly accepted in the course of the following decade.

Durham did not, however, believe that the struggle between the governors and assemblies was the most important element in Canadian politics. 'I expected to find a contest between a government and a people', he wrote: 'I found two nations warring in the bosom of a single state:

I found a struggle, not of principles but of races.' He was the first British politician to understand this, and his analysis of the relations between French and British in Lower Canada is brilliantly sharp and vivid. The burden of it was that the French Canadians were hopelessly behind the times, 'an old and stationary society in a new and progressive world'. There was much truth in this contention. They were essentially men of the *ancien régime*. They had been scarcely touched by the Revolution of 1789—recoiling from it in horror, since it destroyed everything they believed in: the Church, the monarchy, all the ancient institutions of France. And now, side by side with them, a new community was growing up, which seemed to represent all that they disliked and disapproved of: brash, pushing, commercially-minded, Radical and Protestant.

This was clear to Durham, and he had a remedy for it. Firmly managed, the reunion of the two provinces would, he believed, do the trick. It would place the French Canadians in a minority and so secure leadership in the new Government to the British. No doubt the French would resent this at first: but soon they would come to see the merits of British parliamentary government, and insensibly they would abandon their old-fashioned ways of life and thought. It was a miscalculation, springing from a characteristic rationalism. Durham and his contemporaries had hardly yet been obliged, as we have, to take account of the force of nationalist passion.

The reunion of the provinces, put through in 1840, did not reduce the antagonism between the races. Within twenty years a new solution to the problem was being discussed. Durham himself had looked forward to an ultimate union of the whole of British North America, when the Maritime Provinces at the mouth of the St Lawrence could be physically integrated with Canada proper, by a railway, for example, open all through the winter, when the river was closed by ice. That 'Inter-colonial Railway' was begun in the 'fifties, and it went forward side by side with its political counterpart: federation. The reunion of the Canadas might be working badly, but the previous divisions had also proved unworkable. The only other possibility was to split Upper and Lower Canada apart again, to make them separate provinces within a federation.

After long argument, the outline of a federal scheme was agreed between the colonies; and it was put into effect by the Imperial Government in the British North America Act of 1867. This brought Canada and the Maritime Provinces under one federal government, which came to be called, almost at once, 'The Dominion of Canada'. The arrangement excluded two other British territories in North America. Newfoundland preferred to remain outside and did not become a Province of Canada until 1949. British Columbia, on the Pacific coast, was physically detached from the colonies based on the St Lawrence. But its isolation was dangerous, and it entered the confederation in 1871, on one clear condition, however: that a railway should be built forthwith, across the continent, to link it with the other provinces of the Dominion. When this railway—the Canadian Pacific—was completed in 1885, 'British North America' became a reality, not just a grand phrase. It led directly to the opening-up of the prairies over which it passed. The political signs of this were the creation of the new Provinces of Manitoba in 1870 and Saskatchewan and Alberta in 1905. They were peopled in large part, as Ontario had been, by British settlers—more than 200,000 went to Saskatchewan alone in 1901-11. But other immigrants moved up from the United States, and Central Europeans, too, settled on the prairies in substantial numbers.

These were signs of a gradual process that has transformed the racial structure of Canada. Its total population has quadrupled since the beginning of this century, standing at over twenty-one million today. But between the two censuses of 1911 and 1951, the proportion of British Canadians declined by 6 per cent, whilst the Canadians descended from peoples of other European stock increased by 8 per cent. The French accounted for only a quarter of this increase, and this consciousness of being increasingly in a minority has been a factor in the upsurge of Quebec separatism seen in 1970. A mixture of races is, in fact, occurring in Canada—as in the United States, on a far bigger scale, over a longer period. Though the original British and French stocks remain dominant in eastern Canada, they have not the same supremacy in the west. As for the aboriginal Indians and Eskimo, they had dwindled fifty years ago to little more than 100,000; but their decline has been arrested, and there are now some 230,000 Indians and 15,000 Eskimo.

These factors have coincided with a great change in the position of Canada in the world. Among the British Domin-ions she has always held the senior place. She led the way in self-government, in political unification, in developing a foreign policy independent of Great Britain's. She has always had a special part to play in the relations between Britain and the United States. The development of long-distance aviation has given her a quite new outlook. By the polar routes she is the buffer state between Soviet Russia and the United States. Strategically, her interests are now in many ways quite different from those of Europe.

Why then has she not severed her political links with the Old World and joined the United States? The answer to that question can be given partly in terms of current economic and political rivalries. But it is fully intelligible only in the light of history. Canada and the United States may be separated by an undefended frontier that is almost entirely artificial. Yet they are founded on different, even antagonistic, traditions: Catholic French Canada and Puritan New England, British Loyalists and American Republicans. The descendants of these original groups can live on good terms with one another, as neighbours. In instincts and feelings they remain separate; and the separation is deep enough to keep them politically apart.

Latin America

by C. R. S. Harris

Such was the sequel in the North to the European settlement which had begun in the sixteenth and seventeenth centuries. In Central and South America the most remarkable feature of the Spanish and Portuguese colonial empires was the very small number of Europeans by which their immense territories were settled and organised (*see* Chapter 13). By the third quarter of the sixteenth century, Spanish America—the great West Indian Islands, the whole of Central, and a large part of South America—probably contained only about 160,000 persons of pure Spanish descent, ruling over at least eight million Indians. In the Caribbean area so many of the native Indians had been wiped out by war, oppression and disease, that the

POLITICAL DEVELOPMENT OF SOUTH AMERICA

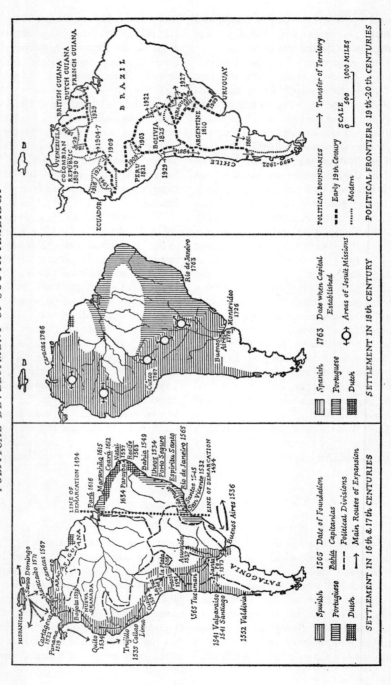

SETTLEMENT IN 16th & 17th CENTURIES

- Spanish
- Portuguese
- Dutch
- 1505   Date of Foundation
- *Bahia*   Capitanias
- - - - Political Divisions
- → Main Routes of Expansion

HISPANIOLA
Santo Domingo 1571
Maracaibo 1567
Cartagena Coracas 1567
Panama 1519
CARACAS
S GUIANA
Bogota 1539
NUEVA GRANADA
Quito 1534
Trujillo
1535 Callao
Lima
1565 Tucuman
Potosi
1541 Valparaiso
1541 Santiago
1552 Valdivia
1565
Asunción 1537
Santa Fe 1573
La Plata
Buenos Aires 1536
PATAGONIA
LINE OF DEMARCATION 1494
Pará 1616
Maranhão 1615
Ceará 1612
Natal
Parayba 1597
Recife
1563
Bahia 1549
Olinos 1534
Porto Seguro
Espiritu Santo
Rio de Janeiro 1532
Santos 1545
San Vicente 1565
LINE OF DEMARCATION 1494

SETTLEMENT IN 18th CENTURY

- Spanish
- Portuguese
- Dutch
- 1763   Date when Capital Established
- ⊕   Areas of Jesuit Missions

Caracas 1786
Cuzco 1787
Buenos Aires 1778
Montevideo 1726
Rio de Janeiro 1763

POLITICAL FRONTIERS 19th-20th CENTURIES

POLITICAL BOUNDARIES
- - - Early 19th Century
- - - Modern
- · · · · ·

→ Transfer of Territory

SCALE
0 500 1,000 MILES

VENEZUELA
BRITISH GUIANA
DUTCH GUIANA
FRENCH GUIANA
COLOMBIAN REPUBLIC 1819-30
ECUADOR
B R A Z I L
PERU 1821
BOLIVIA 1825
PARAGUAY
ARGENTINE 1810
URUGUAY
CHILE

importation of Negro slaves on a substantial scale had already taken place, a process which was to affect profoundly the racial composition of the West Indies, parts of Spanish South America and still more of Brazil.

The attitude to the Indians of the Iberian immigrant, himself often of mixed descent, for both Spaniards and Portuguese had big Moorish and Jewish elements in their ancestry, was in one respect very different from that of the English settler in North America. The *conquistadores* and earliest settlers arrived in the new hemisphere without their wives; quite a number of them married native princesses, and some of them took native concubines. But by the middle of the sixteenth century, the Spaniard had begun to bring his family with him, and the *mestizo* consequently came to be looked upon as the offspring of an illegitimate union. Even so he was separated from the Spaniard not so much by a colour bar as by his social position, which was often little inferior to that of the poorer white. Moreover pedantic purity of blood was never necessary for acceptance in the class of whites. Social position and a reasonably European appearance covered a multitude of indiscretions. In Spanish America these liberal principles were not so readily applied to the Negro. Latin America thus came to be formed of a number of societies containing every band in the spectrum of red, black and white. According to the most reliable estimates, Spanish America at the end of the colonial period (1823) had about seventeen million inhabitants, of which rather less than a fifth were white, nearly a half pure Indians, and about a third *mestizos*, or other persons of mixed blood.

In spite of the black legend of 'the devildoms of Spain', so long current in Anglo-Saxon histories, it is now universally admitted that the civilising mission of the Spaniards, in spite of flagrant abuses, cannot be dismissed as mere hypocrisy. Though the oppression of territorial serfdom and slavery in the mines were notorious, it is doubtful whether the condition of the common people under the Incas was any happier; owing to their limited agricultural technique and resources, their standard of living had been perhaps even lower. Time and again the Spanish monarchs and the Church attempted, mostly in vain, to improve the lot of the Indian. Neither admitted the Aristotelian doctrine of natural slavery, so easily applied to subject races, nor, in spite of the fact that Spaniards were in a small minority, was there any social or spiritual *apartheid*. The history of the missions in the south of the United States, in Brazil, and in Paraguay, where the Jesuits set up a species of Platonic republics, forms a striking contrast to the treatment of the Indian by the British settlers in North America.

There were also two other respects in which the Spanish colonial system differed markedly from the British. The basis of the Spanish system was essentially urban. True to the Roman tradition, the first thing the Spaniard did in landing was to found and lay out a town. In the English colonies the town grew up to meet the needs of the inhabitants of the countryside; in the Spanish, the countryside was organised to meet the needs of the town. But though this urban basis might have been made the foundation of a system of self-government, the absolutist tendencies of the Spanish monarchy worked in the opposite direction. The English colonists from the earliest times started to evolve arrangements for managing their own affairs, but the Spanish colonists were from the beginning rigidly controlled in the minutest details by the monarch through the Council of the Indies. The most important offices were held almost exclusively by Spaniards sent out from the mother-country, who returned to it, like the British Indian Civil Servant, after their period of office was over. Only the minor posts, like membership of the municipal councils (*cabildos*), were open to the creoles (American-born persons of Spanish descent). Of a total of 170 Viceroys between 1535 and 1813, only four were Americans, and of 160 officials of the second rank (Captains-General or Presidents) only fourteen. Of 706 bishops, only 105 were creoles, and those almost entirely of unimportant dioceses. Nor were the grievances of the creoles confined to this preference given to the *peninsulares*. Their trade was restricted by the monopoly granted to the merchants of Seville and Cadiz and by the twice-yearly convoys, as well as by the intermittent though mostly ineffectual prohibition of domestic manufactures. These restrictions were, it is true, tempered by widespread contraband and corruption, but that did not increase the creole's respect for Spanish rule. It was not until the second half of the eighteenth century that a more liberal policy of fostering trade within the Spanish dominions was inaugurated under the Bourbon monarchs—too late to prevent the increase of a resentful conviction of exploitation by the mother-country.

The introduction of European crops, domestic animals, and means of transport had added enormous agricultural resources to the indigenous wealth of sugar, cocoa and tobacco, and to the riches gained from the mining of the precious metals, mostly silver, notwithstanding the persistent legend of *El Dorado*. This wealth was concentrated in the hands of a small class of creole landowners living off the exploitation of an Indian peonage depressed to the bare subsistence level. Its members were often inferior neither by birth

or possessions to the clique of peninsular officials. Round the Viceregal courts was grouped a highly cultivated though limited society whose level of culture was probably a good deal higher than that to be found in the British colonies. Two universities, those of Mexico and Lima, had already been founded before the end of the sixteenth century and there were several more to follow. The creole contribution to Spanish literature was by no means negligible—to mention only the Mexican poetess Suor Inéz de la Cruz. The expulsion of the *peninsulares* thus gave birth to family republics which were more or less narrow oligarchies based on an aristocratic tradition entirely different from the democratic self-governing communities of British America, based on the pioneer farmer.

II

Notwithstanding the vigilance of the Inquisition, the seeds of the French intellectual movements of the eighteenth century had spread from Spain to the colonies in the days of the enlightened monarch Charles III. The impact of the French Revolution, even more than that of the American, profoundly stimulated the more progressive sections of the creoles, but the efficient cause of the independence movement came from quite a different source, the usurpation by Napoleon of the Spanish throne. The administrative chaos which followed this event gave the partisans of independence their long-sought opportunity, and tipped the scales in their favour, though only after some fifteen years of civil war, won by two great military leaders, Bolívar and San Martín.

The revolution broke out in 1810 almost simultaneously in Mexico, Venezuela and Buenos Aires. In Mexico it was a *mestizo* priest, Hidalgo, who raised the 'cry of

Dolores', and another *mestizo*, Morelos, who took up his torch. But the revolution was suppressed, and ten years of war were needed to establish Mexican independence. In the southern Viceroyalty the Spaniards never succeeded in recovering the offensive, though Argentine independence was not proclaimed until 1816, and it was the Argentine leader San Martín, who liberated Chile and a large part of Peru. Bolívar's fate hung long in the balance; Sucre's 'crowning mercy' of Ayacucho only enabled him to complete the expulsion of the Spaniards from South America in 1825. And Spain managed to retain control of Cuba and Puerto Rico till the end of the nineteenth century.

Thanks to British naval supremacy and the Monroe doctrine, the South American republics were permitted to work out their destinies unhampered by foreign interference. The fate of Mexico was very different. At the end of the eighteenth century New Spain stretched from Florida to beyond San Francisco, but American ideas of manifest destiny soon led to its contraction. Before the end of the colonial epoch both Florida and Louisiana had been handed over to the United States, and the annexation of Texas and cessions resulting from the Mexican War (1846–8) reduced the republic to its present dimensions. Emboldened by the American Civil War, Napoleon III established under his patronage the short-lived Empire of the unfortunate Habsburg Maximilian. Nor was American intervention confined to Central America. United States policy would tolerate no European power near its southern shores. The war of 1898 finally deprived Spain of her last American possessions.

III

It might have been expected that common Spanish descent and tradition would have resulted in a Latin United States of South America. But this was not to be, largely because the only sphere of creole activity had been the parish politics of the *cabildo*. Bolívar's dreams of a pan-American federation were quite beyond the comprehension of all but a few of the new leaders. Even after independence had been attained, the rivalries of the local provincial 'bosses', the *caudillos*, constantly threatened to break up the newly formed republics, whose eventual territorial pattern followed closely that of the colonial administrative divisions.

In these circumstances it was almost inevitable that inexperienced oligarchies born of civil war should, in spite of constitutions based largely on that of the United States, fall a victim to dictatorships. During their early years most of them were ruled by a succession of often fantastic, and nearly always, military dictators. But before the century was out, Colombia, Chile and Peru had developed a tradition of fairly stable, albeit intermittent, constitutional government, and Argentina, after 1880, enjoyed fifty years of constitutional government before relapsing. But in many, perhaps in most, Latin American states, it is still true that the changes of government brought about in Western Europe by a general election can only be effected by a revolution. In those states where comparatively stable government has been established, this has largely been due to the growth of a middle class, often of mixed ancestry. The importation of foreign capital—British, French and North American—has also helped to develop a great variety of resources: the agricultural wealth of Argentina and Uruguay, for example, nitrates and copper in Chile, silver and oil in Mexico, and oil in Venezuela.

The social and political pattern of the Spanish American republics has largely been conditioned by their racial composition. In the Andean republics, as in Mexico, the land-hungry Indian, excluded by his illiteracy from political rights and bound to the land in the serfdom of peonage, has constituted a problem which has only begun to be tackled in the present century. In Colombia, Peru and Ecuador, evolution from oligarchy to democracy has met with many difficulties. Perhaps the greatest progress has been made in Mexico, by far the most populous of the Spanish-American states. It is interesting to note the prominent part played by persons of Indian blood in Mexican history. The early leaders of the revolution, as well as the dictator Porfirio Díaz (1876–1911) were *mestizos*, and Jurez, who was President both before and after the reign of Maximilian, was a pure Indian.

In the republics of the River Plate there was no substantial Indian problem. Argentina, after the 'conquest' of the Patagonian desert, had only a few Indians left, mainly in the Chaco, and its *mestizo* element was almost negligible. The population in both Argentina and Uruguay had been built up during the second half of the nineteenth century by European immigrants, chiefly from Italy and Spain. British (and French) capital, which built the only big network of railways in South America and developed their public utilities, made possible the expansion of agricultural resources second only to the United States. There emerged the stabilising influence of a well-to-do middle class, which in Argentina looked like forming the basis for a democratic régime led by a 'Whig' oligarchy of large landowners. But this ordered progress was not to survive the strain of two world wars. Latin America, with the exception of Uruguay, less given to *latifundia*, was to experience a second age of dictators.

Chile, too, absorbed a large stream of foreign immigrants of which a large proportion was German, as well as a large volume of foreign capital (North American and British). But its racial composition was quite different. The Indian problem was comparatively simple, since the only pure Indians, the Araucanians of the south, remained a small isolated element. But there had grown up through the centuries a large *mestizo* population, amounting, in its wider sense, to about half the total population. The poorest part of the community, the *roto*, lived largely at the mercy of a very small class of big landowners, but the transition to democracy has been smoother in Chile than in most South American states, and the development of industrial resources did much to improve the condition of this depressed class.

IV

The history of Brazil presents many similarities to the story of the Spanish colonies. Early institutions were very much alike; the *donatorio* of the Captaincies General was the equivalent of the *adelantado*, the governor, and the *cámara* of the *cabildo*, but conditions were very different from those in Mexico and Peru. In Brazil there were no semi-civilised natives as in Mexico or Peru, who could be made to work for European masters, and the coastal territories of the earlier settlements produced no precious metals. Apart from the wood from which it derives its name, sugar plantations cultivated by imported Negroes constituted the wealth of the colony, and it was not until the very end of the seventeenth century that the discovery of gold and diamonds led to the penetration of the interior. Nor was the centralised control of the Portuguese monarchy, though based on the same principles, as effective, or as powerful as that of Spain. The Portuguese colonists were in their earlier history more than once compelled to defend themselves from powerful foreign aggression. Almost unaided, they succeeded in driving out the Dutch settlers under Maurice of Nassau in the north-western tip of their territory. Trade too was not so restricted, thanks to the British alliance.

The separation between Brazil and the mother-country, which took place without any bloodshed, also traced its occasion to Napoleon, whose invasion of Portugal induced the Regent (afterwards King John VI) to convey his court in British men-of-war to his Brazilian dominions. On his return to Portugal several years after the end of the war, the reactionary colonial policy of the Lisbon *Cortes* led to a revolution. Without his father's formal consent, but perhaps with his tacit acquiescence, his son Dom Pedro was proclaimed Emperor of an independent Brazil whose recognition by the mother country was largely due to British influence. He only reigned until 1831, went into exile, and died shortly afterwards. He was succeeded by his son Pedro II, who after a long regency, reigned until 1889, when he was dethroned by a militarist-republican conspiracy, the final blow came as the result of the abolition of slavery without compensation, which had been ratified by his daughter who was acting as regent during her father's absence abroad, and alienated the great planters on whose support the monarchy was in the last resort dependent. The republic which followed has in most respects maintained the general South American pattern, bouts of dictatorship (surprisingly milder than the Spanish American) alternating with longer periods of more or less constitutional rule.

On attaining independence, the settled portion of Brazil had about four million inhabitants, of whom rather over three quarters of a million were 'white', nearly two million Negroes, mostly slaves, more than half a million of mixed descent, and about a quarter of a million 'civilised' Indians. During the second half of the last century European immigration on a large scale began, chiefly German and Italian, so that after the First World War Brazil contained at least a million and a quarter foreign-born inhabitants. Foreign capital on a large scale was also imported and used, *inter alia*, to develop the coffee industry. By the beginning of the present century Brazil was selling three quarters of the world's supply. The demand for natural rubber, soon to be supplanted by the plantation product of the Further East grown from the progeny of smuggled Brazilian seeds, brought about a short-lived boom, resulting in the exploitation of the Amazonian forest, and the absorption of a number of primitive Indians. True to its traditional policy of assimilation, Brazil became the world's racial melting-pot. Probably something like a third of its present inhabitants have some Negro blood in their veins, and a much smaller proportion some Indian blood. Under the stimulus of coffee, tobacco and cotton, its population rapidly increased, and industrial development was to follow. By 1970 its over ninety-five million inhabitants, of whom not more than about half are 'white', amounted to half the total population of Spanish America.

Finally, a paragraph on Latin-American relations. Until the revolution these were dominated by the rivalry between Spain and Portugal. During the eighteenth century the attempt of the Portuguese to reach the north bank of the River Plate resulted in intermittent war with Spain. This conflict was inherited by their successor states. War also broke out between the Brazilian Empire and the nascent Argentine Republic, concluded by the creation of the buffer state of Uruguay. In the Andean region the break-up of Bolívar's *Gran Colombia* led to a series of wars involving the progressive diminution of Ecuador, and Santa Cruz's fusion of Bolivia with Peru was broken up in 1839 by the martial intervention of Argentina and Chile. The conflict over the nitrate desert involved Chile in struggles with Bolivia and Peru, only settled finally by the League of Nations award of 1929. But the most bellicose record was that of

Paraguay, which, under the dictator Lopez, nearly destroyed itself in a war from 1864–70 waged against the combined forces of Argentina and Brazil. A happier precedent was set, when the growing discord between the Argentina and Chile over the Patagonian boundary was settled by the arbitration of King Edward VII. Since then only one major war, that of the Chaco between Paraguay and Bolivia, has disturbed the harmony of Latin-American relations.

Australasia
by Jack Simmons

Besides settlement in the Americas, the Europeans also peopled other vast territories. Ever since Europeans broke into the Pacific in the sixteenth century, there had been rumours of the existence of a great southern continent, *Terra Australis Incognita* (*see* Chapter 11). Gradually, fragments of this continent, and its outlying islands, were found, by Tasman and Dampier and their successors. It was Cook, however, who first secured accurate and extensive knowledge of the South Pacific. In 1769–70 he sailed round both islands of New Zealand and up the whole of the eastern coast of Australia, to which he gave the name New South Wales. His second voyage (1772–5) systematically demolished all the earlier, fanciful ideas of *Terra Australis* as a vast continent centred on the South Pole.

No immediate steps were taken to follow up Cook's discoveries. But the British Government did not lose sight of them, and at the close of the War of American Independence its interest in them revived. For a time it thought that New South Wales might provide a suitable home for the Loyalists. When they themselves rejected the suggestion,

the country came to be considered for another purpose: to provide a settlement for convicts. Transportation had long been an accepted punishment for crime in all European countries with possessions overseas, and before 1775 large numbers of convicted criminals had been sent to the British colonies in North America, where they were put to work for the planters. The American Revolution having brought this to an end, the Government was urgently pressed to find a suitable new settlement for the convicts, who were confined in ever-increasing numbers in 'hulks' moored in English rivers. In 1786 it was decided to send some of them to New South Wales, and the first party arrived in Sydney Cove in January, 1788.

The plans for the penal settlement had been ill considered and it made a struggling start. It was never intended to be a penal settlement and nothing else. The Government hoped that free settlers would make their way there too. There were some grounds for this expectation. The number of people emigrating from Britain to the North American colonies had shown a sharp increase in the years directly preceding the Revolution. Yet very few free

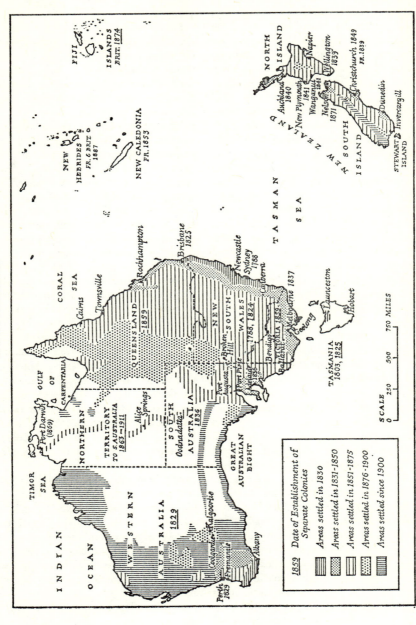

AUSTRALASIA

FIJI
ISLANDS
BRIT. 1874

NEW
HEBRIDES
FR. & BRIT.
1887

NEW CALEDONIA
FR. 1853

NORTH ISLAND

Auckland
1840
New Plymouth
1841
Wanganui
1841
Nelson
1841
Napier
Wellington
1839
Christchurch 1849
Dunedin
Invercargill

NEW ZEALAND

SOUTH ISLAND

STEWART
ISLAND
FR. 1839

TASMAN SEA

CORAL SEA

Cairns
Townsville
Rockhampton
Brisbane
1825

QUEENSLAND
1859

NEW SOUTH WALES
1788, 1824

Newcastle
Sydney
1788
Canberra
Melbourne 1837
VICTORIA 1839

Broken Hill
Bendigo
Ballarat

Geelong
Launceston
Hobart

TASMANIA
1803, 1825

GULF OF CARPENTARIA

Port Darwin
(1869)

NORTHERN
TERRITORY
TO S. AUSTRALIA
1863–1911

Alice
Springs

SOUTH AUSTRALIA
1836

Oodnadatta

Port Augusta
Port Pirie
Adelaide
1836

GREAT AUSTRALIAN BIGHT

TIMOR SEA

INDIAN OCEAN

WESTERN
AUSTRALIA
1829

Coolgardie
Kalgoorlie
Fremantle
Perth
1829
Albany

SCALE
0   250   500   750 MILES

1859   Date of Establishment of
        Separate Colonies

Areas settled in 1830
Areas settled in 1831–1850
Areas settled in 1851–1875
Areas settled in 1876–1900
Areas settled since 1900

(AFTER RAMSAY MUIR)

men went out to New South Wales at first, and those few were of poor quality: 'low mechanics who have failed in business, with long families', wrote one observer. It was not easy for them to make a living. Wheat could not be grown with success in the neighbourhood of Sydney; flax hardly paid its way. Coal was exported on a small scale from Newcastle, a hundred miles up the coast. Though sealing and whaling were more profitable, they did not prove permanently successful trades. Sheep were kept from the beginning, but it was only gradually that the colonists learnt, from John Macarthur, to breed them for wool instead of mutton. Here, in the long run, was the great opportunity of New South Wales: an opportunity that expanded almost without limit after the great pastures across the Blue Mountains had been discovered in 1813. The export of wool began on a commercial basis in 1821. By the middle of the century it was being sent to Britain from Australia in greater quantities than from Germany and Spain together; and still the West Riding clamoured for more.

The colony soon began to change its original character. Transportation continued, but the population of free settlers and 'emancipists'—convicts who had served out the term of their sentences and remained behind in the colony—increased steadily. By 1828 free men and convicts were about equal in numbers. In these circumstances, the iron discipline of a penal settlement could not be maintained without any relaxation. The free colonists began to demand a voice in the government. It was not conceded readily. Although a Legislative Council was set up to advise the Governor as early as 1823, its members were nominated by the Crown. The principle of election was not granted until 1842. Responsible govern-

ment, on the Canadian model, came eleven years later.

New South Wales was the earliest of the British colonies in Australasia, but it did not long remain the only one. Tasmania (then known as Van Diemen's Land) was occupied from 1803 onwards. Like New South Wales, it began as a penal settlement. Before long, however, two colonies were founded on the mainland, from which convicts were specifically excluded: the Swan River Settlement in Western Australia (1829) and South Australia (1836). Both these undertakings sprang partly from philanthropic ideas. Of the two, the South Australian colony was the more successful and it exercised a considerable influence on the subsequent course of Australian history. It owed its origin in part to the ideas of Edward Gibbon Wakefield, one of the few Englishmen of his time who thought with care and imagination about the problems of overseas settlement. His main thesis was simple: that the natural wealth of a colony arose first of all from its land, that accordingly the Government should not give away the land under its control but should sell it at a substantial price, and that the proceeds of this sale should be used to assist further emigration. Wakefield stood for the careful planning of colonial development. His interest was not confined to economics: he concerned himself as closely with the character of the new colonial societies, believing that the Government should take a hand in selecting suitable emigrants, instead of merely helping to find the passage money for paupers. He gave South Australia its momentum, even though he professed himself disappointed by its later development.

He also played a considerable part in the early history of the British colony in New Zealand. This differed from that of any of the colonies in Australia, particularly for one reason. Whereas the indigenous peoples of Australia were small in number and backward in culture, unable to impede the work of the white men, the Maoris were powerful, and secure in their possession of New Zealand. Europeans had to take account of them, to come to terms with them or to fight them. The first settlements were made by men engaged in hunting for seals and whales, by traders and missionaries. Colonisation began in 1840, when a small party arrived, dispatched from England at Wakefield's instigation. The settlers ran into difficulties almost at once. No adequate preparation had been made for them—the land they were to occupy had not even been surveyed. More important still, they quickly incurred the hostility of the Maoris. A praiseworthy effort was made by the first representative of the British Government, Captain Hobson, to define the rights of the two races in the vital matter of the ownership and purchase of land, in the Treaty of Waitangi (1841). But the terms agreed upon there were never acquiesced in by the settlers, over whom Hobson's control was very imperfect; and when they came to be worked out in practice they were not acceptable to the Maoris either.

The settlers and the Maoris first came into armed conflict near Nelson in 1843. In the British Government's view, the settlers were in the wrong: the Colonial Secretary pronounced that they had 'needlessly violated the rules of the law of England, the maxims of prudence, and the principles of justice'. To the Maoris, the important thing was that the Europeans were evidently divided among themselves. The settlers were out of sympathy with the Government, and even more with the missionaries, who were powerfully entrenched in the country. The first Maori War (1845–6) ended in a quick, though not easy, victory for the forces of the British Government, and in the succeeding years its representative, Sir George Grey, worked hard to win the confidence of Maoris, settlers, and missionaries alike. On the surface at least, he succeeded, through charm and patience and integrity. In truth, however, he was pursuing a series of objectives that were incompatible with one another. As the settlers increased in numbers, like all British colonists of their time they began to demand self-government. The missionaries opposed this, largely from concern for the welfare of the Maoris. Representative institutions were conceded, none the less, in 1846, and responsible government ten years later.

These steps were easy to take on paper, and they were welcomed in England, according to the progressive ideas of colonial policy that were current at the time. But if those ideas suited the circumstances of Canada and Australia, that did not mean that they necessarily suited New Zealand, where just and happy relations between British and Maoris were of fundamental importance for the stability of the country. Here responsible government brought not peace but a sword. For it took the control of New Zealand away from the British Government and its officials, who had been well qualified to arbitrate between the interests of the different communities, and gave it into the hands of the settlers. By 1860 the Maoris had come to be outnumbered by the Europeans. They saw their land taken away from them, by processes they did not fully comprehend, their culture threatened; even the protection they had enjoyed from the Government was failing them. They decided to make a fight for it. The consequence was the second series of Maori Wars, which lasted intermittently from 1860 to 1872. They ended with a complete victory for the New Zealand Government; but it was a victory that brought with it sharp lessons. Though the Maoris might be defeated, it was plain to any intelligent European in the country that their rights and wishes could not be set aside; that indeed the future of New Zealand might depend in a great degree on the maintenance of sensible relations between the races. This was clearly understood by Sir Donald McLean, who as Minister for Native Affairs from 1869 to 1876 was largely responsible for the settlement at the end of the wars. His humane and reasonable policy, continued by his successors, did much to ensure that in the long run the Maoris survived, as an integral and important part of the society of New Zealand. For a time it looked as if they would wither away, from contact with the Europeans, like the aborigines of Australia. Although in the 'seventies and 'eighties their numbers fell, the decline was arrested, and during the past half-century the Maoris have steadily increased once more. Recently, indeed, the increase has been striking: from c.100,000 in 1945 to over 220,000 today. If it would be too much to say that New Zealand has solved its problem of race-relations, it has come near to doing so: to finding means of incorporating an aboriginal minority in a community dominated by Europeans, without patronage on the one side or hopeless defeatism on the other.

The settlers in Australia and New Zealand were all farmers and fishermen at the outset. New Zealand retained its agricultural economy, with its market transformed by the development of the refrigerated ship from 1882 onwards: 'Canterbury lamb' became a familiar item in English butchers' shops before the end of the century. The economy of Australia, however, was more complex. This was due first to the discoveries of gold that were made in the south-east from 1851 onwards. These discoveries did not damage Australian agriculture: rather they helped it, by increasing the demand for food for the immigrants at new settlements. They stimulated industrial development, too, and particularly the growth of the Australian towns. The country in which the chief discoveries of gold took place had been separated from New South Wales, to become the colony of Victoria, in 1850. By 1873 its capital, Melbourne, boasted a population of 200,000. It was a mushroom growth and far from stable, but Melbourne had already taken its place as a great town, alongside Sydney and Adelaide.

Here is the beginning of what has become a special feature of the Australian social structure. Today, more than half the population live in its five largest cities, which have in consequence a preponderant political power. It is, moreover, a special characteristic of Australian settlement that it has developed almost entirely from the sea, not by the natural successive extensions of colonies overland. Communications between the colonies were mainly maritime. Accordingly, they all developed in isolation, fiercely jealous of their own separate rights and powers. Their interests, indeed, often differed. Sometimes they were diametrically opposed: after New South Wales had insisted on the discontinuance of the transportation of convicts in 1840, Western Australia was clamorous in demanding their services, to help in the development of a difficult and under-populated country. The colonies went their own way, with little regard to their neighbours. When they built railways, they chose different gauges. Travellers crossing the colonial boundaries could change trains, and goods could be transhipped from one wagon to another; the inter-colonial traffic was not great enough to make this a serious inconvenience.

These separatist tendencies were nourished by responsible government, which was conceded in the course of the 'fifties to all the eastern colonies—including Queensland, detached from New South Wales in 1859. Some people disapproved of these tendencies, arguing that the colonies should combine in a federation, for reasons of security and economy. No one paid much attention to these prophets until the closing years of the century. The military and political weakness of the colonies then became evident, as the European powers, Russia, Japan, and the United States, began manceuvring for position in the Pacific. Slowly during the 'nineties the Australians came to realise that they must combine, at any rate for the purposes of defence and external relations. It was difficult to frame a constitution acceptable to all these tenaciously separate colonies. When it emerged it was a federation in which a very strong position was guaranteed to the States, the powers of the central Government being deliberately restricted as narrowly as possible. This 'Commonwealth of Australia' came into being on the first day of the twentieth century.

Two major independent states thus grew up in the South Pacific. Though New Zealand declined to join the Australian Commonwealth, though in many ways she remained a markedly different kind of country, in her relations with the outside world she usually agreed with Australia. In both states the great majority of the population was of British descent: there was no major community in either that was comparable with the French Canadians. Without hesitation the two Dominions supported Britain in both World Wars. The forces they raised were astonishingly large—almost exactly half the eligible male population of New Zealand served in the first war, for example. In political discussions within the British Commonwealth they stood consistently for maintaining the ties between Britain and the Dominions. Yet though they prize their British tradition, the Australians and New Zealanders are separate peoples, with economic and political interests that are often different from Britain's. The Pacific war of 1941–5 displayed this clearly. They needed now, more than ever before, to preserve a good understanding with the United States; and as the new independent states of South-East Asia emerged, Australia and New Zealand showed themselves anxious to live on friendly terms with them too. At the same time they have long been intensely conscious of their peculiar isolation, as 'European' states with Asiatic neighbours, vastly larger in population, looking sometimes very covetously on the huge under-peopled spaces of Australia. The tendency of the whole history of Australia and New Zealand is to drive them in upon themselves. Yet they recognise, as clearly as any one, that they cannot remain isolated in the modern world.

18 THE TRANSFORMATION OF AFRICA AND ASIA

Africa

by Jack Simmons

The power politics and economic expansion of Europe in the nineteenth century, as in the eighteenth, were as decisive for the old world as for the new. Both in Africa and in Asia the situation was transformed.

The earlier relations between Europe and Africa, from the fifteenth century to the middle of the eighteenth, have already been described (*see* Chapter 12): the discovery of tropical and southern Africa by the Portuguese, the struggle that developed between them and their junior rivals, the English, the Dutch, and the French. The Portuguese had at first hoped to find gold in Africa, and other things of comparable value. They knew that a rich trade existed between the North African ports, in the hands of the Moslems, and the interior; and they were, on the whole, disappointed by what their exploration of the west coast yielded. The trade they were seeking to tap passed, in fact, across the Sahara by caravan. Its source was the great markets of the interior, in the Niger basin, not the comparatively minor places that the Europeans found on the coast. The only really valuable trade that the Europeans developed was the trade in slaves, which were in constant demand for the plantations of the Americas and the West Indies.

The European powers held nothing that can be called a colony in Africa before the nineteenth century. Their interests were limited to trading posts, all of which

had the same purpose. They were markets for the purchase of slaves and other commodities brought from inland, which were exchanged for the weapons and gunpowder and trinkets of Europe. The Portuguese, it is true, made large claims to jurisdiction in the interior; but, as Lord Salisbury once remarked, their character was 'archaeological'. These trading posts were scattered thickly along the shore of West Africa from Senegal to the Bight of Benin. Moving further down the coast, the Portuguese were still established, feebly but tenaciously, in Angola. At the Cape of Good Hope the Dutch East India Company had a station, useful for supplying its ships on the long voyages between Holland and the East. There were a few more Portuguese settlements, further up the east coast; but from Mozambique northwards power was in the hands of the Arabs, with their headquarters at Zanzibar. On the maps, nine-tenths of Africa was a blank, or delineated only by wild conjecture. Europe knew nothing of it, and cared as little.

But in the second half of the eighteenth century, a fresh interest in Africa began to stir. The slave trade was now so valuable that its centres became known to diplomats making treaties; Senegal passed from France to Britain at the Peace of Paris in 1763, and back again to France twenty years later. The great advance in the scientific knowledge of the world

358

that came from the voyages of Bougainville and Cook in the Pacific led to a new curiosity about unsolved geographical questions; and one of the most famous of them—a conundrum going back to Herodotus—was the problem of the sources of the Nile. James Bruce's journey to investigate it (1769–72) was undertaken in a spirit of disinterested inquiry. Though he did not solve the problem, he aroused great interest by his masterly account of

Abyssinia, and he inspired other people to attempt the penetration of the unknown interior of Africa.

But the first planned attack on its problems was made on the other side of the continent. Geographically, it was centred on the Niger. Though that river's existence had long been rumoured, its course had never been traced. Some people supposed that it was in fact the upper part of the Nile, which flowed over from

ROUTES OF EXPLORERS

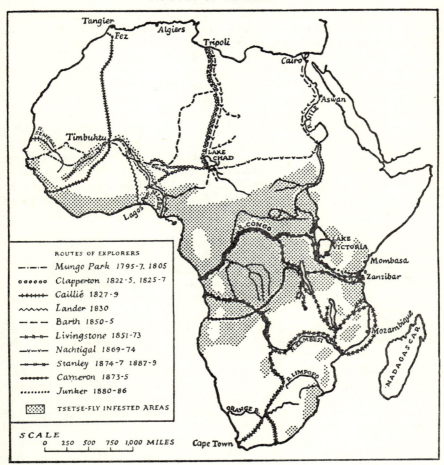

ROUTES OF EXPLORERS	
—·—·—	Mungo Park 1795-7, 1805
ooooooo	Clapperton 1822-5, 1825-7
+++++	Caillié 1827-9
∿∿∿∿	Lander 1830
— — —	Barth 1850-5
-x-x-x-	Livingstone 1851-73
-v-v-	Nachtigal 1869-74
-II-II-II-	Stanley 1874-7 1887-9
••••••	Cameron 1873-5
··········	Junker 1880-86
░░░	TSETSE-FLY INFESTED AREAS

SCALE

0   250   500   750 1,000 MILES

north-western Africa and made a great right-angled turn in the neighbourhood of Abyssinia. A newly founded 'African Association' in London directed the work of a series of travellers towards settling this question. It was solved in two stages. First, Mungo Park reached the river, overland from the Gambia, and travelled along some 200 miles of the middle part of its course (1795–7). On a second journey in 1805 he died, probably at Bussa, about 500 miles from the sea. There was then a pause in exploration. The sources of the Niger were found in 1822, and in the next year three British travellers started on a journey that took them across the Sahara from Tripoli to Kano and Sokoto. Finally, in 1830, Richard and John Lander sailed down the river and out into the open sea. They showed that the 'Oil Rivers', which had long been known to European dealers in slaves and palm-oil, were in fact the Niger delta. They also showed, beyond dispute, that the Niger was not the Upper Nile.

These discoveries were of importance to other people besides geographers. The money required for the expeditions to the Niger came from a variety of sources. The British Government put up the greater part. It did not do so from motives of scientific curiosity, but because it was concerned with a practical problem: the destruction of the slave trade. The humanitarian campaign against the slave trade had its first triumph in Britain in 1807, when the trade was declared illegal to British subjects. But that did not of itself end the business. Illicit British slaving went on and, much more important, other European states continued the trade without restriction. Though all the major powers agreed to forbid it in 1815, to some of them this was no more than a formal gesture. The most effective way to attack the trade in practice seemed to be to cut it

off through naval action on the coast or in the Atlantic, and by agreement with other powers a West African 'slave squadron' was maintained for the purpose from 1807 onwards.

An even more difficult task lay beyond: to strike at the root of the trade in the interior of Africa, from which the slaves were drawn. For success here, two things were necessary. An accurate knowledge of the country was the first, and that could be secured only by exploration. The second was equally important. Any thinking person, not blinded by humanitarian zeal, could see that it would be useless and unjust merely to stop the slave trade, to take away the livelihood—however deplorable —of the African traders, without offering them an opportunity to build up an alternative trade in its place. Hence the interest shown in the development of the palm-oil industry in the early nineteenth century. This proved to be an extremely difficult task, for the truth was that West Africa had no natural product that could compare in value with the bodies of its own people. Here is one of the main reasons why the destruction of the Atlantic slave trade took so long. It was delayed also by the obstruction of the slave buyers, notably Brazil and Spain, but by 1865, with the defeat of the Southern States in the American Civil War, the trade in the West may be said to have come to an end.

In the course of destroying it, Britain had been led to take a much closer interest in West Africa than she ever had in the past. Her trading posts were of less value commercially than they had been in the eighteenth century, when the slave trade was at its height. What she wanted now was a series of positions that would be useful both for attacking that trade and for building up those that should succeed it. She had held Sierra Leone, with its splendid harbour of Freetown, since

1788. With the Landers' discovery, she began to turn her attention, more closely than before, to the Oil Rivers. Much money was spent, wisely and foolishly, on the exploration of the Niger. Many treaties were made with African rulers, to induce them to discourage the slave trade and to develop 'legitimate' trade in its place. These were not satisfactory; and at last the Government decided that it must establish a base of its own in this region. It chose Lagos for the purpose, and occupied it in 1861. Many people at home disapproved of the expansion of Britain's responsibilities in West Africa. But in spite of their criticisms, successive British Governments held on there, maintaining their small centres of political power on the coast.

Meanwhile, greater developments were taking place at the northern and southern extremities of the continent. The French began their colonisation of Algeria in 1830, as some consolation for their weakened position in Europe since Napoleon's defeat. It was an effort of 'colonisation', in the proper sense of the term, involving the settlement of Frenchmen, to build up an extension of metropolitan France across the Mediterranean; and its history belongs rather with the history of Europe than with that of the African continent. To the south, at the Cape of Good Hope, the Dutch colony was captured by a British force in 1806. It was kept by Britain at the peace settlement of 1815, for its strategic value on the route to the East. But even under the Dutch it had begun to expand, as settlers moved away from the Cape to farms in the interior. Though their numbers were small, they quickly came to cover a great tract of territory: for the character of the land and its resources meant that the economic unit of a farm was a large one, some 6000 acres. So there began to develop the characteristic Boer settlement, based on the farmer and his family (including his African slaves), living in isolation, a long day's journey or more from their next neighbours.

The advent of the British administration brought two important changes with it. The new Government thought of the relations between black and white people in terms quite different from those traditionally accepted by the Boers, and it soon began to amend the law in the direction of establishing equality between the races. Moreover, from 1820 onwards British settlers began to arrive in the country, with the Government's blessing. Not unnaturally, the Boers were disturbed. They saw their established ways of life threatened. Before long they might find themselves outnumbered by British immigrants. One remedy was open to them, and a large number of the more enterprising of them took it. In the past, those who had fallen out with the Dutch Government at the Cape had simply moved off—'trekked'—into the interior, beyond its reach. In the 1830s a concerted movement of this sort took place. It was no different in kind from those of the past. But it was more self-conscious, the product of deeply-felt grievance, and it was on a bigger scale than anything that had preceded it. Hence it came to be known as the Great Trek.

The Trekkers ultimately established themselves well away to the north of the effective jurisdiction of the British Government. At first the Government tried to control them. But it had constant difficulties with the Africans on its hands—squabbles dignified by the name of the Kaffir Wars. Its only deep interest in the country was in the security of its coast-line. That was guaranteed by its grip on Cape Town, on Port Elizabeth, and on Natal, which was peopled with British settlers, encouraged to go out there by the Government in the 'forties and 'fifties. In 1852-4 the attempt to control the Trekkers was abandoned, and the virtual independence of the Orange Free State and the Transvaal recognised.

II

So far we have considered the relations between Africa and Europe mainly from the Europeans' standpoint. Their conception of the interior is well summarised in the words of one of the best informed of all British Colonial Secretaries, Earl Grey, who wrote in 1811 that 'South Africa beyond the reach of the white man is one scene of violence and rapine'. This sweeping generalisation was far from true. The slave trade had indeed fomented 'violence and rapine' as the traders moved further and further in search of their prey. But large tracts of Africa were wholly or largely unaffected by it. What strikes one most forcible perhaps in the narratives of the early explorers is not the exceptional murders they witnessed; it is the general stability of the interior, the comparative ease with which traders could move along known highways, paying recognised tolls for protection. And a careful study even of the more primitive societies they portray does not usually reveal tyranny and oppression so much as a well-established system of customary law, by which rulers and ruled were both bound. Nor were all these societies 'primitive', in any sensible use of that word. The Moslem emirates of Northern Nigeria and the Kingdom of Abyssinia were highly-developed political entities, notably resembling at many points the states of medieval Europe. If they are dismissed as not characteristically African, a similar remark can be made of other states to which that objection does not apply: Buganda and its neighbours as Speke saw them, the Matebele Kingdom

described by the missionary J. S. Moffat. There was despotism here, but it was despotism within an ordered and accepted framework.

It was the great achievement of the explorers—though never one that they consciously pursued as an end in itself—to start the interpretation of Africa and Europe to each other. Here Livingstone showed his pre-eminence. As an explorer alone, he stands high. His first great journey (1852-6) displayed almost the whole course of the Zambesi and both sides of the watershed from which it ran; his second (1858-64) brought the discovery of Lake Nyasa; his third (1866-73) a new knowledge of the country beyond Lake Tanganyika. It led directly, too, to the solution of the Nile problem, and the opening up of the Congo basin, by Stanley. But behind all this lay a greater achievement. Livingstone was one of the first Europeans to set himself to understand Africans—dispassionately, with sympathy but without sentimentality. His books reached a wider public than those of any of his predecessors. Henceforth, there was no excuse for treating Africans as pantomime figures or—what was really worse—as backward children. He made them intelligible to his fellow-Europeans as human beings. Though he could not reach Africans in the same way, by the written word, he did much to explain Europeans and their ideas to them. His personal influence over those he met was not forgotten. It has endured through three generations, and it is not dead in tradition even now.

Livingstone directed the attention of Europe, for the first time, to the eastern side of tropical Africa: to the slave trade that was raging there for the supply of the markets of Egypt and Arabia. It was on his initiative that that trade was crushed in the 'seventies and 'eighties, through the joint action of Britain and the Arab Sultan of Zanzibar, who exercised a general suzerainty over the East African coast. Britain's motive here, even more plainly than in West Africa, was humanitarian. Livingstone saw the dislocation and suffering that the trade caused in the Zambesi basin and the neighbourhood of the great lakes, and his formidable, measured denunciation of it did more than anything else to bring about its destruction. The British Government's part in the business was in no way hypocritical: the private writings of naval men, of senior officials in the foreign service, of civil servants and politicians of the Foreign Office itself, all make it perfectly clear that the slave trade outraged their feelings. It was a consequence of the campaign, however, that Britain acquired new political power in East Africa, where neither she nor any other European state had ever enjoyed it before. It was acquired most unwillingly. At this time, in the 'sixties and 'seventies, European politicians seemed almost unanimous in wishing not to extend their colonial responsibilities. The rulers of the new German Empire were pressed by a few enthusiasts and by shipping and commercial magnates to acquire territories in Africa. They refused. A Committee of the British House of Commons urged the Government to withdraw from all its West African possessions in 1865. When the Sultan of Zanzibar offered it a virtual protectorate of his dominions in 1877, the offer was turned down, politely but without hesitation. It seemed possible for Britain to secure all that she wanted without the expense and the liabilities of government. Though France had borne the main burden of assisting the Egyptians with the cutting of the Suez Canal, in the years that followed its opening in 1869 it was Britain that benefited most from the new facilities that it

offered. The policy of the great powers outside Europe was dominated, in general, by trading considerations. So long as these were secure, there seemed no need to extend empires.

III

And yet, in 1884-5 the most spectacular invasion of Africa by the European states began. Many forces combined, to some extent accidentally, to touch off this 'Scramble for Africa': the revelation of the vast Congo basin by Stanley in 1874-84, diplomatic struggles in Europe itself, commercial and maritime rivalries, the activity of unofficial bodies like the Christian missions, the policy of African rulers and traders, understandably anxious to play off one group of white men against another. The German Government allowed itself to be persuaded into reversing its previous policy and plunged without warning into Africa, establishing two colonies in the west, one in the south-west, and one in the east that incorporated a slice of territory hitherto ruled by the Sultan of Zanzibar. The older powers, Britain and France, now saw their interests threatened and, however uneasy they might be at incurring fresh liabilities, felt obliged to make large annexations for their own protection. Almost the whole continent thus came to be 'partitioned' among the European powers.

It was a swift process, practically completed in six years (1884-90). More than anything else, that explains the character of the Partition. It was a rough-and-ready job, done in the crudest way and dictated by the interests of Europeans, not of Africans. The boundaries between the new colonies were drawn on maps in the chancelleries of Europe, to be moved backwards and forwards here and there in a diplomatic game of give-and-take. The maps were far from accurate—how could

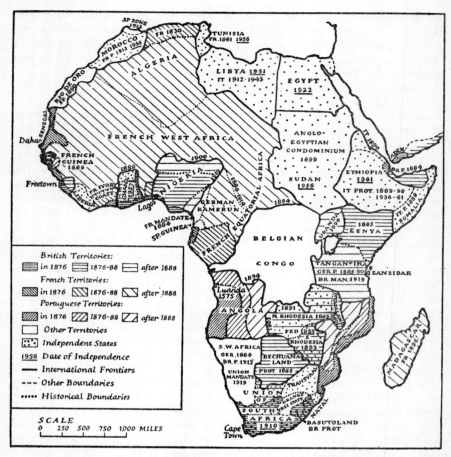

EUROPEAN POSSESSIONS AND SPHERES OF INFLUENCE

it be otherwise, when large tracts of the continent had still never been visited by Europeans who could tell the cartographers what to put on them? And even when a colony had been defined on paper, it was liable to be bartered away for advantages elsewhere: as Germany gave up her claims to exercise a protectorate over Zanzibar in 1890, in exchange for a British surrender of Heligoland—which was of infinitely greater value, lying on her own front doorstep.

For Africa, the Partition was momentous. On a fair view, one is bound to say that at first its results were almost wholly bad. It was so rapidly executed, on a basis of such inadequate information, that the boundaries it established caused widespread hardship. Peoples were split into two, a new and unintelligible barrier dividing relations and intimate neighbours. This happened to the Masai in East Africa. Occasionally the powers in Europe tried afterwards to set things to rights, as when

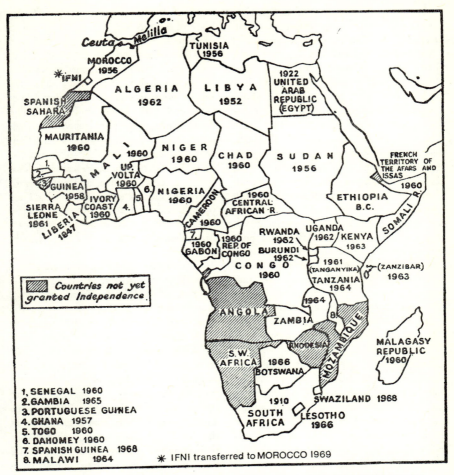

Countries not yet granted Independence

Ceuta Melilla

TUNISIA 1956
MOROCCO 1956
*IFNI
ALGERIA 1962
LIBYA 1952
1922 UNITED ARAB REPUBLIC (EGYPT)
SPANISH SAHARA
MAURITANIA 1960
MALI 1960
NIGER 1960
CHAD 1960
SUDAN 1956
FRENCH TERRITORY OF THE AFARS AND ISSAS
1.
2.
3. GUINEA 1958
UP. VOLTA 1960
6. NIGERIA 1960
CAMEROON
1960 CENTRAL AFRICAN R.
ETHIOPIA B.C.
1960
SIERRA LEONE 1961
IVORY COAST 1960
4. 5.
LIBERIA 1847
CAMEROON 1960
7
1960 GABON
1960 REP. OF CONGO
RWANDA 1962
BURUNDI 1962
UGANDA 1962
KENYA 1963
SOMALI R.
1960
CONGO 1960
1961 (TANGANYIKA)
TANZANIA 1964
(ZANZIBAR) 1963
1964
ANGOLA
ZAMBIA
8
MOZAMBIQUE
MALAGASY REPUBLIC 1960
S.W. AFRICA
RHODESIA
1966 BOTSWANA
1910 SOUTH AFRICA
SWAZILAND 1968
LESOTHO 1966

1. SENEGAL 1960
2. GAMBIA 1965
3. PORTUGUESE GUINEA
4. GHANA 1957
5. TOGO 1960
6. DAHOMEY 1960
7. SPANISH GUINEA 1968
8. MALAWI 1964

* IFNI transferred to MOROCCO 1969

AFRICAN STATES IN 1970, WITH DATES OF INDEPENDENCE

Germany and Britain agreed to adjust the boundary separating Togoland from the Gold Coast. But only very occasionally. The ink that drew the boundaries on those maps in Europe was looked on as indelible.

Moreover, the Partition inevitably involved the Africans in the quarrels of Europeans. Their children were taught to become little Frenchmen, little Germans, little Englishmen, and that divided them as completely as inter-tribal jealousies had ever done in the past. When the World War came in 1914, it brought destruction and suffering to thousands of Africans who knew and cared nothing in the least about the issues that were at stake. And when it was over, millions of them were bewildered to find that they had acquired new governments, with different ideas expressed in different languages, English and French in place of German.

365

Not all the consequences of the Partition, however, were evil. Its long-term results were so complex that snap-judgments of that kind are inadmissible. We shall come later on to consider the total impact of Europe upon Africa. At this point it is important to note one consequence above all others. Whereas in the preceding four centuries Europe had been brought much into contact with certain parts of Africa, she had never become absolutely committed there. Just before the Partition, indeed, it looked as if she might disengage herself from Africa on a considerable scale. On the other side, Africa was not committed to Europe at all. Now that was changed. Europe put money into Africa and built up her power there. Africa received what she had to offer, good as well as bad—ideas, new skill and knowledge that opened up quite new opportunities. Henceforward, there was commitment on both sides; and it was permanent.

IV

A similar issue arose, but in a different form, in South Africa; and largely by accident at the same time. The agreements of 1852–4 that accorded British recognition to the Transvaal and the Orange Free State were designed, as far as the Boers were concerned, to rid them of their connections with Europe. They wanted, above everything else, to live their own lives, on their own. They were uninterested in greatness or wealth: what they valued most was independence, and that for a time they enjoyed. It was disturbed, however, by the discovery of diamonds on the border of the Orange Free State in 1867. After some argument the diamond fields passed under British control; but they drew in a great body of immigrants, who established themselves in and around Kimberley, adjacent to the Free States' territory. The Boers had other rivals

besides to fear: above all the Zulus, a tough body of fighters whom they found it hard to keep at bay. So nervous were they that they decided to accept British control once more, with British military protection. When the clash with the Zulus came, the British were ultimately victorious. After that victory, the Boers no longer needed British help, and they asked for their independence back again. When their wishes were not met they took matters into their own hands, defeated a local British force at Majuba, and put forward their demands as successful rebels. They were granted in 1881, for the new Liberal Government had no mind to embark on a troublesome war to assert a claim which, in any case, it thought unjust.

These troubles were hardly over before new discoveries of minerals were made—this time of gold, in the Transvaal (1884). Before long it was clear that one of the great goldfields of the world had been found there. Like all other discoveries of the kind, it led to the immigration of thousands of prospectors, engineers, and miners. The problems of controlling and policing them were beyond the meagre resources of the Transvaal Government. The Boers could only look helplessly on as this horde of aliens established itself in their country, building up in no time the new city of Johannesburg. They were aliens not only in race and language, but—more important—in spirit. For the immigrants initiated the development of a mechanised industry, financed and equipped from Europe, and the markets they supplied ranged across the world.

To the Boers, they were hateful. As farmers, the Boers detested their machines and their urban-mindedness; as descendants of the Trekkers of the 'thirties, they were furious that their country should be involved by these newcomers in the politics and economy of the outside world.

Yet they could not stop the development they hated and feared. All they could do was to tax the profits of the immigrants—the 'Outlanders', as they called them with a touch of contempt—and grimly to deny them political rights, lest by force of numbers they might get control of the country in the future.

It was not a purely domestic dispute, concerning the Transvaal alone. For the Outlanders were an international force. They were linked, too, in spirit and interest with the British South Africa Company, presided over by Cecil Rhodes. That company had secured powers of territorial government in its charter of 1889, and it was reaching out for control of the country lying west and north of the Transvaal, right up to the Zambesi. At the same time Rhodes was Prime Minister of Cape Colony for five years (1890–6). It is not surprising that the Transvaalers felt that Rhodes and the British Government were engaged in a conspiracy to overwhelm them, by gradually encircling them territorially and using the Outlanders as a Trojan horse to destroy their state from within. Their fears seemed to be confirmed in 1895 by the Jameson Raid, a harebrained attempt to combine a *putsch* in Johannesburg with a supporting raid from the Company's territory. The ease with which they suppressed the raid—and the recollection of the many occasions on which they had successfully defied the British Government in the past—encouraged the Transvaalers to try the fortune of war. All negotiations for a settlement of the questions at issue having failed, war began in October, 1899.

The fighting lasted two and a half years, beginning with a series of quick successes for the Boers and ending with protracted guerrilla warfare in which the British Government forces ultimately won through a patient and implacable policy of attrition. When at last even the Boer irreconcilables accepted terms of peace, they included a promise that self-government should be restored to the conquered territories as soon as possible. It was a Conservative Government that had waged the war from Britain's side and was equally responsible for the peace and the vigorous policy of economic and social reconstruction that followed it. Many Liberals had opposed the war throughout; and when a Liberal Government came back into power in 1905 it set itself to accelerate the process of autonomy. The Transvaal and the Orange Free State received back their independence as self-governing colonies within the British Empire. And with help and the warmest approval from Britain they came together with Cape Colony and Natal to form the Union of South Africa, which was proclaimed a Dominion, like Canada and Australia, in 1910.

This was hailed at the time, and has often been praised since, as a triumphant demonstration of Liberalism at its best. There is substance in this claim, but an exaggeration too that almost falsifies it. The settlement was a good one between Britain and the Boers, magnanimous on both sides. But it was achieved at the expense of ignoring altogether the interests of the African majority. They had not been involved in the war of 1899–1902; it had been agreed on both sides that they should be rigidly excluded from it. Yet behind and beneath the quarrels that produced the war lay the greatest problem of all: that of the position the Africans should hold in the society of South Africa, under the political control of the Europeans. Alfred Milner, who represented the British Government at the Cape before and during the war, perceived that this, and not the matter of the Outlanders, was the biggest issue at stake. The struggle for supremacy in South Africa was vital not only for the control of the goldfields but as a conflict between two totally opposed conceptions of the government of the country. The British believed that the Africans should be associated in the work of politics, slowly, tentatively, as opportunity offered. The Boers were absolute on the other side: Africans, to them, were an unalterably inferior creation, to be ruled as children, for they were and would forever be incapable of ruling themselves.

The settlement of 1902–10 said nothing of this issue whatever. But implicitly it was a victory for the Boer conception. No general political rights for Africans were written into the new constitution at the insistence of the British Government. The electorate in the new Dominion was almost wholly European; and among the Europeans the Boers enjoyed a sure majority. True, they were not united among themselves, but most of them agreed on this fundamental issue. From the very birth of the new Union, the forces were marshalling themselves for the formation of a Nationalist party deriving its traditions from the Trekkers and the Transvaalers of 1899, determined to keep the Africans in subjection. The moderates under Botha and Smuts were in power at first, carrying the Union through the War of 1914 to give valuable aid to Britain and the allies. When the war was over they were turned out by the Nationalists. A struggle between the two parties followed, concluded by what proved to be the decisive victory of the Nationalists at the election of 1949. The policy of maintaining a rigid European supremacy is now securely established.

V

This development in the Union is the exact opposite of what has been happening in the greater part of tropical Africa

during the past eighty years. Indeed, it is partly to be explained as a reaction against the policy of Governments further north. Some ill consequences of the Partition have been discussed already. But if we look at these eighty years as a whole, a different impression emerges. The first business of the new European Governments was to establish a sound administration; and most of them set about the task with an energy restricted only by the very small staffs they could afford for the purpose. Inevitably, this meant that much of the older, traditional African Government remained; that the new administrators worked through it as far as they could, instead of destroying it and replacing it with something brand new. F. D. Lugard in Nigeria developed this expedient into something like a fixed system, which acquired the name 'indirect rule'. His example and his writings were widely influential, not only British colonies but also, for instance, in French North Africa under Lyautey. Indirect rule was a most valuable device in the early years of European administration. It furnished, ready-made, a substantial part of the framework of local government and greatly eased the transition from the old régime to the new. It thus left the Europeans free to concentrate on the chief work that they alone could perform: the technical modernisation of the country.

It is hard to imagine the effect that this had had on the minds of the Africans who have lived through it. The force of the impact of European ideas of the nineteenth and twentieth centuries on peoples who were still living in what were technologically medieval or prehistoric worlds is beyond calculation. The most spectacular signs of the Europeans' work were such things as the railway, climbing over mountains and spanning gorges (bridging even, in the end, the Victoria Falls); the aeroplane, making Paris or London no more than one long day's journey away; the radio; and, in Abyssinia in 1936 and again in 1941, the bomb. But the change is better expressed in smaller things, and in visual terms. It is summed up in the roads that the Europeans built in the forest country, say, of Nigeria. The life of a villager there, centred on a group of huts in a small clearing, was physically shut in to a degree scarcely known in Europe. Moreover, the constriction was permanent, varying not at all with the seasons. There was the forest, impenetrable to the eye, fifty or a hundred feet tall, on every side of him. His only means of movement were the tracks, two or three feet wide, that led to the next villages. The building of a European road transformed his life. It opened up a vision of the hills to the north, hitherto quite unknown to him though only a few miles away. With the bicycle, the motorcar, the bus that went with it, the road offered him an inconceivable new freedom.

Even more important than technical change, the Europeans brought with them new ideas; and gradually, as their schools multiplied and radio sets were imported in bulk, these ideas came to mould the Africans' thinking. They became aware of what was going on, not only in Europe but in other parts of Africa and in Asia. The beginnings of an African nationalism can be clearly discerned in the 1920s, principally in the towns of the west coast. It was fostered by the Europeans; for in reality it was of their own making. That is not to say that they all welcomed it.

Many of them wanted longer to strengthen their administration, which was still flimsy at many points, and to bring forward the more primitive people so as to protect them against exploitation by their more progressive fellow-Africans. For these were all highly mixed societies; and in East and Central Africa, from Kenya down to Rhodesia, there were white settlers also to be taken into account. It is not surprising that many well-intentioned European administrators should have wished to play for time.

But they were not successful. Everywhere in the past thirty years African nationalism has come out into the open, stimulated by the Indian attack on Abyssinia, by the Second World War, by the triumphs of nationalism in Asia and the Arab world, by the example and influence of Communism. It has won its first spectacular victory with the establishment of Ghana as an independent state within the British Commonwealth, on a constitutional equality with Canada—and with the then Union of South Africa. It challenges European supremacy throughout Africa, in the near or the further future, and it is confident of success. When one looks back over the past, what is most interesting is to see how this nationalism itself is the product of European ideas, moulded and developed by Africans to suit their own conditions. Logically, it is the conclusion of the work begun by the Portuguese when they first brought Africa into direct contact with Europe more than 500 years ago.

Asia

by G. F. Hudson

At the end of the eighteenth century, three hundred years after the voyage of Vasco da Gama had opened the Indian Ocean to European navigation, the great civilisations of Asia were still virtually untouched by Western influence. All the oceanic and much of the regional maritime trade of Asia was carried by European shipping, and there were already areas—Ceylon, Java, Madras, Bengal—where European nations had obtained political control. But even in these areas, and much more in the far larger part of Asia which belonged to independent Asian states, the indigenous peoples remained firmly attached to their traditional ways of life and thought.

Except in the Philippines, there had not been any large-scale conversions to the religions of the European intruders, their scientific thought had made hardly any impression and their special political ideas had not penetrated at all. The increase of seaborne commerce had enriched Asian merchants in some localities, but there had been no growth of a native capitalism comparable to the European; the prestige

THE WESTERN POWERS IN ASIA

of European arms by sea and land had caused some Asian states to import arms from Europe and engage the services of European soldiers as mercenaries or instructors, but there had been no changes of military and civil organisation of the kind required for the creation of real power in the age of the industrial revolution.

During the nineteenth century, however, two developments took place which together initiated a profound transformation of traditional Asia. European expansion eventually brought nearly half the population of the continent under the rule of Western powers, while those countries which retained their formal independence were subjected to very strong economic and political pressures and often lost some portion of their sovereignty. The second development, arising out of the first by way of counter-action, was a movement towards Asian revival through adaptation to Western ways and acquisition of the secrets of Western wealth and power. This latter trend in Asia represented at the same time an opposition to Western economic and political ascendancy and a cultural surrender to Western influences; for the Western nations it signified a triumph of their civilisation, yet also the growth of forces which were to put an end to their colonial empires and their industrial monopolies.

In the perspective of world-history this process of transformation appears primarily as one whereby a pre-capitalist and pre-industrial type of civilisation, with many analogies to the ancient and medieval eras of Europe, was suddenly brought forward into an age of developed scientific technology and capitalist economy. It is often more appropriate to speak of 'modernisation' than of 'Westernisation'. But the changes in Asia were due to external stimulus and example rather than to any internal evolution of Asian society and

culture and were very different from the transition to the modern age in Europe. Further, the abrupt introduction of the forms and instruments of an advanced technology into environments of an archaic economic life, without intermediate stages of growth, involved dislocations and disparities sharper than those attendant on economic and social progress in the West, and the effects on traditional custom and belief were even more shattering. Finally, the export to Asia of European liberal-democratic, socialist and communist ideologies involved the Asian peoples in a conflict of political creeds which, even though they could be applied in Asian situations, had been formulated in terms of Western experience and institutions.

II

The territorial expansion of the Western powers in Asia had produced by the end of the nineteenth century five substantial colonial empires—those of Britain, Russia, France, Holland and the United States—and additionally some scattered fragments of territory belonging to Portugal and one small holding acquired by Germany. In area the Russian Empire was the largest, but in population the British was far ahead of all the others, since it comprised the whole of India together with Ceylon and Burma, containing over a third of the inhabitants of the continent; outside this massive core were other British possessions and protectorates—Aden and a group of coastal protectorates in Arabia to the west, Malaya, North Borneo and Hong Kong to the east. All these territories were in communication with Britain and with one another only by sea, and their control was founded on a naval supremacy in the Indian Ocean which had been unchallenged since the last years of the eighteenth century. From coastal or near-coastal bases—Madras, Bombay and Calcutta—the Bri-

N

tish had extended their power by stages over the interior of India, which was divided among a number of contending kingdoms as a result of the break-up of the Mughal Empire; in 1800 the East India Company still only controlled a fraction of the total area of the Indian 'sub-continent', but by 1850, after the Sikh wars, its authority was supreme from Cape Comorin to the Himalayas. Nearly two-thirds of the area with about four-fifths of the population were brought into directly administered provinces, while the rest was left to subordinate Indian rulers. Burma, which had been a separate king-dom, was brought under British rule from India by successive annexations in 1826, 1852 and 1886.

The Russian Empire in Asia differed from the British since it was built by over-land expansion, and also because it invol-ved a substantial permanent settlement of immigrants from Russia, who came in time to form the bulk of the population in a large part of it. The Russians had reached the Pacific across Siberia by the middle of the seventeenth century, but until the middle of the nineteenth they were not established in the basin of the Amur, which was held by the Manchu-Chinese Empire, nor in Turkestan to the south of the belt of steppe between the Caspian and the Altai inhabited by nomadic Kazakh tribes who were only gradually brought under Russian control. The important advances did not begin until 1842, when the Russian frontier in Central Asia was pushed south-wards to the Aral Sea; during the next two decades it was carried down past Lake Balkhash to the east. Tashkent was captured in 1865 and the famous city of Samarkand three years later; the emirate of Bokhara became a Russian protectorate in 1869. Further expansion followed until by the end of the century Russia held part of the Pamirs with only twenty miles of

Afghan territory separating her outposts from the northern border of British-protected Kashmir. Meanwhile in the Far East Russia took advantage of the Taiping rebellion in China and China's war with Britain and France to annex without fighting the left bank of the Amur and coastal territory down to the border of Korea, where the town of Vladivostok was founded in 1861. The empire thus formed was all of one piece territorially with European Russia and there was a ribbon of Russian agricultural settlement across southern Siberia from the Urals to the Pacific. The remnants of the native peoples of Siberia became minorities comparable to the surviving Red Indians of the United States and Canada; Siberia became predominantly Russian by popu-lation as well as by sovereignty. In Turke-stan, on the other hand, the Russians were, like the British in India, a minority of foreign invaders ruling over indigenous peoples of different language, religion and culture.

Of the other Western empires—which were all, like the British, maritime and unaccompanied by large-scale permanent settlement from the metropolitan country —the French domain in Indo-China was formed between 1858 and 1885, and was in some measure a consolation for the French failure to win India in contest with the British in an earlier period. It com-prised the former kingdoms of Annam (Vietnam), Cambodia and Laos. The Dutch Empire in the Malay Archipelago was centred on the island of Java, where two-thirds of its total population was concentrated; it had grown from the first strongholds established by the Dutch in the seventeenth century. In the Philippines the United States replaced Spain as the colonial power after the Spanish-American War of 1898; this group of islands was thus for a second time occupied by invaders ultimately of European origin, but coming across the Pacific from North America—for the Spaniards, sailing from Mexico in the sixteenth century had conquered the Philippines.

III

What was left of independent Asia by 1900 consisted of seven states recognised internationally as sovereign—a western group, all Moslem by traditional culture, comprising Turkey, Persia and Afghanistan, and an eastern including China, Korea, Japan and Siam. All these countries were backward, except Japan; all except Japan lacked native capital accumulation and modern industry, all except Japan were governed by absolute monarchies and all except Japan were deficient for their size in military and naval strength. The Japanese exception was, however, of the greatest importance for all of Asia, for Japan's success in adapting Western techniques and institutions to her own needs and building up thereby a strong, modernised national state was destined to have an immense psychological effect throughout the continent. It showed what could be accomplished by an Asian country with a determined political leadership and dispelled the idea that Asia had been irretrievably left behind in the march of material progress.

The first experiments in imitative adaptation to Western ways had nevertheless been made, not by Japan, but by Turkey—the old Ottoman Empire, which, as a state with Mediterranean coasts and frontiers in Europe with Austria and Russia, had been in the eighteenth century in closer contact with Western civilisation than any other Asian country. A series of military defeats exposing the corruption and inefficiency of the old Ottoman administration induced Sultan Selim III, who began his reign in 1789, to create

new military units on European lines and import European officers to act as instructors. These reforms aroused the suspicion and hostility of the Moslem clergy, who feared infidel influence in Turkey, and of the privileged corps of the Janissaries, whose status was endangered by the innovations. In 1807 the Janissaries mutinied, deposed Selim and set his cousin Mustafa IV on the throne with a promise to undo all the work of his predecessor. But a general, Mustafa Bairakdar, who had commanded an army in the recent war against Russia and saw in the military reorganisation the main hope for survival of an empire that was already crumbling, led a rebellion on behalf of the deposed Selim and marched on Istanbul demanding his restoration. Selim was murdered by the supporters of Mustafa IV, but Bairakdar's troops captured the palace, deposed Mustafa and set up as Sultan his brother Mahmud, who had escaped death at the hands of the reactionaries by hiding under a pile of rugs. Mahmud not only revived Selim's policy, but went much further; he introduced Western forms of civil and fiscal administration, abolished court sinecures and substituted a semi-European style of official dress for the flowing robes and turbans of the Turkish *ancien régime*. When the Janissaries rose against him in 1826, he exterminated them. Although Greece and Egypt were lost to the Ottoman Empire during his reign, the control of the central Government over the rest of the Empire was tightened, so that it was enabled to survive strains and stresses which might otherwise have broken it up before the middle of the nineteenth century.

As long as the aims of the reform movement were clearly to strengthen the Empire against external threats to its existence, the reformers were able to muster enough support in the army and among high officials to overcome the conservative opposition of religious prejudice and vested interests. But the later developments of reform brought about a reaction. To complete the transformation of Turkey into a modern national state on the European model the Government enacted legislation designed to give all Ottoman subjects equality before the law and finally introduced—from above and not under any irresistible pressure from below—a parliamentary constitution. But these changes threatened the dominant position of the Moslem Turks in the Empire without providing any new basis for an Ottoman patriotism. The Empire was a multinational state in which more than a quarter of the population consisted of Christian peoples—Greeks, Armenians, Serbs and Bulgarians—who were grouped in communities (*millet*) according to religion, with private and family law administered by their own ecclesiastical authorities. These communities enjoyed a considerable degree of autonomy in nonpolitical affairs and most of the commercial wealth of the Empire was in their hands, but their status was inferior to that of the Moslems, and they were in effect kept disarmed; Christians on payment of a special tax were exempt from military service, which was obligatory for Moslems. Equalisation of rights and duties might theoretically produce a more compact and cohesive society, but in practice any tampering with the foundations of the Ottoman State tended to unleash forces of national separatism which were now growing among the Christian minorities under the influence of European ideas. Moreover, Turkish official policy in the middle years of the nineteenth century was deeply affected by the attitudes of the European powers, which for various reasons took an interest in the fate of the Christian minorities; in particular, the British, who

wished to maintain the integrity of the Ottoman Empire in order to prevent the aggrandisement of Russia, were at the same time anxious to avoid the reproach of protecting a régime which oppressed Christians, and therefore urged liberal reforms on the Turkish Government. For a while compliance with such pressures paid dividends to Turkey; in the Crimean War Turkey was the ally of Britain and France in a victorious contest with Russia. But in 1877 Turkey had to cope with widespread revolts of the Balkan Christians, was subjected to a Russian invasion and abandoned by the other European powers. This bitter experience convinced Turkish officialdom that liberal experiments could only lead to the disintegration of the Empire and that the better course was to restore the traditional structure of the Empire as an autocratically governed Moslem state. During the thirty years of the reign of Abdul Hamid II no progress was made; the purely material aspects of Westernisation were retained and the construction of railways and telegraphs continued, but there was a determined resistance to Western liberal and constitutional ideas. Abdul Hamid was by no means an incompetent ruler and showed considerable skill in his foreign policy, but his despotism stifled every kind of initiative, political or economic, and produced increasing discontent. The economic development of the Empire was given over to foreign capital, and the building of the Ottoman Debt Administration became a landmark in Istanbul perpetually reminding Turks of the financial bondage into which they had fallen. By 1907 conditions were ripe for a new turn in the struggle between modernisation and reaction, but by that time events originating elsewhere in Asia were also having their effect on Turkey.

During the nineteenth century, despite

all setbacks, Westernisation had gone further in the Ottoman Empire than in any other independent Asian country except Japan. In the Islamic world Persia and Afghanistan lagged far behind; as compared with Turkey, both were deeply secluded by their geographical location from Western influences. Persia, with its desert coastline, had a minimum of maritime commercial contact with the West until the development of its oil resources by British capital began early in the twentieth century; Afghanistan, a mountainous and entirely land-locked country, was even more isolated. It was, nevertheless, Persia which was to make the first would-be democratic revolution in the Moslem world—an event which was due not so much to the strength of the Westernising reformers as to the extreme decadence of the reigning Kajar Dynasty.

IV

In Eastern Asia, China provided the great example of an Asian power incapable of effectively resisting Western penetration and yet stubbornly opposing the influences of Western civilisation. China at the beginning of the nineteenth century had no contacts with the Western world except for a strictly regulated trade through the port of Canton and at one point on the Siberian border, and through a few Catholic priests allowed to reside in Peking because of their knowledge of astronomy. The Empire, which extended westward to the Pamirs and included within its borders a larger population than any other state in the world, appeared outwardly a mighty power; the Confucian scholar-officials who governed it regarded themselves as the élite of mankind, the custodians of the only real civilisation. Yet in the war against Britain which broke out in 1839, China was utterly defeated by very small British naval and military

forces, and another war with Britain and France two decades later was even more disastrous. The Chinese Government was compelled to abandon its policy of self-seclusion, and it became clear to some of its leading men that China would have to make some adjustment to the conditions of the modern world. But the great Taiping rebellion which ravaged China for over a decade from 1853 increased the antipathy to all Western influence among the governing officials.

The Taipings were inspired by an extremely fanatical, persecuting form of Christianity, ultimately derived from the teachings of Protestant missionaries, though strangely modified by their leader, who claimed to receive new revelations directly from God and aspired to found a new imperial dynasty. The result of this association of an intolerant Christianity with a political insurrection was to set the Confucian scholar class against a movement which it might otherwise have been brought to accept—as in previous changes of dynasty in China—and to intensify its resistance to all innovations of Western origin. It is often held that if the Taipings had been successful, their break with Chinese traditions would have led them to modernise China during the later decades of the nineteenth century, and that this outcome was only prevented by the intervention of the Western powers, which preferred to deal with a weak China under the effete Manchu Dynasty. But the Taipings had lost most of the territory they had initially won before the campaign of the foreign-officered force based on Shanghai, and commanded for a time by 'Chinese' Gordon; their defeat must be attributed mainly to the hostility which their alien-inspired fanaticism provoked. During the thirty years which followed the collapse of the great revolt in 1864—when the Taiping Emperor was besieged in Nanking and committed suicide in order to escape capture—the old order in China was preserved with scarcely any change, but Western trade and capital investment penetrated more and more deeply into the Chinese economy, and an increasing number of young Chinese acquired elements of a Western education.

In Japan, by contrast, an initial resistance to Western influences was followed by a rapid and energetic assimilation both of Western technology and of Western forms of economic and political organisation. Japan had been even more secluded than China from contacts with the West, for since early in the seventeenth century permission to trade—and that under conditions of severe restriction—had been confined to the Dutch in the single port of Nagasaki, and no Japanese was allowed to go abroad on pain of death if he returned. There was a considerable potential military force in the shape of the class of *samurai* or hereditary retainers of the local feudal rulers, but their equipment was antiquated and they lacked any system of central command; there was no navy, so that the country lay at the mercy of any power inclined to attack its ports.

After the British had imposed on China the humiliating Treaty of Nanking in 1842—the fruits of which were also acquired by other Western nations under a most-favoured-nation clause—there was talk of forcibly opening Japan also to an extended foreign trade. But the actual initiative came not from any European power, but from the United States, for the creation of a shipping route between San Francisco and Shanghai had made it urgent to have a port of call in Japan. An American naval squadron commanded by Commodore Perry was therefore sent to Yedo (Tokyo) Bay in 1853 with a request, backed by threats, for the opening of commercial intercourse; Perry declared

that he would return next year for an answer. There were acute differences of opinion among high Japanese officials and feudal lords on the question whether to reject or submit to the demands, but the warning of China's recent defeat provided a decisive argument for yielding. The concessions initially made were small, but, as in China, the gate once ajar was forced more and more widely open; the European nations claimed to share in the rights granted to the Americans, and the scope of their demands continually increased. The *de facto* Government of Japan, the Tokugawa family holding the office of *shogun* and ruling from Yedo, the modern Tokyo, incurred the odium of accepting and enforcing terms imposed by foreign powers, and its domestic enemies took the opportunity to demand a restoration of administrative authority to the Emperor who reigned without governing in the ancient capital, Kyoto. An agitation for the overthrow of the Tokugawa was combined with a movement for the expulsion of all foreigners from Japan. Tokugawa rule collapsed in the storm that was thus raised, but the disaster which befell the feudal lord of Choshu when he tried to close the Strait of Shimonoseki to foreign shipping, convinced the leaders of the Emperor's party that Japan was not strong enough to drive away the Western traders, and could only acquire power equal to that of Western nations by learning the secrets of their strength. When, therefore, the Emperor—a boy of sixteen— was at length 'restored' in 1868, his advisers at once embarked on a programme of radical reforms to modernise the basis of the Japanese State and build up an effective army and navy. During the next two decades the semi-independence of the feudal units was abolished and a centralised administration established, a Western system of banking and finance was introduced, and modern industries were started with governmental initiative or encouragement. Japanese students were sent to study abroad and European and American instructors were engaged to teach in Japan; eventually a system of universal primary education was instituted with the inculcation of patriotism and loyalty to the Emperor as one of its main functions. The traditional privileges of the *samurai* were abolished in favour of a national army based on conscription and a General Staff was formed and trained by a pupil of Moltke. A modern navy was created, beginning with British ships and instructors. Finally a parliamentary constitution was promulgated in 1889, a date by which all major European countries except Russia had some kind of elected legislature; but the German rather than the British, French or American model was followed in drafting the constitution, and the powers of the people's representatives were strictly limited.

The practical effect of all these changes was seen in 1894, when war broke out between Japan and China over their rival interests in Korea. Japan won a swift and decisive victory. The Chinese indeed lost more prestige than the Japanese gained, for the contest was still only one between two Asian states, and the West was still unwilling to entertain the idea that Japan might be ready to measure herself against a major Western power. But the war at least demonstrated how great an advantage might be gained by an Asian country through adoption of Western technology over a much larger country which had persisted in traditional ways. The immediate consequences of the war were twofold. On the one hand, the principal Western powers, aware more than ever before of China's weakness and anticipating a possible break-up of the Chinese Empire, began to make all kinds of demands on the

Peking Government and stake out claims to 'spheres of influence' in Chinese territory. On the other hand, the experience of the war led a group of Chinese officials to make a desperate, belated attempt to imitate the Meiji reforms of Japan—so called from the reign title of the Japanese Emperor—through the Manchu monarchy. One of them had the ear of the Emperor Kwang Hsu, and a sweeping reform programme was begun. But it disturbed too many vested interests of the court, and the dowager Empress Tzu Hsi, who had had a guiding voice in Chinese policy for forty years, carried out a *coup d'état* against the Emperor; he was made a prisoner in his palace and the reforms were cancelled. But something had to be done to satisfy popular indignation at the encroachments of foreign powers, so the reactionary court gave its encouragement to a fanatical anti-Western secret society, which came to be nicknamed the 'Boxers' from its Chinese title of 'Fists of Patriotic Harmony'. The Boxers tried to drive all foreigners out of China—traders, diplomats and missionaries—by acts of violence and soon involved their country in an undeclared war, which in the year 1900 caused seven Western nations, together with Japan, to join in sending an expeditionary force to Peking. China was more than ever humiliated, but the disaster led to fresh attempts at reform—this time under the patronage of the dowager Empress; in particular, the immensely old system of competitive public examinations in the Chinese classics for entry into the civil service was abolished and recognition was given to an education of Western type as preparation for an official career.

In 1904, ten years after her victory over China, Japan again went to war, but this time against one of the Great Powers of Europe. Although protected against the hostile intervention of any other European power by an alliance with Britain, Japan fought Russia single-handed and was again victorious. The direct result of the war was to wipe out the dominant position which Russia had gained in South Manchuria and Korea and to substitute a Japanese ascendance in those areas; Korea became a Japanese protectorate and was annexed by Japan in 1910. But even more important than the local consequences was the political effect throughout Asia and in the world as a whole. The Western powers now accepted Japan as an equal, while all over Asia her victory was taken as signifying that the spell of Western invincibility was broken and that Asians need not accept a position of permanent inferiority to the West.

V

What Japan had done, other nations of Asia could do if they would only bestir themselves. New nationalist movements grew up in the independent countries of Asia linking the Western-educated element of the professional classes—by now deeply affected by democratic ideas—with patriotic and modern-minded army officers. From these new movements came three revolutions in the decade following the Russo-Japanese War: the first, in Persia in 1906, deposed the reigning Shah and set up a parliamentary constitution; the second, in 1907 in Turkey, did likewise with Sultan Abdul Hamid II; the third, in China in 1911, overthrew the Manchu Dynasty and proclaimed a republic. The first two revolutions got rid of individual monarchs opposed to reform without removing their dynasties, and sought to limit royal prerogatives by parliamentary powers as in the constitutional monarchies of Europe. The Chinese Republic, on the other hand, marked a much greater break with tradition; it reflected in part the special influence of American ideas in

China—due to American educational activity there—and in part the anti-Manchu sentiment, which sought to put an end to an alien dynasty without having any Chinese candidate for a new monarchical line. The idea of a democratic republic, however, had no meaning for the masses of the Chinese people, and after an unsuccessful attempt by President Yuan Shih-kai in 1915 to restore the monarchy in his own person, China became a prey to rival factions of army generals who fought one another for the control of provinces and of what was left of the central Government. This was the 'era of the war-lords', which lasted until 1927.

The Russo-Japanese War also stimulated nationalist movements in the dependencies of Western powers, particularly in India. In 1857 a last attempt to drive the British out of India had been made by leaders from dispossessed ruling families of the old Mughal and Maratha régimes taking advantage of mutinies breaking out among Indian troops in the service of the East India Company. The insurrection was crushed, the administration of India was made a direct responsibility of the British Crown, and the army was reorganised so effectively that no serious mutiny again took place until the British finally left India in 1947. But from the closing years of the nineteenth century a new type of nationalism arose, no longer connected with the dynastic princely elements of the old India, but based on the new Western-educated professional classes—lawyers, teachers, journalists and clerks. This movement could not hope for army support and had to advance by purely political methods supplemented by terrorism by extremists and later by campaigns of 'civil disobedience'. In the 1920s Gandhi, who combined ability as a political leader with the prestige, nowhere so important as in India, of a religious saint, transformed the nationalism of the Congress party into a mass movement which exerted an ever-increasing pressure on the British authorities. On the British side there was a willingness to concede the principle of ultimate self-government, but a general disposition to regard its attainment as a matter for a rather remote future. Meanwhile concessions were made to Indian nationalism by gradual 'Indianisation' of the civil service and by the institution of elective assemblies in the provinces.

The French and the Dutch were less prepared to yield to nationalist movements in their territories because they had been more influenced in their colonial policies by the Roman idea of empire whereby subject peoples would be gradually assimilated to the metropolitan nation, so that the imperial unity would be permanent and independence of its parts excluded. The Americans, on the contrary, had never developed a consistent doctrine of imperial rule at all and found their possession of the Philippines embarrassing; they were the first Western nation to give a definitely dated promise of independence to an Asian people by an Act of Congress of 1934 which provided for the termination of American sovereignty in the Philippines in 1946.

VI

The so-called First World War, unlike the Second, left the greater part of Asia uninvolved except for indirect effects. Actual fighting was virtually confined to the territory and borderlands of Turkey, and the only important change in the political map of Asia was the detachment of the Arab-inhabited lands of the former Ottoman Empire to form a group of new Arab states under British and French tutelage, together with a National Home for the Jews in Palestine in accordance with promises made by the Allies to the Zionist organisation during the war. But far more significant than any changes of sovereignty were the revolutions, both social and national, that took place in Asia in the years after 1918. The Russian Revolution of 1917 had spread to Asia, both to the Russian settlers and to the subject Asian peoples, with slogans at once of proletarian socialist internationalism and of national self-determination; as a result of complicated civil wars, revolts and counter-revolts in Siberia and Central Asia, the Russian Empire was restored within its former territorial limits, but nominally as a federation with eight Asian constituent republics and native members of the centrally controlled All-Union Communist Party holding office in each. This was a new form of imperialism, unlike any previous form of Western domination, and it was claimed in Communist propaganda as a liberation, in spite of the fact that movements for real national independence among Georgians, Uzbeks or Kazakhs were most ruthlessly suppressed.

In Turkey and Persia the modernising régimes created by the upheavals of the first decade of the century were swept away by fresh revolutions. The 'Young Turks' of 1907, one faction of whom had led the country into war as an ally of Germany, were replaced by the more radically reforming Kemalists, who got rid of the Ottoman Dynasty, disestablished Islam as the state religion and made the Turks write their language with a Latin alphabet. In Persia a revolution swept away the old Kajar régime, but the revolutionary leader, Riza, became himself the founder of a new dynasty. In China the Kuomintang party, trying to carry on the work of the revolution of 1911, reorganised itself and formed an alliance with the Chinese Communist party (founded in 1921) with the aim of overcoming the provincial 'war-lords' who had divided China between them. Marching northwards in 1926, the Kuomintang successively captured Hankow, Nanking, Shanghai and Peking, and thus re-united most of China under its control; it quarrelled, however, with its Communist allies and defeated them in a new civil war. The Communists, with peasant guerrilla forces, continued to operate in outlying parts of China, but remained only a minor factor in Chinese politics until conditions brought about by the Japanese invasion of 1937 enabled them to renew their strength. Outside China, Communism made very little progress anywhere in non-Russian Asia between the two world wars.

From 1931 onwards until 1945, the great dynamic, disruptive influence in Asian affairs was neither Communism nor democracy nor colonial nationalism but the violent imperial expansion of Japan. This reflected an internal nationalist revolution, but one of a special kind, which had no connection with liberalism or with Marxism, based itself, like the reform movement of the early Meiji period, on the tradition of the Japanese sacred monarchy. Aiming at the increase of national power through a 'high-degree defence state' and a 'new order in East Asia', the new Japanese imperialism found its main support in the army, and coerced or intimidated the civil government by acts of violence; strongly anti-Western, it promoted colonial nationalist movements in the dependencies of Western powers and preached a doctrine of 'Asia for the Asians', which implied, however, a subjection of all other Asian peoples to Japan. The movement ran its course, with the conquest of Manchuria in 1931–3, the invasion of China south of the Great Wall in 1937 and the overrunning of South-East Asia to the Timor Sea and the Bay of Bengal from the end of 1941; it ended with Japan's unconditional surrender to the Supreme Commander of the Allied Powers on board the American battleship *Missouri* on 2 September, 1945.

This Japanese adventure, more than any previous event since Vasco da Gama entered the Indian Ocean, was to be a turning point in the history of Asia. The changes brought about in Japan itself by the Allied occupation were to be only a small part of the consequences of the Pacific war. Although Japan had been thoroughly defeated, the effects of the Japanese invasions and conquests had been so far-reaching that nothing could be put back again as it had been. Four years after Japan's surrender the Kuomintang régime under which China had fought the Japanese had been driven from the Chinese mainland by the Communists, who were able to establish their fanatical domination over a society in ruins after eight years of disastrous war. In India and South-East Asia the Western imperial systems were eliminated—in India and Burma by agreed transfers of power without fighting, in Indo-China and Indonesia by armed insurrections and much bloodshed. Within a decade nine new sovereign nations had appeared on the map from the Indus eastward, and the new turmoil of nationalism was spreading to the Arab lands of the Middle East. The days when a European statesman could say that 'the affairs of Asia are decided in Europe' were definitely over.

19 THE INDUSTRIAL AND ENVIRONMENTAL REVOLUTIONS

The Industrial Revolution

by J. M. Prest

The political and social events here recorded from the seventeenth to the end of the nineteenth century and the expansion of European influence overseas had been conditioned and stimulated by fundamental changes in technology. They were to affect the whole world and to create an unprecedented change in the numbers and in the environment of the human race.

Over the last two hundred and fifty years an increasing proportion of mankind has enjoyed a rapidly increasing variety and volume of goods, while doing ever less work to produce them. This process has been termed the Industrial Revolution. Man has always made tools, but he continued for thousands of years to operate them with his own muscles and to control them with his own mind. Under these conditions the productivity of the worker, and the condition of mankind, could be improved only by economy in the use of human labour. One man with a lever could move a stone that could not be moved by several men without. By the principle of the division of labour, by the acquisition of specialised skills, and by the exchange of products whole communities were able to enjoy standards of living that would have been impossible had each man continued to work alone. But at the same time, among nations, no greater increase in power was possible than an increase in manpower; procreation was a duty, and 'civilised' states actually went to war for the sake of the prisoners whom they turned into slaves, with Aristotle's word for it that their actions were just.

The Industrial Revolution, in its widest context, originally developed out of the Neolithic Revolution, and began with the first substitution of animal for human labour, with the replacement of the sentry by the watchdog, the submission of the ox to the yoke and the ass to the bridle. The division of labour raised the productivity of animals no less than that of men, and animals became the object of plunder as much as men and women. To the use of human and animal power must be added, before the eighteenth century, the use of water and wind power. All four, however, had their limitations: slaves tired, only a small number of horses could be harnessed together, and both watermills and windmills were irregular, the one being subject to drought and the other to calm. The windmill worked well enough if there was so much grain to grind, and, on an average, so many fresh winds a year, since the grain that could not be ground today could be ground tomorrow. But it was less reliable for pumping in the fens of Holland or East Anglia, where sometimes when there was most rain there was least wind. Industrially, the world was at a standstill at the beginning of the eighteenth century for the want of a prime mover unaffected by fatigue and independent of the weather. Such improvements as were still possible under the old system—better dieting and selective breeding to produce stronger men and animals, larger mill ponds for storing water, and canalised rivers to speed navigation—could never by themselves have brought about a revolution.

The revolution in power, which was due to European initiative, began in the early eighteenth century, and the story can be divided into two periods. In the first, which came to an end about 1830, the steam engine was invented and developed in Great Britain, and the steam factory and the railway were brought into use. In the second period, which has lasted from about 1830 to the present day, the principles of power working have become understood all over the world, while a new series of inventions in many countries has led to the internal combustion engine and electricity, and to nuclear energy and back automation.

II

Amateurs of technology point to Heron's aeliopile, about two thousand years ago, and Branca's proposed pounding machine of 1629, and ask why the steam engine was not perfected earlier. Their illustrations give the answer. The easy kind of steam engine to imagine was the turbine; but the turbine, to be successful, requires higher steam pressures, and a higher speed of revolution than the boilers or bearings of the seventeenth or any earlier century could withstand, and also a more complicated relationship between the pressure of the steam and the speed of revolution than the science of the day could formulate. The first successful steam engine worked upon very different principles. Scientifically, it was based upon the discoveries that the atmosphere has weight, that nature does not abhor a vacuum, and that between the atmosphere and a vacuum there

is a pressure difference that can be made to do work. Mechanically, it was based upon the discovery that the way to produce such a difference of pressure, and to take advantage of it, was to admit steam into a cylinder underneath a piston, and to condense it there. These principles seem to have been clearly understood by Papin in France, and by other scientists of the late seventeenth century.

But to devise a steam engine, and to set it to work, are two different things. No invention survives unless there is a need for it, as there was in Great Britain in the early eighteenth century. More than any other country, Great Britain was dependent upon coal. For hundreds of years, with every ship built of wood, and every ton of iron smelted and forged with charcoal, the forests had diminished, and domestic and industrial consumers alike had come to depend upon coal. Nowhere else was there such a large or heavily capitalised coal trade as that between Newcastle and London. More coal meant deeper mines, and the deeper the mine the harder it was to drain. By the beginning of the eighteenth century the thousands of horses employed in shifts to work the pumps were fighting a losing battle against the water, even when working continuously.

During the seventeenth century, several patents had been granted in England, and many claims made for the 'raising of water by fire', and Savery, at least, had advertised engines for sale. It was, however, Newcomen who achieved the first successful steam pumping engine in 1708. To one end of a centrally pivoted rocking beam he attached the pump rods, and to the other the engine piston. As the weight of the rods dragged the piston to the top of the cylinder, steam was admitted underneath it. At the top of the stroke a jet of cold water was sprayed into the cylinder to condense the steam and create a partial vacuum. With a partial vacuum below, and the weight of the atmosphere above, the piston returned to the bottom of the cylinder while the pump rods at the other end of the beam rose, raising the water with them. The whole cycle could be repeated several times a minute. These engines, manufactured by arrangement under Savery's patent, which did not expire until 1733, spread rapidly through the British coalfields and to other mining areas all over Western Europe. In 1734 a Swede recorded that a Newcomen type engine was raising as much water as 'sixty-six horse-whims, each drawn by four pairs of horses, or altogether five hundred and twenty-eight horses in twenty-four hours'. Here, at last, was a revolution in power; a machine, many horses strong, in which, from the very nature of its construction, all the horses could not help but pull together. By 1775 there were, perhaps, one hundred and thirty engines of this type at work in Great Britain. If the engine was prodigal of coal, what did that matter? Situated at the pit head, the engine's wants were soon satisfied, and without it there would soon be no coal at all.

It was not the least of the advantages of this engine that it worked efficiently enough to be adopted, and inefficiently enough to stimulate Watt, a mathematical instrument maker at the University of Glasgow, systematically to improve it. Understanding from his conversations with Professor Black that heat was the source of power (though Black himself misunderstood the nature of heat), Watt appreciated the waste involved in alternately heating and cooling the cylinder, and, at length, in 1766, hit on the idea of a separate condenser, which could be kept permanently cool, while the cylinder remained permanently hot. Fortunate, at the second attempt, in his choice of partner, Watt began to manufacture his improved engines at Boulton's foundry in Soho, Birmingham, in 1773, greatly helped by Wilkinson, who could now supply cylinders bored accurately to five-hundredths of an inch. During this period, while still working at low pressures, Watt began to make use of the expansive power of steam. From this point to the use of steam alternately on either side of the cylinder was but a step, and this step, as Boulton knew better than Watt, was timely, for such a 'double acting' engine, running smoothly, and with an even stroke, could be used with crank, or with sun and planet wheels, to produce rotative motion.

It would be unfair to attribute the factory system in textiles wholly to Watt's improvements in the steam engine, for rotative motion is no use without rotative machines to use it. Throughout the second half of the eighteenth century a series of advances took place in Great Britain in the spinning of cotton. Hargreaves' spinning jenny, which was contemporary with Watt's separate condenser, was still hand-driven, but Arkwright's frame, invented in 1768, had to be operated by power. Arkwright hired horses to drive the machine until he had proved its reliability, and then constructed the large water-driven mill at Cromford in 1771. Throughout the 1770s the master cotton spinners jockeyed for position on the better streams. When the rivers ran low in summer they employed the early 'single acting' Newcomen and Watt engines to pump the water back from the bottom of the mill wheels to the top. But this was a roundabout way of obtaining rotative motion from a steam engine, and consequently, when Watt produced his 'double acting' engine in the 1780s, there was a whole industry waiting to receive it. The textile industry could not have expanded far without it, for there were not enough streams. Henceforth new factories, and new centres of population, were to be situated on the coalfields.

The revolution begun in cotton spinning was continued by Crompton, whose mule, perfected in the 1780s, contained features of both the spinning jenny and the frame. In twenty years the revolution spread from cotton to wool, and from spinning it spread more slowly to weaving. Cartwright invented a power loom for cotton as early as 1784, but mechanised weaving was not easily perfected, and it was forty years before power weaving became the rule in cotton, and another thirty years before the same stage was reached in wool, while in the hosiery trade the power-knitted, fully-fashioned stocking came ten to twenty years later still.

Steam power could not reach every country cottage, and so great were its advantages, that it would be tempting to look no further to explain the supersession in Great Britain of the domestic system in industry by the factory. But one should not forget the closer supervision, and the regular hours made possible by aggregated labour. The employer who, under the domestic system, was accustomed to distribute yarn to the weavers in their own homes, was accustomed also to lose some part of it by theft, and to watch impotently while the weavers, after resting on Sunday, took 'Saint' Monday off as a holiday, and 'Saint' Tuesday too, if they liked. These practices alone gave the employer incentive enough to invest his capital in fixed plant, and to concentrate his work under one roof. They account for the establishment of the factory system in other trades, like Wedgwood's pottery at Etruria, in advance even of the application of power. A new sense of discipline and of punctuality came into the world with the factory, in which men worked regular hours, and the work itself proceeded according to a timetable.

The gathering momentum of the industrial revolution was only maintained as a result of changes in the smelting and forging of iron. While Great Britain was undergoing the transition from a wood to a coal economy, it was natural that attempts should be made to smelt iron with coal or coke. The secret was discovered about 1709 by Darby, who for some years kept it to himself and his family. In spite of his precautions, the knowledge spread, and the output of iron increased, stimulated at intervals throughout the century by the demands of the government for cannon. As more iron became available, so man's use of it became more ambitious, and in 1779 the first substantial iron bridge was built, across the river Severn at Coalbrookdale. But the coke-smelted iron had still to be forged with charcoal, and it was not until the 1780s that Cort at Fareham discovered the puddling and rolling processes which emancipated the iron industry forever from the woods, and made possible the partnership between coal and iron which forms the next phase of the industrial revolution.

Watt's steam engines were now applied to work the bellows in the iron industry. With their aid the production of iron in England doubled between 1778 and 1796, and doubled again between 1796 and 1806. Higher temperatures and new methods made better metal, with which the iron industry was now handsomely to repay its debt to steam. Throughout the industrial revolution there has been a recurring theme of new materials making better engines. Watt had started at low pressures because his materials were weak, but he knew that high-pressure steam was more efficient, and by the end of the century better iron had made higher pressures possible. Yet by this time Watt had come to associate high-pressure engines with attempts to break his patents, and when these expired in 1800, and Watt himself retired after making about five hundred engines, this most methodical and ingenious of inventors had become a technological reactionary, opposing the use of higher pressures with all his venerable authority.

The pioneer of high pressure was an erratic Cornish genius, Trevithick, whose skill in making engines was great, though his ability to sell them was small. Low-pressure engines had to be large to be powerful, and being cumbersome they could only be stationary. Trevithick saw that with higher pressures and smaller components there was no reason why the steam engine should not be mounted on wheels and drive itself about, either on a road, or on one of the tram- or rail-ways which were now so common among the collieries of England and Wales. Using pressures of fifty to sixty pounds to the square inch, he discarded Watt's condenser as a luxury, and, exhausting the steam direct to the atmosphere, exhibited locomotives in London in 1803 and 1808. In 1804, in South Wales, one of his locomotives drew five wagons, with ten tons of iron and seventy men, along a railway nine and three-quarter miles long, in four hours and five minutes. It is not easy to see why this demonstration attracted so little attention at the time. Certainly the engine had torn up the track, but there was no technical reason why the iron industry should have taken another twenty years to supply satisfactory rails.

The present generation admires Trevithick, the romantic pioneer who lost interest. The Victorians admired the perseverance of George Stephenson, their copybook hero who succeeded, as presented to them by Samuel Smiles. Despite Smiles, it is doubtful whether Stephenson invented anything, and his first Killingworth engine, built in 1814, was years behind Trevithick's. But Stephenson was a dedicated man, and he improved. By 1820 he had become not just an expert on locomotives, but a railway engineer, understanding not only steam engines, but surveying, and the construction of a track. His fame spread slowly from one colliery to another, and when the promoters of the Stockton and Darlington Railway were looking for an engineer, it was sensible, but still courageous of them to choose Stephenson over the heads of all the great civil engineers in London.

When this line was completed in 1825, Stephenson, dining with his assistants, accurately forecast the great development of railways in the future, and adequately summed up the changes that had taken place in this first century of the industrial revolution in Great Britain. The fortunes of that country, he said, had once been founded upon wool: they were now based upon coal, and the Lord Chancellor ought henceforth to sit upon a coalsack. George Stephenson and his son Robert became the acknowledged leaders of the railway engineers. Together they built the Liverpool and Manchester Railway, and won the locomotive trials at Rainhill in 1829. Between them they completed the marriage of coal and iron. Coal would now drive the iron locomotive from one end of the country to the other: the iron railway would now carry coal from the pithead to the remotest country market town.

One can name a number of other products without which there would have been no industrial revolution—sulphuric acid, for instance, and more accurate jigs and tools in the engineering workshops. This need not amend the picture of a first industrial revolution based upon coal, iron, cotton, and steam, which was one of Great Britain's gifts to the world.

It was, of course, quite natural that this cycle of related inventions should have been completed where it had begun. Britain enjoyed the stimulus to mine coal, a geology in which coal and iron came close together, a competitive society, respect for property, and abundant capital. But with the success of the steam locomotives on the Liverpool and Manchester Railway, the first great cycle of invention came to an end. The mid-nineteenth century is the period in which, while new inventions were germinating, the old inventions were being received. The British settled down to exploit the new processes, and other nations to imitate them—Belgium, France, the United States and Germany.

There had never been such increases in prosperity before. While the population of Great Britain increased from approximately ten millions in 1800 to twenty millions in 1850, and forty millions in 1900, the production of coal rose faster; from about ten million tons in 1800, to over fifty million tons in 1850, and two hundred million tons in 1900. The production of pig iron rose from just under two hundred and fifty thousand tons in 1806, to about three million tons in 1850, while in the cotton spinning trade one man, or his wife, in a power-driven mill in the 1820s was producing two hundred times what he would have produced sixty years earlier by hand. In 1800 Great Britain had engines equivalent to seven thousand five hundred horse power, a revolutionary figure indeed, but one representing less than one horse-power per thousand people. By 1871 there were nearly one million horse-power in the factories under government inspection alone. The Liverpool and Manchester

Railway, opened in 1830, was followed by an additional two thousand miles of track by 1843, and by another six thousand miles by 1855, so quickly did the railways link one great centre of population to another.

These few bare figures illustrate the scale of the progress made, not only in Great Britain, but in other countries. The steam engine, however, had come into a world in which people were beginning to attend both to personal hygiene and to public health. There was no spectacular increase in the birth-rate, but more children were surviving, and the population of the world was beginning to increase very rapidly. Consequently labour was still cheap, and the steam engine had either to be able to do something that men could not do, like draining the mines, or at least to do it very much better, like dragging trains along a railway, if it was to be adopted. At sea, the wind cost nothing, and the transition from sail to steam was slow. In industries such as agriculture, where labour was cheap, and steam was scarcely advantageous, let alone revolutionary, steam made little progress. Many other trades—the building trades, the cobbler's, and domestic service—derived no direct advantage from this new source of power.

So far the steam engine had done little either to lighten or to shorten the day's labour. Typical of the still primitive use of power in the nineteenth century was mining, so admirably described in Zola's *Germinal*. In this great novel there are engines to pump the mines dry, and there are engines to raise the coal and to lower and raise the miners, but underground the coal is drawn by horses, and hewn and loaded by hand. The steam engine had made all this work possible, and was undoubtedly providing the miners with employment, but it had not yet taken their work upon itself. The engine could not face the hazards of fire damp, so the men and women still had to.

In the textile industry, the one great group of trades in which the steam engine was replacing the muscles of the labourer, the consequences, in Great Britain at least, were not all immediately beneficial. There was some substitution of female for male labour, admirable, perhaps, if there was alternative employment for the men, and not so admirable where there was not. For many of the older generation of hand-loom weavers the new power came, in the 1830s, not to lighten their labours, but to put them out of work. Those who remained at work in their own homes, in competition with power, were working longer hours for lower rewards. Too old to change nimbly to the new methods, they fell into poverty, while the younger generation in the factories worked shorter hours for higher wages, and a new, higher standard of living. The tragedy was that while the conditions of work in the factories could be regulated by legislation, and government inspectors appointed to see that the regulations were kept, far greater hardships had to be endured by tailors and sewing girls, sweated in private houses by middlemen whom Parliament was unable, and public opinion unwilling, to reach.

Contemporary observers believed that the steam engine had created not only a factory, but an urban population. Certainly the steam engine did make for concentration, and the census of 1851 showed that the population of England was for the first time more urban than rural, and more northern than southern. But it would be easy to attribute too much to the steam engine. Large towns existed at that time in non-industrial countries like India and China, and towns had flourished for hundreds of years in Europe on trade,

before they began to expand on large-scale industry. Nevertheless, with every depression in the manufacturing industries in the nineteenth century, people deplored what they called 'the divorce of the workman from the land', and schemes were floated to provide allotments for the urban artisan and to settle distressed weavers on smallholdings. Such industrial reaction disappeared with the revival of trade. Employment may have been less certain, but wages were higher in the towns, and on the whole people went to the towns because they wanted to. If, when they arrived, and when they had made good, or failed to, the richer people moved to one quarter, and the poorer people to another, then friendship was as much to blame for that as wickedness. The towns were ugly, and coal can be blamed for the soot that made them dirty, but a social or political, and not a technological reason must be found for the evil jerry-built houses, and the lack of town planning that characterised Birmingham, Essen, and Pittsburg.

In the late eighteenth and early nineteenth centuries the prevailing mood among social and political theorists was one of optimism, and a belief in a natural harmony of interests. To Andrew Ure steam power, the profit motive, and the law of supply and demand promised to become the benevolent despots of the nineteenth century, which would raise the standard of living by providing society with the goods it wanted at the lowest possible cost. Ure was typical of a class which had absorbed enough of the theories of the French physiocrats and of Adam Smith's *Wealth of Nations* to confuse private interest with public good, and of Malthus' *Principle of Population* to believe that the chief cause of distress among the working classes was the number of their children. The 'Manchester School' argued that both capital and labour were commodities—to be bought for as little as possible; that cheap capital and cheap labour stimulated production; that combination, whether of masters or of workmen, was conspiracy or even treason; that any interference by government with the contract of employment or with the terms of trade must be either unnecessary or harmful; and that the universal adoption of these self-evident principles under the general slogan of 'free trade' would be followed by the substitution of 'the contest of commerce for the arbitrament of war'. Men who thought like this sought political power less to 'liberalise' government in their own interest than to prevent government being used at all. Their object was to inaugurate the age of *laissez faire*, in which private enterprise would provide the people with houses, clothes, and food, careers would be open to talent, and the performance of such governmental functions as remained would be auctioned to the lowest bidder. The promulgation of this faith having coincided with technological advances leading to an unprecedented increase in productivity, it was difficult not to believe that the one was the cause of the other, and many of the tenets of this faith were, as a result, exported from Great Britain, with Lancashire cottons, all over the world.

There have always been critics of the social and political conditions under which this first industrial revolution took place. It has even been fashionable among historians to present the whole process as a disastrous conspiracy by which one set of wicked capitalists, called enclosing landlords, drove a formerly prosperous and independent peasantry off their lands into crowded and unhealthy towns, where another set of wicked capitalists was waiting to exploit them and their families under brutal overseers, for long hours, at low wages, in soulless factories saddened by the cries of children being crushed to death by dangerous machinery. But, in fact, the theories of Adam Smith, when developed into 'classical' economics by Malthus and Ricardo, had said almost as much about the conflicting interests of classes in the distribution of wealth, as they had about the natural harmony of interests in its production. As the classes drifted ever further apart, the initiative in discussion passed, in three generations, from Ricardo himself, who thought that little could be done to reconcile conflicting interests, first to Carlyle and Mrs Gaskell, who appealed to the Christianity of rich and poor alike to heal the differences between them, and then to Henry George and Karl Marx, with their respective panaceas, the confiscation by the State of all rent, or unearned income, and the revolution of the proletariat against the capitalists.

All recent critics have been influenced by Karl Marx's analysis of British industrial society in the middle of the nineteenth century. With the fervour of a Jewish Messiah, Marx added the concept of surplus value to Ricardian economics, omitted the idealism from Hegel's dialectic, and showed how history would prove to be on the side of numbers against wealth. He saw society inevitably divided by the ownership of the means of production into two classes, capital and labour, one of which greedily extracted surplus value from the labour of the other. Not only was the individual capitalist strong enough to crush the individual worker, but capital was strong enough to crush the individual capitalist. No man could escape from the morality of his class, and appeals to the charity of the individual capitalist were therefore hopeless. The current political economy, the system of government, and the rule of law were all represented as part of an elaborate confidence trick by which the working classes were invited, or compelled, to submit to being exploited. No less a person than Disraeli anticipated many of the points in this analysis, in a novel called *Sybil, or The Two Nations*, published in 1845. But Disraeli lived to become the leader of a Conservative Government, which, in the 1870s, without making any concession to class warfare by injuring the rich, began to help the poor, and did more than any other single administration to overthrow the doctrine of *laissez faire* and to draw the teeth of Marx's doctrine in England.

III

The steam engine of the early nineteenth century was wonderful, but it was not perfect. It could not be manufactured in fractional horse-power sizes: it took a long time to start: it was relatively immobile: its fuel was bulky and dirty, and was, in any case, not to be found the world over. The two outstanding disadvantages, however, which stimulated further progress, were that the steam engine was thermally inefficient, and that the power generated by steam could not be transmitted over long distances. These two considerations were to lead respectively, in the next cycle of invention, to the internal combustion engine and to electricity.

It was remarkable that nobody knew for certain at this time just how inefficient the steam engine was. Although the discoveries of Newcomen and Watt had been based upon the science of their day, that science still fell short of an understanding of the laws of thermodynamics. Watt had been able to measure the work done against the quantity of coal consumed, but he had not been able to say how much more work a perfect engine would have done in consuming the same quantity of coal. The Stockton and Darlington Rail-

way was completed in the year in which Carnot, in France, postulated the ideal reversible cycle of operation of a heat engine, and trains were running from London and Paris before Joule, Kelvin, Clausius, Helmholz and others were able to relate heat to work, to put forward the concept of energy, and to show how far the actual performance of a steam engine fell short of the ideal. Seldom can man have made so much practical use of an invention before he understood it.

The new cycle of invention which set in towards the end of the nineteenth century was marked by a new relationship between science and industry. Bessemer, Siemens, and Thomas, who revolutionised the production of steel, worked by science rather than by rule of thumb. The laws of thermodynamics led Diesel to search for a design for a rational heat engine. In 1865 Clerk-Maxwell provided a mathematical basis to electro-magnetism before a single dynamo had been installed to light a city, and, at the same time, by mathematical reasoning alone, postulated the existence of wireless **waves** before Hertz discovered them in 1887, and Marconi brought them into everyday use a decade later. The structure of the atom had to be explored for fifty years before a controlled fission reaction could be used to generate electricity on a commercial scale at Calder Hall in 1956. Finally, in the twentieth century, whole teams of scientists have had to co-operate to bring new products into general use.

The first consequence of the scientific examination of the steam engine was a deep pessimism. Not only was a first-class compound engine less than twenty per cent efficient, but it seemed that there was very little that could be done to improve it so long as the heat was generated in an external boiler, and transferred, with losses, to the working cylinder. The obvious improvement seemed to be to generate the heat in the cylinder itself, and to construct an internal combustion engine. This idea has as long a history as the steam engine itself, and Papin had experimented in the seventeenth century with the explosion of gunpowder in a cylinder. Most of the early experimenters failed for want of a fuel which would burn completely and leave no deposit. All found some difficulty in igniting the mixture in the cylinder, for flame ignition was clumsy and set a limit to the speed of revolution, and the electric spark was still unreliable. The first internal combustion engine was put on the market by Lenoir in France during the 1860s. This was a half horse-power, double-acting, two-stroke engine, running on coal gas from the mains with electric ignition. It was light, and easily started, and was used in a number of small workshops in France and England. But it was inefficient, because the mixture was not compressed before it was exploded.

The principles of the four-stroke cycle, which makes it possible to compress the mixture properly before ignition, and to expand it properly afterwards, were laid down by de Rochas in France in 1862, and finally translated into practice by Otto in Germany in 1876. Otto had already greatly improved the performance of the Lenoir gas engine by adding a clutch, and the future of the internal combustion engine was assured when his fellow-countrymen Daimler and Diesel, following his principles, but changing the fuel, began to use, respectively, light and heavy oils. This series of inventions was completed in 1881, when Dugald Clerk, in Great Britain, patented the two-stroke oil engine. By 1900 many of these internal combustion engines were nearly thirty per cent efficient.

The diehard advocates of steam have always said that the automobile waited upon the invention of the pneumatic tyre by Dunlop in 1888, rather than the internal combustion engine. Be that as it may, the different types of engine competed upon fairly level terms while the automobile industry was being established at the turn of the century. The explosion engine may be barbarous, and the clutch and gear-box may be complicated, but no flash tube boiler ever fired as quickly as an internal combustion engine, or showed itself so mobile or flexible. There had been many fairly successful powered carriages since Cugnot's steam three-wheeler ran round Paris in 1769. But the credit for the automobile belongs primarily to Benz, whose first automobile, built in Germany in 1885, included a single-cylinder four-stroke engine, with electric ignition and water cooling, and a differential gear. Endless mechanical and electrical refinements have been made to the automobile since: Benz's single cylinder has become four, six, or eight, and his three wheels have become four or more, but there has been little change in fundamentals. The last stronghold of steam on the roads was the steam roller, used, ironically enough, to prepare the bituminised surfaces which eased the passage of its triumphant rival.

The automobile is one of the great triumphs of the industrial revolution. It is a highly skilled product which, thanks to the division of labour, can be mass-produced by unskilled men who do not understand its working. It can be driven by anyone. Accurately machined and interchangeable parts make it possible to replace any defective part from stock. The demand for it grows with the population of the world, and the only limit to its production is the capacity of the roads to accommodate it. Many people had been set to work by the steam engine, but few people had cared to own one themselves.

It was Ford's genius to see that everyone would want to own a motor-car, and to appreciate the economies of mass production. In the 1890s the automobile industry had developed fastest in France, Germany, and Italy, but the leadership passed to the United States when Ford introduced the assembly line to a works from which, between 1908 and 1927, he supplied no fewer than fifteen million model T automobiles. There had never been production on this scale before.

The influence of the internal combustion engine does not end with the automobile. It has revolutionised agriculture, which steam scarcely touched; it has mechanised war, which, in the age of steam, was still fought with horses, and, with its high power to weight ratio, it has achieved the most revolutionary change in transport, for it has enabled man to fly. Its fuel, being found at first mainly in the under-developed countries of the Middle East, altered the strategy of the great powers, and created a new relationship between industrially advanced and industrially backward nations. The fuel itself needs no mining, and being liquid, can be piped; while the engine, being available in large or small sizes, has decentralised cities into suburbs, and can now be used to dig the suburban garden. Only in the mid-twentieth century have such disadvantages as air pollution and wasteful use of man's oil resources become obvious.

IV

Of much greater significance even than the petrol engine, has been the invention of electricity, which is bringing the industrial revolution to fruition. The two sciences of electricity and magnetism had been throughout the eighteenth century amusing to philosophers. Despite the obvious similarities between them, which were that both electricity and magnetism seemed to have polarity, and that like repelled like and attracted unlike, no connection had been established between them until Oersted in Copenhagen in 1820 discovered that there was a magnetic field surrounding a wire through which an electric current was passing, which would deflect the needle of a magnetometer. If the direction of the current was reversed, then the needle would be deflected the other way. Electricity, so to speak, produced magnetism. But could magnetism produce electricity? It was another ten years before Faraday, in England, showed that it could. The delay may be attributed partly to a misunderstanding of Oersted's experiment. It was not electricity that had produced magnetism, but moving electricity, and moving magnetism, in its turn, would produce electricity. A current could be generated in a loop of wire that was rotated in a magnetic field. From this principle is derived every electric generator in the world today: from the reverse principle is derived every electric motor. From the conversion of electrical changes into magnetic ones, and magnetic changes back into electrical ones, every transformer is derived.

The commercial possibilities of these discoveries were not at once apparent, though Faraday readily assured Gladstone that electricity would one day be taxed. Using alternating current, any voltage can (within limits) be transformed into any other voltage, making electricity much more adaptable than either the external or the internal combustion engine. All that was now required to distribute hundreds and thousands of horsepower across the countryside was just two wires for direct, and, to be safe, three for alternating current. However, the century was far advanced before the generators existed to produce the electricity at one end of the wires, or the motors and electric lamps to burn it at the other, and the only use made of electricity in the middle of the nineteenth century was the telegraph, which was operated by Voltaic cells at the control, after 1843, of a Morse key. At first the telegraphs followed the railway lines, but, with the exploitation of gutta percha as insulation, they were soon going under the sea, where the railways could not follow them. A cable was laid from Dover to Calais in 1850, and in 1866 the first successful cable was laid under the Atlantic to connect the old world with the new. At the same time many people tried to turn the telegraph into a telephone. Reiss managed to transmit sounds in Germany in 1866, but it was not until 1876 that Gray and Bell filed their claims for patents in the United States, and Bell's telephone system went into production.

The telegraphs ultimately prepared the way for power transmission. They gave experience to the cable makers, and encouraged the study of conductors and insulators. Long-distance cables had necessitated the production of primitive relays, and had brought the engineers face to face with the problems of capacitance—though it fell to Heaviside, in Great Britain, later in the century, to unravel many of the remaining mysteries of inductance. By the mid-century the transmission of power waited upon the electric generator. The commutator, which converts the output of an alternator into a series of uni-directional pulses, had been invented in the 1830s, but it was not until 1863 that the Italian, Pacinotti, made the next great advance by dividing the commutator into a number of sections, each of which was connected to a separate coil rotating in the magnetic field. The limit to the output of the generator was now set by the size of the permanent magnet used to produce the field. The

substitution of the electro magnet was made in 1866, and almost immediately Wilde, Varley, and Wheatstone in England, Farmer in the United States, and the Siemens brothers in Berlin all had the happy thought of exciting the magnetic field by feeding back part of the current generated in the revolving armature itself. Provided there was sufficient residual magnetism to induce a current in the armature in the first place, the armature would then excite the field, the field would excite the armature, and there was scarcely any limit to the power that could be taken from an electric generator. Making use of these principles, the Belgian born Gramme led the world in the 1870s in the commercial applications of generating equipment, and he and others were now able, on similar principles, to construct reliable electric motors to use at the one end of the line the power generated at the other.

The early generators were mostly used to supply the demand for electric light. Gas-lighting, invented by Murdock in Great Britain in the 1790s, was never ideal, even after the discovery of the limelight in the 1820s and of the incandescent mantle by the Austrian von Welsbach in 1885, but it had at least enabled many trades to work, in shifts, round the clock. The carbon arc, which had been discovered in 1801 by Davy in England, used too much current for the batteries of the day, and its development waited upon the development of the electric generator. Now that the generators were available in the 1870s, it was soon realised that the carbon arc lamp was too brilliant for indoor illumination, though it was widely used out of doors, in lighthouses, in the streets, in marshalling yards and dockyards, and the great problem of the day became the 'subdivision' of the electric light. Edison in the United States contributed most, and Swan in Great Britain much, to the solution of the problem with the invention of the incandescent lamp. Fairly reliable carbon filament lamps were available in the 1880s, and the first central generating station was established in San Francisco in 1879.

There remained many fundamental problems of distribution. Edison and Brush showed that the electric lamps could be wired in parallel, but it was some years before it was accepted practice to couple generators together in the same way. The relative merits of direct and alternating current were much canvassed in the 1880s and 1890s: direct current equipments had the advantage that they could be used with batteries, which continued to supply the consumer when the generators broke down. Gradually, however, despite phase difficulties, the need for long-distance transmission to connect water power to large cities, and for grids to enable one power station to help another at peak periods, swung the battle in favour of alternating current. The higher the voltage used, the less power is lost in transmitting over long distances, and alternating current, being transformable, can be transmitted for hundreds of miles at a high voltage, and then converted to a low voltage to suit the requirements of the ordinary household.

Alternating currents are a curse unless they are of constant frequency, and the electric generator requires a prime mover to turn it at both a high and a constant speed of revolution. The conventional steam engines could not be satisfactorily geared and governed to achieve this, and, in the 1870s, it was confidently predicted that steam had no future in this or any other field. It was, appropriately enough, in Great Britain, the home of steam, that Parsons in 1884 produced the first success-ful, multiple stage, steam reaction turbo-generator, which, revolving eighteen thousand times a minute, produced seven and a half kilowatts at one hundred volts, and proved the pessimists wrong. Steam turbines are now used in all the coal-, and many of the oil-fired power stations in the world, as well as in most ocean-going ships. At about the same time a Swede, de Laval, was developing an impulse turbine, which was ultimately to do for electricity generated from water what Parson's reaction turbine has done for electricity generated from coal. Similar considerations to those which led to the substitution of internal for external combustion in piston engines have led, in the twentieth century, to the development of the gas turbine in Germany, Italy, and Great Britain. These 'jet' engines have so far been used almost exclusively in aircraft, but it is not impossible that gas turbines will be developed for other purposes in the future.

Continuous development has now raised steam turbine pressures to two thousand pounds to the square inch, and temperatures to one thousand degrees fahrenheit, and a single turbine may now develop nearly half a million horse-power. Nevertheless, all the changes connected with the internal combustion engine and the distribution of power by electricity do not, perhaps, by themselves justify the term revolution. In some fields, as on the railways, all that has happened is the substitution of one form of power for another, while in many factories the independent electrical drive has simply replaced the old steam shafting and belting. The greater flexibility of these new forms of power has, however, brought the familiar increases in productivity to small-scale trades unaffected by the first industrial revolution.

With the many new forms of transport,

by hain, bus and automobile, people no
longer have to live close to their work,
while whole cities can be supplied with
hydro-electricity generated in distant and
hitherto technologically useless mountain
valleys. Mobility of power has largely
taken the place, in industry, of mobility
of labour, which was such an important
feature of the early industrial revolution
in Great Britain, and it is now possible to
carry light industries out into the countryside instead of concentrating them in
large towns. To the nations which began
late, industrialisation has meant internal
combustion and electricity. Saved from
the scourge of soot, they have suffered
the modern plague of accidents on the
roads. Both old and new industrial nations
have realised that the production of electrical energy is the basis of political as well
as industrial power, and, ultimately, of all
schemes of social security. The production
of kilowatt hours of electricity in the
United States, which passed the one
hundred billion mark in the mid-1930s,
had already by the mid-1950s topped
five hundred billions. At this time the
United States produced approximately
forty per cent of the world's electrical
energy, and Russia, the second largest
producer, only ten per cent.

V

But the story of electricity does not, after
all, stop short of revolution. It was apparent
from the earliest days of the telegraph that
messages moved fast, but it was not at
that time clear what carried them. Although Plücker had identified cathode
rays at Bonn in 1859, it is convenient to
trace the story of nuclear energy and
automation from Edison's discovery that
an electric current flowed from the
carbon filament of one of his evacuated
incandescent light bulbs to any second
electrode sealed into the bulb, whenever

the second electrode was positively
charged with respect to the filament.
Thomson, in Great Britain, proved that
this current consisted of the negatively
charged particles which are now called
electrons and that these electrons are
identical with Plücker's cathode rays.

This discovery, and the discovery of
natural radioactivity by the Frenchman
Becquerel in 1896, led to a renewed
investigation into the structure of the
atom, of which the electron is but a very
small part. Clearly, if the electron was
negatively charged, and was a part of the
atom, there must be another positively
charged part, and scientists began to search
for a nucleus. It was 1911 before Ruther-
ford, at Manchester, constructed a model
of the atom, and 1919 before he split a
real one. The Curies, in France, showed
that naturally disintegrating substances
are hotter than their surroundings; the
Swiss, Einstein, defined the relationship
between mass and energy, and, after many
different particles had been used for many
years to explore and to split many different
nuclei, the Italian, Fermi, at last showed
how the liberation of energy from one
atom could be made to liberate more
energy from the next.

The ultimate significance of these
brilliant discoveries is profound. They are
making man independent of the sun for
energy. The coal, the oil, and the hydro
electricity in the world all derive their
energy from the sun. But nuclear energy
is itself the source of the sun's heat and
light, and atomic energy is now available
independently. With it, all the huge
achievements of the industrial revolution
have been put upon a permanent basis.
For the industrial revolution is based upon
power, and with the world demand for
power increasing at the compound rate
of two per cent per annum, all the known
reserves of coal and oil in the world must

soon be exhausted. In 1950 the total world demand for power was two thousand eight hundred million tons of hard coal equivalent; by 2000 the demand is expected to have risen to seven thousand four hundred million tons, and, were it not for nuclear energy, industrial society would face collapse in the twenty-first or twenty-second centuries. With nuclear energy, no limit can be set to the industrialisation of the world, for the weight of the fuel is negligible, and nuclear energy, converted into electricity, can now be carried to any hitherto inaccessible area. The limits to its use are economic, not technological.

VI

The consequences of the discovery of the electron have not stopped here. The infant science, wireless, already used tuned circuits and a crude amplifier called a coherer. Fleming, working in Great Britain for the Italian, Marconi, took advantage of the 'Edison effect' to construct the diode valve, which greatly improved reception, and in 1906, de Forest, in the United States, went one better by introducing a third electrode, the grid, between cathode and anode. A strong electron current, passing from the cathode to the anode of this triode valve, could now be made to move in sympathy with a weak signal applied to the grid. In this way any electrical signal, however weak, could be amplified many times, and, passing through a series of similar circuits, could be amplified, if need be, many millions of times. The oscillation of a tuned circuit could now be maintained and modulated continuously, and wireless, from being a device by which ships communicated laboriously to the shore and to each other, became a means of broadcasting. Television followed.

It is impossible to overestimate the significance of the revolution begun by

electronics, and by the triode valve, which, if it was not the invention requiring the most imagination, was certainly the one leading to the most important immediate consequences since the steam engine. Here is a new dimension in industry, for, compared with mechanical contrivances, electronic ones can operate instantaneously. Mechanical devices could operate, at the most, thousands of time a minute. Here for the first time are instruments capable of operating, under perfect human control, any number of times from once to many millions of times a second. Both the speed of operation and the accuracy of measurement have been revolutionised, and work, which could, in the mechanical age, be performed accurately to one part in a thousand, can now be made accurate to one part in a million. The twentieth century has seen a spectacular increase in the number and sensitivity of detectors—instruments which produce measurements of physical properties in the form of electrical signals. Any signal can be amplified to any size, and any two signals can be compared, and the difference between them used either directly, to do work, or, indirectly, to control it.

The development of electronics has thus led to a great extension in the use of automatic machinery. Automatism is not new, for Newcomen used the movement of the engine beam to open and close the engine valves, and a mechanical co-ordinating sequence can be installed in anything from a musical box to an automobile engine, or an automatic lathe for cutting screws. But such a machine is 'stupid', and a screw-cutting machine will continue to cut screws even when something has happened to make it cut them the wrong shape. For a long time this was thought to be the limit to automatism, but the modern electronically controlled machine is able to go further, by measuring what it is doing, comparing this with what it ought to be doing, and adjusting itself accordingly. A machine can thus estimate the appropriateness of its own actions, and correct its own faults. The vital point is that the back end of the machine should know what the front end is doing, and feed back information continuously in such a way as to control one of the factors determining the result. In this way a machine can be made to adapt itself so as to achieve a constant effect without human intervention. Any tendency in a tinplate strip mill, for instance, to roll the plate too thick or too thin, can be counteracted before a human operator could even have detected the tendency, and the mill can be run without stopping.

After the first phase of the industrial revolution it was still generally true that the best and most accurate products were those made by hand. Machine-made was a term of abuse meaning second-rate. Since the discovery of electronics, the man-made machine has completely transcended the man, until there is no longer any accurate work which the machine cannot do better. Nobody thinks to ask for a hand-made electric light bulb. This marvellous instrument is accurate beyond the power of human hands to construct. The man cannot make one, and the machine makes them by the hundred million. But it is characteristic of this stage of the industrial revolution that the machinery used to manufacture electric light bulbs could not be paid for unless the market for the finished product was vast. The industrial revolution, which has been accompanied by such an enormous increase in the population, is now as dependent upon the people for its momentum as they are upon it for their standard of living. Many manufactured products must wear out quickly, and have to be replaced, while others must be forcefully advertised, if consumption is to keep pace with production.

Small quantity production remains the province of hand labour. It is uneconomic to construct machines to manufacture single articles which are, and are likely to remain, expensive. If, on the other hand enough people want something, they need no longer work to produce it themselves, because it will be cheaper to make a machine to make it for them. The egalitarian implications of this are obvious.

VII

Throughout the course of the changes associated with the internal combustion engine, electricity, and electronics, one can again point to other products without which this second industrial revolution would not have taken place. Iron has been made to yield steel, and without steel and concrete there would have been no revolution in constructional engineering. Without new steels and other metals there would have been no new high-temperature heat engines, and no atomic power stations. Every new development demands, or is preceded by, advances in chemistry. Throughout the course of this second industrial revolution there have been, too, improvements in simple human aids. The bicycle, for example, which is made of steel and rubber, is mechanically no more than a combination of two of the oldest human inventions, the wheel and the lever. But to concentrate on these would be to obscure the significant processes by which man has learnt to operate tools by power, and to control them by electronics, and by which the wealth of nations has come to be measured in megawatts.

Throughout this second period of the industrial revolution, the conditions of employment have continued to vary greatly from one country to another. The individualistic and competitive conditions which existed in Great Britain in the middle of the nineteenth century seemed for a time to have become more necessary than ever after the publication of Darwin's *Origin of Species* in 1859. Darwin proved that the struggle for survival among plants and animals had resulted in the survival of the fittest, the natural selection of species, and evolutionary progress. Although 'social Darwinism' became popular in Great Britain, the United States, Germany, and Russia, Darwin himself was very cautious about applying his theories to the human race. In time the social Darwinists spoilt their own case, for, in addition to outraging many of the better feelings of humanity, they could never make up their minds whether the struggle for survival was meant to take place between individuals belonging to the same society, or between separate societies.

Even while the debate between the advocates of *laissez faire* and public control continued, great changes were taking place in the organisation of industry, banking, and insurance. The principle of limited liability and the development of the stock exchange were giving rise to a larger vested *rentier* interest, but also making it possible for the workman, and for the workman's trade union, to join in the ownership of the means of production, while the growing complexity of industry was doing much to separate the functions of management and finance. Marx had analysed the tendency of capital to combine, and had forecast the growth of the massive capitalism and the monopoly capitalism of the later nineteenth century, though his prediction that ownership would pass into fewer and fewer hands was not fulfilled. As the machinery required for mass production becomes more elaborate, industry becomes more heavily capitalised, and the individual manufacturing unit comes more and more closely to resemble a miniature empire. Competition between rival industrial empires being wasteful, some capitalist concerns prefer to share the market rather than to take their chance of cornering the whole of it.

Similarly, among the working classes, the competition for work has tended always to depress wages, and to eliminate the older and the weaker man. Workmen have countered this by combining in craft or general unions to support each other in illness and unemployment, to agree upon the price at which they will sell their labour, and, if need be, to secure their aims by strike action. Rescued from the absurdities of syndicalism, the 'grand national holiday', and the general strike, organised labour in the West has tended to become reconciled to the capitalist system, and has, indeed, in many countries, invested heavily in it. Labour, like capital, has its own international organisations, and while labour has often blamed international capital for starting wars, international labour has proved unable to stop them.

Organised capital and organised labour grew naturally out of the *laissez faire* conditions of the nineteenth century. In many Western countries governments have encouraged the leaders of industry on both sides to arrange the conditions of employment between them, while in others the State has helped to arbitrate their claims. But arbitration by the State, at the request of the two sides, has to be distinguished from State interference, and from the deliberate attempts which have been made in many countries in the twentieth century to transfer the regulation of the conditions of employment, and the ownership of the means of production, to the State. The immense power concentrated in the hands of the rulers of the rival industrial empires of capital and labour, and their tendency to go to war with each other and to dictate their own terms to the politicians, have led many theorists to advocate government intervention in the affairs of industry in the interests of the nation. Various methods have been tried in Western European countries, and in America, for bringing industry under political control, ranging from the direction of labour, and the fixing of wages by law, to the confiscation of whole industries and their subsequent management by state boards; and from the use of the government's influence as a customer, to government subsidies, systems of licences for the issue of fresh capital, and export, import, and exchange controls.

Against this industrial background of class struggle, and of honest attempts to decide where the control and ownership of the means of production should lie, two hundred and fifty years have passed since the invention of the steam engine. In spite of all the subsequent changes, a majority of the people of the world still work by hand and live in poverty. The alarming and uncontrolled growth of the world population has been matched by industrialisation and rising living standards in some countries, and by apathy and famine in others. The condition of Ireland in the early nineteenth century, and of India, Indonesia, and China in the twentieth, points the grim moral of allowing the people to multiply, without simultaneously raising productivity in agriculture and manufactures. At the other extreme, the easy life of the ordinary man or woman in the United States shows what can be done when productivity increases much faster than the population. An international technological civilisation has been coming to birth, but some countries have grown rich while others have remained poor. The dreams of the nineteenth-century free traders, of the division of labour among the nations, and the co-operation of all countries, seem once more to have faded in the face of fervent nationalism, the new mercantilism, new systems of alliances, and the arms race.

The Revolution in Environment

by J. M. Houston

Although the break with the past which the Industrial Revolutions implied was radical, it was based on previous development. The spread of the plough and the growth of the city had gone together. It would have been impossible to follow up the practical applications of the Technological Revolution without the food base provided by the revolution in agriculture. The effective linkage of coal and iron, railway and plough, food and city, health and population, have since triggered off a whole series of events. They can here only briefly be described. This synthesis of man and resources has been principally worked out around the shores of the Atlantic; stimuli from Metropolitan Europe found a response in the Pioneer World of the Americas, mainly in Anglo-Saxon America, but also in Latin America. This different response is bound up with the industrial expansion which began in the coalfields of Western Europe and extended to the north-eastern United States.

II

In this cross-fertilisation of Europe and the Americas the first important event was the rapid growth of population in Europe. It probably resulted from a decline of the death rates brought about by greater security and gradually improving standards of health, rather than from a sudden increase in the birth rates. It is likely that China and Japan increased their populations a century or so earlier, but it was Europe, not Asia, which discovered the New World. The table overleaf indicates that the European increase of population, which began in the eighteenth century, was greatly accelerated in the nineteenth century.

Estimated Population of the World, 1650-2000
(in millions)

Continent	1650	1750	1800	1850	1900	2000
Europe ..	100	140	187	266	401	947
North America..	1	2.5	5.7	26	81	312
Central and South America..	12	11.1	18.9	33	63	592
Oceania ..	2	2	2	2	6	29
Africa.. ..	100	95	90	95	120	517
Asia	330	479	602	749	937	3870
World Total	545	728	906	1171	1608	6267

This rapid growth, which Malthus had foreseen at the end of the eighteenth century, was accompanied by a much greater expansion of food supplies which he had not expected. The cornucopia of wealth which poured into Metropolitan Europe from the Pioneer World vitalised the Industrial Revolution. This growth of population is unique in the history of the world. The European stock has increased eightfold in the last two hundred and fifty years, whereas that of the rest of the world has grown only half as rapidly. This European expansion reached its climax in the nineteenth century, when Europe increased its proportion of the world population from one-fifth to one-quarter, and its emigrant stock in the

Pioneer World produced another tenth of the global total.

This demographic revolution was made possible by the revolution in agriculture. England, freer from the shackles of feudalism and the Church than the Continent, initiated this movement, although small-scale changes had already started in Flanders. The abolition of the open-field system as a consequence of the enclosure movements, followed by the widespread introduction of the Norfolk system of root crops and the use of rotation grasses launched this revolution. Germany and France followed, but neither was to play such an important role in the emigration overseas. First there was a general increase in the area of cultivated land during the nineteenth century in Western Europe: Germany had a fifty per cent increase, England and Wales about thirty-two per cent, and France some twenty per cent. For the first time in the history of man, yields of cereals began to increase sharply through rotation practices, and later, after the mid-nineteenth century, through Liebig's pioneer work in agricultural chemistry. Wheat yields which had never been more than six to ten bushels per acre, increased in England to over twenty bushels per acre in 1900.

In some countries bordering the Atlantic, which did not share in the agricultural revolution, two American crops were also to revolutionise the carrying capacity of peasant holdings. Maize introduced into Portugal about 1515-25 (in the Coimbra district), spread rapidly throughout the north-western regions of the Iberian Peninsula and gave rise to a great increase of population in what has always been the demographic pulsatory centre of the Peninsula. Ever since, it is the Minhoto and Galician peasantry who have contributed most to Latin American immigration. The potato produced a similar stimu-

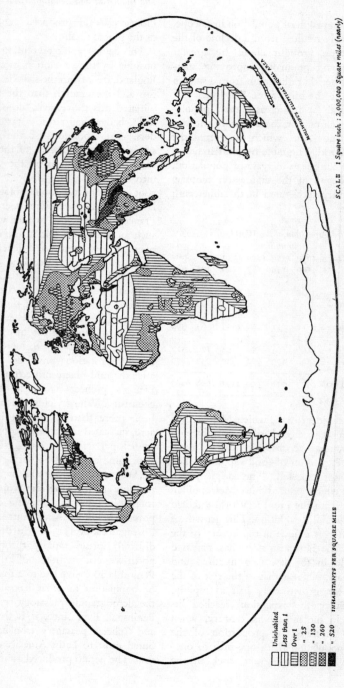

DENSITY OF WORLD POPULATION IN THE MID-TWENTIETH CENTURY

MOLLWEIDE ELLIPTICAL EQUAL AREA

SCALE 1 Square inch : 2,000,000 Square miles (nearly)

Uninhabited
Less than 1
Over 1
"   25
" 130
" 260
" 520

INHABITANTS PER SQUARE MILE

lus to a rapid growth of population, later diverted into the flow of emigration. It was introduced into northern and north-western Spain and Portugal in the eighteenth century, but its most spectacular results were in Ireland. As Arthur Young observed, the Irish potato permitted four times the rural population to subsist on holdings formerly under grain. Marriage rates were intensified and the population of Ireland rose from three millions in the early eighteenth century to over eight millions in 1841.

This growth of European population seems to have been necessary for the subsequent flood of emigration overseas in the nineteenth century. Until then the great flow overseas had been Negro labour. It is estimated that from fifteen to twenty million Negroes were imported from Africa to the Americas between the sixteenth and early nineteenth centuries, whereas the records of Seville between 1509 and 1740 show an official Spanish embarkation of only 150,000 registered persons. Clearly more must have left Spain in this period, as the rise of Spanish colonial towns testifies, but the contrast with Negro labour is striking.

The great flood of European migration gathered force in the hungry years of the 1840s: famines in Ireland, Limousin and Saxony forced thousands to leave the shores of Europe. The movement was accelerated in the 1870s with the replacement of the sailing vessel by the steamship. The results were ultimately fortunate, for only massive emigration saved Europe from gross over-population in the subsequent decades, at a time when the birth rates were not adjusted to the death rates. According to one estimate, the population of Europe in 1910 was eighty-eight millions less than it would have been without emigration after 1800.

Since Jamestown was founded in 1607,

nearly forty-five millions have emigrated from Europe to North America. Over twenty-eight millions have settled there permanently, to account for the present European stock of over 160 millions in the United States and Canada. Some eighteen million Spaniards and Portuguese have settled in Latin America. Today there are over fifty millions who are of European or partly European origin. Of all European countries, the United Kingdom has contributed most, especially from its poorer countries of Scotland and Ireland, sending twelve millions to North America and another three and a half millions to Australia and New Zealand. The causes of migration were diverse: in Western Europe, the enclosures; the redundancy of rural labour; the ruin of domestic crafts by the rise of the factory; a harsh penal code in Britain.

As migration flowed west across the Atlantic, the pivot of origin moved east across Europe. The growth of cities and the rapid industrialisation of the Western part of the continent brought about a decline in migration and a fall in the birth-rate. This fall began in France and then affected all the Western European countries, except Ireland. Meanwhile, at the end of the nineteenth century, growing population pressure and distress owing to primitive agriculture, caused the migrant stream to start from Italy, Central Europe and then the Balkans. Eventually it moved into Russia, and the Ukrainian flood was beginning when the First World War brought it to an end.

It is interesting to consider what might have happened to the Russian flow after the war, had it not been for the Communist Revolution in 1917. Instead, the stream was diverted eastwards to conquer the Asiatic Steppe. True, one and a quarter millions had moved into Siberia between 1861 and 1914, but during the First

World War over three millions were deported into central and eastern Russia, and vast movements have since been organised. It appears certain that the slave labour imported from European Russia to Siberia in the last two decades has at least equalled the number of Negro slaves imported into the Americas in the eighteenth century. Behind all these statistics of emigration, whether European or Russian, lies the epic story of pioneer achievement, and a story of human misery on a colossal scale. The Free World acknowledges the latter in the Statue of Liberty overlooking New York harbour.

III

It has been said that the United States was built upon the railway and the British Empire was created by the steamship. Transport has certainly linked the Metropolitan World with the Pioneer World, providing the latter with labour, the former with capital and raw materials. Today, over three-quarters of a million miles of railways have spread their network over the land surface of the globe, opening up and civilising the continents. Nowhere has this expansion been as great as in the United States and it was started with British capital. In 1830 it had twenty-three miles of railways; in 1850, 9021 miles; in 1880, 93,296; and in the peak year of 1915, 264,378. By the 1880s, 74,720 miles of steel had opened up the Prairies; between 1869 and 1915 fourteen transcontinental lines had been thrust from east to west. Slightly later than the American expansion, 25,000 rail miles opened up the Pampas and, later still, another 21,000 linked Australian settlement. Thus the railway has been essentially the product of Metropolitan Europe, building one-third of the world's rail network within its own countries and over half in the new continents.

These railways have also fed the sea-lanes of the world, another European development. The opening of the Erie Canal in 1825 allowed large quantities of cheap food to be carried by the railroads subsequently brought to the Great Lakes–St Lawrence waterway. The opening of the Suez Canal in 1869 and of the Panama Canal in 1915 must be ranked among the greatest achievements in the revolution of environment. Some eight thousand miles were reduced on the Orient route via Suez to Britain, and the Panama Canal integrated the west coast of North America with its eastern seaboard to an extent which the railway promoters had not envisaged.

Within the last four decades the globe has been further covered by a mesh of air-routes which weave a gigantic web of 1180 million miles around the earth, with some 140,000 commercial aircraft airborne at any one moment. Some fifty-eight million passengers are carried annually on these airways. The extent of the world, which Magellan and del Cano had traversed in the course of three years, has shrunk to a time-distance of as many days.

These technological achievements have not provided all the means man needed to exploit his world. The classical civilisation of Greece and Rome had imported skilled gardeners from the Near East to improve the quality of staple crops already grown, the olive in Attica and the vine in Italy. The Pioneer World produced a challenge much more comparable to that presented by Joshua to the ass-nomads of Israel, 'If thou be a great people, get thee up to the wood country and cut down for thyself there.' The change into a new environment, where the experiences of the old one do not count, was the test of greatness in the Pioneer World. Thus the geographic frontiers of the pioneer settler became more real than the political frontiers of Europe from which he had come. The most successful beginnings were often made in a similar environment to that which the migrant had left. There he could learn to distinguish subtle differences and brace himself for the revolutionary changes beyond his frontier. Thus it was fortunate that the English settler first learnt the techniques of a new life in the deciduous forest clearings and fertile soils of New England, which were not dissimilar to the conditions of temperate Europe. Later, a bigger challenge lay beyond in the prairie frontier, where a distinct climate and chernozem soils had to await the coming of the railway, the mechanisation of large-scale agriculture and the bigger flow of capital. In the far west lay the further challenge of the steppe and the desert, where the new techniques of dry-farming and irrigation had to be learned. But the American conquest of the frontier has been achieved only at great cost to nature's resources. The indiscriminate destruction of forests and the losses by soil erosion have since made the frontiersman more conscious of the principles of nature conservation.

When the environment was more contrasted with the settlers' origin, settlement tended to be less successful. The Spanish attempt to introduce the Mesta into the New World failed; it was defeated by tropical climates. The Dutch never understood the Mediterranean climate of Cape Province and it was some time after the English seizure of the territory in 1806 that the most suitable crops were developed. Swan River and South Australia nearly failed for a similar reason, and were rescued only by the boom in minerals. It is fortunate that the temperate small grains grown by the settler of the Pioneer World have proved more adaptable to climatic variations than many tropical crops subsequently cultivated.

The pioneer fringe, where the emigrant has tried his economy, has also modified his institutions and ideas. Both for the planned colonisation, envisaged by E. G. Wakefield, and for the stampedes of squatters and miners, the geographic frontier has dictated the mould of society. Only in two ways has man combated the frontier with success: by the selective breeding of quick-growing varieties of grain on the cold frontiers of the Northern Hemisphere, and by the control of diseases in the tropics. Otherwise the process of learning afresh in the Pioneer World is by no means yet complete.

IV

The Industrial Revolution could not have worked in a vacuum. It seized on the abundant raw materials upon which the industrial towns and metropolitan cities flourished. Several series of urban growth may be summarised. First, in the nineteenth century came the accelerated growth of the capital cities of Western Europe, such as London and Paris, together with the expansion of the textile, metallurgical and coalfield towns of the industrial areas. The capitals expanded, first by the stimulus of the railways which drew the national resources to the centre, and then by the growth of inter-city communications and other urban services. The industrial towns tended to grow at rates dictated by the nature of their industries, those which could be mechanised earlier growing faster than those of the traditional crafts; the cotton industry, for example, as we have seen, was mechanised earlier than the woollen industry.

A second series of modern capital cities grew up in the Orient. Here dense masses of rural peasantry had already sustained large urban populations for many centuries by the very weight of numbers in their hinterland, as for example, Shanghai. As

o

THE WORLD'S CITY POPULATION IN THE MID-TWENTIETH CENTURY

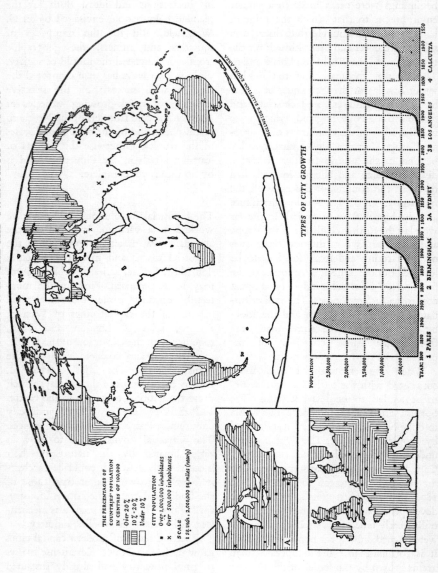

MOLLWEIDE ELLIPTICAL EQUAL AREA

THE PERCENTAGES OF
COUNTRIES' POPULATION
IN CENTRES OF 100,000

Over 20%
10% - 20%
Under 10%

CITY POPULATION
■ Over 1,000,000 inhabitants
× Over 500,000 inhabitants

SCALE
1 sq. inch = 2,000,000 sq. miles (nearly)

TYPES OF CITY GROWTH

POPULATION

2,500,000
2,000,000
1,500,000
1,000,000
500,000

YEAR: 1800 1850 1900 1950 · 1800 1850 1900 1950 · 1800 1850 1900 1950 · 1800 1850 1900 1950 · 1800 1850 1900 1950 · 1800 1850 1900 1950

1 PARIS   2 BIRMINGHAM   3A SYDNEY   3B LOS ANGELES   4 CALCUTTA

A

B

the trade links with the European powers strengthened, their cities expanded.

In the Pioneer World, after the nineteenth century, the capitals of states grew fast. As outlets of the pioneer fringe their primacy was assured. They were portals of immigration, trade and capital. The mineral wealth of northern Ontario fed Toronto, as the prairies fattened New York or the pampas Buenos Aires. In the less developed lands of South America and Australia, the predominance of the capital city, and of a general urban growth, disproportionate to the total increase of population, is producing a regression of the pioneer fringe; vertical integration is replacing horizontal expansion.

In the U.S.S.R. and now in China, an urban revolution is taking place at a speed which is greater than anything ever witnessed before. Between 1926 and 1939, the Soviet cities more than doubled their population, a rate of increase which took the United States about thirty-one years (1856–87), and most European countries, probably a century. Of this urban increase in Russia of 29.6 millions, four-fifths came from rural areas and one-fifth from the natural increase of the urban areas themselves.

A new urban feature has developed on the map in this century—the millionaire city. There are today over 130 cities in the world which have over one million inhabitants in each, of which there are thirty-four in Europe and thirty-two in North America, with a total of 112 in the Northern Hemisphere. A further development has been the growth of what has been called 'megalopolis', the swarming of cities into one vast city region. The first of these has already grown up on the north-eastern seaboard of the United States, stretching for a distance of 600 miles and containing over forty million inhabitants, a fifth of the total population and the wealthiest wage-earners of the nation. It owes its growth to the fruitful rivalry of independent states within a federal government, each city originally developing as a series of independent outlets of trade and manufacture. In the past it was the springboard of continental settlement and ever since it has been the hinge of American economy. The cities of Western Europe between Paris, Cologne and Berlin might also become a second megalopolis with an extension in England between London, Liverpool and Leeds. A federal European state would certainly hasten its growth. Looked at from a world viewpoint, both these urban concentrations of population and power are the product of the cross-fertilisation achieved across the Atlantic and reflect its economic unity.

V

In conclusion, it is worth emphasising that whereas the total population of the world has more than doubled in the last century, manufactures have probably increased fifteen times. This has produced two results. First, some two-thirds of the world population still have standards of nutrition not dissimilar to those of Neolithic society, so that the disparity between them and the favoured minority presents the greatest problem of the modern world. This under-developed world is a dangerous vacuum in the struggle for world supremacy. Secondly, the consumption of the industrial world has reached such alarming proportions that it is doubtful if some of the non-renewable resources of the earth will last another twenty-five to fifty years. It is vital for the future that man has now entered the nuclear age with its renewable resources of energy. This change from non-renewable to renewable resources has also unlocked the greatest source of energy of all—the human will. This means that material progress is no longer sufficient. 'For what shall it profit a man if he shall gain the whole world, and lose his own soul?' Ultimately the fate of mankind must depend upon his victory over himself.

20 WORLD WAR, COMMUNISM AND SOCIAL DEMOCRACY

by John P. Plamenatz

On the eve of the First World War almost the whole world was dominated by Europe or by nations of European stock. There was only one large exception, Japan; and even Japan had made herself formidable by adopting the techniques and institutions of the West. All civilisations, except the European, were static or tributary, or else were adopting, one way or another, European practices. Among the European peoples, the British, the Germans, and the French enjoyed the greatest prestige, political or cultural. Russia was the equal of these three Powers militarily and diplomatically but not as a source of knowledge or centre of ideas. The educated classes in Russia mostly accepted the standards of the West, and acknowledged that by those standards their country was inferior. The United States, already the richest country in the world, kept to herself politically, and culturally was still the pupil of Europe. The emergence of Japan, though it enhanced the self-respect of non-European peoples, was no challenge to the cultural hegemony of Europe, for the only great Power that was not European was, at least superficially, the most Europeanised of Asiatic nations.

The rulers of Germany, Britain, and France differed in their ideas about how subject peoples should be governed, for their domestic political traditions were different and inevitably affected their beliefs about how they should govern

their colonies. Yet they were agreed on the essential point that it was good for non-European peoples to be governed by Europeans, and that, whatever was to become of them in the modern world, it was for their European tutors to guide them to it. These views were not unchallenged, even among the dominant peoples. The Americans disliked or were indifferent to them, while radicals and socialists in Western Europe attacked the 'imperialism' of their governments. Yet the critics of imperialism also accepted, though often unconsciously, the doctrine of European superiority; they believed in 'progress', which is essentially a European idea. The parties of the Left, not least the Marxists, believed in it even more fervently then the conservatives. Europe, they thought, was in the van of progress, and other peoples could make progress only by following where Europe led. Some believed in the force of arms, and others in the force of example; but whatever the methods they advocated or condemned, all the European peoples believed in European superiority. The Europeans were clearly superior in the two things most easily measured, wealth and power, and therefore took for granted their superiority in other things.

The Asians and Africans were both impressed and humiliated by European pretensions. The illiterate poor, the immense majority, were the least impressed and humiliated; they had merely exchanged foreign for native rulers or had acquired new rulers on top of the old ones, often without being much affected by the exchange or acquisition. They were already too poor for any change in the load of masters on their backs to make them poorer. The admiration and the hatred felt for the Europeans were at first confined to the well-to-do, to the old native rulers who had been on top and now had foreigners above them, to the merchants and business men in the towns enriched by expanding trade with the West, and to the students who were the quickest to absorb Western ideas and the first to learn to use them to condemn Western practices. The mass movements were not to come until after the First World War. Already before 1914, the Young Turks, led by Mustapha Kemal, wanted to transform Turkey into a modern state on the European model; Sun Yat Sen had brought down the Chinese Empire and set up a republic in its place (1911–12): and the Indian Congress Party, founded in 1885, was demanding Home Rule for India. These three movements were all 'progressive' in the European sense; their aim was to weaken the hold of the foreigner, not by reverting to a native past, but by setting up a machinery of government strong and efficient by European standards. China and Turkey, though nominally independent, were not really so; they had both (though China much more than Turkey) made such large concessions to the foreigner as no longer to feel themselves properly self-governing.

In 1914 the nationalism of subject peoples was more intense and dangerous to peace in Europe than in Asia. It was directed against two European empires, both of them weak for their size, Russia and Austria-Hungary. The Habsburgs had been unable satisfactorily to convert their dominions into a multi-national federal state, and could therefore not offer to the subject peoples the autonomy which might have made them firmly loyal; they had bought Magyar support at a price that put it out of their power to win the loyalty of the Slavs. The Tsars had pursued a policy of 'russification' so clumsy and brutal as to make it impossible for their non-Russian subjects to trust them.

II

Nationalism, Asian and East European, was not the only challenge to the supremacy of the rulers of the world. Another was Social-Democracy, the many-sided movement created to make good the manual worker's demand for full equality in modern society. Early Socialism in the West had been both reformist and revolutionary, though it had everywhere, except perhaps in France, been in practice much more the first than the second. The expansion of industry, the extension of the franchise, and an improved standard of living and literacy had led, in Western and Central Europe, to the proliferation of trade unions and to the creation of large political parties supported by the manual workers. The largest of these parties, the German Social-Democrats, was avowedly Marxist, and Marxism was already the strongest single doctrinal influence on the French Socialist Party. Marxism purports to be a revolutionary creed; it teaches that the workers must use force to destroy the 'bourgeois' state and then set up their own form of class government to put an end to the capitalist system. It also denounces war as an effect of capitalism, saying that the workers of all countries must unite against the oppressors of their class. The stronger these working-class organisations, the more was conceded to them; so that their leaders, seeing how much could be achieved under the existing system, soon lost their taste for revolution. Yet they were still drawn to the creed they had used to rally the workers to them. More often than not, they continued to think of themselves as revolutionary socialists. In 1914 Western Socialism spoke with two voices. Except in Britain, it was in theory more revolutionary than reformist, and yet everywhere its behaviour showed how deeply it was attached to parliamentary government. This equivocation, in a prosperous and still peaceful Europe, went unnoticed by most people.

The Russian Social-Democratic Party, also Marxist, was quite differently placed. It began as an illegal party in a country without an effective parliament. The leaders quarrelled violently among themselves about the role of their party and they had therefore to decide whether it was to play a subsidiary part as a temporary ally of the middle class, or take control of it. The first course might seem the more in keeping with Marxist doctrine, but Lenin, and also Trotsky, argued for the second. They argued that the world, already dominated by the capitalist West, was fast ripening for a proletarian and socialist revolution. Russia, though backward and still neither democratic nor bourgeois, would therefore not need to stop at a bourgeois revolution, being already caught in the meshes of world capitalism. If the Russian Social-Democrats, backed by the workers in the new factories, could take control of the coming 'middle-class' revolution, they might force their country more quickly through the next stage of development towards Socialism, and might also, by their example, precipitate working-class revolutions in the West. If that happened, the advanced countries, incomparably more powerful than the others, could carry the rest of the world along with them. This doctrine of permanent revolution promised the backward peoples a quick way to industrial power

and Socialism. They were not doomed to be always imitators and followers; they too might play a great part in world history. The world was not aware of the full weight of this doctrine until 1917 and the years after.

III

In late July and early August 1914, Europe, continually at peace (except in the Balkans) since 1871, scarcely believing what was happening to her, slid into war. It was not a struggle between rival political creeds, nor a war between European contestants for mastery outside Europe. If it had been the second, it would have put Britain and Russia or Britain and France into opposed camps; if it had been the first, Imperial Russia would have been the least welcome of allies to the Western democracies. In its causes it was an old-fashioned war, produced partly by traditional enmities, of Russia against Austria and France against Germany, and partly by a recent naval rivalry between Germany and Britain. Even this rivalry was due less to Britain's fears for her empire or her trade than to traditional hostility towards an over-mighty Continental Power. France was relatively weaker than she had been, and so, too, was Russia, especially since her defeat by Japan, while Germany was gaining strength rapidly.

The outbreak of war destroyed several illusions: that the workers in the West had outgrown nationalism and cared more for class than for country; that Europe had grown too civilised to tolerate war; and that democracy and war do not go together. All over Europe the leaders of Social-Democracy, with few exceptions, supported their countries at war; it was at last clear to them, as to everyone else, that they had loyalties stronger than their faith in revolutionary Socialism and international peace. Even in Russia, most of the

Marxists supported the war. But Lenin did not do so. He explained it as a product of decaying capitalism and taunted the Socialist leaders for their betrayal of their class and cause. He condemned the war, and yet also welcomed it, for it would, he thought, exhaust the belligerents and end in proletarian revolutions. As the war, expected at first to end quickly, dragged on, a minority of Western Socialists were attracted by the ideas of Lenin, and at Kienthal in Switzerland, in February 1916, resolved to do their utmost to bring the war immediately to an end. Yet Lenin underestimated the belligerency and solidity of the Western peoples. He was, however, right about his own country. In March 1917 a revolution broke out in Russia and the Tsar abdicated. A few weeks later Lenin, with German assistance, returned to Russia. At that time he had few supporters there; but by 7 November, 1917,* he was already strong enough to take power. Not because the Russian people understood his ultimate purposes or because he had built up a large and popular organisation, but because the whole structure of government had collapsed. Lenin and the Bolsheviks alone undertook to satisfy the most pressing of popular needs: the need for peace and the hunger for land of the peasants. In March 1918 the Bolsheviks made peace with the Germans at Brest-Litowsk.

The United States was drawn into the war partly by natural sympathy with the Western democracies against the Central Monarchies, partly by the German submarine offensive which had cost American lives, and partly by financial interest in Allied victory, for American bankers had made heavy loans to Britain and France. With Russia dropping out of it and Ame-

rica coming in, the war changed character. To the Western peoples it became 'a war to end war' and to 'make the world safe for democracy'. In January 1918 President Wilson published his Fourteen Points proclaiming the right of every nation to govern itself and the need for an international body strong enough to settle disputes which might lead to war.

Ruling circles in Britain and France did not honestly share Wilson's belief in every nation's right to govern itself, for they were themselves governing more foreign nations than all their enemies put together. Yet they could not oppose Wilson. They had encouraged the nations 'oppressed' by their enemies to revolt, and the French were now hoping to use them to set up a chain of states friendly to France east of Germany. There thus emerged in Eastern Europe several new states created by fervent nationalists, supported by France with the connivance of Britain and the sometimes puzzled acquiescence of President Wilson. These new states soon offended against Wilson's principles almost as much as the old ones, for they did not grant equality of rights to all national groups inside them but allowed some to dominate the others, the dominant groups being friendly to the Allies, and especially to France. The Habsburg Empire ceased to exist, and Russia and Germany were considerably diminished. Within the areas vacated by them, there arose a number of small states, economically weak and politically unstable. With Germany and Russia exhausted by defeat or civil war, these states were safe for a time.

An international body to prevent war, the League of Nations, was created by the Treaty of Versailles, but was never strong enough to carry out its main purpose, partly because its constitution made it unlikely that it could take effective action against a Great Power and partly because

* By the old calendar, then still used in Russia, on 25 October. Hence the 'October Revolution'.

the U.S. Senate failed to ratify the treaty, so that the richest and strongest country in the world remained outside the League. The inadequacies of the League, in a world exhausted by war, were not at once apparent.

Outside Europe, the war and the peace settlement, though they had, as we shall see, indirect consequences of vast importance to the world, had an immediate effect only in the Middle East. The Ottoman Empire fell and was replaced by a compact nationalist Turkey ruled by Mustapha Kemal. The Arabs were made free of the Turks and brought under British and French domination at a time when world demand for petroleum, of which there are enormous deposits in the Middle East, was rising fast.

IV

In 1918 there might have seemed to be great hope for the world, at least in the eyes of a Western liberal. On the confines of Europe and Asia two harsh and incompetent autocracies, Tsarist and Ottoman, had collapsed, and inside Europe, the more liberal had defeated the less liberal among the Powers. The British and French, who ruled or dominated half the 'coloured' peoples in the world, were putting themselves forward, alongside the Americans, as champions of freedom and equality; they were 'trustees' for the peoples subject to them, and their purpose, so they said (often quite sincerely) was either to prepare them for self-government or to make them full citizens with themselves in a supra-national democratic state.

The hopes of 1918 faded quickly. There emerged in Russia a tyranny more cruel and efficient than Tsardom; the Social-Democrats failed to make Germany a stable democracy; the French, unable to persuade their English-speaking friends to make defensive military alliances with

them, were drawn into dangerous courses; while the Colonial Powers soon found that their subjects expected larger and quicker concessions than they were willing to make.

Russia had been so exhausted by war and so confused by revolution and irresolute government that the Bolsheviks, though weak, were not seriously challenged for months after they had seized power. But their separate and humiliating peace with Germany quickened opposition to them. They were soon faced with civil war and foreign intervention, and were perhaps saved thereby. For the need to defend themselves against domestic and foreign enemies drove them to courses which fastened their hold on the country; courses otherwise hardly to be excused, even to themselves, let alone to the people generally. When the civil war was over, they had established, almost without knowing how they had done it, a new kind of police state, and a monopoly of power by one party.

The triumph of Bolshevism in Russia had two important consequences for the rest of the world. It split the Marxists and other Socialists in the West into supporters and opponents of Lenin. The supporters thought it their duty to complete the 'world proletarian revolution' inaugurated by the Bolshevik seizure of power in Russia. Later on, when hope of immediate revolution faded, they still thought it their duty to accept guidance from Moscow and to act as if the cause of the oppressed everywhere always squared with the interests of the new Russia. The opponents believed that the Bolsheviks, by rejecting democracy, had made it impossible to establish genuine Socialism in Russia; their aversion to Leninism inclined them to put a higher value on the moral traditions of the West and to give up, in theory as much as in practice, the idea of getting power by violence. This split between Communists and Socialists weakened the Left in all Western countries.

The triumph of Bolshevism created a second European centre of attraction and inspiration. The Bolsheviks, ruling the most backward of great European countries, claimed that they were pushing it forward at unprecedented speed; they denounced Western democracy as a fraud, assuring the subject peoples that there were better ways to prosperity and self-respect than imitation of their masters; they proclaimed the equality of all peoples and races. They had one conspicuous advantage over the British and the French: they did not practise democracy at home and limit it amongst the peoples subject to them. Few outside Russia could know what was happening inside it but millions could see that India and Indo-China were not governed as Britain and France were.

When the Communists, at Stalin's instigation, decided that, though the time for world revolution was not yet come, backward Russia could make herself Socialist without the help of more advanced countries, the appeal of the Moscow gospel was strengthened rather than weakened. For now there could be no 'premature' revolution anywhere, provided local Communists were strong enough to get power and keep it. If they could keep it, they could use it to create a Socialist society.

The defeat of Germany brought power to the German Social-Democrats, who used it to help give their country a liberal constitution. The Russian example served as a warning for it frightened them and prevented their doing all that was necessary to make German democracy secure. Their own revolutionaries, the Spartakists, seemed a great and immediate danger to them, and to avert it they called in the help of groups on the Right, very willing to

destroy the Spartakists but whose loyalty to the new state was doubtful. The Socialists, intent upon the threat from the extreme Left, left untouched the civil service and judiciary which included many people who disliked democracy and the republic. Also, the Socialists, as the rulers of the new Germany, had to take responsibility for signing the Treaty of Versailles, which to most Germans seemed an affront to their nation. Thus the Republic and Socialism were soon associated in German eyes with disorder and national humiliation. Later, there came huge Allied demands for reparations, the runaway inflation ruining the middle classes, and in January 1923 the occupation of the Ruhr by the French and Belgians to punish the Germans for delay in paying what was asked of them. In the five years following the armistice the seeds were sown that later bore fruit in Nazism.

Though Italy had been among the victors, she had received less than she expected at the peace settlement. She was hurt in her pride, and also greatly troubled by industrial unrest. Parliamentary government had never taken firm root in Italy, where there was much more illiteracy and poverty than in England or France. A political adventurer, Benito Mussolini, created a new kind of political movement, Fascism, belonging neither to the Right nor the Left, but exploiting impartially the fears and resentments of all classes. The well-to-do feared disorder, the workers were losing faith in their socialist leaders, and most Italians resented their country's being a Great Power more in name than in fact. Fascism stood for domestic order and national greatness, and also for the duty of the State to care for the workers. It came to power in October 1922, when the King invited Mussolini to form a government. Compared with Bolshevism, Italian Fascism was mild indeed, especially during its early years. Yet its victory was a blow to Liberal Europe.

In spite of these symptoms of unrest in Germany and Italy and the consolidation of Bolshevism in Russia, the years from 1923 to 1929 were years of peace and prosperity in Europe and North America. Germany abandoned her policy of passive resistance to the French, and in 1924 the Dawes Commission made an acceptable plan for the regular payment of reparations, while Britain and France recognised Communist Russia. In the freely negotiated Locarno Treaty of 1925, Germany admitted that Alsace-Lorraine belonged to France, and soon afterwards entered the League of Nations.

This stability and prosperity were precarious. The Germans, borrowing heavily from the Americans, found it easy to pay reparations, and the countries that received them used them to pay their own debts to America. The whole system depended on the free flow of dollars from America to Europe and back again. When the flow stopped, there was universal disaster.

V

The crisis which broke on the New York stock exchange in October 1929 was by far the most extensive and prolonged in the history of capitalism. It deeply affected all the major countries of the world, except the Soviet Union, whose still primitive economy was controlled entirely from the centre and whose dependence on foreign trade was slight.

In 1929 the United States, easily the richest country in the world, produced two-fifths of all industrial goods, and Germany, the next largest industrial producer, was peculiarly dependent on American loans, which stopped when the crisis broke. The United States and Germany were the hardest hit. Whereas no previous crisis had reduced industrial production in Germany by more than six per cent, this crisis reduced it for a time by as much as thirty-nine per cent; and by 1932 there were five million unemployed in Germany. In the United States, unemployment rose from about two millions in 1929 to over twelve millions in 1932 and did not fall below seven millions until 1940. The crisis hit many agricultural and economically backward countries very hard. It proved, most painfully, how much all countries, except the Soviet Union, were involved with one another in an unstable economic system.

The major industrial countries, instead of taking common action against common dangers, tried to insulate themselves from one another. America tried to reanimate her economy while she raised her tariffs, Britain and France took refuge in their dominions and colonies, Germany resorted to all kinds of expedients to force the smaller countries around her into economic dependence, while the agricultural countries set about establishing industries to make themselves less dependent on the world market.

The prolonged depression seemed to many to bear out the theory that there are deep-seated 'contradictions' or tensions in the capitalist system which grow worse as the system grows older. All over the West men were losing faith in the ability of democratic governments to understand and control the societies they ruled. This loss of faith was not equal everywhere nor proportionate to the severity of the crisis. Though America was as hard hit as Germany, American faith in liberal democracy, being older and stronger, was much less impaired.

Though poverty and unemployment made Communism more attractive to the West, the crisis had other and greater effects. The growth of industry in its early stages had increased the relative size of the urban working class, the class of the future in Socialist eyes. But in its later stages this same growth had reduced the importance of the class, enlarging other classes unwilling to make common cause with the proletariat. These people, 'white-collar' workers, shop-keepers, small share-holders, and others, felt they belonged to the 'middle' and 'respectable' classes; socially they had more in common with employees of the state than with manual workers in industry. They envied but also admired the rich and nobly-born, while they looked askance at the workers. When their security was threatened, far from being tempted to throw in their lot with the workers, they looked for a saviour, a strong man or party, to help them preserve their self-respect and sense of social superiority.

In Germany these people found a saviour in Hitler. Yet Nazism was more than just a 'middle-class' movement; it also attracted other people: big business men who wanted a bulwark against Communism, and many of the former ruling classes who thought it the only (though crude) alternative to a decaying parliamentary democracy. The Nazis were recruited from all classes and made proposals to attract them all. Their move-ment was therefore not a class movement; its purpose was neither to save capitalism nor to change it, though it gradually subverted it in the pursuit of other ends. It aimed neither at restoring the old order nor at creating a new order more in keep-ing with long-cherished radical ideals. Nazism exploited Socialist sentiments without being genuinely Socialist; it rejected individualism and responsible government, not only in practice, as the Communists did, but also in theory. In whatever it shared with Fascism, it was the more immoderate and reckless,

especially against Communism. It differed from Fascism in its furious hatred of the Jew and the Slav and its faith in racial superiority, and also in the intensity of its contempt for the Christian virtue of charity. In Fascism there was a larger element of fraud, in Nazism a much larger element of fanaticism.

Hitler came to power in January 1933, and by action and example soon changed the face of Europe. Other would-be dictators found it easier to achieve their ambitions, and almost everywhere they behaved worse, more brutally and cyni-cally, than they had done before. Hitler withdrew from the League of Nations in October 1933, and in March 1936 repudia-ted the Locarno Treaty, sending troops into the demilitarised Rhineland. The French, for a brief moment, thought of using force in reply to this open breach of an interna-tional agreement, but the British declined to support them. The best of all opportunities of calling Hitler's bluff was lost; Germany went from strength to strength, and France gradually lost confidence in herself. Mussolini, mortally offended by the British and French attempt to stop him conquering Abyssinia, eventually became Hitler's ally. The British, bewildered by Hitler's frequent changes of front, did not know what to make of him; they sympa-thised with some of his grievances, were inclined to regard him as the champion of Europe against Communism, and hoped that he might become a tolerable neighbour when the 'injustices' done at Versailles were undone. The Russian Communists, repeatedly insulted by Hit-ler, tried to draw nearer to Britain and France. They stopped attacking the Socialists as 'social fascists', they urged Western Communists to join other parties of the Left to form 'popular fronts' for the defence of liberal democracy against Fascism, they joined the League of Nations in 1934, and in 1935 signed a treaty of mutual assistance with the French. But Soviet Russia and the Western democracies distrusted each other too much to combine effectively against Hitler. The Communists still wanted the eventual destruction of 'bourgeois society', and no one had devoted more thought to the problem of how to climb to power on the shoulders of temporary allies. To get and to keep power, to put an end to dissensions in their ranks, and to make Russia a great industrial nation at break-neck speed, the Bolsheviks had used wholesale and most terrible methods. Not until after the outbreak of war, when they set about exterminating the Jews, did the Nazis resort to methods as bad or worse by the common standards of civilised Europe. To many honest, intelligent, and liberal persons in the West, Communism still seemed, as late as 1939, the more evil, the more unclean, of the two dangers threatening Europe.

Faced by confused opponents who mistrusted each other as much as him, Hitler moved from triumph to triumph. With Mussolini he intervened in the Spanish Civil War on Franco's behalf; in March 1938, he occupied Austria; in September of the same year, at Munich, he coaxed and threatened the French and the British into letting him take the Sudetenland from Czechoslovakia; and in March 1939, he occupied the rest of that country. Never, since Napoleon's time, had one of the Great Powers of Europe treated the others with so much contempt. The British Government were moved to try to make an alliance against Hitler with the Russians, but by that time it was too late. The Russians feared that the British intended to draw them into war with Germany while themselves remaining at peace. They therefore decided to outsmart the Western Powers, and in August 1939

made a pact of non-aggression with Hitler, secretly agreeing to let him take one half of Poland if they could take the other. Thus they hoped to involve him in war with Britain and France, who had guaranteed the integrity of Poland. With the 'capitalist' Powers at war, their own country would be secure from attack and the world revolution perhaps brought nearer.

VI

Meanwhile important developments took place in Asia. In 1919 the Chinese Republic was neither a sovereign state nor a true dependency; it was not sovereign because of the peculiar rights granted to foreigners, and yet no foreign Power was responsible for the good government of China (*see* Chapter 18). Foreigners intervened so much in her affairs that China could not govern herself and was a prey to anarchy. The Chinese nationalist movement, the Kuomintang, led by Sun-Yat-Sen, though by no means Communist, was subject to Russian influences; for the Russian Communists had voluntarily renounced the unequal treaties made with the Chinese and had offered to help them create an efficient administration. With Russian advice the Kuomintang was reorganised by 1927 and gained control of nearly all China. Until 1927 the Kuomintang attracted the town workers, intellectuals, and even peasants, as well as the rising industrial and commercial classes; but in that year Chiang Kai-Shek, Sun's successor, turned against the Communists. He drove them out of the Kuomintang, and proscribed their party. He did not, however, succeed in destroying them, though in 1934-5 they had to withdraw to the remoter frontier provinces.

Having broken with the Communists and with Russia, Chiang sought the friendship of Britain and the United States. With their help, he expanded

China's industries, and in other ways modernised his country, but attempted no drastic social reforms, doing almost nothing for the peasants, the vast majority, who paid high rents to the landlords. Chiang's Western friends, largely from fear of Communism, made concessions to him, abandoning many of the privileges extorted from the Chinese in the previous century. Gradually, nationalist China was becoming a sovereign and modern state.

But Chiang was not left in peace to consolidate his hold on China. Japan, industrial and overpopulated, depending on a large overseas trade, was struck hard by the world economic crisis. She resolved to create for herself a sphere of influence in the Far East which she could exploit economically; she occupied Manchuria in 1931 and the next year made a puppet state of it under the name of Manchukuo. There followed years of desultory warfare between Japan and Nationalist China, the Japanese getting control of the main railways and larger towns without being able to subdue the country districts. Japanese aggression led in December 1936 to a reconciliation between Chiang and the Communists, who accepted him as the leader of a united front against Japan. The Japanese invasion had two other important results: it called attention to the weakness of the Western Powers in the Far East, and it cut off Chiang from the large coastal towns, the wealthier classes, and the West. While his power was centred in the great towns, Chiang had been a reformer, making the kind of reforms, administrative, legal and fiscal, welcome to merchants and industrialists. As a guerrilla leader in the interior of China, he was much less impressive. True, he stood for resistance to Japan, but so too did the Communists, who also stood for other things attractive to the peasants.

In India, as in China, a nationalist movement, at first largely confined to the educated and the well-to-do, began to get mass support during and after the First World War. But India, unlike China, was efficiently ruled by foreigners. She had almost no contact with the new Russia, and was much less affected by Communism. The Congress Party, the great organ of Hindu nationalism, was an oddly assorted body, appealing to classes with very different interests, but it held together in the long struggle against the British. For a quarter of a century it was dominated by an extraordinary man, Gandhi, who added immensely to its strength, and whose philosophy, moral and political, was poles apart from Communism. Gandhi brought self-respect to his people, and taught them methods of non-violent resistance peculiarly effective against humane and law-respecting rulers.

Britain, which had received great help from India during the war, and was no doubt moved also by fears that troubled all colonial Powers since the triumph of Communism in Russia, promised eventual self-government to India. In 1920 she granted a limited autonomy to the provinces, but, as usually happens in such cases, the most she was at any time willing to give was less than the least that would then satisfy the Indians. In 1929, at Lahore, the Congress Party demanded complete independence. Using the methods of Gandhi, the Indian nationalists were able, time and again, to demonstrate their power without reducing their country to anarchy.

The British relied on the support of the princes and the great landlords, and also played the Moslems off against the Hindus. They had done effectively for India what Chiang, during his best years, tried to do for China; they established a clean, just, and efficient administration. But they were too weak to do more. Had they attempted large social reforms, they would have made enemies of the classes most favourable to them. Economically they did little for the peasants, weighed down under a growing burden of debt, or for the artisans ruined by modern industry and European imports.

Asian nationalism was most completely successful in Turkey, where Kemal Ataturk established a strong one-party state. He wanted to make his country independent, in fact as well as in name, by abolishing special privileges granted to foreigners, by buying up foreign concessions, by creating an army, a civil service, and a legal system of Western type, and by making a serious attempt to attach the peasants to the régime by improving their lot. After Kemal's death, his party, unique among parties of its kind, voluntarily gave up its absolute position in the State. Turkey has lived through a popular revolution almost untouched by Communism.

Between the two wars Arab nationalism was strong only in provinces once ruled by the Turks; it was strongest in Egypt, but even there was predominantly middle class. Britain, the dominant Power in the Middle East, had no wish to govern the area directly; she acquiesced in the seizure of power in Persia by Riza Khan in 1921, and in 1922 herself proclaimed the independence of Egypt. Her aim was to keep open the route to India and to get oil on favourable terms; she wanted concessions for herself, military and economic, but was willing to tolerate any native government that respected her 'vital' interests.

Until after the Second World War Communist influences scarcely touched the Middle East and North Africa, partly because Arab nationalism was mostly confined to the well-to-do, and partly because the prestige of the Soviet Union as a world Power was not yet great. Only

in China had Moscow exercised a direct and considerable influence on the course of events. If the Western democracies lost face in non-European eyes before 1939, it was because of their weakness towards Hitler and the Japanese. Yet this weakness was itself partly an effect of fear of Communism.

Communism also bore indirectly in another way on relations between European and non-European peoples. By denouncing 'imperialism' and proclaiming the equality of all nations, it touched the rich democracies where they were most sensitive. They professed to believe in freedom and equality of opportunity. Did they intend these blessings only for themselves? In a world that contained a great Communist Power eager to proselytise, it was no longer safe to treat this question as anything less than urgent.

VII

The Second World War was no more than the First a struggle for mastery between rival creeds. Britain and France would have put up quietly with Nazism if Hitler's policies had not endangered peace; and Hitler had no wish to refashion other countries on the German model. He aimed at German supremacy in the world and not at the spread of German principles among lesser peoples. Hitler was a prophet only in his own country and cared for no other. The Western democracies, while Italy remained neutral, were very willing to concede her right to be Fascist. The British and French Governments still seemed to hate Communism more than Nazism, and most of their subjects probably agreed with them.

France, confused and apathetic, faced by an enemy stronger than herself, was easily defeated in the summer of 1940. Italy entered the war on Hitler's side, and Britain, having lost the greater part of the equipment of her army, was left alone to face an alliance controlling nearly all Europe between Russia and Spain. Her position was dangerous but less so than it seemed; for the Germans had not prepared an invasion of Britain to follow immediately upon the fall of France. The British had several months to recover themselves, they still had a powerful navy, and an air force just strong enough to prevent the Germans from getting the mastery of the air needed for a successful invasion. Above all, the British were united, as the French had not been, by the nearness of danger and the leadership of Churchill. The lonely and successful defiance of Hitler by the country which was the original home of freedom was above all a moral victory.

Though Hitler had to give up the idea of invading Britain in 1940, he was immeasurably stronger than he had been the year before. America was still isolationist, Britain too weak to hurt him, and Russia not yet ready for war. Indeed, Stalin had good reason to be afraid of Germany, for in his frantic hurry to build up Russian industry and agriculture he had brought famine and terror to the people and could scarcely rely on their loyalty. Yet Hitler could not rest on his laurels; for he knew that he would not be left undisturbed to consolidate his hold on Europe. Roosevelt was doing his best to coax and manœuvre his country from neutrality to open support of Britain; it was the obvious interest of Russia to challenge German supremacy as soon as she felt strong enough to do so, and Britain was unconquered. Hitler had two courses open to him: he could either invade Britain the next year or turn his armies against Stalin. He chose the second course, and in June 1941 invaded Russia.

German victories in Europe encouraged Japanese ambitions in the Far East. By seizing the colonies of the Western Powers, the Japanese could encircle and isolate China. But they had to reckon with the Americans, who could not be expected to tolerate the creation of a vast Japanese Empire. The Japanese therefore decided to strike first, which they did at Pearl Harbor on 8 December, 1941. The ease and rapidity of their early victories were astonishing. Within a few months they were masters of all Asia between Burma and Mongolia, except for the areas held by the Chinese Communists and by Chiang. Though the Japanese behaved more brutally than the Europeans had done, their victories were as much admired as feared by the peoples of Asia, for they were Asian victories over Europeans.

What had begun as a European and Mediterranean war was now truly a world war, and Britain's part in it was relatively less important. Hitler's chief enemy was now Russia, and after Russia the United States; and the war in the Far East, after the early battles, was mainly between Japan and America in the Pacific. For a time it seemed that Germany might conquer Russia quickly, for the first Russian armies to face the invader were easily defeated and there was widespread disaffection in the Ukraine and the Caucasus. But the Germans, by their harshness, rallied the disaffected to their rulers, and the war against Hitler became a patriotic war. The German advance was stopped at Stalingrad in September 1942, the Western Allies landed in North Africa in November of the same year, and in February 1943 the Japanese evacuated Guadalcanal. The tide had turned. Russia had proved strong enough to take the full shock of the German army, and the United States, much the greatest of industrial powers, was fast mobilising her immense resources. By September 1943, when the Allies invaded Italy, it was already clear that Germany and Japan were bound to be defeated. After the Allied armies had carried out massive landings in France, and fought their way to the Rhine, the Germans capitulated on 8 May 1945, and the Japanese on 2 September, after two atomic bombs had been dropped on their country.

The prestige lost by the colonial Powers in Asia and Africa was not made good by Allied victory, for the principal victors, the Soviet Union and the United States, were against 'colonialism'. Though, with Japan defeated, the 'white' peoples were stronger than ever before, those of them that ruled the 'coloured' peoples were relatively much weaker.

VIII

Since 1945, there has been prolonged enmity between America and Russia; Asia and parts of Africa have been freed from European rule; there has been great, if precarious, prosperity in the West; and Russia has emerged as the second industrial power.

In 1945, as in 1918, there was much talk of democracy and of the need to organise peace, though the talk was less hopeful, for in the interval there had been many disillusionments. The United Nations Organisation was created to replace the old League, and all the Great Powers, except the defeated, joined it. But the Russians, though they too said they spoke for democracy, for every people's right to govern themselves, and for international co-operation, did not want the West to use these principles against them. They insisted that each of the Great Powers should have a veto which could prevent the United Nations taking effective action against them. They also wanted to extend their frontiers westwards, to establish satellite states along them, and to keep Germany divided, lest united she should join the 'capitalist' Powers. For these ends they used force

where necessary. Their methods alarmed the West, where a cry was raised against Soviet 'imperialism' and conspiracy to make the whole world Communist. To strengthen the non-Communist or 'free' world, the Americans put forward the Marshall Plan in 1948 to restore the economies of states friendly to them, and in 1949 set up the North Atlantic Treaty Organisation (N.A.T.O.) for common defence against Communist aggression. These methods, which the Americans looked upon as defensive, seemed offensive to the Russians, who tried by covert threats and equivocal promises to make them ineffective, using the Communist parties of the West to make difficulties for their governments, and exploiting the desire for peace of a Europe suspicious of American plans to rearm Germany.

Care must be taken when discussing a Communist threat to the world since 1945. True it has been official doctrine in Moscow that 'capitalism' must eventually collapse everywhere, and that meanwhile the 'capitalist' West is inevitably hostile to 'socialist' Russia. True, the Russians have created satellite states and still insist on keeping Germany divided; they still give help (though often less than they are said to do) to foreign Communist parties struggling for power, and use them to embarrass foreign governments. But to believe in the eventual triumph everywhere of Communism and to use foreign Communists to support Russian policy is not in itself to be engaged in actual conspiracy to make the world Communist. Russian aggression and brutality (mostly confined to Europe) have probably been inspired more by the urge to make Russia secure against the West than by any larger ambition. Russian losses during the war were immensely greater than American, and Russia for several years had no atom bomb while America had it. Mistrusting their late allies, the Russians have been pitiless in their hurry to restore their shattered economy and achieve security.

Since Stalin's death in 1953 relations between Russia and the United States have been less acutely hostile. Economically, Russia has much more than made good her losses during the war; she has the atom and the hydrogen bombs; and China, the most populous of countries, is now Communist. Russia is much stronger now than just after the war, and seems also somewhat milder and more accommodating, though not more democratic. The years of feverish industrialisation in fear of war and reconstruction after it are over; the methods that brought millions to the verge of starvation or into slave-labour camps are no longer so often used as they were. There is, however, no evidence that these changes are due to a change of heart or doctrine. It is more probable that Russia's behaviour is milder because she feels stronger and more secure. Even in Stalin's time, Russia treated Red China as an equal, knowing she could not afford to do otherwise.

How China should be treated was obvious; but Russia has been more puzzled about how to treat the lesser European satellites. If she keeps too tight a hold on them, the local Communists may revolt against her, as they did in Yugoslavia in 1948; if she loosens her hold too much, she risks a revolt against Communism itself, as happened in Hungary in 1956. In 1948, Stalin, except for abuse, let the Yugoslavs alone, but his successors in 1956 put down the Hungarians by force, and in 1968 even suppressed 'liberalisation' in Czechoslovakia, thus saving their hegemony in Eastern Europe at the cost of losing many supporters in the West and in uncommitted Eastern countries.

The Americans, too, in spite of their economic generosity, have lost friends through their endeavours to get security against Russia. Communist parties in the West owe some of their popularity to resentment against America for rearming Germany and seeming to conduct her foreign policy as if nothing were more urgent than to defend the world against Russian aggression. In Asia, even more than in Europe, America has been widely blamed for helping to turn the world into two armed camps. The desire to limit the influence of the two colossal Powers has been strong: it was one of the motives leading to the creation of the Council of Europe in 1949, and has largely inspired the foreign policy of India.

IX

By defeating and occupying Japan, America made herself the strongest Power in the Far East. Having granted independence to the Philippines, her only possession in that area, she was far from eager to restore to her European allies the colonies taken by the Japanese. The Japanese victory had destroyed European prestige, and it would now be incomparably more difficult for Europeans to govern Asiatic colonies. The Americans believed that the peoples of Asia ought to be allowed to govern themselves, and that to hold them down by force might encourage the spread of Communism. Yet they could not actively prevent their allies from returning to their colonies; and sometimes, indeed, even supported them against native patriots, when these were already too far gone in Communism. American policy, confused and vacillating, served on the whole to undermine European authority in the Far East. In June 1949 the last Dutch troops left the Dutch East Indies, now called Indonesia, and by the summer of 1954 the French, after a protracted and expensive war, had irretrievably lost Indo-China. The British recognised Burma's independence in 1947, and that of Malaya in 1957 (from 1963 the Federation of Malaysia) and of Singapore in 1959, both the latter remaining within the Commonwealth.

Outside the limits of Japanese conquest, Britain has willingly abandoned vast territories inhabited by hundreds of millions of people, granting independence within the Commonwealth to India and Pakistan in 1947, to Ceylon in 1948, and to the Gold Coast (Ghana) in 1957. Britain has found it easier than France to adapt her policies to her new and diminished position in the world. The very size of her empire has made it obvious to her that she could not hold it indefinitely by force and that the wiser course is to retreat with dignity, which she can do the more easily for the great and honourable part she played in the war. Already, long before 1945, she had associated with her in the Commonwealth daughter nations whose wealth and importance were growing fast, and had announced her intention to prepare all the peoples subject to her for self-government. Her altered position merely obliged her to do much more quickly what she had already committed herself to doing. France's position has been more difficult. Defeated in the war and over-sensitive, she has been afraid that retreat might look like weakness. Her old policy was gradually to assimilate her subject peoples in close union with herself, making French citizens of them; but this policy did not attract these peoples, and she did not contrive to produce an alternative acceptable to them. There were large French settlements in North Africa, especially Algeria, which made it almost impossible to reconcile the claims of the natives with those of the settlers. If a French Government sacrificed the Africans to the settlers, it was faced with rebellion in Africa, but if it made concessions to the Afri-

cans, it provoked the settlers and their powerful supporters in France. Independence for Algeria came in 1962 after bitter civil war.

Britain has been more troubled by Arab nationalism than by the struggle of her colonies for independence. In the line with her usual (though by no means consistent) policy of yielding gracefully to forces she is no longer strong enough to control, she had made many concessions to the Arabs. But the Arab nationalist leaders, eager to make a solid Arab bloc out of several primitive, disparate, and loosely governed peoples, have tried to unite them in hatred of the foreigner: of the British, who dominated the Arab world after 1918; of the Israelis, who with British and American help have created a country of their own in Palestine; and of the French, who fought the Arab rebels in Algeria. Provoked by this hatred and the policies it inspired, the Israelis, the British, and the French invaded Egypt in 1956, but were quickly obliged by world opinion to withdraw their troops. America condemned them because she feared their action might encourage Russia to intervene in the Middle East; Russia made haste to cover up her own aggression in Hungary by crying out against the 'imperialist' attack on Egypt, and the Asian countries resented a European invasion of non-European people. The abortive Suez adventure put an end to British preponderance in the Middle East and added to France's difficulties in North Africa. The adventure failed, not because of Arab strength, but because it suited the two World Powers that it should fail.

So far Communism has made little headway among the Arab peoples. If Russia has influence in the Middle East, she has it, not because Communism is popular, but because the Arab nationalist leaders want to turn the rivalry of America and Russia to their own advantage. Yet Communism may find the Middle East propitious to its growth, for nowhere else in the world are there greater contrasts of wealth and poverty. The Arab leaders care more for power and nationalist politics than for social reform and economic progress. Turkey stands alone in the Middle East as a country strongly opposed to Communism and yet also able and willing to undertake large reforms.

Recent events have shown that economically backward countries are more susceptible than others to Communism but not that they cannot escape it. It has been weak government rather than poverty that has led to Communism, for where government was weak, great and peaceful changes were impossible. India, as poor as China, has been much less attracted by Communism and also much less a prey to anarchy; she has a relatively strong government that rejects Communist methods and is willing to make great reforms.

There were special reasons for the triumph of Communism in China, which knew the evils of irresponsible European interference without the benefits of stable European government. Japanese aggression drove a once 'progressive' Nationalist movement out of the large towns, the sources of its strength, into country districts where the Communists had more to offer the peasants. When the Nationalists regained control of the large towns, they were weakened and corrupted by years of frustration. They got more help from America than Russia could give to the Communists, but in vain, for they could not make effective use of it. By the end of 1949 the Nationalists had withdrawn to Formosa under the protection of the American fleet, and the Communists held all mainland China.

The triumph of Communism in China was widely deplored in the West as a great step forward in Moscow's plan to make the whole world Communist. This impression was strengthened by the attack in June 1950 of Communist North Korea on South Korea. The Korean War, in which Red China intervened on North Korea's behalf, ended only in 1953, without victory for either side, but making bitter enemies of the Chinese and the Americans. After the Korean War Red China was obviously no satellite of Moscow, but increasingly a contender for leadership in the Communist world. Concern with internal reform is rivalled by her mission abroad, as in her involvement in Vietnam and influential aid in Africa, e.g. the building of the TanZam railway.

Montesquieu has observed that a new faith often begins by making wide and quick progress and then comes suddenly to a stop; it spreads where social conditions favour it and then spreads no more. While people are fascinated by its progress, it looks to them everywhere the same; but when it has settled, they begin to notice how much it differs in different places as it takes the colour of its surroundings.

X

Since the early 'thirties Western governments have intervened on an unprecedented scale in economic affairs. Before that time they had seldom done more than assist by tariffs or subsidies, make laws against monopolies, or sponsor agreements for fixing prices to shield weaker producers from the effects of competition. After it, they undertook lavish programmes of public expenditure to stimulate employment, and sought means of controlling investment and regulating the flow of money. Their first attempts were haphazard and often failed of their objects, but they learnt from experience and also from the writings of academic economists, especially from J. M. Keynes' *General Theory of Employment, Interest, and Money* published in 1936. Above all they learnt during the war how they could control the entire national economy to get it functioning as they wanted. After the war it was taken for granted in the West that governments are responsible for maintaining full employment, controlling inflation, and in general keeping the nation's economy healthy. In countries devastated by war governments took it upon themselves to produce plans for reconstruction, and they everywhere admitted their duty to see to it that the transition from war production to peace production was smoothly made. Far from resenting this intrusion of the State, industrial leaders welcomed many aspects of it, though they criticised others; they learnt to work with the State and to lean upon it. Governments also undertook to provide social services on a scale never before attempted, and they put heavy taxes on large incomes and inherited estates. The West has lived through a profound economic and social revolution; and has done so whether or not many industries have been taken over by the State, for nationalisation has been one of the less important sides of this revolution.

This massive change has enormously enriched the West, especially North America. It has also reduced the relative size of the manual working classes, and has increased their real incomes more than those of other classes. The differences and antagonisms that kept the workers apart from the classes 'above' them are now diminished, and new social tensions are emerging different from the old. The class that is now growing fastest is not the 'proletariat' as Marx foretold, but the amorphous 'middle class', a vast assortment of people with widely different economic functions who share certain pretensions and anxieties.

There have been even greater changes in the Soviet Union. There has arisen a vast administrative hierarchy to keep the people obedient to their rulers and to control production. An illiterate and mechanically unskilled people have been taught to read and write and to take care of machinery. The years of desperate industrialisation and reconstruction are over, and it is no longer necessary to use the wholesale and dreadful methods of Stalin. The industrial power of the Soviet Union is growing fast. Yet Russia is still, as much as ever, a one-party and a police state, and differences of income are large and growing.

It is still common form to speak of 'socialist' Russia and the 'capitalist' West, though Russia is even less socialist than the West is capitalist, as these two words were understood before 1914. Socialism used to mean at least two things: the control of production by the producers or the community generally, and nobody getting an income except for doing work useful to society. In Russia production is controlled by the leaders of an irresponsible party, and hundreds of thousands earn their incomes by services to that party, keeping the people docile to it. Capitalism used to mean the ownership and control of the means of production by private persons, with government doing little more than maintain law and order. Western governments now exercise a general control over production and lay heavy taxes on the rich for the benefit of the poor. The important differences between Russia and the West are much more political and moral than economic, and the theories of Marx are as little relevant to the modern world as the classical economies of Adam Smith and Ricardo.

The peoples of European stock, 'Western' and 'Communist', are still privileged above all others. They are growing fast in industrial power and material wealth, and have ample room for expansion. The richest parts of the world, actually and potentially belong to them. If they live in over-populated areas, they can move to Siberia, or to the Americas, or to Australia. These movements are more restricted than they were but are still possible. The peoples of Asia, by comparison, are much less fortunate; they are the poorest of all and suffer most from over-population, and the fertile and still empty lands are mostly closed to them. The cry 'Africa for the Africans' excludes Asia as much as Europe; and Asia for the Asians, if the Asians aspire to the blessings promised either by Communism or Western Democracy, is scarcely enough.

CONCLUSION

by John Bowle

This new outline of world history has extended from the emergence of man into the dawn of the nuclear age. But the beginnings of agricultural settlement go back only ten millennia, and the antiquity of all written evidence is at most six thousand years: even if the Upper Paleolithic age be included, *Homo sapiens* has occupied only a brief space in the history of life.

Yet, looking back over the variety of civilisations here described, at the quality of experience realised and at the variety of environment exploited, much has been crowded into these ages. History, like nature, is ruthless. It is also vivid, many-sided and far flung, and it demonstrates the almost indestructible persistence of human societies. Though the flower of civilisation is delicate, its roots spring up and ramify with the toughness of ground elder. Contemporary discoveries promise a widening of knowledge and power which will make our generation seem provincial, and the astonishing advances of science, by which our age is signalised in world history, obvious achievements.

In spite of formidable doubts and perils, our horizon is expanding. Already we have to take a world view of civilisation and to understand the background which *this* outline has delineated. Pessimism is now all too fashionable; but there is no warrant for it. There is no evidence in history for the defeat of life.

Over the centuries we discern horrible suffering, vistas of boredom, of cruelty and superstition—the rise but also the decadence of civilisations: the murmur of poverty and frustration forms the undertone to the articulate glories of even the greatest states. Yet, whatever the outcome, there has already been a rich variety of experience lived and sometimes recorded. To our prehistoric forebears it would have appeared unthinkable. More precisely, the course of world history from the earliest times demonstrates one incontrovertible fact—man's devious, gradual, but cumulative mastery of his environment and an increase in population which, among the higher species, is without parallel. Biologically and culturally man has been a success. The thought may appear obvious, but it is often forgotten. It is not a matter of opinion whether there has been progress, either in the experience of the human spirit or in the conquest of the earth. It is a fact.

Of this fluctuating experience, and gradual mastery, history is the record. It presents a grave and often tragic picture, but also brilliance, gaiety and much ordinary contentment. It is not without a moral. Its moral is the toughness, the rich variety, the immense range of human societies, and the need to liberate the energies of life. It promotes a humanist view, making for tolerance of human variety and respect for the tireless ingenuity of man's ways. Like the complexity of the animal kingdom of which it is a part, it also promotes awe. Such seems to be the plain significance of world history—not, as Fisher believed, a tale without a pattern, but a record in which two specific trends may be observed from the paleolithic age until today: the gradual mastery of environment, and, out of this deviating but cumulative progress, the realisation of a great and diverse range of human experience.

II

In most of the foregoing chapters political events have been given a subordinate place. Today it is the social, cultural and economic aspects of civilisation that are most interesting. The total impressions of cultures and the comparison between them are now increasingly the concern of historians, who attempt to elicit useful conclusions from such contrasts in adaptation and setting. Sociology and anthropology have invaded history, and history is the better for it.

While this outline has been designed to show the frequent continuity and interdependence of world civilisation, it is intended also to promote comparisons. Contributors have not endeavoured to impose metaphysical patterns on events, or to discover 'laws' of civilisation's progress or decline. They have written independently and from different points of view. But they have endeavoured to trace continuity, to juxtapose an immense diversity of cultures, and to demonstrate that what has seemed overwhelmingly important to Western minds must now take its place alongside less familiar but equally massive and enduring societies. The descendants of these peoples are coming into their inheritance as world citizens, and they will have as great a say in the future as Europeans and their progeny.

To many Western minds the old Chinese or Indian civilisations seem alien, and their own European cultural ancestors remote. Yet a Greek epigram or the verse of a seventh-century Chinese poet can strike home to a Western reader more intimately than many twentieth-century expressions of his own culture.

Certain facts are perhaps worth a retrospective glance.

First is the importance now attributed to the late Paleolithic and Neolithic ages. As Dr Weiner has observed, Upper Paleolithic art implies that among some of these illiterate hunters there must already have been a play of ideas demanding elaborate language. Further, as Dr Lienhardt has demonstrated, the least civilised African tribes—the Pygmies and Bushmen, for example—have shown notable dramatic powers and aesthetic sensibility. The most primitive human was not a slave to routine; he was often a lively and observant hunter. Brisk perception and swift activity, as well as the lust to kill, go back into our earliest ancestry.

The effect of the Neolithic Revolution may have been a blunting of perception; but it was the price of a cardinal advance. As Professor Evans writes, 'Had it not been for these changes, it seems unlikely that any human societies more complex than the small groups, which are all that a purely hunting and gathering economy can generally permit, would have come into being at all'. This basic achievement, first made in the fertile Crescent of the Middle East, was not due to conquest; it was made gradually by peasant farmers—the Natufians of Carmel, for instance, and the villagers of Karim Shahir. The dawn of civilisation was not spectacular. Similarly, the beginning of writing in Iraq was due to the desire to keep records, not to the Zeitgeist.

Whether or not the earliest Egyptian, Indian, or Chinese cities developed independently, there is a common background of Neolithic farming to all the civilisations of the Old World. Moreover, the Mesopotamian temple states grew up from the need for common irrigation.

Old and new myths about the origin of civilisation have dissolved in the light of scientific inquiry, and this crucial common period is no longer dismissed as a dull prelude to the real business of recording the vicissitudes of empires, but placed squarely as the common origin of the entire human story.

Another fact may have seemed striking to Western Europeans. In the light of world history, the period known in Europe as the Dark Ages was not dark at all: it was predominantly a time of high culture. Not merely was the Byzantine Empire at its height, but in the East, writes Mr G. F. Hudson, 'the old Indian civilisation reached its zenith in the days of the Gupta Empire, which flourished between A.D. 320 and 500 . . . the age coincided with the finest flowering of the Sanskrit literature'. When Britain, abandoned by the legions, was sinking into barbarism, in Northern India 'it was the most fruitful epoch in science and mathematics and . . . highly productive of philosophical thought'.

Further, though the West was becoming illiterate, the Far Eastern civilisations were flourishing. For sheer staying power there has been no society comparable to the Chinese: their system of examinations originated two hundred years before the birth of Christ; it continued with some modifications until 1912. A civilisation has been carried on for millennia by means profoundly different from those familiar in the West. And it is also memorable that across the Pacific, during the Western Dark Ages there was even a vigorous, if limited, culture among the Maya in Central America. The foundations of the Peruvian state, too, were being laid at this time, though the Inca domination only began about the twelfth century. But since the rise of civilisation there has never been darkness all the time.

The variety of religions is also important and may even bring reassurance. Societies can carry on over long ages without the inspiration of much other worldly hope, as witness the brilliance of Hellenic Humanism and the long success of the teachings of Confucius. Such is the vitality of mankind that men and women can maintain considerable prosperity under a régime as self-destructive as that imposed by Aztec beliefs. In general, few religions, apart from the universal fertility cult, have been as sanguine as most versions of Christianity. While they may well be considered spiritually inferior to the Christian revelation, they have not led to widespread despair.

Further, the cult of racial superiority now seems quite untenable. This prejudice has, of course, not been by any means confined to Europeans. The Chinese regarded foreigners with particular contempt, and predatory warriors everywhere despised the peasants and townsmen whom they pillaged. It is natural and healthy that vigorous peoples should have their proper pride. But such intolerance must give way before the facts of world civilisation. The widespread Western belief, for example, that Eastern civilisations are static and incompetent cannot survive the evidence. The glories of Salamis and Plataea no longer blind us to the achievements of the Persian administration and to the influence of the Eastern idea of empire on Rome, Byzantium, and even on the Western Middle Ages. Nor can the great Indian initiative in penetrating Malaya and Indonesia and exploiting the seaways of the Indian Ocean be ignored. In spite of the West's recent material supremacy, it has never had the monopoly of enterprise.

But Western initiative has achieved the greatest conquest of environment. It has created the technological basis of a world civilisation. The earliest pre-history shows how skills in stone and flint became world-wide; then primitive agriculture also became all but universal. Beneath the diversity of cultures and religions, the foundation of human societies has generally been similar. The Industrial and Environmental Revolutions are clearly providing a common basis for something new. In spite of the violence of current nationalism and ideological conflict, these technological advances are moving mankind towards a new adaptation to supra-national facts. They are creating a new kind of man whose outlook is bound to be world-wide, and they are likely in time to create a new civilisation which draws its vitality from the many great cultures and different climates described in this survey. The intermixture always characteristic of mankind is also likely to increase; the scale of administration and the range of authority will probably widen, just as within nation states provincial anarchy has been ironed out. Nor is the interdependent economic life of the world likely to be confined indefinitely within the bounds of economic nationalism. These prospects are still distant, but history demonstrates that facts tell.

III

These are only a few of the more notable aspects of world history. Readers will have observed many others. Next to the clear evidence that *homo sapiens* has increased his mastery of the world, the most striking fact of all is the contrast between the disasters caused by war and political disorder, and the benefits derived from creative thought, economic enterprise and hard work. The real makers of civilisation have been men of genius and talent in the arts and sciences, in philosophy, invention and management, and the toiling peoples who have kept the great concern going

since Neolithic times. But the paradox is not due simply to the supposed wickedness of politicians; the causes lie deeper in the dangerous quality of power to those who handle as well as those who suffer it. Centralised political power is necessary, for without it order and safety are impossible; but like a radio-active substance, it can be deadly. It is vital to find means of controlling public power and directing it to biologically reputable ends—to the enhancement, not the annihilation, of life.

Since civilisation has been mainly built up despite military and political exploitation, it seems sensible to direct more interest and energy towards the non-political aspects of society. A reaction against the overwhelming power of modern states and bureaucracies may well be setting in. Men are certainly beginning to hope much less from political revolution and to regard nineteenth-century expectations in that field as irrelevant. The achievements of the human spirit and of the massive organising powers of mankind are more important than the old struggle for domination, product of the economics of scarcity and of the tensions of the subconscious mind. Perhaps, if world order is to come about, it may be achieved through gradually by-passing politics, under the truce of fear that nuclear weapons impose. The exploration of outer space, moreover, already begun with landings on the moon, has opened up a whole new field of interest, which could transcend the earth-bound competition of traditional power-politics. If these extraordinary prospects can be exploited not merely as a strategic aspect of a suicidal conflict, but through the collaboration of scientists working for mankind, attention may be further directed from the obsolescent ideological conflicts which now spell mortal danger. The space-age may hold out a new hope.

Man, who emerged fifty thousand years ago, has still, like the other animals, to adapt himself or perish. Unlike them, he has, by his own mastery, changed his environment, and must now conform to the revolution he has wrought. As mind probes deeper into the uncanny secrets of the universe, new dangers as well as new powers are opened up. The legend of Faust has never been more topical.

NOTES ON THE CONTRIBUTORS

JOHN BOWLE, M.A., Professor Emeritus of Political Theory, College of Europe, Bruges; former Lecturer in History, Wadham College, Oxford. Publications include: *Western Political Thought*, Jonathan Cape, London, and Oxford University Press, New York, 1947; *The Unity of European History*, J. Cape, London, and Oxford University Press, New York, 1948; *Hobbes and his Critics*, J. Cape, London, and Oxford University Press, New York, 1951. *Politics and Opinion in the Nineteenth Century*, J. Cape, London, and Oxford University Press, New York, 1954. *Minos or Minotaur?; The Dilemma of Political Power*, J. Cape, London, 1956; *Viscount Samuel, a Biography*, Gollancz, London, 1957. *A New Outline of World History*, Allen & Unwin, London, 1962; in America *Man Through the Ages*, Little, Brown, Boston, 1962; *Henry VIII*, a biography, Allen & Unwin, London, 1964, and Little, Brown, Boston, 1964; *England, a Portrait*, Benn, London, 1966 and Praeger, New York, 1966.

JOHN BRADFORD, M.A., F.S.A., formerly University Demonstrator in Prehistory, Oxford. Publications include contributions to: *A History of Technology*, edited by CHARLES SINGER, Oxford University Press, London, 1954; *Myth or Legend*, ed. by G. E. DAVIES, G. Bell & Sons, London, 1955; *Proceedings of the International Classical Congress*, Copenhagen, 1958; *Ancient Landscapes*, G. Bell & Sons, London, 1957.

P. R. L. BROWN, B.A., Fellow, All Souls College, Oxford. Publications include: *St Augustine of Hippo*, Faber & Faber, London, 1967.

ANDREW ROBERT BURN, M.A., Reader in Ancient History, University of Glasgow, until 1969. Publications include: *Alexander the Great and the Hellenistic Empire*, English Universities Press, second edition, London, 1959.

LIONEL BUTLER, M.A., D.Phil., Professor of Medieval History and Dean of the Faculty of Arts at the University of St Andrews. Publications include articles on medieval ecclesiastical history and history of the Order of St John, and (with R. J. Adam) English edition of Robert Fawtier's *The Capetian Kings of France* (London, 1960).

JOHN DAVIES EVANS, M.A., Ph.D., F.S.A., Professor of Prehistoric Archaeology, University of London. Publications include: *Malta*, Ancient Peoples and Places Series No. 11, 1959; *Excavations at Saliagos near Antiparos*, 1968 (with Dr A. C. Renfrew); *The Prehistoric Antiquities of the Maltese Islands*, 1969; also excavation reports and papers in various journals.

W. G. FOREST, M.A., Fellow of Wadham College, Oxford. Publications include: *The First Sacred War* in *Bulletin de Correspondance Hellénique LXXX*, Paris, 1956; *Colonization and the Rise of Delphi* in *Historia VI*, Wiesbaden, 1957; *A Chian Wine-measure* in the *Annal of the British School of Athens LI*, London, 1956.

C. R. S. HARRIS, M.A., D.Phil., Reader in Studies in the Humanities, University of Adelaide, S. Australia; former Fellow of All Souls College, Oxford. Publications include: *Duns Scotus*, Clarendon Press, Oxford, 1927; *Germany's Foreign Indebtedness*, Oxford University Press, London, 1935; *Allied Military Administration of Italy*,

1943-1945 in *History of the Second World War*, H.M.S.O., London, 1958.

P. M. HOLT, M.A., B.Litt., D.Phil., Professor of Arab History in the University of London. Publications include: *The Mahdist State in the Sudan; 1881-1898*, Clarendon Press, Oxford, 1958; *A Modern History of the Sudan*, Weidenfeld & Nicolson, London, 1963; *Egypt and the Fertile Crescent, 1516-1922*, Longmans Green, London, 1966.

J. M. HOUSTON, M.A., B.SC., D.Phil., University Lecturer in Geography; Fellow & Bursar of Hertford College, Oxford. Publications include: *A Social Geography of Europe*, G. Duckworth, London, 1953; *The Western Mediterranean World*, Longmans Green & Co., 1964. Articles in the *Encyclopaedia Britannica, Encyclopaedia Americana* and in various geographical journals. Articles in *Geographical Journal, Transactions of the Institute of British Geographers, Town Planning Review, The Advancement of Science*.

G. F. HUDSON, M.A., Fellow and Director of Far Eastern Studies, St. Antony's College, Oxford; formerly Fellow of All Souls College, Oxford. Publications include: *Europe and China: a study of their relations in History before 1800*, Edward Arnold, London, 1931; *The Far East in World Politics*, Oxford University Press, London, 1936; *The Sino-Soviet Alliance Treaty of 1945* in *St Antony's Papers* (Far Eastern series, Vol. I), Chatto & Windus, London, 1957; *The Hard and Bitter Peace*, Pall Mall Press, London, 1967; *Fifty Years of Communism: Theory and Practice*, C. A. Watts, London, 1968.

M. A. JONES, M.A., D.Phil., Lecturer in American History and Institutions, University of Manchester. Publications include: *American Immigration*, Chicago, University of Chicago Press, 1960. *Sectionalism and the Civil War* in *British Essays in American History*, edited by H. C. ALLEN and C. P. HILL, Edward Arnold, London, 1957.

GODFREY LIENHARDT, M.A., D.Phil., Senior Lecturer, Institute of Social Anthropology, University of Oxford; former visiting Professor of Anthropology and Sociology, College of Arts and Sciences, Baghdad, Iraq. Publications include: *Some Notions of Witchcraft among the Dinka, Africa*, Vol. 21, 1951; *'Religion'* in *Man, Culture and Society*, edited by SHAPIRO, Oxford University Press, New York, 1956; *The Anuak Village Headman* (*International African Institute Memorandum*, 1958); *The Political System of the Dinka in Tribes without Rulers*, edited by TAIT and MIDDLETON, Routledge & Kegan Paul, London, 1958.

F. M. H. MARKHAM, M.A., Senior Fellow of Hertford College, Oxford, and University Lecturer in Modern History. Publications include: *Henri de Saint-Simon; Selected Writings* (Editor and Translator), Blackwell, London, 1952; *Napoleon and the Awakening of Europe*, English Universities Press, London, 1954; *Napoleon*, Weidenfeld & Nicolson, London, 1963 and New American Library, New York, 1964.

THE REV. GERVASE MATHEW, M.A., F.S.A., University Lecturer in Byzantine Studies, Oxford. Publications include: *Byzantine Painting*, Faber & Faber, London, 1950. Contributions to *Journal of Roman Studies, Antiquity, Oriental Art*, and *Cambridge Medieval History*, Vol. IV.

J. H. PARRY, C.M.G., Gardiner Professor of Oceanic History and Affairs in Harvard University. Sometime Professor of Modern History in the University of the West Indies, Principal of the University of Ibadan, Nigeria, Principal of the University College of Swansea and Vice-Chancellor of the University of Wales. Publications include: *The Spanish Theory of Empire*, Cambridge University Press, Cambridge, 1940; *The Audiencia of New Galicia*, Cambridge University Press, Cambridge, 1949; *A Short History of the West Indies*, Macmillan, London, 1956; *The Age of Reconnaissance*, Weidenfeld & Nicolson, London, 1963;

The Spanish Seaborne Empire, Hutchinson, London, 1966.

R. H. PINDER-WILSON, M.A., F.S.A., Assistant Keeper in the Department of Oriental Antiquities, British Museum. Publications include: *Islamic Art*, Ernest Benn, London, 1957; *Persian Painting of the fifteenth century*, Faber & Faber, London, 1958; contributions to *British Museum Quarterly*, *Ars Orientalis* (Washington), *Oriental Art* (London), *Encyclopaedia of Islam*, *Encylopaedia Britannica*.

JOHN P. PLAMENATZ, M.A., Chichele Professor of Political Theory and Fellow of All Souls College, Oxford. Publications include: *Consent, Freedom and Political Obligation*, Oxford University Press, London, 1938; *The English Utilitarians*, Blackwell & Mott, Oxford, 1949; *The Revolutionary Movement in France, 1815-1871*, Longmans Green, London, 1952; *German Marxism and Russian Communism*, Longmans Green, London, 1954.

J. M. PREST, M.A., Fellow of Balliol College, Oxford.

JACK SIMMONS, M.A., Professor of History in the University of Leicester; former Beit Lecturer in the History of the British Empire, Oxford University. Publications include: *African Discovery: An Anthology of Exploration* (Editor, with MARGERY PERHAM), Faber & Faber, London, 1942; *Southey*,

Collins, London, 1945; *From Empire to Commonwealth: Principles of British Imperial Government*, Odhams, London, 1951; *Parish and Empire: Studies and Sketches*, Collins, London, 1952; *Livingstone and Africa*, English Universities Press, London, 1955; *Britain and the World*, Studio Vista London, 1965; *The Railways in Britain*, Macmillan, London, second edition, 1968.

MICHAEL VYVYAN, M.A., Fellow and Tutor of Trinity College, Cambridge.

J. S. WEINER, M.A., M.SC., M.R.C.S., L.R.C.P., PH.D., one-time Reader in Physical Anthropology, University of Oxford; Professor of Environmental Physiology, University of London. Publications include: *The Piltdown Forgery*, Oxford University Press, London, 1955; *Human Biology* (part author), Clarendon Press, Oxford, 1964. Papers in *Man*, *The Journal of Physiology*, *The Journal of Applied Physiology*, *British Journal of Industrial Medicine*, *American Journal of Physical Anthropology*, *Human Biology*, Proc. Royal Society, etc.

JAMES A. WILLIAMSON (dec.), M.A., D.Lit. Publications include: *Cook and the opening of the Pacific*, E.U.P., Hodder & Stoughton, London, 1949; *Sir Francis Drake* (Collins Brief Lives Series), Collins, London, 1951; *The Tudor Age*, Longmans Green, London, 1953. Contributions to *Blackwood's Magazine*, *Cambridge History of the British Empire*. Joint Editor of *The Pioneer Histories*.

FOR FURTHER READING

CH. 1. The Dawn of Mind
Fossil Men, by M. BOULE and H. V. VALLOIS, Thames & Hudson, London, 1957.
The Old Stone Age, by M. C. BURKITT, third edition, Bowes & Bowes, Cambridge, 1957.
History of the Primates, by W. E. LE GROS CLARK, fifth edition, British Museum (Natural History), London, 1956.
The History of Man, by C. S. COON, Jonathan Cape, London, 1955.
Mankind in the Making, by W. W. HOWELLS, Penguin, Harmondsworth, 1967.
Stone Age Hunters, by GRAHAME CLARK, Thames & Hudson, London, 1967.
Adam's Ancestors, by L. S. B. LEAKEY, second edition, Methuen, London, 1953.
Man, Time and Fossils, by R. MOORE, Jonathan Cape, London, 1954.
Man the Tool-Maker, by K. P. OAKLEY, third edition, British Museum (Natural History), London, 1958.
Man and the Vertebrates, by A. S. ROMER, Penguin Books, Harmondsworth, 1954.
The Meaning of Evolution, by G. G. SIMPSON, Geoffrey Cumberlege, Oxford University Press, London, 1950.

CH. 2 The Neolithic Revolution and the Foundation of Cities
Courses towards Urban Life, edited by R. J. BRAIDWOOD and GORDON WILLEY, University of Edinburgh Press, 1962.
World Prehistory, by GRAHAME CLARK, second edition, Cambridge University Press, 1961.
Cambridge Ancient History: Revised edition of Vols I and II (Published in Fascicles).
The Neolithic Revolution, by SONIA COLE, third edition., B.M. Natural History, 1963.
The Birth of Civilisation in the Near East, by

H. FRANKFORT, Williams and Norgate, London, 1951.
The Origins of Agriculture: a Reconsideration, by E. S. HIGGS and M. R. JARMAN, *Antiquity*, Vol. XLIII, 1969, pp. 31–41.
Early Mesopotamia and Iran, by M. E. L. MALLOWAN, Thames & Hudson, 1965.
Earliest Civilisations of the Near East, by JAMES MELLAART, Thames & Hudson, 1965.
Early Civilisation in China, by WILLIAM WATSON, Thames & Hudson 1966.
Civilisations of the Indus Valley and Beyond, by SIR MORTIMER WHEELER, Thames & Hudson, 1966.

CH. 3. Mediterranean Culture
The Greek Tyrants, by A. ANDREWES, Hutchinson, London, 1956.
The Greeks, by A. ANDREWES, Hutchinson, London, 1967.
Greek Art, by J. BOARDMAN, Thames & Hudson, London, 1964.
Ancient Greek Literature, by C. M. BOWRA, Thornton Butterworth, London, 1933.
The Greek Experience, by C. M. BOWRA, Weidenfeld & Nicolson, London, 1957.
Pericles and Athens, by A. R. BURN, E.U.P. Hodder & Stoughton, London, 1948.
The World of Odysseus, by M. I. FINLEY, Chatto & Windus, London, 1956.
The Emergence of Greek Democracy, by W. G. FORREST, Weidenfeld & Nicolson, London, 1967.
Greek Architecture, by A. W. LAWRENCE (Pelican History of Art), Penguin Books, Harmondsworth, 1957.
The Republic, by Plato, translated by H. D. P. LEE, Penguin Books, Harmondsworth, 1954.
The Peloponnesian War, by Thucydides, translated by R. WARNER, Penguin Books, Harmondsworth, 1954.

433

CH. 4. Eastern Empires
Iran

Cambridge Ancient History, Vols. I–XII, Cambridge University Press, Cambridge, 1923–39.

Cambridge Medieval History, Vol. I, Cambridge University Press, Cambridge, 1911.

L'Iran sous les Sassanides, by A. E. CHRIST-ENSEN, second edition, Copenhagen, 1944.

A Political History of Parthia, by N. C. DEBEVOISE, University of Chicago Press, Chicago, 1938.

La Religion de l'Iran Ancien, by J. DUCHESNE-GUILLEMIN, Paris, 1962.

Iran from the earliest times to the Islamic Conquest, by R. GHIRSHMAN, Penguin, Harmondsworth, 1954.

Persia from the Origins to Alexander the Great, by R. GHIRSHMAN, London, 1964.

Iran; Parthians and Sassanians, by R. GHIRSHMAN, London, 1962.

History of the Persian Empire (Achaemenid Period), by A. T. OLMSTEAD, University of Chicago Press, Chicago, 1948.

A Survey of Persian Art, edited by A. U. POPE, Vol. I—text, Vol. IV—Plates, Oxford University Press, London, 1938.

East Asia: the Great Tradition, by EDWIN O. REISCHAUER and JOHN K. FAIRBANK, Allen & Unwin, 1958.

Persepolis I and II, by E. F. SCHMIDT, University of Chicago Oriental Institute Publications, Chicago, 1953 and 1957.

India and China

The Wonder that was India. A Survey of the culture of the Indian sub-continent before the coming of the Muslims, by A. L. BASHAM, Sidgwick & Jackson, London, 1954.

Chinese Thought from Confucius to Mao Tse-tung, by H. G. CREEL, Eyre & Spottis-woode, London, 1954.

A History of China, by WOLFRAM EBERHARD, Routledge & Kegan Paul, London, 1950.

China, by C. P. FITZGERALD, Cresset Press, London, 1950.

The History of Buddhist Thought, by EDWARD J. THOMAS, Routledge & Kegan Paul, London, 1933.

CH. 5. Alexander, Carthage and Rome

Alexander the Great and the Hellenistic Empire, by A. R. BURN ('Teach Yourself History' Series) second edition, English Universities Press, London, 1959.

The Cambridge Ancient History (12 Vols.), Cambridge University Press, Cambridge, 1923–39. The chapters on Alexander (by SIR WILLIAM TARN) are in Vol. VI; on the Hellenistic Age, in Vol. VII; on Carthage, in Vols. III, IV, VI, and VIII; on Rome, in Vols. VIII to XII.

Carthage Punique, by Fr. G. G. LAPEYRE and A. PELLEGRIN, Payot, Paris, 1942.

Cambridge Medieval History (Vol. I.), Cambridge University Press, Cambridge, 1911.

The Romans, by R. H. BARROW, Penguin Books, Harmondsworth, 1950.

Daily Life in Ancient Rome, by R. CARCO-PINO, Routledge & Kegan Paul, London, 1941; Penguin Books, Harmondsworth, 1956.

A History of Rome, by MAX CARY, Macmillan, London, 1935.

Roman Readings, by MICHAEL GRANT, Penguin Books, Harmondsworth, 1958.

Alexander the Great: the Main Problems, ed. G. T. GRIFFITH, third edition, Methuen University Paperbacks, London, 1966.

Latin Literature, by J. W. MACKAIL, John Murray, London, 1895.

Hellenistic Civilisation, by SIR WILLIAM TARN and G. T. GRIFFITH, third edition, Methuen, London, 1966.

Carthage, by B. H. WARMINGTON, Penguin Books, Harmondsworth, 1964.

Histoire Politique du Monde Hellénistique, by J. WILL, 2 vols., University of Nancy, 1966–7.

The Phoenicians, by D. HARDEN, Thames & Hudson, London, 1962.

CH. 6. Palestine and the Making of Christianity

Israel among the Nations, by NORMAN H. BAYNES, S.C.M. Press, London, 1927.

Augustine of Hippo, by PETER BROWN, Faber & Faber, London, 1967.

The Dead Sea Scrolls, by MILLAR BUR-ROUGHS, Viking Press, New York, 1955.
Martyrdom and Persecution in the Early Church, by W. H. C. FREND, Blackwell, Oxford, 1965.
Conversion. The Old and New in Religion from Augustus to Augustine, by A. NOCK, Clarendon Press, Oxford, 1933.
Constantine and the Conversion of Europe, by A. H. M. JONES ('Teach Yourself History' Series), E.U.P., Hodder & Stoughton, London, 1948.
The Conflict between Christianity and Paganism in the Fourth Century, ed. by A. MOMIGLIANO, Clarendon Press, Oxford, 1963.
See also the Loeb translations from the Greek of the *Ecclesiastical History* (2 vols.) by EUSEBIUS (Penguin Classics, 1965); *Life of Apollonius of Tyana* (2 vols.), by PHILO-STRATUS; *Lives of the Sophists*, by EUNAPIUS; and the translation from the Latin of *The Confessions* by St Augustine (Penguin Classics, 1963).

CH. 7.   The Arabs and the Expansion of Islam

History of the Islamic Peoples, by C. BROCKELMANN, Routledge & Kegan Paul, London, 1949.
Pre-Ottoman Turkey, by C. CAHEN, Sidgwick & Jackson, London, 1968.
Muhammad and the Conquests of Islam, by F. GABRIELI, Weidenfeld & Nicolson, London, 1968.
Mohammedanism, an historical survey, by H. A. R. GIBB (Home University Library), Oxford University Press, London, 1949.
History of the Arabs, by P. K. HITTI, Macmillan, London, 1949.
The Cambridge History of Islam, edited by P. M. HOLT, A. K. S. LAMBTON, and B. LEWIS, Cambridge University Press, Cambridge (forthcoming).
History of Egypt in the Middle Ages, by S. LANE-POOLE, Methuen, London, 1925.
The Arabs in History, by B. LEWIS (Hutchinson University Library), Hutchinson, London, 1954
Istanbul and the Civilization of the Ottoman

Empire, by B. LEWIS, University of Oklahoma Press, Norman, Oklahoma, 1963.
A History of Medieval Islam, by J. J. SAUNDERS, Routledge & Kegan Paul, London, 1965.
The Rise of the Ottoman Empire, by P. WITTEK, Royal Asiatic Society, London, 1938.

CH. 8.   Byzantium; Rus and Muscovy

Byzantium

Byzantine Studies and other Essays, by N. H. BAYNES, Athlone Press of the University of London, 1955.
Anna Comnena, by G. BUCKLER, Oxford University Press, London, 1929.
The Byzantine World, by J. M. HUSSEY, Hutchinson University Library, Hutchinson, London, 1957.
Byzantine Painting, by A. GRABAR, Skira, Geneva, 1953.
Byzantine Civilization, by STEVEN RUNCIMAN, Edward Arnold, London, 1933.
History of the Byzantine State, by G. OSTROGORSKY, Blackwell, Oxford, 1956.
History of the Byzantine Empire, by A. A. VASILIEV, printed in Madison, U.S.A., 1952.
Byzantine Aesthetics, by GERVASE MATHEW, John Murray, London, 1963.
The Court of Richard II, by GERVASE MATHEW, John Murray, London, 1968.
The Fall of Constantinople, 1453, by STEVEN RUNCIMAN, Cambridge University Press, 1965.

Rus and Muscovy

Lord and Peasant in Russia, by J. BLUM, Princeton, 1961.
The Russian Primary Chronicle, by S. H. CROSS, Mediaeval Academy of America Publication No. 60, Cambridge, Massachusetts, 1953.
Ivan the Great of Moscow, by J. L. I. FENNELL, London, 1961.
Kiev Rus, by B. GREKOV, Foreign Languages Publishing House, Moscow, 1959.
The Art and Architecture of Russia, by G. H. HAMILTON, Penguin Books, Harmondsworth, 1954.
A History of the National Economy of

World History

Russia to the 1917 Revolution, by P. LYASH-CHENKO, New York, 1949.
A History of Russia, Vols. I–III, by V. O. KLYUCHEVSKY (translated), Dent, London; E. P. Dutton, New York, 1911–31.
La Russie des Origines à la Naissance de Pierre le Grand, by C. STÄHLIN, Payot, Paris, 1946.
Avvakum et les Débuts du Raskol, by P. PASCAL, Paris, 1938.
Survey of Russian History, by B. H. SUMNER, Duckworth, London, 1948.
A History of Russia, by G. VERNADSKY, Vol. II: Kievan Russia, Yale University Press, New Haven, 1948; Vol. III: The Mongols and Russia, ibid., 1953.
Tsardom of Moscow 1547–1682, by G. VERNADSKY, 2 vols., Yale, 1969.

CH. 9.   The Nomad Empires of Asia
The Aryans, by V. G. CHILDE, Kegan, Paul & Co., London, 1926.
A Geographical Introduction to History, by LUCIEN FEBVRE and L. BATAILLON, Kegan, Paul & Co., London, 1925.
Le Conquérant du Monde (Vie de Genghiz Khan), by R. GROUSSET, Albin Michel, Paris, 1950.
Travels in Tartary, Thibet and China, 1844–6, by E. R. HUC, Herbert Joseph, London, 1937.
Contemporaries of Marco Polo, by M. KOMROFF, Jonathan Cape, London, 1929. (For travels of Carpini and Rubruck, see also editions with detailed notes by BEAZLEY and by ROCKHILL, Hakluyt Society.)
*Pivot of Asia. Sinkiang and the Inner Asian Frontiers of China and Russia, etc., by O. LATTIMORE, Little, Brown & Co., Boston, 1950.
Chinese Central Asia, by SIR CLARMONT P. SKRINE, Methuen, London, 1926.
On Ancient Central-Asian Tracks, by SIR AUREL STEIN, Macmillan, London, 1933.
A Study of History, Vol. III, by A. J. TOYNBEE, second edition, Royal Institute of International Affairs, London, 1935.

*Or Inner Asian Frontiers of China, American Geographical Society Research Series No. 21, 1940.

L'Empire de Steppes, by R. GROUSSET, Paris 1948.
The Art of the Northern Nomads, by SIR E. MINNS, Proceedings of the British Academy, 1942.
The Scythians, by T. TALBOT RICE, Thames & Hudson, London, 1957.

CH. 10.   The Western Middle Ages
The Mind of the Middle Ages, by F. B. ARTZ, second edition, Alfred Knopf, New York, 1954.
La Société Féodal, by MARC BLOCH, Paris, 1939–40, translated by L. A. MANYON as Feudal Society, 2 vols., Routledge & Kegan Paul, London, 1961.
The Cambridge Economic History of Europe, Vol. I: The Agrarian Life of the Middle Ages, edited by SIR JOHN CLAPHAM and EILEEN POWER, Cambridge University Press, Cambridge, 1940
Vol. II: Trade and Industry in the Middle Ages, edited by M. POTAN and E. RICH, Cambridge University Press, 1952.
The Shorter Cambridge Medieval History, edited by C. W. PREVITÉ-ORTON, 2 vols., Cambridge University Press Cambridge, 1952.
The Dawn of a New Era, 1250–1453, by E. P. CHEYNEY (Vol. I of The Rise of Modern Europe, edited by W. L. LANGER), Harper & Bros., New York, 1936.
The Medieval City State, by MAUDE V. CLARKE, Methuen, London, 1926.
The Legacy of the Middle Ages, edited by C. G. CRUMP and E. F. JACOB, Clarendon Press, Oxford, 1926.
A History of the Medieval Church, 590–1500, by MARGARET M. DEANESLY, eighth edition, Methuen, London, 1954.
The Making of the Christian West, 910–1140, by GEORGES DUBY, Geneva, 1967.
The World of Humanism, by M. P. GILMORE (Vol. II of The Rise of Modern Europe, edited by W. L. LANGER), Harper & Bros., New York, 1952.
The Barbarian West, 400–1000, by J. M. WALLACE-HADRILL, Hutchinson University Library, Hutchinson, London, 1952.

A History of Medieval Europe, by MAURICE KEEN, Routledge & Kegan Paul, London, 1968.

The Making of the Middle Ages, 1000–1250, by R. W. SOUTHERN, Hutchinson University Library, Hutchinson, London, 1953.

CH. II. The Expansion of Europe
The Colonial Period of American History, by C. M. ANDREWS, Yale University Press, New Haven, 1934.

Cambridge History of the British Empire, Vol. I, Cambridge University Press, Cambridge, 1929.

Histoire de l'expansion et de la colonisation françaises, Vol. I, by C. A. JULIEN, Presses Universitaires, Paris, 1948.

The Spanish Conquistadores, Ed. by F. A. KIRKPATRICK, second edition, Adam & Charles Black, London, 1946.

The Fatal Impact, by ALAN MOOREHEAD, Humist Hamilton, 1968.

The Great Age of Discovery, by A. P. NEWTON, University of London Press, London, 1932.

The Age of Reconnaissance, by J. H. PARRY, Weidenfeld & Nicolson, London, 1963.

The Spanish Seaborne Empire, by J. H. PARRY, Hutchinson, London, 1966.

The Portuguese Pioneers, by E. PRESTAGE, Adam & Charles Black, London, 1933.

The Quest for Cathay, by SIR PERCY M. SYKES, Adam & Charles Black, London, 1936.

Short History of British Expansion, Vol. I, by J. A. WILLIAMSON, third edition, Macmillan, London 1945.

CH. I2. The Native Cultures of Africa
Les Peuples et les Civilisations de l'Afrique, by H. BAUMANN and D. WESTERMANN, Payot, Paris 1948 (French translation).

Continuity and Change in African Cultures, ed., by W. R. BASCOM and M. J. HERSKOVITS, Chicago, 1959.

The Golden Trade of the Moors, by E. W. BOVILL, Oxford University Press, 1958.

Old Africa Rediscovered, by BASIL DAVIDSON, 1951.

African Worlds, edited by DARYLL FORDE,

Oxford University Press, for International African Institute, 1954.

For particular areas: the relevant volumes of *The Ethnographic Survey of Africa*, edited by DARYLL FORDE. Published by Oxford University Press, for International African Institute.

African Political Systems, edited by M. FORTES and E. E. EVANS-PRITCHARD, Oxford University Press, for International African Institute, 1940.

The African World, by ROBERT A. LYSTAD, Pall Mall Press, London, 1965.

A Short History of Africa, by ROLAND OLIVER and J. D. FAGE, Penguin, 1962.

African Systems of Kinship and Marriage, edited by. A. R. RADCLIFFE-BROWN and DARYLL FORDE, Oxford University Press, for International African Institute, 1950.

The Races of Africa, by C. G. SELIGMAN, third edition, (Home University Library), Oxford University Press, 1957.

History and Archaeology in Africa. Report of a Conference held in July, 1953, at the School of Oriental and African Studies, University of London, 1955.

CH. I3. The Native Cultures of the Americas
Daily Life in Peru under the Last Incas, by L. BAUDIN, Allen & Unwin, London, 1961.

Mexico before Cortés, by I. BERNAL, translated by W. BARNSTONE, Doubleday, New York, 1963.

The Aztecs under Spanish Rule, by C. GIBSON, Stanford University Press, Stanford California, 1964.

The Handbook of South American Indians (5 vols.), edited by J. H. STEWART, Smithsonian Institution, Washington, 1946–50.

The Handbook of Middle American Indians (4 vols.), edited by W. WAUCHOPE, Smithsonian Institution, Washington, 1964.

The Ancient Maya, by S. G. MORLEY, Stanford University Press, California, second edition, 1956.

The Spanish Seaborne Empire, by J. H. PARRY, Hutchinson, London, 1966.

Agricultural Origins and Dispersals, by C.

O. SAUER, American Geographical Society, New York, 1952.

The Daily Life of the Aztecs, by J. SOUS-TELLE, translated by P. O'BRIEN, Weidenfeld & Nicolson, London, 1961.

Arts of Ancient Mexico, by J. SOUSTELLE, translated by E. CARMICHAEL, Viking Press, New York, 1967.

The Rise and Fall of Maya Civilization, by J. E. THOMPSON, University of Oklahoma Press, Norman, Oklahoma, 1954, second edition, 1956.

The Aztecs of Mexico, by G. C. VAILLANT, Pelican Books, Harmondsworth, 1950, Doubleday, New York, 1957.

CH. 14. Civilisations of India and the Far East

See Chapter 4: Eastern Empires, India and China.

CH. 15. The European Nation State

The Civilization of the Renaissance in Italy, by JACOB BURCKHARDT (The Younger), third edition, Phaidon Press, London, 1951.

The Origins of Modern Science, by H. BUTTERFIELD, G. Bell & Sons, London, 1957 (second edition).

The Origins of Prussia, by F. L. CARSTEN, Clarendon Press, Oxford, 1954.

The Seventeenth Century, by G. N. CLARK, second edition, Clarendon Press, Oxford, 1947.

An Introduction to Seventeenth Century France, by JOHN LOUGH, Longmans Green, London, 1954.

The England of Elizabeth (The Elizabethan Age), by A. L. ROWSE, Macmillan, London, 1950.

Baroque et Classicisme, by VICTOR L. TAPIE, Plon, Paris, 1957.

Imperial Spain, by J. H. ELLIOTT, Arnold, London, 1963.

Cambridge Economic History of Europe, Vol. IV, edited by E. E. RICH and C. H. WILSON, Cambridge, 1967.

Crisis in Europe 1560–1660, edited by T. ASHTON, Routledge London, 1965.

Religion, The Reformation and Social Change, by H. R. TREVOR-ROPER, Macmillan, London, 1967.

Gustavos Adolphus, by MICHAEL ROBERTS, London, 1953–8.

Russia at the Dawn of the Modern Age, by G. VERNADSKY, Yale, 1959.

Russia, A Short History, by M. T. FLORIN-SKY, New York, 1966, Collier-Macmillan, 1964.

CH. 16. The French Revolution, Napoleonic Europe and the Nineteenth Century

Politics and Opinion in the Nineteenth Century, by JOHN BOWLE, Jonathan Cape, London, 1954.

The French Nation, by D. W. BROGAN, Hamish Hamilton, London, 1957.

Napoleon, by G. LEFEBVRE, translated from the French, Routledge & Kegan Paul, 1965–7, and Columbia University Press, New York.

Napoleon and the Awakening of Europe, by F. M. H. MARKHAM ('Teach Yourself History' Series), English Universities Press, London, 1954.

Napoleon, by F. M. H. MARKHAM, Weidenfeld & Nicolson, London, 1963, and New American Library, New York, 1964.

Modern Germany, by K. S. PINSON, Macmillan, New York, 1954.

Britain in Europe, 1789–1914, by B. W. SETON-WATSON, Cambridge Univeristy Press, Cambridge, 1937.

The Struggle for Mastery in Europe 1848–1918, by A. J. P. TAYLOR, Clarendon Press, Oxford, 1954.

The French Revolution, by J. M. THOMPSON, Blackwell, fourth edition, Oxford, 1951.

Europe Since Napoleon, by D. THOMSON, Longmans Green, London, 1957. (This book contains a valuable bibliography.)

England in the Nineteenth Century, by D. THOMSON, Pelican, Harmondsworth, 1964.

Italy, by D. MACK-SMITH, University of Michigan Press, Ann Arbor, and May-flower, London, 1959.

CH. 17. European Nations Overseas
The United States
British Essays in American History, edited by H. C. ALLEN and C. P. HILL, Edward Arnold, London, 1957.
A Diplomatic History of the American People, by T. A. BAILEY, sixth edition, Appleton-Century-Crofts, New York, 1958.
The Rise of American Civilization, by C. A. and M. R. BEARD, 2 vols. in 1, Macmillan, New York, 1933.
Westward Expansion: A History of the American Frontier, by R. A. BILLINGTON, third edition, Macmillan, New York, 1967.
An Introduction to American Politics, by D. W. BROGAN, Hamish Hamilton, London, 1954.
American Economic History, by H. U. FAULKNER, sixth edition, Macmillan, New York, 1949.
The Growth of the American Republic, by S. E. MORISON and H. S. COMMAGER, 2 vols., sixth edition, Oxford University Press, New York, 1969.
America: The Story of a Free People, by ALLAN NEVINS and H. S. COMMAGER, Oxford University Press, New York, 1942.
American Constitutional Development, by C. B. SWISHER, Houghton Mifflin, Boston, 1943.
The Great Experiment: An Introduction to the History of the American People, by FRANK THISTLETHWHITE, Cambridge University Press, Cambridge, 1955.

Canada
Cambridge History of the British Empire, Vol. VI, Cambridge University Press, Cambridge, 1930.
The Durham Report, abridged version edited by SIR REGINALD COUPLAND, Oxford University Press, London, 1945.
The Road to Confederation, by D. G. CREIGHTON, Toronto University Press, 1964.
A Short History of Canada, by G. P. DE T. GLAZEBROOK, Oxford University Press, London, 1950.

Pax Britannica, by JAMES MORRIS, Faber, London, 1968.
The French Canadians, 1760–1945, by M. WADE, Macmillan, London, 1955.

Latin America
The Conquistadores, by JEAN DESCOLA, Allen & Unwin, London, 1957.
The Spanish Empire in America, by CLARENCE H. HARING, Oxford University Press, New York, 1947.
A History of Latin America, by HUBERT HERRING, Alfred Knopf, New York, 1955.
The Evolution of Modern Latin America, by R. A. HUMPHREYS, Clarendon Press, Oxford, 1946.
Latin America. A Selective guide to publications in English, by R. A. HUMPHREYS, Royal Institute of International Affairs, London, 1949.
Latin America, by PRESTON E. JAMES, revised edition Cassell & Co., London (printed in U.S.A.), 1954.
A History of Brazil, by J. CALOGERAS PANDIÁ, University of North Carolina Press, Chapel Hill, 1939.
A History of Mexico, by H. BAMFORD PARKES, Methuen, London; Cambridge, Massachusetts, 1939.
Bolívar and the Independence of Spanish America, by J. B. TREND, Hodder & Stoughton, for English Universities Press, London, 1946.
The Growth and Culture of Latin America, by D. E. WORCESTER and W. G. SHAEFFER, Oxford University Press, New York, 1956.

Australasia
Australian Government and Politics, by J. D. B. MILLER, Duckworth, London, 1965.
Cambridge History of the British Empire, Vol. VII, Part 1, Australia; Part 2, New Zealand, Cambridge University Press, Cambridge, 1933.
Australia, by R. M. CRAWFORD, Hutchinson, London, 1952.
New Zealand, by H. MILLER, Hutchinson, 1950.
The Long White Cloud, by W. P. REEVES, third edition, Allen & Unwin, London, 1924.
An Economic History of Australia, by E.

SHANN, Cambridge University Press, Cambridge, 1930.

A History of New Zealand, by KEITH SINCLAIR, Pelican, 1959.

Empire in the Antipodes, by J. M. WARD, London, 1966.

Cook and the Opening of the Pacific, by J. A. WILLIAMSON, English Universities Press, London, 1946.

CH. 18. The Transformation of Africa and Asia

Africa

Cambridge History of the British Empire, Vol. VIII: South Africa, Rhodesia, and the Protectorates, Cambridge University Press, Cambridge, 1936.

East Africa and its Invaders by SIR REGINALD COUPLAND, Faber, London, 1938.

The Exploitation of East Africa, 1856–1890, by SIR REGINALD COUPLAND, Faber, London, 1939.

Trade and Politics in the Niger Delta, 1830–1885, by K. O. DIKÉ, Oxford University Press, London, 1956.

An Introduction to the History of West Africa, by J. D. FAGE, Cambridge University Press, Cambridge, third edition, 1962.

Africa and the Victorians, by J. GALLAGHER and R. E. ROBINSON, Macmillan, London, 1961.

The Beginnings of Nyasaland and North Eastern Rhodesia, 1859–1895, by A. J. HANNA, Oxford University Press, London, 1956.

A History of South Africa; Social and Economic, by C. W. DE KIEWIET, Oxford University Press, London, 1941.

African Discovery: An Anthology of Exploration, ed. by M. PERHAM and J. SIMMONS, second edition, Faber & Faber, 1957.

An African Survey: Revised 1956, by LORD HAILEY, Oxford University Press, London, 1957.

The Great Trek, by E. WALKER, second edition, A. & C. Black, London, 1938.

Asia

See Chapter 4; Eastern Empires, India and China.

The Making of Modern Turkey, by SIR

HARRY CHARLES LUKE, new and revised edition, Geoffrey Bles, London, 1955.

The Far East in the Modern World, by F. H. MICHAEL & G. E. TAYLOR, Methuen, London, 1957.

Asia and Western Dominance, by K. M. PANIKKAR, second edition, Allen & Unwin, London, 1953.

Japan, by G. B. SANSOM, Cresset Press, London, 1953.

The Western World and Japan, by G. B. SANSOM, Cresset Press, London, 1953.

The British Impact on India, by SIR PERCIVAL GRIFFITHS, Macdonald, London, 1952.

Indian Nationalism and Hindu Social Reform, by C. S. HEIMSATH, Princeton University Press, Princeton, N. J., 1964.

South-east Asia, by LENNOX A. MILLS, Oxford, University Press, London, 1964.

A History of Modern Japan, by G. R. STORRY, Penguin, London, 1960.

The Last Stand of Chinese Conservatism, by MARY CLABAUGH WRIGHT, Stanford University Press, California, 1957.

CH. 19. The Industrial and Environmental Revolutions

The Industrial Revolution

The Industrial Revolution, by T. S. ASHTON (Home University Library), Oxford University Press, London, 1948.

A Concise Economic History of Britain from 1750 to recent times, by W. H. B. COURT, Cambridge University Press, Cambridge, 1954.

An Economic History of Modern Britain, (3 vols.), by SIR JOHN CLAPHAM, Cambridge University Press, Cambridge, 1926–38.

Lives of the Engineers, (5 vols.), by SAMUEL SMILES, 1861–1862, JOHN Murray, London, 1904.

A Short History of the Steam Engine, by H. W. DICKINSON, Cambridge University Press, Cambridge, 1939.

Engineering in History, a symposium, McGraw Hill, New York, 1956.

An Inquiry into the nature and causes of the Wealth of Nations, by ADAM SMITH, 1776, Methuen, London, 1950.

Capital, by KARL MARX, 1867-1894, Kerr, Chicago, 1908; Allen & Unwin, London, 1938.

Capitalism and the Historians, edited with an introduction by F. A. HAYEK, Routledge & Kegan Paul, London, 1954.

The Revolution in Environment

World Population, by A. M. CARR-SAUNDERS, Clarendon Press, Oxford, 1936.

Pioneer Settlement, edited by W. L. G. JOERG, American Geographical Society, New York, 1932.

Man and Nature, by G. P. MARSH, Sampson Low & Son, London, 1864.

The Culture of Cities, by L. MUMFORD, Harcourt Brace & Co., New York, 1938.

The World's Cities, by PETER HALL, Weidenfeld & Nicolson, London, 1966.

Les Fondements de la Géographie Humaine, by MAX SORRE, 5 vols., Librairie Armand Colin, Paris, 1952.

Land for Tomorrow, by L. D. STAMP, Indiana University Press, Bloomington, Indiana, 1951.

Man's Role in changing the Face of the Earth, edited by WILLIAM L. THOMAS, University of Chicago Press, Chicago, 1956.

The Great Frontier: An interpretation of World History since Columbus, by W. P. WEBB, Secker and Warburg, London, 1953.

The Growth of Cities in the Nineteenth Century: A study in statistics, by A. F. WEBER, Macmillan, London, 1899.

World Population and Production, by W. S. and E. C. WOYTINSKY, Twentieth Century Fund, New York, 1953.

CH. 20. World War, Communism and Social Democracy

A History of Soviet Russia, by E. H. CARR, Macmillan, London, 1950.

Histoire Générale des Civilisations (Vol. VII) *L'Epoque Contemporaine*, edited by MAURICE CROUZET, M. Crouzet, Paris, 1953.

Stalin. A Political Biography, by ISAAC DEUTSCHER, Oxford University Press, London, 1949.

American Capitalism. The Concept of Countervailing Power, by J. K. GALBRAITH, Hamish Hamilton, London, 1952.

L'Ere des Tyrannies, by E. HALEVY, Nouvelle Revue Française, Paris, 1938.

The Economic Consequences of the Peace, by J. M. KEYNES, Macmillan, London, 1919.

Capitalism, Socialism and Democracy, by JOSEPH A. SCHUMPETER, third edition, Allen & Unwin, London, 1950.

Two Concepts of Liberty, by SIR ISAIAH BERLIN, Oxford, 1958.

Hitler, a Study in Tyranny, revised edition by ALAN BULLOCK, Odhams, London, 1964.

The Second World War, by WINSTON S. CHURCHILL, 6 vols., Cassell, London, 1954.

A History of the Great War, by C. R. M. F. CRUTWELL, Oxford, 1934.

The Hard and Bitter Peace, by G. F. HUDSON, London, 1966.

Mao Tse-Tung, by G. PALOCZI-HORVATH, Secker & Warburg, London, 1962.

On Alien Rule and Self-Government, by JOHN PLAMENATZ, Longmans, London, 1960.

British Foreign Policy in the Second World War, by SIR E. L. WOODWARD, H.M.S.O., London, 1962.

INDEX

Index

migration—*cont.*
  Europe, from, 399; Germans, Goths, Vandals, Huns, 180 f; Greece, 45; India, from, 276, 277; Yueh-Chih, the, 172
Miletus, 45, 46; capture of, 52
Milner, Alfred, 367
Minoan (*see* Crete)
Minos, 38, 40
Miocene Age, 4
Mirabeau, Comte de, 314 f, 318
Mitanni, 38, 64
Mithras, 66, 100, 112
Mithridates I, 67
M'lefaat, 22
Mohacs, 139, 296
Mohammed, 84, 121–6
Mohammed bin Tughluq, 78, 282
Mohenjo-Daro, 34 f, 35, 70
monarchy: European, 294 ff, 311; medieval, 196 f; Orleans, 324
Monasticism, 147, 190, 201, 206; Russian, 162
money: Byzantine, 146; Greece, 49; Maya, 258; Persia, 66; Rome, 99
mongoloid peoples, 10
Mongols: Carpini on, 177 f; carts, women's duties, etc., 179 f; conquests in 13th century, 150; conquest of China, 181; decline, 184 f; khanates, 290; numbers, 177; Russia, in, 157, 158 ff, 168 ff, 173–86; sack of Baghdad and Aleppo, 182; taste for luxury, 181; taxation, 177; Wm. of Rubruquis on, 179 ff; *yurts*, 179
Monte Circeo, 9
Moscow, 159–62; church, the, 162; hegemony of, 161 ff; organisation, 'the Third Rome', 162 f
Moslem culture, 75, 88; India, in, 280 ff; Spain, in, 190
Moustier, Le, Mousterian culture, 9, 11
Mozart, W. A., 308, 319
Mughals: Empire, 226, 282 f, 291; Grand, the, 153
Munich Agreement, 415
Muscovy (or Russia) Company, 221
music, European, 300, 308
Mycale, 53
Mycenae, **42 ff**
mystery cults, 110 f

mysticism, 151

NAHAL OREN, 24
Napoleon Bonaparte, 312, 315, **316–21**; administrative institutions, 317; consulate, 317 f; continental system, 319; emperor (1802) 318; Leipzig, 319 f; Russian campaign, 319
Napoleon III, 325 f
nation states (European), 294 ff, 311
nationalism: Arab, 421; European, 319 f, 409, 423
Natufian culture, 22
navigation: improvements in, 302 f; medieval, 204 f, 250; Polynesian, 283 f; progress in, 275
Neanderthal man, 4–12, 14, 15
Negrillos, 235 ff
Negroes, 10, 234 f
Nelson, Horatio, 316 f
Neolithic Age, 1, 5, 12, 14, 17–37; China, in, 36 f; Crete, in, 39; farmers, 13; jewellery, 63; objects and economy, how different from earlier, 17–18
Nero, 98, 108
Nestorians, 98, 108
New England, 222, 224, 225, 228
Newfoundland, 218, 231
Nicaea, Council of, 117 f
Nicholas I, 323
Nile, inundation, 31
Nilotes, Nilo-Hamites, 243 f, 244, 245
Nineveh, 26, 64
Nippur, 28
Nizhnyi Novgorod, 161
nomads, nomadism, 19–20, 121, 125, **168–86**; beaten by firearms, 184; Matthew Paris on, 176; pastoral, 168
Normans, 147, 191, 193; kings in England, 193
Norsemen, 216, 218; in Russia, 154 ff
North Atlantic Treaty Organisation, 419
Novgorod, 154 f, 158, 161
Nubia, 249
nuclear power, 307
Nupe, 243

OIRAT, 184
Oldoway type, etc., 10, 11
oligarchy: Athens, 57; Sparta, 49
Olympias, 81

Olympic Games, 43
oracle-bones, 36, 72
Orchomenos, 42
Origen, 115
Ovid, 97

PACIFIC OCEAN, and population in, 283
paganism, 118
Pakistan, 421
palaeontology, 1 ff
Palegawra cave, 21
Paleolithic Age, 1, 5, 10–15, 18, 21
Papak, 68 f
Paraguay, 351
Paris, Matthew, on the nomads, 176
Paris, Peace of, 1763, 229, 232, 342, 358; 1856, 326
Park, Mungo, 360
'Parliamentary Experiment', the, 199
Parthians, 67, 68, 70
Pasargadae, 65, 66
Patrick, St, 190
Paul, St, 87, 107, 108, 112, 115
peasant farming: China, 36; importance of, 19; Middle East, 26; villages in Sind and Baluchistan, 34
Pecheneg, 153 f
Peisistratus, 52
Pekin Man (*Sinanthropus*), 9 f, 11, 12
Pelopidas, 58
Peloponnesian League, 48, 49, 50, 53, 54
Peloponnesian War, 55, 56, 57, 58 f, 89
Pergamum, 83, 92
Periander, 46
Pericles, 54 f, 55, 56, 57
Persepolis, 63, 66
Persia: empire, **62–9**; geography and climate, 62–3; Greece, 50, 52, 54; modern, 375, 379; Moslem rule in, 125 ff (*and see* Iran)
Peru, Spaniards in, 220, 227, 349
Peter the Great, 306
Petrarch, 210
Phaestos, 38, 41
Phidias, 55
Philip of Macedon, 59, 81
Philippine Is., 371 f
Philistines, 102
Philo, 104
philosophy: Greek, 45, 46, 56; Hellenistic, 85 ff; leads to religion, 110

447